A HISTORY OF CHINA'S FINANCIAL THOUGHT

VOLUME 2

A HISTORY OF CHINA'S FINANCIAL THOUGHT

VOLUME 2

Yao Sui
Central University of Finance and Economics, China

Translated by

Wang Yong
University of Shanghai for Science and Technology, China

Wu Zhongxiu
Hanshan Normal University, China

World Scientific

NEW JERSEY · LONDON · SINGAPORE · BEIJING · SHANGHAI · HONG KONG · TAIPEI · CHENNAI · TOKYO

Published by

World Scientific Publishing Co. Pte. Ltd.
5 Toh Tuck Link, Singapore 596224
USA office: 27 Warren Street, Suite 401-402, Hackensack, NJ 07601
UK office: 57 Shelton Street, Covent Garden, London WC2H 9HE

Library of Congress Cataloging-in-Publication Data
Names: Yao, Sui, author. | Wang, Yong, translator. | Wu, Zhongxiu, translator.
Title: A history of China's financial thought / Yao Sui, Central University of Finance and Economics, China ; translated by Wang Yong, University of Shanghai for Science and Technology, China, Wu Zhongxiu, Hanshan Normal University, China.
Description: Hackensack : World Scientific, 2023. | Includes bibliographical references. | Contents: v. 1. -- v. 2.
Identifiers: LCCN 2020040399 | ISBN 9789811223600 (v. 1 ; hardcover) | ISBN 9789811223617 (v. 2 ; hardcover) | ISBN 9789811216800 (hardcover) | ISBN 9789811220005 (ebook) | ISBN 9789811220012 (ebook other)
Subjects: LCSH: Finance--China--History. | Money--China--History.
Classification: LCC HG187.C6 Y36413 2023 | DDC 332.0951--dc23
LC record available at https://lccn.loc.gov/2020040399

British Library Cataloguing-in-Publication Data
A catalogue record for this book is available from the British Library.

This book is published with the financial support of Chinese Fund for the Humanities and Social Sciences.

《中国金融思想史》
Originally published in Chinese by The Shanghai Jiao Tong University Press
Copyright © The Shanghai Jiao Tong University Press 2015

Translated by Wang Yong and Wu Zhongxiu

A HISTORY OF CHINA'S FINANCIAL THOUGHT

Copyright © 2023 by World Scientific Publishing Co. Pte. Ltd.

All rights reserved. This book, or parts thereof, may not be reproduced in any form or by any means, electronic or mechanical, including photocopying, recording or any information storage and retrieval system now known or to be invented, without written permission from the publisher.

For photocopying of material in this volume, please pay a copying fee through the Copyright Clearance Center, Inc., 222 Rosewood Drive, Danvers, MA 01923, USA. In this case permission to photocopy is not required from the publisher.

For any available supplementary material, please visit
https://www.worldscientific.com/worldscibooks/10.1142/11730#t=suppl

Desk Editors: Balamurugan Rajendran/Nimal Koliyat/Nicole Ong

Typeset by Stallion Press
Email: enquiries@stallionpress.com

Printed in Singapore

Preface

At the end of the 1980s and the beginning of the 1990s, I wrote an outline of *A History of China's Financial Thought*. At that time, I felt that China, a great country with 5000 years of civilization, should have its own history of financial thought in addition to its history of economic thought and history of monetary thought (theories). As a teacher in the financial field, I had the responsibility and obligation to shoulder this task. So I made up my mind to use my spare time to draft such a book. After four or five years' endeavor, I finished the first draft and had it published by the China Financial Publishing House in October 1994. After the publication, I felt rather happy, because the book was sold out within a year, which was a good indication of the need for such a book. In the second year, the book was awarded the first prize among the fields of philosophy and social sciences in Beijing, because it filled an academic gap. However, I felt uneasy because my academic accumulation was shallow. Some of the financial thought was not explored in the social environment of its emergence and there wasn't any comparative analysis either. There were some things unsaid, some things unclearly expressed, some things too demanding of the ancient scholars and some things far-fetched in my writing. In addition, there were quite a few wrongly used or inappropriately omitted words, some of which were key words. As a result, readers might have found it hard to comprehend or would easily have misunderstood the text, which could lead to confusion or cause trouble. Moreover, in the postscript to the first edition, I mentioned that I had planned to write about the time before the founding of the People's Republic of China (PRC). But that edition stopped at the May Fourth Movement. My promise to the readers is a debt to be paid off as quickly as possible. During the past 16 years, though I have been quite busy making preparations and amendments, my diligence has not been enough for the task ahead. In this revision of and addition to the first edition, I implemented the following ideas.

First, for each historical period, I have presented the most advanced or representative ideas of the time. I have not made a general introduction. Instead, I have combined key points and less important points to introduce to the readers a more comprehensive picture. For example, during the Wei, Jin and the Northern and Southern Dynasties, the currency minting ideas of the Northern Dynasties were not advanced at all, but they were characteristic of the time and indicative of the unstoppable quality of the trend. Although there were twists and turns in the process, it was impossible to resist the landslide trend forward. Without an introduction, no one would be able to reflect on that historical development. The dispute over money shortage beginning in the Tang and Song Dynasties was related to monetary policy. I had bookishly thought that such a dispute was not academic or theoretical, and a description of such a phenomenon was a profane act. However, ten years of administrative experience changed my naive ideas. I came to realize that while it is important to have pure theoretical or academic enquiry, policy and management thought are of equal importance. On the one hand, Chinese people have never stopped their exploration of problems in the economic and financial fields. Otherwise, the flourishing time of the Han and Tang Dynasties could never have existed, and there would never have been paper money in the Song Dynasty, which circulated in the whole country in the Yuan and Ming Dynasties and even in foreign countries, lasting for five to six hundred years. How can we turn a blind eye to these and think nothing of our forefathers' contributions? Talking always of Western financial thought is lamentably like forgetting our ancestors. On the other hand, Western countries and China have their respective advantages. In the past one hundred and fifty to sixty years, the Western countries became stronger, while China fell behind. That is also true as far as economic thought is concerned. How should we sum up the lessons from our experience? Only when we can correctly treat our history and the present can we have a better understanding of the future and the world, especially in our dealing with the relationship between the East and the West as well as that between the North and the South.

Second, instead of being simplistic and crude, or being subjective, we should study the background and the unique environment of the financial thought carefully and intensively. I was impressed by the way Chohachi Itano, a Japanese scholar, studied the economic thought of Sima Qian. He analyzed Sima Qian against the background of the Yellow Emperor and Zhuang Zi, maintaining that Sima respected nature but supported some decisive measures to retain the dignity of the Han government, because he was a royal historian. That analysis was simply convincing. In my writing, I often wanted to challenge myself and tried to get rid of the simplistic way of thinking. I was determined to learn from masters in this field and followed all convincing suggestions. Unfortunately, I was often beset by my stupidity and ignorance.

Third, regarding citations, in the first edition I tried to be concise in my quotations and avoided, where possible, longer ones. Now, I have changed my ideas and think that this book is not only for myself but also for other people. It is to serve the needs of the readers and offer them a chance to make independent judgment and deeper enquiries. So there is indeed no need to impose my views on other people. Without much adjustment to the overall structure, I have tried my best to cite more quotations and have added my understanding and interpretation when the need arose. The effect of doing this shall be determined by the readers.

Fourth, the thirty years from the May Fourth Movement to the founding of the PRC, though seemingly short, was a period of great change. In order to strive for national independence and prosperity, there had been attempts to save the country by education, science and industry. With many active minds, there had also been different strategies and methods emerging, such as the clash between Marxist and non-Marxist beliefs, the conflicts between old and new ways of thinking, and the collision between internal and external forces. Such a scene was magnificent and unprecedented. As far as financial writings were concerned, research papers not included, monographs, collections of published articles, textbooks and popular writings were already voluminous. According to Hu Jichuang's *A Sketchy History of China's Contemporary Economic*

Thought published in 1982, there were already 60 monographs, textbooks and collected writings. 10 years later, in the financial part of the general bibliography in the Beijing Library of the Republic of China, it was roughly estimated that there were at least 200 similar items. If books related to the reform of currency were also included, there would be more than 300 of them. In the parts I want to supplement, I could only add those representative and influential people. No matter whether they were famous prime ministers, financiers, thinkers, writers, scientists or industrialists, they must have an innovative understanding of finance, a superior consciousness and a spirit of the time. Their pedigrees or ranks would not count. Their viewpoints had to influence policy decisions or the thinking of one or several generations of people. In addition, I also paid my tribute to those people whose deeds were grand and spectacular. Among the four representative figures, two of them had come back from their study in the USA. Chen Guangfu was a representative of the national bankers in the contemporary Chinese financial field. Ma Yinchu was a renowned economist and patriot, known to be tough as nails. Zhang Naiqi was a self-taught banker and financier, one of the Seven Gentlemen in the Anti-Japanese Salvation Movement, and a firm ally of the Communist Party of China. The last one was one of the founding members of the CPC and the one of the first to spread Marxism in China. These four people were basically positively viewed and so far I think no one has outdone them. It also seemed unnecessary to pick out one or two scholars to critique, at least not for the time being. The validity of this pioneering effort still needs to be tested over time. Besides, their financial thought was only introduced vaguely and the comments were also very brief, to be elaborated on in the future.

Fifth, it is challenging to complete the task of combing through the long history of financial thought of at least 2500 years, during which the Chinese currency evolved. In ancient China, there was officially run credit in addition to usury. Besides, there were such ways of exchange as *bianhuan* and *feiqian*, for the purpose of avoiding hardship and the risk of long-distance transportation. As a matter of fact, there were different methods to avoid risks and the money shortage. The local restrictions on the cross-border circulation of currency exacerbated the shortage of money, during which *feiqian* emerged. It still needs to be clarified whether the development of credit catered to the need of money shortage or if something else played a decisive role in the process. The learning from this was that as long as credibility and other technical conditions were present, even if the transactions were carried out in different places and at different times, and the transactions were not in a cash-on-delivery mode, *feiqian* and paper notes would surely emerge, taking the place of coins and functioning as the media of exchange. The key point here was that the credibility of the issuers of these credit instruments should be unquestionable. Otherwise, cash would be required and they could not be used as the substitutes. As a result, it might be safe to say that China's commodity economy was unusual in some regions, such as large cities, political and economic centers, and key waterways and frontier places. Although the whole economy was still a small agricultural economy that was only self-sufficient but not very developed, in these regions, the commodity economy and currency economy were extremely active and developed rather quickly. The advanced development of credit, the vast territory of China, the needs of the border war, the supply of food and fodder, the government procurement and the concentration of taxes all needed corresponding solutions which were suitable for the national conditions of China. If we are oblivious to the achievements of our forefathers, how can we talk about our Chinese characteristics? How can we make other people understand the history of China's financial thought with our vague narration? For the convenience of writing, in this book I used currency to refer to cashable money and paper notes to refer to uncashable money. But both these kinds of moneys were different from the kind of currency issued by Western banks or Chinese banks in later years. There were also differences between the face value and the market value of the currency. Inevitably, there would also be people who manipulated the market and engaged in speculation and profit-seeking activities. In my opinion, we might conclude that the stock market in ancient China was thus born. Besides, because of the prominent feature of the Chinese government-run credit, something similar to trust institutions seemed to have also emerged, though insurance institutions had never appeared. It still needs to be clarified whether that had anything to do with the officially run feature of credit. I think this is probably due to the difference between Chinese culture and Western culture, to which we must pay enough attention. On account of these reasons,

I am deeply aware of my lack of learning, inability to conduct a comparative study and the superficiality of my grasp of China's history of financial system and history of thought, not to mention my ignorance of related things abroad. But I also firmly believe that as long as researchers, me included, start to do research in this field, there would be no need to worry about future success. That day will surely come.

With a somewhat reasonable knowledge structure, I could only turn for help to my predecessors, colleagues and students. I sincerely appreciate the time I am living in. Before the end of the Cultural Revolution, my courage and determination had been tempered, so I am not afraid of hardships and difficulties. Since the Cultural Revolution, we have been living in an era of emancipating the mind. This extremely active atmosphere brought about fruitful and flourishing academic outcomes. Classical literature, which used to be difficult to get, is now easily at hand. Chronicles, biographies, commentary upon people and various other research achievements keep coming out, to the extent that one cannot finish reading them all. The convenience resulting from the compilation of ancient literature made me strive all the more, being afraid that I am not diligent enough. The publication of *Quan Song Wen, Quan Yuan Wen, Xu Zizhi Tongjian Changbian, A Collection of the Writings of Kang Youwei* and *Complete Works of Ma Yinchu* came about so successively that my eyes seemed fully occupied. The *Selected Literature on the History of China's Economic Thought*, compiled by Wu Baosan, presented the literature from the pre-Qin period to the Ming and Qing Dynasties, benefiting researchers in this field and contributing immensely to the study of the history of China's economic thought. The collation and publication of various collections of writings provided firsthand information for research and made it convenient to carry out objective research from a historical materialistic perspective, thus getting rid of the possibility of being wrongly informed or doing ineffective study. We should not treat the ancient scholars as we wish and pay no respect to their thought. We should also not regard history as a little doll to be dressed up any way we like. Instead, we should adopt an attitude of historical materialism and carry out our research without any bias. For that reason, I have revised many problematic points, which were mostly too demanding of the ancient scholars or too imprecise about the general background of the introduction. In general, my basic viewpoints remain unchanged, which is also one of the reasons why there is not much comment in the newly added chapter.

Speaking of *China's Financial History* and the revision and supplementation of this book, I should first of all thank the related leaders and members of the Ministry of Education for their understanding and support. At the beginning of 2003, when a leader of the Ministry of Education talked to me, I submitted my request for my withdrawal from the administrative post to concentrate on teaching and research. With my requirements satisfied, I could only make good use of the time and do my best to repay such good will.

I also want to thank Shanghai Jiao Tong University Press. The press presented me with the chance to revise and supplement the original work and publish this book. At the time of the compilation of *China's Financial History*, Feng Qin, the editor, telephoned to inform me of their intention to republish *A History of China's Financial Thought*, for which I was very grateful. I had mixed feelings because I intended to make revisions but could not start the work at that time. Mr. Feng, the editor, was very tolerant and assured me that there was no hurry. Disappointingly, I dragged on until it was very late to submit my final version of the book. After a thorough reading, I still found many unsatisfactory points, for which I felt very apologetic to the press and the enthusiastic readers. On reconsidering, I realized that my limited scholarship could not be improved within a short time. So I could not keep putting off the publication of the book.

I want to add that I must thank the Central University of Finance and Economics, of which I have been a member, and to be more specific, the School of Finance I am teaching in. Since I came back in 2003, I have not been assigned any specific tasks except the tutoring of my graduate students. I have been offered a very comfortable, quiet and relaxed environment in which I could concentrate on my research. I would like to take this opportunity to express my thanks to the young teachers in the school. They shouldered the heavy task of teaching, scientific research and all kinds of pressure from their families, leaving me a quiet and undisturbed environment. It is only natural that I should say a sincere "thank you" to them.

In the course of writing, my students and my family members offered me help and support from different angles, which encouraged me substantially and could only be repaid by my intensified efforts.

On the publication of this revised edition, I want to say that I am not afraid of being laughed at. My intention is to be a stepping stone for others, so that we can all accumulate experience from such an endeavor. Consequently, I'm looking forward to suggestions from the readers, especially specialists in this field.

Yao Sui
July, 2010, revised in October, 2010

About the Author

 **Yao Sui** is a Professor at the School of Finance of the Central University of Finance and Economics in Beijing and served as the Vice-President of the university from 1996 to 2003. As a PhD advisor, he used to teach courses such as "Money and Banking" and "An Introduction to Finance." His past Chinese publications include titles such as *Money and Banking* and *A History of China's Financial Thought*.

About the Translators

Wang Yong is a Professor of Linguistics at the University of Shanghai for Science and Technology (USST). He has published nearly 20 translations and has more than 20 years of experience in teaching translation. As Director of the Master of Translation and Interpreting (MTI) Center of USST, Wang is also responsible for the translator training program in the university.

Wu Zhongxiu, an avid reader of history and philosophy and English teacher from Hanshan Normal University of South China, has translated and published over a dozen books, ranging from financial works, company management manuals and biographies to popular science books.

Contents

Preface	v
About the Author	xiii
About the Translators	xv

Chapter 8	Financial Thought of the Self-strengthening Movement Period	575
	1. Introduction	575
	2. Theory regarding establishing banks of China	577
	2.1. Conceptions by insightful figures in modern China	577
	2.2. Bank establishment proposal by Li Hongzhang and Sheng Xuanhuai	582
	2.3. Proposal to the Qing Dynasty for alleviating fiscal and financial crisis by forming bank	598
	Annex: Sheng Xuanhuai's theory about monetary systems	600
	3. Insurance theory of Wang Tao	606
	3.1. The bourgeois ideological tilt of Wang Tao	606
	3.2. On insurance	609
	4. Foreign debt theory of Ma Jianzhong	614
	4.1. Theory of commerce begetting wealth	614
	4.2. Views on wealth	617
	4.3. Views on monetary reform	622

4.4. Theory of foreign debts	625
5. Chen Chi's financial theory	632
5.1. Monetary theory	633
5.2. Theory on bank	643
5.3. Theory on insurance	648
6. Zheng Guanying's financial theory	650
6.1. Thought of commercial war	651
6.2. Theory of monetary reform	654
6.3. Theory on banks	659
6.4. Theory of insurance and national debts	667

Chapter 9 Financial Thought During the Period from the Sino-Japanese War of 1894–1895 to the Revolution of 1911 — 675

1. Introduction	675
2. Yan Fu's financial theory	677
2.1. Monetary thesis	680
2.2. Monetary reform	686
2.3. Theory on bank interest	694
3. Qian Xun's financial theory	699
3.1. Monetary thesis	700
3.2. Theory on bank	709
3.3. Theory of national debts	715
4. Financial theory of Liang Qichao	718
4.1. Monetary thesis	721
4.2. Monetary reform	728
4.3. Theory on banknotes	739
4.4. Theory of banks	744
4.5. Theory of national debts	755
5. Kang Youwei's financial theory	766
5.1. Monetary theory	771
5.2. Theory on bank	778

Chapter 10 Financial Thought Between the 1911 Revolution and the May Fourth Movement in 1919 — 799

1. Introduction	799

2. Sun Yat-sen's financial theory	801
2.1. Sun's monetary theory	804
2.2. Theory of monetary revolution	808
2.3. On the reorganization of finance	817
2.4. On the utilization of foreign capital	827
3. The monetary revolution theories of Zhu Zhixin and Liao Zhongkai	830
3.1. Zhu Zhixin's theory of paper note exchange for material objects	830
3.2. The commodity standard theory of Liao Zhongkai	837
4. The monetary theory of Zhang Taiyan	848
4.1. Monetary writings of Zhang Taiyan	850
4.2. On the nature of currency	854
4.3. On the gold standard	859
Chapter 11 The Financial Thought between the May 4th Movement and the Founding of the People's Republic of China	865
1. Introduction	865
2. The financial thought of Chen Guangfu	868
2.1. His theory of finance	874
2.2. The tenet of the Bank of Shanghai	886
2.3. His theory on bank management	899
3. The financial thought of Ma Yinchu	935
3.1. Monetary theory	939
3.2. On the credit system	962
3.3. On the banking system	966
3.4. Theory of financial market	978
3.5. Foreign exchange and foreign investment	999
3.6. The relationship between China's monetary finance and traditional economic ideas	1007
4. The financial thought of Zhang Naiqi	1011
4.1. Zhang's theory of monetary system	1014
4.2. Theory of currency war	1039
4.3. China's financial system theory	1053

	5. The financial thought of Li Da	1084
	5.1. Nature and functions of currency	1088
	5.2. Various currency theories	1090
	5.3. Credit, credit currency and monetary system	1095
	5.4. Financial panic and the collapse of gold standard system	1105
	5.5. The collapse of the gold standard	1113

Epilogue   1123
Postscript   1131

Chapter 8

Financial Thought of the Self-strengthening Movement Period

1. Introduction

From the early 1860s to the mid-1890s, a variety of currencies were in circulation in China. Foreign silver dollars mainly included the Spanish silver dollar, the Mexican silver dollar (folk name eagle silver dollar), the British silver dollar (folk name human image silver dollar or queen silver dollar) as well as the American, Japanese and French silver dollars. These were exquisitely made and convenient for carrying and circulation, and welcomed by all walks of life; their market price exceeded their face value, and Chinese interests were being exploited by foreign countries. The situation got the attention of both the government and the people. In 1889, China minted five types of machined silver dollars (folk name dragon silver dollars), with two categories of silver dollars in circulation concurrently. The standard copper coins, silver dollars and silver in taels were of unlimited legal tender currency. The minting and issuing rights were not centralized, and there were also foreign silver dollars and paper money in circulation; the silver dollar system was not perfected.

This period was the prime time for the development of draft banks, which dominated the financial market of the time. They colluded with government officials of the Qing Dynasty in their profiteering activities. The number of financial institutions increased, and their area of activity expanded, with business outlets spread throughout the country. Financial institutions became the pillar of the Qing government finances, an instrument for raising tax, taking out loans by the government, receiving donation payments for government title purchase on behalf of the government, making warranties, raising fiscal funds, transferring funds, transferring tax payments, advancing payment for the various causes and conducting treasury functions on behalf of the government. These financial institutions were financially solid, and they granted funds to the government, private banks and other financially sound firms with reliable financial track records; however, they did not engage in cash business directly. Private banks, especially those in Shanghai, recorded rapid growth in the eighties. The owners of private banks were compradors of foreign banks or foreign firms, or they took shelter in foreign concessions in Shanghai. In 1876, 60% of private banks in Shanghai were opened in foreign concessions. By the end of the sixties and in the early seventies, foreign banks started to provide loans secured with bank certificates to private banks; the loans amounted to 3 million taels by 1873, which consolidated foreign control over private banks. Private banks also played the role of a hub connecting treaty ports with merchants from further inland; there were countless such banks widely distributed across the country. They used to have the financial backing of draft banks, and they had a secondary backing after the economic aggression of foreign banks. A financial crisis broke out in 1883, and hundreds of private banks in Shanghai went out of business. The crisis ran along the Yangtze River and spread to Hankou in central China; by the end of the year, it expanded to the commerce, agriculture and handicraft industries, and devastated many silver and coin business operations in many places. In 1878, the Yongnian Life Insurance Company, the first insurance company in China to be run by the Chinese, was incorporated. The proponents of the Self-strengthening Movement were attracted by the profit therein and followed suit, with two insurance companies being set up thereby in 1889, namely, Liren and Liji; however, the two soon went out of business.

Before the Sino-Japanese War of 1894–1895, there were nine foreign banks with 58 branches in China, which formed a financial network along the coast and the Yangtze River area. They supported commodity export into China and plundered raw materials from China, starting to make loans to the Qing government. The Qing government borrowed 46 million taels in foreign debt, about 74% made via foreign banks, while the

Hong Kong and Shanghai Banking Corporation alone handled upwards of 63% of the amount of foreign debt made by foreign banks. British citizen Robert Hard grabbed the position of Inspector General of the Imperial Maritime Customs Service and held it for 40 years, which held the great power of overseeing Chinese customs. After the sixties, foreign banks replaced foreign firms in dominating the financial market in Chinese treaty ports. These foreign banks provided financing facilities to foreign importers through international remittance, expanded foreign commodity export to China, plundered Chinese resources and took on the financial business of the overseas Chinese in Southeast Asia. They controlled and manipulated remittance business between different treaty ports, becoming one of the pillars of the financial colony in China. They absorbed money from various classes in China, and made loans to foreign businessmen in their effort to intensify their plundering of China. They created a monetary crisis by calling back or refusing to make loans through private banks and firms. As trade grew, they issued excessive paper money in China, which increasingly became the means of payment and purchase on the market of treaty ports in order to plunder Chinese wealth. They also built insurance institutions to safeguard the economic interest in commodity export and plunder the monetary capital of China. Faced with external pressure, including Western powers entering China to set up their own banks and having gained some growth, in order to retrieve the lost economic right, patriotic Chinese bourgeois representative figures, industrialists and thinkers put forward their keen requests for setting up banks of their own. As China sustained trade deficit and the monetary system was outdated and out of order, the Qing Dynasty pinned its hope on instituting banks to promote minted coin and issue paper money for the purpose of plugging financial loopholes and relieving the financial straits of expenditure exceeding revenue. The newly emerged industries and mining enterprises met with capital shortage, which stepped up the need for the establishment of banks.

2. Theory regarding establishing banks of China

2.1. *Conceptions by insightful figures in modern China*

The bank was an outgrowth of highly developed commodity economy, a product of capitalism. It was a new type of financial institution fit for the capitalistic mode of production, its existence and development greatly facilitated the development of capitalism.

In the 20-odd years from the end of the Sino-British Opium War, starting from 1845 when the first foreign bank was established in Hong Kong to 1897 when China opened its first independently owned bank, the Imperial Bank of China, the imperialists had set up over twenty banks in China. The purpose of foreign powers setting up banks in China was definitely not to transform China into a capitalist country; quite the contrary, they wanted to transform China into a semi-colony or colony of theirs. The establishment and growth of foreign banks in China became a key means of capitalist countries for conducting economic aggression and plunder, exporting capital and grabbing the wealth and fruits of labor of the people of China. Their activities upset China's economic and financial markets, the normal order of monetary circulation, monopolized China's financial market and controlled China's economic lifeline. When foreign banks flocked to China and pinched its economic livelihood, insightful Chinese figures encouraged the people to set up banks of their own from various perspectives and at various times.

In the year following the establishment of the Oriental Bank in China, Wei Yuan, a forerunner in learning from the Western countries in transforming China and a bourgeois reformist, put forward the enlightening patriotic slogan of "surpassing foreigners by learning from them", which echoed the sentiment of the time and national ethos. Regarding finances, he introduced banking practices of Great Britain including bonds, banknotes, remittance, saving and loans under the caption "The Pacific — General Survey of England in Records and Maps of the World". He wrote, "in London, the British capital, there is one such Bank. After the war with France, England incurred a principal debt of more than 4,241,410 *liang* of silver, and an interest debt of more than 169,270,000 *liang* of silver. All these money was paid in the following years according to the documents signed." In *Selected Notes on Foreign Affairs — General Annals of Trade*, he compared the economic foundations between China and the West, and arrived at the conclusion that one was founded on agriculture and the other on commerce. He then made a brief introduction of the financial institutions of Western countries. He also compared briefly paper money, banks, checks and insurance companies of Western countries with those of China, with general qualitative descriptions provided. For instance, "paper money, like that in China, is issued by the monarch, and retired in scheduled time, circulated in the country with solid credibility, hence it benefits both commerce and the country. Banks, like silver stores in China, accept silver and interest be accrued thereon, however only the monarch could set up banks which accept silver deposit or withdrawal and borrowing, or issue checks." He displayed obvious admiration for these arrangements. He was not only the earliest one to call for learning from the West, but also the earliest in introducing new-style Western banks into China.

In 1859, Hong Ren'gan, the Ganwang Prince of the Taiping Heavenly Kingdom, put forward his proposals of setting up banks, issuing paper money and developing modern financial economy: For starting banks, if there is a home of solid means amounting to a million, it shall first declare its estate and ownership title to the government repository, and then get approval for issuing one point five million silver notes, such notes shall be exquisitely painted with delicate flowers and grass, affixed with state seal and signets. It is allowed to exchange commodity with silver, or silver note with silver, a profit of three *li* per tael is allowed. It may be jointly issued by three or four wealthy houses, or by one house exclusively. This move will greatly benefit the merchant, the scholarly class as well as the people; convenient for carrying, it will not be noticeable even if one carries 10,000 taels. When such is sunk in river, then the loss is limited to the person alone, while the bank stands to gain, and the treasure still remains. Even if robbers are encountered, it will still be difficult for them to be taken away." Hong Xiuquan, the Heavenly King, remarked, "This is a practical strategy." Rong Hong also made a suggestion to the Taiping Heavenly Kingdom to establish a banking system; however, the Taiping Heavenly Kingdom soon failed before such a suggestion could be implemented.

After the sixties, along with the birth and growth of new-style modern industry and commerce in China, there arose an increasingly pressing need for financing, a call for establishing a new-style credit system, and activities quickened. Activities of establishing banks by the Self-strengthening Movement proponents who were enthusiastic in starting industrial businesses and emerging national businessmen were underway, and their understanding was deepened and enhanced by the day.

The *Shenbao* (Shanghai News) reported on March 18 and April 3 of 1876, respectively, that the renowned comprador, general manager of the China Merchants Steamship Navigation Company and business giant Tang Tingshu and the governor of Fujian Ding Richang planned to incorporate a bank in South China via collective funding and set up branches in several cities of Japan and London. Its function was to provide financial services to companies engaging in trade. When Chinese businessmen in foreign countries were in need of funds, it would provide finance to them and to overseas trade and international shipping; the planned capital subscription was established at the amount of 2 million *yuan*. The *Shanghai Courier* also reported that some Guangdong businessmen had subscribed almost all capital required to the amount of 300,000 taels.[1] This plan ultimately did not materialize. Similarly, Guangdong businessman Mr. Chen initiated the establishment of Rongkang Silver Store; he planned to first open offices in Guangzhou and Hong Kong, then successively in Shanghai, Shantou, Fuzhou, Tianjin, etc. The planned capital subscription was set at two million *yuan*, and half of the amount was to be paid up in advance. The purpose thereof was to facilitate "remittance of Chinese merchants", enable Chinese businessmen doing businesses overseas to compete for economic right and keep them abreast of their Western counterparts.[2] However, the initiative ceased operation by 1877 due to insufficient capital subscription. In the late seventies and early eighties, proposals and activities of setting up new-school banks in cities including Tianjin and Shanghai emerged; however, none of them were carried out.

Around 1892, Chen Chi and Zheng Guanying (please see Sections 4 and 5 for details), bourgeois reformists, conducted comprehensive and profound discussions and expositions of the functions, roles, and positions, as well as the necessity and special significance, of setting up banks in China. In 1895, Hu Yufen advanced a theory in *Memorial on Improving National Strength through Reformation*, stating, "now that China does not set up banks of its own, issue paper money or mint silver coin, the

---

[1] Wang Jingyu, *Studies on Tang Tingshu*, China Social Sciences Publishing House, 1983, pp. 187–188.
[2] Huang Yiping, *Economic Changes in Modern China*, Shanghai Chinese Classics Publishing House, 1992, pp. 426–427.

westerner may produce an elaborately printed certificate the size of a few inches and make it worth thousands or even tens of thousands of silvers." In the following year, Wang Kangnian also proposed, "The key to revitalization further lies in promoting the use of capital and commodities. If the use of capital is to be promoted, the commerce must be stimulated ... companies are to be started, silver coin minted, banks set up ...." "Without banks being established, then there would be no way to reduce taxes, without establishing the law of lending, capital would not be able to circulate unburdened."[3] Sun Luqin of Qiantang (in Zhejiang) remarked in *Wealth Management*, "mining, building railway, setting up post service, and putting up manufacturing businesses, the multitudes of important activities suffer from lack of financial resources; where so long as the bank has fund available, it could raise fund in their stead gradually, hence the bank is the foundation for all business activities, and when the bank accrues a small profit, the multitude of new businesses prosper, and the economic rights of China can be retrieved."[4] In *Exhorting Tongzhou Business Society to Incorporate Collective Saving and Regular Commercial Bank*, Zhang Jian also pointed out, "the mind of the Chinese people has yet to be enlightened, and the learning of commerce underdeveloped, how could the various types of banks be established simultaneously? If a plan is to be worked out for the industry, then it must start from banks. For the sake of the bank, the priority must be placed on the business of saving, while regular commerce be conducted concurrently, regular commerce shall be financed by saving, and the interest of saving shall come from regular commerce. Both functions are to be concentrated in one bank, such arrangement would be very flexible and stable."[5] Hence, this sufficiently indicated that they both had fully understood the close relation between developing businesses and establishing banks. Businesses could not work without banks, and banks had to be in place first. Banks could not work without businesses as their source of profit; since banks obtained the highest interest rate, once the bank assumed both functions, the whole economy could operate flexibly and stably, and the day of recovering the

---

[3]*Last Words of Wang Xiangqing*, vol. 1.
[4]*Collection of Works on Governance of Qing Dynasty*, vol. 18, Finances II.
[5]*The Ninth Record of Zhang Jizi*, vol. 2.

lost economic right would be around the corner. This view represented the opinions and expectations of the emerging national bourgeois class.

Li Hongzhang, a leading figure in the Self-strengthening Movement, planned to set up state banks, and Sheng Xuanhuai, his subordinate, planned and established the commercial Imperial Bank of China. In order to clear the straitened financial situation, the Qing Dynasty attempted to establish the bank of the ministry of revenue, which created great excitement for a considerable period of time. An assessment thereon shall be conducted hereinbelow successively.

2.2. Bank establishment proposal by Li Hongzhang and Sheng Xuanhuai

Li Hongzhang (1823–1901), courtesy name Shaoquan, was born in Hefei of Anhui. He was a leading figure in the modernization movement of China, an actual leader in the movement and an unyielding promoter of the Self-strengthening Movement. Li Hongzhang passed palace examinations and quelled the Taiping Heavenly Kingdom uprising, and supervised foreign, military and economic affairs of the Qing Dynasty. He was the leader of the Self-strengthening Movement. Li Hongzhang advocated starting Western-style industries so that China may attain self-reliance and independence. He held that "the self-reliant may attain independence, and things might not turn out well without self-reliance."[6] In order to attain self-reliance, "foreign powers must be pacified, and the domestic laws must be reformed."[7] Hence, reformation for self-reliance was the general platform of Li Hongzhang's economic thought, and also the banner for the Self-strengthening Movement. Starting from the 1860s, a slew of modern military and civilian industries were started. The cause of the Self-strengthening Movement for self-reliance was gaining traction. He signed the Sino-French Treaty, the Treaty of Shimonoseki, the Sino-Russian Secret Treaty and the Peace Protocol of 1901. His key works were compiled into the *Complete Works of Li Hongzhang*.

---

[6]*Complete Works of Li Hongzhang — Reply to Governor Liu Zhongliang the Imperial Censor*, Essays Communicated with Friends and Colleague, vol. 15.
[7]*Complete Works of Li Hongzhang — Reply to Wang Renqiu*, Essays Communicated with Friends and Colleague, vol. 19.

Li Hongzhang pinned his hopes on foreigners and establishing joint-stock banks with foreigners. This concept had long been under deliberation. In the process of setting up westernized industries, capital was constantly needed, which hindered the development of the cause, and limited the room of enterprise establishment for the Self-strengthening Movement proponents, which further restrained the materialization of the grand dreams cherished by modern Chinese politicians. Hence, the concept of setting up banks came into being. Regarding starting banks alone or in joint stock, Li believed that if a bank was to be started by the government alone, it would have low credibility and few would have faith in it. As regards whether it was doubted by the merchant, the people or government officials, he did not specify. Besides, there was a grave shortage of capital; hence, he noted in the abridged *Memorial on Planned Establishment of State Bank* in 1885, "if the bank is to be set up by the ministry of revenue or any provincial entity, it is feared that there would be the issue of creditability, and capital is starkly lacking, such enterprise must be conducted with joint efforts from both Chinese and foreign businessmen so that it may last."[8] He reported the idea to Empress Dowager Cixi with the articles of association and plans for setting up banks in Beijing as demanded by William Keswick, of the foreign firm Jardine Matheson.[9] The project was

---

[8] *Complete Works of Li Hongzhang*, Essays Communicated with the Translation Bureau, vol. 19.
[9] Keswick and Mick pointed out, "The bank shall have the right to compel houses of various sizes of means to deposit their silver in the bank." "And the existing silver in state repositories may also be deposited in the bank, and withdrawal therefrom may be made wherever necessary." "It will no more be necessary for the state to take in and distribute physical silver, all transactions shall be conducted via the bank. That is, transactions shall be conducted via silver note, and the state shall be relieved of such exacting efforts." "There are often issues of monetary transactions with foreign entities, the bank can serve as an agent therefor. When huge sum of loan is to be borrowed, no other bank is allowed to be involved." It specifically stipulated the following: "(1) State loan and payments for military weaponry, machinery purchase as well as remunerations to ministers on overseas trip shall be handled and remitted by the bank. (2) All tax silver from all provinces with customs bureaus shall be deposited in the bank. (3) The bank shall be allowed to write silver checks, and the amount shall be at the discretion of the supervisor, physical silver can be withdrawn at any time against such silver checks. The taxes and customs duties from the various provinces can all be submitted in the form of silver checks. (4) In a period

approved by Empress Dowager Cixi but opposed by ministers represented by Elehebu, and was also opposed by the ministry of revenue. The opposition for it stated that "the various items proposed by the said foreign businessmen are actually out of ulterior motive of gobbling up the market and jeopardizing both the state and the people in the name of making profit for us." Hence, the plan did not materialize.

On June 3, 1887, Li Hongzhang wrote in the Essay Communicated with Zhou Fu, Sheng Xuanhuai and Ma Jianzhong, "As the superintendent of commerce, I think the various key enterprises of railway, mining, textile, infrastructure must be conducted in turn, and the bank being the pivot upon which hinge the various enterprises. The said American businessmen proposed to start joint business with Chinese businessmen, it is a fair and equitable proposal, I would like to pledge for such cause." Li was being extremely definitive in his understanding of the importance of banks and attitude toward establishing a Sino-American joint bank. On the 27th of the month, Li reiterated in *Two Issues Regarding Starting Bank with Foreign Loan*, "Gold dollars are universally used in the United States, tens of millions of silver dollars are deposited, there is no way to put these to use, they apply for setting up banks jointly with Chinese of solid means at the various treaty ports. If the state takes out loans of tremendous amount, an annual interest of three or four percent shall be applied thereon, and five or six percent on loans taken out by the merchant and the people, hence it would eliminate such circumstances where the various foreign banks monopolize the financial market and profit therefrom … Mitkiwig is a leading figure in American business circles, and now that banks of various countries are set up in the various treaty ports, it would naturally be unreasonable to forbid American businessmen to set up banks; besides, they would partner up with Chinese merchants and preliminary negotiation has been conducted, which is particularly well justified."[10] Li's ideas were as follows: (1) Setting up joint-stock

---

of 50 years, the bank shall have exclusive right to the interest stated in the preceding three paragraphs, no other entity may have any interest therein" (Quoted from Li Hu, *Studies on Chinese Economic History*, Hunan People's Press, 1986, p. 243).

[10]*Complete Works of Li Hongzhang*, Essays Communicated with the Translation Bureau, vol. 19.

banks could eliminate the situation where foreign banks corner the market and profit therefrom while China could do nothing to get rid of the ills. (2) Even if the Chinese government refused to partner up in setting up the banks, foreign banks could still be set up in China. (3) Setting up joint-stock banks would benefit the Chinese government, the merchant and the people. Based thereon, American businessman Mitkiwig visited China and tried to start the Sino-American Bank (originally named National and International Hybrid Bank), headquartered in Tianjin, with branches to be set up in Shanghai and Philadelphia, with a capital of 10 million *yuan*, split equally between China and the United States. Americans were to exclusively take up the position of Chairman, with staff comprised of half Chinese and half Americans. This plan was disclosed by foreign businessmen in newspapers, and Li Hongzhang was soon impeached by 81 disciplinary governors jointly and people submitted a slew of memorials accusing him of three misconducts as follows: (1) By awarding monetary issuing right to a foreign entity, the bank would be able to institute a gold and silver minting division, and had the right to write gold and silver checks. (2) The Beiyang Minister (superintendent of trade for the northern ports) was promised an interest-free loan, while the central government could only obtain loans with interest; this stark contrast between private and public loans was outrageous. The bank promised to advance Li Hongzhang, the Beiyang Minister, a loan of 500,000 *yuan* interest-free, to be repaid after a year, while the Qing government could obtain a loan of 1.5 million *yuan* on an annual interest rate of 30%. (3) China was to raise capital of 500 million *yuan*, and America was to make up for any shortage for the specified amount at an interest rate of 30%; that is to say, the Chinese were required to make a payment of 1.8 million *yuan* for no cause annually, and such cost was to be repaid in apportionment by the Qing government thereafter.

Against the backdrop of public denunciation, Li Hongzhang was compelled by the Qing government to explain himself. "Misled by the foreigner's erroneous remarks, some of my colleagues were spreading false information, which caused the concern of your majesty … Now that the public does not approve the plan, and his majesty feared that this might give rise to some vice, how dare I do not follow the instructions of his majesty? And I would telegraph the American businessmen to stop the project of starting a Sino-American bank."[11] The plan of starting a bank jointly with foreigners fell apart, and the plan for starting a Chinese bank also fell apart. However, starting banks concerned the economic right of the state. Foreign banks in China or joint-stock banks issuing money on behalf of China, handling national treasury revenue and expenditure, monopolizing borrowing and lending transactions of the Qing Dynasty, and having access to the various privileges in China could jeopardize the national rights and interests of the Chinese economy and were the most sensitive issues, and would most naturally arouse public outcry. Such circumstances would also most easily stimulate the keen desire of the Chinese to start banks of their own; meanwhile, it would also further accelerate the sense of urgency to start banks of their own. The issue of starting a bank historically fell on the shoulders of Sheng Xuanhuai.

Sheng Xuanhuai (1844–1916), courtesy name Xingsun, style Yuzhai, was born in Wujin of Jiangsu. He was reputed to be "the father of modern industries in China", and was a patriotic industrialist who had "tremendous effect in driving the development of modern Chinese economy" (Xia Dongyuan); he established the first Chinese bank, the Imperial Bank of China, and "the steamship, electricity, mining and road companies he established were all fundamental items of a country" (Chen Sanli). However, he was conservative politically, and his guiding principle for starting modern enterprises was "trying to do something of grand scale while remaining in high-ranking position". In order to bring prosperity to national capitalism, he transformed himself from a capitalist with strong national character to one with powerful government backing, engaging in state-owned businesses, on whom the national economic livelihood hinged. He joined the team of aides and staff of Li Hongzhang in 1870, and first took up the post of superintendent of the China Merchants Steamship Navigation Company and director of the China Telegraph Company. In 1896, he took over Hanyang Iron Works and Daye Iron Works, held concurrent positions at Pingxiang Coal Mine, handled the building of the Beijing–Hankou Railway, supervised China Railway, started the China Merchants Bank, was awarded the privilege of submitting special memorials to the emperor, and was later promoted to the positions of deputy

---

[11] Quoted from Li Hu, *Studies on Chinese Economic History*, p. 244.

minister of the ministry of punishment and associate commerce minister. He basically controlled all major civil industrial enterprises during the Self-strengthening Movement. His major works included *Extant Essays of Yuzhai, Unpublished Correspondences of Sheng Xuanhuai* and *Selected Works of Sheng Xuanhuai's Archival Materials*.

Sheng's financial thought was explained in theorization on banks, *Opinions on Setting up Banks* (1895), *Memorial of Itemized Stratagems on Self-Reliance* (1896) and the attendant *Petition for Setting up Banks, Petition for Unifying Monetary System before Promoting Central Bank* (1909), as well as deliberation on monetary systems and monetary law. There were three groups of telegraphs written by him, *Opinions on Setting up Banks, On Minting Silver Coin* and *To Zhang Zhidong* (1899); he also touched on the subject in his memorials on banks. He was neither a theorist nor a thinker; however, he learned from books and from society and discussions with colleagues and friends out of love for his country, his people and the desire to get back the economic right and to get rid of foreign control so that the objectives of "enriching the country and the people" and "managing wealth for the entire country" could be reached.

As an industrialist who was both a government official and a businessman, Sheng noted, "if the country is to be enriched, commerce must be developed; if the commerce is to be developed, the top priority lies in setting up banks."[12] This understanding came from his relatively in-depth research on banks before his meteoric rise (1896). In *Opinions on Setting up Banks*, he made a concise argument: "Western countries all have a slew of banks, such banks could circulate the wealth between the government and the people, the far and the near, revitalize the commerce and are a key hub for wealth management in the world." These words indicated that banks abounded in the Western countries from which they had originated. The function of the bank was to circulate the capital and wealth between the various social classes and various areas for the purpose of revitalizing commerce, managing wealth for the entire country and to become a hub of wealth management for the entire society. Of course, "a key hub for wealth management of the entire society" did not refer to commercial activities exclusively; it included the industrial, commercial, agricultural,

---

[12] *Extant Essays of Yuzhai*, vol. 12, p. 32.

political, military, foreign affairs, cultural, educational spheres and even the individuals, and became the center of wealth management for the entire social. In *Memorial of Itemized Stratagems on Self-Reliance*, Sheng wrote, "Westerners pool the wealth of the entire country and employ the capital for commerce and industry, entrust such in the bank as a hub thereof." This statement could not be made more specific. Westerners pooled the capital strength of the entire country and employed the foundation benefiting the commerce and the industry, which could regulate the supply and demand of capital, and only the bank could function as a central hub.

According to Sheng, the bank was beneficial to both the government and the business: "silver dollars minted by the government could be employed for payment and the concern of stagnation is eliminated; paper money produced could be universally circulated, there is no fear of its being laid waste; money movement from outside the capital could be made without additional charge for movement; the government could deposit temporarily any backup fund and obtain interest thereon; silver may be converted into the pound when ships and machinery are purchased, and the pound may be converted into silver when foreign payments are collected, such accounts could be double-checked and inspected at all times so that latent loss may be eliminated. These are the benefits for the government. There are banks in the treaty ports and the various provincial capitals. The travelling businessmen or shop owners would deposit their surplus capital, and borrow fund to make up any shortfall; silk, tea, commodities could be employed as collateral for loans, and they would be free from extortion of foreign businessmen; when the peasant and the craftsman have any surplus fund, they could make some incremental saving and avoid spending such randomly. Now that the government would promote commerce and production industry, the bank is an indispensable entity in meeting each other's needs, depositing or borrowing funds for terms of various durations. These are the benefits for the business." He itemized the various business activities, including deposit, loan, exchange and intermediate business involved in banking, from the government sector to the commercial, from the public to the private life, in his analysis in a clear and logical manner, making his work both easy to understand and thorough in exposition. His work introduced the basic functions of the bank, including financing, regulating and handling. However, he placed the footing thereof on state-run commercial businesses, failing to do justice to the productive industrial and agricultural activities on which the national economy hinged; this defect indicated the inherent drawbacks of state-run commercial businesses, which developed into a deep-entrenched problem in the long run.

Sheng Xuanhuai learned from the West and discarded all banal customs and traditions, carefully examining the mechanism of economic operation and development of European countries and Japan, arriving at the conclusion that "if the country is to be enriched, the commerce must be developed; if the commerce is to be developed, the top priority lies in the bank." He came to the understanding that the bank brought both tangible and intangible benefits to the country: "economic livelihood is revitalized, which benefits both the merchant and the people, the benefit is intangible; when more benefits spring up, the government will also have more to gain therefrom, such benefit is tangible." "And when the Imperial Bank of China brings substantial success, then activities such as the Zhaoxin Stock, building road and mining, solicitation for stock subscription could all be handled via the bank like that of the Western countries, which is more convincing than causes run by the government and there would be no more such ills as credibility issue. Hence banks are held in important place in the Western countries and Japan, and their governments render all necessary support thereto."[13]

In comparing traditional Chinese financial institutions such as private banks and draft banks with new-style banks, Sheng held that "China used to have money shops with capital not more than a few scores of thousand taels, few would have faith therein; if a silver store collects capital of several hundred thousand taels, a little more would have faith therein. If there is a bank with capital amount to a couple of million taels, and branches thereof are to be set up in the various provinces according to the rules of the west, then it would be of a grand scale, the hub would naturally work smoothly without a hitch." In his opinion, the amount of capital limited the credibility of traditional Chinese financial institutions and checked their credit growth, and had an impact on setting up outlets and its key

---

[13]*Extant Essays of Yuzhai*, vol. 2, p. 31, 32.

position and function in socio-economic order. Therefore, Sheng went straight to the point in *Petition for Setting up Banks* and remarked, "Banks originate in the west, the grand purpose thereof is to circulate the commodity and wealth of a country, and meet the supply and demand requirement of both the government and the people, and their laws in this respect are better than those under which Chinese draft banks and private banks operate, the state renders protection thereto, hence the bank could be operated without failing." Obviously, if his remarks were to be understood the other way round, it would exactly indicate the fact that the philosophy and purpose of traditional Chinese finances were both imperfect and the state rendered inadequate protection thereto. These difficulties surfaced from his statements. On April 23, 1892, in a letter to Yan Zhimei, he laid bare his mind, "I have private discussion of this issue with the *Zhongtang* (Grand Secretary), and we concluded that banks are after all more dependable than private banks, and feared that private banks might fail."[14] These remarks cannot be denounced as fawning over foreigners and negated as such. Sheng not only advocated but actually personally engaged in planning and organizing a bank of China's own. It is probably wise for us not to belittle and denigrate his thoughts and actions.

In view of these, in *Petition for Setting up Banks*, an attachment to *Memorial of Itemized Stratagems on Self-Reliance*, Sheng forcefully laid out the necessity for and major significance of "the urgency to set up a bank of China". He wrote, "lately many scholars from home and abroad with insightful understanding put forward proposals for setting up banks, claiming it to be a hub whereon commerce is hinged; now that a railway of grand scale is to be built, without a bank of China's own being established, neither the vitality of Chinese businessmen could be put through nor monopoly by foreign businessmen be eliminated." Sheng believed that the urgent necessity or significance of setting up a bank of China was based on the internal and external aspects. It was the inevitable trend of the times; the traditional Chinese financial institutions could not meet the historical mission. Nothing but the bank could circulate the commodity and wealth of a country and meet the supply and demand of both the

---

[14]Xia Dongyuan, *Extended Compilation of Sheng Xuanhuai's Chronicles*, Shanghai Jiao Tong University Press, 2004, p. 378.

government and the people; with proper legislation such would be the foundation benefiting both the commerce and industry, becoming the economic hub of the entire society. "None of the countries use the bank as the hub for business transactions between the government and the merchants."[15] The bank was both the livelihood of Chinese businessmen and one of the keys to China's self-reliance. "A country is free from ills with banks established, the commerce and learning are prosperous, perfection of craftsmanship is encouraged, and silver coin is minted." As a key figure in the Self-strengthening Movement and a powerful character among the industrialist faction, Sheng was keenly aware of the fact that "the benefit of the railway is remote and meagre while the benefit of the bank is close at hand and substantial,"[16] especially from his railway-building practice. Hence, he vowed in 1885, "I will exert my life energy to assist the Grand Secretary (Li Hongzhang) in building railway, setting up banks, post, textile enterprises." "Over a period of three years, a surplus profit shall be cumulatively increased, foreign debts paid up, and the world will be all notified of the fact that steamship company and telegraph company are beneficial without attendant drawback, and then mining, railway, bank, post could all be started successively."[17] That is, things shall be started according to the urgency and difficulty, with less urgent and less difficult things to be started first, more difficult things to be started successively. At that time, he planned and developed these causes methodically and with full confidence. He believed that he would be successful so long as he did it methodically. After the Sino-Japanese War of 1894–1895, in a telegraph to Zhang Zhidong in 1896, he displayed the mentality of needing urgent banking help due to financial straits: "railway bureau authorized by imperial edict has failed to enlist businessmen over the years; when cause thereof is investigated, it is discovered that there is no Chinese bank available, the merchant and the people have nowhere to attach their capital, hence it is easy for capital to scatter and difficult to accumulate."[18] He laid bare his mind: "railway must be built for the sake of iron works, and bank

---

[15]Xia Dongyuan, *Extended Compilation of Sheng Xuanhuai's Chronicles*, p. 728.
[16]*Extant Essays of Yuzhai*, vol. 89, Addendum 66, p. 26.
[17]Xia Dong Yuan, *Extended Compilation of Sheng Xuanhuai's Chronicles*, p. 452.
[18]*Extant Essays of Yuzhai*, vol. 89, Addendum 66, p. 28.

must be set up for the sake of railway." "Three difficulties" existed in building the railway in China at that time, of which two are enumerated below. The first was that "soliciting stock subscription must start from the bank, in inchoating period, everything hinders progress. Perseverance alone could make progress and success may be effected step by step."[19]

As for eliminating foreign monopoly and extortion, Sheng believed that if China had a bank of its own, "and makes it creditable with the merchant and the people, the money could circulate without end, debt raised from the people could replace debts raised from foreign banks. Hence China could get rid of the extortion of hefty interest rate, and no more loss arising from pound conversion, the so-called curbing the ill of benefit flowing overseas, and the country would be free from want, this was the first point thereof."

According to the estimation of Sheng, the second point was that "HSBC takes in Chinese deposit in the amount of over sixty million *yuan*, moves it to India, and soon returns for more." Therefore, he pointed out in *Petition for Setting up Banks* and remarked, "if Chinese bank could obtain 10 more percent profit therefrom, then the right of 10 more percent would be taken back from foreign firms." His patriotism overflowed in his lines.

These two points were exactly what Sheng repeatedly emphasized, appealed, and expounded: "it is of great urgency for China to imitate Western practices and establish bank, stem up the extortion by foreign banks." In summarizing historical experience, he wrote, "since the powers came to China for trade, the Chinese failed to engage in this industry, and the banks of Great Britain, France, Germany, Russia, Japan arrived at China to grab the tremendous profit from China."[20] When he "heard that Hart[21] coveted setting up a bank", and planned to enlist Chinese stock subscription in setting up a Sino-British bank, he said, "Hart has the customs in his hands, and Chinese businessmen would certainly be enlisted thereby."[22] He hastily reported this to Li Hongzhang and was certain to

---

[19]Xia Dongyuan, *Extended Compilation of Sheng Xuanhuai's Chronicles*, p. 561.
[20]*Extant Essays of Yuzhai*, vol. 1, p. 14.
[21]Hart (1835–1911), British, took up the post of Inspector General of Chinese Maritime Customs Service in 1863, and returned to England in 1908.
[22]*Extant Essays of Yuzhai*, vol. 25, pp. 5, 13.

establish a successful bank. He further noted, "a bank functions particularly as the hub for all activities, circulating commodities and meeting each other's needs, how could it be reasonable for British, German and French banks to hold the economic right to accumulate wealth from Chinese businessmen and the people while no Chinese bank handling the businesses of its own and still claiming it could satisfy the need of both the country and the people!"[23] His outrage was beyond concealing. After the Imperial Bank of China was established, foreigners still did not give up meddling therein. On August 14, 1903, in a telegraph to the Foreign Affairs Bureau, Sheng was categorically opposed to the attempt of merging the Imperial Bank of China with banks from Austria and France. In order to safeguard the state interests and national dignity, he diametrically opposed foreign monopoly of the Chinese banking industry and combated foreign businessmen in securing the right to erect banks in China, keeping the industry from depending on foreign businessmen. It could be said that he spared no effort in his conduct, which required not only insight and courage but also wisdom and relevant expertise to accurately and flexibly grasp the situation.

In *Memorial of Itemized Stratagems on Self-Reliance* written in 1896, Sheng Xuanhuai proceeded from the macro background of social development and reality in China, and put forward three closely interrelated key issues: self-reliance necessarily entailing training soldiers, training soldiers entailing wealth management and wealth management entailing cultivating talents. The key to wealth management lay in two points: "increasing revenue and decreasing expenditure". He concluded through analysis that "Westerners pool the wealth of the entire country and employ such as the capital for commerce and industry, entrust such in the bank as a hub thereof. It is of great urgency for China to imitate Western practices and establish banks, stem the extortion by foreign banks." These statements fittingly catered to the mentality of the people of the time; the pivotal position and function that banks held in socio-economic life could be well inferred therefrom. In *Petition for Setting up Banks*, he compared traditional Chinese private banks and draft banks with foreign banks, pointing out the advantages of foreign banks; he also compared the advantages and disadvantages of foreign banks in China with setting up banks

---

[23]Xia Dongyuan, *Extended Compilation of Sheng Xuanhuai's Chronicles*, p. 548.

by the Chinese, and pointed out the necessity of setting a bank of China's own. Therefore, he proposed, "Banks originate in the west, the grand purpose thereof is to circulate the commodity and wealth of a country, and meet the supply and demand requirement of both the government and the people, and their laws in this respect are better than those under which Chinese draft banks and private banks operate, the state renders protection thereto, hence the bank could be operated without failing. Since the powers came to China for trade, the Chinese failed to engage in this industry, and the banks of Great Britain, France, Germany, Russia, Japan flocked to China to grab the colossal profit from China. Lately many scholars from home and abroad with insightful understanding put forward proposals for setting up banks, claiming that it is a hub whereon commerce is hinged; now that a railway of grand scale is to be built, without a bank of China's own being established, neither the vitality of Chinese businessmen could be put through nor monopoly by foreign businessmen be eliminated." "Hence China could get rid of the extortion of high interest rates, and stay away from the loss of currency exchange, thus enriching the country by cutting losses to the foreigners."[24] His purpose in resisting foreign banking forces and changing foreign monopoly of Chinese economic right was very clear.

His purpose in setting up banks also came from the understanding that "Chinese businessmen must have a bank and railway started side by side to ensure success. Now that a railway must be built for the sake of iron works, a bank must be set up for the sake of the railway." Since the railway was to be built, and the resolution of setting up a bank before engaging in erecting an industrial entity had been made, success was a guarantee no matter how difficult the process.

With respect to specific measures on organization and management, Sheng Xuanhuai proposed the following:

First, banks had to be established by businessmen, and such should have the privileges of state banks. The practice of "stock solicitation and operation to be conducted by businessmen, with the government offering protection without involvement in actual management," was to be invoked in bank incorporation and operation, that is, "businessmen operate on

---

[24] *Extant Essays of Yuzhai*, vol. 1, pp. 6–7, 14.

government sponsorship". His reasons were that "the bank is a business concern. If the businessmen have no faith in it then there would be no pool of strength, without a pool of strength the cause will fail. If the project is to be commenced prudently and wound up successfully, then incremental progress must be made for grand achievement." "Bank must be run in accordance with Western business practices, and managed by the board of directors on their own," so that "the strength of businessmen may be pooled in conducting the bank for the country." Hence, he demanded that the bank should be started by businessmen, and was actually opposed to government-run businesses. His pretext was that the time for establishing a state bank was not mature: "when both the government and the businessmen have won the faith of the people, internal and external political situation are both ready, then establishment thereof may be implemented." He feared that the government may meddle in the project, interfere with the operation activity of the Imperial Bank of China, reap all profit and taint it with ills of government politics which may adversely affect its business activity. This was only one aspect of the issue. On the other side, if there was no support from the government or government held no stock in the bank, it would be impossible for the bank to win faith of the people and the society, and such would only incur ridicule from foreigners. Then the Imperial Bank of China would fail, which equally concerned Sheng. He needed the privilege delegated by the country, such as handling national debts, issuing money (paper money, minted coin), handling remittance, and collecting, making and depositing government payments, so that it may compete for a footing with financially solid and powerful foreign banks in China, and win the faith of the people, soliciting stock subscription and capital deposit from businessmen. On the Chinese financial market under the strangling pressure of monopoly by foreign banks, in order to survive and develop, it would have no other resort but to turn to the country for protection, hence his remark, "soliciting stock subscription from Chinese, and interest will not flow out; making it a commercially operated concern, then ills will not generate therefrom."[25] This fact grew more conspicuous after the Imperial Bank of China went into operation, as foreign banks "have grown to a grand scale, and have deep entrenched

---

[25] *Extant Essays of Yuzhai*, vol. 25, p. 6.

foundation. Not only transaction payments by foreign businessmen all went to foreign banks and Chinese banks could not touch any of these business, but bulk trade conducted by Chinese businessmen went to foreign banks too due to long standing transactions and faith cultivated therewith."

By February 1909, Sheng remained unchanged in his principle of "joint operation between the government and businessman." In a memorial titled *Exposition of Measures on Central Bank — Daqing Bank* attached to the *Petition for Unifying Monetary System before Promoting the Central Bank*, he laid out a rhetorical question, asking why it should be necessary to enlist the strength of commercial capital for Western and eastern state banks. His answer was that "the concern is that if the country needs funds too urgently, or it orders the bank to issue more convertible certificates to relieve financial difficulties, or the bank issues more money than the market needs, when these issues lead to peril, shareholders thereof may consider electing directors to put some checks on the bank." Then the chairman appointed by the government would have to negotiate with directors to stem small defects and convince the entire country. Hence, it would be known that "the government and the businessman may cooperate and support each other."[26] His purpose was to prevent the government from sacrificing bank reputation and jeopardizing the interests of the people, by engaging in unrestrained issue and driving prices up, leading to market turmoil for the purpose of satisfying fiscal needs. He demonstrated the rationality of bank from the historical perspective.

Second, Western practices had to be followed for all management and operations. In plain terms, everything had to be conducted in accordance with the rules and regulations of HSBC: (a) Notes had to be printed on fine-quality paper with machines according to the amount of silver deposited therewith, readily available for withdrawal. (b) When government bodies at the provincial level took out a loan from the bank, a contract for such a loan could not be authorized before the head office of the bank could report the issue to the ministry of revenue and a repayment source could be designated. (c) To issue notes to raise debt on behalf of the state, the bank should not rely exclusively on its own capital when making loans to the state, and interest rate must be negotiated per the prevailing market

---

[26]*Ibid.*, vol. 14, p. 25.

rate. (d) Funds originally transported from the provinces to the capital could be remitted via the bank, and public backup funds could be deposited therein temporarily. (e) The charters of association of HSBC had to be the guiding principle for all personnel regulations. (f) In terms of organization layout, Shanghai had to be the headquarters for banks to facilitate trading activities between China and foreign countries as it was the first treaty port in China.

Third, the Daqing Bank had to be incorporated and run with reference to the various central banks of countries. With regard to the articles of association of the Imperial Bank of China, it was exactly like what Zhang Zhidong had remarked, "the original approved articles of association were neither like a government entity nor a commercial one, while resembling both a government entity and a commercial one; it was neither like one of China's nor one of the western's, however it was also resembling both a Chinese one and a Western one, it was really difficult to determine the advantage and disadvantage therein."[27] The new-style bank originated in Europe, and the best-run banks were also in Europe. In modeling after Western banks, following Western business practices should not be faulted. However, it remained unclear what he meant by saying modeling after and referencing Western banks. In *Memorial on Measures Regarding the Daqing Bank* in April, 1909, Sheng Xuanhuai said, "the Daqing Bank shall be incorporated and run with reference to the various central banks of the countries ... businessmen seek their respective private interest, hence one must particularly count on the central bank for controlling the hub of national financial institutions: (1) To stimulate monetary activity and decrease interest rate; (2) To complement the inadequacy of the companies and banks; (3) To handle the businesses of national treasury. What merited special attention was that it may make the monetary systems for gold, silver and copper coins uniform, make the exchange of paper money effective throughout the country. Such important issues herein mentioned shall be the exclusive responsibilities of the central bank. There are three sources of capital, namely, the stock shares, the deposit and the interest generated from issuing paper money. Upon inspection, it is found that Japan has the best system, and its effect extends to companies and banks;

---

[27] *Ibid.*, vol. 27, p. 12.

the benefit is monopolized by the central bank, which is an extraordinary privilege. Supervision is a must when privileges are entrusted thereon, there are also three important items in it: (1) Qualifications of shareholders are to be specified by the law, approval from the ministry of revenue must be obtained for anyone desiring to be a shareholder; (2) When the president appoints vice president or designates director, such shall first be elected by the shareholders and confirmed by the ministry of revenue, and the ministry of revenue shall oversee the whole process; (3) Where a bank business violates the regulations, or the government deems such business as detrimental, such may be prohibited." Learning from the Western countries did not mean clinging on to the practices of any one of the countries, nor copying it in entirety slavishly; it simply meant to pick the best and the ones most suited to the situation in China and learn therefrom.

2.3. Proposal to the Qing Dynasty for alleviating fiscal and financial crisis by forming bank

After the Sino-British Opium War, the war expenditure and huge war reparations had depleted the treasury silver of the Qing Dynasty and incurred a huge pile of debts thereto, which led to fiscal straits for the Qing Dynasty. The Qing government had no other means but to step up extortion of the people and took out loans from the powers secured by customs duties, salt tax, etc., which were desperate moves. However, the exorbitant interest rate and the hefty loss arising from pound conversion further aggravated the fiscal and financial crises of the Qing Dynasty, and started a vicious cycle.

In order to get rid of the financial difficulty, some officials claimed that expanding financial resources inevitably entailed developing industries, while developing industries further inevitably entailed developing banks. This could be classified as a positive and encouraging proposal. Others proposed to follow the beaten track by issuing paper money via banks, which was a passive move. Proponents of the former proposal included Zaitian (Emperor Dezong (1871–1908)) and imperial censor Zhang Zhongxin, and for the latter Shengjing general Yiketanga. In 1895, in *Memorial on Petitioning for Forming Bank with Specially Designated*

Official, Zhang Zhongxin noted, "I privately considered that the country has been extremely worn out as of today.

… No source is greater than business in terms of producing profit, and nothing is more important to business than establishing banks. I used to make such remarks to people, some were shocked, they thought the issue was of great significance and could not be easily realized, and so much funds could not be readily raised. I don't think any of these issues difficult. I fear that if a decision is not resolutely implemented and the privilege entrusted thereon not exclusive, it might not work. However, if the decision is resolute and privilege exclusive, then the bank could be erected within a year, and all businesses prosper within three years."

In March of 1897, Zhang Zhongxin further remarked, "the establishment of a bank is naturally a vital path to prosperity and wealth …. If China does not establish a bank of its own, and leaves foreign countries to establish banks as they will and grab the economic right of China, this will not be a move that lasts long."[28]

In 1898, Yiketanga[29] remarked in *Petition to Enact Monetary Law and Establish Bank*, "Now that the situation is of dire urgency, it will definitely not last long. There is no other way but to enact paper money law to amass billions of wealth, and reap billions of profit. If paper money law is to be implemented, there is no other way but to set up a bank to win faith of the people." In 1905, Peng Shu made a similar remark, "in my view, the times are hard and financial means are depleted. The way of wealth management lies in pursuing those that are easy and of instant effect, while issuing paper money alone is the most appropriate." The ministry of revenue also fueled the fire in deliberating over the issue, "we found that the bank is the hub of finances, while paper money is the hub of the bank."[30]

The entire Qing Government unanimously and wishfully pinned their hopes desperately on issuing paper money to tide over the financial straits. Such ignorance and banality of understanding were really pathetic!

---

[28] *Records of the Qing Dynasty — Records of Dezong Emperor*, 1897.
[29] Yiketanga (?–1899), courtesy name Yaoshan, born in Manchu, was appointed the Shengjing General in 1895.
[30] Quoted from *Studies on Chinese Economic History* by Li Hu, p. 250.

The corruption of the Qing Dynasty manifested not only in their negligible accomplishment in politics and economy but also in their simplistic equating of the bank with monetary issuing institution without the least knowledge thereof. In their views, so long as the bank was established, there would be unlimited supply of money; they simply combined the bank with the government finances, and believed that they could absolutely subject the bank to fiscal needs and their fiscal difficulties would cease to exist. Repeating the failed path was exactly the indication of a situation beyond redemption, which was also a great taboo in banking. There were very few in the modern Chinese government who had a sober understanding and categorically resisted such practices, and it was also extremely difficult for anyone to do so.

The Qing Government was prepared to unify the monetary system, promote silver coin, regulate silver price and also had the intent to set up a state bank. In 1904, the ministry of revenue submitted a Memorial titled *Planned Trial Bank Establishment and Promoting Silver Coin for the Purpose of Sustaining the Finance and Expanding Financial Resources by the Ministry*, which stated, "In times of the monetary systems requiring regulation, it is of urgent necessity to set up a bank as the hub for policy implementation. We have deliberated the issue many times, it is planned that the ministry of revenue shall work out measures to raise stock capital, following the articles of association for banks of the various countries; with some adjustments made, a trial establishment of bank shall be implemented, which shall be established as the hub for monetary circulation." After that, the ministry of revenue remarked in the *Memorial on Planned Articles of Association upon Deliberation Following the Imperial Edict to Trial Form a Bank* that "upon our investigation, monetary systems and the bank complement each other, no smooth circulation of money would be possible without banks, this is a proven law."

Annex: Sheng Xuanhuai's theory about monetary systems

In his ideas on self-strengthening activities, Sheng Xuanhuai was keenly aware that China had to have a monetary system of its own, and the monetary system should be uniform across the entire country at that. Therefore, he proposed, "in my opinion, the monetary system of a country has already been created by that specific country, none has followed the system of another country slavishly."[31] Hence, he appealed forcefully, "if the monetary system is in chaos, how could the country remain stable?"[32] This forceful questioning was exactly an accurate judgment of the monetary system of the time, and clearly defined China's monetary problem. "If China does not implement its own policy on the monetary system and mint silver dollar to circulate alongside silver dollars coming into China from other countries, when the multitudes of silver dollars from the UK, France, Germany, Russia, America and Japan come to China and infiltrate into the inland via the foreign concessions, there would be no way to stop the development of the situation and substantial profit shall be shared with and grabbed by foreigners, this is one ill." In *Memorial of Itemized Stratagems on Self-Reliance*, he criticized, "Mexican silver of 90% purity is minted into silver dollar and shipped into China, traded with Chinese silver of 100% purity; the loss arising therefrom is almost approximating into the trillions."

In a telegraph to Zhang Zhidong, Sheng made a further analysis, "when Mexican silver is shipped into China, its price rises when the market is under-supplied and drops when oversupplied. Its price is not based on its weight, hence it is a commodity, not money. The dragon silver is valued with reference to the Mexican silver, and its price is lower outside the capital; though it may be used across the provinces and municipalities, its minting is followed as a norm, you also know that this situation is not acceptable."[33] Hence, it could be seen that silver dollars were minted simultaneously by the capital minting bureau and the provincial minting bureaus. If silver dollars instead of silver taels were minted, it was still impossible to discard the tael for the dollar; sometimes it may cause a situation of "no silver left available to be minted with", which was the second ill thereof. When the ministerial repository accepted a proportional payment scheme, fen was still employed as the standard; for instance, if 100 yuan was transferred into the repository, it could only be converted to seventy three taels of silver. Hence, the purity dropped from 100% to 90%

---

[31]*Extant Essays of Yuzhai*, vol. 1, p. 7.
[32]*Ibid.*, vol. 34, p. 29.
[33]*Extant Essays of Yuzhai*, vol. 34, p. 30.

in the conversion process, and there was no way to make up for the discrepancy, which was the third ill. When such was employed for military pay, it had to be converted into seventy three taels of silver; if the market value for Mexican silver dollar had dropped to seventy tael, then the dragon dollar could also only bring about seventy taels. For instance, the dragon dollar could only be converted into six qian and eight fen in the imperial capital; this was the fourth ill.[34]

Without the precondition of a unified and independent monetary system, when the Qing government minted silver dollars, foreign silver dollars would infiltrate into China from the various foreign concessions and encroach on China's interests, and silver dollars minted by the various provinces also competed with the central government for interest. Silver dollars were used in market circulation as standard, while government repositories used tael as the standard. Under the rule of good money being driven out by bad money, when two types of moneys circulated on the market, that is, silver dollar and dragon silver dollar, or silver dollar and silver tael, dragon silver dollars and silver tael would be purchased by foreigners and retired from circulation or would be then shipped overseas, incurring losses to China for which there was no remedy. This situation occurred in 1899. In order to safeguard the independence of China's monetary system, Sheng Xuanhuai proposed to implement a uniform silver dollar system where one silver dollar weighs one tael across the country for the purpose of resisting the invasion of foreign silver dollars into China. Obviously, Sheng Xuanhuai was being impractical and too idealistic, but this also indicated that he was far from profound and thorough in his understanding of monetary systems. On July 13, 1901, in his telegraphs to Liu Kunyi and Zhang Zhidong, he openly expressed his willingness to relinquish the proposal for minting silver dollar weighing one tael and shifted his position to "coins of silver dollars weighing seven *qian* and two would be convenient, the proposal being the most appropriate."[35] This indicated that Sheng constantly modified his theories and understanding in his relentless pursuit to establish a reasonable monetary system for

---

[34]*Ibid.*, p. 33.
[35]*Ibid.*, vol. 55, p. 26.

China, turning the ideal into reality, instead of adhering stubbornly to his entrenched views.

Without discarding the tael standard and moving to the dollar standard, it would be impossible to cease minting one tael silver dollar; without stopping the minting of one tael silver dollar, it would be impossible to unify the monetary system, and outflow of economic right would remain unplugged. The reason was simple and clear. Besides, there were also precedents of failure clearly in view: "no reform would serve any good purpose without addressing the origin. This is the irrefutable proof of futility of slavish learning from the west."[36] Starting from the origin meant the Qing Dynasty should start from the ministry and bureau, and all payments to be made or received should be shifted from the tael standard to the dollar standard; otherwise a monetary systems not unified would lead to a predicament where it would be particularly difficult to have independence and unification and difficult to plug the loophole to protect the economic right. Sheng's patriotism was made abundantly clear.

Hence, on March 25, 1904, Sheng telegraphed the ministry of foreign affairs stating that the principle guiding negotiation with American financial expert Jeremiah W. Jenks going to Shanghai should be as follows: "the exclusive purpose is to reform the national currency, a consensus should be reached within the delegation and it must be ensured that no obstruction remains. Because monetary system reform is definitely not something easily attainable, self-reliance is particularly important, no foreigner is to be allowed to meddle therewith, so that the sovereignty is safeguarded and interest protected."[37] There would be no problem of counseling foreigners and who were allowed to air their views; however, they were not to force their opinions on China. The issue of monetary system allowed no foreign interference so that sovereignty may be safeguarded and economic right be preserved. These were his consistent philosophy and principles.

In February of 1908, the Qing Dynasty was preparing constitutional reform due to public pressure. Sheng Xuanhuai was consulted "for issues concerning monetary system". In "the area where constitutional system

---

[36]*Ibid.*, vol. 55, p. 27.
[37]*Ibid.*, vol. 64, p. 8.

counts on the most", Sheng aired his principle and views on "promoting central bank and unifying the monetary system to relieve financial strains." Hence, it could be seen that the purpose of unifying the monetary system was not for the sake of the market nor for benefiting the commerce and the industry, or facilitating domestic and international trade, but for the sake of the central government finances. Then, how should monetary systems be unified? That is, "if monetary systems are to be unified, monetary laws are inevitably to be instituted, and instituting monetary law inevitably entails the employment of decimal system." Following the experiences of Japan's monetary system reform, having summarized lessons from that of China, he concluded that "the foundation must be first consolidated before the outcome could be regulated, the central bank is actually the foundation for national monetary issuance." The remark was accurate. He believed that the central bank was responsible for such basic functions as issuing money and national money could only be issued by the central bank; hence, he said that the central bank shall be held as the fundamental, and the money the peripheral. If the unified monetary system was to be implemented, a central bank had to be established first, as without a central bank, there would be no foundation, and without a foundation there could be no peripheral. "Without a central bank, how could one get comprehensive knowledge of the market situation and control the national money; the former dragon silver dollar failed to fend off the Mexican silver, followed by minting of copper coin, which further aggravated the poverty of the people. All these ills were out of the making of officials; such conducts were detached from the merchant and the people, which were ills arising from the situation where there was no bank to manage these items."[38] He was saying that governmental conduct did not take the merchant and the people into consideration, neither consulting the merchant and the people nor seeking comments; such persistent conduct without regard to opinions from other parties violated the law of the market. Governmental conduct refused to respect the law of monetary circulation, further failing to "unify and consolidate the bank and the monetary bureau and oversee the entire process." "Advantages and disadvantages for the country should be explored, investigation shall be made before

---

[38] *Ibid.*, vol. 14, p. 32.

each law is to be enacted and promulgated; unreserved comments shall be solicited from the people, and important comments thereof be addressed, hence no issue of compatibility concerning people shall occur." If the national money was to be circulated across the country in exactly its original form without distortion, then "trust of the people must be obtained, there must be control by the central bank so that the entire country may follow its instructions as one."[39] This was the monetary and banking theory arrived at by Sheng after monetary system reform research, which utilized his lifelong effort, incorporated experiences from home and abroad, and was valuable and commendable, deserving recognition. However, pitiably, on its last legs, the Qing Dynasty faced a devastating catastrophe, and the foundation of the central government had been undermined; it had no time to attend to investigation, and it was impossible for the outstanding plan proposed by Sheng to be implemented.

However, from the angle of the history of thought, it deserves introduction for research and reference. Sheng proposed the following: (1) The minting bureau should be placed under the supervision of the ministry of revenue to eliminate possible dispute. (2) Paper money printing should be placed in the capital to facilitate research and inspection. (3) If gold coin minting could not be effected immediately, it is appropriate to have preparation made and procedures fixed. (4) Paper money issue should be immediately assigned to the country to prevent outflow of economic right. (5) Gold dollar should be minted on a trial basis and deposited in the bank as reserve to prevent used gold from being shipped overseas. (6) Silver dollar and gold coin should be minted and launched into circulation in stages to facilitate circulation. (7) Silver and copper fractional coins should be minted in stages as the situation requires, with no excessive minting allowed. (8) As white brass coin brought the most profit, it must be treated with greatest care to prevent private minting. (9) Additional new copper coins should be minted discretionarily, so that circulation of the existing copper coins may be unaffected and immediate effect may be attained. (10) Used silver bullions should be purchased in stages and minted to be recirculated as currency. (11) New coins should be quickly minted to facilitate circulation on loans taken out. (12) Gold, silver,

---

[39]*Ibid.*, vol. 31, pp. 31, 32.

copper resources are best to be mined as quickly and on as big a scale as possible to facilitate minting. (13) The customs should accept primary money exclusively in accepting duties according to new treaties. (14) Acceptance and transfer of taxes and taxes in kind by the prefectures and counties should be made in the original money to save both the people and the government from incurring losses.

Having written an expansive article of 5,000 words, Sheng concluded, "with the objective firmly set on upholding the advantage and eliminating the disadvantages, all decrees to be promulgated shall be of lasting effect without being revoked, then monetary system can be implemented soon, and financial measures may be determined and established, it will not only be greatly conducive to promoting the constitutional cause, but also ease the difficulty of raising funds for the army and the navy."[40]

3. Insurance theory of Wang Tao

3.1. *The bourgeois ideological tilt of Wang Tao*

Wang Tao (1828–1897), original name Li Bin, courtesy name Lanqing, was born in Changzhou of Jiangsu. He lived in a coastal port city of China, had visited various Western countries and was a new-generation scholar engaged in cultural activities. He was among the first-generation intellectuals devoted to translating Western works in China. He visited Italy, France, the UK, etc., and had firsthand knowledge of the economy, politics and culture of the Western countries. Compared with contemporary reformers such as Feng Guifen, Zheng Guanying, Ma Jianzhong, Xue Fucheng, Song Yuren, and Chen Qiu, he was not discussing China within the traditional Chinese perspective; instead, he proceeded from a unique perspective, observing China from an overseas angle. With different insights and criticisms, his assessment of the future would also be somewhat different.[41] In 1864, he started *Xunhuan Daily* in Hong Kong, reviewed current affairs and advocated reform self-reliance and learning from Western laws and starting

---

[40]*Ibid.*, vol. 14, p. 33.
[41]Zhu Weizheng, *New Compilation of Taoyuan Essay — Introduction*, San Lien Book Store (Hong Kong), 1998.

commerce. His major works included *Appendage to Records of Taoyuan Essays and New Compilation of Taoyuan Essay*.

Wang Tao was one of the representative figures of modern China reformists in the early stage. He denounced the conservatives as "being slavish to the history without knowing the necessity of accommodation," while pointing out that "it is an unswerving trend to reform the ancient practices to suit the current situation."[42]

Wang Tao's principle of learning from foreign countries was one of "learning the fine practices and ridding those bad practices". From the sixties onward, the advantages of machine production and overseas trade were emphasized; by the seventies and eighties, Confucian culture was changing. Wang Tao believed that the military had to be restored and improved before the Confucian ethics may thrive again.[43] Then, he engaged in discussing economic modernization at great length. He first preached building powerful cannons and formidable warships and then shifted to the proposition of "first getting rich and then be powerful"; he shifted his position from eliminating social ills to increasing projects which brought about benefits. He sharply criticized the mentality of valuing agriculture at the expense of commerce as "knowing exclusively measuring farmland and collecting taxes, tolerating and encouraging wily petty officials to extort and pillaging the people, they are nothing but predators on the peasant"; he proposed to "treat commerce as the foundation of the country", proclaiming that "wealth and strength are the goal for administration."[44] He was resolutely opposed to foreign economic aggression, and believed that foreign capital at the time, especially British aggression on China, had shifted from the military field to the realm of commerce, which resulted in outflow and gradual depletion of China's economic right. He firmly demanded that the economic right of China should be returned to China, forcefully proposing to attain self-reliance

---

[42] *Appendage to Records of Taoyuan Essays* (hereinafter referred to as "Appendage") — Reform First Part.

[43] *Epistles from Taoyuan — Letter Submitted to Governor Ding* contained remarks, "when the military is well furnished, virtues are properly esteemed, when the armies are strengthened, the ritual prospers."

[44] *Appendage to Records of Taoyuan Essays — Erecting Beneficial Projects*.

through reformation and contention with the West. He specifically set developing independent national industry and commerce as the core of his entire economic thought, "following Western practices", by starting profitable causes including mines, textiles, shipbuilding, railway, machinery, banks, and insurance. He also definitively proposed to implement a system in which capital employs labor, demanding that "the people shall be allowed to set up companies on their own", "making the wealthy contribute capital and the poor contribute their labor."[45] He specifically stated "that government-run businesses are inferior to that which are commercially run."[46] However, he still cherished impractical expectations for the theory of "commercially run business supervised by the government" as held by the Self-strengthening Movement's proponents.

What concerned Wang Tao the most was the Western powers' economic aggression. He particularly pointed out that British invaders engaged in activities "based on commerce, complemented by the military", and "the two operate side by side."[47] He particularly emphasized the danger of economic aggression ("commercial strength"), believing that the Western powers always started from engaging in trade, then proceeded to military occupation and finally made the occupied a colony thereof. He was convinced that China should "employ the military power and the commercial strength concurrently,"[48] then it might be free from the concern of surprise. Therefore, he forcefully appealed, "it's still not too late for revitalization if China has the resolution." His modernization theory values first the great strength of the nation, followed by the prosperity of the people. He brilliantly combined developing national economy with withstanding foreign aggression and revitalizing China, anticipating the advent of the theory of commercial war advanced by Zheng Guanying. Meanwhile, he proposed to "befriend the UK, Japan, enlist these as reinforcement, forge a close relation of interdependence therewith."[49] The

---

[45] *Appendage to Records of Taoyuan Essays — Valuing the People*, Second of Three Parts.
[46] *Appendage to Records of Taoyuan Essays — Ghostwritten Letter Submitted to Governor Feng of Guangzhou*.
[47] *Epistles from Taoyuan — Letter Submitted to Governor Ding*.
[48] *Appendage to Records of Taoyuan Essays — On the British Valuing Commerce*.
[49] *Appendage to Records of Taoyuan Essays — Fending off Russia through Concerted Efforts of China and Foreign Powers*.

foreign powers were allowed to add commercial ports and engage in commercial activity in the inland area.

Different from the views held by Huang Zongxi at the beginning of the Qing Dynasty, and also from the theory of enriching both the foundation and the peripheral as held by reformists of the landed class, Wang Tao represented neither the interest of the city-dwelling class nor the interest of the landed class which had close relations with industry and commerce, but the interest of the early bourgeois class. He challenged the bigoted old liners and challenged the traditional Chinese mentality. He was particularly appreciative of the constitutional monarchy, and criticized the tyrannical regime for impoverishing both the country and the people, partitioning the monarch and the subjects, and instituting tyranny of multiple layers. Many reformist thinkers during the Reform Movement of 1898 were influenced by his theories as he was a reputed reformist thinker in the early stages of the movement.

3.2. On insurance

In *Ghostwritten Letter Submitted to Governor Feng of Guangzhou*, Wang Tao energetically proposed to develop independent national capitalistic industry and commerce which may bring about profit; meanwhile he proposed to adopt the use of paper money, set up national banks and develop related financial institutions such as insurance, with the expectation that financial institutions of China's own would guarantee and facilitate the development of national industry and commerce in order to realize the objective of "upholding the dignity of the country and expanding the national strength". However, he did not go into great depth in discussing the bank, whereas he dwelled in great detail on insurance. The following is an introduction thereto.

The Origin and Essential Purpose of Insurance: Wang Tao believed that "the topmost advantage of Western businessmen lies in ocean-faring. There are unexpected events in braving the ocean waves, hence an insurance company is incorporated to modulate the perils. Two or three percentage points are taken therefrom; the company would obtain a meagre profit when things go well, and businessmen would have something to resort to when an accident takes place, no great loss shall be borne thereby; this is indeed a measure of great virtue." The purpose of setting up an insurance company was to reduce and eliminate risk, prevent the occurrence of accidents and loss, and make economic compensation when accident and loss did occur. The following few words summarized the nature of insurance as a means of plain and simple economic compensation: "Compensation is immediately made when loss is incurred, faith is demonstrated thereby"; "Having something to resort to, with no great loss sustained". Generally, accidents are rather the exception, "a two or three percentage point is set aside", and employed as a means of modulation. The company would obtain a meagre profit when things went well, and businessmen would have something to resort to when accidents took place, and no great loss would be borne thereby. Hence, individual enterprise would not fall into desperate situations when hit by accidents and one may restore production and operation within a short period. When economic compensation for the loss was in place, the businessman would not be forced into bankruptcy, the workers would not get laid off, the loss from the production and circulation may be kept to a minimum, and the business could be brought back to normal operation quickly.

Wang Tao's understanding and interpretation of the function of insurance was pretty clear and specific. Meanwhile, he also indulged in a high-sounding exposition and laid bare his mind on "setting up insurance company and facilitating business." The so-called facilitating business referred to the fact that "without insurance the vendor would not have enough courage to ship goods", while with insurance in place "the vendor would have faith and confidence in shipping goods far and for long time". The benefits arising from establishing an insurance industry were compensating loss, ensuring safety, reducing risk, facilitating communication, benefits for the establishment and development of China's seagoing shipping industry, benefits for conducting foreign trade, safeguarding maritime rights and interests of China, and benefits for the stability of social and economic life.

Functions of Insurance: First, insurance facilitated establishing and developing national industry, especially meeting the needs for inland water transportation. Under the constraints of foreign powers conducting economic aggression in China via insurance, water transportation and insurance businesses were all monopolized by foreign capital. It was impossible for China to build and develop its own independent national insurance industry: "currently we have to rely on Western insurance exclusively, we are not only dependent on them for a living but could not set up a business of our own." The development of national industry and commerce would still be strangled. Industry and commerce in domestic and foreign trade still had "to register westerners as ship owners before an insurance could be taken out. In this way, many areas will be placed under the duress of foreign powers." In Wang Tao's view, in order to develop China's water transportation in both inland rivers and outgoing seas, China had to establish its own insurance industry; if independent and self-reliant national capitalistic industry and commerce were to be established and developed, an independent and self-reliant national insurance industry had to be established. "Investment solicitation and insurance shall go side by side and complement each other." The establishment of a national insurance industry would not only promote the establishment and development of national industry and commerce but also prevent outflow of economic right. "Insurance companies could be started and in operation within a period of two or three years. Insuring Chinese goods with Chinese insurance company, Chinese would not have to go to foreigners for insurance, while all profits could be retained in China." This was exactly what the national capitalists pursued in earnest as the foundation for patriotism and pursuit of survival.

Second, insurance was required for conducting foreign trade. The development of national industry required not only a domestic market but also an overseas market, entering international markets and gaining markets in other countries. When national industry entered international markets, the shipping industry would be required to expand correspondingly from inland waterways to the open seas, which would further require the development of China's national insurance industry. This required not only establishing branches and conducting businesses in China but also conducting maritime insurance in order to accommodate the developing needs of foreign trade.

Third, there was the function of insurance. According to his research, overseas Chinese people were spread out widely across the globe, with some living in places as close as Singapore, Penang Island and islands of Southeast Asia and some living in places as far away as California in the

United States, Havana and Australia. Every single overseas Chinese living abroad missed their relatives back home: "they pray that the dignity and strength of the heavenly kingdom reach them and render protection thereon." However, if China could make use of shipping and commerce, and set up insurance institutions in different places then, "though it is an activity of asserting trading right, it is by no means not also an activity of asserting the dignity and strength of the country." Trade would be conducted in places densely populated by overseas Chinese: "insurance business is to be set up to insure goods circulating from China"; "men of outstanding repute to be elected to oversee said businesses, who would also serve as a source of information." Hence, the function of insurance could be expanded to areas beyond economic activity; it could represent the Chinese government and bridge the communication gap between overseas Chinese and the motherland. "When a consulate is established later on, and a consular appointed", such cause could employ businessmen from afar, and "the overseas Chinese originally overseeing insurance business could all be brought under the discretionary employment thereby."

Wang Tao cited the fact that Great Britain engaged in foreign expansion and reigned supreme overseas on the backs of "ships and insurance"; it first colonized America and later focused on India, setting up the East India Company. He cited the history of the prosperity of Indian commerce thereafter to demonstrate his point; he also very optimistically believed that so long as "China reforms its law and implements such, prosperity thereof would reach within a short time." He could not tolerate the fact that with such bountiful financial strength, such an immense population, unfathomable intelligence and skill, superior materials and fine workmanship, China fell under the manipulation of the Western countries! He bitterly detested the foreign aggressors who were pillaging his motherland and manipulating its economic livelihood; therefore, he was determined to learn from the West, follow their path and strive to bring China to self-reliance through reform. The problem was that the foreign powers had already extended their aggression into the decadent and declining China, so following the development path of Great Britain would inevitably meet with fierce resistance from reactionary forces from home and abroad. This path was doomed to fail in China. Hence, this type of imitation or learning could only go skin deep and would fail to get the essence therefrom. This idea appeared too naive and detached from the conditions of China and the trend of capitalist development of the time. He only proceeded from an empty concept of economic common sense and made a purely abstract inference; he would definitely have run up against a stone wall for each and every one of his proposals.

Operation of insurance industry: Wang Tao proposed to conduct the insurance industry in the manner of commercial operation under the supervision of the government, believing that so long as "businessmen contribute capital and the government conducts oversight", "all business activities conducted by the businessmen" would get "government assistance and protection instead of government ailing the business." His conception was diametrically opposed to the monopoly policy on new-style industrial and mining enterprises by the bureaucratic group from the Self-strengthening Movement. He attempted to reduce the resistance to and pressure on enterprise establishment by national capitalists by invoking the form of commercial operation under government supervision. This could at least "deter petty government officials from overtly seeking bribe and local officials from setting up items to seek private interest." Under protection of government-run business, their vested interests may be shielded from encroachment, and their initiative in developing production may be kept from being upset. His proposals represented the interests of some national capitalists prepared to invest and having invested in new-style enterprises. He believed that "the commissioner and the businessman naturally could work in harmony for the same end, and there would be no difficulty created thereby," reflecting the fact that Chinese national capitalists were too feeble to stand up against and break away from the old liners, let alone fight to the bitter end with Western powers. This was exactly the fatal weakness of China's national capitalists. At the same time, it also reflected that the ills of enterprises already established and launched in the form of commercial operations under the supervision of the government, for instance, the China Merchants Steamship Navigation Company, had not been fully exposed. Further, national capitalists had not expected the bureaucrats of the Self-strengthening Movement to attempt to monopolize non-military industries through the form of commercial operation under the supervision of the government, or repress private capital for the vicious purpose of controlling and pillaging wealth through the form of commercial operation in name and government supervision in essence. It was no wonder that the people at the time had yet to see through the facade and cherished illusions on the scheme of commercial operation under the supervision of the government.

Of course, Wang Tao was not the first Chinese in modern China to advocate setting up the insurance industry. Before the appearance of modern national capitalist enterprises, Hong Rengan (1822–1864), Prince Ganwang and prime minister of the Taiping Heavenly Kingdom, promulgated "New Compilation of Government" upon approval by Hong Xiuquan in 1859, emulated Western practices and proposed thirty-four items of reform, which included starting insurance companies.[50] Wang Tao dedicated expansive discussions to insurance, and his understanding of Western insurance business and theory was basically accurate. He engaged in active dissemination and promotion in a China out of touch with the contemporary world; soon after that, the China Merchants Steamship Navigation Company set up the Renhe and Jihe insurance companies in 1858. Wang Tao's public dissemination and promotion had little bearing on them.

His intense national confidence and passionate patriotism profoundly affected and edified the Chinese, admonishing that "when the great profit of insurance is engaged, sea-faring merchants would not have to face great loss; while the profit of Chinese still gets circulated among Chinese, no westerner will have exclusive right to the profit." This resounding declaration is still haunting; it is still of no little significance in the grand wave of revitalizing China.

4. Foreign debt theory of Ma Jianzhong

4.1. *Theory of commerce begetting wealth*

Ma Jianzhong (1844–1900), courtesy name Meishu, was born in Dantu (in present-day Zhenjiang). Ma was a modern enlightenment thinker and Self-strengthening Movement activist. He lived in an era where China "faced a formidable foe not known of for thousands of years", faced "a situation

---

[50]*Collection of Historical Data of Modern China*, the Taiping Heavenly Kingdom, Book 2, Shanghai People's Press, 1957, p. 563.

unheard of for thousands of years", and was further affected by the warfare of the Taiping Heavenly Kingdom. He enrolled in a French missionary school in Shanghai in 1853 and stayed there until 1870. He participated in the second Opium War. In order to seek the path to prosperity and wealth for the country, he dedicated himself to the study of Western learning, studying English, French, Latin and Greek classics.

In 1876, Ma joined the staff and aide team of Li Hongzhang, assisting in the managing of self-strengthening causes. Upon Li Hongzhang's recommendation, he went to study in France and held a concurrent position as translator to the minister to France. He studied at the Paris Institute of Political Studies and received a doctoral degree therefrom, being the only Chinese, aside from Rong Hong (1828–1912), to receive Western bourgeois science and cultural education directly and having had a taste of Western politics and economy as well as social customs. He was a concurrent translator to the Chinese ministers to France and the UK, and had visited France, the UK, Germany, Austria, Switzerland, Belgium and Italy.

After returning to China, Ma submitted memorials to Li Hongzhang repeatedly to state his views on matters regarding "taking out loans, building road, building navy, conducting commerce, mining, starting schools, setting aside materials as reserve."[51] He was one of the able aides to Li Hongzhang in conducting self-strengthening activities. He went overseas (India, Korea, Japan, etc.) on business trips to perform diplomatic missions for Li Hongzhang, and held positions including assistant president of the China Merchants Steamship Navigation Company and president of Shanghai Mechanical Textile Bureau. His key works included *Remarks from Shikezhai, Travelogue from Shikezhai* as well the epoch-making language and natural science masterpiece *Collection of Essays on Arts*.

Ma Jianzhong's economic thought and proposals were mainly reflected in *Remarks from Shikezhai*, which was published in 1890. He believed that "state governance should be based on bringing prosperity and strength to the country, while prosperity shall be prior to the pursuit of strength for the country" and "preaching prosperity shall be based on

---

[51]*Drafts of the History of Qing Dynasty — Biography of Ma Jianzhong.*

protecting chamber of commerce, while popular will shall be the key to strength seeking". The highlights of his economic thought included valuing commerce, enriching the people and strengthening the country. He energetically proposed to develop modern industry and commerce in an all-round way, and was convinced that the prosperity and strength of a nation lay not only in powerful cannons and advanced warships but also in building a modern foundation for industry and commerce, and only in this way could a country attain prosperity and strength. Commerce was the source leading to prosperity, and countries including the UK, the United States, France, Russia and Germany "have all attained prosperity though this way."[52] Proceeding from the theory of balance of trade, he considered striving for trade surplus in foreign trade as the central link to enriching the people, emphasizing that "the key to the wealth of Western countries … lay exclusively in protecting chambers of commerce."[53] On the one hand, he proposed to develop new-style industries, "producing fine products unique to China", "imitating foreign products to compete with them on the market"; on the other hand, he advocated the policy of tariff protection, "imposing heavy duties on imported products and light duties on exported products,"[54] modifying unequal "tariff agreements", fighting to retrieve tariff autonomy to expand export and restrict import. The major move was to discard *lijin*, a kind of local business tax. "All the *lijin* collecting facilities shall be eliminated" to benefit Chinese businessmen. He was opposed to the monopoly policy implemented by the Self-strengthening Movement's proponents, proposing that "merchants pool stocks to set up company", and such a company should be run by merchants alone. Large-scale enterprises could be incorporated in the form of joint stock between the government and the businessman, the two parties pooling capital in such enterprises. He even pinpointed Li Hongzhang in his criticism, attacked the peremptory policy of "no more textile company may be set up in 10 years" and demanded publicly that "new textile companies be set up". However, he still cherished great illusions of support and protection from the proponents of the Self-strengthening Movement.

---

[52]*Remarks from Shikezhai — On Wealth of the People.*
[53]*Remarks from Shikezhai — Memorial Submitted to Li Hongzhang on Studies Overseas.*
[54]*Remarks from Shikezhai — On Wealth of the People.*

4.2. Views on wealth

The economic views of Ma Jianzhong were extremely close to those of Western mercantilists, both considering gold and silver as the only form of wealth. He compared coal and iron with gold and silver, concluding that although coal and iron were of the greatest use to humans, they were not considered wealth, only a means to wealth. In *On Wealth of the People*, he stated confidently, "there are a multitude of minerals, while the topmost useful are coal and iron. However, coal and iron are means to wealth instead of wealth; what constitutes wealth is nothing but gold and silver."

Hence, wealth and money (gold and silver) naturally formed the relation of one begetting two and the relation of two in one, gold and silver being the wealth and the wealth being gold and silver.

Then, how could the wealth of the society be increased? Ma Jianzhong first focused his attention on the field of circulation, on foreign trade. "The likes of the UK, the United States, France, Russia, Germany, India of the UK all attained prosperity through commerce"; "the source of wealth is exclusively limited to commerce." That is to say, a country can only attain prosperity through commerce by obtaining trade surplus while money is not shipped abroad. The cause of silver depletion and poverty of the people of China, in his opinion, were due to the fact "that exported silver is no less than thirty million in excess of imported silver in a year." Hence, "if China is to get rich, nothing works better than exporting more and importing less. Exporting more and the wealth scattered could be amassed again; importing less, then the wealth not scattered will stay not scattered." He was firmly convinced that so long as China embarked on the path of developing commerce, prosperity and strength would be attainable. Next, he turned his attention to gold and silver mining. In his mind, it was difficult for the scattered wealth to be amassed again; opening up mines and exploiting proprietary wealth seemed to be a better move. Hence, he set a very high store by mining gold and silver, and demonstrated with the practical examples of the UK and the United States that "countries including the UK, the United States all engaged in foreign trade, however it is impossible to be profitable in both import and export, hence they opened up mines to exploit the natural endowments and make up for the trade deficit." It could be seen that he viewed foreign trade as a source of wealth, while gold and silver mining was a complement to foreign trade.

However, Ma attributed the tremendous change and rapid development resulting from the industrial revolution brought by the application of steam engine in the capitalist countries exclusively to "the successive discovery of new gold mines in places like Los Angeles." He believed that the United States that had been founded for less than a century, and had people who were all of mediocre talent, and British Australia that had been developed for less than a century, both had a dense web of railway network erected, and agriculture was highly developed and the wealth thereof topped the world; "these are all the outcome of amassing wealth from mining gold." Taking Los Angeles alone, for instance, it was a period of about 400 years from the discovery of America in the mid-Ming Dynasty to the reign of the Daoguang Emperor during the Qing Dynasty, and it was a period of not more than 20 years from the Daoguang reign to the 10th year of the Tongzhi reign (1871); however, gold and silver mined over the 20-year period amounted to 1.2 billion taels, and the amount was already twice that mined from the previous 400-year period. From the 10th year of the Tongzhi reign to the time of Ma's analysis, with the introduction of novel and convenient mining machinery, mining output had more than doubled.

Ma's emphasis on gold mining also came from the understanding of the global trend of money development. Silver coins were to be minted to unify currency circulation and satisfy domestic demand; gold coins were to be minted to stay consistent with the gold standard implemented around the globe, resist foreign plundering and bring convenience to China in international trade. At the time, throughout the west and the east, only China and India still adhered to the silver standard: "foreign countries use gold and silver concurrently, therefore there is an increasing amount of silver, more silver inevitably leads to silver price drop"; "a huge loss is incurred in trading silver for the pound." China incurred an increasing amount of loss resulting from pound conversion, which ran counter to the original purpose of attaining prosperity through trade, a trend which could not be sustained: "it is urgent to have concurrent gold coin for circulation, set up a checks and balance mechanism between the parent and the offspring, eliminate the ills of exorbitantly high or exorbitantly low prices, only in this way could the loss of at least up to 10 million be made up for unobtrusively."[55] Otherwise, against a backdrop where gold coins were circulated among the Western countries, China had "lost control over the mechanism of the checks and balance between the parent and the offspring, and has been under the manipulation of foreigners for long."

If China mined gold extensively, the gold price would necessarily drop due to increase in the amount of gold: "it would be a huge benefit for transaction payments and trade conducted by Chinese businessmen."[56] In the beginning, foreign silver dollars could also be employed in the opening up of Chinese gold mines, and gold mined could be used in purchasing foreign silver dollars, exactly what was called "fending off your spear with your shield". "Such a petty amount of silver as interest shipped overseas annually was from Chinese businessmen in name only; in essence it is still obtained from foreign businessmen. Where is the outflow of national interest?" So long as this proposal could have been actually followed through, silver outflow could have been stemmed. The problem was whether the old and new colonists would meekly allow themselves to be ordered about by the Chinese.

"There is a limit to the amount of gold and silver, however there is none in the use thereof." Ma proposed to issue paper money in a restricted manner, referring to the practices of the UK and France for the amount of issuance: "a treasury reserve of 40 million silver could afford the issuance of 60 million paper money."[57]

The view of wealth by Ma Jianzhong was extremely similar to that of mercantilists. First, mercantilism confused the two concepts of money and capital. Its representative figure Thomas Mann (1571–1641) believed that "money begets trade, trade expands money."[58] Similarly, Ma Jianzhong believed that gold and silver were wealth and wealth was also gold and silver. Hence, trade deficit led to money being scattered beyond the

---

[55]*Remarks — Memorial Submitted to Li Hongzhang on Reconsidering Navy Establishing Memorial* by He Ruzhang.
[56]*Remarks — Memorial to Li Hongzhang on Matters Concerning Mining in Mohe.*
[57]*Remarks — Memorial Submitted to Li Hongzhang on Reconsidering Navy Establishing Memorial* by He Ruzhang.
[58]See *Encyclopedia of China — Economy*, p. 644.

national boundary, that is, wealth got scattered; hence, in the situation where silver was depleted, the people were impoverished. Second, mercantilism believed that commercial activity could bring about more money. In order to increase national wealth, they held foreign trade highly, believing that so long as export exceeded import and trade surplus was realized, there would be net income and the country would become richer. Similarly, Ma Jianzhong was a supporter and disseminator of the theory of trade balance. He had made specific statements regarding this theory: "the source of wealth is exclusively limited to commerce"; "it would be beneficial when export exceeds import, it would be also beneficial when export equals import, however, it would be detrimental when import exceeds export." He proposed to energetically uphold and develop silk, tea, cowhide, wool, cane sugar, straw-plaited articles, cotton, chinaware, etc., all originally produced in China as the competitive products of China: "timely rectification shall be made, all of these are the so-called finely produced articles for export; hopes are pinned thereon to restore the scattered wealth of China." Meanwhile, import would be reduced and imitation would be employed to substitute foreign products to meet domestic market needs, which referred mainly to imported cloth and imported yarn, "to retain the wealth not yet scattered." Restricting foreign goods from being imported and going all out in developing the domestic manufacturing industry were the propositions for ensuring that trade surplus in foreign trade was identical to those of mercantilism. In conclusion, the money valued by mercantilists was not wealth in the sense of general goods and materials, but wealth existing in the form of capital. They equated money with wealth in the perspective of capital.

Mercantilism set special store by examining the circulation process. It was because "commercial capital was the earliest free form of capital itself" and also due to the fact that "it had produced sweeping impact in the earliest period of feudal production transformation, that is, the germination phase of modern production."[59] However, they failed to unravel the secret of how commodities brought about extra money after being sold in the field of circulation, and erroneously believed that it was "assigned profit" arising from buying low and selling high. Hence, proceeding from

---

[59] *Karl Marx and Frederick Engels*, vol. 25, p. 376.

that phenomenon, what they concluded was that the process of circulation was the source of wealth generation. At the same time, Ma Jianzhong attached great importance to circulation, especially foreign trade, while he valued production mainly from the perspective of foreign trade to serve the purpose of "retaining wealth not scattered".

Early mercantilists attempted to keep gold and silver in the country, and proposed to regulate gold and silver exports, while later-period mercantilists held the opposite view, and did not propose restricting gold and silver export; in their eyes, so long as export exceeded import in foreign trade, national wealth growth could be guaranteed. The views of Ma Jianzhong were close to later-period mercantilists. He did not propose prohibiting silver exports for the purpose of stemming outflow; he only proposed to reduce imports and increase exports in order to attain balance and surplus in international trade.

Of course, the mercantilist views of Ma Jianzhong were somewhat different from those of the mercantilist in terms of specific content and characteristics. Mercantilism was an economic theory for the period leading to modern capitalism; it served the purpose of primitive capital accumulation in cooperation with colonialism, featuring aggressiveness and expansionism. While Ma Jianzhong lived in a semi-colonial and semi-feudal China, the national bourgeois were newly born at the time; the mounting pressure of the feudal forces and oppressive repression of foreign colonists made them extremely weak and they could barely gain a foothold. National capitalists were stuck in a complex situation, being competitively weak on the international market, while having to guard against capital flight and the occurrence of economic crisis, striving to win the protection and support of the country to ward off the powerful invasion of Western powers on Chinese market and endeavoring to create a relatively sound environment for development.

The major means of economic aggression by the Western powers was commodity export. Ma Jianzhong was keenly aware of the havoc and profound crisis created by the tremendous trade deficit and silver outflow in the Chinese economy; hence, his mercantilist opinions featured resistance to foreign aggression, denunciation of the Western powers in engaging in economic aggression and a variety of privileges enjoyed thereby in China as well as various discussions of anti-aggression. Mercantilism represented the interest of the commercial capital in the closing period of feudal society in Western Europe. It had been employed by the newly born centralized governments to protect the interests of commercial capital and absolutism regimes, and to advocate protection and intervention in economic life by the state authority. On the contrary, Ma Jianzhong represented the interest of commercial capital which was diametrically opposed to the feudal society in China. Hence, China was both oppressed by its own government and rejected by foreign capital; it had to combat both the Western powers and domestic feudal forces, and was characterized by its fight against feudal bureaucratic monopoly. His views preached economic freedom in economic policy, and opposed government interference, oppression and monopoly by the Self-strengthening Movement proponents.

4.3. *Views on monetary reform*

In order to withstand aggression of foreign banks, reduce or avoid wastage from minting, unify the national monetary system, mint gold coin, issue paper money and adapt to the monetary development trend of the times. He Ruzhang reflected his core views on monetary system reform in a paragraph from the *Memorial Submitted to Li Hongzhang on Reconsidering Navy Establishing Memorial* written in the winter of 1881.

Regarding the ills of the monetary systems at the closing period of the Qing Dynasty, Ma Jianzhong cut straight to the point: "silver bullions are employed as money, however of varying purities and weights."

"What's more, among the big countries in the world, only China and India use silver coins." Monetary systems around the globe had followed the trend of adopting a gold standard, making gold the accepted form of money. "In recent decades, gold has been extensively used across the five continents, and production thereof has been on the increase." "Ever since opening up ports for trade, a tremendous amount of gold and silver has flown out, as all countries around the globe use gold as money, while China uses silver exclusively for money, the mechanism of the checks and balance between the parent and the offspring has been laid waste, and China had been under foreign duress for long."[60]

---

[60]*Remarks — Memorial to Li Hongzhang on Matters Concerning Mining in Mohe.*

On the contrary, the price of silver dropped more when there was more silver available. In international transactions, for instance, foreign trade, debt liquidation, reparations, etc., gold must be used: "converting silver into the pound, wastage increases by the day." When conducting foreign trade, China should "use gold coin proportionally, maintaining the mechanism of checks and balances between the parent and the offspring so that the ill of exorbitantly high or exorbitantly low prices may be eliminated. In this way the wastage made up for could be at least up to 10 million." In other words, under the silver standard, the Qing Dynasty wasted 10 million taels for nothing on this count alone.

Faced with a chaotic, outdated monetary system, Ma Jianzhong expounded his plan of monetary system reform from the following three perspectives:

(a) "Following the practice of Tibet minting silver and coin, the government shall mint silver and coin of various values, all tariffs, taxes, payment transfers shall be made in silver and coin." Tibet silver and coin were already the money of account, being government-minted money with a fixed form, weight and purity, and were no longer simply money by weight of silver. Going from money by weight to money of account was already progress; as it proceeded from the necessity to verify purity and weighing to minting in accordance with a fixed form, purity and weight and counting by the number of coins, a huge development at that, it was favorable to give play to the function of intermediary exchange through money, favorable to promote commodity production, expansion and development of commodity economy. Further, "production cost of at least two or three million taels could be saved therefrom, and profit from the practice of adulterating copper therein is beyond measure." Using impure silver would definitely bring about a substantial sum of profit arising from such minting activity to the government, and the government would naturally be attracted thereto. The problem was "now that silver and coin are to be minted by the national treasury, it would be out of necessity to have them minted in the same weight, and the people would be willing to use such." This was the other aspect of the same problem; the government might not have scrapped the rule of uniformity for the sake of some meagre advantage, and people would loathe to accept or use minted silver coin of inferior make. The end result would have inevitably run counter to the purpose and the future of the monetary system reform would have been forfeited for the sake of a small advantage.

(b) Against the backdrop of silver coin being readily accepted by the people, paper money, substitution of silver coin, could then be issued: "the government may produce paper money to substitute it; paper money of sixty million may be produced on the repository reserve silver of about forty million. The paper moneys of the UK and France are circulated around the world without promotion." So long as silver coin enjoyed repute among the people, paper money could be issued in the ratio of three units of paper money against two units of silver coin reserve, and such paper money would be able to circulate around the world like the paper moneys of the UK and France.

"If paper money is circulated in this manner, profit in the amount of scores of million could be obtained." As he noted in *Memorial Submitted to Li Hongzhang on Overseas Studies*, "There is a limit to the resources of gold and silver, while the use thereof is boundless. Substituting coin with paper money, restraining such with faith, and a *qian* could beget the use of hundreds of *qians*." Actually, the history of paper money issuance in China was sufficient to demonstrate the reason, so why bother invoking the Western practice for reference; this was exactly the proof of modeling after the West.

(c) China should proportionally employ gold coin in circulation. As stated above, on the condition of engaging in commerce with Western countries, and in considering that the world had instituted a gold standard or gold and silver dual-standard system, only a couple of countries including China still adhered to the silver standard. In conversion between national currency and foreign currency, wastage and loss of tremendous amount were incurred, and China definitely had to "employ gold coin in circulation proportionally"; that is, it should not stay out of the global trend, but keep itself abreast of the trend of development in standard system, while maintaining "checks and balance between the parent and the offspring, eliminating the ills of exorbitantly high and exorbitantly low prices", making up for the wastage loss in an unobtrusive manner. Of course the issue tolerated no delay, nor did it permit any bigoted course, nor should it have been cursorily conducted or allowed to take its own course.

Ma pointed out not without concern, "however, people do not trust the story because the peril has not been exposed. When people are at the end of their resources, there would definitely be someone who would rise to take to arms." He expected that the government may adapt itself to and avail itself of the trend of the times, take hold of the shift of destiny and implement laws for the revitalization of the country, disseminating and implementing with utmost care. If such was the case, then there would certainly have been no concern that the gains may be outweighed by the effort; over the period of a few years, the poor could have been transformed into the rich, and it goes without saying that when the people are rich the country would necessarily be powerful.

4.4. *Theory of foreign debts*

Ma Jianzhong was the first to systematically discuss raising foreign debt for the purpose of bringing the country to prosperity and strength. He disseminated debt theories of the West. He held that "debt is what regulates the surplus and the deficit, connects the have and the have-not, holds a position as important as the mechanism of market."[61] It was something out of unalterable principles and an extremely regular matter. Private debts, national debts and market transactions were equally important and indispensable. This interpretation did not treat debt raising as a havoc-wreaking issue, nor did he dismiss it as an ill without merit, instead he assessed it in a lauding tone and on the positive stance of developing a macro commodity economy. "Almost all the Western countries are billions-deep in debt, while the UK, France, Germany and Russia still remain as powerful as ever."[62] Raising debt did not hinder the Western powers from rising to prominence in the world; it was naturally not something bad. These countries developed at an abnormally fast pace, and the secret of "the ever refreshing development of railway, machine factory, telegraph and the like of the European countries and the United States" lay in the fact that "loans are exclusively made for

---

[61] *Remarks — Theory of Raising Debt to Build Rail.*
[62] *Remarks — On Railway.*

frequent large payments."[63] This insight was uniquely different from that in China where traditional views and practices were deeply rooted; it was really refreshing for his readers.

The purpose of raising debt determined its success: "debt raising will benefit the country when properly handled, otherwise harm will be brought about thereby." "Before the loan is advanced, the borrower is required to explain to the lender the cause for such loan."[64] There had to be a rigorous and scientific feasibility study and implementation plan for the effect of debt use, whether it was beneficial or detrimental, whether the country benefited or sustained loss therefrom. Ma believed that starting new-style enterprises belonged to the former category, while military expenditure the latter; that is to say, a distinction was made between production and non-production, as the two brought about different economic benefits to the creditors and would have dramatically different outcomes regarding their willingness to subscribe.

It would be beneficial for the country to raise debt to build roads, reclaim mountains, and dredge rivers. The situation thereof is fundamentally different from that of raising debt for the purpose of funding the military. Hence people all scramble to subscribe, subscription comes unsolicited as clouds gather, because people count on the fact that repayments of the both the principal and the interest are secured." Raising debt for productive public utility was fundamentally different from that for the military and war.

Raising debt for production was opening up a new source of income for the country, which became a new means of subsistence for the people; the principal and the interest could both be repaid in installments. Such debts were solvent, and there was no reason why people would not rush to purchase. In order to demonstrate this issue, he examined the historical evolution of debt in Western European countries. The earliest form was "individual lending to individuals", with national debts coming into being after the Persian Empire invaded Greece, that is, "debt lent by the people to the country". After the Qianlong and Jiaqing reigns, the form of debt of "country lending to country" and "a country borrowing from the people of

---

[63]*Remarks — Theory of Raising Debt to Build Rail.*
[64]*Three Records from Eastward Trip.*

another country" appeared. During the reigns of the Xianfeng and Tongzhi Emperors, debt was beginning to be employed in productive investment, expanding productive scale and introducing new production capacity, which led to radical progress of new technology and new production capacity.

Ma forcefully proposed to raise debt for the development of national capitalist industry and commerce. He did not endorse raising debt by the Qing government, but proposed that debt should be raised by the people on the market of Western countries according to international business practices, and the government should furnish guarantee thereto. He believed that China "may employ the capital of foreigners to attain the livelihood of Chinese, to obtain ever-growing benefit and to repay a diminishing interest".[65] Within a few years the objective would be reached: "transforming the poor into the rich, the people would be wealthy and the country self-reliant."[66] Transforming the backward situation of China over a short period of time since it lagged in development for so long by availing itself of foreign finances was a dream modern patriotists had struggled for their entire lives. However, when the proposal of raising foreign debt was published, the people wondered why debt should not be raised domestically: "raise fund from national treasury"; "raise fund from the people". Why should foreign debt be raised? His reply was that "nine out of ten houses in China were financially depleted, even the national treasury was battered out of shape, and even if there are a couple of houses of solid means, it is after all a cause winning little enthusiasm."[67] For one, there was no such extra financial strength for the treasury and the people to purchase bonds, and even if there were a few investors, these could hardly make any difference. For another, the traditional mentality and legal system were unfavorable to bond issuance. The traditional Chinese mentality was that there should be neither domestic debt nor foreign debt; Chinese were wont to the mentality "the likes of debt raising activity harms the national dignity."[68]

---

[65]*Remarks — On Railway.*
[66]*Remarks — On Wealth of the People.*
[67]*Remarks — On Railway.*
[68]*Ibid.*

Legally speaking, when there was no serious and complete legal remedy for the solution of dispute of rights and interests between the creditor and the debtor, it would be difficult to raise either domestic or foreign debt. These two issues, especially the second one was unavoidable and had to be settled, otherwise it would not only hinder domestic investment but also dampen enthusiasm of foreign investors.

Erecting Projects with Raised Debt: The issue Ma was most concerned about was the railway. He affirmed that "nothing could work better in terms of bringing prosperity and strength to China."[69] Favorable conditions for China to build railways included the time of the situation, terrain, iron ore mines and manpower; what was lacking was funding alone. "Now that China is deliberating building a railway, the topmost issue goes to raising fund, shall the fund be raised from the government while the treasury has already been hard up for a variety of expenses, or shall the fund be raised from the people while such practice is unheard of and very difficult to carry out? There is no other way but to raise foreign debt."

As for specific measures on introducing foreign capital, Ma stayed very vigilant of foreign capital aggression and economic infiltration, and he was specifically opposed to enrolling foreign businessmen in stockholding. He learned from the lessons of foreign businessmen subscribing stock that raising foreign debt was different from accepting stock subscription of foreign businessmen. The first difference was that stock subscription could bring annual dividends, while raising a debt entailed only annual interest. The second was that "when China builds railways traversing the interior land of the country, how could foreign businessmen be allowed to subscribe to the core interest of the country?" Wasn't it an act of inviting the wolf into your house and handing your weak point over to the adversary? The purpose of erecting a railway system was to bring benefit to the people: "what's the point of bringing harm to the country?" He also cited the examples of Turkey's railway, the Suez Canal and the Panama Canal to demonstrate that "no foreign subscription may be enlisted in railway stock."

Principles of Debt Raising: Ma believed that three principles in "the way of debt raising" should be followed if debt raising was to be con-

---

[69]*Ibid.*

ducted successfully, that is, "collateral on which repayment is grounded", "methodology in raising debt" and "a term of repayment in place"; he believed that "it depends on the person for the debt to be made".

"Collateral on which repayment is grounded": This was the basic condition for debt raising. "One must have something to count on when taking out a loan from others." The collateral for a loan was not to be based exclusively on the size of wealth of the country; when weighing the difficulty of taking out a loan, a treasury minister may not count only on the balance of government revenue, just like a merchant prince may not count exclusively on his savings, a rich man his land and property, the state its revenue. If loans were to be taken out to make up for military expenditure, and there would be no collateral for such cause, no interest could be repaid, the enthusiasm of the creditors would be dampened and the government would have to increase interest rates to attract buyers. However, if loans were taken out for expanding financial resources, such bonds would have collateral for security and interest for repayment; hence, bonds issued for establishing railways had always been thriving, be it in the Western powers, such as the UK, France, the United States, Austria and Italy, or the enervated countries, such as Peru and Tunisia. "People scramble for purchase without solicitation as though clouds gather and fog closes in." This was sufficient to demonstrate that the success of a debt-raising project was determined by the purpose instead of something else. Ma repeatedly emphasized that "in a world where the monarch and the people are in one, debt may not be raised for military purposes, and cannot help but be for commercial purposes."[70]

"Methodology in taking out a loan": It could be seen that from comparison of the history of loan raising and different modes of loan raising, prior to the Jiaqing reign, the Western countries "were troubled by the petty amount available from the people and difficulty to gather at short notice when a loan was raised from the ordinary people; and it was thought that the wealthy would be exorbitantly demanding when a loan was raised from the wealthy." Supply of funds was limited when a loan was to be taken out from the bank.

---

[70] *Remarks — On Wealth of the People.*

Hence, those who were good at raising debt "would engage the bank, befriend the wealthy, and then debt may be instantly raised when urgent need arises; otherwise, there would be little chance that they would not be extorted." In practice, the first and biggest threat arising from raising foreign debt to build railways lay in embezzlement by the handling individual; therefore, such debt must "be handled on our own." This was a practice exercised by both the UK and France; the government officials of each country would meet officials from the government and private banks in the capitals of the UK and France in person to prevent extortion by foreign banks: "interest rate and price shall be fixed by us to eliminate manipulation by the handling bank." The second was to raise funds directly in foreign countries, that is, "purchasing foreign products with foreign silver directly, ridding of the cost of conversion and the concern of monopoly." In this way, the conversion loss could be eliminated when Chinese loans were repaid and transferred abroad, and China may break free from the control of foreign banks. The third was that the materials purchased with commercial credit should be appropriated in annual installments upon completion thereof; this may reduce the amount of loan required and reduce wastage. What was to be guarded against was only "that they might jack up the value, or pretend to handle it in our interest, borrowing silver and repaying silver would be far more direct and convenient." The key lay in requiring the handling party "to show understanding and treat the matter discretionarily, accommodate the situation as the case may be and seek the optimal strategy coping with the situation." The fourth was that no customs duty should be set out as collateral to win the faith of foreigners. According to the practices of European countries and the United States, loan for railways could be taken out so long as "a well-trained supervisor conducts meticulous inspection and assessment, credit could be gained by producing such inspection and assessment report to the foreign countries." The fifth was that the specific practices of the West may be imitated because they had unregistered bonds with numbers marked thereon only; once the railways recorded gains, bonds could be then recalled gradually in batches to prevent foreigners from reaping too much profit from the Chinese railway.

"Term of repayment in place": This was different from the previous two principles; it absolutely allowed no arbitrary interpretation and accommodation. A repayment plan was fixed before the loan was made; that is, "a scheme of repayment is to be worked out in advance". A repayment method for commercial credit was apportioned either to the principal and interest or to liquidating the bonds by lot-drawing.

Bonds Issuance: In Ma's opinion, a small-scope trial could be conducted as the first step, for instance, a railway from Tianjin to Beijing as a pilot project. There were three advantages in this plan: it could furnish a practical instance for domestic market, gain publicity and make its name on the foreign financial market.

Before the Sino-Japanese War of 1894–1895, Western powers forced their investment in China through privileges, which seriously hindered the development of China's economy. Ma Jianzhong devised a complete set of ideas, from motioning to raise foreign debt to drafting principles for debt raising and measures of debt raising as well as procedures of implementation. He executed his promises, stating, "building railway with raised debt is an innovative measure, if the Western practices are not imitated and modified, how could perfection and an ill-free scheme be attained!"

Ma was both forceful in proposing to raise foreign debt for building railways and resolute in safeguarding the state sovereignty and national interest. He proposed to "take hold of the shift of destiny and revitalize the country," refusing to sit on the golden opportunity, while at the same time having to cope with the force of habit and resistance from the government; he had to find a way to win the trust and support of foreigners, and at the same time guard against manipulation by them. In order to seek a way to accumulate wealth and strength for the country, he engaged in active planning and repeated demonstrations, which adequately indicated his familiarity with modern Western financial market theory and practical knowledge as well as passionate patriotism. In 1886, he had made a suggestion to Liu Mingchuan, the governor of Taiwan, to establish a bank for the purpose of developing Taiwan;[71] however, he received no response and the proposal failed to materialize. In the following year, when he suggested to Li Hongzhang to take out a loan to implement new government causes, his first suggestion was to set up banks. The purpose of "raising debt to erect profitable projects" was to satisfy the capital need for developing modern

---

[71]Huang Yiping, *Economic Changes in Modern China*, p. 427.

enterprises and growing modern China's economy. The precondition for development was naturally the reformation of the domestic financial system and establishment of shareholding joint venture banks. However, many of his ideas were out of touch with reality; he especially failed to see the true nature of the Western powers and the nature of modern China, cherishing unrealistic illusions and a confounded understanding. He strove to win the support of the government domestically, expecting the government to furnish guarantee for a debt-raising scheme; internationally, he strove to utilize foreign debt on equal and reasonable terms. From there, he further pinned his hope of revitalizing China on building the railway and commerce, attempting to lay the foundation of China's path to "prosperity and strength" on foreign debt. How could these not run up against a stone wall!

5. Chen Chi's financial theory

Chen Chi (1855–1900), former name Jiayao, courtesy name Kechang, was born in Ruijin of Jiangxi. He was one of the representative figures of modern Chinese reformists. He passed the imperial examinations in the Guangxu reign, and was appointed to positions including department chief, director, councilor of the ministry of revenue, secretary to minster of punishment, and secretary to the grand minister. Since coming of age and starting his teaching career, he was observant of current affairs and dedicated to finding a path to prosperity and strength for China, absorbing modern Western thought and culture eagerly. He extensively read Chinese translations of Western works, visited coastal ports in person, especially Hong Kong and Macao under colonist rule, and inspected "the ills and strength of the world". In 1893–1894, prior to the breaking up of the Sino-Japanese War of 1894–1895, he wrote the *Book of the Mean*, proposing the implementation of measures to bring prosperity to the country, revitalize commerce and withstand economic aggression by the Western powers; he initiated the organization of society to strengthen China together with Kang Youwei, Liang Qichao and others.

In 1896, in order to save China from its enervated situation, he published *Measures of Enriching China Revisited*, a book containing 64 items (including agriculture, forestry, animal husbandry, fisheries, water conservancy, industry and trade, weapons, mining, lighting, water supply, business, banking, currency, insurance, etc.), which proposed imitating Western economic practices. He was a very active forerunner in thought in the Hundred Days' Reform movement, and his works are currently available in *Collection of Works by Chen Chi* compiled by a present-day individual.

Chen Chi's financial views were mainly embodied in the Monetary Law, the Jiaochao Paper Money, appendages to the *Book of the Mean*, and Theory of Sifting Sand for Gold from *Measures of Enriching China Revisited*. Like Zheng Guanying, he also upheld the banner of patriotism and nationalism, absorbed advanced Western financial knowledge and set special store by minting coins and the function of bank. There were both merits and demerits, and the succession of old and new elements in his theory. However, in his emphatic demonstration of the necessity of establishing banks and urgency for reforming the monetary system, there were also partial and out of place areas in his argument, which was typical of reformists' writing.

5.1. *Monetary theory*

Among the reformists, Chen Chi's exposition on money was pretty voluminous. He proposed to mint metal coins and implement a system of three categories, mixed with a complete system of monetary reform. In the demonstration, he proposed his own monetary theory, the gist of which was as follows: "minting our own metal money as the foundation, mixing it with paper money to facilitate circulation, and minting a great amount of silver coin and copper coin to broaden its circulation"; "retaining the right is like grabbing the core link"; "it would be impossible for it to remain not rich and not powerful".[72] In short, "economic right shall be retrieved by issuing paper money and minting metal money".[73] The purpose was to bring prosperity and powerful military prowess to the

---

[72] *Memorial of Itemized Exposition of Minting Silver*, submitted on 1895.
[73] *On Establishing Banks*.

country in order to fend off the economic aggression by the Western powers.

He poignantly pointed out that, since the closing period of the 19th century, the Qing Dynasty had lifted the ban on trading with the West, which resulted in the economic phenomenon of rocketing gold and copper coin prices against plummeting silver price. Rocketing gold price was because "they lured us to trade our gold with their surplus goods, which led to tripling of gold price and depletion of our gold". Rocketing copper coin price was due to "the situation where copper coin is traded for with silver, after repeated cycles of transactions, the amount of standard copper coin is dwindling, while the price thereof is rising, hence comes copper coin depletion".[74] Plummeting silver price was "due to excessive supply of silver. Then, why is there a surplus of silver in China? The answer is, over twenty million taels of silver have been shipped into China from the European and Asian countries annually".[75] "Silver has been shipped in annually, and silver has been employed to trade away our commodities and gold, hence the prices of China's gold and commodity rise by the day, while silver price drops by the day".[76] When there is excessive silver, circulation would be made inconvenient: "if silver coin is not minted, there would be a variety of ills, including inconvenience for use, varying values and purities, defrauding the people, and ailing the country; the most convenience this situation brings about is that wily and corrupt officials could extort and pillage the people".[77]

The gold standard system was universally adopted across the globe, with Great Britain being the first to adopt it in 1864, with only China and India still adhering to silver standard at that time. On the trend of rising gold price against dropping silver price in China, there were four ills to the people's livelihood and the national interest. The ills to the people's livelihood were that it impoverished the rich of China; "as the treasure of a country", the Western powers did not place a price limit when purchasing gold, while wealthy Chinese merchants and powerful people scrambled

---

[74] *On Mining and Banning Copper.*
[75] *On Minting Copper Coin Benchmarked against Silver.*
[76] *On Universally Accepted Pound.*
[77] *On Mining and Banning Copper.*

to sell their gold hoard. Hence, "there is no more gold holding in Chinese, suppose any unexpected event occurs, how could we fend it off?" This was the first ill. The second ill was that it impoverished the poor of China. When the prices of daily necessities rose, "nothing remains affordable, the poor goes starving". The third ill was that it corrupted the government officials. Hence, "corrupt officials run rampant, even capital punishment could not deter them." The fourth was that it uprooted the livelihood of the Chinese people. The situation of rising gold price and plummeting silver price seriously threatened the livelihood of the people, and even resulted in the impoverishment of the entire nation; the national treasury was depleted, the regime got corroded and disintegrated, and the society was undermined in its foundation and collapsed. The other four ills were that the Western powers incurred huge conversion loss to China through the price spread between gold and silver, and hence could manipulate China's financial market, control the economic livelihood of China and hold in their hands the destiny of China.

Analysis of the critical situation by Chen Chi: Chen Chi's first point was that with regard to loss sustained in national debts, when the repayment date of national debts neared, the pound would inevitably appreciate, and the loss would amount to over 20% or 30%. As to the expenditure for coastal defense, "all must be purchased with pound that means we sustain losses from each and all of these purchases." The second point was that it harmed commerce. As commerce had to be conducted by converting pounds into silver, silver was cheap and the pound expensive: "all Chinese remittance firms, private banks, pawnshops count on foreign businessmen for living, it is easy to trade pound for silver, but difficult to trade silver for pound." The third was that it harmed the bank. When a Chinese bank was established, if it conducted business with foreign firms, "it will definitely sustain a loss in either buying or selling pound, the situation is similar to that of national debts." The fourth was that the livelihood and financial market were all held in the hands of others. "Now that China opens up gold mines, and does not ban shipping gold overseas, the practice amounts to handing the enemy a sharp weapon."[78] He believed that national debt alone would "incur billions of implicit loss from pound conversion, which obvi-

---

[78] *Memorial of Itemized Exposition of Minting Silver.*

ously ails China." This was definitely a serious warning, calling out the economic loss incurred by China from pound conversion. It was simply too great and too grave a threat politically to go unnoticed by the people in general and the government. However, his ideas were also suggestive of glossing over by the government, making plummeting silver price a scapegoat for the corruption and incompetence of the Qing Dynasty, which was inconducive to monetary system reform and revitalizing of China.

Theoretical grounds for the foregoing analysis: In Chen Chi's opinion, "the more valuable could move the less valuable, and the heavier could move the less heavy, while it is definitely impossible for the lighter to move the heavier and the less valuable to move the more valuable; this is an established law of nature. Even the sage coming back to life could do little to the law." The so-called more valuable and less valuable, or heavy and less heavy, referred to the domestic monetary materials: "without the three categories being all balanced, they will not live up to the requirements for the use by the people". With respect to the material money was made of, internationally, foreign countries employed gold, while China employed silver: "the material employed abroad is more valuable than that employed by China, and heavier than that in China, it is inevitable for China to be controlled." Otherwise, if "ours is more valuable and heavier than that of foreigners, we could definitely be able to control others." He predicted that such a situation would be very difficult to bring about, and hence proposed that "if theirs are valuable and heavier, ours should be valuable and heavier too, though there is no way for us to control others, we could at least stand on our own feet."[79]

However, well-meaning wishes could not ultimately replace the scientific significance of theory. The first reason was that the economy, finances and commodity prices of China were under the control and manipulation of Western powers, which definitely could not be turned around by monetary system reform. Against the backdrop of a corrupt and incompetent Qing government, the Western powers stepped up their political, economic, military and cultural aggression, and engaged in "all military, political, economic and culture oppressive means to step by step reduce China to a semi-colonial country and finally a colony." The process

---

[79]*Ibid.*

whereby they controlled China's market was one wherein they fully utilized the inexpensiveness of machined products and transformation in shipping and transportation as powerful weapons, and one wherein they dumped cheaply made commodities, took up China's market, made loans, issued paper money, opened up banks and monopolized China's finances and financial market: "hence, they not only crushed the national capitalism of China, but clutched the throat of China in the areas of financial market and finances."[80] He imputed all the ills to the outdatedness of the monetary systems. At the same time, he exaggerated the function of the gold coin, attributing Great Britain's domination and reigning supreme over the world to their use of gold coins, even ridiculously hinting that such a situation was "implicitly coinciding with the law of Prince Zhougong" to pacify his imbalanced mentality. "When the way of balance between the valuable and the less valuable, the heavy and the less heavy is abided by, one may dominate the world and enjoy exclusive economic rights. The various countries sustain implicit losses thereby, they could not but seek independence of their own."[81] Based thereon, he believed that "the strength of the country, the prosperity of politics, the wealth of the people" hinged on monetary systems. Hence, the enervated state of China "originated in the ills in monetary system when the root cause is traced down; if the ill is to be treated when the proper symptom is diagnosed, then the ill of the monetary system could be rectified with one solution."[82] The ensuing monetary system reform conducted by the Kuomintang Government spoke volumes on this issue, which exactly exposed the weakness and shortsightedness of Chinese capitalist reformists in politics.

The second reason was that the choice of monetary material depended on the level of commodity economy development of the market of a country that was restrained by the level of commercialization and the volume of commodity transactions, determined by the demand for the amount of commodity value to be represented in money and to be realized. The exchange process would ultimately decide on a commodity value

---

[80] *Selected Works of Mao Zedong*, Pocket Edition, Bound Volume, The People's Press, 1967, pp. 591–592.
[81] *Memorial of Itemized Exposition of Minting Silver.*
[82] *On Mining and Banning Copper.*

entity to assume the role of monetary material appropriate for the frequency of commodity exchange and quantity of transaction. This was not to be determined by any sage or great king. In the *Poverty of Philosophy*, Marx made caustic remarks on Pierre-Joseph Proudhon who had made a similar mistake; he wrote, "Thus, the whim of sovereigns is for M. Proudhon the highest reason in political economy." "In his view, the entity which endowed value to money was monarchs instead of trade." Marx expounded a key principle in materialism, "Truly, one must be destitute of all historical knowledge not to know that it is the sovereigns who in all ages have been subject to economic conditions, but they have never dictated laws to them."[83] This worked equally well with Chen Chi.

The third reason was that gold outflow and pound conversion loss were directly affected by the huge foreign trade deficit, the non-autonomous situation of foreign exchange management and customs administration. Based on the foregoing situation where the Western powers controlled the economic livelihood of China, it would be impossible for China to achieve balance in international trade or even trade surplus without the independence and strengthening of China's foreign exchange management and customs administration. Chen Chi got down to the crux of the issue of gold outflow and pound conversion loss; however, he failed to offer an accurate answer to the root cause of the issue, and hence was unable to provide a correct solution to the problem.

Based on this, he was convinced that "their moneys are all expensive, while our money is cheap, isn't that due to the fact that they are rich and we are poor!" The reason the Western powers used gold coin in circulation was that they were productively advanced and their transaction volume surged; hence, they had to use a precious metal of greater value as their unit of account, which naturally indicated the great wealth of these countries; on the contrary, China's productivity stagnated over a long period, and their transaction volume underwent little change, so the baser metal silver would suffice, which naturally indicated that China was poor. "Their products are all cheap, while our products are all expensive, is the situation due to the fact that they have unobstructed circulation while ours is obstructed?" The Western powers mass manufactured cheap products

---

[83] *Karl Marx and Frederick Engels*, vol. 4, pp. 121–124.

with their advanced machines and equipment, dumped them on the Chinese market, occupied the market and pillaged the wealth and materials of China, which was an extremely unreasonable international division of labor and abnormal international order. "They are rich and we are poor, we have to look up to them for living, and China has produced no wealthy businessmen. They have unobstructed circulation while China has a stagnant one, which brings them great profit daily and which created a situation where petty Chinese businessmen would not be able to exist in China." "Once economic right is bestowed to others, then poverty and hardship will ensue and we would have to toil for life."[84] This misfortune was beckoning China. Wouldn't that alert every Chinese with a patriotic conscience?

In the eyes of Chen Chi, monetary system reform was an extremely urgent matter, tolerating no delay. His guiding principle for monetary system reform was that "it is not necessary for the countries to follow the practice of the UK, however none could afford to not model after the practice of minted coin of the UK." Specifically, the measures to be taken included reclaiming economic right, revitalizing business and minting gold money, the weight of which was to be after that of the pound; three categories of money were to be established and proportional paper money used, that is, "laying down the foundation with domestically minted gold money, mixing such with proportional paper money to facilitate circulation, minting silver coin extensively and copper coin to widen its use." The domains of circulation for the three categories of money were different, and hence the level of their circulation would also be different. The reason was to "fend off foreigners", and use silver coin for "pacifying the people"; when the two were compared, minting gold coin would be in the first place: "weighed in terms of valuableness and heaviness as well as the current state of the situation, then minting silver coin is still less urgent than minting gold coin to make up for the urgent need." Copper coin could "be used to move small articles, the odds and fractional, which is of great benefit to the livelihood of the people."[85] Paper money circulation would "benefit both the government and the

---

[84]*On Universally Accepted Pound.*
[85]*Memorial of Itemized Exposition of Minting Silver.*

people", which stands in a "complementary relation to the three categories of coins, and may remain viable."[86] A gold coin equals 10 silver coins (converting to seven taels of pure silver), and 10 thousand copper coins. When the conversion rate was fixed, "it does not fluctuate as the foreign exchange market moves up and down, nor does it follow the movement of the market price; the three categories of coins are mutually balanced, China exercises the law of China, by this way the foundation of the country may be strengthened."[87] Actually, this was nothing but a beautiful dream, which could not be realized in the least. The first reason was that though the statutory conversion rate could be held unchanged under the state authority, the market conversion rate could not be held unchanged. The second reason was that the three categories of coins were mutually balanced, and it could be considered as gold, silver and copper assuming the role of primary money simultaneously, but there was no such relation as the primary and the fractional between them. He specifically emphasized that "the three are the most convenient thing in the country, it is due to the fact that the valuableness and heaviness thereof are appropriate for its weighing and measuring function, which is naturally the unswerving way." This is similar to the situation of bimetallism in modern monetary systems; only an additional primary money was introduced which made the conversion rate of currency value more complicated and out of date. On the condition that the three categories of coins were simultaneously employed, the law of good money being driven out by bad money would come into operation, contrary to the real intent of the architect. Then, how could the foundation of the country be strengthened, the strength, politics of the country be improved, the wealth of the people increased, and the order of society maintained? The third reason was that self-minted gold coin became the focus, because this would be adapting to the great trend of global monetary system development, accommodating to changed times and creating a smooth path to business travel: "even a sage has no way to restrict

---

[86]*Monetary Law*.
[87]*On Mining and Banning Copper*.

such."[88] In his opinion, this could not only eliminate four ills but also bring about four advantages.

Eliminating four ills referred to the situation where there was no outflow of national treasure, there were sufficient resources for the people, there was no corruption among officials and the moneyless China suddenly transformed into a moneyed China. The four advantages were "ceasing converting silver to pound to avoid implicit loss, eliminating losses from the currency exchange when buying and selling pounds, and getting the foreigner's money by selling them Chinese products, thus improving people's lives and building up the national strength." These statements were rather biased. The first reason was that China did not "produce the most amount of gold, or the least amount of silver in the world," nor could it be said that the sole reason why the Western powers split China and demarcated their sphere of influence was to take hold or pillage China of its gold. Actually, the Western powers aimed to obtain privilege for buying low and selling high, including non-productive opium trade in China. The second reason was whether the entire economic right of the world would come to China if China tried to mint gold and gold coin at the earliest opportunity possible; the issue was definitely not that simple. The third reason was if the price criteria of China's money should follow that of the pound closely. Actually the price level of the money of the various countries embodied the productivity and the level of the commodity economy's development; pegging China's currency to that of foreign countries would amount to premature human intervention and be harmful to China's commodity economy development and the money relation thereof. Besides, under the condition of metal money circulation, global money was actually commodity money stripped of its national uniform — the entity proper of metal. The fourth reason was that China was an ancient civilization, which usually shaped the mentality of its people to one of admiration for the past glory of the country. The ultimate purpose of monetary system reform proposed by Chen Chi was to effect a situation "where all their money will be our money", which was nothing but a typical statement of this ignorance.

Chen Chi also analyzed issues such as the inevitability and principles of issuing paper money and the issuing management. Regarding the

---

[88] *Monetary Law*.

former, he advanced that for one it was convenient to carry: "Having currency circulated around the country, obnoxious cost of shipment could be entirely eliminated." For another, it could increase the currency circulation volume, and satisfy the need for commodity circulation and national finances: "in terms of fiscal revenue, for a fiscal revenue of 10 million, paper money in the amount of 10 million can be produced, when such is circulated among the people, the principal and the paper money are equal, there will be no abusive ills any more. While silver and paper money are circulated side by side, the use of twenty million taels could be obtained therefrom." His proposal of issuing 10 million was not based on the commodity circulation need for metal money, nor based on gold and silver as issuance reserve, but on the fiscal need of the government, suggesting issuance in the ratio of 1:1 between the reserve and paper money issuance. Hence, paper money issuance was still a measure affiliated to serving the finances, instead of serving commodity circulation, which was naturally wrong. He proposed two principles for paper money issuance. The first one was that "with creditability it works, without creditability it does not work." The second was that "it works with reserve for paper money set aside, and does not work without reserve set aside."[89] As mentioned above, the so-called issuance reserve was based on "annual revenue", and such a principle was as illusory as a castle built on sand and as perilous as piling eggs. On the latter issue of organization and management of paper money issuance, Chen Chi advanced his conceptions from the following five perspectives:

(a) "Laws governing officials' appointment": Chen Chi believed that the ministry of revenue should set up a separate department in charge of paper money and a special minister should be designated to preside over the issue; the paper money administrative office was to be set up in the various provinces and ports. The issuing method for paper money was to be made with reference to remittance firms and banks, and a relation of the interior and the exterior was to be set up between the commercial administration and the monetary system. (b) "Method of setting aside reserve": The ministry of revenue was to set aside two million taels of silver from

---

[89] *Jianchao Paper Money*.

the total fiscal revenue, in a term of 5 years: "where there is bank run of treasury fund, accommodation shall be made thereto, and prompt repayment is required to settle the account." This was to ensure the integrity of the issuance reserve. (c) "The law of employing paper money": Revenue and expenditure for both the government and the people had to be made in an evenly split proportion of silver and paper money. (d) "The law of retrieving right": remittance firms, bank outlets, and bank branches were "required to pay the paper money administrative department several hundred gold for handling charge annually" as a token of obligation to the government. (e) "The law of enriching the country and facilitating the people": Where the poor could deposit a small sum of savings for interest in accordance with the articles of association of Western banks, "collateral shall be required for appropriation and loan, and a low interest rate shall be charged thereon"; a huge amount of fund could also be raised to alleviate the need of the country: "low interest shall be charged as a token of fairness." His proposal of bank accepting small-sum deposit was pretty insightful.

5.2. Theory on bank

Chen Chi paid special attention to the concept of setting up banks of China's own. He was convinced that the bank was not only a necessary condition for developing production, expanding circulation and conducting commerce but was also a necessary condition for guaranteeing fiscal expenditure and revenue, and raising military expenditure. In consideration of the prominent role played by the bank after the five treaty ports were opened up, he boldly proposed to "set up a bank". He was keenly aware of the fact that "the bank is the genuine source leading to the prosperity of commerce".[90] Since "there is neither a bank in China nor does the government feel any urgent need to establish one, then it would be difficult for the government to raise funds, which would not be an issue for foreign countries, but it would obstruct commerce in China while it

---

[90]*Prologue to Perils of Flourishing Age.*

facilitates commerce in foreign countries."[91] The precondition for setting up a bank should be consistent with the origination of the bank. The bank was originally the product of highly developed commodity economy, especially the credit system. It did not have to follow a certain government need; of course the bank could serve as a channel for fund-raising for the government after it came into being, and would receive redoubled attention from the government. However, there was no reason to hold the opinion that a bank came into being for the purpose of answering the fund-raising need of the government. Chen Chi might have made these statements in order to arouse the enthusiasm of the Qing government in setting up a bank, urging it to render support and attention to the banking cause of China's own. This exactly fitted the characteristics of commercial capital at the closing period of the Qing Dynasty, having close relations with the government in policy promotion, though such a position could hardly stand theoretically.

The first reason Chen Chi held such a high opinion of establishing a bank was that he had absorbed experiences from the setting up of banks by Western countries in the opened up ports of China; he was well aware that the function of banks was to raise and regulate funds and they had the function of "benefiting the commerce and the industry as the real source, bringing practical effect of effecting long distance travel". That is, it was the source for the money capital required by industry and commerce development, and it would bring about the practical effects of expanding communication and developing international trade. It could be ensured that the bank could accumulate funds, accommodate capital surplus and shortage, speed up capital turnover, provide additional capital to expand the scale of production and circulation, and ensure company requirements for supplemental funds; that is to say, he already had some understanding of the intermediary role of credit. Just as he wrote, "the problem that commercial fund could not be accumulated could be rid of by circulation of money." Businessmen with business acumen could grow their businesses to a great scale and become very prosperous; however, they did not require a great amount of funds. The

---

[91] *On Establishing Bank*, No more citations shall be provided for further quotes from this book hereinbelow.

secret was in speeding up capital turnover and accommodation of funds; otherwise, the businessmen would still be equally helpless and lost.

Chen Chi believed that the banks in the Western countries could "circulate their funds and act as the hub of the financial market," functioning as the hub and intermediary in accommodating funds. This was an issue of critical importance. Of course, the functions of the bank analyzed by Chen Chi were conducted in two aspects: the need for replenishing funds in fund circulation and the possibility of fund provision. He still had yet to directly demonstrate the functions of a bank, and his demonstration was only limited to "commerce", failing to touch on the "industry", and only limited to the circulation process while failing to touch on the production process, which reflected the fact that commercial capital was highly developed. However, it should be acknowledged that his exposition on bank functions was accurate and insightful, and he figured prominently among the reformists in the history of modern China.

The second reason was regarding international relations. Against the backdrop that the country had opened up to the world and engaged foreign countries in trade, Chen Chi was convinced that it "would absolutely not do" if no bank was established. Of course, it would still be acceptable if the country could be reverted to the circumstance of blocking itself up; otherwise, "there would not be a single tile left for shelter in case of heavy wind and pouring rain; this would definitely not do." It seemed that the urgency of setting up a bank came from the exterior instead of the interior, in other words, from the threat of economic aggression by Western powers instead of maturity of objective conditions for setting up domestic banks. As institutional economics put it, it was by no means the result of induced institutional change, but rather the result of enforced institutional change; that is, under the oppression of foreign powers, against the general background of survival of the fittest, many an upright Chinese citizen with lofty ideals rose to the occasion. Hence, he demanded that the fund-regulating function of the bank should be put into play, which should accumulate idle money and capital in society to guarantee the tremendous temporary fund requirement in China's international trade and guard against any contingency, providing the people of reduced means with a way of making a living and revitalizing China's commerce. He explained the situation with a telling simile that, compared to the Western powers, China was "actually like an invalid combating a brawny man, how could it stand any chance of winning!" The conclusion was self-evident. This understanding fit the national situation of China at the time well; however, such a disadvantage could by no means be turned around by simply setting up a bank. Before deep-level barriers, such as the independence and development of politics and economy, were tackled, the function of banks in China could hardly be brought to full play, which has been proven by the history of modern Chinese finances. Domestically, he believed that the money shops in the various provinces and draft banks run by Shanxi merchants had already conducted businesses including issuing money note and remittance, which benefited both the government and the people. The purpose of setting up a bank was, "now that commercial relations have spread across the globe, trips covering tens of thousand miles by land or water transportation …. The more vast the area of land, the more populous the people, the more frequent the use of money, the more inconvenient the carriage and use of money." Hence, he proposed that "without prosperous commerce then the country could not be unified, without bank then travel and communication across the country would be inconvenienced." However, he failed to understand the fact that banks of any country were inevitably the product of the highly developed credit system of commodity economy in that country; if the economic conditions and economic needs for setting up banks in that country were not in place, no foreign force whatsoever could drive it to find the inherent ground for setting up a bank of its own and transform such into reality. This was the first point. The second point was that the need for productivity in the Western powers was mainly embodied as the need for industrial capital; however, be it the usury and commercial capital in ancient Chinese society or those in medieval times, these were all commercial capitals of the closing period of feudal society, different from industrial capital. Industrial capital alone was the product of highly developed commodity economy, and hence modern banks corresponding and providing service thereto did not come into being because commerce was conducted or must be set up for that purpose.

Chen Chi's understanding of the main banking businesses was relatively more systematic. He was the first to raise the points that "westerners opened up banks extensively in the various treaty ports, and there are six key businesses in banking." He pointed out the six basic banking businesses, namely, issuing money note, handling remittance, raising fund and soliciting stock subscription, organizing deposit and making loans. Zheng Guanying had made an exposition on these issues, but without such concise terms and brevity. The specific interpretation of Chen Chi was basically accurate. The first business was "issuing money note, draft, stock, deposit, charge, loan." As the bank engaged in honest money note issuance, finely produced paper money won greater credibility and widespread acceptance due to the difficulty of counterfeiting, and the people would use money note instead of silver and deposit money note instead of silver. "The use of twenty million taels could be obtained from 10 million taels." There was flattery in the remarks, and it was biased statement at that. The second was writing drafts: "be it the need for the use of 1,000 or 10,000 taels, a small piece of paper would do the work hands down." With a meagre charge you could "travel around the world without carrying a single coin on you, never has it gone wrong." Safe and convenient, how could it not gain universal welcome? The third was raising stock; so long as there was a bank, "an amount up to millions or tens of millions would be raised instantly as though one already has it on him, once it is called for, responses from all walks of life rush in." He believed that the reason for the prevailing phenomenon that Chinese companies have to raise money from the people was due to the lack of banks. Actually, the reason was the underdeveloped situation of China's commodity production and that the investment awareness corresponding thereto had yet to take shape; when the people had accumulated money, they would either stash it away, purchase real estate, engage in business or lend, and they had neither knowledge nor interest in establishing a factory. The fourth was absorbing deposits of varying durations and amounts. "Current deposit at monthly interest rate of three percent could be withdrawn at any time, term deposit of three months draws a four percentage interest rate, term deposit of five or more months draws a five percentage interest, amount as small as three or five *yuan* could all be deposited." This scheme benefited both the wealthy and especially the poor, and the bank managed the money for the public and raised funds from extensive sources. The fifth was making loan on collaterals. He believed that "pawnshops take articles, while banks take property." The difference between the two was extremely distinctive. Banks could mobilize the stagnant, provide a livelihood and revitalize the commerce. The sixth was credit loan. If the government carried out major investment projects against the backdrop of inflexibility of tax and revenue which could not be increased at no cause, banks could raise national debts and issue bonds on behalf of the government and this "is a source inexhaustible, and of instant success." How could this not be fatally appealing to the financially exhausted Qing government? However, once the government considered banks as an inexhaustible source of revenue, especially when the government was in financial straits, then the establishment of integrity and guarantee of paper money issuance reserve could all be discarded, and credit risk or social crisis would burst into being and haunt the originator of such a scheme.

5.3. Theory on insurance

Insurance was no longer a dispensable item at the time. Water and land transportation each had its respective risks. Chen Chi explained the function of insurance from the general concept thereof. Indeed, the so-called insurance could turn risk into safety, eliminate disaster and prevent risk at a small cost. He noted, "insurance policy is first taken out for goods shipped, later clients consigning the goods would also proceed to take out insurance policy, and vehicles carrying people would also take out insurance policy." "Shipped goods, factories, wealthy businessmen, wealthy houses, government premises, anything privately appreciated but hard to come by could be appraised and insured." This was the first point. The second point was that life insurance fit the traditional Chinese mentality of "sustaining the old and poor", which embodied the great virtue of "self-help, guarding against peril": "it is of the utmost importance to keep things intact". Relatively speaking, Chen Chi believed that "the items that matter especially greatly are maritime, fire and transportation insurances for goods." "Out of everyone that is indemnified, a hundred or thousand do not need indemnification, therefore the insurance company still reaps great profit." Along with the expansion of the scope of insurance, "articles to be covered grow by the day, the profit of insurance expands, and the number of insurance company increases." It would naturally not be an issue for the insurance industry to develop and prosper.

Along with the development and growth of the Self-strengthening Movement, there were already insurance companies which had been incorporated by Chinese businessmen, and the Renjihe insurance company was one among them. The companies covered "maritime risk for the surplus profit." However, in the eyes of Chen Chi, insurance companies incorporated by China on its own fell far behind the need of the circumstances, as a great many insurance businesses were controlled by foreigners, and the benefits were "reaped exclusively thereby".

Chen Chi paid special attention to the insurance gap in the textile industry. Having conducted in-depth investigation and analysis, he concluded that life insurance was in great demand. This situation greatly affected the nationalization of the textile industry. The second issue was an additional export tax was required to be made on top of the customs duty. When Chinese businessmen purchased scores of thousand bales of imported cotton, they were required to take out an insurance policy, and they were still required to take out an insurance policy for purchasing imported yarn, which was as much as "five percent on top of cost, literally an additional export tax paid to foreigners in the customs." The third issue was that foreigners exclusively reaped the benefit from price fluctuation.

So, why could China not conduct insurance in the textile industry and set up insurance companies of its own? Chen Chi believed that there was distrust between the government and the businessman in China, and between the businessmen, few could think outside the box. In his opinion, if the government really intended to set up a bureau of commerce administration, set up insurance companies and exclusively take the insurance premium of Chinese businessmen, they had to "conduct businesses in sincerity and frankness, conduct concerted effort, insure the property of the people, and reap the profit from the various ports; in terms of insurance alone, the strength of Chinese businessmen would develop into grand scale, and the overall situation of China would be revitalized." He ultimately pinned the prospect of learning from the West on the corrupt and rigid Qing government, which was doomed to failure. On the condition that no regime shuffle occurred, it was perfectly normal that his expected objective failed through such a weak reform.

6. Zheng Guanying's financial theory

Zheng Guanying (1842–1921), former name Guanying, courtesy name Zhengxiang, style Taozhai, was born in Xiangshan (present-day Zhongshan). He was a successful comprador, a businessman participating in the government-run Self-strengthening Movement, a government representative, a leading figure of the capitalist movement, a thinker and a political theorist in early phase of modern China. He lived in Macao in his early years, traveled throughout Southeast Asia and received a Western education. He gave up on gaining a social station through the imperial examinations: "at first I learned trade from foreigners, and later engaged in commercial war with foreigners, hoping to retrieve economic right and stem up interest outflow" (*Collection of Works* by Zheng Guanying, Second volume, p. 620). In the years after 1861, he worked in two main British companies, Dent & Co. (ceased operation in 1868) and Swire Shipping, as a comprador. In this period, he also conducted business of his own and invested in enterprises. He was appointed as general manager of the Shanghai Telegraph Company (1881), assistant manager and later general manager of the Shanghai Textile Company and deputy manager of the China Merchants Steamship Navigation Company (1882) by Li Hongzhang and Sheng Xuanhuai successively. He also assisted in the management of Changjiang Electric Wire (1883). He assumed these senior posts in the dual capacity of business representative and commercial operator under government supervision. He did not take part in politics and assumed no government role as this would "be overstepping my place and soliciting reproach"; however, he was an active thinker and debater. He supported constitutional reform and participated in the preparatory constitutional convention in Shanghai after the 1890s. In the first year of the Republic of China, he opposed Yuan Shih-kai's ascent to the throne and Zhang Xun's restoration out of abhorrence for the tangled war among warlords. He laid stress on system reform and developing commercial reform. At first he set as his personal mission "to be steeped in studies of politics and the tangible" and bringing prosperity and strength to the country. He published *Key Points for Salvaging the Times and Reformed Remarks* in 1880. His five-volume work titled *Words of Warning to a Prosperous Age* came out in 1894, which was richer in content and more famous, and included three volumes dwelling on three areas: national debts, minting silver and banks. In 1895, a 14-volume revised and expanded work came out, which was an expansion in both scope and space and marked his transition from a Self-strengthening Movement political theorist to a reformist advocate. He energetically participated in the debate between the reformists represented by Kang Youwei and Liang Qichang and the revolutionaries led by Sun Yat-sen after the Sino-Japanese War of 1894–1895.

"Insurance" and "Studies on the General National Bank of England" were added to his financial work. *Words of Warning to a Prosperous Age* was published in 1900, which was a year rife with outrage and grief among the reformist thinkers, which resulted in emancipation and freedom of Zheng's mind and spirit, indicating that he believed the current social crisis was not due to demarcation of China by foreign powers, but the disintegration of the society itself. He also introduced a section on "monetary law". His main works included *Collection of Works* by Zheng Guanying compiled by a present-day compiler.

6.1. *Thought of commercial war*

Zheng Guanying had been a senior comprador. He assumed senior posts in new-style enterprises started by the Self-strengthening Movement proponents, and also started enterprises on his own with his personal investment. He was the first generation of national capitalists in China. He withdrew from society and lived in seclusion in the period from 1886 to 1892, compiling his *Words of Warning to a Prosperous Age*. He gradually consolidated his reformist thought during this period, and established his theory upholding social reform.

Before the Reform Movement of 1898, *Words of Warning to a Prosperous Age* was printed and distributed on imperial edict by the Guangxu Emperor. The work had been widely read along with the *Protests from Xiaobinlu* by Feng Guifen, which had also been translated into Japanese and Korean, gaining a great readership. His political thought hinged upon the core of "saving the country by bringing prosperity and strength thereto." He believed that "if foreign forces are to be expelled, one must first be self-reliant; if self-reliance is to be attained, one must first obtain wealth; if wealth is to be obtained, one must first revitalize industry and commerce; if revitalization of industry and commerce is to be attained, schools must be first established and improved, constitution instituted, ethics held in high esteem, politics improved."[92] His economic thought centered on commercial war. He classified the foreign aggression of Western countries into two types, military aggression and economic aggression, and considered the social consequences from the latter far more serious than the former: "military annexation was a peril easily discerned, whereas commercial carve-up would enervate a country without leaving a trace."[93] Because today's world was one of commercial war, a country of prosperous commerce was a country of strength, and a country of stagnant commerce a weak country. He was convinced that commercial war was inevitable, and it was necessary to "found the country on commerce". This so-called commerce was not commerce in the narrow sense, but commerce including industry, especially the machine-manufacturing industry. He woke up to the fact that "in order to revitalize commerce, laws of nature must be worked out, and production must be finely conducted"; "when the origin of commerce is traced, manufacturing stands out; while machine figures prominently among modes of manufacturing."[94] In *Words of Warning to a Prosperous Age*, special discussions were dedicated to commerce, industry, agriculture, mining, shipping, telegraph, insurance, bank and fiscal tax revenue. We cannot be sure that he could thoroughly grasp the fields discussed and accurately theorize such topics. Faced with aggressive activities of the Western powers, he was the first to hold up the banner of commercial war, which would suffice. The so-called commercial war in his words referred to the competition of the various domestic economic departments including capital production and circulation against foreign capital,

---

[92]*Epilogue to Words of Warning to a Prosperous Age* — Author's Statement.
[93]*Commercial War.*
[94]*Business Five.*

withstanding economic aggression of foreign capital, developing and strengthening the industry and commerce of domestic national capitalist. If the commerce in his words was to be understood as the function of economic foundation to a country, then the relation between the commerce and the military was that of economy and politics, and his basic view regarding commercial war and military warfare was very insightful and commendable for the time. His understanding of the nature of foreign capital aggression was more insightful than that of other reformists, including Wang Tao, Ma Jianzhong, Xue Fucheng and Chen Chi. Hence, his call for fighting against foreign economic aggression was more urgent and determined, and he equated directly developing domestic national capitalist commerce with the survival of the country.

He demanded that all privileges of foreign aggressors in China should be restricted and cancelled, such as tariff agreements, inland water transportation, building of roads, setting up factories and mining. He proposed that all the key positions in the various port customs such as the inspector general and assistant managers should be taken up by the Chinese in order to realize the objective of "holding these privileges in our hands". He bitterly denounced the ridiculous remarks that "Chinese are corrupt and mean, less honest or upright than foreigners" as preached by the treasonous elements, questioning them, "if no Chinese is as good as foreigners ... would it not follow that the governorship of the provinces should also be taken up by foreigners?"[95]

His writing touches on a wide array of monetary financial theories. Among the twenty essays in the *Reformed Remarks*, there are only three essays on the subjects of Minting Silver, National Debts and Borrowing; in *Words of Warning to a Prosperous Age*, essays on businesses were expanded to six, covering businesses including banks, monetary systems, direct financing and intermediary business, namely, First Volume and Second Volume On Bank, Minting Silver, Monetary Law, National Debts and Insurance. Though it could not be said that a self-contained complete system of financial theory had taken shape in his work, it was doubtless that he was different from Wang Tao and Ma Jianzhong who skimmed a few subjects and discussed one or two specific businesses relating to

---

[95] *Tax Code — Excerpt Appended.*

finances, either insurance or debt raising; he covered the basic contents of the whole of Western finance, and his groundbreaking effort could not be overemphasized.

6.2. Theory of monetary reform

The monetary system reform proposed by Zheng Guanying was mainly reflected in the two essays, "Minting Silver" and "Monetary Law". He was convinced that China's monetary system should and could adapt to the general trend in global monetary system development, setting gold as the standard while concurrently circulating silver dollars. He was convinced with intense awareness and patriotism that China should and could resist the rampaging and pillaging of foreign silver dollar — an instrument of aggression for foreign countries in China. He strongly advocated minting silver dollars on China's own, dissecting in great detail the defects of China adhering to the silver tael system, the convenience of foreign silver dollar, the jeopardy of foreign silver dollar circulating in China, the advantages of minting silver dollar on its own as well the great significance of getting back mintage, and forcefully laid out his conception of eradicating ills. His monetary system reform proposal was progressive, patriotic and could not be accused of sticking to the old ways or inappropriateness.

There were many disadvantages in using silver instead of foreign silver dollar which was more convenient. The first was excessive wastage: "extra charge, subsidiary cost, and purity discount." The second was the varying weights. Foreign silver dollars could "be circulated on the market without obstruction, without loss arising from discount." His specific analysis of this disadvantage in the Monetary Law was unprecedented and unsurpassed by anyone expounding on the ills of the Qing Dynasty's monetary systems. Silver weight standards in China varied; in addition to the pass standard, and treasury standard, the provinces had their own respective standards. There were also the water transportation standard, capital standard, etc., while minted silver of varying purities made the universal acceptance of such silver impossible. The third was price being manipulated for profit and loss incurred from circulation. The fourth was that it was cumbersome to carry and difficult to use, while foreign silver dollar was "easy to carry, relieved of the concern of cumbersomeness, it is really convenient compared with silver."

If foreign silver dollars were circulated, the people would naturally find it convenient. Actually, even people from the remote countryside could benefit from it; however, he considered such a situation "bringing about boundless perils". There were mainly four ills. The first was impurity. Most foreign silver dollars were of 90% purity, some even under 90% purity; however, all were calculated at the price of seven *qian* and two *fen* in China. No weight verification would be conducted, the price thereof fluctuated on the market and the invisible wastage was literally beyond computation. If China made silver dollars of its own, profit of several fens could be obtained from each piece: "the profit is so substantial." The second was exemption of import duty. Such money could buy millions of Chinese products; though there were price fluctuations along with market movement, there was no improvement in purity. The third was that foreign businessmen could mostly get Chinese silver with their products. They would mint and sell foreign silver dollar to make profit in an endless cycle. The fourth was that if they raised the price of silver dollar by a few *fens*, the cumulative sum fleeced from such a stealthy exploitive practice would be staggering. In short, the circulation of foreign silver dollar in China was "leading to great silver outflow"; "they trade our hundred percent pure silver with their silver of discounted purity, we suffer an implicit loss therefrom, and they trade such silver dollar with bloated price for our a-hundred percent pure silver, we further suffer ostentatious loss on a rapidly changing market."[96] The foreign silver dollar was employed as an instrument in pillaging the Chinese people, and it was readily accepted by the Chinese people. It was convenient as a means of payment and purchase for the people, which further enhanced its deceptive nature and the intensity and extent of the exploitation and extortion, the risk thereof was beyond imagination. The problem did not stop there. Zheng determined that money was a national treasure, and the national treasure of a country should be country specific. How could the treasure of one country be adulterated with treasure from another country? They came under false pretenses and unjustified, overthrew the rightful host, inflicted loss to the

---

[96]*Commercial War*, First Half.

country and ailed the people. He was outraged by foreign aggressors using foreign silver dollar in exploiting all weaknesses of China, conducting explicit or implicit fraud, exploiting at multiple levels via vile and vicious ruses, and his grief and indignation over the fact that the motherland suffered endless exploitation and bullying were beyond concealment. His genuine hope of restoring the autonomy of the national currency in circulation burst was evident. The key was that "the economic right to profit is held in the hands of foreigners." China's financial power was held in foreign hands, which amounted to saying that the life of China was held by foreigners. If this situation continued, wouldn't China as a country and its people perish? Mintage was the economic livelihood of China and also the economic autonomy of China. How could any righteous Chinese remain unoffended and unconcerned by the fact that these were held in the hands of foreigners!

Zheng Guanying was convinced that there would be four advantages to replacing foreign silver dollar with domestically minted silver dollar. The first was "that it will be sufficient to strip foreigners of these economic right." If China mints more silver dollars, then foreign silver dollar inflow into China would naturally diminish, and the privilege of foreigners plundering Chinese interest with foreign silver dollar would also be terminated. The second was to "protect the financial resources and dignify the sovereignty." If domestically minted silver dollars were widely circulated, then the outflow of silver would naturally be stemmed, and the national strength would improve; no country would dare to intimidate China when its national strength was improved. The third was "no concern for wastage." Since silver dollars did not require 100% purity, as long as there was minting there would be surplus, so after deducting all expenses there would still be some surplus. The fourth was that "it will facilitate the merchants and the people and maintain operation of the market." The uniformity of purity and weight of silver dollars as well as equal value and price would be favorable to stabilize and expand the market. He had firm faith in these four advantages and "if these four disadvantages could be eliminated, then what can hold us back from implementing them?"

Regarding the specific issue of domestically minting silver dollars, Zheng Guanying believed that "there is a superb move, nothing works better than mandating minting of gold and silver in the various provinces and in two types of purity; the make of such money shall be exactly resembling that imported. The minted money shall be distributed; silver, silver bullions of various forms from the people shall be collected by a mandate and be melted in the various coin minting bureaus; the people shall be compensated with gold and silver coins equivalent to the amount collected therefrom upon conversion." By waging a coin-minting war, replacing the spurious with the genuine, and routing the superior strength of foreign silver dollar in China, China could reap the social effect of killing two birds with one stone. "As time goes, there will not be a variety of silver bullions, the people would have to use the universal money."[97]

In *Reformed Remarks* and *Minting Silver* from *Words of Warning to a Prosperous Age*, Zheng Guanying refuted accusations of "entailing too much production cost" on domestically minting silver dollars. He pointed out that the concern for domestic minting was not insufficient funds but that "Chinese are greedy and faithless, without chemist's supervision, hundreds of ills arise". The failure of minting pie-shaped silver by Lin Zexu in Jiangsu was irrefutable evidence.

Zheng Guanying sharply pointed out that an increasing number of countries around the globe shifted to using gold, while the number of countries still adhering to silver dwindled. The price of silver dropped substantially, and the market for silver-producing countries narrowed significantly. Only China, India and Mexico still adhered to silver standard, and it was likely that all silver standard countries would shift to using gold. It would be difficult for China to survive if it did not urgently conduct monetary system reform. China sustained great loss in conducting transactions with foreigners, raising foreign debts and even greater loss in collecting customs duties. Take the price ratio between gold and silver for instance, before 1876, a pound could be converted to three or four taels of silver, but by 1892 the conversion rate rose to four or five taels a pound, and further rose to seven or eight taels per pound by somewhere around 1900: "the rate redoubled compared to twenty years ago". If the customs imposed a duty at the rate of 5%, import tax on foreign goods excluding

---

[97]*Commercial War*, vol. 1.

medicine would have recorded five million taels less, while Chinese-specialty products and export and domestic sales would have recorded five million less: "if the two items of foreign products were taxed in pound at the rate of five percent, the sum total would result in an increase of 10 million revenue." Because of the outdated monetary systems, China could not avoid incurring a great loss in international trade, and had its national livelihood strangled and national sovereignty threatened. Meanwhile, the national fiscal revenue diminished while expenditure expanded, the national treasury was depleted and the country's financial strength drained, which was like an enervated person whose fate was in the hands of others, a formidable and terrifying situation. Zheng Guanying could not help but proclaim that the government must "choose a fine model and follow, make preparatory arrangement"; "tailor measures to suit the situation, it is urgent for us to imitate the gold pound circulated in the countries, and ban the use of foreign silver dollars to dignify the sovereignty and stem up outflow of economic benefit" (*Monetary Law*). He was by no means deceiving or deliberately mystifying, nor entertaining a groundless concern and fussing about nothing. Instead, it was the assertion of patriotism by righteous people fighting for national monetary autonomy and economic independence when faced with the unrestrained pillaging and rampant misconduct of foreign aggressors.

Issuance of paper money: In the second volume of *On Bank*, Zheng Guanying discussed issues such as the face value, production and quantity of paper money. The so-called face value was to be classified into three categories: large denomination note of 1,000 taels and 500 taels; intermediate denomination note of 100 taels and the 50 taels; small denomination note of 10 taels and five taels. He held that the amount of issuance must be kept within the amount of silver deposited: "paper money to be issued would amount to several million, the amount of reserve set aside in the bank must correspond to the quantity of paper money to be issued. Government officials shall conduct inspection and verification thereon to ensure that paper money issuance does not exceed the amount of silver set aside so that faith of the people may be maintained and the scheme may last." By doing so, the paper money issuance of China could differ from that of Western countries in that all fiscal funds would be deposited in banks, "established as the foundation, while paper money is issued as voucher." The fact was that all "Chinese government revenues are deposited in the various repositories conducive to embezzlement and appropriation by officials." The cause of evil for excessive issuance of paper money lay in the government. If paper money was to win the confidence of the people, Western practices had to be followed in managing banks and issuing paper money. However, he failed to realize that it was absolutely impossible to count on the corrupt government to shoulder the critical task of monetary system reform. The Qing government was already on its last legs, having exhausted its financial resources. How could it withstand the final indignity in the form of issuing paper money through banks? However, this proposition was doubtless a superficial cure without touching the core of the issue.

6.3. Theory on banks

Arguably, the earliest theoretical discussion on banks in China was by Zheng Guanying. However, it was Hong Rengan, Prince Ganwang of the Taiping Heavenly Kingdom, who first proposed to start banks; he proposed it in his *New Compilation of Government* as an item imitating the Western system. However, he did not make any theoretical exposition thereon. Zheng Guanying expounded the position and function of banks, the necessity of setting up banks, the special implications for China, and the organization form and issues which must be emphasized at the incorporation of a bank. A relatively well-formed understanding regarding theoretical issues and practical issues of bank had taken shape in his works.

He came to understand the prominent position and function of bank in the multitude of industries, that is, its critical position and function in the national economy. "The bank is employed in the maintenance of commerce, to fully bring out its function as the hub of the multitude of industries, expand financial ("wealth") resources and maintain the general situation." As the general hub of the national economy, the bank could regulate the funds of the society, ensure that the various departments in society have their financial needs met in order to maintain the smooth performance of production and circulation, and maintain the stability of the market. He considered the bank as "the general account house for all."

When private funds were deposited in the bank, the risks of pointless spending and theft could be done away with. Zheng Guanying illustrated the reason that the bank became a general account house for the entire society from different perspectives, taking into consideration the interest of fund depositors, rendering convenience thereto and accommodating fund for customers. His contemporary Chen Chi talked in general terms on the same topic, but was far less comprehensive and profound than Zheng Guanying.

The so-called "wealth" must have referred to funds. In the first volume of the eight-volume *On Bank* published in 1900, Zheng Guanying inserted the following paragraph in his introducing remarks: "Nothing is better than for the wealth of the world to be circulated, and nothing is worse than when it is stagnated. When wealth gets circulated, it grows by the day, benefiting both the owner and the borrower; when wealth gets stagnated, the market is undersupplied, the owner would claim that such a situation benefits himself and harms others, however, the truth is that it harms the owner too." This understanding was quite extraordinary, and he insightfully pinpointed the basic characteristics of capital, that is, accrual and movement of capital. The relation between the two was that capital accrual required movement as it accrued and accumulated through movement; on the contrary, there would be no capital accrual without capital movement, and concern of capital insufficiency would surface time and again, which would incur capital loss by the day. In the essay titled *On Bank*, Zheng Guanying touched on the concept of capital as he expounded its essential characteristic, which indicated that he already had some pretty profound understanding of the special relation between the bank and the capital. This understanding had not taken form when the 14-volume work *Words of Warning to a Prosperous Age* was completed or elevated to such a height. The final touch arrived in the eight-volume edition of the same work, as this type of attainment came from two aspects, namely, book knowledge and practice, which was by no means attainable overnight. He further distinguished money and capital; though he did not make any argument on the difference between the two, he did make a distinction in using the two terms. When he talked about China opening up treaty ports to engage in commerce with foreign countries, he pointed out that what flowed out of China was money, instead of capital; when he talked about the financing function of the bank, he used the term "expanding financial resources, pooling the fund of the entire country" instead of "money", which should be acknowledged as a remarkable progress in understanding.

As to questions regarding how this capital came about and how it accrued, he did not elaborate. However, his eagerness for setting up banks had made its impression. This reflected the eagerness to develop national industry and commerce by first-generation national capitalists of China. He was aware of the bank's role as pillar in "benefiting both the people and the country"; if an entity "benefits us but harms others" "or benefits the people but harms the country", then "it could not be called an entity bringing about great benefit". The unspoken words were that only starting a bank constituted great benefit, and preparation for bank establishment had to be conducted immediately, which equally reflected his eagerness as a national capitalist, striving to bring prosperity and strength to the country.

Zheng Guanying analyzed the advantages of starting banks to benefit both the country and the people. First, he elaborated on the 10 functions of banks in China's national economy as follows: (a) The success of banks implicitly concerned the sovereignty as it connected the government and the people, the far and the near, "pooling the wealth of the country and reaping a great benefit, very responsive without the least cumbersomeness". It was very convenient for fund accommodation, and situations such as fund shortage or fiscal straits would not occur again in China. (b) "When the country conducts something of grand scales, such as building railway, shipyard, various projects, it could raise funds therefor." (c) If there was urgent need for funds, such as for military affairs and relieving refugees from various catastrophes, instant fund accommodation could be effected and the need addressed. (d) There would no longer be the need to pay heavy interest on loans by the country; the bank had its own rules regarding business operation and there would no longer be such ills as embezzlement of public fund. (e) When the country has multiple loans, in the case of which there might be a lack of money, it could still get loan elsewhere, without the need of the use of collaterals.[98] Foreign debts

---

[98] Bill of lading after customs duties are cleared, which could be used as a collateral in taking out a loan.

could be taken out to safeguard the integrity of sovereignty. (f) "The bank could turn around the situation so that market situation does not deteriorate, and commerce could be supplemented thereby."

Where industrialists, silver stores and private banks of solid means were found to be short of funds, which hindered the regular operation and circulation of social reproductive fund, the bank may render great assistance thereto. By so doing, the social market order would be maintained unaffectedly, and commercial activity could be expanded and developed. (g) When the bank worked or conducted business on behalf of the financial treasury, public funds of the various provinces were deposited in the bank (annual interest of scores of hundreds of thousands taels accrued on the funds of customs duty, government silver stores), and withdrawal thereof could be made readily available, which was little different from depositing such in the treasury, and the annual interest income would still go to the public fund, making it impossible for corrupt officials to embezzle and appropriate such. (h) Remunerations of government officials and savings of private citizens could accrue interest, which eliminated the peril of "more likely to incur loss than generate interest" when such was deposited in small money shops and private banks. (i) It would no longer be necessary for overseas Chinese to consign their remittance funds to foreign banks for processing, and their company incorporation activities would no longer be under the stranglehold of foreigners. (j) "When the market is faced with monetary contraction, drafts issued by the bank could be circulated instead to ease such monetary constraint" and regulate the market. Second, based on the beneficiary of the 10 functions stated above, the following four categories could be made: (1) Safeguarding the national economic sovereignty from encroachment by resisting foreign economic aggression and interference ((e) and (i)). (2) Increasing financial revenue and reducing expenditure, hence easing the fiscal crisis ((a)–(d) and (g)). (3) Safeguarding the normal order of production and circulation, facilitating capital circulation, proper turnover of social reproduction and the stability of the social economic order ((f) and (j)). (4) Safeguarding the rights and interests of city dwellers from encroachment (h). Finally, though Zheng Guanying did not directly expound the function of banks, the basic businesses of banks, saving, loan, remittance and exchange had all been included in his elaboration. He was convinced that banks were the general hub or general account house for the "livelihood of the people and the country". Out of consideration for the Qing Dynasty, he strove to safeguard the national political and economic order, which both stood for the interest and requirements of the newly emerging national capitalist and was conducive to establishment and development of new-style industrial and commercial enterprises. However, how could he understand that the bank was exactly the product of capitalist modes of production? Facilitating the development of newly emerging productivity and modes of production was the rightful social effect expected of the bank's function. It was highly unlikely for a bank of China to be established and developed without transforming the social form, which was in conflict with the purpose of maintaining the old, traditional superstructure and economic foundation; such ambivalence was the inevitable reflection of the duality mentality of Chinese reformists. Hence, he made the same mistake as Chen Chi, and overemphasized the function of the bank as a support to government finances and as an inexhaustible, magic source of income, which correspondingly debased the role it played in promoting the expansion and development of production and circulation, especially its role in satisfying the need for sustained development of advanced commodity monetary economy.

The function of the bank to be established by China at that time differed drastically from that of Western countries, that is, withstanding the financial aggression and pillaging of foreign capital in the form of foreign banks in China. Zheng Guanying thought that there were three vested interests for foreign banks in China. The first was that they stopped at nothing, unrestrained by China's government regulation. "The silver notes employed by foreign businessmen are not subject to verification by Chinese and foreign officials; they do everything as they please and stop at nothing." The second was that they reaped substantial profit; the British HSBC alone issued over a million in paper money in Guangdong: "the bank has obtained profit in excess of two million." The third was that they solicited and accepted Chinese stockholders, but did not render any help to Chinese businessmen. "Even though Chinese businessmen hold stocks in them, they have no transaction with Chinese businessmen. Chinese businessmen could by no means obtain any mortgage loan even with company stocks of solid Chinese companies as collateral, while foreign companies could take out mortgage loans on both goods and stocks." In using the money deposited by the Chinese to pillage the Chinese, the hideous image of colonialists was vividly depicted. This situation directly jeopardized the survival and development of China's national industry and commerce, and undermined the soundness and stability of China's market, which was "a situation of handing over the enemy a formidable weapon." "A proposed move for today's China, nothing could salvage the market and maintain the market situation but setting up a bank with a great sum of money raised." This categorical statement came from the heart of the first Chinese national capitalist; it was both a forceful cry and a vow. "Nothing figured more prominently than commerce in strengthening the Self-strengthening Movement, and nothing more urgent than banks in consolidating commerce." The importance and role of the bank in bringing prosperity and strength, salvaging the country, and developing a national capitalist industry and commerce stood out vividly, which also reflected the importance and function of the bank in national economy. However, what he neglected to mention was that he faced a traditional, corrupt and diehard old-school government, and hence his proposal was naive and rife with illusions.

Upon assessment of the various aspects, he was convinced that "there are more than what meets the eyes in the profit the bank reaps", which could be summarized in the following six points: (a) The bank was of substantial capital, which was by no means comparable to private banks. Taking Chinese private banks, for instance, they employed capital not more than a few scores of 1,000 taels; however, their profit amounted to 20,000 or 30,000 taels: "the banks are of more substantial capital, and conduct businesses of bridging China and foreign markets, profit reaped thereby is conceivably huge." (b) The bank could absorb foreign deposits. It could accommodate and save the situation in times of fund shortage, which was unlike private banks "which would be bogged down in dire financial straits". (c) The bank could issue paper money. When scores of hundreds of thousands or millions of silver dollars were circulated in the market, such was an advantage beyond comparison by any other industry, "which was a profit generated without any cost attached thereto". (d) Interest accrued on deposit and profit generated thereby was conceivably large, which formed a stable substantial income for the bank. Interests on term deposits of 1 year, 6 months, 3 months and premature withdrawal were 5%, 4%, 3% and 0%, respectively, and 2% on current deposit. On the contrary, interest on loans was up to 7% or 10%. The interest spreads were 2% at least and as high as 8%, and the profit arising therefrom was credible. (e) Expenses arising from items such as rent and fire insurance premium for depositing collaterals in the bank were considerably lower than those charged by other industries. (f) Operation of the bank was particularly free from perils.

Zheng Guanying's analysis was convincing, and he was convinced that the bank "brings out so many conveniences and brings in such a huge profit, it is indeed a cause unparalleled in benefiting the world." Anyone intent on starting commerce and imitating Western practices to salvage the deteriorating situation of China would inevitably miss the point and go astray if he failed to gain a full understanding of establishing banks, which would be as much as "attending to the trifles to the exclusion of the essentials".

As for organization of the bank, the forms of Western banks Zheng Guanying introduced included the following: "government banks, commercial banks and small-sum banks." The small-sum bank was introduced in the 14-volume edition, and he elaborated with over 200 words: "as peddlers go after small meagre profit, it is feared that they would squander away their hard earned money, and savings of poor people such as hired laborers … and it would be particularly easy for soldiers to empty their purses on liquor and gamble; if such people deposit their savings in banks, many a little makes a mickle, and such accumulated savings could be employed to fend off poverty, and it would make an extensive and thoughtful measure to benefit the people." Zheng found it hard to let go of the issues faced by agriculture, the rural area and the peasants of China. In 1913, at the advanced age of 73, he wrote *Proposal of Preparing for Famine Time and Enriching the Peasant*,[99] proposing to start a small-sum bank, "there is no better means than this in enhancing the social position of the peasant." In the country, the peasants "often found their circumstances hardened up in crop sowing season, they could not find financial means to purchase crop seed, many have to idle their land, this is due to the fact that there is no grassroots financial institution." The incorporation

---

[99]*Collected Works* of Zheng Guanying, Second Volume, pp. 1155–1158.

of small-sum banks could do the following: (1) It could "accommodate the urgent needs of the poor with savings accumulated in the same village ...." (2) The peasant could be freed from being reduced to an impoverished state, "to prevent their land being merged by the powerful." (3) It could "help them prosper and get rich". Since small-sum banks had so many benefits, "immediate incorporation thereof should be conducted." Then what would its incorporation philosophy be? Zheng held that "such shall be employed to regulate the have and the have-not, relieve the poor, make loan in spring and recover repayment in autumn, yield interest on fund deposited, stash away wealth among the people, and be easy to carry out. Facilitating the people shall be the first priority for the law of encouraging saving." Regarding the mode of incorporation, a rural union or national bank would be employed in the organization of banks. A minimum amount in excess of 100 *wen* could be deposited, and a meagre sum could yield interest. With a small minimum amount set on deposit, and a low criterion on interest accrual, such measures "are in conformity with the way of mutual assistance among the people and becoming the principle of local autonomy. The measure of exhorting the people to save tolerates no delay, and such shall be proceeded from accumulating loan capital." In conclusion, "it seems plausible to start national financial institutions to facilitate the people to deposit their savings, small-sum banks shall be incorporated to accommodate the need of the people."

He also believed that obstructions and social ills had to be eliminated before banks could be set up. Only by absorbing beneficial practices of the Western countries, pooling the insights of the people, taking the values of the people as the benchmark, eliminating social ills and reforming social ethos could banks be successfully erected. Zheng did not introduce the subject from the variety of forms as the central bank and commercial bank, and it seems unnecessarily to complain about this point. As no Chinese bank had been set up and there were only foreign banks in China, he was not at fault for proceeding from the practical standpoint.

Zheng Guanying was worthy of the appellation of an accomplished first-generation Chinese capitalist and worthy of the name of patriotic capitalist with national integrity. He proceeded from the practical situation of China, treated the subject with great care, conducted in-depth investigation, and proposed specific procedures and implementation measures for setting up banks in China instead of basing himself on wishful expectations and illusions, or singing high praises and engaging in pointless talk, let alone mechanically duplicating the established rules of Western banks, which was rather exceptional and unprecedented in the traditional old society in the closing period of the Qing Dynasty.

6.4. Theory of insurance and national debts

In the essay titled *On Insurance*, Zheng Guanying made some observations on the insurance business, which he introduced as, "there are three categories of insurances, marine, fire and life insurances. Marine insurance covers goods shipment, fire insurance house and warehouse and life insurance the life and diseases." He introduced the category, functional characteristics, history of development, and attached three articles of incorporation of marine, fire and life insurances, which made it more accessible for people to conduct in-depth examination of insurance businesses. The Chinese insurance market at the time was monopolized by British insurance companies, with all terms and conditions, rates relating to insurance, etc., being fixed by foreign companies. Hence, "it could be verified that insurance activities originated in 1523, and Italy followed suit, all were insured by the state." "While fire and life insurances originated in 1701. By 1762, an insurance company specializing in life insurance was set up in London." In 1885, Li Hongzhang, the leading figure in China's Self-strengthening Movement, decided that the China Merchants Steamship Navigation Company would set aside 200,000 taels of silver to set up two insurance companies, Renhe and Jihe, to insure all warehousing and commodity transportation businesses of the company.

Since Great Britain started the Guangzhou Insurance Company in Guangzhou in 1805 (originally known as the Canton Insurance Company), the first insurance company in China, in a period less than a century ago, it was of great necessity to popularize and disseminate financial and insurance knowledge. It could not be denied that the immense popularity of *Words of Warning to a Prosperous Age* had great bearing on the situation.

In *Proposal of Preparing for Famine Time and Enriching the Peasant*, Zheng specifically proposed, "preparing and instituting agricultural insurance, so that the ordinary people could rid of concern even in years of flood and draught; building agricultural granaries to amass and distribute agricultural produces. It seems that the central government should set up a general insurance administration to oversee the industry; an agricultural saving union shall be set up in the various villages, and small-sum banks be set up in the various counties to handle insurance business, the two institutions, when combined, could form a big institution. The cause entailed great benefits and little cost, in compliance with ancient systems, conducive to the current time, indeed a great strategy to prepare for contingencies and enrich the people." Zheng was concise and went to great pains in elaborating the founding philosophy, purpose and principle of performance; what remained was only the appointment of personnel and implementation when time and conditions ripened.

Regarding the discussion on national debts, Zheng Guanying had set out specific essays in *On Loan* from the 36-volume edition *Reformed Remarks* and *National Debts* from *Words of Warning to a Prosperous Age*.[100]

Notion of Debt: He believed that China held different notions on this topic from those of Western countries. None of the Western countries "have national debts"; so long as "the parliament approves of taking out a loan upon deliberation, even if the country is conquered by another country, the debt is still to be repaid." Western countries would constantly borrow from the people in the amount of many millions when they engaged in initiating great projects, waged great wars or the fiscal revenue fell short of expenditure requirements. Opposite to this practice, the traditional Chinese notion of "(being) free from any national debt" ran deep in China. In order for the government to overcome financial crisis and solve the problem of insufficient fiscal revenue, national debt had to be raised. He believed that the notion of being free from any national debt was handed down from the story of the Nanwang King of the Zhou Dynasty who was burdened with piling debts and had become "a laughing stock". It should be acknowledged that his understanding was authentic; having investigated the evolution of China's debt culture, however, we have not found any material reason for the formation of this notion. Piling debt was

---

[100]No more citations shall be provided for further quotes from the two essays hereinbelow.

only the phenomenon; the cause thereof should be attributed to the small-scale production mode of the times. Government bonds were the product of modern economy development. In *The Origin of the Family, Private Property and the State*, Engels specifically noted, "As civilisation advances, these taxes become inadequate; the state makes drafts on the future, contracts loans, public debts."[101] The germination and development of national debts were closely related to the semi-feudal and semi-colonial economy of the Qing Dynasty. National debt preceded foreign debt in germination, and based its development on foreign debt. Foreign debt preceding domestic debt was a path of development correctly summarized in Ma Jianzhong's theory; however, Zheng Guanying held an opposite view.

Theoretical grounds for raising national debts: Zheng Guanying remarked, "wealth is like water, blockage thereof is constantly feared, while circulation thereof is not." The theory that wealth and funds were best put into circulation rather than stashed away was an outstanding insight of Zheng Guanying. Different modes of circulation entailed different outcomes. Accommodating both the government and the people was diametrically opposed to interest grabbing by both the government and the people. In the former, the needs of the government and the people were accommodated and regulated, production and life went on in an orderly manner; in the latter, resources of both the government and the people were exhausted, the entire country was in chaos, both the country and the people were worn out, and production and circulation were disrupted.

If the purpose of accommodating both the government and the people was to be achieved, Zheng Guanying believed that "great impartiality must be demonstrated and maintained with great faith." On the aforesaid condition, the purpose of the debt was a core issue. He cited the words of a certain minister of the Qing Dynasty to Great Britain, "these creditors are glad to make loans. If a country raises debt to build railways and electric lines, conduct mining, conserve water, etc., projects leading to prosperity, such loans would bring about great interest and the price of the coupon would go firm. They are reluctant to make loans to people who would engage in squandering activities. Lenders would particularly loathe

---

[101]*Karl Marx and Frederick Engels*, vol. 21, p. 195.

that a borrower raises debt for military purposes, which turns silver and coin into fire powder, ammunitions, if such leads to the demise of the country, the loan would be a lost cause and irrecoverable; what is at stake is not limited to the interest." In fact, he had made a distinction between debt-raising for a productive purpose and loans for non-productive purposes. Productive purpose loans would enrich the country and benefit the people, repayment of principal and interest would not be an issue, and everyone would be happy to invest therein. On the contrary, non-productive loans and loans for military purposes were especially detested because the prospect of a war remained unpredictable; not only would the repayment of principal and interest of the loan be difficult but the fate of the country and the person would also hang in the air. This was exactly the reason why he repeatedly emphasized that raising foreign debt was but a temporary measure. Of course, compared with accepting funds for purchasing government posts, raising debt was arguably a better measure. He was convinced that if debt raising could be put into practice, then raising funds from the people to ensure fiscal expenditure, and as an established fine practice for coping with contingencies, was far better than "raising funds by selling government posts, borrowing foreign debts by harming the country, harming the people by installing tariff passes". If evaluated in isolation and from a static point of view, this understanding was by no means bad; the national vitality of countries such as Turkey and Persia was enervated due to heavy debts and hefty interest which resulted in their economic rights being deprived.

Zheng Guanying optimistically believed that such circumstance would by no means occur in China, as China was of vast territory, with rich mineral resources, "which far surpassed that of the Western countries"; "China has a huge revenue with little debt, and could obtain a big loan without the need to pay a high interest." Moreover, "Chinese and foreigners rush to purchase China's debt coupons". Such reasons would make a country of ancient civilization with a history of several thousand years complacent intoxicated and even boastful: "though China produces little gold, the situation is still under control". "Previous foreign debts entailed interest rates up to seven, eight percent or even more, if not for the fact that these loans were embezzled by foreign firms handling such", they would have deserved little attention, and should be dismissed lightly. Such blind optimism, the savage conduct of aggression and pillage by Western powers that China sustained and the corruption and incompetence of the Qing government constituted a stark contrast, which was extremely jarring and unacceptable.

Raising foreign debt: This was a practical issue of critical importance, which could not be avoided or equivocated. In Zheng Guanying's opinion, raising foreign debt was nothing but incurring one debt to pay off another: "it temporarily eases urgent need, but should be permanently stopped; even though it could be employed to meet urgent need while other fund could be temporarily employed to make up for the shortfall, it is best not to be borrowed." Raising foreign debt was only an inferior move, a contingent move to cure fiscal deficit, definitely not a fixed policy for long-term implementation. "China has already sustained huge loss from pound price fluctuation", that is, the so-called pound conversion loss. While Western countries had adopted the gold standard, China still adhered to the silver standard, and the price ratio between gold and silver fluctuated on the market; usually the trend was for gold to appreciate while silver would depreciate. Chinese payments were made based on the exchange rate of the pound, and the rise of the pound rate meant more silver payment; hence, a loss was incurred. China had already sustained huge losses on the conversion rate between gold and silver, and it still had to surrender several items of tariff duties as collateral for debt repayment, several items of tariff duties, which further jeopardized the national sovereignty and undermined the national foundation; hence, he called for "permanently stopping borrowing any foreign debts thereafter." This was only his personal subjective will; such will was but meaningless talk and failed to have any practical significance unless founded on the actual situation of China's national circumstances of the time. The basic financial policy he fixed for himself and the people was to "tailor expenditure to revenue which is the eternal law of nature". Generally speaking, that was correct. However, after the Sino-British Opium War, China faced an increasingly impoverished financial situation; the Taiping Rebellion (1851) brought the financial revenue and expenditure situation of the Qing Dynasty to an extremely perilous state. How could balance be maintained!

The Sino-Japanese War of 1894 and an aggressive war waged by the Eight-Nation Alliance forces in 1900 had forced the Qing Dynasty into the Treaty of Shimonoseki and the Peace Protocol of 1901 with Japan and the Eight-Nation Alliance forces, respectively. The principal of war reparations alone reached 1.2 billion taels of silver. By raising foreign debt, China lost customs autonomy, then control of salt administration, and lastly finances fell under the control of the Western powers. China then further conceded the rights to start banks, conduct mining, build railways and erect factories. Therefore, Zheng Guanying stated theoretically, "unless absolutely necessary, when foreign debt has to be raised again, comprehensive organization of the entire situation must be examined, prudential preparation be made, no further handling by the foreign banks in China be entrusted so that repeated process and embezzlement and jeopardy of taking out loans can be eliminated." This was a clear understanding of the risk of raising foreign debt as arrived at by him after Ma Jianzhong, a complicated understanding from a conflicted mentality, that is, it would be impractical not to raise foreign debt and that heightened attention must be paid to certain issues if foreign debt was to be raised.

In Zheng Guanying's opinion, directors of foreign banks in China conducted fraudulent activities and profiteered in the process of handling foreign debt raising; hence, it would be better to issue bonds directly to domestic and foreign businessmen. In the eight-volume edition, he even straightforwardly proposed to place orders with renowned foreign factories with foreign debt so that repeated handling may be reduced. It could be seen that he attempted to cut down on the intermediate procedures to reduce expenditure and safeguard national interest, bringing the maximum rights and interests from raising foreign debt to the country. What tested his forbearance the most was loans secured with customs revenue: "such huge economic right is granted to foreigners instead of Chinese citizens, and it is granted not to foreign houses of solid means but to wily foreign brokers. This is the reason why raising foreign debt has been the greatest economic right outflow after the time of opening up commerce with foreign countries." "This shameful situation of selling out national sovereignty and incurring humiliation to the country had been ridiculed by insightful foreigners and must not be allowed to continue." However, if raising foreign debt had to be resorted to, he held that loans could be taken out directly with foreign businessmen and it would not be improper to secure such loans on customs revenue. He also proposed that "compared with raising national debts from the Great Britain, Russia and

France, it is better to raise debt from the United States. And if foreign debts must be raised, then scores of billion is better than a few billions, debt denominated in silver better than in pound."

He thought that it was better to raise debt from the United States than from Great Britain, Russia and France. This was because the conceded territories of the three countries were adjoined to China, so if conflict with them arose, China would be under coercion thereof. On the contrary, the United States had no territory adjoining China, so there would be no such concern. Zheng Guanying even proposed to borrow more foreign debt instead of less, because a smaller amount of several billions would entail an interest rate of 4–6% or 7%, but if the loan amounted to scores of billions, the interest rate thereon would drop to not more than 3%. Therefore, he proposed to replace old debt of a higher interest rate with a new debt of a lower interest rate: "if such a huge sum of funds is obtained, China could revitalize the multitude of dilapidated causes", which indicated the fact that he cherished some expectations of the Western powers and harbored impractical naive illusions, which were some of his conspicuous limitations. While acknowledging the progressive viewpoints of Zheng Guanying, it is equally our responsibility to point out his weaknesses, his dependence on the government and foreign aggressors, and the lack of thoroughness in his arguments.

Chapter 9

Financial Thought During the Period from the Sino-Japanese War of 1894–1895 to the Revolution of 1911

1. Introduction

This was the most chaotic period of China's monetary systems with an excessive variety of foreign silver dollars, copper coins and paper money circulating simulataneously in China. After the Sino-Japanese War of 1894–1895, the types of foreign silver dollars circulating in China amounted to several scores, while domestically minted silver dollars were mainly divided into two types: the one tael type and the seven *qian* two *fen* type. Silver dollars minted by the various provinces varied in purity and weight with varying prices. The coexistence of silver dollar and silver tael brought about conversion difficulty domestically which led to rampant speculation; the fluctuation of international settlement caused a huge loss to China. In 1900, Li Hongzhang tried minting copper coins while serving in the capacity of Governor of Guangdong and Guangxi, which gained widespread acceptance, and the government benefited therefrom; hence, the Qing Government decreed that the various coastal provinces and provinces along the Yangtze River should follow the minting practice. In 1909, the exchange rate between copper coins and silver dollars rose from 1:110 to 1:130–140. In the late Qing Dynasty, the circulation of banknotes was in an extremely disordered manner, and foreign banks engaged in issuance of paper currencies which encroached on China's sovereignty and jeopardized China's society and economy. Domestic banks each had their own way; there were the state-run Daqing Bank, Bank of Communications, the various commercial banks and local banks, with circulation of government cash and private banknotes, paper money, silver tael note, silver dollar note and silver-backed note. There was neither a circulation quota nor a circulation reserve in place.

The period from 1897 to 1911 was the birth stage of China's banking industry; draft banks grew to the height of their development, while private banks survived this period. After the Sino-Japanese War, China's national bourgeois capital gained some development; the financial aggression of imperialists roused the desire of national bourgeois capital to start banks, and the Qing government also planned to incorporate banks out of fiscal requirements. The first bank in China, the Imperial Bank of China, was established in 1897, the Bank of Revenue Ministry was established in 1905, and the Bank of Communications established in 1907, and some government banks and money shops as well as commercial banks of local nature were established thereafter. Draft banks were hand in glove with the Qing government, and financed the Qing government with their full financial prowess in 1900. They emerged financially more solid thereafter, and their businesses prospered; they handled businesses on behalf of the national treasury, were in charge of remitting and repaying interests and principals of some foreign debts, and their business arms spread overseas; however, they were in their death throes starting from the last years of the Guangxu Emperor. The strength of private banks was preserved, solely attributable to the special position they held in import and export trades. Foreign businesses used private banks to expand capital export and increase commodity exports into China, whereas private banks availed themselves of the opportunity to consolidate their position on the financial market; besides, private banks provided small- and medium-sized businesses with necessary funds in a flexible and convenient manner. They also manipulated the "rate of tael vs. silver" (the prevailing rate for converting Shanghai silver dollars into Guiyuan dollars); for instance, if the rate stood at 7.225, it meant that each silver dollar could be converted to seven *qian*, two *fen*, and 2.5 *li* of the Guiyuan, or 7.225 *qian*. They also practiced "Inter-bank Borrowing" (inter-bank borrowing interest rate). Speculation by private banks led to the Draft Discount Chaos of 1897 and the Rubber Chaos of 1910, which resulted in the bankruptcy of a slew of private banks.

In the same period, the imperialist financial industry stepped up investment in China. During the period from 1895 to 1913, thirteen more foreign banks were established in China, with 85 branch institutions. Their investment focus was on capital export. Their banking presence in China turned into hubs for the various acts of economic aggression by the foreign powers. In addition to actively increasing direct investment, continuing operation in depositing and lending businesses, monopolizing foreign exchange, issuing paper money and manipulating the financial market, they also brokered loans to the Chinese government, and invested in railways, shipping, trade, industries and mining, which strengthened their financial expropriation of China. Take foreign exchange manipulation for example. HSBC raised the foreign exchange rate to pay less silver when making payment to China's government and suppressed the foreign exchange rate when collecting interest from China so that it could collect more silver.

Therefore, when the bank consortium composed of the UK, France, Germany and the United States brokered the Monetary System Industrial Loan, they grabbed about 73,700 pounds through pound exchange manipulation from the Qing government, and they also interfered with China's monetary system reform and enjoyed broad concessions of conducting land reclamation, livestock husbandry, tapping forest and mineral resources in the three northeastern provinces. They had conducted practices including accepting banknotes, lending money to private banks, controlling settlement and controlling China's financial institutions.

2. Yan Fu's financial theory

Yan Fu (1854–1921), former name Chuanchu, other name Zengguang, courtesy name Youling, Jidao, was born in Houguan of Fujian. He was an enlightenment thinker in modern China, pioneer and forerunner of comparative cultural studies of Chinese and Western cultures. He received tutoring in the classics from an accomplished scholar in his hometown from the age of 10. Graduating from Fuzhou Navy School in the 10th year of the Tongzhi Emperor (1871), in the 3rd year of the Guangxu Emperor (1877), he went to study at the British Greenwich Naval College, also known as the Old Royal Naval College. When he was at home, he had had contact with English teachers; when he was abroad, his experiences propelled him to explore the secret behind the prosperity and power of the UK. This focus guided Yan Fu to earnestly investigate the British political, economical and social systems and he finally settled wholeheartedly on the then prevailing British thought (Schwartz). In the period from his return from England in the 6th year of the Guangxu Emperor to the 26th year of the Guangxu Emperor, he served in Fuzhou Navy School as instructor, dean, vice president and president successively over a span of up to 20 years. During this period, he had started a newspaper and school jointly with others; he worked as the general manager of the Translation Bureau under the Imperial University of Peking, as the Anhui Higher College supervisor, Fudan Academy supervisor and editor-in-chief of the Noun Review Division under the Ministry of Education. In 1912, Yan Fu assumed the role of the president of Peking University, but he soon resigned, as he considered that the basis for authoritative thought of republic government was not yet available. Therefore, he initiated and endorsed the Confucianism Society in 1913, participated in the initiation of the Chou-An Organization in 1915 and attached himself to Yuan Shikai for the purpose of restoring monarchy. A collection of eight masterpiece translations by Yan Fu is currently in print (Huxley's "Evolution and Ethics", *Primer of Logic* by Jevons, *The Wealth of Nations* by Adam Smith, *The Study of Sociology* by Spencer, *On Liberty* by John Mill, *A History of Politics* by Jenks, *The Spirit of the Laws* by Montesquieu and *A System of Logic* by John Mill) along with the *Yan Fu Collection*.

Yan Fu scoured through Western cultures and thought in search of a recipe dealing with the various social ills of China. He was a devout follower of Spencer, had faith in social Darwinism, criticized China's traditional civil administration and politics, and was convinced that the Western values that were absent in China's traditions were exactly the key to the success of the wealthy and powerful Western countries. In his opinion, the optimal means to make China powerful was to improve the various abilities of the Chinese, namely, fully developing the intelligence, physical strength and morality under a free social environment. After the Sino-Japanese War, the national situation of China was getting more perilous by the day, and he suddenly awoke to the deep-entrenched illnesses of the imperial examinations and threw himself into the realm of political reform. In the 28th year of the Guangxu Emperor, the translation of bourgeois economics classics, *The Wealth of Nations*, came out. The first half of the translation was completed before the Reform Movement of 1898 and the other half was finished thereafter. Yan Fu was the first to introduce the bourgeois classic economics and vulgar economics into China.

His economic thought was sporadically seen in the comments inserted into the translations, especially in *The Wealth of Nations*;[1] there were over three hundred comments, amounting to over sixty thousand words. His ideas were coherent throughout, which approved, modified or disputed the statements of Smith (1723–1790), and he conducted in-depth comparison of both ancient and modern, Chinese and foreign economic works. Analysis and critique on China's historical and current economic problems manifested his economic views and theoretical perspectives. He was strongly opposed to the official policies and other economic intervention policies of the Qing Government, holding that these policies brought nothing but harm. He maintained that "matters concerning the livelihood of the people is best left to the people to decide", and upheld the policy that industry and commerce were to be run by the people, and held that economic liberalism and laissez-faire are the unshakable laws of economics. Those who violated them would suffer a crushing defeat. According to Yan Fu, the way of rescuing the country and the present situation fell into two categories, the difference between treating the symptoms and curing the ill, that is, wealth management was a temporary solution, whereas resolution of the root cause lay in instituting policy, raising talents, enculturing customs and pacifying the people. When the matter was an urgent one, the symptoms could not but be treated first, whereas for a less urgent matter, the root cause could be investigated. Therefore, there were different measures depending on urgency and the differences between the symptoms and the root causes. He expressed his own financial viewpoints

---

[1] *An Inquiry into the Nature and Causes of the Wealth of Nations* retranslated by Wang Ya-nan and Guo Da-li, thereafter *The Wealth of Nations* for short.

through translating and interpreting the thoughts conveyed in *The Wealth of Nations*, demonstrating that the establishment of the monetary system must follow the necessity of the commodity money relation development, which could not be forced. It analyzed the objective necessity and prospect of China's monetary reform, introduced banks into China, revealing that interest was part of the profit. However, the translation of *The Wealth of Nations* "was too intent on profundity and elegance, deliberately emulating the style of pre-Qin Dynasty writings, which made it very difficult to understand for those who are not too well versed in the classics" (Liang Qichao). Further, there were many deletions in the translation, and there existed great differences between the social, economic and cultural environments discussed in the book and those of China during the late Qing period; China's traditional monetary thought, the times and the class limitations were also somewhat embodied in the book. The book failed to draw sufficient attention and the expected repercussion after its publication.

2.1. Monetary thesis

Functions of money: Yan Fu summarized the functions of money into two main ones, "one is as a medium for trade, the other is as a measure of value".[2] According to a note by the original editor, the former was a "medium for trade" and the latter "a yardstick for value". Namely, the former functioned as a means of circulation, and the latter as a standard of value. Obviously, he understood the two basic functions of money very well, and paid more attention to its function as a means of circulation; hence, the function was presented first and the function as a standard of value was a bit less important and therefore presented later. These were based on the supply and demand theory of monetary value and the nominal theory of money.

On the supply and demand theory of monetary value, Yan Fu wrote, "the intrinsic value of gold and silver is the same as that of other commodities, depending on the fluctuation of supply and demand, regardless of the amount of such item." White gold (silver), for example, is more scarce;

---

[2]On page 22 of *The Wealth of Nations*, the Commercial Press, 1981. When this book is cited again, the page number alone will be indicated, the book title shall not be given again.

however, it is less expensive than gold. More than half of the 40-odd metal elements among the chemical elements are extremely difficult to obtain, but their prices are not high. The reasons lie in the fact that the demands for platinum and other metals are less than the demands for gold and other metals. Meanwhile, "where a country is poor in minerals, gold and silver have to be imported from without, the values thereof are tied to the commodity wherewith they are traded, however this phenomenon can still be placed under the rule of supply and demand" (p. 179). That is to say, the prices for general commodities not only depended on the supply of monetary metals but were also decided by the market demand quantity for monetary metals, that is, the ratio between monetary supply quantity and demand quantity. Hence, when it comes to embodying the function of "a yardstick of value", it may not necessarily be gold. In ancient times, it was said, "gold has four virtues, portability, non-perishability, ductility, and no quick change in value."

The situation was different in Yan Fu's time: "as trade expands on a daily basis, and minerals extracted across the world mount up, therefore the fourth virtue is hardly tenable anymore." It was exactly the change in the supply and demand relation for gold coin which induced value instability.

What did he mean by the phrase the worth of commodity in "the price depends on the worth of commodity with which it trades"? What are the differences between the worth of commodity he advanced and the monetary theories advanced by Adam Smith and David Ricardo? These questions can only be thoroughly answered through comparison.

Regarding the differences between his theory and the monetary theory of Adam Smith, Yan Fu refused to accept the statement of Adam Smith that the "true value" of a commodity depended on the "amount of human labor invested therein". He believed that such an argument stating that the value of a commodity depended on the difficulty and amount of human labor invested therein was "something though sounds reasonable, still a Homer's nod". A fine theory without being carried out in practice was but nothing. The reasoning was simple, "There is no constant value in an article; its value purely depends on the interaction between supply and demand. When supply falls short of demand, the commodity becomes expensive for its rarity; whereas if supply exceeds demand, the commodity gets less expensive for its easy availability" (p. 25). The price of a commodity depended on the difficulty of obtaining, difficulty in obtaining such commodity did not entail much human effort, and easy availability did not mean less labor. This view was not originally from Yan Fu; ancient sages had proposed the supply and demand theory in "Qing Zhong" from Guan Zi, which stated the same rule. Though Yan Fu was the first to introduce *The Wealth of Nations* of Adam Smith to China, and introduced the bourgeois classic economics, he failed to embrace the advanced Western theories of value; instead, he adhered stubbornly to the traditional Chinese theories, which was the tragedy of Yan Fu.

Compared with David Ricardo, the consummator of the Quantity Theory of Money, Yan Fu also differed in his theory of supply and demand of value. Specifically, there are four points:

The first is the difference in theoretical foundation. Of course, the Quantity Theory of Money proposed by David Ricardo conflicted with the Labor Theory of Value. Yan Fu only admitted that the value of money was decided by the quantity thereof, and explained that, viewed from the perspective of domestic gold production, if the gold production exceeded the required quantity of money in circulation, the relative value of gold would drop, and commodity prices would rise. Hence, gold production would drop to accommodate the circulation requirement for money, and the relative value of gold trended back to suit the regular value quantity; otherwise, gold production would pick up, until gold value dropped to the regular value quantity. Viewed from the perspective of international gold flow, gold was distributed according to the industries and wealth requirements in the various countries, and therefore money had the same value quantity in the various countries, and there would be no import or export of money. Where a country discovered a gold mine, money quantity in circulation would be excessive, and commodity prices would pick up, money value would drop below the metal value thereof, and there would be gold export or commodity import, until monetary circulation was restored to its normal level; on the contrary, the money value would rise above the metal value, and there would be gold import and commodity export. The theory was advanced in support of his free trade argument. Yan Fu was educated in the tradition of Chinese supply and demand theory, and held that a commodity was expensive when it was hard to obtain and inexpensive when it was easily available, regardless of the human labor and quantity involved; what mattered was only the change in ratio between the supply and demand of commodity in circulation. When a commodity was oversupplied, its price dropped due to easy availability; otherwise, it would be undersupplied, and the commodity price rose due to the rarity of it. In other words, when the supply of a commodity in circulation fell short of the objective demand, the price for such commodity would rise due to difficulty in acquiring such commodity, whereas if the supply of a commodity in circulation exceeded the practical demand, the price for such commodity would drop due to easy availability. For instance, "a lot of land the size of one *mu* (Chinese unit of measurement for area, about 667 square meters), if located at the remote area, it will not sell even for a few silvers; whereas if the same is located in the metropolis, it will soon be sold out even for ten thousand silvers; are there any differences in human effort?" Money quantity in circulation here was not involved; it only stated that the land price difference was brought into existence by difference in land supply and demand. By the same token, "for fruits from the same tree, those from the sunny side will bring about fair price for its sweetness and larger sizes, whereas those from the shaded area are discarded for its sourness and smaller sizes; are there any differences in labor here?" He concluded that "value is worth, and it is the equivalence between two equivalent names" (p. 25).

The second is the difference in the concept of value. Yan Fu had no idea of the theory of value; the value in his mind was actually the price, namely, the so-called the worth of commodity, and there was no constant value in a commodity, that is, the commodity price, and there was no fixed price for a commodity. He could not tell the difference between price and value, so he completely confused the two, and simplistically determined price solely on the supply and demand relation; he thought "the measure of value" might not necessarily be gold. Under the circumstance that trade expands on a daily basis and minerals extracted across the world accumulate by the day, it was inevitable for money value (actually commodity value) to undergo rapid change. On the contrary, David Ricardo based his theory of money partially on the Labor Theory of Value. He considered precious metals as a special commodity, and held that its "value is only proportional to the labor quantity necessary for the production and transportation of the commodity." He also thought that the value difference between silver and gold lay in the quantity difference between the two involved in the production thereof, and definitively noted, "Gold is about 15 times more expensive than silver; this is not due to greater demand for gold, nor due to 15 times more supply of silver than that of gold, it is solely due to the fact that it costs 15 times more labor in the acquisition of gold than that for the acquisition of silver."[3] It was as if this statement was specifically stated to Yan Fu. As a Chinese citizen who had studied British classic economics, Yan Fu had read quite some David Ricardo; however, he failed to get rid of the constraints of traditional Chinese concepts.

The third were the differences in prerequisites. The Quantity Theory of Money advanced by David Ricardo was based on the prerequisite of excluding the factor of change in supply and demand. The focus of the theory was placed on the comparative relation between commodity and money quantity which finally emerged after having encountered a series of mistakes. In comparison, Yan Fu paid attention to the change in supply and demand relation exclusively, be it between commodities, between metal currencies, or between commodity and metal money, and he acknowledged only the relation change between the "interaction of supply and demand".

The fourth was the difference in the similitude of mistakes. The mistakes of David Ricardo lay in the fact that he assumed that money was forever in circulation as a means of purchase to the exclusion of the function of money as a store of value. Similarly, in discussing the interaction between supply and demand, Yan Fu excluded the function of money as a store of value. However, their conclusions were different; on this account, David Ricardo failed to tell the difference between metal money and paper money, and confused the circulation law for metal money and that for paper money, and therefore arrived at the Quantity Theory of Money. On the contrary, Yan Fu based his observation on the apparent phenomenon of price change, and only saw the difference between the easy availability and difficulty of acquisition, and hence arrived at his supply and demand theory of value.

---

[3]David Ricardo, *On the Principles of Political Economy and Taxation*, the Commercial Press, 1962, p. 301.

On the nominal theory of money, Yan Fu thought that "the reason that money is only a denomination of property instead of real property is that if the stuff that it denominated and exchanged perishes, then the three categories of metal are nothing but dirt" (p. 22). Money is "an article for exchange", i.e., a medium: "it is like the stakes in gambling, those that are few in number denominate greater value, whereas those that are great in number denominate lesser value, what matters here is only a token, not the actual value of the stakes" (p. 168). This meant that money was not a commodity, it was not real property in society, but only a stake used for denomination, a stunt for wealth. Provided that the overall quantity of wealth remained constant, the money quantity was in inverse proportion to the wealth quantity it stood for, once it ceased being a token of wealth or the commodity it was required to exchange ceased to exist; that is, once it was removed from the exchange object, it was nothing but a pile of dirt. Then, what were the differences between gold, silver, copper and dirt? The physical value of metal money was not different from the token of value or paper money which stood for money.

Hence, Yan Fu concluded that the wealth of a country should not be judged based on the quantity of money it possessed, that is, not from the quantity of gold and silver it held. Hence, the statement, "even a country hoards a huge amount of gold, it may not necessarily be rich, this is an ultimately obvious fact." Actually, it was an ultimately obscure fact. Theoretically, he criticized those who engaged in mining gold and silver and earning foreign exchange as "preaching wealth management while they themselves are totally confused, which is hardly different from those who know nothing about the nerve network and instruct on excision of tumors, and they seldom fail to have people killed." Comparing it to killing people, the purpose was to criticize the fetishism of money tendency in mercantilism, striving to divert attention from the realm of circulation to the realm of production. He tried to undermine the importance of gold and silver from the perspective of economic policy, striving to find a means of livelihood for China, which was in dire shortage of gold and silver; such an effort was of positive significance. Policy based on erroneous theory was seldom successful in practice. The growth of capitalist economy, aggression against China and the economic reality had deepened people's understanding of the unrivalled might of money as the representative entity of social wealth and wealth in its entirety, which was not to be undermined by Yan Fu.

In conclusion, the monetary theory of Yan Fu was the weakest link in his financial theory in his absorbing advanced theories of Western bourgeois classical economics. There was not much innovation in his theories, for the fact that he refused to absorb new Western theories and failed to break away from the limitations inherent in traditional Chinese theory of money. Though he advanced many resounding arguments, he was also not free from mistakes and weaknesses.

2.2. *Monetary reform*

His demonstration of the relations between monetary systems of economic development, commodity and money, and bad money driving out good money stood out most distinctively from among the reformers and his overall monetary thought.

Yan Fu held that "establishing a monetary system" was inherently an artificial process, but the determination of monetary metal must "follow the natural course and let people have their hearts' desire" (p. 35). He surveyed the process in which the various countries established their legal tender money: "all established out of necessity, regardless of gold or silver, starting from the judicious decree of their respective predecessors, all contributing to the adoption thereof" (p. 34). Bimetallism ("coexistence of gold and silver money") grew into gold monometallism ("gold standard"): "it is not a result growing out of the forethought from those of high positions", it was actually the necessary development of commodity exchange. When Great Britain started to establish a modern monetary standard system, both gold and silver were legal tenders, and thereafter "no transaction is not conducted without the office of gold"; hence, the state decreed gold as the standard money; on the contrary, in France, Germany, Austria and Italy, no transaction was conducted without the office of silver, and only in modern times, the standard money of "silver has been replaced by gold". Therefore, he concluded, the selection of monetary metal in commodity exchange had to follow its inherent and necessary law, "there is a tendency that cannot be otherwise." Before such an inherent and necessary law, neither government nor the ruler could do anything about it, nor could anyone "bend the natural law to suit my will, or distort the law of nature." The function of a government lay in officially instituting the metal functioning as money in circulation via legislation, which was the rightful attitude of following the objective natural law and respecting the fact. Veritably as Marx once noted, "... that it is the sovereigns who in all ages have been subject to economic conditions, but they have never dictated laws to them."[4] The opinion held by Yan Fu exactly conformed to the statement.

There had never been a lack of writers theorizing on the economic phenomenon of bad money driving out good money in China, but none had conducted positive analysis by citing the history of the modern Western monetary system development as Yan Fu had done. He meticulously delineated the development and process of Great Britain promoting gold standard system from gold and silver bimetallism, as well as France, Germany, Austria and Italy promoting silver standard from bimetallism.

In the 56th year of the Kangxi Emperor (1717) of the Qing Dynasty, the statutory conversion rate in Great Britain was one gold guinea to 21 silver shillings, but it was actually converted to less than 20 silver shillings and 8 pence; hence, gold coin became the bad money and silver coin became the good money. Plus there was an abundance of gold and lack of silver in Europe in the Qianlong period, so using gold money was more profitable, and therefore gold coin functioned as the standard money. People generally stashed away silver and put out gold in exchange, when there was new silver shilling issued: "such silver coins were instantly stashed away, or exported to foreign countries, while those that were retained in the country in circulation were all worn down over years of use, and the weights of which were discounted." In the 39th year of the Qianlong Emperor (1774), the British parliament decreed that "where people desire to pay their taxes and debts by the number of coins, such payment may not exceed five hundred shillings, that is, twenty five pounds, any amount exceeding said number shall be paid by the weight thereof." The decree also stipulated that one ounce equaled five shillings and two pence. In the 21st year of the Jiaqing Emperor (1816), the conversion rate for state-minted silver coin was changed from 62 coins to

---

[4]*Karl Marx and Frederick Engels*, vol. 4, p. 121.

66 coins per pound, while one guinea was still converted to 21 silver shillings, and hence "the move necessarily reversed the prior disadvantage associated therewith, gold was stashed away while silver was put out for use, therefore gold coin found no cause of establishment" (p. 32). As stated above, the British parliament then decreed that gold was the unlimited legal tender, while silver the limited legal tender. On the contrary, in France, Germany, Austria and Italy, a gold Louis d'or was statutorily converted to 24 silver livres, but in practice one gold Louis d'or was converted to 25 livres and ten sous. Therefore, gold became the good money and silver the bad money: "when people pay taxes and debts, every ten Louis d'or are converted to one livre and ten sous, hence none is transacted without using silver." Which clearly indicated that there was a great difference between the actual prevailing conversion rate ("the real rate") and the statutory rate ("the stipulated rate"): "families paying taxes or debts will absolutely use the money whose nominal value exceeds its real value, and those currencies whose nominal value falls short of their real value would either be hoarded and melted or collected and exported to foreign countries, even draconian law failed to eliminate such practice" (p. 35).

That is to say, those currencies with higher conversion rates in practice, what we call good money, were hoarded, or destroyed, melted and shipped abroad, and finally driven out of circulation; on the contrary, those metal currencies with higher statutory conversion rates, what we call bad money, monopolized the circulation. Such a monetary phenomenon was not what the draconian law by the government could prohibit, and therefore bimetallism was only in nominal existence.

The analysis conducted and conclusion reached by Yan Fu were very insightful, and he negated the proposals that China should institute bimetallism, or even trimetallism as some people advocated, and his understanding was more insightful than scholars such as Chen Chi and Zheng Guanying. His amendment to Adam Smith's statement of "when more than one standard is instituted, through the interaction among the currencies, the money with the highest statutory rate prevails" (p. 34) was also correct. This reflected the fact that Yan Fu was intensive in his research into Western theories of money without slavish following thereof, which was an adequate proof of his superior perspective and determination as well as rigorous attitude.

Based on these observations, Yan Fu proposed that "if China ever strives for prosperity and wealth, then the top priority both the civilian officials and military commanders must tackle" was monetary system reformation. The defects in the current monetary system had already caused deep trouble, and China could learn from the Western countries, especially from Great Britain. Because Great Britain was the first Western country "instituting gold standard", "which is ultimately rewarding", the instance was most convincing and practical. In his opinion, the gold standard of Great Britain could be summarized into the following four points: First, gold was the unlimited legal tender, whereas silver was not a legal tender money, and the amount of taxes or debts people paid with silver may not exceed 40 shillings. Second, the government minted shillings within a certain quota to prevent value debasement due to oversupply; copper coin was an inferior money, and the amount of payment made with one-pence coin may not exceed one shilling, namely, 12 pence, and payment with farthings may not exceed half a shilling, that is, 24 farthings. Third, the government minted gold coins without increasing or decreasing the value thereof, and all costs of minting and coal related thereto should be recovered from the shilling and the penny. Fourth, forging with precision molds, the edges and reticules as well as intaglio patterns were uniform and compact, making private minting "impractical unless in large scale, however once minted in large scale the cause will soon be exposed."

"Two key points in the state minting of money: One is that coins should be of equal weight (fixed weight), two is that coins should be of equal purity (different coins may not be of varying purity). And hence three virtues generated therefrom: One is convenience, two prevention of malpractice, three edifying the customs" (p. 22).

Therefore, in Yan Fu's opinion, the reason for the eradication of private minting and private selling of coins in Great Britain lay "not in its effective disclosing of irregularities and implementation of draconian law" (p. 32), but in the rigor and reasonableness of the British laws.

Yan Fu promoted the modern monetary system of Great Britain without distinguishing it from the monetary system of the semi-colonial and semi-feudal society of China, and prepared to introduce it into China. In his opinion, in China "there exist three categories of metals, yellow gold (gold) is the superior, white gold (silver) the intermediate and pink gold (copper) the inferior; the three metals are in circulation side by side which is a phenomenon seen in the Great Britain, France, etc., in the current world. When the Kingdom of Qin unified China, coins were classified into two categories. Yellow gold was called pure gold, was deemed a superior money; copper was inscribed as half tael, its name indicates its weight, an inferior money" (p. 19). In practice, the three categories and two categories of money of China were all different from those of Great Britain and France. None of the three categories, superior, intermediate and inferior money, or two categories, the superior and inferior money, of China stood in the relation of primary and secondary money, or the relation between unlimited legal tender and limited legal tender. Though some division of labor took shape in the exchange process, precious metals were mainly used in large-amount payments, the paying and receiving activities among upper, ruling classes, whereas base metals were mainly used in small-amount payments, in the exchange among the lower classes and civil activities. The government did not decree which money was the primary money and which one was the secondary, which one was the unlimited legal tender or a limited legal tender, which one could or could not be freely converted and minted through legislation. As for chaos in pricing criteria in areas of pricing standards, weight and purity, minting and issuing, chaos was the rule rather than exception. These were the prominent features of a pre-modern monetary system in which the monetary system of modern and contemporary times had not taken shape and established. How could the two be mentioned in the same breath, and compared without any common grounds in sight? This was something Yan Fu failed to see.

Countries around the globe successively adopted the gold standard system, while China alone adhered to the outdated silver standard system and was hampered by the situation in which the silver was too cheap and gold too expensive, and the national strength dwindled by the day; trapped in a perilous situation, China was reduced from a grand and prosperous country to an inferior country. "In the last decade, the great change of gold appreciation and silver depreciation in East Asia is unheard of in history. Measured in gold, silver almost halved its value than that of ten years ago." "Roughly speaking, the cause of this situation is that silver mines are producing more and more by the day, this being the first reason; Eastern and Western countries have all discarded silver and switched to the gold standard system, this being the second reason" (p. 354). Regarding the cause of the continued depreciation of silver, Yan Fu conducted an in-depth analysis, which few could rival. In his opinion, "the loss of silver value of China, compared to that of thirty years ago, amounted to almost one third. What our people have strived thrice the effort to have accumulated, to date only two thirds remain. Whatever wealth has been accumulated in the form of silver sees the loss, if the combined amount of the twenty strong provinces of China is calculated, then it could be seen how extensive the loss of silver depreciation has incurred to the national wealth, how can the number be insignificant! How can the number be insignificant?" (p. 213). "Trapped in the situation, China is incapable of making a change, hence becomes an inferior country, and from the past to the present commodity prices underwent drastic change" (p. 355). "The more time lapses, the more difficult for monetary system to change, this is the most worrisome issue China faces" (p. 455).

What was the way out for China's monetary system? "The officials currently in high offices strive to maintain the stability of the values of gold and silver, this is naturally an issue they could not but promote, however great prudence must be made in planning so that the change may be incremental and smooth, this is the matter of great stake of the state" (p. 213). Hence, it could be seen that a bimetallism of gold and silver would not work. What about the fate of promoting monometallism of gold? Yan Fu was equally negative on this proposal. He said, "now that the various countries have adopted the gold standard, while China alone remains unchanged. Though there is huge disadvantage in the situation, if China abruptly discards silver and embraces gold, it would be something beyond its national strength." Since China had insufficient financial strength, a reckless move would cause inconceivable consequences; hence, by blind imitation without taking into consideration the national situation and without mobilizing the national strength comprehensively, monetary system reform cannot but fail. Hence, came the predicament, it would be impossible not to reform but huge obstacles would lay on the road to reform, so where was the prospect of China's monetary system reform? Yan Fu was at a loss and had to write cautiously, "This is a matter of great significance, from issues as significant as the emoluments of governmental officials to matters as insignificant as exchange between merchants, all suffer from the situation. Anyone aiming to right the wrong in a grand way should not fail to read extensively and deliberate repeatedly" (p. 172). Regarding promoting the issuance of paper money, he showed keen interest; there was the benefit of portability in issuing paper money. He made four complements to the "convenience" feature suggested by Adam Smith. Metal money "becomes heavy and unwieldy when in great amounts, and difficult to transport, this is one disadvantage; and it involves weighing, measuring and calculating, a very complicated process, which leads to malpractice, this is the second disadvantage; ill-thought way of concealment tends to invite theft, this is the third disadvantage"; in areas of great trade volume which rose and fell as though the flood tide and ebb tide of the sea, sometimes the need was urgent and sometimes unhurried, metal money cannot properly suit the market demand for money quantity to be circulated in ever changing environments; there were often situations where the supply failed to meet the demand. For paper money, the situation was different: "the quantity of production and issuing thereof can be immediately addressed as the situation requires." It could meet the market demand anytime, and furnish the market with sufficient exchange vehicle in a timely manner; this was the fourth point. Therefore, issuing paper money was due to "the ever deepening governance and civilization process, the ever broadening exchange among merchants, the medium of exchange, it is practically impossible even though one specifically desires to implement a monetary system of three categories" (p. 270). This was the necessary outgrowth of ever-deepening, ever-broadening social development and economic exchange; no country across the globe, neither the east nor the west, could stay outside the trend. This was a very penetrating insight.

Issuing paper money is an evitable outcome of money exchange, but such practice is not without its shortcomings. Yan Fu endorsed David Ricardo's opinion, remarking that "there are two points that may concern us, one is that when the demand is urgent and greater while the issuing is insufficient, then the value of the paper money will exceed that of its face value; the other is that circulation without redemption will decrease the value of the paper money below its face value." That is to say, if market demand surged and the quantity of paper money issued lagged behind the demand, then the real purchasing power would exceed the nominal purchasing power, and the real value it stood for would exceed its face value; on the contrary, when such paper money cannot be redeemed, the surplus paper money will get stuck in circulation, then the real purchasing power would fall short of the nominal purchasing power, and the real purchasing power would drop below its face value. The two situations both reflected the unstable purchasing power of paper money: the amount of value it stood for varied and the money value was unstable. That is to say, in the former situation paper money appreciated because of deflation, whereas in the latter it depreciated due to inflation: "the two situations are both evils to the people, and the latter is especially vicious to the people." As stated above, deflation "can be immediately dealt with", whereas inflation without a redemption remedy was absolutely not something that could be cured immediately. In order to prevent the occurrence of the latter situation, the requirements for the monetary system had to be followed: freedom of redemption; melting and forging guaranteed; trading gold for paper money allowed, "no brutal refusal is allowed, when people bring paper money to redeem gold, even though gold stock in the bank is not high, it may not refuse to cash the paper money with gold, and pay the paper money bearer with gold of the weight and purity specified by the monetary bureau. Only in this way could the paper money be established as an adequate instrument for the purpose, and there would be no premium any more" (pp. 270–271). Veritably as Marx once said, "Identity has already entailed its opposite — possible nonidentity; redeemability entails its opposite — irredeemability; appreciation entails depreciation, in Aristotle's words, implicit entailment."[5] When Yan Fu discussed the disadvantages of issuing paper money, his support for and emphasis on redeemability were correct. However, in order to maintain the stability of paper money's purchasing power, it would be inadequate to simply guarantee the freedom of paper money redemption; the key lay in whether the paper money issue quantity could be placed under strict control. In his words, the banknotes issued by the banks were different from the paper money issued by the state, and the purpose of paper money issue was not to satisfy government financial

---

[5]*Ibid.*, vol. 46, Book 1, p. 77.

requirements, it was to meet the requirement for the circulation of drafts. Therefore, "These do not rest upon the circulation of money, be it metallic or government-issued paper money, but rather upon the circulation of bills of exchange,"[6] and are regulated and governed by a law totally different from that of paper money circulation. These were reasons neither David Ricardo nor Yan Fu understood.

Yan Fu was consistently opposed to the abusive issuance of paper money by the government. He enumerated the facts that in many areas of North America, unrestrained paper money issue brought about mounting problems to the nations and untold suffering to the people. Domestically, since the Southern Song Dynasty, whenever the government faced financial problems they would try to issue paper money to tide over the situation, but only at cross-purposes, ultimately failing in their attempts. When investigating the reasons thereof, people erroneously assumed that "With the unlimited power of a state government, it can beget something from nothing, and produce paper money to be forever circulated in society, without anyone questioning when such can be converted into real money." By placing excessive faith in the power of government without restraint placed on issue quantity, assuming no responsibility for redemption, the people would be worried and concerned, and monetary system would be in chaos, which would ultimately be detrimental to the state. "All old and new were of the same flock, and few know how many countries they have jeopardized" (p. 681). Though the paper money discussed here was different from the above-mentioned paper money, one was redeemable and the other irredeemable, one was a credit money or banknote, the other paper money; the two related but different concepts got confused here. However, his understanding of the cause of oversupply of paper money could be said to be profound.

2.3. Theory on bank interest

In order to develop production, there would be the need for sufficient capital support, while expanding capital source depended on the banks to absorb unemployed capital in society. Therefore, Yan Fu expounded on the points that establishing banks was beneficial to both bringing

---

[6]*Ibid.*, Vol. 25, p. 451.

prosperity to the country and convenience to the people. Saving banks especially had special positive functions different from other banks.

Yan Fu drew inspiration from the history of Scotland in establishing banks. He thought that "in the period between Kangxi Emperor and Yongzheng Emperor, Scotland started to establish banks, engaged in making loans, which greatly benefited the people, and the nation became increasingly rich." Scotland was located in a remote, desolate and cold place; the land was barren and the people rough. Its taxes could not meet expenditure requirements. Compared with England, it was the fertile to the barren, the rich to the poor. Due to the fact that it made progress annually, in 100 or 200 years, it had gained strength comparable to that of England and France. One of the drives that propelled the unlimited development of Scotland was its sound banking system. For instance, when making loans, the bank required an applicant to be secured by several people (at least two people) jointly, "which is called security. A security determines the amount of a loan, usually the loan ranges from a hundred pounds to a thousand pounds." The security has "the right to ban the loan, increase or decrease the size of the loan" (p. 85). The lender can terminate the loan anytime according to the ability of the applicant and diligence manifested thereby. In this way, saving banks can both stimulate the people to apply themselves to work and provide them with financial safeguarding and security, and therefore can work the practical effects of guiding the people to prosperity and motivating them to apply themselves to work. Judging from the way Yan Fu sang the praises of the economic takeoff of Scotland, detailing the security and reliability of its lending method, the advantages of supporting economic growth and facilitating the national prosperity, we can conclude that he was endorsing the establishment and growth of private banks in China to raise capital and support the development of national industries, facilitate economic prosperity and make China a country of wealth.

Saving banks deserve special mention. In Yan Fu's opinion, setting up saving banks "is not only the ultimate strategy of making a country wealthy, it can also edify the people in the process." Starting saving banks was not for the sole purpose of transforming the people from poor to rich, it could also transform customs, encourage the formations of social conventions of frugality and accumulation, and convert people's ideas; by doing so, the virtues it renders would be boundless and peerless. This was the significance of setting up saving banks.

Functions of saving banks: In Yan Fu's opinion, its functions were to "accept consigned property and offer interest in return". Its characteristics were "that the amount of loan can be extremely small, and the term can be extremely short", that is, many a little makes a mickle, it had the effect of extending the short into a long, stimulating the stagnant into a flow. Money or monetary capital scattered among the individuals used to be neglected due to its smallness of size and brevity of duration; they had been employed in places which generated no return. The appearance of saving banks offered the ordinary people a convenience; all their money could be deposited in the bank, regardless of how small such an amount was and how brief the duration was. "Therefore the people benefited and prospered, cattle flocked, after a few years, the once poor families turned into houses of moderate means" (p. 250). He surveyed the issue of capital from the perspective of Western economies, and held that so long as capital stayed in circulation people would get rich, otherwise people would get impoverished. Therefore, he forcefully appealed, "stagnant property leads to poverty, which is more detrimental than luxury." He was firmly convinced that the evil cause to India and China's transformation from former wealthy countries into poor countries lay exactly in it, because hoarding property "neither grows nor yields interest", be it a big national government or a small businessman and ordinary people; in short, it did not accrue. If the country has the need "to build something and to mobilize money, then it would face the dilemma of inability to raise sufficient capital and has to pay exorbitant interest, which will yield national interest to hostile nations and foreigners, how can a country in such a situation not be besieged by great troubles" (p. 249).

Theory of interest: Yan Fu aired his personal views on issues including the concept of interest, the determining factors and usury interest rate.

The concept of interest by Yan Fu's definition: "What interest refers to is part of the profit". "Therefore the interest is the price for purchasing the right to employ the property." That is to say, interest was part of the profit; it was the price of purchasing the right to utilize the capital (property). This definition clearly indicated the source of interest, and therefore disclosed the essence of interest, which was a penetrating insight of the writer. However, his definition was inevitably influenced by classic economics, and the statement of interest as price contradicted with his previous argument. Viewed from that angle, it indeed displayed the value movement form unique to lending behavior; it was both the right to use capital and also a capital appearing in the form of commodity, and therefore also had a price. However, the price was only a price in form, different from the real price. Yan Fu failed to distinguish the form from the essence, took the phenomenon for essence, concealed the real source of interest from the perspective of price, and ultimately concealed the exploitative nature of interest.

Factors affecting interest rate: In Yan Fu's opinion, "all prices are the results of the interaction between supply and demand, how can the policy makers force their rules thereon?" That is, the supply and demand of lending determined the level of interest rates. He emphasized that interest was regulated by the law of market supply and demand; it could not be controlled and manipulated by the rulers. Theoretically, when the government exercised control on interest rate, the higher the interest rate the heavier the exploitation sustained by the people. This was because a higher interest rate arose out of a situation where the borrower was in great need of a loan, and the lender would be reluctant to make a loan on a lower interest rate; however, "high interest rate violates the law and incurs punishment, now that an offence is committed, then further insurance is required to cover such risk over the usury loan." That is to say, there would be further charge on the interest, and therefore the resulting interest rate would be heavier than usury; hence, he argued that the government should let the interest rate follow its natural course, whereas arbitrary imposition of policy "makes a great chaos in wealth management" (p. 84). The problem was that interest rate on loan capital differed from usury interest rate; in addition to being susceptible to the change of market supply and demand, the most important factor affecting interest rates is the average profit margin. However, if one excluded the average profit margin and emphasized the function of the supply and demand relation, it would be as much as barring value and discussing supply and demand alone in determining commodity price; both failed to touch on the essence of interest rate.

So long as it can uphold the benefits and bring prosperity to the people, it would be unnecessary to weigh the interest rate level. In correcting Adam Smith's argument that if "a poor country exits regulation and then usury loan will be rampant", Yan Fu noted that the European and American countries were of vast territory and abundant resources, and there were many more benefits to be explored; the people were earnest in their needs for loans, and the profits were tremendous and interest rates high, "because there are a great many unemployed benefits, there are also handsome return on usury loans, the policy bringing about the highest profit is due to the era of the situation." The interest rate at the time in China was very high: "half of the reason lies in that people do not trust each other, and half in that many matters are waiting to be done." The interest rate would trend higher thereafter. Because "railways of great length are being built, annually there emerged new unemployed benefits, hence the interest rate on usury loans would necessarily rise substantially." According to his speculation, if such substantial rise did not materialize, the situation was necessarily out of two reasons. One was that "China set up banking houses on its own with detailed and sound charters of association, and the people deposited their stagnant property without scruples"; the other was that "people of sound means deposit their wealth in foreign banks, and lend such via selective security thereby, and there is nothing to worry about." In his opinion, "the former benefits China, whereas the latter injures the interests of China" (p. 223).

Foreign banks in China accepted idle money and intermittently idled money capital, and then reinvested in China for the purpose of pillaging and controlling the country, which was a grand threat to and loss of China's economic rights and interests, and indeed required "the officials in high offices to examine and review". This was the specific manifestation in the financial realm of the strategy of using Chinese resources to subdue China by the Western powers; Yan Fu uncovered the situation and sounded the alarm, which was indeed a praiseworthy deed.

Usury interest rate of ancient times: Yan Fu did not approve of the argument that "interest rate in ancient times was higher due to the fact that higher profit margin could be obtained then". That is to say, a higher interest rate in ancient times did not mean a higher profit; if one was to prove the argument, the first point to prove was that there were more borrowers in ancient times, otherwise it would be futile to prove the existence of a higher profit on the basis of a high interest rate. He held that there were two factors determining high interest rate, "one, depending on the relative greater number of lenders and borrowers, two, depending on the credit of the people of the time, neither had anything to do with profit margin" (p. 275). That is to say, first, it was determined by the supply and demand situation for usury capital, and then it was determined by the credit situation; it had nothing to do with profit margin. The conclusion that usury interest rate of ancient times was not determined by profit margin was correct. However, he did not produce sufficient proof in support of his argument. "The form of interest is older than that of profit. The level of interest in India for communal agriculturists in no way indicates the level of profit. But rather that profit as well as part of wages itself is appropriated in the form of interest by the usurer."[7] On the top limit of usury interest rate he said, "Hence the usurer knows no other barrier but the capacity of those who need money to pay or to resist."[8] Moreover, historically, "Profit thus appears originally determined by interest. But in the bourgeois economy, interest is determined by profit, and is only part of the latter. Hence profit must be large enough to allow of a part of it branching off as interest."[9] Therefore, the relationship between usury capital and loan capital is different from the relationship of domination between interest rate and profit margin; this fact should not be confused or mixed up.

3. Qian Xun's financial theory

Qian Xun (1853–1927), courtesy name Nianqu, was born in Gui'an of Zhejiang Province (present-day Wuxing). In the 10th year of the Guangxu Emperor (1884) he entered the service of Xue Fucheng, the Ningbo-Shaoxing prefecture governor, and after the 16th year of the Guangxu

---

[7]*Ibid.*, Vol. 46, Book 2, pp. 381–382.
[8]*Ibid.*, Vol. 25, p. 677.
[9]*Ibid.*, Vol. 46, Book 2, p. 382.

Emperor he followed Xue on official visits to the UK, France, Italy, Belgium, etc., in the capacity of backup county magistrate in Zhili Province. In the 24th year, he was reassigned to the post of Supervisor of Hubei students studying in Japan, in the 31st year as counselor to the commissioner studying overseas constitutional government, in the 33rd year to the post of ambassador to the Netherlands, and he became ambassador to Italy in the following year. He returned to China in the 1st year of the Xuantong Emperor (1909), and in 1914 he worked as a member of the Council of State and was emeritus editor of Peking University. His works include: *Fifty-five Memorials Submitted to the Emperor during My Two Years' Ambassy in Two Countries* and *Four Pillars of Finance*.

In the 27th year of the Guangxu Emperor (1901), Qian Xun wrote the *Four Pillars of Finance*. "Four Pillars" referred to tax and rent, money, bank and national debt. With over a hundred thousand Chinese characters, the book was divided into four volumes, and the two volumes on money and bank took up over fifty-five thousand Chinese characters. The money volume included eight sections: ancient currencies in the world, functions of money, materials of money, minting of money, money systems, money standard, the law of money circulation and paper currencies.

The bank volume included five sections: the origin of bank and evolution, categories of bank, business of bank, paper currencies of bank, and issuing of paper currencies, cause of panic and remedy thereof. In the author's preface, he claimed that he knew "no oriental writing (Japanese), nor could I understand the profundity of it, I recorded herein four pillars according to what students have described to me." However, the book was substantial in content and systematic in method, absolutely not something which could have been compiled upon dictation, so he must have researched extensively. As far as what we know today, this should have been the earliest book comprehensively theorizing money and bank based on the Western monetary banking study of the time.

3.1. Monetary thesis

Money is a creation of wealth managers (economists). Qian Xun believed that commodity was the product of commodity exchange, a hallmark of human civilization. "Civilization evolves and commodities emerge, division of labor appears and exchange begins." Meanwhile, he thought that money has been created by economists who thought that exchange of articles "gradually failed", "absolutely inapplicable" to meet the requirements of commodity production and the development of exchange; they "created a third item to be the medium between the seller and the buyer, hence came the money. As money emerged, the inconvenience of article exchange was dissolved." Money indeed overcame the inconvenience of article exchange, was a product of the progress of exchange, and was far from being the ingenious product of a few people.

Functions of money: Qian Xun thought that money had four functions, as an exchange medium (means of circulation), as a value yardstick, as a means of payment for lending and for borrowing (means of payment) and store of value (means of value storage). The domestic understanding of the four monetary functions was adequately sound; what remained debatable was only an order of sequence and naming, which revealed his omissions and mistakes under the influence of Western economics.

Qian Xun definitively specified the relation between measure of value and price. "Measure is established on price, price is created for measurement." He also defined the order relation between commodity price and exchange; commodity price comes first and then exchange, "if there were articles without measure thereof, then there was no proper exchange." However, he confused the difference between price standard and value measure, and mistakenly regarded that price standard was "the basis for monetary study". This was hardly strange, because his understanding of value was still rather superficial; he merely argued that "value is to be researched from among the measure, and generated therefrom", "when money meets commodity, value emerges; otherwise money holds only an empty name of value." He even erroneously thought that once people changed their credit and habits, "gold and silver will naturally extinguish their values." In his opinion, the value of money was not an inherent property of monetary commodity, and only obtained such property in comparison to other commodities.

"Because monetary value has commodity purchasing power, therefore it has the advantage in exchange, however commodity value also has the money purchasing power in return." Because the monetary value is the purchasing power of the money, money has commodity purchasing power, and hence the commodity acquires the money purchasing power and the purchasing power is reciprocal. Qian Xun saw the common property of money and commodity, but failed to see the difference between the two, especially failing to understand the particularity of money as a universal equivalent. Hence, he confused the purchasing power of money and monetary value. In conclusion, he failed to understand what value was.

Qian Xun understood that the metal that serves as the material of money can only apply to a certain function of money, and cannot serve all the four functions. Article A might serve as a means of circulation, Article B might serve as a measure of value, or Article C might serve as a means of payment, yet still Article D might serve as a store of value. "If there is one thing that serves four functions simultaneously, it should have been an extremely convenient matter, however the fact is that in most cases four functions cannot coexist in one article, but appear in several articles separately, that is what necessarily is the case." Separation of the functions of money like this was due to the fact that he failed to understand the functions of money as one interrelated integral unity; they may not be divided and considered in isolation, and he erroneously placed the means of circulation in the first place and mistook the characteristics of the means of circulation (practical, valuable and not necessarily of full value) as the common properties of money.

Qian Xun noted that, as a medium for the exchange of articles, money should have seven essential material properties, that is, the properties necessary for the material of money. Satisfying the common interest of the people, it possesses the advantages of portability without the perils of wear and loss, it has all the conveniences of same quality, same form, ease of division, counting and distribution, little change in value and ease of identification in quality and form. Except that the first property is a social property, the remaining six are all natural properties, and they are roughly identical to the properties including homogeneity, separability, combinability, small size with big value, and ease of storage, roughly equivalent to the functions and properties such as fit for representation and value measurement that people talk about today. What small size with big value referred to was the second, sixth and seventh properties, ease of storage the third, homogeneity the fourth, and separability and combinability the fifth. Weighed under this perspective, through historical choice, such metal materials as copper, iron, lead and tin had been eliminated, and only "gold and silver are the most appropriate ones." "All countries adopted gold and silver standard as long as it aspires for progress." That is to say, the gold standard or silver standard was historically inevitable, and was the general trend of world money development.

The monetary system evolved from weighing monetary systems to counting monetary systems. In discussing the weighing monetary system, Qian Xun quoted the words of a Japanese economist, "China has instituted monetary systems in ancient times, and could have been called advanced civilization in the world, a country of the earliest monetary system. However the country still employs weighing monetary system, it is really an odd phenomenon." What he called an odd phenomenon was that the countries around the world had evolved to counting monetary systems, while China, the oldest civilization, still adhered slavishly to the outdated weighing monetary system and refused to move one step forward, unable to keep up with other countries and follow the trend of the world. In his mind, "counting monetary system is naturally a more advanced system than weighing monetary system. All civilized countries have adopted it; even those half civilized countries also flocked to foreign money of counting measurement because they were keenly aware of the inconvenience of the weighing monetary system." Obviously, China indeed lagged behind.

Bimetallism: Qian Xun wrote, as "bad money drives out good money, the so-called Gresham's Law has gained great popularity." It was truly a rarity in history when the statutory conversion rate of gold and silver matched that of the prevailing market rate. Under the bimetallism, if the market price for gold coin exceeded the statutory price (expensive), then the money in circulation would be silver coin, which would inconvenience traveling businessmen as it was difficult to carry; on the contrary, if the market price for silver coin exceeded the statutory price for gold coin, then what was circulated would be gold coin, and small businesses would see losses. Bimetallism would necessarily lead to the situation where expensive metals were melted and exported, whereas the base metal money functioned alone in the circulation realm, and the outcome was necessarily that bimetallism existed in name only, and ultimately would be replaced by the unitary gold standard system. However, a unitary gold standard system also gradually revealed its inconvenience. The materials for precious metals were of higher prices, inconvenient for small-amount business payments and division, whereas the materials for base metals were of lower value, insufficient for making large-sum payment; therefore, even under a single monetary standard, composite standards would gradually emerge, that is, the statutory money should be for proper money use, and complemented by other money. There was a difference between "a bimetallism complemented by a composite standard system" and "a unitary standard system complemented by a composite standard system". The latter took "precious metal as the proper article (the standard money), and the base metal as the complement (fractional money), regardless of its statutory price or market price, the conversion rate is fixed without fluctuation." There was a statutory limit for payment with fractional money; they are coins of inferior quality minted with low-value base metals. The composite standard system under the unitary standard system was actually a unitary standard system, "even in countries adopting a gold standard system, gold does not monopolize monetary circulation; under such a system, gold is employed as the statutory standard money, however, it still has to be complemented with silver and copper etc." This adequately proved that there was no difference between the gold standard system and composite standard system; what he failed to understand was that the gold standard system was a system wherein gold coin was the primary money, and other coins were fractional money, and it did not equal sole metal money in circulation to the total exclusion of other metal money.

Paper money was the inevitable outcome of money development. "When transactions were increasingly frequent, businessmen craved for credit, especially the advantage of portability, when people had this in mind, even with the portability of hard metal money, people still considered it too heavy and inconvenient for carrying and trading. Therefore there arose the fine practice of exchange purely based on price, and there were personal checks as well as paper currencies. All simply trended to simplicity and convenience." "There are four reasons for paper money replacing metal money in circulation." The first was portability. "Coins are not portable, unlike the portability of paper money." The second was saving interest and value gain on capital. "Transactions on the market are all conducted via paper money, while the substance of metal can be used separately as a capital, which is to free up the money in substance for an interest." The third was the benefits of safety and lower risk. "When there was no paper money, people held metal money, they would surely store it in an impenetrable house and had it guarded with a loyal servant." Study on the origin of banks of England revealed that, there was indeed the factor of storing and safeguarding. The fourth reason was free from damage and loss from wear and tear. "The price (value) of coins necessarily decreases in the long run, whereas paper money could maintain the price (value) of the hard money."

Redeemable paper money and irredeemable paper money: Qian Xun noted that there were three advantages in the circulation of redeemable paper money. The first was portability: "it is more portable than gold, and way more portable than silver." The second was the ability to increase the amount of money. The experiences of paper money issuance in history proved that "only a fraction of money should be set aside as reserve, whatever the difference between the amount of paper money issued and the amount of hard money is, such difference can put into adequate use." The third was elasticity ("elastic property"). It may "expand or contract according to the degree of social demand." This was the "biggest advantage" of redeemable paper money. There were both advantages and disadvantages in the elasticity of paper money, and there were different understandings of this issue between monetarism and free bankerism.[10]

---

[10]Opposing monetary and financial schools and theories of the mid-19th century in Great Britain. Representatives of the former include Samuel Jones Loyd (1796–1883), Norman (1793–1882) and Peel (1788–1850) who claimed that the issuance of banknotes should be strictly limited and backed by full amount of gold reserve. They thought decentralized bank-issuing right is the real cause of the financial crisis, and advocated issuing right to be centralized in the Bank of England. On the contrary, representatives of the banking school such as Tucker (1774–1858), Fullarton (1780–1849) and Wilson (1805–1860) emphasized that banknote issuance should be adapted to the elastic needs of the economy and be flexible, that banknote issuance should be adapted to industry and commerce requirement for credit; if the market did not need such banknotes, they would flow back to banks. It was impossible for banks to issue banknotes without any restraint, and they were opposed to the idea of full reserve and opposed to setting a limit on the quantity of issuance.

His conclusion was that "the monetarism sounds more reasonable, whereas bankerism advocates the advantage paper money brought about, however speculation arises, financial circle is disturbed, trade suffers, additional issuing of paper money cannot but take the blame. If the banks are vested with the right of issuance, demand would absolutely surge, while the competition for issuance knows no bounds." Of course, he could not have understood the two theories in a profound manner.

The advantages and disadvantages of irredeemable paper money were more obvious. In Qian Xun's opinion, "if elasticity is skillfully employed, and its nominal value is maintained, then the country would reap no little benefit therefrom." The benefit might exceed that of gold. Specifically there are three benefits, the first of which is reduced cost. Under general social credit conditions, it "is sufficient to mark the price for regular exchange, with little difference from hard money". The second is the small value and great variation, very convenient for division and calculation in payment. The third is that, if there was sound government credit, with proper issuance and regulation, it was the best means of payment. However, with advantages came disadvantages, of which there were five. First, there were no natural constraints like that of gold and silver coins in the amount of issuance. The amount of paper money issuance "might be two times or three times, depending solely on human will", without considering the requirements for production and distribution, and it could be issued entirely depending on fiscal requirements, which was more dangerous compared to gold and silver coins. The two could not be mentioned in the same breath.

Second, there would be an increase in issuance whenever an accident occurred. For instance, if "the government is involved in upheaval in infrastructure, trade," or "fiasco in war, invasion by foreign enemy, occurrence of catastrophe such as flood or drought, which prompted increase in paper money issuance, then great harm would be incurred thereby." Nothing could have been more convenient for the government, but nothing could have been so harmful to the people: "to increase taxes and rent is extremely difficult, however issuing paper money by simply affixing a governmental seal on it would be an extremely easy matter." "If the ruler covets this convenience, it would definitely set the country and the people in utter misery." Third, it was easy to issue money but it was difficult to halt issuing; there was a danger that the more that was issued, the more difficult it would be to halt issuing.

It could not be used on the international market beyond the borders of a country; when additional paper money is issued "such issuance accumulates and stays within the border, prices rise by the day, once the government tries to check the its dwindling financial strength and engages in additional issuance, there would be no limit to the issuance." Fourth, even if there is not much additional issuance, it would still impact trade and production on no small scale. Fifth, there would be price fluctuation and unpredictable market movement; when there was additional issuance, prices would surge, while when there was insufficient money, prices would plummet. Therefore, Qian Xun argued that irredeemable paper money "would absolutely bring about myriad evils including financial constraint, business suppression, credit plummeting and property damage and loss." A country would not issue such money without having been absolutely cornered. In order to prevent it from causing very serious damage, it should be adopted only as a temporary expedient measure, and it may never be adopted as a long-term application ("the fiscal policy makers are advised not to adopt this inferior measure unless absolutely necessary, even if this measure is adopted it must be quickly disposed of, then its damage might not be that great").

Qian Xun particularly emphasized that the biggest victim of increasing issuance of irredeemable paper money was the general public ("the likes of employees and ordinary workers, the so-called labor society"). Irredeemable paper money was the optimal means for the fiscal agency to skillfully extort wealth. First, it was as much as increasing taxes and rents without incurring criticism; second, it was as much as issuing national debt without the need to pay interest. Among the different social strata of different classes in society, "the labor society benefits the most from money circulation, and also suffers the most from the vices of paper money. Laborers get their value for their labor, and depend thereon for their liveliness, once the value of paper money changes radically, the value differs in the short span from morning to evening, then the conversion ratio between labor and salary will surely suffer a loss, and the people will find it difficult to maintain their livelihood. While only those unscrupulous speculating merchants will profiteer from all these irregularities.

Whereas the laborer who can take advantage of nobody else are but to be taken advantage of by others. When such poverty and hardship come to a head, revolution ensues, the repercussion ripples to the political realm, therefore philosophers liken paper money to the damages of exorbitant taxes and tyrannical government." He warned the rulers, "no ingenious fiscal policy may be employed without consideration of the social effects caused thereby."

Qian Xun also introduced the classification of banknotes proposed by the British economist Jevons, namely, the total reserve (full reserve), the classified (amount) reserve (partially secured with public bonds, negotiable securities for issuing collateral, the rest secured with gold and silver), minimum amount reserve (minimum reserve for cash), proportional reserve, maximum quota on issuance amount, elastic issuing (taxing the amount in excess of the maximum quota issued), security reserve, real property reserve, foreign exchange reserve (issuing or halting issuing depending on surplus or deficit in foreign exchange), unrestrained issuing, same price for metal and paper money (set identical price on both paper money and metal money; if the paper money decreases in value, then reduce the amount thereof in circulation), tax payment (irredeemable paper money to be considered as metal money in paying tax), exchange postponement (pre-arranged redemption period) and non-exchange (non-redemption). He argued that it was very difficult to determine which method was the most appropriate one; "none of the methods set out in the first through the tenth is not accompanied by a slew of advantages and disadvantages, none can be judged as the best." Japanese economists had the view that "it is best to combine the use of classified amount reserve and the elastic issuing." If surveyed positively, the then practices of Germany and Japan were the most convenient ones: "security reserve issuing, that is, setting the maximum amount and following the practices of classified amount reserve and maximum amount reserve, striking a compromise between the two and taking advantage of both, and adopting elastic reserve in practice, when additional amount is issued without corresponding reserve being set aside, such additional amount can be converted into taxes so that the system is maintained operational." The key to the practice was that rulers should apply appropriate measures to suit the times.

3.2. Theory about bank

The bank is "the hub whereon hangs the repletion or depletion of a country's financial resources." The function of the bank is "of great importance to the prosperity and decline of agricultural, industry and commerce of the industrial society, whereas on the prosperity or decline of the industrial society hinges the wax and wane of national strength." Qian Xun compared banks to blood veins in the human body. The blood of a country circulates via it. Once it is blocked, the industrial society suffers, and the country suffers in turn; on the contrary, if the bank is properly regulated, money circulates smoothly, industry prospers and the country benefits therefrom: "the bank is of great importance to the country." The banks in a country were "actually the embodiment of skillful maneuver of the finance", "serving as the general office of the central government".

In classifying banks, Qian Xun placed the central bank in the first place, then introduced agricultural bank, saving bank and national bank.

Central Banks: Qian Xun first theorized on the nature of the central bank. First, it was a bank of banks and did not compete with other banks: "its business often embraces the concept of managing finance for the country." It provided the various banks with loans at low market rates and was the mother of banks. Second, it was the bank of "exclusive privilege". It had the privilege to issue paper money: "this is naturally a special responsibility, a responsibility regular banks may never aspire to". This is what is meant by the term issuing bank. Third, these are banks with "special obligations"; these banks engaged in receiving and making payments for the national treasury, managing and raising government bonds, paying interest on public debt, discounting fiscal negotiable securities, stabilizing the financial market, collecting taxes and rents from across the country, and wiring such into the national treasury. Obviously, they were conducting the businesses of state banks.

The central bank regulated interest rate. Qian Xun held that the lending rate of the central bank "actually originates in the Bank of England, the central bank of Great Britain, because the central bank is the bank of banks." Actually, there were two aspects to the interest rate, public advertisement and actual lending: "in public advertisement the price might seem exorbitant, however in actual lending and borrowing practices, there are exceptionally low interest rates." Maintaining a low interest rate was the "obligation of the central bank". In practice, the lending rates in Great Britain were relatively high, for which there were two reasons: "it is set up as the reward for preventing speculation, and a prevention for the reduction in reserve." In his view, the national situation of Japan was different from that of Great Britain, as Great Britain was the world financial center, whereas Japan was a primitive country in terms of wealth; none of the private banks of Great Britain were without ample capital, whereas private banks of Japan were generally very insufficiently funded. The Bank of England lay at the center in executing a central supervising and regulating function relative to the various banks, whereas Japanese banks held the position of a central subsidizing and regulating agency. Great Britain practiced free policy, whereas Japan practiced protective policy. Therefore, "Japan must institute a big central bank to execute the function of appropriate subsidization, a necessary function. Now that it functions specifically as a subsidizing agency, it may not but provide low interest rate loans, these are the reasons Japanese banks differ from British banks."

Agricultural Banks: These were also variously known as the land mortgage bank (Italy), the industrial bank or farmers bank (Germany). They granted loans secured by land: "it is nothing than a financing institution for farmers." Agricultural banks differ from other banks in the characteristics of providing "long term low interest rate loans, banks may not require the borrower to repay the loan in a lump sum". The reason was simple; land improvement must be incremental, and it would not be able to generate substantial yield, so there must be many years of operation before any surplus can be obtained therefrom. Therefore, only an "incremental repayment plan of taxes, splitting the principal and interest in repayment could work." The working capital of an agricultural bank may not depend on capital solely: "the emphasis is especially placed on good market for bonds"; "the necessity for bonds issuance is out of the same policy as the necessity for the central bank to issue paper money."

Saving Banks: The purpose of such banks was for the ordinary people to conveniently deposit money. The capital it absorbed was to be used in "lending, or buying government bonds, securities, stocks, etc., or to invest in other safe causes to obtain various benefits." The functions included, "One is to foster a virtuous trend, the other is to meet some urgent needs, which is of great benefit to the society of a country." Therefore, it could not be dispensed with. There were three special provisions reflecting the business characteristics of saving banks: One, there may not be a limit on the minimum amount. Two, there was a maximum amount limit on deposit. For instance, in France, the maximum deposit amount was one thousand francs, and a single deposit could not exceed three hundred francs. In Switzerland, any individual could not have deposit in excess of fifty pounds, a single deposit could not exceed ten pounds, and could not be withdrawn in twelve months. Such individuals were required to apply three months in advance before actual withdrawal. Three, the capital was mostly deposited by ordinary people.

Small-Sum Banks: The purpose was for people to conveniently find employment and promote the prosperity of commerce, agriculture and the myriad industries. This bank was dedicated to granting small loans to ordinary people and facilitating their employment. Different from regular banks, capital contributors thereof were bank stockholders, and a combination of stockholders constituted the bank, benefits going to the people constituting the composition. A small-sum bank could introduce capital at any time, to be paid in a lump sum or in monthly installments; if its capital failed to meet the lending requirements, it could take out a loan from big banks on the back of its credit.

The bank business Qian Xun introduced included four types, depositing, lending, discounting and overdraft, two of which are discussed below.

Deposit Business: Qian Xun particularly emphasized that some banks sought temporary interests, and heeded little their reputation being tarnished, confusing the difference between banks absorbing deposit from society and taking loans, engaging in defrauding and deceiving the world. He argued that, examined from the legal perspective, there was no difference between withdrawing deposit and returning loan, and the depositor can be considered a lender. However, when inspected in actual practice, the difference cannot but be distinguished. From the perspective of the bank, it held the initiative in the former, while it played a passive role in the latter. When a depositor brought in gold and silver to deposit, the initiative was in the hands of the bank regarding whether to accept the deposit request or not, whereas the depositor was in the passivity; as a borrower, the bank sought a momentary advantage in the capacity of a capital keeper, and the bank assumed the obligation to repay capital and interest. In this situation, the bank requested another party to lend money to it. Regarding whether a loan was made to it, the bank was in a passive situation, whereas the initiative stayed in the hands of the counterparty. From the perspective of interest, "deposit interest rate is low while lending interest rate is high." The loan might also require a guarantee or mortgage, whereas the deposit would involve no such issues. Therefore, from the perspective of banks, absorbing deposits was much more graceful than borrowing funds; besides, the amount of deposits from society also involved the credit of the bank, "hence banks tend to report a certain amount of deposits they have gathered as deposits from customers, when in realty these are mostly loans taken out at a high interest rate." "Sometimes banks enter borrowed funds under the name of deposit in deposit report." "If deposit is somewhat withdrawn, there would be panic and run-on."

Deposits were classified into six types: "current deposit", term deposit, "deposit at notice", "special current deposit (special current deposit, at a high interest rate, with a bottom limit on amount)", "saving deposit" (saving deposits) and "deposits under other names". The loan business included "mortgage" and "credit loan", with the former further divided into "pledge mortgage" and "guarantee certificate mortgage". "Pledge" referred to the performance of handing over the originals such as a certificate of government bonds or stock to the lender; "guarantee certificate" referred to the performance of handing the original certificates of land, property, etc. to the lender.

Note discounting business: This business differed from making loans; one was based on mortgage of notes to obtain a loan, while the other was solely conducted against notes with no consideration to the person. Commercial paper can also be circulated after being endorsed. Qian Xun acknowledged that this indicated the prosperity of the commerce in Europe and the United States. He also pointed out the defects therein; "sometimes when a merchant requires financing while he has no goods to trade, hence a check of huge amount is issued without the least collateral provided, then panic of speculation arises time and again." Hence, there was also a difference between a secured guarantee and unsecured guarantee.

Qian Xun not only introduced positive functions of banks but also set out a special section to discuss financial panic. The so-called financial panic referred to the situation "where a bank incurs excessive loss and could no longer sustain itself, and it goes bankrupt when it could not make ends meet". Therefore, it led to the situation where "party A forces party B, and party B presses party C to recover a debt, business environment undergoes radical change, participants who get trapped in the forced situation go bankrupt." That is to say, the discontinuation or closing down of a few banks and bankruptcy of a few capitalists led to a chain reaction that affected the entire banking industry, industry and commerce and even the entire society, and a production and circulation crisis ensued.

Qian Xun noted that there were three causes for the occurrence of financial panic. The first reason was "too much speculation for profit leading to overproduction". In Western society, business relations were interconnected like an interlock; when one went bankrupt, the ripple spread to the rest. This was true of the banks; if one went bankrupt, the rest got shaken. Besides, banks and businessmen were interconnected, so when businessmen went down, banks followed. Due to financial constraints, trade stagnated, prices plummeted, quite a few businessmen sustained loss, and obviously banks also sustained loss in turn. The second reason was that "working capital transformed into fixed capital, which reduced the amount of money." Take the case of the excessive laying of the railway for example. The circulating capital available on the market shrunk substantially due to railway laying, and the money capital could not be recovered immediately; when there was a capital constraint on the market, enterprises naturally looked up to banks for loans. However, bank capital had been tied down in railway construction; if such railway stock was pledged out as collateral, when stock price plummeted, banks also inevitably sustained the extraordinary harm. The third reason was that if "the outlets for goods are suddenly blocked, radical change ensues." Money plays an extremely important role in the market; neither the buyer nor the seller, neither the borrower nor the lender may go without it. If the money circulation amount decreased, then outlets for good would be blocked and market prices would suffer an extraordinary drop; if metal money got exported abroad in a great amount due to war or other accidents, then it would induce domestic panic and a similar panic would arise due to unrestrained paper money issuance.

As a strategy for remedying financial panic, Qian Xun argued that there were two ways: banks increasing loan making and increasing interest rate. The former was based on the presumption that "the market is stagnant and if financing is to be maintained unobstructed, the most effective and convenient way is to encourage banks to expand cash lending." He analyzed the problem from the apparent phenomenon that when market and finance were constrained, there was a tendency that it would be impossible to recover whenever cash was released; therefore, he absolutely opposed the strategy of retiring cash from circulation. When in financial constraint, withdrawers came hot on the heels, while no one showed up to repay their loans; so in order to meet the money demand of the market, the bank was forced to seek help from other banks so that both may tide over the crisis, otherwise the bank run would surely spread and jeopardize others. Here, the central bank tried to expand credit by increasing money issuance against the statutory power of the state; this practice was naturally very convenient, but the central bank had to take precautions in inspecting the reports submitted by the various banks to check out corrupt practices which encouraged speculation. The idea of "raising interest rate" was based on the understanding that "banks have the biggest room for maneuvering the money in terms of adjusting interest rate". In order to prevent financial panic, the banks took the emergency measure of raising interest rates and alluring depositors not to withdraw their deposits due to the increase in interest so that such depositors might even urge others to make deposit. This measure could even attract foreign capital to flow in, and foreign money could be utilized to remedy the domestic panic due to shortage of cash. He criticized the view that raising interest rate could only raise people's suspicion, and noted that "gold and silver were no different from ordinary goods, they all flow to the place where price is higher"; "therefore when domestic prices of gold and silver are low, they flow out of the country; when domestic prices of gold and silver are high, they flow back into the country; when banks are about to panic, interest rate should be raised to absorb gold and silver from home and abroad to consolidate their reserves, this is the optimal strategy."

3.3. Theory of national debts

Qian Xun defined national debts as "the debts borne by the country". Creditors included nationals, foreigners, individuals, collectives (company) and governments of other countries. The obligations assumed by the state are further assumed by the citizens. This is the concept called joint responsibilities. The nationals are both enlisters and debt-sharers. The amount of credit right would be distributed according to "the size of private property", whereas debt would be apportioned among the public. In his opinion, "the private rights and public justice of the nationals are two distinctive areas, they are absolutely unrelated." However, the country may not conduct the matter without extreme caution, no national debt may be issued without proper justification. The Germans must follow the law and the Japanese must first pass an agreement through the imperial council, otherwise no national debt may be issued. Therefore, he considered the theory of national debts as the study of deliberating the remedy for annual state revenue and expenditure. Imbalance between annual national expenditure and revenue, or annual national expenditure exceeding the revenue, or the annual national revenue exceeding the expenditure, was studied under this theory. In his view, the latter was not a dreadful issue and could be ignored; what merited serious treatment was the former, because it was "definitely not an easy measure, one mishap in conduct, the country would be set in a perilous situation."

Reasons for annual expenditure exceeding annual revenue: Qian Xun said that there were three reasons for this. The first reason for the imbalance between expenditure and revenue was the financial structure of expenditure first and revenue second. "In the fiscal year budgeting, it is very hard to balance the expenditure and revenue, the period of expenditure and the period of revenue differs in a year, therefore some mismatch is incurred in the process." The second reason was that the fiscal revenue was negatively affected by natural calamities and manmade disasters, which resulted in imbalance between annual expenditure and revenue: "extraordinary upheavals including natural calamities and wars as well as market panic in business which result in drop in revenue." The third reason was an increase in treasury expenditure due to unexpected upheaval and big expenditure projects, which led to the imbalance between expenditure and revenue. Though there was no change in revenue, "when pressing matters arise or the government plans to carry out huge causes, mismatch between expenditure and revenue occurs," and a remedy may not be left out.

Reasons for highly developed government debts around the world: Qian Xun proposed two reasons. The first one was that the development and perfection of the financial industry promoted the development of national debts. "The smooth operation of the financial market, in old times when the financial market had not been established, there was no hub for the concentration and distribution of capital, capital was spread across the various industries, even if the government wanted to have the scattered capital consolidated and take out a loan therefrom, it would be extremely difficult to perform such a task." "Things are different nowadays, there are already institutions for the concentration and distribution of capital, it is naturally easier to raise capital." The second reason was the strengthening of government credit. He argued that national debts were fully based on credit, and if credit was established, it would be easier to get things done, be it by an individual or the state. National debts could not be raised solely on the appeal of patriotism: "The amount of national debts to be raised solely depends on the regular credit of the state." Therefore, he emphasized that if a government practiced tyranny and went back on its words, it would meet its failure whenever it tried to raise the matter, and would be unable to raise it again. On the contrary, if there was political prosperity, the people had the right to participate in politics and there were sound property rights, the nationals would be glad to help the government. It was to the extent that if a country was of sound finance, not only the nationals but also foreign capitalists and bankers would compete to offer assistance. This manifested the importance of credit. It could be seen that he had intuitively realized the intimate relation between national debts, finance and credit; they determined the rise and fall of national debts. However, he failed to specifically point out that national debts were the embodied form of national credit.

Differences between national debts and taxes: Qian Xun thought that there was a constant in taxes, "there is a limit, if further taxes are imposed for no justifiable cause, vices will necessarily arise." The situation was different for national debts, as it was only an operational investment, and the government assumed not only the obligation of repayment but was also required to pay annual interest on it. So long as the government enjoyed sound credit, there would be no problem with debt issuance. Otherwise, the government would suffer a fiasco even for a single issuance. Hence, he pointed out that payment for war expenditure may not depend solely on national debts, otherwise the country would be placed on perilous grounds. Once the government credit suffered, the foundation for government finance would be undermined. Once war was started, none of the various industries of a country would be unfazed by the threat; the people would store away their capital and refuse to part therewith. Even those businesses that had thrived thus far would undergo contraction, let alone national debts whose recovery hung in the balance. So it would be unreasonable to expect people to answer the fund-raising call. Whenever the country had a big engineering project, such as dredging riverbeds or building bridges, though these activities concerned the interests of the people, they were ultimately public affairs of the state. Therefore, raising tax as a policy was out of the question; the optimal means was to issue national debts to absorb idle capital in society and issue temporary government bonds.

Qian Xun also introduced topics regarding categories, management and repayment of government debts for common knowledge. National debts were classified into three categories, according to nature, form and duration. Classified according to nature, there were four types of national debts: coercive national debts (to coerce the people to answer the call for raising capital), persuasive national debts (also known as patriotic public debts, raised by patriotic rhetoric, with a low interest rate), arbitrary national debts (the regular national debts, commercial national debts) and covenant national debts. Classified according to form, there were three national debts: fixed national debts, floating national debts and annuity national debts. Classified according to duration, there were four types of national debts: permanent national debts, termed one-time repayment national debts, timed national debts repayable at any time and termed fixed amount repayment national debts. There was a difference between issuance at par and discount issuance in placement of national debts. There was a difference of indirect issuance and direct issuance in national debts issuance; the former could be further divided into delegated issuance and authorized issuance.

4. Financial theory of Liang Qichao

Liang Qichao (1873–1929), courtesy name Zhuoru, style Rengong, other styles Cangjiang and Ice Drinking Chamber Master or Master of Yin Bing Shi, pen name Jitianjin, was born in Xinhui of Guangdong. He was an important representative of modern reformists, a thinker and a scholar in China. He won candidacy for palace examinations at the provincial examination, but failed at the palace examination in the 16th year of the Guangxu Emperor (1894). When he stopped by Shanghai on his way home, he read some translations of Western books and "he was much appalled by the contrastive signs of powerful foreign countries and enervated China". He studied under Kang Youwei, assisting him in compiling books including *A Restudy of the Literary Issues in Traditional Chinese Classics* and *Confucius as a Reformer*. In the 21st year, he mobilized the Gongche Shangshu Movement together with Kang Youwei. In that August he assumed the position of secretary in the Society for Strengthening China. He hence became active in politics and in September he started *Domestic and Foreign News* (issued in affiliation to the *Peking Gazette*), and was appointed as a secretary by British missionary Timothy Richard. In July of the following year, he worked as the editor-in-chief for the *Newspaper of Current Affairs* in Shanghai, mainly engaged in criticizing the current policies and advocating reform. Thus, he started his life as a propaganda master. In October of the 23rd year, he was appointed as the president of Changsha Academy of Current Affairs, and participated in the Reform Movement; on the 23rd day of the fourth month of the following year on the Chinese calendar (June 11), he was granted the title of deacon, and organized the preparation for the establishment of a Translation Bureau under the emperor's decree. On the 8th day of the sixth month of the Chinese calendar (September 21) he fled to Japan after the reform movement debacle; on November

1st he started the *China Discussion* at Yokohama, and on January 1st of the following year he started the bimonthly *Xinmin Collection* and *New Novel* magazine, which stopped publication on October 15th of the 33rd year. These brought about a tremendous impact among the then intellectuals, which became the "outstanding ones" among the media, affecting the literary style of an entire generation. He engaged in promoting the various schools of Western thought, fiercely attacked the corrupt and benighted Qing Dynasty, criticized despotism and its ethics, and advocated for new wisdom, new virtues, new force of the people and new ethics of breaking away from tradition and emancipating the mind. In July 1899, he started "Datong School of Higher Education" in Tokyo, which provided higher education to overseas Chinese, and took up the role of president. During his exile in Japan, under the influence of the Japanese, Liang was "fond of talking about wealth management", "really zealous in discussing monetary systems and financial affairs" (remarks by Lin Zhijun). This laid the foundation for his later focus, commentary and participation in the monetary system reform, establishing the banking system and consolidating finance. He organized the Political Information Society, secretly organized "Society for the Friends of Constitutionalist", and became the leader of constitutionalists. In the 2nd year of the Xuantong period (1910), when *Xinmin Collection* stopped publication, he started *National News*. After the Revolution of 1911, he organized a progressive party, a research institution, which adopted the policy platform of "uniting Yuan Shikai". In 1913, he assumed the role of attorney general, and general manager of the monetary system bureau in the following year. Though he applied himself to attain something, Liang ended up achieving nothing, and found nowhere to employ his talent with all his grand plans. He proposed a monetary system reform and planned to establish a banking system, but the supreme ruler ignored these, and all his ambitions could only turn into idle theorizing. He resigned by the end of the year and then served in the Council of State.

In 1915, Liang took up the post of editor-in-chief for the monthly *Greater China*, resolutely opposed Yuan Shikai ascending the throne, and masterminded and organized the "War of Protecting the State". In 1917, he opposed the Zhang Xun restoration, and on July 10th he took up the post of minister of finance in the Duan Qirui administration. Under mounting pressure from the warlords, the monetary system reform and policies for consolidating and regulating the finance that Liang proposed at the beginning of his term failed again. On November 15th, the Duan Qirui administration resigned and Liang left the capital in sorrowful silence. In December 1918, he served as an extra-delegation counsel to the Paris Peace Conference Delegation and visited various countries in Europe.

In 1920, Liang returned from his overseas visit, took leave from officialdom and dedicated himself to the cause of culture and education, serving as a mentor in Tsinghua Academy. He was a scholar of encyclopedic perspective, broad vision, desultory reading, healthy curiosity and quick wit; in the field of modern Chinese cultural thought, few could come up to his accomplishments. His areas of study included philosophy, history, literature, sociology, library science, economics, finance, financial study, law, religion, education and many other disciplines, and he had written a great variety of books, compiled into *Combined Collection of Works from Ice-drinking Chamber*.

In popularizing and spreading Western financial theories, Liang exerted himself greatly, and thought that "the top priority in resurrecting and bringing prosperity to China lie in consolidating and regulating money, and setting the finance in motion." His theoretical knowledge and practices in Western finance were far superior to those of Ma Jianzhong, Yan Fu and his teacher Kang Youwei in terms of both breadth and depth. His writings were smooth and passionate, simple and forceful. He published *The Evolution History of Economics*, the first book systematically introducing Western economics in China, in the 28th year of the Guangxu Emperor, and then the publication of *Citizen and Bank* in the 10th year of the Republic of China (1921). His publications were mainly concentrated in two periods, that is, around April 6 of the 2nd year of the Xuantong period (1910) when the Qing Government promulgated the Ordinances on Monetary System and the period when he served as the general manager of the monetary system bureau in the 3rd year of the Republic of China. He wrote and published over twenty articles and speeches on finances, which topped writers in terms of quantity in the modern period of China. As time elapsed, a few of his views or conclusions underwent some change, but his overriding ideas remained unchanged — of attacking Western powers conducting aggression against China through their banking presence in China, money and financial instruments, which exposed the corruption and financial chaos of the Qing Government and the Yuan Shikai government. He strove to consolidate and reform China's monetary systems to create favorable conditions for the development of a modern national economy. His positive role and contribution in developing an independent national economy and theory cannot be ignored.

Of course, Liang Qichao was an important representative of modern Chinese reformists after all; he insisted on reforming political organizations as the top priority and of greatest importance, or in other words his understanding was that if there was no reformation of political organizations, then all other reformations would be in vain. On the eve of the Revolution of 1911, he definitively pointed out in "Notifying Industrialist Debaters in China" published in the 2nd year of the Xuantong period (1910) that "If China is to resuscitate its industries, how should it proceed, the answer is, the first priority is to set up a constitution. ... How to proceed with the first priority, my answer is this: reform political organizations." The second and third priorities also depended on political organizations. The reason was that "if political organizations can really be reformed, then all matters pending handling shall proceed successfully in succession. Whereas if political organizations are not reformed, then one more thing dealt would be one more irregularity introduced. Such matters are better left unattended to rather than being dealt with." Of course, the so-called political organizations to be reformed were limited but to the council of state and the responsible cabinet,[11] which will be not commented upon hereinbelow.

In what follows, only his theories on money, banks and utilization of foreign capital shall be briefly introduced and preliminarily analyzed.

4.1. Monetary thesis

Liang Qichao had conducted repeated discussions on the functions of money, the foremost one being published in the *Study on Ancient Chinese Coin Materials* in the 34th year of the Guangxu Emperor, in which he

---

[11]*Collection Composed in the Ice Drinking Chamber*, Vol. 20, reprinted by Zhonghua Book Company, 1989, p. 58. Hereinafter referred to as the Collection.

wrote, "There are four functions of money: (a) exchange medium, (b) yardstick of value, (c) payment standard, (d) store of price."[12] Elsewhere, he also wrote of money as transaction medium, price measure, vehicle for borrowing and lending, and store of value, which were what we called the means of circulation, measure of value, means of payment and store of value, respectively. In *A Brief History for the Excessive Minting of Copper Coins by the Various Provinces* published in the 2nd year of the Xuantong period (1910), he specifically noted that "The most important function of money lies in its role as a price measure. All prices of articles must be made with reference to the money as a standard." That is to say, the measure of value as he understood it differed from our normative connotations; his concept of price was that "it necessarily follows the statutory stipulations without the least deviation (mistake)." That is, "for instance, based on what the law decrees as a tael of silver coin, each and every coin must contain a full tael of silver in both quantity and quality; so long as there is no change in the price of silver bullion, there would be no change in the price of silver coin."[13] How could this be a measure of value? Obviously it is a standard of price, that is, the quantity of monetary metal contained in a unit of money stipulated by the government. He confused the two different concepts, which was adequate proof that his understanding of value and price, measure of value and price standard, was not accurate. In *Preliminary Question of Policy Concerning National Debts* he wrote, "Things in the world, only those which can be put to use are valuable, which is a grand principle in economics."[14] Value was the undifferentiated expenditure of human labor; the use value was the effective use of goods. Proceeding from this phenomenon, he rashly concluded that the functionality of money was a constant monetary unit of weight with name matching its essence, and the so-called value reflected and weighed by it was actually the price thereof; on the contrary, if money was not formed into bar-shaped precious metal with fixed weight and name matching its essence, then such may not be called minted coin, and was only goods instead of money. Hence, he argued that money by weight was still not

---

[12] *The Collection*, Vol. 21, pp. 121–122.
[13] *ibid.*, p. 14.
[14] *ibid.*, p. 45.

money yet, and counting money alone was real money. Following from this statement, he said the difference between money and minted coin was that the so-called money "is to set a unit as price standard, and implement it across the entire country, there are times of amount of money beyond the standard and fractions of amount of money below this standard. A system is formed therefrom with a neat order built around it, then it can be called money." That is, "there must be fixed form, fixed value, the number of the unit is the standard easily attainable as a means of exchange, which is used to weigh the prices of the various items."

In Liang's view, it was natural to conclude that there was only copper coin and no other money in the thousands of years of monetary history in China, and no conclusion like the so-called three categories of metals by the ancient sages, "turtle, cowry, leather, coin, cloth, silk, fowl, livestock, instrument, pearl, jade" could be arrived at. In the *Monetary Issue in China* published in the 30th year of the Guangxu Emperor (1904) he lamented, "Alas! From Taigong of the Kingdom of Qi (the founder of the Kingdom of Qi), to date, in a span of close to three thousand years, China has still adhered to copper standard system and could not get away from the situation. Alas, I am too ashamed to talk about this!"[15] Therefore, in the article published in the 1st year of the Republic of China titled "Our Views on Irredeemable Paper Money", when confronted with question of whether China was a country with the institution of money or a country without, he answered categorically, "No money!"[16] Needless to say, "in most areas in China, raw gold and raw silver are used; however, raw gold and raw silver are among the category of goods, they could not be designated as money."[17] Actually, Liang regarded the Western practice as the standard and measured ancient Chinese monetary systems against modern monetary systems, so it was no wonder that he arrived at such a conclusion.

---

[15]*The Collection*, Vol. 16, p. 106.
[16]*Ibid.*, Vol. 28, p. 4. This theory originated from the Western cultural perspective. Hegel once asserted, "What is shown before us is the oldest country, however it has no past. … The current situation of this country is identical to the ancient situation we knew of. Judging from this sense, China is a country without history" (Quoted from (US) Cohen, *Discovering History in China*, Zhonghua Book Company).
[17]*The Collection*, Vol. 28, p. 4.

Regarding the choice of materials for money, Liang held that they must have the following eight virtues: "(a) that it is valued by all, and no one would refuse to accept such; (b) portability; (c) solid quality, no peril of damage or destruction; (d) that it is of appropriate price; (e) severability, and such severance harms no value thereof; (f) homogeneous quality of all composite parts; (g) press mark can be affixed on their surfaces; (h) that it is of stable price which does not undergo radical change." Historically, only "turtle, cowry, leather, coin, cloth, silk, fowl, livestock, instrument, pearl, jade, etc., had served as money materials, or "with some features present and other features absent, however they are ultimately disqualified." Only metals with these eight virtues complete in them could "monopolize the field." Base metals were inferior to precious metals, "therefore copper and iron are inferior to gold and silver, and silver is inferior to gold." In these scores of years, the supply and demand of silver is off balance, silver price fluctuated radically without predictability, failed in the eighth virtue for money material, while gold "has these eight virtues complete in it."[18]

In conclusion, Liang Qichao's understanding of money had both correct aspects and incorrect aspects. He correctly pointed out that money had four functions domestically, discovered that measure of value was the most important function of money, and that money serving as measure of value must have eight virtues and have a constant metal weight with name matching essence which must be statutorily stipulated. This understanding deserves recognition, which is beyond doubt.

What Liang was incorrect about was, first, his vague concept of money. He thought that "money in nature is but a stake available on market".[19] Too many stakes of course would be useless, but too few would equally not work. In his view, during the 1921 Beijing Money Agitation, the problem was not that there were too many stakes on the market but too few available. To him, money was not a special commodity separated from the commodities to serve as a universal equivalent, not the crystallization of human labor; it did not contain the output of tangible and

---

[18]*Ibid.*, Vol. 20, p. 71.
[19]*Ibid.*, Vol. 37, p. 30.

intangible human labor, and no difference between the socially necessary labor and the private labor was embodied therein.

In his opinion, money was but a token for calculation, "hence, paper money was only the decreeing of paper to stand temporarily for money statutorily."[20]

Of course, this was indeed well said, but it was also Liang's words that money was but a token for calculation, except that it was valued by the people for "its merit as a transaction medium", it "was neither edible in time of hunger, nor wearable in time of coldness", "if its merit as a transaction medium is extinguished, then how does it differ from dirt and rocks?"[21] "Gold, silver and wealth are necessarily not the same things. What is called money is but one of the exchange hubs, when there is nothing to exchange, then how does it differ from tile debris and dirt."[22] Besides serving as a medium for exchange, it had neither use value of any sort, nor embodied any human labor. As regards how and why it became a token for calculation, he failed to arrive at a correct and reasonable answer. According to his monetary theory, value refers to the "effect of money as an exchange medium", that is, the average use value the society invested in money. He totally failed to understand that money was a special commodity with special use value, and that money is the independent form of value which transforms the original opposition between value and use value of a commodity into the opposition between commodity and money. He eliminated the boundary between money and regular commodity, value and use value.

Second, Liang erroneously thought that what determined the price and the purchasing power of money was not the contrast between the value contained in the commodity and money, but the quantity of money. In his opinion, "If a country has excessive money, then price must be dropping by the day; this does not happen alone to silver, it is the same with gold."[23] He did not understand the fact that price was the monetary reflection of commodity value; that is, it reflected the comparative relation

---

[20]*Ibid.*, Vol. 28, p. 4.
[21]*Ibid.*, Vol. 16, p. 112.
[22]*Ibid.*, Vol. 12, p. 20.
[23]*Ibid.*, Vol. 22, p. 28.

between money value and commodity value. Similar to Yan Fu, he also confused price and value, arguing that with regard to "things in the world, only those which can be put to use are valuable, this is a grand principle in economics." He just observed that "The law of price is no other than the complement between supply and demand, price drops when the market is oversupplied, price rises when the market is undersupplied; the law works for all articles, money is no exception."[24] His theory of money quantity was not limited to explaining domestic monetary circulation but also extended its circulation abroad. The automatic adjustment function of free trade would also affect international market, and jeopardize the input and output of money along the border; commodity price would rise and fall accordingly, "when there is too much import, then the store of a country's money decreases that is a natural phenomenon. However, the bigger the decrease, the higher the price of money would be, and commodity article price falls accordingly. When commodity price falls, export increases of necessity and money returns. When there is too much export, then the store of a country's money increases, that is a natural phenomenon. However, the bigger the increase, the lower the price of money would be, and commodity article price rises accordingly. When commodity price rises, import increases of necessity, and money gets dispersed. As an article, the nature of money is the same as those of the articles, it follows the trend of supply and demand, fluctuates as driven by supply and demand, and has the natural tendency to revert back to the median."[25] He was restating the theory of David Ricardo, with nothing new of his own.

Third, he confused some basic categories relating to money. As stated above, with regard to money and minted coins, value and price of paper money, measure of value and price standard, payment and loan, means and standard, he used these categories randomly as the occasion suited, and this random use brought about confusion. Under the circumstances of well-developed commodity economy, an advanced modern monetary system came into being, and we can neither deny that it was more perfect and advanced than previous monetary systems nor deny the existence of previous monetary systems. It followed that, regarding countries which had not

---

[24] *Ibid.*, Vol. 16, p. 112.
[25] *Ibid.*, Vol. 12, p. 43.

joined the ranks of advanced commodity economies, we could not simply deny the existence of their money and dub these countries as being without money. Similarly, regarding those materials which had served as materials for money, we could not deny that they had the physical properties and social properties attached thereon fit for assuming the role of materials for money and relegate them to ordinary goods. Internationally, coins minted by the various countries would slough off their national systems and be reduced to its bar form of metal. However, Liang Qichao mistakenly argued, "there is no national boundary in economy, therefore money and goods are often circulated internationally, even minted coins are made in accordance with the entire wealth of a country, in the import and export process, things will turn out naturally, contrary to people's expectations."[26] In Western economic works, the concepts of measure of value and price standard were often confused, and the use thereof extremely chaotic. The remarks Marx once made in *Das Kapital* by quoting John Fullarton's *On the Adjustment of Means of Circulation*[27] were more than adequate to prove this point. Besides, the evolution of the price standard for money indicated that name by weight was the most primitive unit name of money; later, due to historical causes (such as inflow of foreign money), money acting as the measure of value was replaced by precious metals and minted coins of insufficient value, which led to the gradual separation of unit name and weight name, and then price standard which started from the initial customary standard evolved into a basic calculation unit containing a fixed amount of gold (or silver) stipulated by state laws, which was the standard system money. Liang Qichao unreasonably split the *yuan* and the tael, contrasting the two as unrelated, totally different concepts; he thought that "the *yuan* is a name of the monetary unit, whereas the tael was the name for gold bullion, silver bullion weight, they may never be confused."[28] He emphasized that minted coin had the characteristics of price standard in his theorization without justification, denied the monetary nature of gold and silver bul-

---

[26]*Ibid.*, Vol. 28, p. 58.
[27]"Value of this description may be made to answer all the purposes of intrinsic value, and supersede even the necessity for a standard, provided only the quantity of the issues be kept under due limitation" (*Karl Marx and Frederick Engels*, Vol. 23, p. 148, Annotation 84).
[28]*The Collection*, Vol. 8, p. 33.

lions, and denied one of the most important parts in China's monetary history — silver — in spite of the fact that it had been serving as the primary money from the Ming and Qing Dynasties.

4.2. Monetary reform

Based on the foregoing understanding, he considered monetary system reform as an extremely urgent matter, allowing for no delay. In the 4th year of the Republic of China (1915), he pointed out in *My Financial Policy on Monetary System Reform*, "I think that China remains a country of no money to date, how I hope that our generation exerts ourselves to bring it into a country of money, then both the country and the people would benefit substantially therefrom."[29] The real meaning of his idea of advancing China into a country of money was nothing but scrapping the tael and replacing it with the *yuan* system; the reform of scrapping the tael and replacing it with *yuan* conducted by the Treasury of the Kuomintang Government was promulgated in March 1, 1933 and implemented in October. It could be seen that upon the effort of Liang Qichao that, though a dual system was still in place as ever, it did actually work some effect in preparing the public opinion and providing a new theory.

Liang Qichao's understanding of monetary system reform could be divided into two stages. In the 30th year of the Guangxu Emperor, faced with the 17 articles of *Memoranda on A New Monetary System for China* proposed by American monetary commissioner J. Jenks (1904) for the Qing Government, Liang remarked that monetary system reform was the general trend that swept all along with it. One reason was that, considering from the economic prospect of China, if China did not carry out monetary system reform, then there would never be a day of economic prosperity; the earlier the reform, the earlier China would benefit, the later the reform, the more China would suffer from the vice. Another reason was his blind faith in the plan designed by foreigners. The advanced development of Western economy, the systems as well as theories thereof virtually enthralled Liang. Jenks's program had been implemented in India, Japan and the Netherlands, "all went smoothly without drawbacks, how can

---

[29]*Ibid.*, Vol. 32, p. 40.

China be an exception", so naturally it would be beyond question and hesitation. The third reason was that he started from the state of a China of entrenched poverty and underdeveloped circumstance,[30] and thought that if China could engage in reform proactively, then it could take the initiative of reform into its own hands and benefit therefrom; otherwise, if China continued to follow the established systems and stick to the old tradition, in a few years, the Western powers would interfere with China, and coerce China into reforming; by then, China would be a big market for the powers to grab and compete for, "and the current monetary system remained a big obstruction to its competitiveness."[31]

In 1914, Liang took up the post of the general manager of Monetary System Bureau and strove to attain something, after receiving appointment from Yuan Shikai; he soon instituted the bureau and assumed duties on March 10. His philosophy for regulating monetary systems was extremely clear. In *Building Banking System* he noted, "The present day national treasury and people's livelihood are both in a very precarious situation, the cause of it may be very complicated, however the chaos in monetary systems and imperfect banking system are really two of the primary causes thereof." Liang proposed a monetary system reform plan as follows: The first point was that China should implement the gold standard, but the silver standard was still needed as a transition for the time being, and gold standard would be ultimately installed, though not for the present. The second was that one primary coin and two fractional coins were to be minted, the primary and fractional coins would complement each other, and a decimal system would be employed. The third was that the primary coin would be allowed to be freely minted, but a high mintage would be charged thereon. The fourth was that the officially minted one-*yuan* silver dollars were temporarily allowed for circulation as national money, and the old fractional coins were allowed to remain in circulation at market prices. The fifth was that the amount of issuance for paper money was to be limited to the range of not exceeding the annual tax revenue, which was a guarantee for not inducing any trouble. Meanwhile, Liang Qichao also

---

[30] On the colonial nature of China, though having a deep personal understanding, Mr. Liang refused to acknowledge it.
[31] *The Collection*, Vol. 16, p. 123.

headed the drafting of *Regulations on National Coin and Rules for the Implementation of National Coin*, which temporarily put an end to the debate on monetary systems reform theory, and entered into the stage of plan implementation. His emphasis at this stage was that monetary system reform was the top priority to save China from collapsing and to bring prosperity. Such an understanding was very popular during the late Qing period and early period of the Republic of China. Among the scholars theorizing on money we have thus far studied, from the constitutional reform and modernization supporters to revolutionists, every single scholar was placing high hopes on monetary system reform, and none failed to put forward far too optimistic slogans or platforms; their inflation of the significance of monetary system reform indicated the fact that they failed to clearly understand the position, function and interrelation of production, circulation and distribution in social reproduction, and failed to correctly grasp the relation between commodity and money. Of course, this situation also manifested the fact that China at that time faced grave circumstances including fiscal crisis, monetary system chaos, runaway prices, silver coin outflow, decentralized coin minting, dwindling purchasing power of the people, and the people hardly being able to sustain their livelihood. Faced with these problems, Liang penned with deep emotion, "since the time I lived in Japan, I've been fond of analyzing world affairs, I used to think that when it comes to saving China from demise and resurrecting it, the first priority for this issue, nothing is more urgent than regulating money, circulating the finance, which is the hub of finance, on which attaches the livelihood of the people."[32] Before the demise of the Qing Dynasty, he cried out with a burning heart, "on the pace of the promulgation of the monetary system hinges the survival of the state."[33]

Liang even wrote specifically on this subject without exaggeration, "Things waiting to be dealt with are more than one, however the most urgent one is no other than promulgation and deciding on the monetary system." If there was a day's delay in promulgating the monetary system, "the difficulty will be increased by the day, while a few years later, even if we want to promulgate such a system, it would not be possible any

---

[32]*Ibid.*, Vol. 32, p. 40.
[33]*Ibid.*, Vol. 22, p. 1.

more."[34] He found that these words still failed to express his full intention, and he further deliberated in the *Deliberations on Monetary System* by dividing it into three sections (the people's livelihood, finance and politics, foreign policy) and eighteen subsections. In short, without a fixed monetary system, there would be endless peril.

Having a good monetary system meant the survival of the country. Liang considered that there were four reasons relating to monetary system which directly contributed to the existence of the country. First, a chaotic monetary system incurred foreign intervention in China's finance and control of China's economic lifeline. Second, the people could hardly maintain their livelihood, "engaging in desperate conducts, swarming thieves and uprising factions avail themselves of the circumstances." Third, the ordinary people lived in dire circumstances. Fourth, all Chinese prostrated before foreign capitalists and financiers for their livelihood. How could the country stay alive? The indirect cause for the demise of the country was that the monetary system was too chaotic which "further corrupts the governance of officials, and the people have no way to exercise financial supervision, which rendered the constitutional polity an empty name." Upon analysis, some of the causes he proposed were cause and effect reversed. For example, as for the relationship between underdeveloped livelihood and the monetary system, it should be the relationship between economy and money; therefore, in order to suit the requirement of economic development, it should be that the level of economic development determined the level of money development and monetary system. Money had reactive effect on economic development, but the effect can never be a deciding factor. It seemed that this cause–effect relation should not have been reversed. Similarly, comparing foreign intervention and chaotic monetary systems, it should be that foreign intervention was the direct external cause of the chaotic monetary systems in modern China instead of the other way round; that is, it was the chaotic monetary systems in modern China that incurred foreign intervention. Some were overgeneralizations, inflating the importance of monetary systems without justification, such as unstable governments, successive revolutions, incessant wars and nominal constitutional polity; these were all early signs of the social system

---

[34]*Ibid.*, Vol. 19, p. 109.

represented by the Qing Government and the regime itself sliding to death and decadence. These grand trends of historical development were absolutely not something that could have been swayed by monetary systems. Of course, some dissection and analysis were pretty sound, or quite correct, such as market chaos, surging prices, the fact that the budget plan could not be compiled and implemented, finances drying up by the day, people being unable to maintain their livelihoods, etc.

Since monetary system reform was given critical importance; having the effect of bringing back to life the dead, the final effort that attained a great achievement, it would have been a panacea for the dying Qing Dynasty. Of the relation between monetary system reform and politics, chaos in monetary systems was the source of political chaos: "monetary system concerns the survival of the state." Liang seemed to have reversed the cause and effect, but he repeatedly emphasized the importance of monetary system reform in politics, economy, foreign affairs and finance, which also showed his insightfulness. Therefore, after the Revolution of 1911, in order to heal war wounds, rectify social and economic order, a multitude of issues had to be dealt with, and monetary system reform was the topmost issue haunting the profound modern thinker.

In the second year of the Xuantong period, Liang proposed three criteria for the selection of monetary standard in *Deliberations on Monetary System*: "The first is to investigate the nature of materials for money to examine which best suits the function, the second is to examine which best suits the level of people's livelihood, the third is to investigate which best suits exchange with the neighboring countries."[35] Judging from the first criterion, he concluded that "silver is inferior to gold, which is a universally acknowledged law." Therefore, having examined the world around, gold standard replacing silver standard was already a foregone case, and only underdeveloped countries like China would still weigh the merits and demerits of silver standard system. According to the second criterion, the fundamental conditions and level of development of the various countries varied. In countries of well-developed industry and commerce, trade contacts "often involve huge quantity, only gold can be of great value at a

---

[35]*Ibid.*, Vol. 22, p. 11.

small amount and convenient for carrying"; however, this requirement "is not a necessity for countries with underdeveloped industries."

The third criterion, international exchange or internationally accepted money was the irresistible trend naturally, and it could not have been otherwise, or a country would suffer and get cornered. The three criteria were worked out with perfect reasons, and the second was the most important one. Actually, the first and the third criteria were both worked out centering on the second point.

His views on monetary system reform had undergone three major changes, but he should not be viewed as irresolute, with no constancy of the mind, or flirting with the idea, or trifling with the issue. In 1915, he pointed out in *My Financial Policy on Monetary System Reform*, "I indeed advocated gold exchange standard, and proposed that silver standard shall be instituted as a transition over a very short period. In the early days of the founding of the Republic of China, the government had floated a proposal of borrowing sixty million pounds foreign debt, I was then not in China, unaware of the real situation, thought it might work, hence I advocated the implementation of full-fledged gold standard." However, "the implementation of full-fledged gold standard requires waiting for an opportunity in some other days, while implementing gold exchange standard can be performed anytime."[36] While in the post of the Monetary System Bureau general manager, Liang was convinced that it was appropriate to implement the gold standard or gold exchange standard in China upon careful analysis and comparison of the advantages and disadvantages of the different monetary systems; however, China still needed silver standard as a transition over a short period. The reasons were that, first, bimetallism had failed the test in many countries. Second, though it was common knowledge that gold standard was the most perfect system, China "could not immediately adopt it" due to the fact that the gold China possessed "is in fact insufficient for coin material use." Third, the gold exchange standard was "mostly employed by the suzerain in its colony, it is difficult for China to copy the practice." Actually, this was self-deception. Fourth, silver standard was neither the best standard nor could it last long without failure.

---

[36]*Ibid.*, Vol. 38, pp. 38, 40.

However, given the financial strength and material resources of China today, as an interim measure for the present, silver standard still remained the most practical and easy-to-implement system. He repeatedly emphasized that "the future objective of the government is to naturally shift to gold standard, however for the moment silver standard is best temporarily adopted as a starting point for regulation."[37] Therefore, the monetary system reform he advocated was nothing more than the continuation, complementation and perfection of the late Qing period monetary system reform.

In attempting to understand and evaluate the silver standard and gold exchange standard, Liang firmly adhered to the principles of Western monetary systems, and stuck to the silver standard. He insisted that the standard money must be "a type of money whose name matches its essence", whereas fractional money was a type of money "whose real price is less than its nominal price, it is only employed as a supplement, and its application must be restricted." Paper money "may be held to exchange for real money, it may not be otherwise."[38] He particularly emphasized that the government may not consider minting as an instrument for raising fund, and he was adamantly opposed to the implementation of an inflationary policy. He argued that "no matter how difficult it is to manage the finances, funds could only be raised from elsewhere; resorting to minting bureau is absolutely out of the question." Because a country's real purpose of minting primary money was not to make a profit but make it a sheer expense, while the profit obtained from minting fractional money was to make up for the loss arising from minting the primary money. If the government considered minting as an instrument for raising funds, it would mint fractional money without restraint. Then, the quality of fractional money would deteriorate by the day, weight thereof would diminish by the day, while private minting would increase by the day, and money price would drop by the day, and the amount of bad money would grow by the day. According to Gresham's Law, good money would ultimately be driven out by bad money.

Since the late period of the Daoguang Emperor, monetary systems had been in a chaotic situation, and those farsighted were deeply

---
[37]*Ibid.*, p. 3.
[38]*Ibid.*, Vol. 21, p. 107.

concerned. In the previous few decades, "the official copper coins circulated across China were deteriorating in quality by the day, the conversion rate dropped to two thousand coppers for one tael, the value of which halved compared with that at the reign of the Kangxi Emperor and Yongzheng Emperor; the corruption of monetary systems was beyond remedy."

"Inevitably, money with lower real price cannot guarantee its face price, that's a universally acknowledge law, it is not something which can be enforced by the power of the state." "Then its pernicious influence is ten times more harmful than imposing irrational tax and depriving people of their property." Historical lessons like these were extremely profound, which were considered by money theorizers as "tangled silk could not be untangled, and a slew of tracks of overturned carts". If a country was intending to make a profit from minting. It would incur extremely excoriating consequences, more severe than fierce floods and savage beasts, and worse than unprecedented famine and war turmoil. "Property and lives of the millions and the strength of the country fostered over a span of hundreds of years are to be lost in an instant."[39] If every government took minting as a state administrative obligation without the intention to make profit therefrom, the monetary system would necessarily be perfect, the people would be rich and the state would enjoy dignity and prosperity; on the contrary, if the government took minting as a means of making profit, and the administrative organizations did not rectify the situation, and heeded not the private sectors, infighting would be increasing by the day and demise would ensue in the end.

This did not mean that Liang was against government using monetary system to raise money. The precondition he emphasized was that the stability of the monetary system must be maintained. For instance, if there was reserve of one billion yuan, then the amount of coin certificate issuance could be in excess of three billion *yuan*. He also thought that issuing paper money "is indeed a perilous way, however, if it is properly employed, such arrangement often is sufficient to meet the urgent need of the country." For China at that time, issuing the amount of three hundred

---

[39]*Ibid.*, Vol. 21, pp. 14–16, 23.

or four hundred million non-convertible paper money would of course not have been an issue.

Liang believed in the virtual gold standard, that is, gold exchange standard. In the 30th year of the Guangxu Emperor (1904), Jenks, an American citizen, arrived in China and submitted a memorandum to the Qing Government, attached with an exposition of scores of thousand words advocating that China should institute "gold exchange standard".[40] Liang made an instant response, specifically writing an article titled "China's Money Problem", energetically promoting and explaining the issue, and approving the proposal in principle. However, *Deliberations on Monetary System* written in the 2nd year of the Xuantong period was the article in which he truthfully employed the principle of gold exchange standard and explained China's monetary systems according to the practical situation of China in a manner which made the profound issue simple.

His reason for establishing a gold exchange standard in China was grounded in the fact that China was in great need of an established monetary system. Which monetary system was to be adopted in China thereafter and which money would be employed as the standard money? In his opinion, based on the global trend, "the force favoring the adoption of the gold standard will be ultimately irresistible." However, having intensely scrutinized China's national situation, he genuinely felt that there was a problem in adopting the gold standard. The first reason was the underdeveloped economy: "inland tenant earns no more than a few scores of coppers for its daily service, it is feared that replacing copper with silver would not be appropriate, let alone gold." The second reason was the insufficiency of gold reserve, as it had taken foreign countries more than a decade to prepare for the adoption of gold standard, China would not have the national strength to abruptly implement this system. Then how about silver standard? Liang had been of this opinion for a long period of time, and he observed that "judged from today's understanding, it was nothing but the erroneous opinion of the mercantilist a hundred years'

---

[40] At first, Liang Qichao's concept of gold exchange standard was muddled, and he would not have people get a clear understanding out of this muddled thinking. The result would be understandably confusing; therefore, he had not yet advanced this concept when he wrote China's Money Problem.

ago."⁴¹ It would of course be most favorable for China to adopt the silver standard, and it would be most appropriate for the "national living standard"; internationally "it would be easy to maneuver, sometimes it might work miraculous effect". However, there might be defects. When silver import exceeded output, silver price would drop and commodity price would rise by the day and the people would suffer. Besides, foreign debts denominated in gold amounted to several billions, interest on the debt alone would reach a staggering number, and there would be a conversion rate loss arising from silver versus the pound conversion, all of which would have far-reaching consequences. There was great speculation in foreign trade, while silver price fluctuated unpredictably, and interaction of the drawbacks of the two factors would bring more detriment to China. Therefore, Liang argued that he should not adhere to the entrenched opinion of the silver standard. As for gold and silver bimetallism, he stated, "people arrived at consensus on its impracticality." Since none of the three monetary systems discussed above were to be adopted by him, he naturally said, "what I advocate is gold exchange standard only."

He annotated his work with remarks citing Western economists, "the system of gold exchange standard is a sustaining soup for dying economy of poor and weak countries."⁴²

It should be acknowledged that Liang's understanding of the gold exchange standard was roughly correct, and he was perfectly clear of the vicious ambition of American expert Jenks who tried to control China's finance through monetary system reform. He deplored the monetary system reform proposed by Jenks, saying, "in the past they dared not to speak out in such a flagrant manner in intervening in our finance, nowadays they introduced this privilege on the account of monetary system, hence such monetary system reform is really not something that benefits our country, but something that jeopardizes our country. Judging from this point, I could not believe it if there is not ultimate ambition in the proposal submitted by Jenks and the various countries approving it." The provision that he opposed the most was that Jenks' proposal stipulated that one foreigner should be commissioned as the controller of money, and an appropriate

---

⁴¹*The Collection*, Vol. 16, p. 107.
⁴²*Ibid.*, Vol. 22, pp. 10–11, 14.

number of foreigners should be appointed to management "who have the right to submit proposals to China concerning rectifying finance". Liang questioned in the article, "In a country as big as China, populated by four hundred million, how come not a single individual capable of the post could be selected therefrom." How could this not be a grieving situation and fill people with indignation? He acutely sensed that the danger of the matter lay in "creating another Robert Hart"! Besides, Hart's authority was limited to customs duties, areas beyond the Yangtze River and the coast were not under his sphere of influence, whereas the controller of money "bears a close relation to the internal affairs, the slightest move thereof would be adequate to doom us."[43] Therefore, he fiercely opposed the move and argued that the power of foreigners must be constrained in two aspects even if they were appointed out of absolute necessity. The first one was to prescribe their powers; they were only allowed to manage the minting affairs across China; and their powers should be limited to handling overseas agency remittance and conversion. They were not to intervene in the implementation of new money, staff appointments, bank establishment and paper money issuance. That is, they would only be in charge of the technology and excluded from participation in government affairs. The second measure was to set a term limit to their appointments; for instance, setting a tenure of 3 or 4 years, after 5 or 7 years their affairs would be returned to China to be dealt with by China on its own. These were adequate points of evidence that Liang Qichao did not betray the national interests and state sovereignty in his support of gold exchange standard.

After Liang Qichao vigilantly alerted the country to Jenks's aggressive nature, he noted, "now that Jenks is gone." The original hidden troubles would be eliminated, there would be no necessity to give up a great cause for small troubles. Based on the sage model of "Zichan put Zheng Xizi to death but adopted his bamboo penal code",[44] he declared that the practice of

---

[43]*Ibid.*, Vol. 16, pp. 123, 121.

[44]Zichan (?–BCE 522) was regent in the 22nd year of Jianggong in the Kingdom of Zheng during the Spring and Autumn Period (BCE 543). Zheng Xi (?–BCE 501) was a senior official in the Kingdom of Zheng, living in the same period as Zichan. Zheng Xi reproached the political arguments of Zheng Zichan on multiple occasions, and worked out

"bury its overall soundness for its partial ambition" was inadvisable. He would not allow himself to place his country and nation on the same footing with Korea and Egypt mentally and psychologically. However, the then China had already fallen into the realm of a semi-colonial state of country. He often warned the Qing Government, "Even if not for the people's livelihood, you should still make preparations for your own sake. Even if not preparing for the future overall situation, you should still make preparation for the present reparations."[45] Exhorting it to conduct itself well was nothing but sounding the enduring alarm and a different delineation of the dependency situation of China. Hence, if China did not fundamentally change the dependency on the Western powers, where was it to find the second way out to China's monetary system reform other than the gold exchange standard? Starting from the stance of national bourgeois, he was in conflict with the powers; however, at the same time, there were a myriad relations existing between him and the Western powers, and the situation was also a troubled case of disentangling the entangled silks. He was both disgusted by the image of the aggressor presented in the Jenks program and also totally won over by the life-sustaining soup prepared thereby.

He was dissatisfied with the ever-enervating and ever-impoverishing situation of China, which was being bullied and trampled by other powers; in the meanwhile, he also exerted himself to maintain the current political and social systems, opposed revolution, and insisted on reformation. These reflected the class limitations and time limitations of the class he represented.

4.3. Theory on banknotes

Liang Qichao took great pains in introducing redeemable note or paper money and irredeemable paper money.

---

the "Bamboo Penal Code" which was adopted by the Kingdom of Zheng. Zheng Xi was later put to death by Sizhuan (Zichan), the regent of the Kingdom of Zheng. Books including Xun Zi–You Zuo, Lushi Chunqiu–Li Wei, Huai Nan Zi–Fan Lun, etc., recorded that Zheng Xi was killed by Zichan.
[45]*The Collection*, Vol. 16, pp. 123–124.

He forcefully advocated the issuance of paper money, considering it a necessary step in fostering production, vitalizing the various industries and increasing national wealth. If there was a reserve of one billion *yuan*, then redeemable paper money issuance could exceed three billion *yuan*, that is, "if redeemable note of reserve totals four billion *yuan*, then promissory note, draft, check etc. currencies can be expanded to an amount in excess of 10 billion."[46] Since reserve was a preparation for issuance, how could it be counted as money in combination with the redeemable paper money issued? This was sufficient to indicate his confusion in concepts.

On irredeemable paper money, Liang said, "paper is temporarily decreed to stand for money by way of legislation." As an article, irredeemable paper money was of no value itself; the power it had in marking price depended fully on the mandatory authority of the law. However, the force of law did not go beyond the national boundary, and hence once the national boundary was crossed over, the value of the irredeemable paper money would be entirely extinguished.[47] His understanding of the nature of irredeemable paper money was convincing. He especially noted the point that the circulation of paper money depended entirely on the mandatory force of the state, and once it was outside the sphere of influence of the regime, the force of circulation disappeared automatically; this understanding was absolutely correct. He had also made the following provisions elsewhere: irredeemable paper money was one of the "negotiable securities. All negotiable securities are in nature capable of increasing the capital."[48] He also said, "The nature of paper money is not different from taking in silver deposit and issuing an invoice, and the depositor must offer interest whereas paper money does away with interest."[49] This understanding was incorrect. Paper money is generated from the means of circulation, and is a token and representative for money, whereas negotiable securities are a certificate of capital ownership or certificate of creditor's rights with a certain face value, and are a type of fund-raising in modern Western society. The two are of different natures, generated from

---

[46]*Ibid.*, Vol. 22, p. 75.
[47]*Ibid.*, Vol. 28, pp. 4, 7.
[48]*Ibid.*, Vol. 22, p. 91.
[49]*Ibid.*, Vol. 8, p. 41.

different sources, which should not be confused. In the 1st year of the Republic of China, in *Our Peers' Views on Irredeemable Paper Money*, Liang made a distinction between irredeemable paper money and redeemable paper money. He argued that it was very difficult to control the amount of the former in circulation, which might flood and jeopardize the market; on the contrary, redeemable paper money had no such issue, and had the biggest effect on balancing the supply, regulating the market supply. "When there is undersupply of money, more might be issued to make up for the insufficiency; when there is an oversupply, the people would cash them. Whereas such oversupplied money will return to the bank." Things were different for irredeemable paper money: "those money issued do not return to the national treasury by way of tax or revenue of state-run businesses. If the authorities slacked in the slightest way, then a portion of the oversupply would spread pernicious influence on the market and could not be eliminated." This was indeed an important difference between redeemable paper money and irredeemable paper money, which then led to their entirely different effects on social and economic life. He was not opposed to irredeemable paper money, but he thought it "difficult to adopt abruptly, if forced implementation is performed, the defect will immediately be revealed."[50]

However, for the interests of the government, irredeemable paper money issuance could not be prohibited: "it is extraordinary political means, just like the poisons, though they could be incorporated into medicine to treat the illness, how can a charlatan use such without great precautions!" Therefore, Liang had to remark that issuing paper money "was indeed a perilous way, however, if such is properly employed, it often is sufficient to meet the urgent need of the country."[51] In short, issuing irredeemable paper money was, after all, a shortcut to tide over the financial straits of the country.

There was no need to verify this issue with various countries, as there was no lacking of precedent in China alone. Irredeemable paper money "was constantly related to excessive money supply, and this point stood

---

[50]*Ibid.*, Vol. 28, pp. 6, 3.
[51]*Ibid.*, Vol. 22, pp. 90–91.

out prominently in debtor nations."[52] Obviously, the problem lay in that the debtor nation could not repay its debts; the government faced financial straits and had to issue paper money to make up for the deficit. It was not the purpose of irredeemable paper money to meet the requirements of circulation; besides, there were inadequate means for the withdrawal thereof; when the oversupplied paper money remained in circulation, the result would be a decrease of its purchasing power. The pernicious consequence of excessive issuing of paper money also lay in the fact that foreign banks engaged in issuing redeemable paper money in great quantity, taking advantage of the occasion when the statutory money of China would lack credit; the result was that "except for a portion of cash getting exported abroad, the rest was all concentrated in foreign banks." Redeemable paper money issued by foreign banks were increasingly permeating into China's market; these foreign banks included HSBC, Crédit Agricole Corporate and Investment Bank, Deutsch-Asiatische Bank and Yokohama Specie Bank, and they conducted themselves as though they were the central bank of China. With more foreign banknotes issued on the Chinese market, there would be less room for the issuance of domestic banknotes. Issuing paper money was originally the privilege of the government of a country. How can it be shared with foreign banks? Besides, once this privilege was monopolized by foreign banks, the government maneuverability for urgency would thus be lost, and it could only seek approval of foreign banks, which meant that the sore spot of China's finance would be in the hands of foreign banks, and China's economy would in turn be contained by foreign countries. Therefore, in a final analysis, Liang stated that excessive issuance of paper money was a move which both wrecked the country and mutilated the people. Could the government shoulder censure like that? In response to the issues raised above, he put forward policies and conditions for issuing irredeemable paper money. It could only be adopted as an expedient measure for a short period of time, as the ultimate objective and fundamental guiding principle should be fixing the issuance of paper money. The most pressing matter was "to remove China away from the state of a debtor nation", and the

---

[52]*Ibid.*, Vol. 28, p. 5.

next in importance was that "the issuing agency is the banks, if the two issues are not fixed, nothing further could be talked about."[53] That is to say, the preconditions for issuing irredeemable paper money were to liquidate debts, transform China's status from a debtor country to a debt-free country or even a creditor country, and paper money had to be issued only by banks. Based on these principles, there were two principles that banks had to follow when issuing irredeemable paper money, that is, no overissuance was allowed, all issuance was to be withdrawn from circulation, and plans for redemption and retiring plan for such issuance had to be worked out in advance.

Liang argued that these series of questions must be discussed so that the conditions for monetary system could be established. The monetary system had to be decided first and then irredeemable paper money could be issued: "What can we do if irredeemable paper money is issued today? Therefore the first move should be deciding on the monetary system. Once the monetary system is decided, the system is fixed, and the paper money standing therefor has a statutory price to be grounded on."[54] Discussing irredeemable paper money issue without first having decided on a monetary system was nothing but causing trouble for people with irredeemable paper money. Actually, he was also being too pedantic; in October 1915, the Beiyang Government promulgated Rules of Banning Paper Money, and the Bank of China and the Bank of Communications issued redeemable notes. However, in 1916, within a year of promulgation of the Rules, the government should have declared ceasing redeeming banknotes, and departments including the customs, post and telecommunications which were under the control of Western powers should also have refused to accept banknotes issued by the Bank of China and the Bank of Communications. That is to say, after the promulgation of instituting the new monetary system, the government could still issue irredeemable paper money, harm the interest of the people, and still ignore these preconditions and principles when issuing paper money.

---

[53]*Ibid.*, Vol. 10, pp. 10–11.
[54]*Ibid.*, p. 5.

4.4. Theory of banks

Liang Qichao's theory of banks evolved around the issue of money, and the subjects he discussed include the urgency of setting up banks in China, the types of banking systems, the then situation of the banks of China, and banking policies.

Setting up banks was the most pressing matter in China. In Liang's view, "financial institutions are the livelihood of the national economy"; only Wang Anshi had been versed in this law in the entire history of China, "the myriad industries declined due to this defect."[55] The people had to resort to usury because the capital the people needed for production and funds needed for making up for the shortfall for living could not be solved elsewhere. While usury lenders took advantage of people's vulnerability, the usury hacked a hefty portion of the producers' funds, so producers had to continue taking out more usury loans. "These were the reasons that the people got more haggard by the day, and the national economy got more constrained by the day."[56] Liang wrote in the opening remarks in the banking policy section of *A Private Investigation into China's Reform on Finance*, "Banks are the general hub of national economy, what it concerns is not finance alone. However if the national economy is underdeveloped, there is nothing that can be done in finance. When finance is talked about, the source must be traced back to banks."[57] In September 1913, Liang drafted the *Proclamation of Government Fundamental Principles* for the cabinet talents headed by Xiong Xiling, wherein he advanced a complete set of plans for developing capitalism, of which special attention was placed on rectifying the finance and thereby increasing national treasury revenue, so that a capitalist financial system may be established favorable to domestic commerce. In conclusion, the reasons he held that China had to establish its own financial system and institute banks were as follows: The first reason was that bank establishment was a must for resuscitating the economy. "America and Japan were indeed the proven experience of success." Having investigated the Meiji

---

[55]*Ibid.*, Vol. 27, p. 74.
[56]*Ibid.*, p. 68.
[57]*Ibid.*, Vol. 8, p. 41.

Restoration of Japan, he proposed not without profound feeling that the reason why Japan's national economy was well developed was because it learned from the United States and put up government bonds and set up banks, while the wealth of modern America was most likely attributable to this reason. These two matters were inseparably related, and the miracle lay in issuing government bonds and setting up banks by the people. If a bank wanted to obtain the right to issue banknotes, it had to be secured with government bonds, as the greater the security the more the issuance, and the people would rush to purchase government bonds, and government bonds would be circulated on the market, thereby leading to the establishment of more banks. That is to say, starting banks could provide double benefits; one was the interest generated from the bonds and the other was the interest generated from the notes. This would also be a great deed for the people, as from the micro perspective, such banknotes were backed by the state and would be as stable as Mount Tai; from the macro perspective, it would serve as the hub for the revitalization of China's industry and commerce, when the new banknotes were circulated, monetary policy was eased, the various causes showed vitality and embarked on the track of great prosperity. The greater the number of banks, the fiercer the competition, and the lower the interest rate, making it more convenient to investors: "our people may excel the international commercial circle."[58]

The second reason for China to establish its own financial system was that banks were the fundamental means to turn around the passive circumstances of the state finance. In *Building Banking System* published in the 3rd year of the Republic of China, Liang noted, the present-day national treasury and people's livelihood were both in a very precarious situation. The cause of it may be very complicated, but the chaos in monetary systems and the defective banking system are really two of the primary causes thereof.

He was convinced that "if the government goes all out to improve these two issues, then after one or two years, a majority of the perils the country faces will absolutely be removed."[59]

---

[58]*Ibid.*, p. 46.
[59]*Ibid.*, Vol. 32, p. 8.

These words were spoken to the Beiyang Government; however, Liang's words fell on deaf ears, and he could not convince the warlords who were engaged in expanding arms and preparing for wars and grabbing territories. Nonetheless, he demonstrated that conducting monetary system reform and establishing a banking system were of critical urgency and importance in the modern process. However, this understanding seemed inadequate, or not accurate enough, because outdated monetary systems and financial system were indeed detrimental to the modernization progress of China's economy, unfavorable to the development of national bourgeois capitalist industry and commerce, unfavorable to the enhancement of competitiveness in international trade; however, the fundamental reason for the passive situation of the late Qing period finance was neither the monetary systems nor the banks. After the Sino-Japanese War of 1894–1895, the Western powers took control of the fiscal revenue and expenditure and financial administration of China via extorting reparations, loans, government bonds, funds and manipulating the various factions of warlords, and China's financial situation took a sharp turn downward. Meanwhile, in 1916, a situation and trend of local finances breaking away from the central government took a more distinct shape, the process of finance decentralization deepened, and the difficulty the central finance faced further deteriorated. Therefore, in order to fundamentally turn around the passive situation of the national finance, there were three moves to be made. The first was to radically change the semi-colonial nature of China's finance, the second was to further concentrate the financial control and strengthen the national financial strength, and the third was to consolidate and clean out the old sources, tapping new sources and cutting costs. Otherwise, it would but be ridiculously insignificant measures. If the government engaged in issuance to make up for the fiscal deficit, the situation would further deteriorate and a vicious cycle would come into being. This was something that Mr. Liang opposed energetically. How could he go back on his own words?

The third reason for China to establish its own financial system was that it was necessary to rectify the monetary systems. In the 5th year of the Republic of China, Liang published *Proposal of Expanding Fudian Bank to Salvage China*, in which he pointed that there were two matters which troubled merchants of China, one of which was the chaotic situation of money and the other the lack of financial institutions. In order to rectify the monetary systems, a survey of the experiences of the countries around the globe was conducted which indicated that every single country relied on "banks as a hub". Banks could mint new money with capital accumulated and cash to be absorbed thereby. What a great convenience it would bring to the people and the merchants if it unified monetary systems and recalled variegated money and the like, or even salvaged the military notes whose credit had already collapsed. The issuance and circulation of modern money could not be separated from the business activities of banks, while the banks also had the function of creating credit money. Therefore, setting up banks naturally became the necessary condition for rectifying monetary systems.

Liang's views that "the essential livelihood lies not in the government but in the market"[60] were very important, but he failed to elaborate this point theoretically, making further comment on this unnecessary.

Types of banking systems: Regarding what type of bank system to be adopted, Liang argued that "it is quite difficult to come to a conclusion if one is not versed in the national situation and taking into account the current circumstances." One must be thoroughly acquainted with the histories of the various countries and national situations, then meticulously deliberate, and then a final solution may be arrived at, with appropriate timing and tailoring, and only then a bank system may be implemented. "If one adheres too rigidly to the established law without appropriate accommodation, I think a small misstep would lead to colossal consequences." The reality in China was that it could practice neither a unitary bank issuance system nor a multi-bank issuance system, but a "compromise between the two, and settle on an accommodative measure", that is, establishing a pure unitary bank system as the ultimate goal while adopting a multi-bank system as a transition. The actual implementation would be divided into two steps. The first step was to "adopt the practice wherein the central bank and national bank coexist side by side, till the national bank sees substantial development and further consolidates its foundation in the future"; the second step was that the issuing right could then be withdrawn and concentrated in the central bank, and a unitary system would take form.

---

[60]*Ibid.*, Vol. 37, p. 29.

Liang analyzed the banking systems of the various countries and concluded that there were roughly two types: "one is the unitary bank issuance system, the other is the multi-bank issuance system."[61] The former was the central bank system; theoretically, "it is inherently the most perfect one", which stood detached from the multitude of banks and regulated the finance of the entire country.

In his opinion, in adopting such a bank system, "there must be a majority of robust private banks in place in a country, before the central bank may display its effect thereon." Further, "when the national livelihood has attained substantial growth for a substantial period of time, and most private banks have accumulated solid capital and tremendous deposit, they have built firm foundations, even without the benefit obtained from issuance they would still be able to stand on their own feet." That is to say, on the basis of a developed credit system, the banking system had taken firm root, and the private banks ceased to mainly make their profits from note issuance, and then the issuance system would trend to a unitary one. On the contrary, the credit system of China at that time was far from attaining this level, for which there were five reasons. The first one was that there was not much unemployed private capital in China, and deposits were not well harnessed. If the government did not delegate the issuance benefit, it would be very difficult to arouse the investment enthusiasm of the businesspeople in starting banks. The second reason was that China was a country of vast area while the outlets of the central bank were limited; "how could it take care of the entire market without omissions?" The third reason was that the central bank issuing loans directly was an extremely perilous practice. The past failure was not far removed, and the history of the Daqing Bank had almost fallen to a state beyond remedy. The fourth reason was that the facts of American Civil War and Japanese Meiji Restoration both demonstrated that if the domestic demand for government bonds was to be aroused, national bank system must be introduced: "hence once the use of domestic government

---

[61]Mr. Liang called it the National Bank System in the article "Prerequisite Problem Regarding Government Bonds Policy" published in the second year of the Xuantong period (*The Collection*, Vol. 21, p. 47).

bonds was initiated, fund-raising would naturally be an easy issue;"[62] this would be one of the means benefiting finance. The fifth reason was to remove the paper money issued by the various provinces from circulation. If the merchants and people were allowed to purchase government bonds with paper money, and if banks were allowed to be started so securely and paper money issued, the merchants would naturally rush in to buy paper money and purchase government bonds. The government would then be able to remove the paper money issued by the various provinces from circulation without mobilizing cash. This was exactly how the United States eliminated the greenback notes and Japan stopped the use of Dajo Kansatsu, which were measures beneficial to finance.

Starting Banks: In Liang's view, banks "by nature were to be started privately, and not fit for being started and run by the state." The reasons were that "in today's world, even the central banks of the various countries were started with raised funds, only that the governments administered strict supervision thereon. Whereas with other banks, big and small, none is not entrusted to the people in the beginning." Learning from the prevailing international practices, this was the first reason. The second reason was that state-run banks did not satisfy the operation mechanism. He said that the state-run banks in the Qing Dynasty "are now all administered by the government, with officers appointed thereby conducting personally even the tiniest matters relating thereto, which was absolutely inadequate to perfect the management. This practice had been experimented by the European countries, the defects far outweighed merits." The third reason was the unshakable principle of free competition. Liang rejected socialism as the situation where "the state being the sole capitalist, the only enterprise, there was no second one competing therewith". Proceeding from this conclusion and carrying on this inference, "the current situation favors the arrangement of placing all operational functions in the hands of the state, even if the state is competent, the perils would be more pernicious, let alone the fact that it is incompetent."[63] We may set aside his misunderstanding and distortion of socialism for now. We could not help but acknowledge the inherent

---

[62] *The Collection*, Vol. 32, pp. 8–11.
[63] *Ibid.*, Vol. 27, pp. 78–79.

reasonableness of his emphasis on the opposition between state-run and privately run banks, but it cannot be denied that his theory was one-sided. Faced with the powerful conservative force, entirely rejecting state-run banks was but pointless talk, and then it would be highly unlikely for private banks to be started nor could they continue in business.

In *Fair Appraisal of Foreign Debts* published in the 2nd year of the Xuantong period, in addition to putting forward the concept of commercial banks, Liang also advanced the conception of the establishment of emigrant banks and agricultural banks. Establishing emigrant banks was out of two reasons. The first reason was national livelihood. The provinces in the central region were already overpopulated, while the provinces of Mongolia and Manchu were underpopulated and devoid of proper regulation. Hence, mobilizing people to reclaim waste land was a move favorable to economic development and naturally very important for social security. The second reason was for the sake of foreign policy, as foreign countries had long been coveting the provinces of Mongolia and Manchu. Therefore, it was necessary for China to set up emigrant banks in the manner of Germany to solicit volunteers from the central land, and grant loans, lands thereto so that the frontiers may be consolidated, and several benefits may then be reaped from the move. The problem was whether these measures could be implemented and practical effect be worked out; he proposed that such banks shall be established by the state with borrowed foreign capital. As capital required thereby would be 10 million at the minimum, and capital recovery would span over a period of at least 50 years, if the state did not step in to establish it, merchants and the people would not have the strength to back such a cause. In the same way, he also proposed that the state should establish an agricultural bank so that "agriculture may be improved". China was a country founded on agriculture, and its underdeveloped agricultural sector was a key point encumbering the development of the entire national economy, and recovery of capital in agriculture was especially drawn out. Therefore, even if the country granted privilege and authorized the issuance of exhortation debentures to raise funds therefor, it still was extremely unlikely that any private individual would invest therein, so such banks must also be initiated by the state with raised foreign funds. Ordinary commercial banks were the lifeline of the national economy and people's livelihood, and the establishment thereof should be entrusted to the people and not monopolized by the government. He also advocated the idea of establishing saving banks and proposed the promulgation of a banking law.

Duties and Responsibilities of the Central Bank and National Banks: In order to carry out the two-step establishment plan for banking systems in China, Liang had done in-depth preparation and planning in the functions of the two types of banks. In general, the duties and responsibilities of the central bank were to "regulate the financial hub of the country at ordinary times, and assist the government in the operation of finance when issues arose; if appropriate people were employed in the posts, then the national strength would be enhanced thereby, and the sovereignty would thereby be enhanced, that would be the situation where the law is ultimately good and intention perfect."[64] He had made such an exposition in the article titled "Biography of Guan Zi" published in the 1st year of the Xuantong Emperor (1909). The reason that the central bank could have brought the national financial hub under control was the function of money; so long as the "real" money[65] was in appropriate proportion relative to paper money, "one could manipulate articles with money, and manipulate real money with paper money". "Real money sometimes is stored in the central bank, sometimes distributed in the market, the expansion of the function thereof is but to regulate the balance."[66] Of course, the central bank can also "recall and release government bonds, one of the miraculous means of manipulating the finance." (In the Constitution Defense War of 1916, he planned to expand Fudian Bank into a state bank, prescribing its privileges as follows: the stocks shall be distributed equally between the state and merchants, redeemable paper money be issued, money be rectified, branches and subsidiary firms be set up, and such banks shall engage in dealing government bonds and local government bonds). The unique properties of issuing banks, state banks (rectifying money and dealing in government bonds), and bank of banks (not engaging

---

[64]*Ibid.*, Vol. 21, p. 1.

[65]That is, metal money, the so-called "money of modern world fulfilled by metals such as gold, silver, and copper, these are what are called real money" (*The Collection*, Vol. 28, Biology of Guan Zi, p. 61).

[66]*The Collection*, Vol. 28, p. 61.

in ordinary banking businesses) were all embodied herein. This indicated that he had a comparatively profound understanding and overall mastery of the function of the central bank, and therefore Liang made an indelible mark on the popularization of financial institutions and the central bank in early modern stage in China.

Liang held the view that the businesses conducted by Bank of China and Bank of Communications were in conflict with the foregoing principles. From the scope and category of business, they were not different from commercial banks, and they were inadequate to be the central banks; from the perspective of issuance, they were different from commercial banks, and hardly was there any difference between them and the central bank. The Bank of China did not perform the least duties and responsibilities of a state bank, with the earmarked funds withdrawn and appropriated by the government, capital not employed in conducting proper business operation; the monetary systems not rectified, insufficient branches instituted, credit being inadequate, and redeemable note failing to gain wider acceptance.

What was more aggravating was the behavior of the government, which took "the banks as external branches of government, it is determined to 'engage in unrestrained pillaging', some powerful people from the government department even started their own banks and exploited the government with usury."[67] The banks assisted the government in the stealing and the bank ledgers showed profit every year; however, the profit was but an empty account and the truth was that the bank collected the wealth of millions of people and then passed it on to the government. If the government went bankrupt, the entire society would be dragged down into bankruptcy by it. This understanding did not come solely from his service in the ministry of finance but also came from his profound understanding of the usurer nature of the Beiyang Government. Having reviewed the history of Daqing Bank, he asked, "How could people still have faith in them? Its interior corruption and instability defied description, the knowledgeable have already seen through its ruse."[68] He attempted to imitate the Western practice; that is, the government would promulgate decrees and

---

[67]*Ibid.*, Vol. 37, p. 39.
[68]*Ibid.*, Vol. 21, p. 42.

regulations on how to issue government bonds, and the parliament would legislate rigorous procedures to discipline banks to not make excessive loans to the government. However, if the nature of the government was not changed, Liang's conceptions would remain but empty words; though they may be high-sounding phrases, what good would they be?

Banking Policy: In *A Private Investigation into China's Reform on Finance* published as early as in the 28th year of the Guangxu Emperor, Liang raised the issue along with monetary policy. The banking policy in his writing was the strategy that the government should adopt in vigorously supporting and developing the banking industry in response to the social atmosphere that the people in China were of indifferent financial awareness; the trend of people starting banks and depositing their savings in the bank had not been formed. He elaborated the issue from two aspects. The first was "what method shall be adopted to make bank notes circulate across China", and the second was "what means shall be adopted so that the people would benefit from the banks and be free from its harm." The first aspect concerned how to popularize and urge the people to participate in the investment of starting banks. He argued that though issuing paper money was not the main business of banks, they should enjoy such issuing right with certain restrictions. He was well conversant with the national situation, and deeply aware that the people lacked financial awareness: "in uncivilized regions, the wealthy would rather put their property in boxes and store them away in the ground than deposit such in the bank. If one is to start banks, in addition to the capital required, there is no way to have the capital circulated."[69] This was an important reason why the banking industry would never be highly developed and prosperous in China. If a bank had issuing right for paper money, and also had a million *yuan* of paper money for circulation in the market, if it was well managed, it could make a profit of 12%, and the annual profit would be 120,000 *yuan*. Once the trend was set in motion, the banking business would transform in a favorable direction, and banks would thrive and deposit would increase. Interest on the loan would also be sufficient to sustain the banks, and they would not single-mindedly count on the benefits from issuance.

---

[69]*Ibid.*, Vol. 8, p. 41.

The second aspect was to legislate for banks. Liang outlined six rules for China's banks with reference to the rules of American and Canadian national banks as well as rules of Japanese state-owned banks. In view of the characteristic that some small foreign banks in remote areas did not have more capital than China's private banks, he specified that the bank capital "may not be less than fifty thousand *yuan*", so that it may facilitate the popularization of banks. Even if a bank went out of business, the government could still sell its bonds to pay off the debts, and therefore no loss would be incurred and the people would not incur loss therefrom. In reference to Japanese regulations, an issuing bank is required to retain no less than 20% of the total paper money it issued; however, if the ratio was set too high, it might affect the growth of the banking industry.

As stated above, the one who started a bank would gain double interest, that is, the national bourgeois capitalist industry and commerce would gain development, while the old-style private banks and silver firms would naturally die out; meanwhile, foreign banknotes totaled no more than 3 million *yuan* and the circulation of which was limited to the treaty ports. Paper money issued by banks of China enjoyed privileges of all sorts, and foreign banks "do not have any of these privileges, therefore they would ultimately be unable to compete with China's banks, and will ultimately be wiped out."[70] There was no sense in delaying implementing such a great cause. However, Liang overlooked the fundamental change of China, which was that it had been reduced to a semi-colonial society after the Sino-Japanese War of 1894–1895, and the national bourgeois capital had suffered double impoverishment at the hands of foreign powers and the Qing Government. So how could the modern financial industry of China undergo rapid growth?

In the 2nd year of the Xuantong period, in *Fair Appraisal of Foreign Debts* when he mentioned China's banking policy a second time, he stated frankly that he "vehemently opposed the simple central bank system, and advocated the concurrent adoption of national bank system."[71]

As to corresponding strategy for the traditional Chinese financial institutions and their future, such as the private banks, Liang held that

---

[70]*Ibid.*, Vol. 8, p. 46.
[71]*Ibid.*, Vol. 22, p. 76.

"judged from reason, they should be banned"; however, proceeding from the practical circumstances, it would be best to "wait till they die out naturally". In his opinion, "the operation of traditional private banks is most prone to jeopardizing public order and peace." They issued silver notes and paper money on their own without authorization, in amount equal to their capital, and the government was kept in the dark and would not bother to investigate; only one time-honored firm usually kept its promises for the sake of long-term interests, and most other banks engaged in excessive issuance for the petty short-term interests, which led to "bad debts being frequently incurred, the market was shocked".

If such was abruptly banned, it would surely create market panic across the board, everyone would request to withdraw their money, and then the traditional private banks will surely "all die out". Along with "establishment of new banks and conducting competition therewith, these traditional private banks will naturally die out." No one with any sort of vision would refuse to gladly amend their conducts to comply with the government stipulated perimeters and enjoy eternal benefit.[72] As long as articles of association for banks were promulgated, "within a few years, there would surely emerge a few banks of substantial scale in China". The high tide of China's banking industry seemed a bit belated, but its inception did occur, and the elimination of traditional private banks was not that simple.

4.5. Theory of national debts

Liang Qichao's work on national debts was mainly published over the period from the 30th year of the Guangxu Emperor (1904) to the 2nd and 3rd year of the Xuantong period (1910–1911). His main works included *History of China's National Debts*, *Fair Appraisal of Foreign Debts*, and *Issue of Foreign Capital Inflow*.

Liang discussed the nature, function, issuing principle and issuing conditions of domestic debt,[73] the merits and demerits, cause and origin,

---

[72]*Ibid.*, Vol. 8, pp. 43, 46.
[73]He believed that there was no inherent difference between domestic debt and foreign debt. If a difference needed to be made, then fund raised from domestic market was called domestic debt and fund raised from foreign market called foreign debt; debt to be settled

principles to be followed in borrowing foreign debts, etc. The breadth of his coverage and depth of his discussion were unprecedented in China.

Negotiable securities: Liang believed that foreign debt, national debt, local debt, social debt, stocks, corporate bonds, etc., all fell into one category, and it also included redeemable banknotes, promissory notes, drafts, checks, etc., or anything whose purpose was to enhance the function of capital, of which, stock and national debts were the most important ones. Circulation of negotiable securities in the market made finance brisk and unobstructed, and there had to be two major institutions for assistance, "one is joint exchange company, the other bank"; "the former is stock exchange, which serves as the hub for buying and selling, and banks are at the downstream of mortgage."

Stocks forever relied on the mediation of the two institutions to be able to circulate in the market. "China lacked both". Therefore, Liang demonstrated that China was in urgent need of establishing a security exchange of its own, the main reasons of which were to provide facility to buy and sell stocks, to help joint-stock companies in issuing stocks and raising capital, and to promote stock transaction and expand social capital.[74]

The nature of government bonds: Liang believed that, "taking government bonds as an item, the debtor is the state and the certificate bearer the creditor." A government bond "is a type of negotiable security, it is the livelihood the civilized countries could not go without for a single day."[75] It could "enhance the effect and use of capital". However, government bonds were virtual capital instead of real capital, or a paper replica of capital (Marx); it could not play any role in the social reproduction process. It was quantitatively different from the real capital, did not directly reflect the change of actual capital, and could expedite the concentration of existing wealth. This was something Liang Qichao failed to understand.

---

in domestic money was to be called domestic debt and debt to be settled in foreign money called foreign debt.
[74]*Ibid.*, Vol. 21, pp. 118–122.
[75]*Ibid.*, p. 45.

Comparing government bonds and taxes, it could be seen that the common features the two shared were that they were both collected from the people and to be borne by the people; the difference between the two was that "taxes influence the present and bonds the future; taxes function only once, while bonds function several times. By nature, government bonds are nothing but splitting a part of our present obligations and handing them down to posterity."[76]

Liang refuted Adam Smith's view that losses incurred in governments bonds would burden posterity, which was no different from using revenue and taxes today borrowed from posterity of scores or hundreds of years later. He pointed out that if there was no huge investment there would be insubstantial profit coming, while the benefits of some big engineering projects would be continually reaped over a span of scores or even hundreds of years instead of being solely reaped by the present generation. Hence, "what the present generation brings benefit to the posterity, the expenditure incurred thereby shall be shared by the posterity."[77] This point is basically correct.

The functions of government bonds: Liang profusely praised the wonder-working effect of government bonds. "Grand policy may be implemented without exhausting the strength of the people, while the present people are not driven to assume unbearable burden, part of the burden may be passed down to future generations, then the cause may be retained without being scrapped and the people are not overburdened, it is a move killing two birds with one stone." It was a move that did not impose more burdens on the people and also achieved its goal, veritably a move killing two birds with one stone, and a miraculous one at that.

As to the livelihood of the people and the national economy, the first point Liang made was to transform cash into capital and produce yield therefrom. The second point was that the state may have the use of the cash and get projects up, while the principal can yield interest. The third point was that businesses could be started and the principal could similarly

---

[76]*Ibid.*, Vol. 25, pp. 34–35.
[77]*Ibid.*, Vol. 25, p. 35.

generate yield. "Therefore they circulate in repeated cycles, the same cash can be ultimately employed by scores and hundreds of people concurrently", which was beneficial both to the country and the people. Otherwise, the livelihood of the people and the national economy "would get stuck and unresponsive, constrained and not expanding."[78] He exaggerated the positive effects of government bonds, and believed that the government bonds in the Western countries were the investment object; without government bonds, the finance of the country may not be conducted, and foreigners considered government bonds in the same breath as clothes, corn, etc., which they could not live without for a single day. This understanding sounded quite partial; he failed to see the negative effect of government bonds, and did not know that as the biggest means of transaction in the market, it may aggravate inflation and credit inflation, deepen social and economic crisis.

Principle of government bonds issuance: The principle Liang raised was that "it is strictly prohibited to raise debts to fund routine expenditure of the country; only extraordinary expenses may be financed with debt."

What were called fixed items of expenditure were regular expenses, which should be collected from taxes; if taxes were insufficient for such expenses, then they should be reduced to fit the revenue. As the nature of fixed expenses determined that they would not gain value, and as such were often spent without a corresponding or accompanying return; hence the principal and interest thereof could not be repaid, and therefore such debt-raising items would not be compatible with the purpose of raising debt. Next came repeated extension of use; after a few years, even if half of the debt was employed, it would still be insufficient to pay off the interest of the debt. Then, what else would be left to benefit the country? This was again incompatible with the purpose of raising debt. Of course, extraordinary expenses referred to putting up items whereon the eternal interest of the country was hinged and the expense whereof was beyond the financial strength of the people for a period of 1 or 2 years such as the following: building railways, building and repairing river and coastal structures, regulating and rectifying the finance, reforming the administration,

---

[78]*Ibid.*, Vol. 22, p. 42.

enhancing military readiness, responding to hostility and offences, conducting state funerals, handling riots and calamities, exhorting the people to the pursuit of livelihood, encouraging, reserving and the like. All these required raising debts, and could not be done without it. The third point Liang made regarding people's livelihood and the economy was that "people's livelihood was the standard, maximum economic return at the minimum labor cost."[79] The last two principles are valid to date, and his findings should be acknowledged.

Necessary conditions for government bond issuance: Liang summarized the lesson from Yuan Shikai's failure in issuing government bonds, and proposed that there were five indispensable conditions as follows: "(a) the government should financially attain the trust of the people; (b) the management of government bonds should be meticulous, thorough and well thought up; (c) widening the uses of government bonds, (d) setting up institution in charge of the circulation of government bonds, (e) most people should have the capability to answer the call for fundraising activity."[80] These five conditions were inseparable from each other, and none could stand without the others. In his opinion, China did not have these conditions available at that time. The first referred to the situation wherein the government should properly work out its financial plan; the financial foundation was solid, the revenue and expenditure transparent, and the people were convinced that the government finance would not go bankrupt due to loss or debt, and interest thereon would definitely be repaid on maturity. There would definitely be no mishap arising from lack of security. Nowadays, money of dubious source are naturally appropriated without being retrieved. Though appropriation was prohibited, who would still have faith therein? The second referred to the principle that it was best handled by national banks and postal offices. Since it was handled exclusively by the official monetary bureau, the administrators were equipped with neither knowledge nor dutifulness in the execution of their responsibilities, and the issuance would naturally sour. The third referred to the situation wherein the merchants and the

---

[79]*Ibid.*, Vol. 22, pp. 43–46.
[80]*Ibid.*, Vol. 21, p. 101.

people in Western countries regarded government bonds as necessities like clothes and foods which they could not go without for a single day. If the government settled all government bonds, all institutions of society would cease to operate. The reason the public purchased government bonds was not for the repayment of the principal, they purchased government bonds on a meager profit with a view to obtain the various business facilities associated therewith. These were absolutely impossible in China. The realization of the fourth was absolutely dependent on the stock exchange company for the resale of stocks and on banks for mortgage. If these two institutions were missing in society, then application of government bonds would never be a smooth operation. While the people of China knew only the official monetary bureau in handling money affairs, the social atmosphere was one where people were afraid to deal with government officials, and stock exchange institutions were non-existent, the circulation of government bonds was naturally out of the question. The fifth was even more miserable beyond description. China had been in a dire situation where the people were poor and wealth depleted, and most people could not make ends meet. Where could they get the surplus money to put up for the debt-raising activity? Their being patriotists would be of little help. Therefore, while this measure had been one benefiting the country and bringing convenience to the people in Western countries, in China it would have been one that jeopardized the country and burdened the people. Actually, the myriad new deals Yuan Shikai implemented were of this nature. This analysis was incisive and vivid, the exposition hearty and unrestrained, and the understanding profound and correct.

Liang Qichao advocated that the fundamental purpose of raising domestic debt was to rectify monetary systems, stimulate the finance, and develop modern nationalist industry and commerce. In order to protest the excessive issuance of government bonds for its lavish spending, he quoted a Western saying, "No taxation without representation".

He sternly warned the Chinese, "Without supervisory right over the finance, no payment of the apportioned principal and interest on the government bonds shall be made by the people."[81] This understanding was of

---

[81] *Ibid.*, Vol. 25, p. 39.

historically progressive significance, and was far from anything that the regular reformists could have hoped to attain.

Nature, advantages and disadvantages of foreign debts: In Liang Qichao's opinion, there was neither right nor wrong in foreign debt itself, and the sole difference lay in the government which had raised the national debts. By nature, foreign debts and domestic debts were identical, and there was no difference between the two: "(Economic) livelihood finds no borders", international circulation of domestic and foreign debts obliterated the border, and there would be no such issue as the domestic debt being benign and foreign debt being vicious, and still less necessity to be frightened at the mention of foreign debt. "To be fair, foreign debt was not evil by nature, even if there is, it would still be slight, and far from being beyond remedy. All matters of the world come accompanied by both advantages and disadvantages, how could that happen to foreign debt alone. However foreign debt was fingered as an evil instrument, it was but a political evil." The sole difference lay in the government which issued and purchased the bonds slanted the bonds politically, and brought about different consequences. This understanding sounded more rational than some reformists and revolutionaries at the time, and more reasonable in its exposition, especially under the historical conditions of China at that time, and the analysis and understanding were of some progressive significance.

Foreign debts brought huge profits to some countries, such as France, Italy, Russia, America, and Japan, whereas some other countries suffered huge losses, such as Egypt, Persia, and Argentina. Liang believed that seven reasons concerning foreign debt expedited the demise of the debtor country. The first one was that the creditor countries were necessarily rich and powerful, and they were not afraid of defaulting on the side of the debtor country: "their forces were sufficient to secure the debts." The second was that a country of financial chaos must be politically corrupt beyond description, as once it raised foreign debt, there would be no end till the entire country was lost. The third was the fact that things would be fine when no foreign debt was obtainable, but once it was obtained, it would be a huge amount and would came abruptly: "the ruling class would forget the perils in enjoying the comforts and stepping up their luxurious expenditure"; "which ultimately led to incapability of repaying the debt and resulting in foreign interference." The fourth was that the entire country would embark on enjoying luxury resulting from raising foreign debt: "the original purpose was to obtain benefit from the borrowed capital, however it is soon consumed up." The fifth was that the nationals were ignorant of economics, and had no management experience in modern enterprises and organizations: "investment in such businesses would be like throwing a stone into water, the result would be complete annihilation of both the principal and the interest." The sixth was that the sudden influx of foreign capital would lead to domestic inflation, and a private business craze would instantly ensue, and panic would be created; industries would stagnate and not recover over years and debt would not be serviced, which would then incur interference by the creditor countries. The seventh was that once a country was oversupplied with money, prices would surely climb up sharply, commodity import would surge and trade deficit would ensue; then money would outflow, price would plummet, which would result in finance and price disturbing the national economy and people's livelihood or incurring unexpected losses thereby. There would be nothing to prevent the occurrence of these things, and the country hence would not recover from the impact. In Liang's opinion, the first three evils originated in the government, which were unique to countries which had lost credibility of the people thereof: "it was actually a political evil of a country, and foreign debt was a means whereupon it was revealed."[82]

These were the main reasons of foreign debt causing the demise of countries. The latter four were caused by foreign debt itself, as they occurred in all debtor countries. So long as government policies were correct, they could be avoided.

For a well-managed enterprise and country whose economy had taken off, further development thereof would be checked by shortage of capital and financial constraint, then foreign debt on these occasions would not be something to be feared. National economy in general was like private social economy; if it did not have sufficient operating capital, it had to borrow, and so long as it was properly managed, profit generated from the business would be able to repay the principal and interest year by year, and

---

[82]*Ibid.*, Vol. 22, pp. 55–57.

it would ultimately accumulate some surplus money. Similarly, so long as a country was richly endowed in terms of natural resources but the people faced insufficient capital, it was inevitable for it to resort to foreign debt.

"Where a country suffers from extraordinary event, and the finance thereof is constrained, none can be better than employing foreign capital to mitigate the situation." Factors including whether the state's politics were corrupt, whether its finance was solid, and whether it was appropriately employing its finances were of utmost importance in utilizing foreign capital. However, some countries which were unfit for borrowing foreign debt had to give up borrowing domestically and were forced to raise foreign debts, for which there were some reasons. The first reason was to relieve the national treasury of the heavy burden of exorbitant interest, which benefited the treasury interest directly and relieved the burden of the people indirectly. The second was that it gave up raising domestic debt to avoid depriving funds for private enterprises, protecting tax sources passively from drying up. The third was that it reactivated the financial market by applying foreign capital, rewarding enterprises, fostering tax sources actively, making it grow gradually and increasing fiscal revenue.[83] Countries engaged in mass capital export were the Western powers, which were experiencing domestic capital surpluses. These countries sought a second destination ("lower reaches") for their tremendous profit-seeking capital where the land was vast, the people multitudinous and the capital drained. Of all the countries around the globe, "no country fits these conditions better than China; this is the fundamental source for which the foreign powers invaded China." Liang strongly condemned the act of aggression by the Western powers, pointing out that "the destination for foreign capital inflow is a place where the right of livelihood is transferred to foreigners, that is, the place where political power is transferred to foreigners, this is a situation anyone with some insight would deplore."[84] Economic aggression and political aggression complemented each other, and the two areas advanced simultaneously. This situation could be left unguarded and required serious treatment.

---

[83]*Ibid.*, Vol. 22, p. 49.
[84]*Ibid.*, Vol. 16, pp. 63, 77.

Principles and relevant policies regarding raising foreign debt: Liang Qichao was not opposed to raising foreign debt. However, he only argued that principles for utilizing foreign capital and raising foreign debt must be followed. (a) The purpose of borrowing money must be considered, as it could only be used for production. "Where foreign capital is borrowed for utilization in production, the benefit of utilizing foreign capital is often reaped; where such is not employed in production, the evils of utilizing foreign capital are necessarily incurred." (b) The management method shall be prepared in advance, overall planning should be made and installment repayment should be arranged. "When a foreign debt is taken out, if an overall plan for management method thereof is worked out and a staged repayment schedule arranged, then even if it were a huge amount, it would not do any harm; otherwise it would lead to a dead end, the misery of which is beyond imagination."[85] (c) The effect of utilizing foreign capital should be considered. This was similar to raising domestic debt; it should "attain the maximum effect at minimal labor expenditure." Liang set special store by the capability of repaying foreign debt, considering it the first priority in borrowing foreign capital. If debt was employed in finance, when the future source of tax was the source for repaying the debt, then debt could be raised when there was indeed such a tax source, otherwise debt could not be raised; if debt was employed in the livelihood of the people and the national economy, then the profit of the enterprise was the source of debt repayment, and when there was indeed profit, debt may be raised; otherwise, debt could not be raised. He emphasized that raising foreign debt must be conducted according to the capability of the industrial development of the country and capability of the enterprise. The background circumstances at the time were that "the people lacked enterprise management capability, now that the circumstances are like that, I am afraid that nine out of ten enterprises would fail, however, due to the fact that the capital is borrowed foreign debt, such investment once performed could never be recovered, and money invested in non-production areas, as well as the likes of graft and waste by the government."[86] His analysis was not far from the truth, was very practical and to the point. His

---

[85]*Ibid.*, p. 83.
[86]*Ibid.*, Vol. 22, pp. 42, 69, 72.

analysis was helpful for the people at that time and later decades to understand the effectiveness of utilizing foreign capital; it was indeed a very profound insight.

Reasons for China to raise foreign debt: Liang elaborated from two perspectives, the finance and the livelihood of the people and the national economy. The first was that China's finance had dried up beyond remedy, and the annual deficit reached about one hundred million. If this trend had continued, payment of official emoluments and military expense would have been frequently delayed, the government would have been reduced to the point where no fund could be resorted to in fostering clean government, and formidable upheaval would have occurred.

If the situation deteriorated to this state, then vicious tax, vicious money, vicious domestic debt would arrive, and the wealth of the people would be further plundered: "the entire country is reduced to a corpse, and an upheaval is still urgent and unavoidable. If foreign debt is employed as a complement, then the evils currently faced might be mitigated a little." However, this was an expediency wherein the remedy was worse than the evil; it was indeed not a move which was justified and reasonable. The second perspective was that in terms of the livelihood of the people, the things China was richly endowed with were resources and human power, and what it lacked was capital. The land and labor of China failed to be productive due to lack of capital. Therefore, he believed that "if there is a government with adamant adherence to its explicitly defined responsibility in China, and policy plan overseeing the entire circumstance is instituted, then in finance, old debts may be sorted out by raising foreign debt, and expenses for reforming administration is secured; in terms of the livelihood of the people, foreign debt can be raised for the building of transportation facility, and establishing financial institutions, these are all pressing matters to be done, and benefits therefrom can be passed down to the infinite posterity." Hence, the most fundamental prerequisite for the issue on whether China could raise foreign debt was whether it could conduct political reform, whether there was an ideal leader. If the answer was yes, then foreign debt could be raised. Where the best could not be attained, the second best to be resorted to was that a parliament and a responsible cabinet were the absolute indispensable conditions; otherwise, "there is no room for debate on whether foreign debt could be raised." Making do with what was available with the sole purpose of tiding over the crisis at that time would not only be far from salvaging the country from bankruptcy but would also expedite its demise. That is, "I am both a supporter of raising foreign debt and an objector to raising foreign debt. While my support or opposition depends on whether political organizations could be reformed. In my opinion, raising foreign debt by the present government would be all evils without any benefit."[87] Of course, the so-called reform that Liang meant was highly unlikely to be a real and thorough political system revolution.

Liang advocated forcefully that "it is better raising foreign debt than accepting foreign involvement in stock; rather raising foreign debt by the merchant than by the government." In his view, a Sino-foreign joint stock was the worst move, a self-deception. According to the situation of China at that time, a Sino-foreign joint-stock contract was "a creditor's certificate whereby foreigners held China's Achilles' heel, we all consider it as a public enemy of the country."[88] Therefore, conducting joint stock was inferior to raising foreign debt. By raising foreign debt, China could both utilize foreign capital and withstand the aggression of foreign capital, that is to say, the relation herein was one of utilization; only one aspect was involved in raising foreign capital. Therefore, it could be withstood and utilized. Since it was withstood, utilization thereof would bring about no peril, "the principle states that we should withstand them, while it is our right to utilize them."[89] "Withstanding foreign economic aggression was the unswerving way we must adhere to, whereas utilizing foreign capital at our service was our right." His understanding that withstanding and utilizing were not contradictory, not mutually exclusive, not in opposition, was very brilliant and insightful.

5. Kang Youwei's financial theory

Kang Youwei (1858–1927), former name Zuyi, courtesy name Guangxia, style Changsu, was involved in the Reform Movement of 1898. He

---

[87] *Ibid.*, Vol. 22, pp. 57–58, 60, 90.
[88] *Ibid.*, Vol. 16, pp. 94, 95.
[89] *Ibid.*, p. 98.

participated in the Zhang Xun restoration and then restyled himself as Gengshen; in his later years, he styled himself Tianyouhuaren, and people called him Mr. Nanhai. He was born in Nanhai County of Guangdong Province.

He was the standard-bearer in the Reform Movement in the late Qing period, a progressive figure in pursuit of truth from the Western countries in modern China. Out of passionate patriotism and an intense sense of historical responsibility, he called out forcefully for reform and sought to salvage the country, fighting for independence. He was a social reformist in pursuit of prosperity for the country.

He was well versed in both Chinese and Western learning, engaged in expounding the classics and annals from a new perspective and strove to save society. He was a thinker, philosopher, educator and man of the letter who attacked fiercely the traditional thought, traditional concepts and traditional culture. He began to accept traditional Confucian education at an early age. At the age of 22, he switched from the old school of learning to the new school. In the 8th year of the Guangxu Emperor (1882), he purchased a substantial amount of Western books, came into contact with modern Western natural sciences and social, political theories, and gradually transformed from a feudal scholar to a bourgeois reformist. In the 14th year of the Guangxu Emperor, he submitted a ten-thousand-word petition to the emperor, saying he was "painted an extremely perilous picture of the current social situation", and requested the government to stage a reformation on established laws and grasp the sentiment of the people. Since then, he embarked on a journey as a representative of reformation. In April of the 21st year of the Guangxu Emperor, he united over 1,300 palace examination candidates from the eighteen provinces who were then at Peking and submitted a petition (historically known as the *Gongche Shangshu* Movement), opposing the signing of the Sino-Japan Treaty of Shimonoseki; he also advanced proposals of salvaging the dying country and finding a way of survival for China. In the same year, he passed the palace examination and was assigned the post of director in the ministry of works, but he did not take up the post. He actively participated in disseminating reforming information, organized the Society for Strengthening China and the Society for Salvaging China, and also started newspapers (*Wan Kwoh Kung Pao*, later renamed *Briefs of Home and Abroad*). On May 6th, he submitted to the Guangxu Emperor a proposal with measures of "enriching and rehabilitating the people, cultivating scholars and drilling the military", measures of enhancing national strength and avenging national disgrace. In September of the 23rd year when he learned that German troops had stormed and occupied Jiaozhou Bay, he rushed to Peking and submitted a fifth proposal to the emperor, putting forward the suggestion of "learning from the practices of Russia and Japan to settle national issues." In the beginning of the 24th year, he submitted yet another proposal in answer to the imperial calling, appealing for overall planning, summoning the ministers for the settlement of national issues, instituting a system bureau inside the government for elaboration of a new system, and instituting bureaus such as the law bureau dealing with affairs in connection with the people to implement new policies.

On April 23rd, the Reform Movement commenced, in which he served as a non-commissioned assistant supervisor in the Ministry of Foreign Affairs, and submitted memorials repeatedly. After the reform failed, he fled to Japan with Liang Qichao, and refused to cooperate with the revolutionary Sun Yat-sen who was dedicated to the cause of overthrowing the Qing Dynasty. He later went to Canada and organized the Royalists Society, advocating constitutional monarchy and opposing the democratic revolution. During his 16-year exile, he visited 32 countries, investigated the political situations of the various countries, and educated himself on the latest Western political, economic, philosophical, and educational thought and thought of science and technology, which laid the foundation for the new leap in his later stage of ideas. He returned to China in 1913 after the Revolution of 1911; he was opposed to democracy and republicanism and advocated republicanism with nominal monarchy. He started the periodical *Bu Ren*, organized the Confucian Association, and proposed that Confucianism should be established as the state religion. He lashed out at the fake democracy tricks of Yuan Shikai and the scrambles for power and benefits of the people at large. In July 1917, he participated in the Zhang Xun restoration, and when the endeavor failed, he focused his attention on writing and lecturing, and occasionally spoke out opposing the conduct of betraying the country, striving for national rights or appealing for the establishment of constitutional monarchy. In *Trend-Following and Restoration*, Lu Xun wrote, "He (Kang Youwei) headed the *Gongche Shangshu* Movement and led the Reform Movement of 1898, he had been trendy ... later when the times changed, he turned out to be a pure sage. However, bad luck was hot on the heels, and Kang Youwei was forever established as the founder of restoration." He had written scores of works, including *Poem Collection of Kang Nanhai*, *Memorials of the Year of Wuxu* (1898), and *Book on Great Harmony*, and currently there is a redacted edition of *Complete Works of Kang Youwei* available.

His economic thought was mainly reflected in the various memorials he submitted to the emperor during the reformation period, and embodied in works published after the reform failed, including *Theory of Salvaging the Country with Substance*, *Theory of Salvaging the Country with Gold Primary Coin* and *Theory of Salvaging the Country with Wealth Management*. His financial theories were mainly embodied in *Theory of Salvaging the Country with Gold Primary Coin* and *Theory of Salvaging the Country with Wealth Management*. As recorded in *A Sequel to the Self Compiled Chronicle of Kang Nanhai*, in October of the 34th year of the Guangxu Emperor (1908), he wrote the *Theory of Salvaging the Country with Gold Primary Coin*, comprising 30 articles. In it, he outlined that the United Kingdom and France were involved in financial chaos: "great revolutions ensued. In the closing periods of Yuan and Ming Dynasties, both dynasties met their demise due to increasing taxes on financial strains. Nowadays, when all countries shifted to gold primary money while China adhered to the old system, and silver price is on the decrease by the day, the people are getting poorer by the day, there is no way to collect taxes and maintain the livelihood of the people; will the country demise on this issue ... in the fall of 1910, banks of Shanghai, Tianjin, Peking, Guangzhou collapsed in a slew, and great upheaval would arrive before the end of the year; hence I published this article, I would say that every word I wrote was accompanied by a tear drop and I could only hope that readers pay attention." These could be regarded as the background, motivation and purpose of *Theory of Salvaging the Country with Gold Primary Coin*.

In *Theory of Salvaging the Country with Wealth Management* published in October of 1912, the 1st year of the Republic of China, he stated, "after the Republic of China was founded, the finance was in dire straits, foreign debt reached an amount of 600 million taels, and was under the supervision of foreigners, the entire country was shocked and dismayed, no country around the globe has been founded on loans. In the demised Qing Dynasty, the people would riot even for a small amount of foreign debt for building railway, while nowadays banks frequently engaged in huge amount of borrowing, nobody would oppose it; the reason was that foreigners had deep understanding of our financial constraints, after years of development, the situation deteriorated and their effort of partitioning China accelerated. What is nowadays urgently needed is to establish a big national bank with joint stocks, with Shanxi bankers coming out as the principal contributor and assisted by the various money firms and private banks. Then we would have a big national bank, and thereafter can China have the foundation of self-reliance. I have inspected an article written several months ago, *Theory of Salvaging the Country with Wealth Management*, excerpts closely related to the current affair were published for viewing by the people." In November of the same year, he said, "Outer Mongolia, Tibet declared independence successively, and the various provinces took law into their own hands and carved up China … after the Republic of China was founded, the provinces sought after military expenditure on army buildup, all available resources had been exhausted, the only way was to raise foreign debt to tide over the situation; in spring six hundred million taels was borrowed, and supervision was imposed by foreigners; in winter a further constraint of six-country bank consortium was instituted; it was like drinking a poisoned wine, the measure was adequate to wreck a country. I wrote the 'Refutation of Raising Grand Debt', denouncing Yuan Shikai as 'a person that wrecked the country, which nobody shall talk about, therewith nobody shall associate'. Accepting the borrowing conditions was like 'placing one's head in a noose to kill oneself', 'emptying the water of the Xijiang River could not cleanse the gross disgrace'."

Meanwhile, he made minor modifications to the *Theory of Salvaging the Country with Wealth Management* and published it. He believed that "China was in a pernicious and constrained situation; all functions of the government were dysfunctional, while the lack of capital was the fundament peril." The key to tiding over the crisis and turning the corner lay in whether wealth could be properly managed. "There is no such knack in wealth management but proper utilization of banks"; "it is nothing but ingeniously utilizing the bank as a hub, and putting intangible stuff such as paper money and government bonds into practical use in circulation, uncovering stashed away gold and silver which were of solid value as reserve, minting and issuing uniform gold coin as the symbol."

5.1. *Monetary theory*

In the 14th year of the Guangxu Emperor (1888), 10 years before the Reform Movement of 1898, Kang Youwei had already taken an interest in the monetary issue, and conducted some research. He ghostwrote *Memorial on Money* (currently known as *Memorial on Petitioning the Minting of Silver Money*) on behalf of disciplinary minister Tu Renshou, in which he commented directly on the evils of the then money of China, and how it had deteriorated in both name and essence; he petitioned the government to reform the silver coin in order to maintain the monetary law. Kang then analyzed the signs, causes and ills of a deteriorated monetary law, and highlighted the importance of the urgency of reforming monetary law. Monetary law concerned the security of the country, the wealth of the people, "times between the past and the present are different, application requires change", that is to say, monetary law could not remain unchanged forever, even the ancestors would not have done that. In the early period of the Qing Dynasty, silver coin had been minted. In the 26th year of the Qianlong Emperor (1761), Gaozong of the Qing Dynasty (the Qianlong Emperor himself) decreed that silver coin of three categories be minted (the big one *qian* and five *fen*, the intermediate one *qian* and the small five *fen*). He argued that since the founding emperor had set an example, "it seems appropriate to follow the law of the ancestor and carry it out." The accusation of ruining the ancestor's law hardly held water. He wrote of the nearby rugged island country of Japan, a small island nation; after 10 years of application of minted money, the Japanese only attained self-sufficiency, "but their money also outflew to China, there is a great amount of small silver coins, its finance is sound and the country prosperous"; "whereas in the grand country of China, how can China leave the control of right and power to the hand of foreigners?" Therefore, accommodating the change and suiting the changing circumstances were "the key to monetary law of the ancient times and today", home and abroad. The so-called key to monetary law, in Kang's view, was that "application shall be tailored to the time, the proportion of metal content in small and big coins shall be adjusted according to the changed circumstances of the times, coins of different weights shall be used concurrently." If timely change was not made, and monetary law was not reformed, then "the dynasty will demise, strength and interest will be exhausted, people's use will be obstructed, the evils thereof are beyond description." The consequences were inconceivable, beyond description. He remarked, that "if today's monetary law is corrupted beyond remedy, the credit, the essence, the use thereof are all lost"; "if expedite plan is not worked out, it would surely deplete China's silver while foreign silver dollars would be spread all over the central land of China."

In the 21st year of the Guangxu Emperor (1895), in his *Second Memorial to the Qing Emperor*, Kang devised a "money law" as one of the six conceptions of building a wealthy and prosperous country. When "China was at the extreme of poverty", Kang conceived that the perfect way "which may pool the wealth of the country and benefit the entire country" was monetary law. So long as the traditional private banks declared their amount of capital and deposited all silver into the Ministry of Revenue and government repositories of the provinces, the Ministry of Revenue would make exquisite money, and "increase half the amount" over the silver handed in thereby, which was to be used in rents, taxes, emoluments and military expenses, "facilitating its circulation and manifesting its credibility". The entire country could obtain a hundred million, which could instantly make the country a rich one. Yet another conception was to mint silver dollar. Foreign silver inflow and losses from many areas were called big loopholes. China's "shoe-shaped gold ingot and silver bullion are defective in many ways, the shapes are difficult to hold and carry, the weight not fixed, and there are the differences of extra wastage charge, discount in weight, purity, etc., and there are also the differences of national treasury specified weight standard, statutorily specified weight standard, Hunan specified weight standard and canal transport specified weight standard; it is very difficult to settle on the weight and there is too much wastage." On the contrary, the foreign silver dollar featured a "fixed weight standard, round shape for easy holding, convenient for use, and conducive for circulation." None of the

Western countries allowed circulation of foreign silver domestically: "China should mint its own money and benefit from the mintage"; "the benefit is pretty substantial."[90]

The evils China would suffer if gold primary money was not implemented: Kang Youwei noted pointedly that if measures to implement gold primary money were not adopted, there would be six main evils to the people and four perils to the country domestically and internationally. These could be summarized into three evils. The first peril was that it would "impoverish the people by the day". Silver price would drop by the day, article prices would rise by the day, plus given the fact that tax payment discounted both the weight and purity of silver, and government officials were prone to engage in malpractice and fatten themselves, the people would suffer even more. The second was it would make commerce a perilous activity. Silver price and copper price were manipulated by gold, which resulted in unstable article prices, unpredictable prices, leading to chaos in the market. Under chaotic monetary systems, weight and purity discounts would differ in different markets. National bourgeois capital would hardly make any difference in the domestic market, and internationally, China's silver price and article prices would be manipulated by foreigners, causing more difficulty to the livelihood of the people.

The third was the draining of national finance and national strength getting depleted. When fine gold flows abroad, there would be little left in China; article prices would rise by the day and silver price would drop by the day, tax revenue and expenses would consequently incur loss, and the fiscal revenue would be insufficient to cover expenses. In repaying interest on foreign debt, great loss would be incurred in the pound exchange rate. There would be import surplus and China would suffer great loss. Further, the financial power would be controlled by foreigners, and China would be in a situation where the livelihood was held by the foreigners. In summary, if China did not shift to gold as a primary money, "then the country gets poorer and the treasury depleted and finance be plunged in financial straits, and neither navy nor army could be built, foreign debt could not be

---

[90]*Complete Works of Kang Youwei*, Vol. 2, Shanghai Chinese Classics Publishing House, 1990, pp. 86–88.

repaid; and finance shall be under foreign supervision, the country might demise. The people suffer, article prices run high, and if the people could not purchase living necessities, they would take laws into their own hands, engage in stealing and looting, the country may demise. Even if this is not the case, the entire China lives servilely under the situation where financial power is controlled by foreigners, it is worse than living in a conquered state." Kang also said, "the livelihood of the people of China hangs on these two years. If China successfully shifts to gold coin and manages well, then China may survive; and it will perish if it refuses to shift to gold coin and adheres to the established old law." The situation was so pernicious that it left no room for not reforming. However, if he only talked about the monetary system problem, his understanding fit the reality, and his conclusion held water, because China alone exercised silver standard, wherein the price of gold rose by the day, and the price of silver dropped by the day, and the loss arising from the pound exchange rate fluctuation led to poverty, hardship of livelihood, and difficulty in commerce, which in turn further escalated the fiscal straits. However, if these were said to be entirely the direct consequences of the outdated monetary systems of China, or that they might even lead to the pernicious situation where the state might perish, such conclusions could hardly stand. If the purpose of these alarming and high-sounding statements was to draw attention, then its scientific value was substantially debased.

Proposals on monetary system reform: The following measures were required: adopting gold standard, minting gold primary money, decreeing a statutory conversion rate between gold and silver, decreeing silver as the fractional money and nickel-copper as auxiliary money, issuing paper money and prohibiting the circulation of foreign money in China. The shift to gold standard required "reserve bank" and "accumulating gold in advance". Accumulating gold required collecting gold from the overseas Chinese and redeeming gold from the people by setting up banks. However, Kang was also acutely aware that "China is poor, accumulating gold is very difficult, and minting too." This was because, first, if China resorted to foreign countries, gold price would surge to an inconceivably high level; the second reason was that, if the service of the treasury was to be employed, the treasury did not have the financial strength to purchase such a huge amount of gold. The third reason was if government bonds were resorted to, in addition to the difficulty in issuing, the funds might be appropriated for other uses. The fourth reason was if the people were resorted to for redeeming gold vessels, how long would it take, and how much gold would be obtained therefrom? These issues all hung in the air.

The fifth reason was that with a long-term trade deficit, minted gold would be depleted in a short period of time. The sixth reason was that China did not enjoy financial autonomy and could not restrain the use of money. This analysis was pretty objective, and not as optimistic as that put forward in the *Theory of Salvaging the Country with Wealth Management*. Kang decided to temporarily adopt the "indirectly beneficial and usable" new method, that is, the cure-all measure which could bring the dying China to life — statutory gold exchange standard. It would create the condition for transitioning to the gold standard, "otherwise it would be sitting for sure death beyond salvation." Under the gold exchange standard, the state decreed gold as the primary form of money, and stipulated the conversion rate for gold and silver (1:20); no gold coin would be minted, paper money should be denominated in gold unit, and silver coin and paper money should be circulated domestically.

Response to Zhang Zhidong's criticism: *The Memoranda on A New Monetary System for China* proposed by American commissioner Jenks met with oppositions from all sides in China. Zhang Zhidong, governor-general of Hunan and Hubei, pointed out that "The proposal of Jenks offered us an empty mintage benefit and grabbed our substantial financial power, a very wicked strategy, and with manifest perils."[91] He believed that giving up silver standard and mandating the gold price at 32 (gold silver conversion rate at 1:32) "is a move entailing extreme peril, the trial of which may not be lightly attempted." Kang Youwei deplored Zhang Zhidong's ignorance in economics, and his failure to understand that it was natural that the government could not fix the market price for gold and silver but it could fix the conversion rate of gold and silver; the dire consequence from Zhang Zhidong's opposition was that "over a span of ten-year, nowadays useless foreign silver flooded in, and foreign

---

[91] *Compilation of Modern Chinese Monetary History*, Vol. 1, Book 2, pp. 1188–1194.

debt grew by the day and more reparations were made, the two overlaid on each other and greatly routed the finance, if the situation is not improved, in two or three years' time the entire country may go bankrupt and perish, it would be the fault of Zhang Zhidong." So, was the proposal of Kang Youwei perfect? Actually, there were obvious mistakes and loopholes in it. His understanding of the nominal gold exchange standard was limited, and he erroneously believed that raising statutory silver price would increase its paying capability in international settlement; as for silver coin assuming the role of fractional money, no restrictive provision on silver content in silver coin should be stipulated when the statutory price was higher than the actual value in order to stablize exchange rate, "if their exchange rate is lower then we will fix our rate higher, and if their exchange rate is high then we will fix ours lower, then the risk of over-inflation is avoided, and it would be difficult for foreigners to drive the rate in wild fluctuation." As to how adjustment was to be controlled, he did not elaborate or make any specific investigation thereof; therefore, the issue was left unfinished. Moreover, gold exchange standard was not originally proposed by Kang Youwei, and he failed to make any in-depth discussion therein, as it seemed to be not that important.

Issuance secured by government bonds: Kang Youwei believed that the practice of securing issuance by government bonds would "be of substantial benefit with little disadvantage"; it was "a fine method in issuing paper money." He was convinced that if the country issued government bonds in the amount of five hundred million *yuan*, "the country would obtain the use of five hundred million out of nothing, and the banks obtain the reserve security of five hundred million yuan out of nothing, and the people obtain five hundred million of capital out of nothing, and if such is circulated in the country and among the people, both can acquire boundless benefit therefrom."[92] This point was incorrect on several counts: (a) The government bond was fiscal revenue obtained by the country in accordance with credit principles; it was an extra amount of tax collected in advance. As a complement to the fiscal revenue, it was not obtained out of nothing; as it was a loan obtained from the laborers in the

---

[92]*Theory of Salvaging the Country with Wealth Management.*

form of credit by the country, it was a means of plundering the people by the state in old China. Hence, it was neither a boundless benefit to the country and the people nor was it that miraculous and attractive. National debts contributed to the prosperity of security speculation and domination by modern banks. National debts and the national debt system contributed to capital concentration which formed the starting point of modern society; at the same time, as a necessary complement to the national debt, the modern tax system, together with a certain degree of money concentration, in their plundering of the peasant and the handicraftsman, created the proletarian which constituted the inseparable precondition for modern society. (b) The government bond was a type of negotiable security issued by the government to make up for non-production expenses. As a virtual capital, it stood for past capital and was a reliable certificate for yield payment. The money value of the capital it stood for was also entirely virtual; it only stood for the right to receive benefit, but did not stand for capital.

Therefore, it could not serve as issuance security for banknotes. If Kang Youwei's proposals were implemented, it would surely have led to inflation and depreciation of paper money. The bankruptcy of paper money issued by the Republic of China officially declared the failure of Kang Youwei's monetary theory.[93] (c) The amount of banknote issuance was restricted by the issuance reserve and amount required for circulation. If the amount issued exceeded the objective amount required for circulation, there would be flowback into banks via redemption; if the issuance amount was in substantial excess of the reserve, while bank redemption and circulation pace failed to regulate the situation, then there would be depreciation of paper money. So, a new balance between the amount of commodity available and purchasing power of money would need to be struck, and there would never come the advantage of boundless benefit with little disadvantage. (d) The banknote differed from metal money in that it was a token of value; when it was issued substantially in excess of

---

[93]During the War of Resistance Against Japanese Aggression, most government bonds were handed to Sichuan in the form of coupons for a subscription by the Kuomintang Government, and became the security for issuing paper money thereby; then Sichuan appropriated the fund and advanced such to the Kuomintang Government.

the objectively required amount for commodity circulation, it did not mean the abundance of capital, or bore no direct relation to the prosperity of agriculture, industry, commerce and mining. The prosperity of agriculture, industry, commerce and mining required the corresponding increase in the amount of banknotes in circulation, but the increase of banknotes in circulation was not the direct outcome of the prosperity of agriculture, industry, commerce and mining.

5.2. Theory on bank

According to *Study of Kang Youwei's Thought* written by Xiao Gongquan, Kang Youwei had proposed the conception of establishing a new-style bank as early as in 1895, stipulating that all traditional private banks should declare their amount of capital and deposit physical silver in the Ministry of Revenue and the various repositories of the provinces. Such deposits would be held as the reserve for issuing paper money by the Ministry of Revenue. The total value of all paper money would be 1.5 times the total price of silver deposited with the government, and the entire amount of government silver in circulation in the 18 provinces would total one hundred million taels. The objective of the proposal was to become "somewhat like the national banks of the United States of America incorporated in 1864." In order to prevent foreign silver dollars flowing into China from taking advantage of the full-weight silver of China, Kang energetically proposed that China should mint silver dollar of its own to plug the loophole.[94]

In the 45th book (*Book Catalogue of Japan*) of *Newspaper of Current Affairs* published on the 24th day of the tenth month of the 23rd year of the Guangxu Emperor (November 15, 1897), there was a Business Division — Book of Banks: 15 Categories, in which there ran an abstract written by Kang: "Blood serves as the vein of people, when vein is unobstructed, the body will be strong; wealth serves as the vein of a country, when wealth runs unobstructed, the country will be powerful. Bank is the vein of a country. With banks, the country can circulate its wealth, the commerce can circulate its wealth. Obstructed and the strength will be

---

[94]Ma Honglin, *A Critical Biology of Kang Youwei*, Nanjing University Press, 1998, p. 267.

depleted, unobstructed and the strength will grow, that is the ultimate significance. Therefore, the great sage named it a fountain, which indicated that circulation is valued. All the revenue China collected is deposited in the Ministry of Revenue, and repositories of the provinces and the customs; however, there had never been arrangement made therefor. Not only the interest thereof had never been obtained, the significance of circulation was also lost; interest was not obtained for aversion to talking about benefit. The practice of rank purchase reaches the pertinent supervisory officers, heads of the localities slight the intellectual, trade honors, and exploit the people without restraint, both the name and the essence are lost, which is far worse than talking about benefit … all countries have banks, the bank issues paper money according to the amount of money deposited therewith at a ratio of 1:1.5. Merchants and the people rush to deposit their money, when there is bank failure, damages shall be covered by the Ministry of Revenue. Therefore, there is little risk of bank loss and failure in the entire country. What is circulated in the society is all paper money. All physical silver is deposited in the national treasury, and shall be used in purchasing foreign items, one is turned into the use for two.

Hence, the country is suddenly enriched and the people are not harmed. Just like Western banks are employed for the service of the country and the armies, the benefit is universally known. When banks could have our provinces, prefectures, counties purchased and to spare with a roll of paper, what else can our country be founded on? And what is the point of being averse to talk of the benefit of banks?"[95]

After the failure of the Reform Movement of 1898, Kang visited Italy. When he paid homage to the ancient relics in Italy, he was convinced that the nub of the great Roman power in holding its vast dominion lay in its strategy of strengthening the boughs and weakening the twigs, controlling the areas of easy access. Compared with Rome, there were two areas wherein China could not excel, one of which was that China had not established a national bank. He believed that since Rome had reigned over the countries, it must have had financial power under control. And they established national banks, deposited taxes in the banks. There were even

[95] *Complete Works of Kang Youwei*, Vol. 3, Shanghai Chinese Classics Publishing House, 1992, p. 893.

the lending banks, facilitating the poor in business to shake off poverty. And the finance of the entire country thrived, the circulation was under perfect control to fit the intent. "In Kang's view, the reasons for the prosperity and powerfulness of the Western countries were four grand measures, namely, laying emphasis on the capital and the provincial centers, building roads, expediting postal and communications service, and establishing banks, as well as the universal implementation of law across Europe."[96] In comparison, for thousands of years, the Chinese knew only to deposit gold and silver in repositories without the knowledge of establishing banks, and hence there was no knowledge of either interest or the convenience of circulation. With tens of millions in hand and mountainous piles of physical silver, the Chinese still knew only crying and wailing in poverty and even sold ranks and engaged in gambling! The righteousness of interest has long been held as evil. He lamented that "the prosperity and powerfulness of the various countries all depend on the mediation and circulation of the banks; now that China undergoes such upheaval, we finally come to know this rule."

The law of wealth management lay in proper employment of banks. On the issue of building a prosperous China, Kang Youwei believed that the key lay in "getting up businesses" and "properly managing wealth". The key in wealth management lay in following the rules and adhering to the proper way. He was convinced that "if the law of wealth management is attained, the livelihood of the country will not be trapped in straits, and the people will not be worried about the straits of livelihood." "In one year the scale will be up, in three years the effect will be obvious, in five years the livelihood of the people and the national economy will be out of straits, in ten years the country will be rich and powerful, invincible in the world." The path to wealth management lay solely "in ingenious employment of banks as the hub", which was the central argument in the *Theory of Salvaging the Country with Wealth Management*, and naturally was the core of Kang Youwei's wealth management thought.

Theoretical basis of ingenious employment of banks: The reason Kang Youwei valued the function of banks so highly lay in his incorporation of

---

[96]*Travelogues of Eleven European Countries*, Yuelu Press, 1985, pp. 158–159.

the theoretical and the practical as the basis, which had strong practical significance. He pointed out that the difference between the ancient times and modern days was that "physical gold was used in ancient times with limited application", whereas "in modern times virtual gold is used to boundless applications." The so-called physical refers to metal money, gold is physical in circulation and is the basis; the so-called virtual refers to the shadow of metal money, that is, paper money and government bonds. Gold and silver bullions manifest their shapes, whereas paper money is their shadow, and shadow can be bigger than the shape, and government bonds further copy the shadow. The relation between the physical and the virtual is that without the physical there would be no foundation whereon the virtual stands, and without the virtual the physical would not reach far. If there is only the physical without the virtual, then there would be no such thing as copy and extension, and no multiplying effect; if there is only the virtual without the physical, then there would be nothing for the virtual to be attached to, and no circulation would be possible. Therefore, the relation between the physical and the virtual is a relation of one and two, where "one is the foundation, and two the application. One is the defense and immobile, two the hand-held and the mobile, they complement each other and extend to infinity. One may beget two, and both originate in one, unite two into one, repeat the process and it begets the millions. Therefore if there is one there is existence, and if there is two there is sublimation."

Banks mediate "to work wonders". The banks set aside gold ("the physical") as the foundation to issue paper money ("the virtual"), the state offered government bonds to the banks; the banks purchased government bonds from the state with paper money ("the virtual") as security ("shadow rubbings") for paper money issuance, that is, issuing paper money ("the virtual") in exchange for gold ("the physical"). In this process, the treasury was in the banks, then gold ("the physical") was in the banks, disbursing paper money(virtual) also comes from the banks,therefore the banks and the state were actually one as though the shadow follows the object though appear in the form of two. They are different in shape and spirit but are not separated. The key to the issue is how the state employs the banks to make them the hub for the circulation between the physical and the virtual, gold and paper and government bonds "in a relation which operates infinitely and beget the great multitudes".

Kang was convinced that if this was properly employed, "then no fear that replacing gold coin with paper money might not work; shifting to gold as the primary money to incorporate silver coin without worrying about its consistency; regarding purchasing government bonds as storing gold without worrying about its absorption. The solvency of military coupon in the form of copper coin which has ailed the people is no longer worried about."

If this was really the case, the special functions of banks would be in full play. This is a special function "as magical as the philosopher's stone".

So long as the country could give the bank the full play to work its philosopher's stone effect, it could work the magical effect of "generating something from nothing, transforming the empty into the full, and the small into the big, enriching the country and the people, the society will be civilized and tranquil."

Could the bank work the special effect of the philosopher's stone? The answer should be positive. How did it possess such effect, and was the effect infinitely great? The answer should be negative. The bank had special functions in creating a credit circulation vehicle; it could not only transform small and scattered funds into capital but also guide the production with consumption, and could also raise monetary supply according to the needs of production development and expansion of circulation. This is indeed like the touchstone in Kang Youwei's words, but it differs in that it could not issue any amount as it pleases unchecked, could not create something from nothing, transform the empty into the full, and enrich both the country and the people without restriction.

Financial system: Kang Youwei was the first to advance the strategic thought of establishing a relatively sound financial system in China. He extensively investigated the banking systems of Japan, European countries and the United States, and was convinced that they were all different on their own terms with each having its own distinctive features. However, categorically, they could only be classified into two broad groups, the exclusively monopolizing state bank and the decentralized national bank. The state bank system was practiced among the European countries, whereas the United States adopted the national bank system. Japan modeled after the United States in the beginning and later shifted to a state bank system. Other forms of bank included the specie, privilege, industrial and exhortative. The reason why different forms of banks were adopted in different countries was the different national situations of the various countries. The European countries were of smaller size; it was convenient and flexible for them to raise and allocate funds, and only one state bank was required for regulating paper money issuance, government bonds sales and finance control of the entire country, and then "everything was under perfect control". China needed such a unifying state bank, "which in the macro aspect could finance the country and in the micro aspect benefit the people, and deal with foreign affairs at the intermediate level, nothing was inappropriate." At that time, China had a vast territory, with a road system underdeveloped, and places too far apart to be covered over months on the road; so a single state bank would definitely have been inadequate to regulate, accommodate and finance funds across the country. Therefore, it would not do to simply imitate the practices of the European countries and the United States. As Kang saw it, China resembled the United States in that both were of vast territories and had difficulty of traffic but China faced more inconveniences than the United States. Besides, traditional private banks across China were issuing paper money, and such a practice coincided with the practice of national banks of the United States. However, there was no security for issuing paper money in China (such as government bonds, promissory notes, and stocks), and the government did not interfere therewith, nor did it supervise or inspect the issuance activities of the private banks, and therefore the value of such money was not as stable as the US dollar. As for national banks, they were conducive to the spreading and adverse to the concentration of financial strength, the interest rate across the country could freely fluctuate, credit could expand or contract freely, and bank closing was not an infrequent event due to poor domestic or international support. Implementing a unitary national bank system would have been equally inappropriate in China, as simplistically learning or introducing any banking system would be in conflict with the national situation of China; if China was to establish a banking system of its own, it had to "incorporate the practices of Europe, the United States, Canada and Japan and make appropriate adaptation to suit the vast territory of China, so that it might be a move enriching the people and harnessing the rich resources, wherein overall planning must be made taking into consideration the circumstances of the entire country, measures tailored to suit the circumstance so that it may be comprehensive and perfect, will a fine strategy be with us?"

Kang Youwei's conception of establishing China's complete financial system could be divided into the upper, the intermediate and the lower levels. The upper level was the central state bank, domestically "overseeing the hub of paper money", internationally "regulating, handling remittance and raising foreign debt". The intermediate level was the composition bank, engaging in communication of credit-dealing activities between the country and the people. The privilege bank system was instituted to develop resources of the remote areas. Such banks were empowered with the privilege of issuing paper money. Government bonds would be raised to fund the people, to set up banks fostering industries and business, and stock exchange would be established to improve commerce flow and circulation. At the lower level was the national bank, which mainly engaged in issuing government bonds and absorbing funds.

State banks: This had to be incorporated first as it held a special position in the entire financial system and played a special role. The "Central State Bank" is the "mother of all banks, a bank of banks, it has the power to regulate the finance of the entire country, whereas paper money issuance is assigned to the national treasury, the state bank shall render assistance when the finance is in need." Kang's understanding of the central bank's functions was basically correct — the bank of banks, a bank of issuance and the bank of the state. He made a comprehensive exposition without omitting anything in these areas. The function of the central bank was to regulate and control the financial activities of the entire country, regulate paper money issuance, and handle the finance and the treasury business. In the central bank systems of various European countries, if non-state banks plan to issue paper money, they had to obtain authorization from the ministry of finance, endorsement from the money controller and signature of the bank general manager.

On the contrary, in China, traditional private banks were allowed to issue paper money (banknotes) without supervision; there was neither government supervision or inspection, nor cash reserve, nor signature by the person in charge. Once the bank collapsed, there was no recourse. Because credit was in tatters and the political situation unstable, wealthy families would deposit their funds in foreign banks, and the national financial strength would thus be drained. Funds deposited under the security of foreign banks alone amounted to five or six hundred million *yuan*, which resulted in domestic financial stringency and business destitution. The consequence was "first it is difficult to cope with, second it is difficult to conduct comprehensive evaluation, the country and the people would bleed to death." When the financial strength was scattered and could not be concentrated, the "overall situation and the soundness and fitness of" finance of the country were totally unknown, and accordingly the activities could not be regulated and controlled, and wealth management would naturally face many levels of obstacles. Once there was a fiscal crisis, loans had to be obtained from foreign banks, and stringent conditions which endangered the national rights and interests would have to be accepted. Kang arrived at the conclusion, "Finance is the livelihood of the people, the country should absolutely not exercise the power without instituting corresponding supervision and regulation." Within the financial system, the central bank was of ultimate importance, "it relates to the life of the finance across the country, if it is appropriately managed and the country thrives, if it is inappropriately managed and the country fails." If China set up its own central bank, "then the great foundation for wealth management is in place", "and then rights relating to hiking and cutting interest rate, raising and repaying debts can be handled by ourselves and we can recover the right to fix interest rates." By laying a foundation for economic independence, the independence of politics, economy and culture can be guaranteed. These remarks were very reasonable.

National bank: This was employed at the lower level. Kang observed that in establishing central banks, if China pursued the route of reorganizing private banks, it simply would not work: "then there is the problem that no private bank in China has enough capital to warrant a national bank, none is fit for the role." If China embarked on the route of joint investment with the people, then it would not be implemented due to the fact that tens of millions of bank capital could not be allocated from the depleted national treasury. Further, raising foreign debt could lead to the national sovereignty being betrayed and it definitely would not work: "having our national bank daily supervised and examined by foreigners, it would not only be humiliating but there is no such reason in the world." Regarding government bond issuance, he claimed that the people had long lost faith in it and few would buy government bonds; issuing stocks and offering it to people for discretionary purchase would also not work because the people were unemployed, with little savings and they were simply waiting for their inevitable doom in months or years. Donation and raising fund also would not work, as it was a time just after upheaval, and this move was feared to lead to depleting the source and harming the foundational strength.

As regards learning from the history of foreign countries, in the Civil War period, in order to cope with military expenses, the United States mandated that all banks purchase government bonds with one third of their capital, and the government granted them the right to issue paper money, resulting in "benefiting both the country and the people." Kang Youwei proposed that, in addition to the practice "that national banks are only allowed to purchase government bonds as the practice of the United States and Japan", "the national banks are further required to contribute to the capital stock of the central bank": the national banks and traditional private banks were required to purchase government bonds equal to a quarter of their capital, and to contribute one twentieth of their public reserves as contributions to the capital stock of the central bank. Those which did not want to contribute to the central bank's capital stock were required to purchase government bonds with one tenth of their capital, and they were required to double the amount of their purchase of public reserves and government bonds. The pawn, hypothec, gold and silver shops would be required to pay one fortieth of their capitals as stocks of the central bank, and double the foregoing amount as public reserves. Those shops that purchased government bonds issued by the central bank would be allowed to issue an amount of paper money equal to the amount of government bonds purchased, and those that voluntarily purchased government bonds issued by the central bank could issue paper money, or they could resell such privilege to others; on the contrary, those that did not purchase government bonds would not be allowed to issue paper money, and if they became insolvent, the court would not accept a case lodged thereby. All paper money privately issued previously would be prohibited from circulation. He believed that the advantages of such practice were as follows: First, it could facilitate the establishment of the central bank so that the finance across the country could be regulated, and the various banks could obtain both long-term interest wherein most could obtain a premium and short-term interest of capital circulation. Second, the various banks could acquire rights and interests in issuing paper money, hypothecating and selling government bonds and stocks, and there would be great benefit and little harm. Third, it seemed that the various banks would incur a loss by contributing capital to purchase government bonds, but they would acquire the privilege to issue paper money: it is as though "transferring the capital from the internal warehouse to the external warehouse, which is as much as not contributing a single coin." They would receive solid stocks, which is a particularly great benefit. Fourth, contributing capital in establishing the central bank is a cause pooling the rich in an effort to jointly establishing a state bank; all share the burden and hardship, no one will be accused of being "ultimately unrighteous". The state bank would get rid of the financially constrained situation by adopting this method on the preconditions that national interest is guaranteed, the immediate interest of the investors would be protected from harm, and greater long-term interest would be promised; only in this way can this system benefit both the country and the people.

Compositional central bank system: This type of bank was instituted to suit the characteristics of China where there was vast territory, poor transportation networks, unimaginably long distance between the capital and the frontiers, and weak communication between the various local banks and the central bank, especially the underdeveloped situation of capital allocation and financing. Compositional banks were first incorporated in Canada. The so-called compositional bank referred to a bank consortium incorporated with a certain proportion of capital contribution from the various banks of the capital, the major metropolises, counties and municipalities. Closing of such banks seldom happened, and the people benefit greatly therefrom. The United States imitated the practice and incorporated many compositional banks. Kang Youwei argued that a three-tier credit compositional bank system should be established (provincial capital to be the upper, prefecture and county the intermediate, and town the lower) with capital proportionally contributed by banks and private banks from provincial capitals and major cities; one tenth of its principal would be used in purchasing capital of the central bank, and the amount of paper money to be issued would be 30% or 70% of their capitals. Outside the imperial capital, it would represent the central bank in issuing paper money, raising government bonds, implementing the monetary system, collecting state tax and local tax, scouring and purchasing gold and silver, and conducting various credit activities. It would enjoy certain powers, as an entity equivalent to a branch or sub-branch of the central bank in the locality. It would have the duties of organizing the mortgage banks and industrial banks in the localities to facilitate management, supervision and review conducted by the central bank, "as though they are branches of the central bank, perfectly stable and reliable."

Specie bank: It served as an auxiliary to the state bank. It was incorporated abroad and mainly engaged in businesses such as raising foreign debt and conducting foreign exchange. Branches and sub-branches of it engaged in scouring and purchasing gold and silver. This function was assumed by the state bank in the various European countries, while Japan established the Specie Bank to take up this function. Kang Youwei proposed that "in the initial period, banks shall be first established in New York, and then in Paris and London, to conduct foreign exchange and stabilize financial prices, and banks shall then be extended to other areas."

Privilege banks: These banks were to be established in the remote areas, "in order to broaden resources and facilitate reclamation and colonization." Britain, Germany, Switzerland, Japan, the United States and Mexico had all established banks in this way. Kang Youwei believed that China could incorporate banks in twelve places including Tibet, Xinjiang, Mongolia, Jilin, Fengtian, Yunnan, Nanning, Qiongzhou and Dajianlu, with a capital requirement of two million and five hundred thousand, possibly in the form of paper money. Then, "the geographical advantages of the frontiers can be tapped, resources could be enriched, agriculture, husbandry, forestry, mineral could yield bountiful produces. Garrisoning troops or peasants can all be attained." This was a critical move in managing the frontier.

Household land mortgage bank: "Banks managing principal assets of the people which subsidize the people" first originated in Germany. The land there was barren and the people poor. The big land owners from the various regions came together and organized an association, issuing debt coupons secured with their homesteads and land and selling such to the middle class, with all proceeds generated from the sale being deposited into the association. The coupon bearers could apply for loans to set up agricultural and industrial businesses. France, Sweden and Japan imitated the practice. China boasted of ten thousand miles of land, countless homes and mansions, but the Chinese engaged solely in selling to the total ignorance of mortgage. They knew no way to obtain money for conducting industry and commerce, rectifying and handling land and crop, and deplored the lack of capital despite all the land and property. Therefore, few businesses thrived and none could find a way to succeed in China. Kang could not help but lament, "having such land and such property, how could people get so desperate and get reduced to such poverty, to the state of being enslaved and perishing?" He advocated that provincial and county exhortative banks be established, and business offices be set up in the towns. The government would advance two hundred million as capital, and the provincial banks could issue bond coupons at a ratio of 1:15 to the capital thereof, while 1:10 and 1:5 were to be the ratios for county and town exhortative banks, respectively: "taking out loans secured by public, private homestead and land, so that capital may be obtained." Besides, with the exhortation by the newspapers, capital and bonds would not be an issue, even if there were some difficulties in the beginning, since there was to be a stipulation that loans could only be made against bond coupon purchase, and no loan could be made without bond coupons; hence, capital would flock in to purchase bond coupons. In his opinion, the situation in China had just been unstable, and the people were particularly poor, the land and the homesteads were particularly cheap, which was a poor comparison to the past; however, if exhortative bank subsidization was properly employed from above with industrial bank encouragement from below, secured by real estate, businesses including trams, power plants, railways, ships, water works, gas lamps, drainage canals and canal excavation, road mending, and railway building could be conducted, and then industry and wealth would further create industry and wealth, thereby shaking off poverty and embarking the country on a road to prosperity. This would surely be better than waiting for relief from the state: "when there is a reliable source for acquiring a capital, in the time of a year, the entire country would see improvement, in the time of three years there will be of sizable effect, in the time of five years, the people would thrive, in the time of ten years the businesses of agriculture, industry, commerce and mining would dominate the land." Then, the day wherein the country is prosperous and the people well off would not be far off.

Stock exchange: China faced sluggish commerce and capital shortage. While everyone knew that a country cannot not attain prosperity without a thriving industry, few knew that "capital begets industry, while capital can be physical and virtual." There are great differences between circulated stock and uncirculated stock. While the former can make one into ten thousand, the latter can only be taken as one, so it is of no use due to the fact that it begets nothing; therefore, for the same amount of money capital, there is a world of difference in proper management and poor management. Confronted with the accusation that "this is speculation, how can it not jeopardize the people", Kang Youwei was convinced of the truth in the lesser of the two evils; judging from the ratio between those who made it and those who failed to make it, i.e., a ratio of 3:1, it could be seen that the gains naturally outweighed the losses. The tremendous development of the New York Stock Exchange in the United States over the previous 30 years demonstrated that indisputable fact. Before stock transactions were available, there were only about a hundred millionaires, and next to none multimillionaires; nowadays, there are several hundred multimillionaires, while millionaires number in the thousands. The failure of banks resulting from market speculation would definitely lead to bankruptcy, and "when losses amounting to great amount, the business would be over". However, in the face of great benefit, stock exchange is "as usual and more thriving." In Europe and the United States, ultimately they had not banned it due to the defects associated therewith. The reason was simple; those who manipulated the market controlled over half of the stocks, and only those few directors could manipulate the enterprise production and management, the precondition for their speculation being that the company is profitable. If such a company was unprofitable, then few would pay any attention to the stock, and they would not be able to sell stocks; on the contrary, if the company often recorded profit, then the stock price thereof would not be depressed, and if anyone would like to dominate its fluctuation, it could be allowed. So long as the price fluctuation was not too violent and the purpose thereof was not deception, then the half-true half-untrue, half-real, half-unreal fluctuation could be allowed. Not only can normal commercial profit be obtained therefrom but likely also boundless profit. It is exactly "this move incorporating both the physical and the virtual, turning one into two, into the myriad that makes it easy to make a fortune." Failure in stock trading may also jeopardize the national interest, but the government may ban or restrict it anytime; if anyone is deeply concerned over such defects, it would be like "someone ignorant of the extreme poverty of China tries to promote equalizing wealth in society", which is as good as saying "that it is versed in preventing the defects without the knowledge of its positive effect in encouraging creating wealth, which is even worse than those who put the cart before the horse." The insightful remarks on stock market by Kang Youwei were unprecedented in history.

In conclusion, Kang Youwei believed that wealth management was the foundation for a country, the core of it being in "brilliant employment of the bank" and "proper utilization of virtual money". Regarding the brilliant employment of the bank, Kang was convinced that "the top priority is to establish a state bank, so that capital may be concentrated in the central bank to issue government bonds and then issue paper money; then, compositional bank is set up in the provinces, counties, towns to facilitate the communication among the people; and there would be exhortative banks, industrial banks, stock exchanges to enrich the people; still there would be specie banks to conduct foreign exchange, engaging in raising foreign debt internationally; and there would be privilege banks to expand resources and help consolidate the frontier; when these moves are implemented, poverty would never again worry the Chinese." Regarding his banking theory, we can make the following comments:

First, Kang Youwei preached "republic with nominal monarchy", and "Respecting Confucius and Studying the Classics" in politics; he became an old-fashioned hardliner. However, in economics, especially in banking theory, he was an adamant advocate of adopting the Western financial system. He preached that financial institutions be employed in raising funds, bringing into play their special function of financing and circulating funds, putting into practice the method of wealth management, "making the empty full, making the simple sophisticated". It was considered the "top wonder works of enriching China, the Chinese, and salvaging China". He tried to find a broad way for China to get rid of capital shortage, fiscal straits, maintain economic independence, revitalize industries, train talents and benefit both the country and the people; it reflected the interest and demand of national bourgeois capital in developing a modern national enterprise.

Second, when Kang Youwei learned and introduced the Western financial system, he did not engage in slavish copying; instead, he deliberately studied the difference between China's situation and that of foreign countries, and proceeded from the national situation of the time, "incorporating the systems of different countries and creating a special new system." Uniform supervision and inspection as well as control had to be ensured, while flexible regulation had to be made. Therefore, he proposed to implement an overall financial system featuring multiple levels and multiple forms, wherein funds were to be raised from multiple channels, the purpose whereof to uproot or turn around the backward situation of China wherein "China was in jeopardy and the businesses stagnated". After many years of deliberation, he devised a system: "at the upper level the European banking system of central state bank is to be adopted", "complemented with the specie bank practices of Belgium and Japan", "at the lower level the national bank system of the United States is to be employed", "at the intermediate level there are the compositional banking system"; the "privilege banking system practiced in England, Scotland, Germany and Korea", "the exhortative bank system and industrial bank system of Germany, France and Swede are to be set up", and "the stock exchange system is to be instituted." This design program was very detailed, but too many subjective elements also found their way into it, and there were also areas not well thought of, as well as errors in understanding. Nonetheless, we shall not negate his benign motive, "to fit the vast territory of China, and offer a strategy which might enrich both the country and the people"; his subjective motive was "to work out an overall plan embracing the situation of the entire country, creating a special system to be employed in China, all-embracing and thorough, will all hinge on this?" This principled stance of learning and introducing advanced foreign knowledge and achievement is still full of significance and guidance value to people of today.

Third, concerning the issue of saving the country, Kang Youwei indulged in discussing wealth management, primary gold money and rescuing the country via material production, which was entirely impractical without taking into consideration the reformation of the social, political, economic and cultural systems. The theory was advanced around 1905, and doubtless it was opposed to the revolutionary movement; he pinned hopes on the resurrection of the dying Qing Government and turning the table of the national situation. Four months after the Revolution of 1911, an article came out officially denouncing the shameful conduct of Yuan Shikai in handling the aftermath of the revolution, equating which with national betrayal and humiliation. Kang indulged in discussion of rescuing the country via wealth management, which was nothing but veiled indignation and criticism against the collusion between the new warlords and the powers.

Fourth, Kang's theory reversed the relations between wealth management and wealth production, bank and rescuing the country. He exaggerated the functions of wealth management and banks.

He believed that banks must be counted on in rescuing the country, enriching the people, regulating the navy and army, and implementing new law. "In one year the scale thereof will be up, in three years the effect will become obvious, in five years the livelihood of the people and the national economy will be out of straits, in ten years the country will become rich and powerful, invincible in the world." Hence, he wrote not without sadness, "If the Qing Dynasty could have employed it, the country may have been saved." In monetary system reform, he made similar mistakes, believing that if China did not adopt the gold standard the country would perish, and if the country shifted to the gold standard system, then the country could be rehabilitated. The fact is that, between making money and managing money, making money is the foundation and managing money is a condition; without making money there would be no money management, and managing money without s discussion of making money is water without a source or a tree without roots. Of course, wealth management plays a facilitating and guaranteeing function in production. Proper wealth management leads to improved efficiency, so that more may be created in a better manner, that is to say, the same amount of money can have more things done in a better manner. Establishing banks and rescuing the country, enriching the country and the people stand in a similar manner: under the conditions of an advanced commodity economy, the creation of banks could facilitate and guarantee the purpose of enriching the country and the people, laying a solid economic foundation and firm material strength for the consolidation of state power. However, the bank can neither dominate the country-rescuing effort nor determine the realization of the enterprise of enriching the country and the people. Without first discussing the foundation and precondition, the existence of the bank itself would be an issue, and the function of the bank would be nonexistent. However, in Kang's words, the function of wealth management in making money, of bank in enriching the country and the people, and even of instituting a complete financial system of China as well as a monetary system of gold standard was so important as to determine the survival of China; these remarks bordered on overstatement and inappropriateness.

Fifth, the nub of Kang Youwei's measure of rescuing the country with wealth management was that the Qing Government faced "dire financial straits", and his theorization of bank, paper money and government bonds all centered on this. Therefore, he thought that the basic function of the bank was a credit intermediary, which had been discussed specifically by Chen Chi, and in which he was not interested at all. The only point that aroused Kang's intense interest was "the philosopher stone" effect, the satisfaction of fiscal requirements. Following this line of thought, only issuing paper money, raising government bonds, raising foreign debt, conducting foreign exchange, seeking and purchasing gold, silver, etc., were touched upon, and no effort was spared in seeking a source of finance for the dying Qing Dynasty. Compared with his forerunners, including Zheng Guanying, Chen Chi and Yan Fu, Kang Youwei was particularly eager for immediate results, and his discussions sounded more subjective. For instance, he considered that there were four immediate urgencies to be dealt with after the establishment of the state bank: "the first is to borrow a little foreign debt as capital injection; the second is to issue paper money and government bonds to expand circulation and obtain guarantee; the third is to mint gold primary money, recalling old silver coin, paper money, and copper coins to unify money; the fourth is to energetically scour and purchase gold and silver to expand reserve for cash." We can get a clear picture from his remarks of the first and the fourth tasks. He believed that establishing banks and borrowing foreign debt as reserve for issuance were different from borrowing foreign debt to start projects or businesses which were not profitable; foreign debt could not be borrowed for non-profitable activities, as profitability hangs in the air in starting businesses, and there was considerable risk in it. Foreign debt could only to be raised for starting banks, "the more the better". Because "finance of China is extremely drained, neither the country nor the people has capital for getting up businesses, and hence nothing could be done." At that time, China recorded an import deficit of 70 million *yuan*, 50 million *yuan* interest on reparations, totaling 120 million *yuan*, with overseas Chinese possibly remitting back to China a few scores of million *yuan*: "if no foreign debt is taken out, then the pool will be drained, and the reserve for the state bank would be drained, wouldn't that be an extremely perilous situation!" However, since the central bank had not been set up, foreigners did not trust the Chinese, which resulted in supervision by foreigners, a "gross disgrace and peril, no borrowing should be allowed." He argued that one hundred million in reserve would suffice for starting the central state bank, and hundreds of millions in foreign debt must be raised, of which one hundred million was to be deposited in banks of Europe and the United States as reserve, and the amount actually borrowed would be no more than one hundred million. He planned to bypass the six-country bank consortium to avoid harsh terms including supervision and take out loans from other banks of Europe and the United States. In order to make an overall plan incorporating the entire situation and settle the issue once and for all, he emphasized that foreign loan borrowed shall serve as issuance reserve. So long as the foundation for the first year was properly laid, two or three hundred millions more may be borrowed in the following year and the year after that to expand the reserve and increase the capital. Then, there would be more paper money, and with skillful maneuvering, the country could set up grand engineering projects, expand railways, build ships, and the people could also start businesses of all types; taxes would be in less straitened circumstances, and neither the country nor the people would be worried about poverty. He delineated an enticing wonderworld, but he neglected an important fact: under the circumstances of aggression by the Western powers, the Chinese financial industry had already been dominated by foreign banks. So what effect could it work by miraculously exaggerating the function of the central bank abstractly in isolation? Besides, starting banks was a gambling activity; the wonder-working maneuvering was a disastrous technique, and was not a panacea to both the country and the people, but an extreme risk!

In order to increase issuance reserve, Kang advocated scouring and purchasing gold and silver. Because the aforesaid two hundred million reserve was by no means sufficient, if "credit is to be expanded and dry bones are to be benefited", then grand-scale scouring and purchasing gold and silver should be established as the top priority. Purchasing internationally would lead to a surge of gold price, therefore domestic scouring would be made. The surrendered and purchased gold would be deposited in domestic banks; gold and silver held in pawn and jewelry stores, mining of gold and silver, scouring and purchasing private holdings of gold and silver, and conducting and expanding overseas Chinese remittance business would all be accomplished. Of the four channels of collecting gold and silver, "none excels that the people selling their gold and silver holdings to the state bank." Private trading of gold and silver would be prohibited, and newly mined and existing gold and silver would be concentrated in the state bank, hence more government bonds and more paper money could be issued, thereby enriching the country and benefiting the people. It would definitely not be an issue to compete against the United States. He argued that in the replacement of gold with paper money, paper money only carried credit, and so long as there is a reserve set aside for withdrawing, nobody will withdraw. What a bold and naive idea!

After the failure of the: Reform Movement of 1898, Kang Youwei started businesses with part of the donations from overseas Chinese with a view to make money to support and expand the activity of the Royalists Society. These business projects included the following: Shanghai Guangzhi Bookstore, Guangxi Zhenhua Company on the mainland;

Chinese Business Company, China Hotel and Huayi Company in Hong Kong; Huamei Bank, Qiongcai Hotel in the United States; and real estate, trams, railways, Huamo Bank and shipping companies in Mexico. Except for the Shanghai Guangzhi Bookstore, which had published a batch of influential books and magazines, the rest of the businesses failed either due to poor management, bad staff, internal strife or change of political situation.[97] Kang may have inadvertently demonstrated the fact that a theorist, thinker, intellectual or even a revolutionary might not necessarily guarantee success in business. Eloquence in speaking and brilliance in writing did not equal practical ability. On the contrary, this demonstrated the fact that he and his followers had broken out of the mold which had constrained traditional scholars, broken away from the banal ideology held by such traditional scholars who rejected commerce and felt ashamed at the mention of profit and commerce, which also demonstrated the tortuousness and difficulty of the path they had embarked on. As to how far they could travel, that would be a totally different issue.

---

[97]Ma Honglin, *A Critical Biology of Kang Youwei*, Nanjing University Press, 1998, p. 273.

Chapter 10

Financial Thought Between the 1911 Revolution and the May Fourth Movement in 1919

1. Introduction

In February 1914, the Beiyang government of the Republic of China promulgated the *National Currency Act* and established the Currency Bureau, which was responsible for the minting and issuing of new silver coins. Popularly called the Yuantou coin, the new silver coins were identical in shape, weight and purity. They soon took the place of dragon dollars. After the May Fourth Movement in 1919, they also replaced Mexican silver dollars, becoming the sole standard coin in circulation. Under the reign of the Beiyang government, with warlords occupying different places, copper coins were minted by different provincial bureaus, leading to sharp differences in material and purity. The serious disorder in minting and issuing made copper coins very untrustworthy, some of which circulated only in a couple of cities and counties. The circulation of Chinese and foreign currencies was even more chaotic than during the late Qing Dynasty. After the 1911 Revolution, especially during World War I, with commercial banks playing a leading role, the Chinese banking industry developed rapidly. They undertook to sell public bonds because the high rates of interest and substantial discount not only solved the problem of capital but also offered them opportunities for speculation. Many banks were set up for the selling of public bonds, while quite a few banks collapsed due to failure in bond speculation. From 1914 to 1921, 96 private banks were established. After Yuan Shikai's failure to restore a monarchical government, Bank of China and Bank of Communications, as the financial pillars of government, faced the threat of bank run. On May 12, 1916, the government declared that the two banks would stop honoring their bills. As a result, people started panic buying by dumping the notes of the two banks, which came to a stop in March 1920, when the government bond to straighten out the finance began to be released. Under the control of foreign banks, the branches of the two Chinese banks were scattered quite unreasonably over several provinces and cities. With the fall of the Qing Dynasty, draft banks lost their support and started to deteriorate. Old-style Chinese private banks, after reforming, entered a new stage of development.

Foreign banks partitioned China into "spheres of influence". Hong Kong and Shanghai Banking Corporation focused on the Yangtze River valley and the Pearl River valley. National City Bank of New York centered on Shanghai, spreading its business actively to Tianjin, Hankou, Chongqing, Changsha, Fuzhou and Guangzhou. Banque de l'Indochine had a presence in provinces like Guangxi, Yunnan and Guizhou, while the business of Yokohama Specie Bank Ltd was concentrated in major cities. By the end of 1926, there were 65 foreign banks with over 250 branches in China. Big powers like Britain, France and the United States at first contended and then cooperated with each other on the issue of loaning to China. After the 1911 Revolution, the foreign consortium that emerged in the beginning of the twentieth century had among itself fierce contention. The four-nation consortium (England, France, Germany and the United States) later became a six-nation consortium (with the addition of Japan and Russia). In March 1913, the United States exited the consortium because America didn't get the expected benefit, resulting in a five-nation consortium. When World War I broke out, Germany was expelled. After the October Revolution, Russian banks quit. In May 1918, the new four-nation consortium was composed of 71 banks of the USA, England, Germany and Japan. Through the "Chinese Government Reorganization Loan", the five-nation consortium (England, France, Germany, Russia and Japan) took control of all the salt tax and a share of the customs duties. Only the interest earnings from the guardianship of salt taxes amounted to 42,850,000 pounds. The circulation price for the Reorganization Loan bond abroad was 90% of its face value, and the final gain was 84%, generating a profit of 2.5 million pounds, not including various commission charges. Between 1917 and 1926, though the salt taxes and customs duties added up to 1,660 million *yuan*, the government could only put 20% to use, roughly 360 million *yuan*.

2. Sun Yat-sen's financial theory

Born in Xiangshan county (now Zhongshan county) of Guangdong Province, Sun Yat-sen's (1866–1925) childhood name was Dixiang and adult name was Wen. His style names were Zaizhi and Deming; his other name Rixin was similar to Yat-sen in pronunciation. In 1897, he chose Zhongshan Qiao as an alias while in Japan, and was thus known to the world. He was a great patriot, democratic revolutionary, statesman and thinker. At the age of 12, he went to Honolulu with his mother to join his elder brother Sun Mei and started to receive Western education. At 18, he came back to China and at 21 he began to study medicine. He practiced medicine in places like Macao and Guangzhou, gradually getting involved in revolutionary activities. In 1894, he went north to Tianjin by way of Shanghai to present a proposal to Li Hongzhang, a high-ranking official of the Qing government, pleading in vain for the implementation of Western laws and regulations to rejuvenate the country, because he thought the Self-strengthening Movement had failed to fend off foreign humiliation and vitalize the country. In October of the same year, he organized the Revive China Society in Honolulu to reenergize China and set up, for the first time, the banner of "Expelling Manchus, Reviving China, and Establishing a Unified Government". In 1895, he planned an uprising in Guangzhou but failed. While in London, Sun was kidnapped by the Chinese legation and held captive. Rescued through the collective efforts of the public, he caused a sensation in Europe with the publication of his own account of the event, *Kidnapped in London*. In league with other revolutionary groups, Sun established, and was elected director of, the Revolutionary Alliance in 1905, whose aim was "to Expel the Manchu Barbarians, to Revive China, to Establish a Republic, and to Distribute

Land Equally Among the People". With the Three Principles of the People as its political guideline, the Revolutionary Alliance organized more than ten armed uprisings, which, though unsuccessful, rocked the reactionary Qing government. After the Wuchang Uprising in 1911, representatives from 17 provinces elected Sun the provisional president of the Republic of China. Sworn into office in January 1912, he promulgated the *Provisional Constitution of the Republic of China*. Under the big powers' political and economic pressure, he soon relinquished the presidency to Yuan Shikai and began to think that economic construction should take priority over revolution. In August of the same year, the Revolutionary Alliance was reorganized into Kuomintang, and Sun was chosen as the director. In 1913, Sun staged the Second Revolution against Yuan Shikai, which also failed. In 1914, he founded the China Revolutionary Party in Japan and was nominated director. In 1915 and 1916, Sun put out two declarations denouncing Yuan Shikai's restoration efforts. In 1917, the Congressional Extraordinary Session held a meeting in Guangzhou, which led to the establishment of a military government for the protection of the *Provisional Constitution*. Sun was elected Marshal of Army and Navy, pledging to launch the Northern Expedition. After the failure of the Constitutional Protection Movement, Sun established residence in the concession area of Shanghai and wrote *Memoirs of a Chinese Revolutionary*. In the book, he summarized the lessons from his experience and developed his Three Principles of the People into the New Three Principles of the People, which consisted of "Working with the Soviets, Working with the Communists and Helping the Farmers". The New Three Principles of the People had in itself anti-imperialistic and anti-feudal elements. Nationalistically, it opposed imperialistic oppression. Democratically, it maintained the people's control of the government instead of a minority control. As to social welfare, it held the policy of land to the tillers and regulation of the capital. On March 12, 1925, Sun died in Peking. His writings were collected into *Complete Works of Sun Yat-sen* and *Selected Works of Sun Yat-sen*.

Sun was the one who named the Chinese discipline of economics. Though he wasn't an economist himself, in the course of planning for the rejuvenation of China, it was only natural that he would touch upon economic issues and expound his revolution as well as reconstruction theories. His active acquisition of the latest Western theories, including Karl Marx's *Das Kapital*, laid the foundation for his economic and financial thought. In his judgment, economics "originated from China", because in ancient China, under the administration of talented economist Guan Zi, benefiting from fishery and the salt business, the State of Qi became the richest state in the world. Because of the absence of the term "economics" and the disorderliness of academic enquiry in China, it hadn't become a scientific discipline then. The word "*Jingji*" (economy) had existed since ancient times. For example, in the Ritual and Music chapter of *Theory of the Zhong*, there was a sentence as follows: "They all knew the law of *Jingji*, though they didn't have the chance to hold office." It referred to the administration of the people and governance of the country. In modern China, the translation for the word "economy" varied a lot. At first, there were *Fuguo Ce* and *Fuguo Yangmin Ce*. Later on, there were *Licai Xue, Ji Xue, Shengji Xue, Ping Zhun, Zisheng Xue*, etc. In Sun's opinion, these expressions "were not adequate to depict its connotation, while *Jingji* seemed much closer in meaning."[1] Under the influence of his fame and prestige, "*jingji*" as the translation of economy finally won universal approval and acceptance. As the core of Sun's economic thought, the connotation of the Principle of the People's Livelihood evolved with the changing times and the development of his revolutionary cause. Before the Revolution of 1911, it was only "to distribute land equally among the people", but later it extended to the issues of capital, industry and commerce, as well as education, which constituted the four areas of Sun's Principle of the People's Livelihood. Sun's financial theory included mainly monetary theory, theory of monetary revolution and theory of using foreign capital. His monetary theory was mainly expressed in his "Open Telegram Advocating Monetary Revolution and Opposing Russia" ("Monetary Revolution" for short),[2] which came out in December 3, 1912, and the second chapter of his *Fundamentals of National Construction*, the title of which was "Citing the Use of Money as an Example."[3]

---

[1] *Complete works of Sun Yat-sen*, vol. 2, p. 510.
[2] *Ibid.*, vol. 2, pp. 544–549.
[3] *Ibid.*, vol. 6, pp. 159–246.

2.1. Sun's monetary theory

After carefully studying Karl Marx's writings and works on Western classical economics, Sun gained a good deal of enlightenment. His exposition of the nature of money unfolded directly from a significant question: "The relations between man and money are so close, and the mode of its use is so universally accepted — yet I ask: 'How many people are there who know what money is and what is its functional peculiarity?'" "Ancient and modern, Chinese and foreign, people who use money but don't know its nature can be found everywhere." This is reminiscent of Marx's citation of William Gladstone in *A Critique of Political Economy*, which was more academic and humorous: "Not even love has made so many fools of men as the pondering over the nature of money."[4]

On the origins of money: In *Psychological Reconstruction*, Sun wrote, "Once there was an 'assembly in the market-place at midday', exchange took place very easily, as many commodities were set out on view before the crowd. At the same time this gave great economy of human labor, and also aroused an increase in the desire to buy. Previously people exchanged only the most necessary and essential commodities, now they pay more attention to the exchange of elegant articles. Before commodities were themselves exchanged, they were exchanged even earlier for elegant articles, and the latter exchanged in their turn for commodities. Elegant articles, such as shells, precious stones and pearls, began to represent the value of commodities." Money originated from the development of commercial exchange, since the practice of bartering gradually gave way to commercial transaction. Sun's understanding accorded with the historical development of money and was very much to the point.

On the nature of money: In Sun's view, "There is an old definition that money carries out the functions of exchange (for commodities). Western economists also say that money itself belongs to the category of commodities, and is capable of determining the two important peculiarities, first, exchange at the average value of a commodity, and second, to be a measure of all commodities. The writer takes them into account, calls

---

[4]*Complete Works of Karl Marx and Friedrich Engels*, vol. 13, p. 54.

money 'established value.'"[5] Established value had the connotation of universal equivalent, but it wasn't simply equal to the latter, because universal equivalent was concerned with the value of commodity, while established value focused on the agency role. Universal equivalent could function as a criterion of evaluation, but this function couldn't be seen as equal to price and criterion of price. On the contrary, it was clear that established value didn't differentiate between the two. This indicated that Sun approved of the Western bourgeois classical economists' explanation about the nature of money, understood its commodity feature, and knew clearly that human production was the source of commodity ("The same was the case with the fisherman, hunter, woodcutter, blacksmith and, in fact, all craftsmen: they brought their surplus for exchange for what they needed"). It was to his credit that Sun could understand the commodity nature of money and the derivation of commodities from human production.

But the belief that "money is but a kind of commodity" does not seem well-rounded. It is fair to say the money is a commodity, a kind of merchandise, as well as the outcome of production. Nevertheless, money is no ordinary commodity. More importantly, it is a special commodity, possessing not only use value derived from the nature of ordinary commodity but also value of social utility, which stems from the social nature unique to this particular commodity. Unaware of this distinction, Sun simplistically equated money with common commodity without any further elaboration. In addition, he confused the function of metal currency with that of paper money.

Money was only "the symbol of commodity and property". Its emergence was because "symbols of the money alone can fulfill some of its functions, which give rise to the misunderstanding that money is a pure symbol."[6] We must bear in mind that "money is no symbol" and that money "crystallized from the exchange value produced in the process of commodity exchange."[7] The self-negation in Sun's monetary theory was apparently behind the times, because he considered money a pure symbol of material wealth, without any special and magical power. "The power of

---

[5] *Complete Works of Sun Yat-sen*, vol. 6, pp. 173, 170.
[6] *Complete Works of Karl Marx and Friedrich Engels*, vol. 23, pp. 108–109.
[7] *Ibid.*, vol. 13, p. 38.

gold is drawn from the process of exchange of commodities. If there is no process of exchange of commodities, gold would be transformed into sand and dust. Even if there are commodities, but without trading, gold would also lose its significance."[8] That viewpoint was inappropriate. Emphasizing the commodity nature of money, his refutation of the omnipotence of money and money fetishism was right and praiseworthy. But even without transaction, money only ceases its function as universal equivalent, which means it is still a commodity, not as worthless as sediment. This doesn't mean that the commodity nature of money isn't acknowledged. If money is purely symbolic, then there is no sense in its being money. At the same time, he denied the social nature of money as universal equivalent and denied the symbolic nature of wealth. Going from one extreme to another, this was like throwing the baby out with the bathwater.

Money served two basic functions: medium of exchange and standard of price. That understanding was unquestionable and had been elaborated on by other Chinese scholars before Sun. Like his predecessors, Sun paid far more attention to the function of medium of circulation than of measure of value. So he didn't have a thorough understanding of the inner logic of money's emergence and development, and his conclusions were rather simplistic. It never occurred to him that, without the theoretical preparation of measure of value, money could never function as medium of circulation, let alone as a transaction intermediary. Besides, his understanding of the other functions of money was also not so profound, usually only a passing remark, and thus rather superficial and disregardful.

Social pattern and exchange of currency: With reference to the stages of exchange and currency evolution, Sun divided the growth of civilization into three stages: the production of necessities, the production of conveniences and the production of luxuries. He believed that there was already division of labor in the stage of the production of necessities. At that time, producers bartered their production for what they needed (means of production and means of subsistence). What producers and swappers wanted most was the satisfaction of their need of livelihood. So this stage was characterized by the production of necessities. In the second stage, transactions developed further. Since "playthings like turtles,

---

[8]*Complete Works of Sun Yat-sen*, vol. 6, p. 171.

shells, beads and jades were transformed into the evaluation criteria of commodities", money entered the stage. With money becoming the evaluation criteria of commodities, human beings began to desire more and used money for their comfort. "With prosperous culture and flourishing material life, the progress of civilization quickened." Human beings reached the stage of the production of conveniences. The third stage was made possible by the invention of machinery. This stage saw the overproduction of commodity and development of industry. Countries with a strongly developed industry tried to extend their market and to export their manufactured goods. People tended to maintain the point of view that only articles of luxury could bring benefit to mankind. In the case of block trading, money wasn't as convenient and there wasn't much money in circulation, so credit (checks, bills) took the place of money. After World War I, "many countries did away with gold and introduced paper money in place of it." Free from the limitation of gold and silver, monetary wealth increased substantially and human society began the age of luxury. The evolution of currency was the result of development of exchange relation. It was in accordance with and served the specific stage of commodity exchange. On the contrary, the exchange of commodity was under the influence of commodity production, which was determined by the development of productivity. The form of currency could indeed reflect the productivity of different stages of development, which illustrated that "different forms of money can fit in with the needs of different stages of social production."[9] Social patterns varied with the change in production mode. Different production relations would lead to different social patterns and determine the essential feature of that period. There was no doubt that Sun's viewpoints were shaped by the methodology of Western economists, but some of them remained open to question.

On the inevitability of paper money's replacement of specie: In Sun's opinion, "in industrially and commercially underdeveloped countries, money generally takes the form of gold and silver, while in industrially and commercially developed countries, where the wealth and commodities exceed the quantity of gold and silver by tens of millions of times, money has usually taken the form of paper notes. Just as, in the past, gold

---

[9]*Complete Works of Karl Marx and Friedrich Engels*, vol. 46, Book 1, p. 64.

and silver replaced cloth, shells, and knives and became money, so, too, paper notes will replace gold and silver as the money of the future. This is a matter of natural evolution, a thing dictated by reason, the course things must take."[10] That is to say, with the development of productive forces, it was only natural that paper money would take the place of specie, which was an objective law not to be changed by human effort. After the invention of modern machinery, human society went forward much more quickly, and material conditions flourished even more. "This invention created an entire revolution in industry and ushered in a new world, while money gradually began to lose its force." Trading activities "went beyond the bounds of the sphere of money". Business transactions which used to be paid in cash could be finished with credit obligations. Transactions involving large sums of money were "the purest waste of time and energy, and moreover caused much trouble". "By eliminating the necessity of the double transmission from the seller to the buyer and back, bills and mortgages preserved money from such dangers as theft, loss or accident. It reduced the cares and time spent on commerce while ensuring the safety of the transaction, thus producing unthinkable advantages for society."[11] This was his analysis of the emergence of credit currency in cash's process of being a medium of exchange. As was pointed out, his discussion was mainly concerned with credit currency, without any analysis or exposition of the causes and process of the advent of paper money.

On the relation between currency and capital, Sun's view was very clear: "Capital refers not exclusively to money. Both machine and land are capital."[12]

2.2. Theory of monetary revolution

After the 1911 Revolution, taking advantage of the serious financial straits of the Beiyang government, Russia orchestrated Mongolia's independence. Within such a context, Sun published his open telegram, *Monetary Revolution*, proposing to "carry out a monetary revolution to resolve our

---

[10]*Ibid.*, vol. 2, p. 545.
[11]*Ibid.*, vol. 6, pp. 174–175.
[12]*Ibid.*, vol. 2, p. 521.

financial difficulties". His proposal was that "gold be withdrawn from circulation and bank-notes be introduced to lighten the burden of the state finances and to develop industry and commerce,"[13] with the purpose of resisting aggression of Western powers and fostering national economy. His plan was fivefold: First, "the government was to accept as money only paper notes designated as such by national decree"; paper notes had to be used for all national revenues and expenditures as well as for all market transactions. Second, the government was to reduce gold and silver to the status of commodities; "the use of gold and silver coins should be strictly prohibited. The metal currency in circulation would be exchanged for paper notes only at the bureaus issuing paper notes; they would not be allowed to circulate on the market." Third, "as for the standard, we could emulate Japan and designate gold as the standard", and use silver and copper coins as fractional currency. Fourth, the issuing and retrieving of paper notes would be based on the financial and commodity conditions of the country. Fifth, under special circumstances, for example, if the country had an urgent need, measures could also be taken. "The people's representatives have only to decide on a budget and then hold the citizenry responsible for providing the amount necessary. Either taxes can be increased, or a per capita contribution can be solicited. As soon as an order is promulgated, the issuing bureau will issue notes in the same amount to meet the nation's needs. When the notes expire, the tax department will retrieve and cancel them."[14]

Lessons from the issuing of paper notes: At all times and in all countries, "paper notes were initially a great convenience, but ultimately they resulted in infinite problems that ended only with their natural and inevitable elimination."[15] "Reckless issuing of paper notes would disturb the national finance and harm both the military and the civilian, so it must be handled with care."[16] The reason was that paper notes were not like gold and silver. Though both were tokens of commodities and had the same function, "gold and silver were valuable per se and difficult to obtain",

---

[13]*Ibid.*, vol. 6, p. 175.
[14]*Ibid.*, vol. 2, pp. 545–547.
[15]*Ibid.*, p. 545.
[16]*Ibid.*, vol. 1, pp. 308–309.

while paper notes "were cheap and easily printed". Consequently, "even when gold and silver lost their character as tokens of commodities, they still had value per se and could still circulate on the market without causing problems." "As soon as paper notes ceased to represent commodities, they would lose their value, and problems will arise if they continue to circulate on the market." The devaluation of paper notes lay in that fact that they had next to no intrinsic value. On the contrary, gold and silver had their own value. So there were different social and economic influences in their circulation. Paper notes might cause problems which could be avoided by the circulation of gold and silver, because they were issued on credit. As a result, "as soon as paper notes were issued, they would be sure to inspire immediate confidence and will circulate widely and without hindrance. At that point, finances can be properly conducted."[17] Without credit, the existence of paper notes was but pointless and as good as useless. "If a government discredited its own paper notes, and yet forced everyone else to trust them and accept them, that was surely a mission impossible."[18] As a revolutionary leader, Sun was no monetary expert. His insightful discovery must have derived from his diligence, his reading of modern works of Western economics and his deep enquiry into social and economic life, Chinese and foreign, ancient and modern. But he wrongly considered paper notes to be the same as gold and silver, all tokens of commodity. Their different natures determined their different functions. With gold and silver in circulation, paper notes could only perform the function of money when they represented gold and silver (to act as a medium of circulation and means of payment). Besides, only gold and silver could function as a measure of value, a medium of storage and world currency.

Sun proposed that two organizations should be set up in order to carry out monetary revolution effectively, one charged exclusively with issuing notes and the other with retrieving and destroying them. With the issue of notes under the exclusive control of the central government, the two organizations were responsible for the issuing, retrieving, and destroying of notes, thus regulating the paper notes in circulation. He devised two

---

[17]*Ibid.*, vol. 2, p. 545.
[18]*Ibid.*, vol. 6, p. 176.

channels for the issuing of paper notes. One was the financial channel: "For example, suppose the central government of the nation collects total annual tax revenues of 300 million *yuan*. Then, when the tax department has received its budget, it can proceed to issue debt certificates for the same amount to the note-issuing bureau, which in turn will issue notes in the same amount in order to meet the nation's financial needs." "Under this system, after the bureau issuing paper notes receives debt certificates from the tax department, it will issue notes in the same amount. Because responsibility for these paper notes is assumed by the people, the notes are valid and are called *live notes*." The other was the circulating channel: "The paper money circulating in society must all be remitted by the issuing bureau. The paper notes retained by the issuing bureau are not yet valid. In order to be valid, they must be exchanged for gold, silver, commodities, or industrial properties." There were also two channels for the withdrawal of paper notes from circulation. One was the financial channel: "At the end of the period, the tax department will turn the 300 million *yuan* it has received over to the note-canceling bureau and thus cancel the debt certificates." "On the other hand, because they have fulfilled their function of representing total tax revenues, the notes with which the tax department redeems the debt certificates (using tax revenues) are no longer valid; they are called *dead notes* and should be destroyed." The other was the channel of commodity: "The commodities received by the issuing bureau in exchange for its notes will be stored in public warehouses, which will sell those goods locally or ship them elsewhere for sale. Only paper money, not gold and silver, will be accepted as payment. The notes exchanged for the goods in the public warehouses will lose their value because they no longer represent commodities and will immediately become dead notes. All dead notes will be handed over to the cancellation bureau to be destroyed."[19]

Sun's theory of monetary revolution was met with vehement opposition. After the theory went public, "reproaching voices can be heard everywhere. At the instigation of political parties in Beijing, some people claimed that this was no other way than a political struggle. Out of jealousy of China's reform, some foreigners worried that they would not be

---

[19]*Ibid.*, vol. 2, p. 546.

able to control China as before."[20] There was public uproar because no one thought it practical. Contrary to the expectation of his opponents, Sun held a firm belief. He called attention to the fact that, after World War I, "some countries did away with gold and introduced paper money in place of it, exactly what I proposed." But some people put forward this objection: "During China's Yuan and Ming Dynasties, paper money was also issued, but it only hastened their downfall. During the Civil War in the United States, the issue of paper money also produced similar result." Sun's answer to this was quite straightforward. That was because they issued money in unlimited and excessive quantities. Some people thought that the government stopping the payment of cash on its bonds was the abolition of money and would result in "panic and predicament". Sun was quite rational about this. According to his understanding, "when issuing that decree, the government copied only part of the measures adopted in other countries. In other countries the governments did not pay on bills or cheques in specie, but at the same time they did not accept specie. The Peking government acted otherwise. When promulgating the decree, it thought that it would not pay in specie to the people, but that this did not exclude the possibility of not accepting the bank-notes it had issued itself. This was only deceiving the people by worthless and valueless paper."[21] That penetrating comment hit the nail right on the head. The Peking government's failure lay in its accepting the banknotes without paying in specie to the people. The issue of paper money was aimed at people's gold and silver. When the United States stopped paying on account of its bills, the government at the same time stopped accepting specie. When the government issued a national loan, it was also paid in paper. To pay their taxes or purchase commodities, those who had specie had to exchange it for paper banknotes at the banks. As a result, the Peking government's practice was equivalent to proclaiming bankruptcy, while everyone was glad to use the paper money issued by the American government.

On keeping a stable currency and avoiding the repetition of former mistakes, Sun discussed two essential aspects. One was to balance the issuing of paper notes with the circulation of commodities. Since paper

---

[20] Liao Zhongkai, *Collected Works of Shuangqing,* p. 294.
[21] *Complete works of Sun Yat-sen*, vol. 6, p. 176.

notes "serve as representatives of commodities", "they must be backed by the commodities they represent or by the citizenry before they can have validity". "Notes in circulation always represent other objects. The more commodities there are, the more notes there will be, and even if there is a profusion of notes, it will not result in problems." Since the issuing of paper notes was in accordance with the commodities in circulation, the purchasing power of paper notes would naturally vary with the increase and decrease of commodities. So, there would not be any imbalance of "paper money in unlimited and excessive quantities". The other aspect was the joint guarantee of the issuing of paper notes by gold, silver and commodities. To prevent the devaluation of paper notes and the failure of issuing, Sun further pointed out, "The paper notes retained by the issuing bureau are not yet valid. In order to be valid, they must be exchanged for gold, silver, commodities, or industrial properties." That is to say, paper notes in circulation must be ensured by goods. After the monetary revolution, gold and silver would be downgraded into commodity and treated likewise. The government "should speedily enact laws" and "set up public warehouses and factories where people can exchange their products or labor for paper notes."[22] Commodities from the exchange were the guarantee for the issuing of paper notes. The exchange of labor for paper notes meant that the addition of new paper notes was based on the future increase of commodities. As we all know, money in circulation reflects the value of commodities in circulation, so the ideal issuing of money should correspond to the commodities in circulation. After the founding of the People's Republic of China, the stability of the *Renminbi* was ensured not only by the foreign exchange reserve of gold but also by the quantities of commodities under government control. From Sun's insightful observation during the early period of the Republic of China, we can infer that he had a profound understanding of the relation between money and commodities in circulation. This was due partly to his repeated enquiry into domestic and foreign theories about the relation between currency and commodities, partly to his penetration and farsightedness as a statesman. Of course, the attainment of this goal was no easy thing at all. First of all, there needed to be an advanced commodity and credit system.

---

[22]*Ibid.*, vol. 2, pp. 546–547.

Correspondingly, there had to be a sound and meticulous organization of the amount, structure and price of the production, circulation and distribution, so that the quantity, structure and distribution of the circulation of commodities and currency could be balanced. This was a complex and systemic project, not so easy to put into practice, and China was lacking in the required conditions at the time. In addition, there were loopholes in his plan. For example, in terms of circulation (encashment), using industrial properties as guarantee of issuing paper notes was incomparable with gold, silver and commodities. It was indeed a rigid practice to issue paper notes for circulation after the exchange of commodities of equivalent value. Earlier scholars had considered it unnecessary, so Sun's proposition was a theoretical retrogression. Even the withdrawal of paper notes from circulation was flawed, because there was no need to destroy them all. Those in good condition could remain in circulation so as to cut down circulation expenses. The crucial part of issuing paper notes was to control the amount and to ensure their withdrawal, which would prevent the occurrence of inflation and devaluation. Theoretically, in modern times, Sun was the first to propose the substitution of commodities for gold and silver as the guarantee for issuing money, which was both insightful and significant.

In terms of the prevention of inflation, Sun spoke approvingly of Sang Hongyang, the counselor to Emperor Wu of the Han Dynasty: "He introduced the measure of the lowering of the prices of commodities down to their nominal value, in order then to release commodities for proper circulation. Collecting them in a normal period, he threw his reserve supplies into the market when prices rose, and thus lowered prices again to their normal value. When there was a superfluity of some commodity and therefore its price fell, he was able to transfer his supplies from one place to another, thereby regulating commodity prices and benefiting the state." Sang brought into full play the positive function of national constitutions in the allocation of commodities and regulation of their prices. In Sun's view, Sang "could be said to know the real meaning of money". Following the example of Sang, he proposed the establishment of public warehouses for the purchase and storage of commodities, which could be sold if conditions permitted. He opposed the accumulation of wealth and the issuing of large amounts of paper notes backed by governmental forces, because "the wealth or poverty of a nation by no means depends on the quantity of money, but rather on the quantity of commodities and their wide circulation."[23]

Motivation for monetary revolution: Sun's purpose was to solve the government's financial difficulties. On November 3, 1912, the Russians signed the *Russo-Mongolian Agreement* and thus took "advantage of our financial crisis and the unsettled state of our reconstruction efforts to grab our Mongolia". The whole nation swore unanimously to defeat Russia. He lamented, "our financial difficulties are the major reason we are now unable to even consider going to war." At the early period of the Republic of China, the troubled financial situation made it hard for the government to function properly. In addition to the failure to obtain loans from the six-nation consortium, there was the Russian disaster. "China's survival is at stake, and I am forced to propose extraordinary measures in order to cope with the situation." Although China's finances were in a state of crisis, "our financial resources have remained the same, and our production has increased. What has created our current poverty is a lack of money." That is to say, the nation was deficient in currency instead of commodities. Though it made some sense, that understanding was fairly partial indeed.

Goals of monetary revolution: First, "the market will never have to be concerned with financial crises."[24] Since paper notes took the place of gold and silver, "the export of gold and silver will no longer affect our economy", "even if there is no gold or silver in the entire country". The reason was that paper notes were different from gold and silver, whose stock and production were under the restriction of natural reserve and productive power. With gold and silver in circulation, once their quantity decreased, there would certainly be a crisis. While foreigners would send their gold and silver abroad, the Chinese might bury theirs underground in preparation for worse circumstances. Consequently, gold and silver would become even scarcer at precisely the time when the country urgently needed them. While unscrupulous international bankers would attempt to monopolize specie, "Chinese poverty will feed on poverty". The opposite

---

[23]*Ibid.*, vol. 6, p. 176.
[24]*Ibid.*, vol. 2, pp. 544–546.

was true in the case of paper notes. In the issuing of paper notes, "the solicitation of a per capita contribution" would be very easy. People could draw on it, either through their labor or in exchange for their products. When applied to the market, this situation would definitely lead to a state of all-round prosperity. As managed currency, unlike gold and silver, the issuing of paper notes wasn't so strictly limited by natural and producing conditions. The one and only tight control needed was the amount of supply of paper notes.

Second, China's industry and commerce would develop a lot. Sun believed that after the monetary revolution was accomplished, finances would certainly operate smoothly. Undoubtedly, the industry and commerce of China would develop, and China's exports would exceed its imports. Since foreign goods would not be able to compete with local ones, foreigners would have to turn over their gold, silver and jewelry to make up the difference. As the Chinese would be in need of money, it would be advisable to abolish gold and silver, and to issue paper notes to meet the demand of commodity circulation. This would satisfy the market's need for money, ensure the capital flow in production and circulation, and increase China's export, thus breaking away from the control of the foreign banks. But without a change of the semi-colonial nature of China, how could a monetary revolution alone break the shackles of foreign powers on Chinese economy? Moreover, at that time China was not only in need of money but also in the worse situation of weak economy, fragile industry and struggling handicraft industry, without any hope of "taking great leaps forward". The overexpectation and overoptimism precisely demonstrated the partiality of his understanding.

Third, "to sum up, once we have carried out this revolution, our finances will immediately be regenerated",[25] and the financial difficulties would be overcome straight away. Theoretically, the series of measures in the issuing of paper notes proposed by Sun was aiming not at making up the financial deficit, but at acting as advances for financial expenses. The purpose was not to trigger inflation, but to avoid the excessive issuing of paper notes, and keep the balance between financial issuing of money and tax. Even the issuing of urgently needed paper notes was backed by

---

[25]*Ibid.*, p. 547.

increased tax and per capita contribution, so the advances of paper notes could be withdrawn safely. The issuing of paper notes for social circulation was backed up by commodities, gold and silver, as well as factories, so disorder and deterioration in their circulation would not be expected to occur. But in actual economic operation, the circulation of paper notes was not as easy as he thought. If the budgetary revenue could not be collected in time, and the government would have to increase taxes and per capita contribution, then the issuing of paper notes as advances for financial expenses would never attain the goal of assimilating the purchasing power of circulating currency and withdrawing paper notes. If the rise of taxes and per capita contribution increased people's burden, negative social and economic influence would ensue. At that time in China, Sun's design was more idealistic than practical.

2.3. On the reorganization of finance

After the 1911 Revolution, Sun paid close attention and devoted major effort to the reorganization of finance, because he thought it most urgent to set up new financial institutions. In his judgment, China's vast territory was very fertile, but since the founding of the Republic, there had not been any growth in the produce of Southeast China, while the famine of Northeast China remained the same. The reason was that "there wasn't any specific financial institution handling the circulation of capital."[26] Playing a pivotal role, finance should enhance the circulation of capital on the market. It seemed to have an influence on the price of commodities, the stability of market, and the balance between supply and demand. It was inconceivable that economy and politics could do without finance. China was a big country abounding in natural wealth, so the need for different kinds of banks was imperative, and "the more banks there are, the better".[27] With the country's finances in chaos, it was difficult to get expected loans through customary procedures.[28] After the representatives of bureaucrats and former big shots joined the revolutionary forces, they

---

[26] *Ibid.*, vol. 2, p. 275.
[27] *Ibid.*, vol. 3, p. 7.
[28] *Ibid.*, p. 124.

got the support of foreign loans. When they reenergized a little, they began to consolidate their standing. Some people even unleashed all their ferocity, attempting to bring down the Republic for the restoration of monarchy. "Ennobling one family while enslaving the masses, they are the so-called public enemy and should be duly punished."[29] In the office of provisional president, Sun commenced the establishment of the central bank, bank of agricultural prosperity, bank of farming, frontiers bank and Sino-Western Joint-ventured bank. He also planned to raise capital by floating shares to set up China Bank and Chinese Industrial Bank in Southeast Asia. After the Northern Expedition, he issued orders in 1924 to maintain the credibility of banks of Guangdong Province and quickened the establishment of the central bank of the government. At the opening ceremony of the Central Bank in Guangzhou, he made a speech, calling on "the military, political, agricultural, industrial, and commercial circles" to support it. We can well perceive that Sun, as a statesman, was greatly concerned about the revitalization of Chinese agriculture and industry and the development of border areas. For the rejuvenation of China, all possible means available could be adopted, including the introduction of foreign investment and capital from overseas Chinese. In short, to mobilize all the forces for the reconstruction of the country, China needed all types of banks, especially banks of its own.

With his ideas scattered mainly in related speeches, letters, instructions and orders, Sun didn't have any monographs on the rectification of Chinese finance. During the period between 1912 and 1913, and the period between 1920 and 1923, he repeatedly suggested the establishment of banks, the rectification of finance and the issuing of a single currency in China. As an outstanding revolutionary and a great pioneer, he not only had such an insightful understanding but also put his understanding into practice; he not only publicized his plan to party members and the general public but also participated in the formulation and implementation of related policies. His overall goal was "the success of revolution and the prosperity of China". "As the hubs of financial operation, banks are the key to the development of commerce. They are directly related to national

---

[29]*Ibid.*, pp. 285, 299.

economy and of an extreme importance, so I must be cautious and conscientious."[30] That is, banks were the hubs of social capital's financing. They could "smooth the operation of finance", so were of direct relevance to such important national issues as sovereignty, civil interests and people's livelihood. In fierce competition, there must be a perfect handling of the operation of banks. Sun came to realize that at that time "foreign bankers controlled the medium of exchange of Chinese commercial centers". Consequently, foreign banks such as HSBC "played a decisive role"[31] in China's internal struggle. When government officials negotiated with foreign consortia for loans, they met with all kinds of obstacles resulting from the foreigners' presumptuous demands.[32] China's independence was out of the question without getting rid of foreign financial control.[33] In a speech on the Principle of Nationalism, in order to help the audience gain a deeper understanding of foreign banks' colonial plundering in China and reach a consensus, Sun analyzed paper notes, capital transfer and money deposit in detail, giving them a penetrating revelation. According to his analysis, Chinese people's mentality "was poisoned by foreign economic oppression", so they trusted only foreign banks instead of Chinese banks, resulting in the inferiority of Chinese silver to foreign paper notes. As a matter of fact, it never occurred to them that the paper notes of foreign banks were nothing but tens of millions of pieces of printed paper at the least amount of cost. Using these paper notes in exchange for Chinese commodities, he asked, "Can you image how serious a loss we are suffering?" As to the transfer of capital, since the foreign banks were transferring capital on behalf of the Chinese, the Chinese "had to endure the loss caused by their high fees and discounts."[34] In addition to the 5% remittance fee, they would charge extra from the two sides involved and profit from the exchange from silver to paper notes, adding up to over 2% of the total capital. For example, the transfer of 10,000 *yuan* from Shanghai to

---

[30]*An Extra Collection of the Writings of Sun Yat-sen*, Shanghai People's Publishing House, 1990, p. 355.
[31]*Complete works of Sun Yat-sen*, vol. 3, p. 108.
[32]*Ibid.*, vol. 2, p. 549.
[33]*Ibid.*, vol. 3, p. 108.
[34]*Ibid.*, vol. 10, p. 542.

Guangzhou would result in a loss of 200 to 300 *yuan*. "One way or the other, after at most thirty-odd transfers, all the capital would come to naught." Because these were foreign banks with outlandish signs, people felt immensely assured and deposited all their savings therein, caring very little about the interest rate. After the 1911 Revolution, royal families and bureaucrats of the Qing Dynasty feared that the revolutionary party would confiscate their properties, so they deposited all their money in the foreign banks in Peking. Infested with money, the foreign banks stopped paying interests and began to charge fees for the safekeeping. "An investigation shows that at the time the deposit of Chinese people in the foreign banks in China amounted to around 2,000 million *yuan*." "With the deposits as capital, the foreign banks granted loans to small businesses of China and charged high interest. The least interest per year was 7–8%, sometimes even more than 10%." Consequently, "combining the paper notes, remittance, and deposits, the profits of foreign banks would probably amount to 100 million *yuan*."[35] As the representative of the government, Yuan Shikai was only the foreign banks' proxy. On behalf of the interests of foreign forces, the warlords also manipulated China's finance and caused the devaluation of paper notes and panic of the general public. The traitors of the revolutionary army deliberately dumped the currency of local banks collected from the market, and forced the banks of Guangdong Province to pay the newly issued paper notes. Their perverse manipulation of the finance made the public fatigued and desperate.[36]

Meanwhile, Sun proposed that "while industries are the foundation of a country's prosperity, bank is the mother of industries."[37] Banks were the pivot of the economy and controlled its lifeline. Banks were also the foundation of industry and the root of real economy. The position and function of banks were paramount and incomparable. The establishment of banks was closely linked to the revitalization and development of industries, commodity circulation, society and economy, and national strength. This reflected clearly that Sun, an outstanding patriotic revolutionary, had modernity and economic awareness. Without turning back, he marched

---

[35]*Ibid.*, vol. 9, pp. 204–206.

[36]*A Detailed Chronology of Sun Yat-sen*, Book 2, Zhonghua Book Company, 1991, pp. 1458–1460, 1544.

[37]*Complete Works of Sun Yat-sen*, vol. 3, p. 77.

forward courageously with this historic mission. On October 13, 1916, in his "Letter to Comrades of the Whole Nation", he poured out his heart: "Since my announcement of stopping military activities, I have intended to put my hand to industries, in the hope of revitalizing economy and preventing the loss of economic rights to foreigners. My first step is to set up banks to assist the development of industries. But this is an influential and grand project, in need of large amount of capital and a detailed charter. It is now still under discussion."[38] He explained explicitly the relation between banks and industries, the considerable relevance of banks to the revitalization of industries, and the essential conditions for the establishment of banks. As to the relation between banks and revolution, Sun gave an elaborate elucidation at the closing of his "Speech at the Founding Ceremony of the Central Bank in Guangzhou": "Now that you have understood the governmental nature of the Central Bank, you should try to keep the bank in operation, which means you are supporting the government. Supporting the government means you are supporting the revolution. Supporting the revolution, in turn, means you are supporting the transformation of China from poverty to prosperity."[39] This served to show distinctly his understanding of the decisive part banks played in the success of the Chinese revolution. With flames of war raging across the country, amid the bustling military activities, Sun was diligently making preparations for the establishment of banks and publicizing his proposition, without any slackening of his effort.

Sun expounded the function of banks in different ways under different occasions. To sum up, the banks were meant to "revitalize the industries of China from depression and guard against the covetousness of foreigners."[40] The meaning of this assertion was twofold: one was the revitalization of Chinese industries; the other was the resistance against foreign banks. "Finding a way out can help China break away from all kinds of interference."[41] As far as the revitalization of industries was concerned, Sun held that modern China was poor and weak, with industry and commerce still in the budding stage, and the ships, railways and mines just

---

[38] *Ibid.*, vol. 3, p. 377.
[39] *Ibid.*, vol. 10, p. 544.
[40] *Ibid.*, vol. 3, p. 79.
[41] *Ibid.*

making a start. To develop transportation, industry, commerce, agriculture and other businesses, the first priority was to solve the problem of capital shortage. "Only when China has its own banks could we borrow money with ease", so that the capital for construction "could be injected", and hardships and obstacles avoided. Therefore, "it is imperative to publicize the establishment of banks."[42] The promotion of the establishment of banks was a top priority indeed.

Because the government was then lacking funding, its finances were in straitened circumstances, and both the military and the political circles were short of money. Many soldiers didn't have enough food and clothing and faced the danger of dying of illness. All these posed a grave threat to the new regime in Guangdong. Costs like medical fees and funeral expenses were nowhere to be raised. If the political circle raised a sum of money, it would immediately be diverted to the military expenditure. All the administrative undertakings stopped due to the lack of funding, and even the day-to-day operations of the government were not smooth. Setting up the Central Bank, "the government intends to run businesses", in the hope of making big profits with a small amount of capital. Therefore, "protecting the Central Bank is like protecting the seed for development" and "the potential is enormous."[43] Meanwhile, "the economic strength of this bank will be greatly enhanced. Chinese economic forces also will not be controlled by foreign banks anymore."[44] China would become self-reliant only after gaining its independence and autonomy.

Resisting the control of foreign banks was a matter of national sovereignty, dignity and destiny. In modern China, people considered it a noble and sacred undertaking. In Sun's point of view, while negotiating with foreign banks for loans, we "met with all kinds of obstacles" as a result of their presumptuous demands. The reason was that in China there wasn't any big bank with the capacity of handling such loans.[45] If China wanted to overcome these obstacles and put an end to their demands, "we must have the big bank of our own, which could shoulder the task of making loans to support the new regime." Take large remittance as an example:

---

[42] *An Extra Collection of the Writings of Sun Yat-sen*, pp. 348, 355.
[43] *Complete Works of Sun Yat-sen*, Vol 10: 541.
[44] *Ibid.*, p. 543.
[45] *Ibid.*, vol. 2, p. 549.

"foreign banks charge much remittance fee and discount expenses, so we Chinese will suffer losses transferring money in foreign banks."[46] Should the Chinese have their own exchange offices, then "the profit will not be earned by foreign banks and things could be easily handled."[47] Therefore, the legitimate rights of Chinese people could be protected from violation only when the government set up their own banks. On this basis, it was possible to "make it convenient for the overseas Chinese to remit money and overseas Chinese businessmen to deposit money, and facilitate the development of industries." In summary, this could achieve the goal of "revitalizing economy and preventing the loss of economic rights to foreigners."[48] So resisting the control of foreign banks was for the better revitalization of industries, since it would lead to the creation of a favorable external environment.

In the early years of the Republic, Sun's idea of rectifying the finance was also based on such a judgment. In the operation of banks, stability was the first priority because the slightest indiscretion would disrupt the market. At that time, the financial institutions of China were incomplete. The country was repeatedly in a state of turmoil. As a result, the wealthy merchants of the past went bankrupt one after another, living a miserable existence. In addition, the Qing government before the Republic was negligent of financial regulation. Consequently, though the Republic was founded, the financial resources of the people had been exhausted. In the final analysis, the most effective remedy was the rectification of finance and the protection of industries. Faced with high pressure and harsh conditions of foreign consortia, Sun, the provisional president, proposed the establishment of a Sino-Western bank with global influence. He believed that "established in coalition with big capitalists of the world, the Sino-Western bank will become the parent bank of Chinese banking industry and have world-wide influence. It will surely help China break away from the six-nation consortium's restraints and lead to the prosperity of the nation."[49] He even paid attention to the drafting of the administration Code of the Central Bank and had the founding plan designed. A presidential

---

[46]*Ibid.*, vol. 10, p. 542.
[47]*Ibid.*
[48]*Ibid.*, vol. 3, p. 413.
[49]*Ibid.*, p. 7.

instruction stipulated that "Nanjing shall be the capital of the Republic of China. Of prior considerations are the rectification of finance, the establishment of banks and the issuing of a single currency."[50] In March 1920, with the publication of *The Means of Introducing Local Self-Government*, Sun listed the important issues to be dealt with by the local autonomous community, among which were cooperative banking, cooperative insurance and so forth.[51] At the end of 1920, he paid tribute to the establishment of national banks by claiming it to be the newest and most effective governing measure by European governments after World War I. He suggested that "China should follow suit quickly to improve people's livelihood."[52] Based on the situation in China, Sun advanced his plan of establishing different types of banks.

The Sino-Western joint bank was the first on his list of banks to be established. Sun argued strongly that "the sole purpose is to bring in foreign capital. The direct effect is the revitalization of Chinese industries, while the indirect effect is the resistance against the four-nation consortium."[53] The prerequisites were as follows: "First of all, the bank shall be registered in China and its operation should abide by Chinese law. Secondly, all the members of the board of directors will be Chinese, while Westerners will act as advisors. Thirdly, in the first 10 years, a Westerner will hold the post of the director-general of the bank; after 10 years, Chinese could hold this office. Fourthly, each party of the joint bank will choose two supervisory managers. The director-general will always act in accordance with their request."[54] He further noted that, at the time, China had been at an obvious disadvantage in national strength, financial resources and intellectual perceptiveness. "The terms of cooperation should be more favorable to us at present. In the future the two sides could be treated equally, otherwise there will emerge unthinkable malpractice."[55] In that case, it would be against the original intention of its founders and those in power. The new bank would be nothing more than a new

---

[50] *A Detailed Chronology of Sun Yat-sen*, Book 1, p. 645.
[51] *Complete Works of Sun Yat-sen*, vol. 5, p. 224.
[52] *Ibid.*, p. 447.
[53] *Ibid.*, vol. 3, p. 78.
[54] *Ibid.*, p. 9.
[55] *Ibid.*

Russo-Chinese Bank, without much significance. How could it "benefit the country and the people?" "Foreigners will never submit to our request." "We will never regain our extraterritorial rights." In addition, if such a precedent was set, other countries might follow the example. In consequence, using a certain country's capital would mean obeying that country's law without one's own sovereignty. China would never have the chance to recover its extraterritorial rights. Because it was a matter of state system and national rights, this issue had to be discussed with frankness.[56] Sun believed that "if the dozens of Chinese banks are incorporated together to set up a giant Sino-foreign Bank", it might be possible to overcome the inadequacy of "without much nation-wide influence resulting from dispersion."[57] Furthermore, when it came to the issuing of bonds, there was no need to put a limit to the inflow of foreign capital, because "the financial hub is under governmental control and even government loan will be out of question". So "China will free itself from unlawful pressure and foreign banks will never obtain the profit therein."[58]

With agriculture as the foundation of the nation, Sun maintained that even if the farmers solved the problem of land and irrigation, they would still be incessantly plagued by the shortage of funds. In his opinion, the government had to set up special institutions, such as banks catering to farmers to regulate the distribution of agricultural capital. That would be a great help when farmers were in urgent need of capital, otherwise they would sink into lifelong debt as a result of usury. "Then the farmers can enjoy the joy of life."[59]

As for the Central Bank, on January 1, 1912, in *The Declaration of the Provisional President,* Sun clearly stated that "from now on, the allocation of national funds, the collection of taxes, and the distribution of welfare, shall conform to the financial laws. Special emphasis will be laid on the reform of social and economic organizations to make people savor the enjoyment of life. That is called the unification of finance."[60] The establishment of the Central Bank was among the priorities of the

---

[56]*Ibid.*
[57]*Ibid.*, vol. 2, p. 550.
[58]*Ibid.*
[59]*Ibid.*, vol. 9, pp. 120–121.
[60]*Ibid.*, vol. 2, p. 2.

government. With the authority of central government over provinces, the government would take control of finance, credit and loan, government bonds and the clarification of monetary system, thus facilitating currency remittance and attaining financial sufficiency. The special circumstance of the time was that "there wasn't any reliable source of revenue. To meet the urgent need, the only way out is the issuing of military currency and government bonds. That can't be done without the aid of financial institutions." So "the establishment of the Central Bank is the first priority of financial operation." He came up with three points about its specific operation: First, banks were of great socio-economic relevance. Most Chinese banks were then quite small. If there was a remittance of 10,000 *yuan* from one province to another, or from China to another country, they weren't able to handle it at all. The profits from the dealings between the Chinese were earned by foreign banks and there was much inconvenience. In addition, "overseas remittance is the pivot of international trade and the key to a country's economic development." "In times of financial straits, the fees of international remittance can alleviate the financial inadequacy, expand business operation, and improve the difficult situation."[61] This explicitly revealed the unquestionable urgency for the founding of the Central Bank. Second, the government had the privilege of issuing paper notes. Different from those issued by previous governments, these paper notes had a foundation fund of 10 million *yuan*. The credit of paper notes lay in their convertibility. The Central Bank's way of issuing was through the exchange of cash for equivalent paper notes. So these paper notes had ready cash as collateral and could be converted to cash at any moment. Sun called this way of operation "cashing". He thought that these paper notes were creditworthy and free from the defects of those issued by the provincial banks of Guangzhou, because they "could be converted anytime" and had a large amount of issuing fund as collateral. Third, the revenue of all the financial institutions "should be deposited in the Central Bank, in preparation for their use."[62] It was indeed the responsibility of the Central Bank to act for treasury. During financial difficulties, it was quite necessary to concentrate the

---

[61] *Complete Works of Sun Yat-sen*, vol. 2, p. 251.
[62] *Ibid.*, vol. 10, p. 553.

limited revenue on major or urgent issues, but the government should guard against all kinds of retention and misappropriation, as well as people with evil intentions, in case they feather their own nest. For the intended purpose, it was also important to have comprehensive and effective supervisory and precautionary rules.

2.4. On the utilization of foreign capital

Around the time of the 1911 Revolution, while planning the development of the national economy, Sun suffered a very embarrassing situation: "The people were poverty-stricken"; as to the development of industries, "there is no capital" and "people are anxious" (lacking in funding, technology, talent and time). "The only solution is to raise foreign capital."[63]

He insisted on taking the God-given opportunity to introduce a large amount of foreign capital, because international capital was keen for ways of investment after World War I. In his opinion, China could learn from the United States, which ranked the first in the world after enduring about a 100 years' hardship in its painstaking development. Citing the example of Japan, he argued that after the Meiji Restoration, "thanks to the use of foreign loans", the smallest, poorest and weakest country also became a major power. His point was that China should utilize the foreign capital "for the industrial production", in the hope of "enhancing national strength". Consequently, China would surely "keep abreast of the United States and European countries in strength and prosperity", prevent the big powers from partitioning its territory, overcome the plight of the nation and solve the problem of people's livelihood.

But in an era like that, it was complex and painful to introduce foreign capital for the revitalization of industries. On the one hand, there was the mentality of "being alone on an uninhabited island". He had to condemn the pedantic traditional notion of "parochial arrogance, self-seclusion," and "blind opposition to everything foreign". "Fearing foreign debt as if it is poison, we don't understand that it is harmful to seek out foreign loan to engage in nonproductive activities, whereas it is beneficial to seek out

---

[63]*Ibid.*, vol. 2, p. 431.

foreign loan to engage in productive activities."[64] On the other hand, there was the need to oppose the slavish mentality of worshiping foreign things and betraying China. Those people abandoned national interests and gave up national sovereignty, causing serious detriment to China's politics, economy and culture. Sun exposed solemnly the betrayal and surrender of the Qing government in utilizing foreign capital, denouncing their loss of sovereignty, excessive utilization and the practice of offering collateral.

Three principles of using foreign capital: In Sun's judgment, "Firstly, there shouldn't be any loss of sovereignty. Secondly, there shouldn't be the need of collateral. Thirdly, the interest rates should be rather low." He repeatedly admonished the Chinese, "we must confine ourselves only to the use of foreign capital and talents, while the sovereignty of China should never be given up. If everything was done of our own accord, there will never be any danger."[65] "Survival lies in our mastery of the way of development. Foreign manipulation of our development will lead to disaster."[66] In the matter of foreign debt, he fulfilled his promise and maintained his position. In 1912, the four-nation consortium intended to negotiate loans on the condition of financial supervision, or the use of tariffs and provincial transit duty as collateral, but Sun flatly said no to their design. In 1924, when he went to North China via Japan, the big powers placed him under pressure again with enticement of loans, only to be rejected.

Means of using foreign capital: In Sun's view, "of two devils choose the lesser. In comparing options of using foreign capital, we should choose the one with the fewest disadvantages."[67] He urged that the use of foreign capital should be in the way of non-governmental economic exchange, which was free from governmental involvement. This would avoid diplomatic disputes and the interference of foreign governments, since it would be inappropriate for them to bother about the loans. On the issue of railroad building, to which he had devoted a large share of his effort, he imposed even more concrete requirements. On the signing of

---

[64]*Ibid.*, vol. 2, p. 322.
[65]*Ibid.*, vol. 5, p. 623.
[66]*Ibid.*, vol. 6, p. 248.
[67]*Ibid.*, vol. 2, p. 499.

contracts for example, he said, "all contracts will include the following provisions: (1) The project will be purely commercial in nature, without the slightest political implication; (2) the company will have the right of inspection at any time; and (3) if, at any time before the expiration of the contract, China has sufficient funds, it can redeem any railroad."[68] Only in this way could China avoid failure. He advocated the mastery of relevant fields and the preparation of the prerequisites for developing industries because while doing business in the world economic market without professional knowledge and without the employment of consultants to train talents and pass on experience, Chinese companies would be defrauded and end up taking a loss. He also stressed the urgency of development, reminding the people to treasure and seize the godsent opportunity so that they wouldn't be penny-wise but pound-foolish. Sun listed three options for the use of foreign capital: "(1) borrowing money to develop Chinese industries; (2) setting up Sino-foreign joint companies; and (3) contracting with foreigners for the construction, under the condition of ownership reverting to China at the end of the term."[69] In his view, the third option suited China best. "Should China choose to develop this way, there will surely be tremendous success." As a matter of fact, these practices had been recommended and tried by members of the Self-strengthening Movement like Zhang Zhidong and Zhang Jian. Zhang Zhidong held "borrowing" to be "the top choice", while Zhang Jian considered "Sino-foreign joint company" to be "the most common way of using foreign investment". Sun was more inclined to empower the foreigners to take on those tasks, because he was convinced that this could not only put foreign capital to use but also overcome the inadequacy in technology and managerial expertise. Looking forward to the introduction of the capital of overseas Chinese, he called upon them to contribute to the future of the industries of the motherland.

Before the founding of the People's Republic of China, it would have been utterly impossible to achieve Sun's goal of using foreign capital for the development of industries. Without a complete change of the nature of the society, China would never have any autonomy of political, economic

---

[68] *Ibid.*, p. 500.
[69] *Ibid.*, vol. 2, p. 481.

and cultural development. Without the independence of China, all his plans and theories were nothing but kindhearted aspiration and beautiful dreams. In our time of socialist construction, we should conduct a careful and serious examination of Sun's monetary and financial theories to draw nourishment for China's advancement.

3. The monetary revolution theories of Zhu Zhixin and Liao Zhongkai

3.1. *Zhu Zhixin's theory of paper note exchange for material objects*

Popularly known by his courtesy name, the surname of Zhu Zhixin (1885–1920) was Dafu. He also had pseudonyms such as Zheshen, Xianjie, Qufei and Qianjin. He was born in Panyu of Guangdong Province, and his ancestral hometown was Xiaoshan of Zhejiang Province. As Sun Yat-sen's right-hand man, Zhu was a radical revolutionary and thinker in modern China. In 1902, he began to study in Jiaozhong School and, in collaboration with his classmates, organized the Political Study Society to explore the ways of salvation for China. In 1904, with the support of a government fund, he went to Japan to pursue further studies (the second grade of a crash course at Hosei University in Tokyo). In addition to the required courses, he also committed himself to the study of economics. Meeting Sun Yat-sen and other revolutionaries in Tokyo, he joined the Revolutionary Alliance the following year and became secretary and commentator of the Review Department. Writing articles for *Min Bao*, he took an active part in the heated debates against the reformers, defending and elucidating Sun's Three Principles of the People. In November 1905, he published articles in *Min Bao* to introduce *The Communist Manifesto*, *Das Kapital*, and the life and doctrine of Karl Marx and Friedrich Engels. In early 1916, he translated and edited a brief biography of Marx and some excerpts from *The Communist Manifesto* and *Das Kapital*, making him one of the first revolutionaries to translate *The Communist Manifesto* in China. Coming back to China in 1906, he taught successively in Guangdong Higher School, Guangdong School of Law and Politics and Fangyan School. Meanwhile, he was actively involved in revolutionary publicity and secret activities, and even the uprisings staged by the revolutionaries in Guangdong. After the Revolution of 1911, he assumed the office of the counselor-in-general of the Guangdong military government, concurrently supervisor of the Appeasement Department of Guangzhou and Yangjiang, director of the Accounting and Auditing Office, and director of the Department of Military Law Enforcement. In 1913, he joined in the Second Revolution against Yuan Shikai. After the failure of the Second Revolution, he fled to Japan to continue his anti-Yuan activities and joined the China Revolutionary Party. During the Constitutional Protection Movement in 1917, as one of the key assistants of Sun Yat-sen, he held the position of military liaison officer and secretary of confidential matters. He did a good job in the editing of *Republic Daily* and *Construction* magazine and was temporarily in charge of the editorial work of *Shi Bao*. Expressing his brilliant understanding as a radical democratic, he contributed his effort while Sun Yat-sen was writing the well-known *Fundamentals of National Construction*. On September 21, 1920, he died unfortunately while revolutionaries at the Humen Fort of Guangdong instigated an army of Guangxi to turn over. His writings were collected in *Works of Zhu Zhixin*.

Zhu Zhixin's monetary thought was the elucidation of Sun Yat-sen's monetary theory. In October 1919, he published "Paper Notes in Ancient China", written the previous month. In March and April 1920, he published "On Dr. Senga Tsurutaro's Abolition of Gold Standard" and "A Criticism of Rice Standard", respectively. He not only drew on Western monetary theory but also conscientiously summed up the historical lessons of the emergence and development of paper notes in China, which contributed a theoretical basis to China's currency reform and paved the way forward.

(1) *On the value of different forms of currency*
Zhu divided the development of money into the stage of metal currency and that of paper notes, and subdivided paper notes into convertible notes and unconvertible notes. He made a comparative study of the value of money, convertible paper notes and unconvertible paper notes.

On the origins of metal coins: With reference to Zhu's judgment about the money of ancient China, there were two origins of money. "One derived from decorative luxuries like shells." "The other evolved from things that were conducive to human existence, for example, cloth and silk."[70] As it happened, metal coins approximately belonged to the category of luxury and their main function was "representing goods not yet at hand". In his view, "scholars attributed the circulation of money probably to its lack of change in value, universal appreciation, easy exchange, and lasting un-damageability. But we must bear in mind that money was commonly agreed on to exchange for other commodities."[71] He claimed that money "would never play the role of currency" without this function or special feature. He also believed that the function of money was inseparable from its purchasing power. Metal money (such as gold, silver, copper and iron) itself could be consumed, because it had "its own value, in other words, the final function derived from its purchasing power." But while functioning as currency, metal money, though of no practical use, could be exchanged for commodities with practical use.[72] Only after losing the function of currency would its consumptive value come up.[73] His idea was that the currency function of gold and silver was contradictory and mutually exclusive with the value of itself. He quoted the equation of exchange of Irving Fisher, a prominent American economist, to illustrate the value of money: "with reference to the money in circulation, the velocity of circulation, and the transactions in the area, if we divide the multiplication of the amount of money in circulation and the velocity by the amount of transactions, then we have the price of the currency."[74] He agreed that while the money in circulation was under governmental control, the amount of transactions and the velocity of circulation depended on the situation of national economy.

The origin of paper notes: Likewise, Zhu maintained that there were two ways of development which merged into a unified money system. One was the convertible paper notes which stood for metal money; the other was the unconvertible paper notes which represented commodities. "Historically, the above-mentioned two kinds of paper notes existed side

---

[70]*Writings of Zhu Zhixin*, Zhonghua Book Company, 1979, p. 778.
[71]*Ibid.*, p. 427.
[72]*Ibid.*, p. 699.
[73]*Ibid.*, p. 451.
[74]*Ibid.*, p. 445.

by side and were compatible with each other."[75] An example of the former was *jiaozi*, while *chayin* and *yanchao* were examples of the latter. His understanding of *jiaozi* was as follows: "Before 1094, there wasn't any depreciation of its value. It can be inferred that its acceptance was guaranteed by not only the ready cash, but also the credibility of the government. Moreover, the credibility of a nation was nothing more than the guaranteed levy of millet, silk, gold, silver and tax. Therefore, it is obvious that though it was institutionally the symbol of metal currency, *jiaozi* was in fact the embodiment of commodities." Different from *jiaozi*, *chayin* and *yanchao* were not media of exchange, but they were clearly "certificates for the exchange of commodities". After the reform in 1071, both the government and common people began to use *yanchao* as the substitute for money, resulting in the circulation of *yanchao* on the market. Later, changing the regulations concerning *yanchao*, Cai Jing invented *qianyin* and put it in circulation in Shanxi. The *jiaozi* in Sichuan was replaced by *qianyin*. "So the two origins of the past merged into *qianyin*." "Now it was the lawful national currency."[76] That is to say, *jiaozi*, *chayin* and *yanchao* were all paper notes and the symbols of commodities. As a matter of fact, *jiaozi* was the symbol of metal money. The issuing of *jiaozi* was backed up with commodities, but it wasn't the direct representative of commodities. *Chayin* and *yanchao* were certificates of purchasing. In a particular area, under specific historic conditions, they could act, together with paper notes, as the media of exchange and means of payment. But they were, after all, only certificates for purchasing and negotiable securities, thus quite different from paper notes. Zhu didn't catch the difference and confused the value basis of paper notes with the guarantee of paper money issuing. Attention should be paid to the fact that the former refers to the true value of paper notes, while the latter is concerned with the way to stabilize the value of paper notes, a totally different question.

Differences in the ultimate effectiveness between convertible paper notes and unconvertible paper notes: In Zhu's opinion, "while money stands for commodities not yet at hand, paper notes stand for money not

---

[75] *Ibid.*, p. 428.
[76] *Ibid.*, pp. 429, 431.

yet at hand."[77] This was only about convertible paper notes. The ultimate effectiveness of money that they represented was the ultimate effectiveness of convertible paper notes. On the contrary, unconvertible paper notes "don't exclusively stand for money", so their ultimate effectiveness depended on the expected value of the commodity to be exchanged for them. The reason for the circulation of unconvertible paper notes without a specified way of retrieving was that people believed the government that issued them had its yearly revenue and could guarantee its circulation. So if the bank had some capital, the paper notes could be retrieved. "If the paper notes are used to pay off debt, then the payer must sell his commodity (or via someone else to sell his commodity) to acquire these paper notes. Therefore, whatever is the value of the commodities of the payer is the ultimate effectiveness of these paper notes. The eradication of paper notes depends on commodities. It is the same as the way banks redeem the paper notes with commodities."[78] Zhu's so-called ultimate effectiveness wasn't the value basis we talk of, but the purchasing power of the money.

The purchasing power of convertible paper notes wasn't as stable as unconvertible ones. First of all, as a kind of commodity, "the value of metal currency fluctuates widely with the change in economic situation." While metal currency was fulfilling the function of currency, "if there was an excess of currency, there would also be an excess of gold and silver. So the ultimate effectiveness of metal currency would be lower than the expected ultimate effectiveness."[79] Consequently, the purchasing power of the currency would decrease. Since convertible paper notes were the symbol of money not yet at hand, their purchasing power would certainly decrease, just like the metal currency, ending in less ultimate effectiveness than unconvertible paper notes. The unconvertible paper notes were for the exchange of different kinds of commodity. "These commodities have varied uses and will not become excessive as a result of being exchanged for paper notes. That is, their value will not decrease with the vanishing of paper notes."[80] Unconvertible paper notes were based on a definite assurance that after a certain period, they could be used in exchange for certain commodities and

---

[77]*Ibid.*, p. 428.
[78]*Ibid.*, pp. 429, 451.
[79]*Ibid.*, p. 452.
[80]*Ibid.*

thus wouldn't depreciate. Second, for unconvertible paper notes, "there are other ways of retrieving, but there probably isn't any way of retrieving for convertible paper notes."[81] Zhu even argued that "nowadays the depreciation of unconvertible notes in China isn't as sharp as that of the cash in the United States and Japan. This is enough to shatter the illusion of convertibility that has been in existence for hundreds of years." This was indeed unreasonably taking a part for the whole. Third, his conclusion was founded on his erroneous summary of historical experience. He maintained that "the history of Chinese convertible paper notes was a history of failure."[82] "The history of the Yuan Dynasty's unconvertible paper notes was a history of success."[83] He blamed the failure of convertible paper notes on the government: "The government failed to hoard money for the exchange of the paper notes issued."[84] He attributed the success of unconvertible paper notes to "the government's reserves of commodities in preparation for their exchange". In his final analysis, he stated that the retrieval of unconvertible paper notes was in fact part of the tax collected, the same as the buying of commodities, because, with little exception, the collection of taxes was from manufacturers and traders. Originally levied through the collection of material objects, taxes were now in the form of money. "Then the money could buy back the commodity that was supposed to be handed in. The change from money to paper notes was like using paper money to buy back the commodity that was supposed to be handed in. So the retrieval of unconvertible paper notes could be done in the form of commodities."[85]

(2) *On the preparation for issuing paper notes (material objects for exchange)*

Zhu stated, to "get out of the predicament of paper money, it is imperative to lay the basis of paper notes on the commodities they represent." He insisted on the issuing of unconvertible paper notes, totally ignoring the issuing of money exchange. He believed that the government should retrieve paper notes with reference to its reserve of commodities. So when

---

[81]*Ibid.*, p. 448.
[82]*Ibid.*, p. 447.
[83]*Ibid.*, p. 455.
[84]*Ibid.*, p. 454.
[85]*Ibid.*, pp. 449–450.

the paper notes in circulation exceeded the need for them, paper notes would naturally flow back to the treasury and the prices of commodities would not inflate. To avoid the defect of using one kind of commodity as the material object for exchange, he suggested the use of eight kinds of commodities as the material objects for exchange, which included such life necessities as rice, cotton, silk, tea, salt, oil, coal and sugar. If other life necessities were found essential in the future, addition could occur anytime. After weighted average, these eight objects for exchange of banknotes could be used as the price index of commodities. "This index can indicate to us the purchasing power of each *yuan* (if this term was adopted), and it will remain the same for quite a long time."[86]

The amount of commodities prepared for exchange should accord with the need of the paper notes in circulation. The retrieval and exchange should be done on a monthly basis. If the paper notes were not put into circulation all at once, then there wouldn't be any fluctuation in the amount of paper notes in circulation, so their value would be stable. But with the exclusion of precious metal (gold and silver) currency, it was difficult to prepare the eight kinds of life necessities for the exchange because Sun Yat-sen held that the prerequisite for the issuing was to get gold and silver, commodities and industries ready, while the plan of Liao Zhongkai included 12 kinds of commodities, gold and silver included. First of all, whatever kind of position Liao put gold and silver in, objectively they could still function as the general equivalent. They could meet the demands of different levels on the market without the restriction of important life necessities. Second, Zhu's understanding of a complete guarantee of the preparation of commodities in proportion to the amount of paper notes in circulation was as partial as that of Liao Zhongkai. Third, in addition to monetary factors, non-monetary factors would also have influence on the stability of currency value. Moreover, it was fairly idealistic and unpractical to think that the weighted average of eight kinds of commodities was the purchasing power of money.

The stability of the value of paper notes: Zhu's idea was that paper notes had the basis of several commodities. That explanation was indeed original and refreshing. If the exchange value of rice increased, then the

---

[86]*Ibid.*, p. 775.

increase could be calculated with reference to the market price, so the amount of rice used for exchange should decrease proportionately. In proportion to the price index, if there was a 1% increase in the price of rice, then the rice used for exchange would be 99% of the original amount. "So there will not be any fluctuation in currency value." If the price of silk went down to 99% of the original, then there should be a 1% increase in the silk used for exchange. Though the price of silk varied, the value of paper notes remained the same. "This kind of adjustment will free the currency value from the influence of the time. As a result, the price of commodities would be affected only by its production and consumption. The so-called financial adjustment of these days can probably be abolished."[87]

Shortly after the founding of the People's Republic of China, when scholars discussed the value basis of *Renminbi*, there emerged echoing voices of Zhu's thought and Liao Zhongkai's theory of commodity standard. They seemed to have their new allies and successors. It may be safely assumed that the theory of use value and the so-called theory of using 100 kinds of commodities as standard were further developments of their theories under new historical conditions.

3.2. The commodity standard theory of Liao Zhongkai

Formerly known as Liao Enxu, Liao Zhongkai (1877–1925) had an alternative name, Yibai, though he was popularly known by his courtesy name. He also had two pseudonyms, Tufu and Yuanshi. His ancestral hometown was Guishan (now Huiyang) county of Guangdong, but he was born in San Francisco. He studied in Japan, at first the preparatory courses in economics in Waseda University, then in the department of politics and economy of Central University. In 1905, he joined the Revolutionary Alliance and served at the headquarters as the secretary of the Foreign Affairs Department. After the 1911 Revolution, he took the office of counselor-in-general of Guangdong military government and was concurrently in charge of the finance of the government. After the failure of the Second Revolution against Yuan Shikai in 1913, he sought refuge in Japan in the company of Sun Yat-sen. Joining the China Revolutionary Party in May

---

[87]*Writings of Zhu Zhixin*, p. 774.

1914 in Tokyo, he became the deputy director of the Department of Finance. After the failure of the first Constitutional Protection Movement in 1919, he focused his attention on research into revolutionary theory. In the same year, working together with Zhu Zhixin and Hu Hanmin, he started the publication of *Construction* magazine. They elucidated and actively disseminated Sun Yat-sen's theory of the people's democracy and of the people's livelihood, exploring ways to solve China's problems. In 1921, he became the vice-minister of the Ministry of Finance of the Republic of China (ROC) government and the head of the Guangdong Provincial Department of Finance. He devoted himself to the rectification of finance and the collection of expenditure to contribute his share of effort in fighting Lu Rongting, warlord of Guangxi Province. In 1922 and 1923, he went to Japan on behalf of Sun Yat-sen, to negotiate with the Soviet envoy Adolph Joffe. He was a strong supporter of the restructuring of the Kuomintang. After the reorganization, he was elected standing member of the Central Executive Committee, member of the Political Committee, head of Guangdong Provincial Finance Department, and concurrently held the office of such important positions as head of the Workers Department, head of the Farmers Department of Kuomintang, party representative of the Whampoa Military Academy, director-in-chief of the Department of Military Supplies, and Secretary-General of the generalissimo. After Sun Yat-sen's death in March 1925, he faithfully carried out Sun's policy of "Working with the Soviets, Working with the Communists and Helping the Farmers". He participated in the eastern expedition to punish warlord Chen Jiongming, and the suppression of Yang Ximin and Liu Zhenhuan's rebellion, who colluded with the imperialists. On August 20 of the same year, he was assassinated by the Kuomintang rightists. His writings were collected in *Works of Liao Zhongkai* and *Collected Works of Shuangqing* (a collection of the writings of Liao and his wife He Xiangning).

Liao published two essays to publicize, elucidate and carry out Sun Yat-sen's monetary theory advanced in *Monetary Revolution*. "Monetary Revolution and Construction" was published between September and October 1919. "More on Money Revolution" came out in April 1920. The two articles firmly supported Sun's idea of the abolition of gold and silver, the employment of paper notes, the implementation of commodities standard and the implementation of the paper currency system. With both theoretical development and institutional design, he clarified three issues: "The first priority is to analyze the nature and function of money, and the incompetence of precious metal as money. Secondly, there is the need to discuss the requirements of China's special economic situation. Thirdly, there is a description of the alternative choice we have been advocating."[88]

(1) *On the functions of money and monetary revolution*
Like Sun Yat-sen and Zhu Zhixin, Liao held that the role of money was to facilitate business transaction and its functions were threefold: "(1) medium of exchange, (2), standard of price, and (3) the storage of purchasing power."[89] In the process of commodity exchange, the three functions were indispensable. Without the function of medium of exchange, transactions wouldn't be smooth. "The need of the demand and the supply cannot be satisfied, while the benefits of the division of labor cannot be enjoyed." Without the function of standard of price, there wouldn't be any measurement of the price of the commodity and the gain or loss of the transaction. Without the function of the storage of purchasing power, there wouldn't be any representation of the value of the labor embodied in the commodities. It is fairly obvious that this assertion was partial and not scientific. The materials selected to mint coins shared "four advantages". "They are of fixed value, easy to carry, endurable, and easy to split up." Because "people all consider them to have the four advantages",[90] gold and silver around the world were the first choices when it came to minting coins.

Liao was convinced that gold and silver currency couldn't ensure the stability of price. Gold and silver standards "undoubtedly will not serve the expected purpose" and "are by no means the paramount institutional option". Liao recognized the value of gold and silver as standards, but considered them valueless when functioning as money. As to the intrinsic value of the monetary unit, he frankly claimed that "it was in fact the purchasing power of each individual monetary unit". Drawing support from the nominalistic theory of national approval, he criticized the position of

---
[88]*Collected Works of Shuangqing*, Book 1, p. 308.
[89]*Ibid.*, p. 308.
[90]*Ibid.*, p. 309.

metal as currency. "Its falsehood lies in mistaking the value of the metal for that of the money. Money is one thing, while gold or silver is another thing. They are different by nature."[91] He warned that "with paper notes in wide circulation, that theory is irrelevant now."[92] The purchasing power of money derived "either from the public consent, or from the national legislation. It is not dependent on valuable things." He insisted that "it is a historic outcome" resulting from "the earliest exchange with commodity as the medium in ancient times."[93] He also used the quantity theory of money to explain price, saying that the price was determined by "the total currency in circulation and the velocity of circulation of the currency, as well as the total transactions at the time." In other words, if there was a sudden increase in the amount of currency in circulation, no matter in the form of gold coins or paper notes, and if the total transactions and velocity of circulation remained unchanged, "then the purchasing power of currency will decrease in proportion to its increase in amount, as a result, the price will rise accordingly."[94]

The evolution of money: Liao was convinced that "the more advanced the national economy becomes, and the more prosperous domestic and foreign trading grows, the less likely coins will be widely in circulation." In modern times, with ways of production changing rapidly and mechanized production taking the place of manual labor, the volume of transactions was never heard of before. The exchange of commodity for money was the highlight in economic circles. As a result, "gold and silver coins amount to less than 1% of the money in transactions, while paper notes, bank notes, checks, and promissory notes take up more than 99% of the total."[95] Therefore, in countries whether with gold and silver standards or gold exchange standard, metal currency was only fractional currency with the least amount of face value, and the transactions involving larger volumes than the value of a currency unit would be dealt with via paper notes. Those involving even larger volumes would be dealt with via

---

[91] *Ibid.*, p. 367.
[92] *Ibid.*, p. 366.
[93] *Ibid.*, p. 367.
[94] *Ibid.*, p. 310.
[95] *Ibid.*, p. 309.

checks and promissory notes. The standard money would be stored in banks or the treasury, out of circulation. He asserted that with "the change of ways of production and trading", money would also change accordingly. That was "a natural development which cannot be influenced by human efforts." This was a fairly comprehensive and accurate understanding. He believed that "the nature of money will surely change in compliance with the socio-economic development." When he talked about "the nature of money", he was referring to the material of the money. That is, originally gold or silver coins stood for a certain amount of gold or silver. The paper notes he talked of now stood for important commodities. So by "nature of money", he was referring to the form of money. The forms of money included commodity money and metal money, as well as coined money deriving from its being a medium of circulation, credit money resulting from its being a means of payment, and standard money, fractional money, and paper money circulating in a certain area. Despite the difference in form, their nature was the same, while the difference only lay in their material nature, of which he wasn't aware at all.

Paper currency: In Liao's view, paper currency (credit money, including paper money, banknotes, etc.) was the latest and most important commodity standard practice. It was most in accordance with economic principles. He realized that the development of the credit system and the wide employment of credit instruments provided prerequisites for the replacement of metal currency by paper currency, and that the inherent disadvantages of metal currency were removed, because paper currency was "the latest, most important, and most in accordance with economic principles."[96] In ancient times when the credit system was underdeveloped, only gold and silver were free from the defects of "changing over time, weighing much but of little value, and becoming useless after segmentation". As a result, only gold and silver currency could function as money in circulation. In his times, paper currency was universally accepted around the world, because it was convenient to carry and to split. As to durability, currency of gold and silver standard also wore off. In modern times, the governments of the world all stipulated that after a certain number of years

[96]*Ibid.*, p. 316.

of circulation, the metal currency would be retrieved for reminting. Because the broken and illegible paper notes and banknotes would also be replaced according to regulations, there wasn't much difference between metal currency and paper currency. Paper notes were themselves valueless, but as the symbol of money of gold and silver standard, their value was the same as gold and silver. As discussed earlier, since the value or purchasing power of gold and silver currency fluctuated and couldn't function as price standards, it would be more practical and scientific to use gold, silver and other social necessities as standard and paper notes as symbol, rather than use gold or silver as symbols and paper notes as standard. He exaggerated the merits of credit currency, and even mistook the disadvantages of paper notes for advantages, for example, instability for stability, and mentioned only in passing its disadvantages, such as easy wearing. But he linked, very naturally, credit currency and credit system, and discussed them together under the overall socio-economic and political development. That was more profound and comprehensive than others and to be commended.

Significance of monetary revolution: China's lack of a modern monetary system would inflict serious harm. "The discrepancy in the price exerts enormous influence on national economy as well as domestic and foreign trade."[97] The determination of price standards would clear away obstacles and lead to more life opportunities. Consequently, beggars and vagrants would disappear. Paper currency could be transformed into circulating capital and fixed capital for "road-building, canalizing, and the producing of all kinds of commodities. So products and paper currency would increase in proportion." Should China develop in this way, within 10 years, "even if it's not the rival of the United States or Britain, China's economy would become self-reliant. China would never fall victim to capitalist countries again, and the hard-won wealth of the people would not fall into the hands of foreigners. This is an urgent need of modern China."[98] This assertion was by no means wrong, but to some extent it exaggerated the effects of monetary revolution. Monetary revolution could never easily solve the above-mentioned socio-economic and politi-

---

[97]*Ibid.*, p. 306.
[98]*Ibid.*, p. 315.

cal problems once and for all. Furthermore, the issuing of paper currency should be adapted to the objective needs of economic development and in proportion to the growth of commodities, not vice versa. His misunderstanding might have resulted from his insufficient mastery of basic monetary theories.

The urgency of monetary revolution: How should China carry out its monetary revolution? Should China simply follow Western countries (European countries and the USA, as well as Japan) and adopt the gold standard? Or should it follow the example of colonial countries (the Philippines, India and Southeast Asian nations) and adopt the gold exchange standard? Liao considered both options unacceptable. Then how about continuing with the existing silver standard and unifying it? It was also unacceptable. His defense was as follows: "Replacing silver standard with gold standard isn't fundamental at all because it is the same as replacing gold standard with silver standard. The only difference is the nature and the value of the metal."[99] If silver standard was put into practice around the country, and "the existing silver money was standardized", it would mean the gross neglect of the national construction and people's livelihood. It would only "solve the immediate problem and blind the whole nation", so it was a temporary quick fix to the monetary problem. Fictitious gold standard and real gold standard were also "incomplete reform". The long-term passive situation in international trade couldn't be changed only by an appropriate monetary system. The hinge point was that "in international trade, the first priority is to maintain the balance between export and import." This important understanding was very insightful and surpassed earlier scholars. He put a counterquestion to the advocates of gold standard: "If China's production, export and import remain unchanged, and if we only replace silver with gold, how should we compensate for the excess of import?"[100] Moreover, in the United States, the world's financial center, the abolition of gold standard was already widely advocated. He had a conviction that the world was shattering the superstition about gold and treated it equally with common commodity, so it wasn't as valuable as before World War I. This judgment was indeed far

---

[99] *Ibid.*, pp. 307–308.
[100] *Ibid.*, p. 307.

ahead of those of the rest of the world. At that time, China's commodity–money relationship and credit system weren't, as he predicted, advanced enough for credit currency to take the place of metal money. China's political and economic conditions couldn't sustain the development of commodity–money relationship and the credit system to an unprecedented level. Globally speaking, his prediction didn't come true in any of the developed countries until the end of World War II.

(2) On the monetary system based on commodity standard

Liao suggested the implementation of a monetary system based on commodity standard. The core elements were that the standard money "will not be limited to precious metals. Necessities of social life can also be options". He put forward twelve kinds of commodities "to function as monetary standard", which were "gold, silver, copper, iron, coal, rice, wheat, bean, sugar, salt, silk, and cotton". These commodities wouldn't be used as the medium of exchange. "They are just for reserve, while an equivalent amount of money will be in circulation."[101] The commodities the government kept in reserve would be of the same value as that of the money in circulation. After exchanging the commodities in reserve for paper notes, the paper notes retrieved would be destroyed except the surplus. To be more specific, first of all, wherever the government could exert its authority, the issuing of banknotes should be terminated. The circulation of silver coins should be prohibited after a certain deadline. They would be retrieved in exchange for newly issued money and reminted into silver ingots, which would be treated equally with common commodities and kept in reserve. Second, the government would collect its revenue in newly issued money and copper coins would serve as fractional money. Denominations bigger than the unit of *hao* (a former silver coin of the Guangdong and Guangxi Provinces) should all use paper money. The monetary unit should be one *yuan*, or the use of *yuan* should be abolished. *Hao* and *fen* were smaller in denomination than *yuan*. Third, there wouldn't be a fixed unit of currency. The unit of currency would be determined by the value of commodities, which, in turn, would come from the authorities' monthly or weekly statistical index resulting from the analysis

---

[101]*Ibid.*, p. 362.

of the supply and demand of commodities in the market. Fourth, the government would establish the Ministry of Currency, which would be independent of the Ministry of Finance, so that financial reasons wouldn't shake the foundation of currency. Under the ministry there would be the departments of minting, issuing, supplying and destroying. The Department of Minting would be responsible for the papermaking, plate-making, printing and issuing of paper currency. The Department of Issuing would investigate and make plans for the production and deliver the commodities to the Department of Supplying for exchange. The Department of Supplying would look into the circulation, supply and demand of commodities on domestic and foreign markets, so that the exchange of commodities in reserve could be ensured. The Department of Destroying, in turn, would see to the destruction of paper currency and the calculation of gains and losses, and allocate the gains to the treasury to fill up the financial funds. Fifth, in order to maintain the stability of prices, "the government will purchase more of the commodities whose prices are lower than usual and less of the commodities whose prices are higher than usual." If some commodity was in short supply, the government would empty out its reserve to meet the social demand. Sixth, the profit from these transactions would be used for the building of roads, the cutting of canals and the production of commodities. The more surplus there was in the preparation of money, the more paper notes would there be for the government's distribution and allocation, and the more undertakings the government would carry out to benefit the nation and the people.[102]

The points cited above demonstrate that Liao and Zhu Zhixin were both elucidating and publicizing Sun Yat-sen's theory of abolishing the use of gold and silver currency, issuing paper currency and using commodities as guarantee for money issuing. Trying to adopt a commodity standard, they planned to cast off the connection and dependence relation between paper and metal currency, and overcome the discrepancy in purchasing power between different moneys. They both emphasized the establishment of the commodity reserve system, and the replacement of gold and silver reserve with commodity reserve. With the issuing of paper currency in proportion to the government's reserve of commodities

---

[102]*Ibid.*, pp. 316–318.

instead of the need of the commodities circulating on the market, the issuing of paper currency could be ensured against the satisfaction of financial demand, but the stability of the value of the paper currency still couldn't be ensured. The commodities in circulation and those in reserve were totally different and couldn't be expected to be the same. They believed that there should be a timely adjustment of the exchange ratio of paper currency and commodities for exchange.

Nevertheless, compared with Zhu Zhixin, Liao had his own understanding of the commodities standard, which manifested itself in the following specifics:

Liao held that the price criteria of commodity standard "will not fluctuate". That is, there wouldn't be any inflation or deflation. His explanation was that gold and silver currency "have fixed value, so their purchasing power varies, while under commodity standard, there isn't any fixed unit value. The amount of commodities accords with the value of the commodity. The value of the commodities, in turn, would be determined by the authorities. They will make up an index on a weekly or monthly basis, in reference to the supply and demand of commodities on the market, just like the practice in market."[103] In other words, the weight of metal currency was fixed and its purchasing power would fluctuate with the price of commodities. In periods of inflation, the purchasing power would drop, and vice versa. On the contrary, the currency under commodity standard wasn't constant, and the amount of commodities it represented would vary with the change in price. As a matter of fact, that wasn't Liao's original idea, but a refurbished version of the Western price index standard. This was the first point to be noted.

The second point concerned the specific reasons why the value of the universal equivalent wouldn't change. In Liao's opinion, although the price fluctuated, the criteria wouldn't vary. As long as they were representing commodities, both precious metals and life necessities could be exchanged through the authorities anytime. Under gold or silver standard, the only option for exchange was gold or silver. In the case of unconvertible paper currency, it would be a dud check. Furthermore, with commodities as standard, the production of commodities would mean the circulation of paper

---

[103]*Ibid.*, p. 315.

currency and the consumption of commodities would mean the elimination of paper currency. It was inevitable that the prices of some commodities would vary with the change in demand and supply, but there would never be any "discrepancy between money and production, which would result in the trouble of some lowered price". Since paper currency was in accordance with commodities, and the issuing of paper notes conformed to the demand of production and trade, the purchasing power of money would be stable. In fact, this wasn't the case at all. The variation of the price generally was under the influence of not only the amount of money but also productivity, the value of commodities, the supply and demand on the market, as well as the value of the currency itself and the change in its rate of turnover.

The third point was that monetary revolution would "enhance the increase in production and enrich the people. It isn't intended to provide the government with non-productive expenditure and compensation for financial deficit". This guideline was of paramount importance, because Liao proposed a reasonable relation between monetary revolution and the national economy and stressed the irrelevance of monetary revolution to the compensation of financial deficit. The governmental expenditure should rely solely on such ordinary financial means as rents, taxes and public bonds, without any possibility of resorting to the issuing of paper currency. Of course, monetary revolution would indirectly lead to the increase of government revenue, because the stability of the currency, the regulation of the order of production and circulation, and the profits submitted to the treasury from the issuing of money would naturally promote "national economic development and give rise to the increase of tax funds. The government can balance its revenue and expenditure, while the people will be willing to shoulder the burden."[104] Even more unconventional than that of Sun Yat-sen, this observation seemed fairly penetrating and reasonable and was therefore approved of by quite a few leaders after him.

The fourth point was that though he thought highly of commodities standard, Liao"s comprehension of monetary revolution was exceptionally dispassionate and impartial. He seemed to deify the commodities standard: "If it is carried out in China, the tyranny of gold and silver in the past thousands of years can be overthrown, and monetary revolution will

---

[104]*Ibid.*, p. 316.

bring about substantial results. It is unheard of that the country and the people cannot hence become rich and prosperous."[105] The promotion of foreign trade and the banking industry was also beyond question. It seemed that the implementation of commodities standard would result in a radical change and all the country would take on a new look. In fact, the wording of commodities standard was open to question. The so-called standard was about the measure of value, so it was exclusive. With twelve kinds of commodities as standard, wouldn't it end in utter chaos? It was just like Marx's critique of Darimon: "You want to abolish the privilege of gold and silver and degrade them to the rank of all other commodities. Then you elevate all commodities to the position of money. That is, you want to equip every commodity with the specific attributes of money, which is exclusive."[106] He also confused the preparation for the issuing of money with the basic monetary unit which performed the function of measure of value. He didn't simply think about monetary revolution in isolation. In his opinion, "monetary problem is but one of the economic problems in need of urgent settlement. Without a reform of the major economic issues, the adjustment of certain aspects of the monetary system will be of little consequence. So in China, the monetary revolution should go hand in hand with economic revolution, industrial revolution and the revolution in transportation. After that, monetary revolution will make a significant difference in the country."[107] This comment was just sound and beyond most of the commentators in the field of monetary reform. Needless to say, in addition to the modern economic doctrines of the Western world, he was also profoundly influenced by the economic theories of Karl Marx.

4. The monetary theory of Zhang Taiyan

Formerly known as Zhang Binglin, Zhang Taiyan (1869–1936) was from Yuhang of Zhejiang Province. Also known by the surnames Xuesheng and Jiang, as well as by the courtesy name Meishu, he was commonly known

---

[105]*Ibid.*, pp. 318–319.
[106]*Complete Works of Karl Marx and Friedrich Engels*, vol. 46, Book 1, p. 69.
[107]*Collected Works of Shuangqing*, Book 1, p. 313.

by the alternative name Taiyan. Before becoming a member of the Society for National Strengthening in 1895, he was under the tutorship of Yu Yue, a well-known philologist. At the end of 1896, he bade farewell to Yu Yue and began to compile *Shiwu Bao* and *Jingshi Bao*. In the spring of 1898, he participated in the compilation of *Zhengxue Bao*. After the failure of the Reform Movement of 1898, his name was listed among those to be arrested, so he sought shelter in Taiwan in December and became a staff writer of the *Taiwan Nichinichi Shimpo*. In June 1899, he went to Japan and got acquainted with Sun Yat-sen. At the end of July 1900, in a rally organized by the "Chinese Parliament" at the Zhang Garden in Shanghai, he exited after cutting off his braids, declaring his break with the reformers. In the early summer of 1902, he arrived in Japan again. In 1903, he published "Disputing Kang Youwei: a Letter on Revolution" and wrote a preface for Zou Rong's pamphlet *The Revolutionary Army*. These writings gave vent to his opposition to constitutional monarchy, recommendation of democratic revolution and denunciation of the Guangxu Emperor. Being one of the key participants in the anti-Manchuism efforts of *Su Bao*, he was arrested in Shanghai. In 1904, he wrote letters to Cai Yuanpei and other scholars, instigating the establishment of the Restoration Society. After his release in 1906, he went to Japan for the third time. There he joined the Revolutionary Alliance and became the editor-in-chief of *Min Bao*. When the 1911 Revolution was over, he came back to China, arguing that "with the uprising of the revolutionary army, the revolutionary party should vanish", and requesting the dissolution of the Revolutionary Alliance. In the winter of 1912, he was appointed frontier officer of the three northeastern provinces, but he resigned soon after. He was under house arrest in Peking from 1913 to 1916, the year Yuan Shikai died. In July 1917, he joined the Constitution Protection Movement and was appointed Minister of the Guangzhou Generalissimo. After the May Fourth Movement, gradually turning conservative, he propagated the appreciation of Confucius and the mastery of Confucian classics, because he was unfriendly to the New Culture Movement. When the September Eighteenth Incident of 1931 broke out, he aired his protest against Chiang Kai-shek's policy of non-resistance. In 1933, he issued a declaration to condemn the Japanese imperialists for the occupation of Northeast China. In the same year he settled down in Suzhou and established the National

Studies Society to spread the quintessence of Chinese culture. In 1935, Zhang deplored the Kuomintang government for their crackdown of the students' December Ninth Movement against Japanese invasion, reproaching Chiang Kai-shek and Song Zheyuan for their persecution of patriotic youth under the pretext of anti-communism. His writings were collected in *Selected Political Writings of Zhang Taiyan* and *Collected Writings of Zhang Taiyan*.

4.1. Monetary writings of Zhang Taiyan

The monetary writings of Zhang were published mostly around the time of the 1911 Revolution. "On Minting Currency"[108] was written before January 31, 1900, and was included in the first edition of *Qiushu*. In 1907, while editing *Min Bao*, he published *On Five Non-beings*.[109] "On Whether or Not to Have a Representative System of Government"[110] came out in 1908. After the founding of the Republic of China, he published "Speech on the First Convention of the Federation of the Republic of China"[111] on January 3, 1912. In March 1913, he wrote the "Industrial Plan for the Eastern Provinces."[112] In 1914, he published "On Punishing Counterfeit Money."[113]

Zhang's monetary writings could be divided into three periods. In the first period, when he was inclined to support the reform, he wrote *On Coinage*, touching upon a popular economic topic in modern China. He commented on the two reform plans of currency headed by Wang Liu and Wei Yuan, respectively. In his opinion, Wei's opposition of Wang was "misleading the people". As to Wei's plan of "imitating foreign coins to suppress them" and using jade and shell coins to "make up the shortage of silver", he considered it pedantic and impractical. Zhang thought that

---

[108] *Collected Writings of Zhang Taiyan*, vol. 3, Shanghai People's Publishing House, 1984, pp. 276–278.
[109] *Collected Writings of Zhang Taiyan*, vol. 4, pp. 431–432.
[110] *Ibid.*, vol. 3, p. 307.
[111] *Selected Political Writings of Zhang Taiyan*, Book 2, Zhonghua Book Company, 1977, p. 533.
[112] *Ibid.*, pp. 626–629.
[113] *Collected Writings of Zhang Taiyan*, vol. 3, pp. 570–575.

there were three disadvantages if jade was used as money: "The first disadvantage is that it's difficult to standardize the shape. The second disadvantage is that it breaks easily and devalues the moment it is broken. It is much more time-consuming than the minting of gold. If a jade pendant or jade ring is used to stand for a certain amount of money, there is no standard at all. That is the third disadvantage." In other words, jade was fragile, difficult to carve and evaluate, and thus was unfit for circulation. It was impossible to use jade for the achievement of a unified currency system. On the contrary, he fully approved of paper notes because they could satisfy the demand of circulation. "They are convenient to use for transactions" and "easy to carry around". But he firmly opposed Wang Liu's plan of promoting the use of paper money. Wang's idea was that "the government can print paper currency at will", while Zhang held that government should always abide by the principle of "issuing money on the basis of trust". At the time the Qing government was "in financial shortage. Officials at all levels are lacking of funds. It is groundless to issue paper currency all of a sudden."[114] Therefore, the reform of the currency system "should be carried out in an appropriate time". First of all, the government should mint gold and silver coins to win the confidence of the people. When the credit of metal coins was established, paper money "could replace gold and silver coins". The point of doing this was, "though the government temporarily still needed money", the circulation of commodity and the social order wouldn't be endangered, "while the government would be able to grapple with Western businessmen". The reform of the currency system must "begin with the less important aspects, because the least important aspects would follow naturally". That was "of vital importance". The revised edition of the article further illustrated that he no longer had illusions about the Qing government. He acutely pointed out that the Qing government knew only "usurpation". The so-called *dragon yuan* of 16 *zhu* "weighs less than 12 *zhu*". As a result, "only revolution could make a difference", and "there is an urgent need for late-comers to do something."[115] Without overthrowing the reign of the Qing government, monetary reform would never become effective. It would be a long strug-

---

[114]*Ibid.*, pp. 276–277.
[115]*Ibid.*, p. 278.

gle in need of constant and continuing effort. It was very clear that Zhang linked monetary reform with social and political revolution and believed that political revolution should precede monetary reform. By contrast, some other democratic revolutionaries exaggerated the outcome of the revolution of the monetary system, even to the point of abstract concepts and meaningless talk.

In the second period of Zhang's monetary writing, he argued for democratic revolution and was against constitutional monarchy. But inside the Revolutionary Alliance he was losing favor with the members as a result of his disagreement with Sun Yat-sen. He was also losing faith in the Western system. Turning inactive, Zhang gradually planned to retire in seclusion. The article "On Five Non-beings" was a combination of anarchic and Buddhist thought. On the one hand, it was preaching the illusiveness of government. On the other hand, it was planning the advancement of material civilization. The article criticized the government for the issuing of paper currency as a way to fool its people, and denounced the private banks' right of issuing money, because "they are enjoying the same privilege as the government". In his opinion, under the republic system, there was still a large gap between the rich and the poor. "Without the dispersion of financial rights and the prevention of counselors, the republic system is no better than autocracy."[116] In 1908, after a careful examination of the plan for national reconstruction after the success of revolution, he made the suggestion of opposing the constitutional fraud and building "a true republic", in the hope of overcoming the shortcomings of European and American Parliaments. As to the currency system, he emphasized that "instead of paper, the government should use gold, silver, and copper in the coinage of money to get rid of easy forgery." The government should mint metal money and the money should be standard and authentic, so that prices wouldn't rise, and traders and producers of medium and small scale wouldn't go bankrupt. In short, he was repeatedly presenting his views on behalf of the middle and lower classes.

In the third period of his writing, Zhang clamorously advocated increasing the revenue of the national government. He believed that the

---

[116]*Ibid.*, vol. 4, pp. 431–432.

affluence of people took priority over the prosperity of the country, and the former relied on the development of national economy, so there should be a regulation of financial institutions. Consequently, he said, "the unification of monetary system and the establishment of a national bank are in dire need." While holding the post of frontier officer, he invited some experts to Changchun and asked them to carry out topographical surveys and field inspections, the outcome of which was his preliminary draft of "Industrial Plan for the Eastern Provinces."[117] There, he saw with his own eyes the "extreme financial disorder", and found that the disarray in the Heilongjiang and Jilin Provinces was extremely severe, and people were "unable to carry on even for a single day". "In the course of time, copper coins became scarcer, while *diao* (a coinage unit) was only a nominal denomination. The more *diao* there was in circulation, the less valuable it became. Initially three *diao* was equal to a tael of silver, but now eleven *diao* is needed." "The price of silver rose day by day. For the exchange of one tael of silver, the price grew from eight *diao* to eleven *diao* in the end. Folks with banknotes lost two-thirds of their wealth. Voices of discontent are heard everywhere, and the department stores are quite deserted." "The people of the two provinces protested in crowds." Faced with such a situation, Zhang submitted his solution. "Banks should be set up first of all. The banknotes and silver should be put into circulation. Surplus gold from the mines could all be purchased by the banks. If the banks have 5 million *yuan* in gold and can print 15 million *yuan* of paper notes, then they can use roughly half of that as the capital for purchasing gold. The banks can then mint coins with the gold as the reserve of the banknotes previously put in circulation. In this way, the banks would be firmly founded and, like weights and measures, the currency system would also be unified." He further pointed out that the program "was not exclusively designed for the northeastern three provinces". It could be carried out nationwide in every province to save the country from its desperate financial straits. For months he spared no effort in putting his industrial and monetary plan into practice, only to meet with obstruction and containment from the Yuan Shikai government. His plan ended in failure.

---

[117]*Selected Political Writings of Zhang Taiyan,* Book 2, pp. 533, 626–628.

"On Punishing Counterfeit Money", Zhang's monetary thesis in the third period, was intended to rebuke the Yuan Shikai government's overissuing of paper money. His "punishing" was intended as a warning, and the so-called "counterfeit money" was referring to paper money. In his opinion, "using these empty notes as silver currency is the practice of witches and ghosts", "only to fool the people". He exposed the dirty tricks of the Yuan Shikai government, condemning their use of paper currencies, which were printed at will, to "entice the metal money from the pockets of the public into the depleted treasuries of the state" (Engels). He believed that the "setting-up", "bullying" and "cheating" behavior by the government was no better than the Qing government, who, in collusion with wealthy businessmen, issued paper currency excessively to "deceive its people". It was obvious that he was dissatisfied with the Yuan Shikai government. He was also very indignant and worried that, among the ruling clique, "those benefiting from nepotism are oppressing and exploiting the people for their well-being, but they don't have confidence in the country and don't run any business. Their metal currency is deposited in the foreign banks." "The most shameful thing of China is, while the traders and businessmen don't make much profit, most officials can become rich all of a sudden. Half of our country's money was in the possession of the aristocrats."[118] He reiterated his plan of gold standard, gold mining and the development of industries. However, during the 10-odd years from "On Minting Currency" to "On Punishing Counterfeit Money", though the social system underwent a change, his monetary plan didn't change much. Nevertheless, his monetary theory was more developed and thorough than before. Compared with his contemporaries, he had a much more brilliant understanding of the nature of money, which shouldn't be underestimated in terms of both its scientific significance and its profundity.

4.2. *On the nature of currency*

Elucidation of the theory of monetary value: Zhang's understanding of the value of money was neither from the angle of purchasing power nor from the perspective of use value, but rather from the understanding of the relationship between commodities and the value of money, that is, to

---

[118] *Collected Writings of Zhang Taiyan*, vol. 3, pp. 570, 575.

measure the labor consumed on these things. The labor varied: "The great labor was consumed by the building of cities and roads and the small labor was very too subtle to mention. But all the labor would consume energy."[119] As a result, the value was different. Similarly, gold, silver and copper coins were also the products of labor, obtained by the work of human being. "Though born of nature, they were the products of tens of thousands of laborers."[120] For this reason, "using these coins to exchange for commodities was like exchanging cloth with silk." He believed that the comparison between different labor consumptions and between different values was what we called exchange value. Essentially, the exchange of money for commodities was no different from the practice of bartering. Besides, metal currency can be divided and combined. "Their quality was like that of the leather, the division and combination of which was up to human beings to decide. So they were suitable measurement of all commodities." They were also the best materials for minting coins. This issue was already being discussed in "On Minting Currency". We can also see that Zhang Taiyan was already familiar with the theory of labor value. The theoretical basis for commodity exchange and currency purchase was that they all contained the common "work" of human beings and were all different "works", whose manifestations were "the value". So the prices would vary according to the differences of value or work. The value couldn't be created out of thin air. It meant that value was not a product of fiction, imagination or subjectivity, but an objective reality. It was the expression and comparison of human labor. That was the first point. The second point was that the principles of commodity exchange and currency purchase were equivalent. "The length was based on the longness, the weight, heaviness, and the volume, size."[121] The metal currency also had its intended value. What deserves our special attention is that he explicitly pointed out that money and commodities were both products of labor, and that commodity exchange was a measurement of the relative amount of labor. 400 years had passed since Qiu Jun made similar observations; Zhang Taiyan was the second elucidator of the theory of labor value, and

---

[119]*Ibid.*, p. 572.
[120]*Ibid.*, p. 570.
[121]*Ibid.*, p. 573.

his insights were outstanding among the modern Chinese democratic revolutionists. Of course, his understanding of value and labor was not deep enough. He didn't answer such questions as how labor determined value, why goods must be represented as value, why it was necessary to use money to fulfill transactions and what was the nature of money. Therefore, though he was closer to the theory of labor value than other monetarists, he still didn't have a thorough understanding of the issue and his perception was limited to the initial stage of outward representation.

The nature of paper currency: The analysis of this issue had both cognitive implications and political significance. Zhang's discussion of the nature of metal currency was for the analysis of the nature of paper currency and to serve the purpose of "punishing counterfeit money". Therefore, although incomplete and unsystematic, his analysis was quite profound, especially in patriotic and people-oriented aspects.

Paper currency was "nominal money, but in fact they were certificates". Such an understanding captured the essence and key of paper money. Zhang went on to analyze the production of paper currency and demonstrated the value it represented. "Right now with a slight labor and the help of carving technique, it was possible to print much money. There were no more serious frauds than this."[122] "Nowadays the making of paper currency is different from the mining of gold, silver and copper. And the making of one gold coin was similar to the making of ten gold coins, as far as the labor involved is concerned."[123] The production of paper currency was incomparable with the production of metal coins. "One involved the toiling of ten thousand people, while the other, with the help of carving and other techniques, could turn out countless paper money." So paper money was only "symbolic of metal coins, not to be used directly as the substitute of metal coins." There were no more serious frauds than this. Even "mistaking wood as a man and a horse as a deer" would be no match to the printing of paper money as far as fraud was concerned. The nature of paper money could be summed up in six points: The first point was that "though paper money was nominally currency, it couldn't take the place of

---

[122]*Ibid.*, p. 570.
[123]*Collected Writings of Zhang Taiyan*, vol. 3, p. 573.

metal coins."[124] The second point was that "paper currency was only the symbol of metal money, with no purpose of replacing the latter." As a result, "the heavy one would be substituted with the light one, for the purpose of convenient circulation. The reason for putting much paper money in circulation was that using low-quality currency to substitute the high-quality metal coins", there was the need to guarantee the success of the issuing of paper money. The third point was that paper currency was value-free. That is, the denomination of the paper money wasn't the same as its value. The government "had paper currency in circulation but its value wasn't that solid." He also seemed to be aware that the paper currency didn't have the function of the measure of value, but he didn't delve into the issue. The fourth point was that that it could only circulate in the country. In international transactions, gold coins had to be employed. "Paper money would only be used inside the country. In international businesses, we can only rely on gold coins."[125] The fifth point was that preparations had to be made before the issuing of paper money. "Paper currency must have the support of the treasury. There was no exception to this rule. Nowadays though the West differs from the East in many ways, the treasuries of all the countries are the same." The issuing of paper currency was dependent on the trust of the people, but as far as the finance of the Qing Dynasty was concerned, "the situation was utterly awkward because there wasn't any ready money", and "the government could only make do with it."[126] The sixth point was compulsory circulation. With "the dictatorship of the government", "nowadays many paper notes were printed and used as real currency, like the magic of wizards."[127] The government "used its authority" to issue the paper money for the satisfaction of the financial needs. "For the purpose of controlling all the profits in the country, the government fooled the people with cunning tricks."[128] Paper currency "was of a small size, and not much different from a piece of old paper, but was worth 100 gold coins. The government's fooling of the people was too

---

[124]*Ibid.*, p. 570.
[125]*Ibid.*
[126]*Ibid.*, p. 277.
[127]*Ibid.*, p. 570.
[128]*Ibid.*, p. 573.

much indeed." "Enjoying the same rights as the government", private banks also issued paper money. As a result, "money was devalued and the prices were high. People whose income was below the average went bankrupt."[129] How profound was his exposure of the ruthless exploitation and looting by the ruling class by the use of paper money.

At that time, merchants were not making much money, while most eunuchs were upstarts. In China, those suffering the most from currency depreciation and the skyrocketing prices were ordinary people and small- and medium-sized traders, while the noble officials, crafty sycophants and favorites at the court were controlling half the property of the nation, although they did nothing to contribute to the country and managed no business at all. They deposited their gold and silver coins in foreign banks. By way of contrast, Zhang Taiyan exposed the extremely unreasonable malpractice to the public and pointed out clearly, "If such things would not perish, there would be endless trouble!"

With the existence of coins arose different classes. That was a major issue of monetary theory touched upon while Zhang Taiyan elaborated on his anarchic views in *On Five Non-beings*. He stated very clearly, "The fight for coins would naturally lead to the emergence of classes." It can be asserted that he believed that money was the root cause of class divisions. He believed that the existence of currency led to the contention for it. Conversely, to put it another way, money induced the emergence of private interest, unfairness and fighting, which resulted in the formation of different social classes. In this way, the relationship between currency and private ownership was reversed. At the same time, money became the root cause of class. Money became the scapegoat and was very much guilty. Such an understanding of taking cause for effect was wrong. When discussing the demise of currency, he put forward the following idea: "If people share everything, then there would be no need for trade, and money would be abolished."[130] Such an idea was generally plausible, because when the private ownership of the means of production was replaced by public ownership, there wouldn't be any exchange of commodities. Consequently, trade would be cut off, there would be no need for money,

---

[129]*Ibid.*, vol. 4, pp. 307, 431.
[130]*Ibid.*, p. 432.

and the social, economic and cultural life of the whole society wouldn't be interfered with. In China, Zhang Taiyan was the first person to talk about the class nature of currency and was also the first person to predict the demise of currency.

4.3. On the gold standard

While writing his *On Coinage*, Zhang pointed out that the significance of "minting gold coins" was threefold. The first point was that it was beneficial to the national economy and the people's livelihood, "the big destiny of the country". "China has now a big destiny, concerning not only the customs and national debt. Without gold coins, in foreign exchange, China would use silver coins, but Western countries would use gold coins. Taking advantage of the cheapness of silver and expensiveness of gold, Western countries would formulate an unreasonable ratio of exchange, which would lead to China's big loss and Western Countries' substantial gain." "With the daily mining of gold, the smelting of gold became even expensive. For Western gold, one *liang* was equivalent to 15 *liang* of silver. But when they exchange the Chinese silver, one *liang* of their gold was equivalent to 30 *liang* of silver, a double return. In consequence, the Western countries would gain and China would lose covertly. Such a loss was endless." If China minted its own gold coins, in foreign exchange, "we could use gold coins instead". Even if Western countries "tried to bring down its price, there wasn't much for them to do." So they wouldn't be able to bring harm to China by taking advantage of the price of gold coins.

The second point was that it was advantageous for the issuance and circulation of paper currency. Zhang wasn't against the circulation of paper money. What he objected to was the issuance of money without any guarantee. In his opinion, the first step was to mint ample gold and silver coins to enhance the public's confidence in the government's coinage and ensure the circulation need of the market. After that, paper currency would take the place of metal coins. "I will mount a high platform to announce: 'paper money would circulate!' After some time, paper currency would be used as the substitute for metal money and reach all corners of the country for people to use in their transactions." Besides, he required that the gold and silver coins minted should have uniform quality and specifications. The government wouldn't be allowed to bring in "impurities" and common people wouldn't resort to deception either. Once falsification was spotted, the offenders would "be punished without any leniency".

Third, it was conducive to economic development and prosperity. Zhang believed that as long as his plan was carried out, the credibility of the government's currency could be established, and the commodity economy would develop rapidly. "The merchants of China were too many and very prosperous. They would surely become a great conglomerate."[131] At that time, China would be able to contend with the major powers. Therefore, the issuance and circulation of paper money were prosperous avenues for people's success.

Until the publication of "Industrial Plan for the Eastern Provinces" in 1913, Zhang was firmly convinced of these points. He maintained that "to unify the currency system, it is necessary to cast gold coins first of all". Though the purpose of gold coins was the same, his understanding of the role of different coins was even clearer, that is, with gold coins as the base currency and silver coins as the fractional currency. In the past, he did not give any account of the relationship between gold and silver coins. But later "to cast gold coins as the base currency" meant that silver coins were clearly undervalued fractional coins. "There is nothing to say in favor of silver coins. The purity of silver coins was inferior, and people will not have much credibility in them. With no change in their purity, foreigners will buy silver coins for the purpose of destroying them, which was only inevitable … Whether their purity is good or bad, there isn't much difference in their exchange with gold. As a result, the purity will continue to deteriorate, but the credibility would remain the same. So their destruction would never occur even though there isn't any law forbidding it." In this way, the intention of implementing gold standard was expressed without delay and beyond doubt. As the frontier officer of the three northeastern provinces, at that time, Zhang Taiyan had an even more profound and realistic consideration of the gold standard, the aim of which was the unification of the currency. He thought it imperative to exploit gold mines to make preparations for the minting of gold coins. According to him, the

---

[131] *Collected Writings of Zhang Taiyan*, vol. 3, pp. 277–278.

Huma River in Heilongjiang had the richest gold deposits, and the deposits of Donggou and Beigou of Jilin were inferior. "The three provinces have a yearly output of gold roughly equivalent to 7 million of silver coins." However, a large share of that gold was previously exchanged with the Russians for their rubles. "Chinese people were toiling all the year round, only to serve others. What makes one sigh is that the gold mines managed by the Chinese people were in fact turning out gold for the Russians." In order to cope with this extremely unreasonable situation, it was necessary for China to set up its own banks to purchase alluvial gold and enhance the foundation of the Chinese currency system, for the purpose of expelling foreign capital from the Chinese financial market. With the paper money and the silver coins circulating in an exchangeable way the output of gold mines would all be purchased. If a bank had a fund of 5 million *yuan*, it could issue a warrant of 15 million *yuan*. So the purchasing cost of the alluvial gold would be roughly 1/2 of the original cost. After the minting of coins, the paper currency of previous days had its reserve. In this way, "the bank would be deeply rooted, and the currency system would be unified. The two would be complementing each other."[132] As a result of this, he carried out a systematic analysis and planning of mining, setting up banks, issuing paper money and changing the currency system, for the purpose of enriching the country and people, developing the economy and setting up new businesses. Very sharply, he pointed out the serious consequences of not doing this. "The devious people would issue low-quality paper money, which was like cheating people of their possessions and couldn't be stopped at all. Take the paper money issued by Guangxin Company of Heilongjiang and the official banks of Jilin as an example." "If it was forbidden to circulate, the Russian Rubles would become rampant and our nation would suffer." On the contrary, "if left alone, the real silver wouldn't be used in the circulation process, and ordinary people would suffer even more."

In his article "On Punishing Counterfeit Money", Zhang also mentioned other gold-producing areas in China, including Yunnan, Sichuan, the Tibetan region, Mount Tianshan and Liaodong. In everyday life, gold was also used in many ways, such as "women's rings, earrings. These

---

[132]*Selected Political Writings of Zhang Taiyan*, Book 2, p. 627.

things were made from gold, and such things were not forbidden in the market." According to Zhang's opinion, instead of gold, the Japanese used silver in such ways because Japan was a country without much gold reserve, thus the prohibition. China, on the contrary, "though rich in gold reserve, how could we use gold with abandon?" His emotional sigh was connected with his thought of making every effort to make China a prosperous country. So he was saying that in very step, from consumption to production, care must be taken to increase the output while the use of materials should be economized.

Of course, the prime motive of Zhang Taiyan's implementation of the gold standard was to prevent "the flowing away of precious gold and silver to foreigners", for the purpose of reducing the grave threat of financial shortage and eliminating the long-standing difficulties besetting Chinese economy. He held that in foreign countries "there were famous utensils and exotic devices". If China wanted to buy these things, "there was a net of virtual money, but in the international trade, real currency must be used for the interaction. If the government could not, like what they did in the Ming Dynasty, prohibit the use of gold and silver, real money would have to be used to pay the foreigners." "With the virtual money much in circulation, the fine quality gold would be looked down like rubble." He called such practice "the flowing away of precious gold and silver to foreigners". Such an understanding might not be correct and shouldn't be explained by Gresham's Law. The outflow of China's gold and silver shouldn't be attributed to the flooding of paper money, but to the fact that China had long been in a passive position in international trade and the imports exceeded the exports. Besides, first of all, the Chinese government had been corrupt and incompetent in political and military aspects. After repeated failure in the fight against foreign invasion, the heavy reparations were too much, leading to a long-term deficit of the international balance of payment. Second, Zhang Taiyan believed that foreign countries sold their famous brand instruments at high prices, which was for the purpose of "benefiting the workers". If China could "regulate the workers", then "we can do that easily, without the need to turn to foreigners". Third, as was discussed previously, paper currency could only circulate domestically, so gold and silver must be used in international trade. With these three points in consideration, it was illogical and paranoid to conclude that "with paper money much in circulation, good quality gold would be disposed of like rubble". We must bear in mind that the more paper money there was in circulation, the tighter the control over gold and silver by public and private institutions. The aim was to prevent the outflow of such currency, so the kind of situation as mentioned by Zhang Taiyan was never to happen.

Zhang Taiyan touched upon the choice of monetary material when he discussed the unification of the currency system. He quoted a sentence from *Huainanzi*: "From something came nothing and from nothing came something." This sentence, with its naive dialectic viewpoints, summed up his concept of development of monetary material. In his opinion, the currency materials must first of all "be between useful and of no use". The so-called "being useful" meant that they were the life necessities of common people. For example, "grain and silk were of paramount importance to people's life, so they were not suitable to be used as currency". The so-called "being of no use" meant that as far as gold, silver and copper were concerned, "gold and silver were not as sharp as iron in terms of their being the edge of a knife; though they were shiny, gold and silver were not as good as copper in terms of their being used as material for musical instruments. But the less useful gold and silver were, the more useful they became in being monetary material. Consequently, iron and copper, though useful as materials for weapon, were not as useful as gold and silver in terms of their use as monetary materials. And our Lord used the gold of Zhuangshan and the silver of Zhuti to mint coins." The inevitable result of the development of money was the use of "things of no use", that is, paper money. "Though of not much size, paper money would be sufficient for the use of daily life."[133] It was undeniable that his theory of "being between useful and of no use" was indeed a factor to be considered in the historical selection of monetary materials. But it was not the only factor, nor was it the decisive factor. The monetary material had to be useful and have use value, otherwise it would not qualify. What mattered was not the use value, or its position in human life, but the factor that monetary material must adapt to the requirements of different phases of exchange of goods for general equivalents. Therefore, it was common to

---

[133]*Collected Writings of Zhang Taiyan*, vol. 3, pp. 277, 573–574.

have life and production necessities as the first monetary materials, such as cattle, sheep, grain, knives, farming tools and coins. The reason for the use of shells as currency was that they were a kind of exotic ornament, particularly favored by people and with the natural advantage of being the monetary material. In later times, the monetary materials were gradually transformed to the use of different metals. Second, monetary materials must be easy to "cut" and shape. "If the shape of the material could be easily changed, then the material could be used. If not, not." It wasn't so easy to change the shape of pearls, so it was not an option as monetary material. On the contrary, gold, silver and copper could be easily forged according to the will of human beings to various forms. As to paper currency, he believed that "it was easy to carry around and most easy to change its shape." In fact, paper currency couldn't be considered equal to other metal currency, because it was only symbols of metal money, not monetary entities.

In short, paper money was the representative of currency and the two could not be lumped together. From Zhang Taiyan's analysis we can see that his understanding of the nature of currency and paper money, as well as their relationship, was both unique and wise, and sometimes shallow and unclear. In addition, his language was archaic. But, like his contemporaries, he was loyal to the motherland, conscious of the backwardness of China and the need to keep pace with developed countries, and vigilant of the possible dangers from the Western countries.

Chapter 11

The Financial Thought between the May 4th Movement and the Founding of the People's Republic of China

1. Introduction

Between the May 4th Movement and the founding of the People's Republic, China went through the second half of the Northern Warlords Government, the first 10 years of the Nanking Kuomintang government, the War of Resistance against Japanese invasion and the ending of the rule of the Nanjing Government. Politically, it was the darkest and most chaotic period of the Beiyang Government in modern China, since the fighting of the warlords caused great social turbulence and impeded economic development. The Western powers fought against each other with both open and secret means to further their interests. After the First World War, with the Chinese nation awakening, the foreign powers in China were weakened, but the Japanese and American financial forces gradually expanded in the country, though the British dominance began to waver. With the development of the financial industry in China, the banking industry saw a large number of high-profile national capital commercial banks. The state banks began to commercialize under the influence of the run of banks; the provincial monetary bureaus were mostly restructured into banks and became financing instruments for local governments. Non-bank financial institutions also made considerable progress.

In the first 10 years of the Kuomintang-led Nanjing Government, it established the main body of the national financial monopoly system, forming a pattern of "Four Banks, Two Bureaus, and One Treasury". On October 5, 1928, the Nanjing Government amended the *Central Banks Regulations* and it revised the *Bank of China Regulations* on October 26th. On November 1, the Nanjing Central Bank was set up. In the same month, the Bank of China was restructured. On November 16, the *Bank of Communications Regulations* was revised. In 1935, the *Bank of China Regulations* and the *Bank of Communications Regulations* were revised again. In March of 1935, the Bank of China was officially restructured. With the addition of official shares, public and private shares took up half of all the shares. The restructuring of the Bank of Communications also led to the addition of official shares, resulting in a structure of 60% public shares and 40% private shares. The Imperial Bank of China, the Siming Commercial Savings Bank and the National Industrial Bank of China merged. The branches of the Bank of China and the Bank of Communications, as well as banks like Guangdong Bank, were under the control of the government. By 1936, the total capital of the Bank of China, the Central Bank, the Bank of Communications and the Farmers Bank of China accounted for 42% of the total national capital, 59% of the assets, 59% of the deposits and 78% of the notes issued. On March 2, 1933, the Ministry of Finance promulgated a new regulation to abolish the silver tael and establish the *yuan* as the sole monetary unit. On March 8th, the Ministry issued a bulletin requesting the use of *yuan* instead of silver tael from April 6th. On the evening of November 3, 1935, the legal tender notice was issued. Thus, the abolishment of two *yuan* was realized and along with the legal tender system, the Government unified national currency. The monopoly of the right to issue money officially started. Shanghai became the country's real financial center where there were gold markets, silver markets, exchange markets, securities markets, interbank lending markets, discount markets and insurance markets.

During the War of Resistance against Japanese invasion, the domestic situation changed rapidly, and the financial pattern that met the wartime needs was gradually formed and established. In order to adapt to the difficult war environment, the national government implemented financial control measures, such as limiting deposit, implementing a new remittance system and a wartime foreign exchange control policy. As the highest financial monopoly organ of the Kuomintang government, the Headquarters of the Four-Joint Banks was set up in August 1937 and was revoked in October 1948. In order to meet the wartime financial and economic needs, the power of the bureaucrat capital bank was constantly expanded. On the contrary, the establishment of the new commercial banks was restricted, the supervision of the general banks was strengthened, and restrictions and control were implemented. During this period, financial deficit was becoming increasingly serious, the issuance of legal money was increasing and inflation became more serious. The measures adopted by the national government such as the price fixing policy, saving policy and gold policy were all exhausted and unable to stop inflation. Taking Chongqing workers' wages as an example, from January to June in 1937, the wage was 100 *yuan*, but in 1940, 20 *yuan*, in 1941, 28 *yuan* and in 1942, 20 *yuan*. However, bureaucratic groups developed monopoly capital and expanded bureaucratic capital.

In the early 1930s, in the northeast of China, Japanese militarism had concentrated on China's finance. By June 1931, a Sino-Japanese joint venture and Japan-funded head office had 12 banks in the Northeast in addition to the Yokohama Specie Bank Ltd and the Korean Bank. After encroachment on the three northeast provinces of China, North China and Eastern China, the Japanese first took the destruction of the credit and circulation of the legal tender as their strategic objectives. As a result, they set up forged banks and issued counterfeit banknotes.

In the years before the victory in the War of Resistance against the Japanese and the founding of the Republic of China, with the major changes in the domestic political, military and economic environment, the financial situation of China had undergone profound changes, the bureaucratic financial capital had been greatly expanded, the financial monopoly system had developed to the peak and the national capital bank had rapidly declined after a brief boom. The Kuomintang government launched the civil war, which resulted in extensive military expenditure. Legal tender was issued without restriction, inflation rapidly increased and the legal tender depreciated day by day. On August 19, 1948 and July 4, 1949, the Kuomintang government replaced the legal tender with gold vouchers and silver *yuan* coupons, which were rejected by the people, leading to the complete collapse of the currency system. Foreign banks represented by the United States increased their participation in and control over China's finance, and finally withdrew from the mainland with the failure of the Kuomintang regime.

2. The financial thought of Chen Guangfu

Chen Guangfu (1881–1976),[1] childhood name Hui Zu, later named Hui De, styled Guang Fu, was born in Zhenjiang (Dantu), Jiangsu Province. As the director of the Trade Committee, he was one of the most successful bankers in modern China, one of the most influential business leaders in the Republic of China, and one of the main representatives of chaebols in Jiangsu and Zhejiang Provinces. In 1892, he arrived in Hankou with his father. He was apprenticed to the customs office and learned English there. In 1899, he was hired by the Hankou customs post office. He realized the superiority of the Western management system and strictly adhered to the rules and regulations. In 1904, due to good knowledge of English and business, he became a member of the Saint Louis International Exposition in Hubei Province. In the next year, he went to the United States and got to know Sun Yat-sen and studied abroad with an official grant. He graduated from the University of Pennsylvania Business School in 1909 and practiced in the Broadway Trust Company for two months. After returning to China, he served as the English secretary of the Jiangsu governor (Cheng Dequan), the foreign minister of the Nanyang Commodity Exposition, Deputy Supervisor and manager of the Bank of Jiangsu Province, and the deputy director of the financial secretary of the governor's office of Jiangsu. During his stay in the Bank of Jiangsu, a new theory and modern guidelines for management of commercial banks were used. He moved the bank to Shanghai, quoted the new management methods and bookkeeping, gave up the right to issue paper money and set up a warehouse. He advocated savings, enhanced the credit of the bank and

---

[1]Yao Songlin, *Life of Chen Guangfu*, November 17, 1880, during the sixth year of Guangxu, Qing Dynasty (Note 1 of p. 7 of *Taipei Biography Literature*, 1984).

paid attention to the training of the staff. The measures he adopted changed the old customs of the provincial government's banks and introduced a new atmosphere and ideas to China's finance. However, under the oppression of Yuan Shikai's northern powers, Chen was dismissed for refusing an order of providing a list of depositor names. But he gained the favor of Sun Yat-sen. However, he began to hate bureaucrats and bureaucratic practice. He believed that only private enterprises were conducive to giving full play to personal initiative. In June 3, 1915, Zhuang Dezhi, Li Fu, Wang Xiaolai and Chen gathered more than 70,000 *yuan* and 7 staff and established Shanghai *commercial savings bank* (hereinafter referred to as "Shanghai bank") on Ningbo road, Shanghai. With Chen Guangfu as the general manager, with him mastering the administrative and business tasks of the entire business, under his modern business philosophy, continuous learning, keen innovation, careful management and proper management, the "small bank" became the best of the national commercial banks in less than 20 years of effort. At the beginning, the bank "focused on savings and intended to help the Bank of China and the Bank of Communications to become its subsidiaries".[2] But now the bank had developed substantially and became the norm of China's private banks. Chen boasted that he was not a member of the "official circle", but in order to realize his dream, he had many part-time jobs, and the more jobs he had, the more powerful he became. The better the impression the US and British people in China had of him, the more he became America-oriented, protected the Bank of Shanghai from being swallowed up by bureaucratic capital. On behalf of the Beiyang Government, he was present at the International Reconstruction Conference (1925). After 1927, he served as director of the Jiangsu and Shanghai Finance Committee, director of the central bank, executive director of the Bank of China, director of the Bank of Communications, director of the Chinese National Goods Bank, member of the national finance committee, senior adviser of the Ministry of Finance, chief representative of the China's currency system delegation, Standing Committee member and chairman of Cotton Control

---

[2]*Chen Guangfu Ana*, p. 5, edited by the Bank of Shanghai in January 1949. Hereinafter referred to as *Ana*. With the help of Mr. Hong Jiaguan, I had a chance to read it personally, otherwise, I don't really know how I could have known anything about this.

Committee of National Economic Commission, executive member of Bank of Shanghai Union, chairman of the Trade Committee of the Ministry of Finance, chairman of Sino-US and Sino-UK Foreign Exchange Stabilization Foundations, chief representative of the government at international trade conferences in the US, committee member of government, etc. He moved to Hong Kong in 1949 and died in Taipei in 1976.

In terms of economic thought, in the beginning, Chen Guangfu believed that China's most urgent need was to develop mineral resources and build railways for transportation. During the War of Resistance against Japan, he promoted a unified economy, which highlighted problems, such as unbalanced development of China's economy, survival problems and the fact that agriculture mainly relied on the weather. He put forward the northwest development plan and other strategic ideas and compared Chinese and Western cultural backgrounds. In terms of finance, he proposed abolishing *liang* and using *yuan*, reforming the currency system, establishing the central bank, establishing the bill exchange, formulating the banking law and improving the current account system. Besides, he discussed money issued by the Bank of China and Bank of Communication, shortage of money in Shanghai and the capital flow into Shanghai, as well as the matters that needed attention from the Central Bank. His financial thought mainly focused on the concept of running a business, the consciousness and spirit of management, new theories and so on. Most of his thoughts were collected in Mr. Chen Guangfu's Speech Set (1949), published by the Bank of Shanghai, *Shanghai Commercial Savings Bank Historical Materials* (Shanghai People's Publishing House, 1990 edition), edited by the financial research institute of the Shanghai branch of the People's Bank of China, *Chen Guangfu Diary* (Shanghai Book Store, 2002 edition), edited by Shanghai archives, and *Chen Guangfu and the Bank of Shanghai* published by the China Literature and History Press in 1991.

According to Chen Guangfu's personal statement, his motivation for the establishment of Bank of Shanghai can be summed up as follows[3]:

---

[3]According to Song Chunfang's analysis on *First Draft of the 20 Years History of the Bank of Shanghai*, the subjective factors have been stimulated by four factors when Chen Guangfu established the Bank of Shanghai. The power of Shanghai's financial circle

1. **The life pursuit of regarding pain as happiness:** After starting the Bank of Shanghai, he once said, "there is a true happy thing in our life, which is not warm clothes and enough food, not freedom, wealth and power. It is setting up a goal, starting up a business, and when you achieve them and gain success, it is happiness. This kind of happiness comes from hardship, thus lasts permanently and occupies memorable value[4]." "During our life, we should try to serve the society[5]." This was Chen's outlook on life and values, which was inseparable from the hardships and poverty of China at that time and his own experience of poverty, as well as the knowledge of Chinese and Western thoughts.

   He earnestly warned his colleagues and young people, "The happiness from warm clothes, enough food, wealth and power has no aftertaste, and people will be in a state of anxiety, this is not real happiness. If we gather knowledge and strength from the masses to make our bank successful, that is our success, and the happiness is really precious. At present, after 15 years of operation, although our bank has a good reputation, comparing with the foreign banking industry, it is still having a long way to go."[6] He had a broad vision, and believed in diligence, self-improvement and self-encouragement.

2. **The theory of evolution means that if you do not move forward, you will be left behind:** In a very chaotic world where the market was greatly affected, Chen believed that "at this time we are given the opportunity to reform, and we should be able to work together and

---

makes China's banking industry the third largest, with foreign banks ranking the first and money shops the second. Chinese people are bullied by outsiders on their own land; the treatment of the Chinese and the foreigners was extremely unfair, and the management methods by outsiders were indeed superior to those of the Chinese; gentry and the government colluded with each other and the interests of businessmen were ignored. The oppression of the foreign merchants made recovery action brook no delay. It was not easy for Chinese bureaucrats to run banks on the right track. To open up a new situation, they must start from "complete commercialization of banks". Moreover, due to environmental relations and the current situation, it emerges.

[4] *Ana*, pp. 30–31.
[5] *Chen Guangfu's Diary*, p. 111, hereinafter referred to as *Diary*.
[6] *Ana*, p. 31.

make persistent efforts to move forward, we should take the responsibility and achieve it",[7] so as to avoid the disaster of "social development having its own natural performance".[8] It shows his courage and determination to transform China's traditional finance with new knowledge and new technologies. It shows that he was self-reliant and wanted to do a great deal of business. He would never let himself down and stay behind others in the world; he would never stop fighting.

3. **Redeeming China's rights and interests to develop industry and commerce:** Chen was depressed by China's poverty, weakness and decline. The foreign businessmen, with their privileges, strong capital and the modern management ideas and methods, had deep-rooted basic advantages, while China's industrial and commercial organizations were in shambles, with immature plans, poor capital and a lack of talent. He felt that "If we do not try to restore the rights and interests, the country will become weaker, the resources will become increasingly poorer and the future is unthinkable. If we want to redeem the rights and interests, we have to the develop the industrial and commercial industry by our own strength with sound financial institutions." At the opening ceremony of the Bank of Shanghai, Chen pointed out that the slump in China was due to the block of financial institutions.[9] "If citizens lack of foresight, then there is no place for them to stand. Now that our industry is enlightened in the immature age, we must have a sound financial institution at the beginning".[10] "Mr. Chen's vision is so broad that out of reach by normal people. This is the motive for the establishment of the bank."[11] This was by no means an imaginary adornment.

4. **The desire to establish national capital enterprises in China:** Chen was struggling for free-competition capitalism, and his ambition was

---

[7]*Ibid.*, p. 6.
[8]*Ibid.*, p. 40.
[9]*Historical Data* of *Shanghai Commercial Savings Bank*, p. 6, hereinafter referred to as *Historical Data*.
[10]*Historical Data*, p. 8
[11]*Ibid.*, p. 6.

to create capitalist private companies in China, such as those in the US and Europe. At the time of the birth of the new China, he expressed it clearly, "the capitalist economy" was "self-profit" and "competition", and therefore, it developed into disparity between the rich and the poor due to monopolization, all of which were antisocial. The strong foundation of socialism was based on this. The voice of communism and control spread all over the world. Enlightened private capitalists have been aware of this and have changed in recent years, understanding that the most important pursuit is to serve society. In other words, the purpose of private enterprises is not only for profit but also for ideals. The simplified idea is not only to increase the convenience of the society but also to improve the productive capacity of mankind and to benefit the general employment standard. This is the direction of Western enlightened capitalists, different from what they did in 1920. Private enterprises in China have not yet been able to reach this level. Due to the lack of political clarity, the feudalism of the society and the incompatibility of the people's knowledge, private enterprises cannot be compared with the west, and most private enterprises, in addition to their profit and enjoyment, have no so-called "ideals".[12] In other words, Chen had ideals, but his ability to realize them was constrained by environmental conditions.

Chen established the Bank of Shanghai as one of the "Three Banks in the South of China" and was called "a free entrepreneur who is full of ideals, bold in innovation, steadfast in practice and with a deep sense of the state" (Yao Songling). He earned a good reputation in the world. As an outstanding representative of Chinese bankers, he received formal higher education and a modern financial education in the United States. Besides, he, against the imperialist economic aggression, had the consciousness and long cherished wish to develop national capital in China. He created miraculous achievements in the Bank of Shanghai and proved that his financial thought, management and development concept, as well as the concept of development strategy, were consistent with China's national conditions and suitable for the trend of the times. His financial thought

---

[12]*Diary*, p. 214.

can still provide inspiration and reference, and some of his ideas still play an indicative role. Chen Guangfu especially advocated honesty and hated hypocrisy. We should obey this rule when reviewing his financial thought.

2.1. His theory of finance

Chen Guangfu's financial concept covered his understanding of the status and role of finance, banks and commercial banks, and his understanding of the adaptation and innovation of the financial institutions based on the environment, as well as their continuous change.

At the opening ceremony of the Bank of Shanghai, Chen declared to the world that finance is a hub for the development of industry and commerce. Therefore, in order to develop domestic industry and commerce, we must first develop our own financial industry and have a perfect financial institution. He said, "the development of a country's industry and commerce depends entirely on financial institutions. Now that our industry is in the childish age, we must have a sound financial institution at the beginning."[13] In his view, the status and role of finance in the development of modern economy are very important.

On the relations between the state and the banks, in January 1933, Chen made a four-point speech entitled "The State and the Bank": "(1) The history, organization and operation of British banks are far ahead of our country's, while the common people may still have misunderstandings, let alone our bank. In a society with a relatively low level of people, how should we work hard and make efforts to serve the people so that they can have a good understanding of our work and show their sympathy? (2) Banks are the depositors' banks instead of the banks of directors and directors' shareholders, so how can we make steady use of the deposits of more than 100 million *yuan* so that we can meet client's expectations? (3) Banks can confidently seek benefits for the nation and society. Under the security conditions, the bank should take the funds to assist the industry and commerce, the rural economy and civilian class, and confer the real achievements on the people. (4) The higher the status of banks, the

---

[13]*Ana*, p. 5.

more prudent our bank should be, so that others will not have loopholes."[14] People's understanding of banks needed to gradually change. Even in Britain, there were misunderstandings related to banks, let alone China, which was in its financial infancy. In order to eliminate the misunderstanding, it was necessary to publicize the knowledge of the bank and push aside the business work of the bank so that the people would gradually gain a good understanding of the bank's business activities, especially answering questions such as "what is the bank" and "to whom is the bank responsible", which are related to the bank's responsibility positioning and its characteristics. Chen acknowledged the bitterness of founding a bank from the British, and naturally was able to cope with the situation of China's banking industry. He said, "recently, the society is quite dissatisfied with banks, probably because banks have too much money, but cannot invest as much as possible in industry and commerce. However, the funds used by banks are not owned by shareholders, but entrusted by depositors, they have to be cautious in accordance with the rules."[15] Chen worshiped the American bank management model and respected the British bank management system, so under the total score system, "his ideal banking business has gone away from the orthodox British bank, which specializes in commercial finance, and adopts a new management way of the American bank, the 'department store' style. This is the first step in China's commercial banking system. He is leading the new trend." With great attention to detail and advanced thought, Chen held many events, such as foreign exchange, industrial finance, agricultural finance, civilian finance, trust business, insurance business and travel business.[16] Chen put forward three concepts, as well as the idea of turning the bank into a "civilian"[17] bank. He proposed the slogan that "our bank is the Bank of the people, they make us"[18] and encouraged staff to work together to reach goals. He also believed that the civilian banks should take the initiative to pay attention to the flow of funds and the security of credit, as

---

[14]*Ibid*, p. 125.
[15]*Ibid*, p. 125.
[16]Yao Songlin, *Life of Chen Guangfu*, p. 37.
[17]*Ana*, p. 56.
[18]*Ibid.*, p. 29.

"finance is alive in circulation, while the circulation is all dependent on credit. Credit can be received at any time after its release. If you feel that there is risk of cash withdrawal, credit will be interrupted. Banks make use of the surplus funds to support the legitimate cause of society and credit is the prerequisite."[19]

In Chen's view, the central bank could not be equated with the state. On October 15, 1928, he wrote in *Diary*, "The central bank is very important; it is an indispensable financial institution. People in China do not know much about the nature of this bank, so they believe that the central bank is the national bank. They take the words too literally so misunderstanding is caused. The national bank is the fundraiser of a government. I would like to mention briefly what should be done by the central bank. (1) Central bank should maintain transcendental status and stay out of political relations. First, the state and the government are different. The state bank serves the state and the society. If it is misunderstood by the people, they may think that it is a government bank and doesn't investigate its abuses. Don't make the central bank a profit organization. Second, there is no such thing that the minister of finance served as president. Third, restrictions on government borrowing are tight. The restrictive measures are mostly in the regulations, or made by the congress. (2) The issuing of exchange coupons should be supervised by the local law. (3) The standard currency should be determined, *liang* should be abandoned and *yuan* should be adopted. (4) Cash should be concentrated in order to adjust finance. (5) The central bank should assist ordinary banks instead of competing with them. The central bank is the banker's bank, because it makes up the shortage of the other banks with its expertise. The role of the central bank is to regulate finance, assist businesses, and concentrate cash to offer low interest loans to private banks. Therefore, the central bank cannot regard making profit as the purpose. Otherwise, it is not really a banker's bank."[20]

Chen believed and publicized that "finance is in circulation and circulation depends entirely on credit." For so-called circulation, the bank was the depositor's debtor; all funds could only be transferred by the

---

[19]*Ibid.*, p. 120.
[20]*Diary*, pp. 63–67.

wishes of the depositors. Due to the psychological role of the depositors, they transferred money as soon as an accident happened. If depositors wanted to "withdraw deposit", banks "will have to listen to them and scale back lending, banks will not be able to resist it. Therefore, it can be seen that banks can't concentrate cash on the city; now, it is not the power of banks alone to make cash dispersed." According to this, he criticized the times, the old business ethics that were destroyed, the new business ethics that were still evolving, the old laws that were not applicable and the new laws that were insensitive. In the past, "it was a shame to borrow money without repayment, but now, rich people are proud of it, especially when they encountered some accidents. Credit is not worth as much as before."[21] He deplored that behavior, but his words were not biased.

As for the mission of commercial banks, he thought that as an important part of the financial sector, it could be used to help business development and the revitalization of agriculture and industry. "However, developing business didn't mean the bank itself runs business, and revitalizing agriculture and industry didn't mean the bank invests them. The funds retained by banks come from the society of the masses and serve them. We should do the duty of good management, not only for their safety, but also for their activities."[22] This was the auxiliary function of commercial banks in society and its function of keeping funds. Whether for the development of business or the revitalization of industry and agriculture, banks were only supposed to play an auxiliary role and could not exceed their duties. That was the positioning of commercial banks in the development of agriculture and commerce; besides, commercial banks kept funds on behalf of depositors to ensure that they were safe and could be extracted at any time. Only in this way could one establish the credit of banks and ensure that deposits were available at any time. This was determined by the basic social function of its credit and debt business and its operation characteristics.

---

[21]*Ana*, pp. 119–120.
[22]*Historical Data*, p. 885.

Chen believed that commercial banks should take the interests of depositors as their "supreme duty".[23]

"A bank has a bank's mission and bounden duty, and if it wants to accomplish its mission to exercise its bounden duty, it will be very difficult."[24] "To do one's duty, one must use it effectively; to use it effectively, one must make progress. It is a matter of success and failure; therefore, great attention must be paid." As for the role of commercial banks, "its revenue has a considerable source. In the past, commercial banks had many sources of income, but the most important one was from interest upon loans. For now, the role of commercial banks is focused on assisting industry and commerce. Therefore, the benefit from it becomes more and more important, and the technology of lending cannot be ignored. The environment affects the operation of commercial banks. The nature of its role has changed. In the past, the role of commercial banks was to provide a wide range of services to the community, which paid more attention to quantity rather than quality, and the service cost needs no accurate calculation. But now, things are different. Although there are many kinds of services provided by commercial banks, they are still run by government banks. The emphasis is not on providing different services, but on good services. The service cost must be calculated precisely. Therefore, in order to adapt to the change of the environment, all the commercial banks must try to improve the essence of their service, lower the cost of their services, and reach the level of 'high quality and good price', only in this way can they be in an invincible position."[25] By comparing the role of commercial banks in the past and present, Chen found that most of the income sources in the past had come from the interest of commercial lending. In the future, he wanted it to focus on assisting industrial and commercial production, and lending technology; in the past, it had paid more attention to diversified services and quantity, but Chen thought that it should pay attention to good service and the service cost must be calculated precisely, so that in the face of fierce competition, it could stay undefeated with good service and maximize efficiency.

---

[23]*Ana*, p. 173.
[24]*Ibid.*, p. 109.
[25]*Ibid.*, p. 184.

Chen believed that when setting up a commercial bank one should stick to two beliefs. In 1937, when he reviewed his more than 20 years of hard work in establishing and operating the Bank of Shanghai, he mentioned the two beliefs: "First, anything useful to society is possible to exist; economic value, based on utility, is valuable only when it is useful, and exists only when it is valuable. Second, everything under heaven is moving forward, and no environment can be fixed. If the environment is fixed, there is no hope of human progress. If the environment changes all the time, it is necessary for the useful cause to innovate at all times to adapt to the environment. In other words, if any cause can constantly innovate and adapt to the changing environment, it will continue to exist and develop. Therefore, those who are afraid of running causes care about its inefficiency and lack of progress; if it is utility and makes progress, it will not fail."[26] At the beginning of the establishment of the Bank of Shanghai, the power of the money shop was still strong. Quite a few scholars preferred to be the leader of the money shop rather than the manager of the bank. After more than 20 years of efforts, there had been no significant change in the operating methods of the money shop. However, in order to adapt to the needs of the majority, the commercial banks absorbed the general hot money, the lending focused on the content credit and commercial banks promoted foreign exchange deposits and trusted business at home and abroad. With the revitalization of industry and commerce and the change of the environment, commercial banks could finally make corresponding changes, and their effectiveness continued to improve. The advantage of maintaining civil capital was visible. This development told the world that commercial banks had made great progress and could represent the interests and requirements of most of the national capital. Considering its original causes, one has to admit that commercial banks are useful and they can meet the needs of the environment.[27]

Chen thought that financial institutions should change with the environment. "Banking operations must be governed by the environment."[28] The so-called environment was nothing more than a political environment,

---

[26]*Ibid.*, p. 182.
[27]*Ibid.*, pp. 182–183.
[28]*Ibid.*, p. 187.

an economic environment and a financial environment. In the so-called political environment, generally speaking, political enlightenment was considered very different from political chaos, characterized by the outbreak of civil war, corruption among officials, the in-separation of soldiers and bandits, and the harsh disturbance of people. Banks had to concentrate their cash, shrink their branches, seek redressal in the face of trouble and seek refuge from political chaos, during which their survival and development would certainly be affected. The so-called economic environment meant that the financial industry could separate itself from the national economy and could feel the shock of accidents.[29] For example, the occurrence of a big flood and the bad operations of the manufacturer would cause a bank to suffer from unnecessary rumors, as well as uneasy business. Banks could do business if China's balance of payments could be offset. In short, although "we should strive to move forward, we must develop our business in a sound way so as to benefit the national economy and fulfill the bounden duty of the financial sector. However, this method still depends on steady environment, the improvement of business habits and the stability of local public security. Otherwise, we have to be patient and try our best to work hard in the environment.[30] The financial environment means 'no currency system, no finance, and no finance, no business'."[31] At the beginning, the currency system was not unified, and the financial sector was less organized, the competition was among the same sectors, which were out of touch with reality. Before the War of Resistance against Japan, Chen thought, "Now we should admit that the financial environment has changed, and we should admit that this change is a good thing, a thing that cannot be avoided."[32] "We must not oppose the unification of currency because of the interests of commercial banks and oppose the establishment of Central Reserve Bank." "Therefore, we should welcome the improvement of the environment and promote it at any time. We must not complain about the environmental changes. Even if we complain, the transformation of the environment cannot be

---

[29]*Ibid.*, p. 186.
[30]*Ibid.*, p. 161.
[31]*Ibid.*, p. 67.
[32]*Ibid.*, p. 183.

stopped."[33] "Since all businesses must adapt to the environment to make progress, this is the so-called survival of the fittest in natural selection, or those who suit their actions to the times are wise. When we open a bank, we should be wise enough to make it keep up with the times and understand the transformation of the environment and seek the way to adapt at any time."[34]

Exchange shops and money shops, China's traditional financial institutions, were eliminated by history because they could not adapt to the environment at any time. In the past, when there were no banks in China, exchange shops controlled the finance and were responsible for remittance. They made friends with the government and were estranged from the merchants. Gradually, they lost their positions due to the changing times.[35] Therefore, the money shop came into being at a historic moment. "Since the 20 years of the Republic of China (1931), the banks replaced the banks, the mainland banks went bankrupt in succession, and recently the credit of so-called deep-rooted Shanghai money shop was also shaken." There are "two main reasons, the first one is to stick to stereotypes and lack creativity; the second is to seek personal gain only and lack responsibility. They only make credit loans and real estate mortgage loans as they stick to the stereotypes. Once the economic downturn comes, most of the loans will be lost. As they only seek personal gain, they often take advantage of deposits to do speculation.[36] The new banking industry has developed very well without relying on the environment and has the potential to replace the old financial institutions." Why? "Banks can adapt to the changing environment." In his view, this was true. In principle, "those who are responsible for banks have the spirit of creation and responsibility". In particular, "the old-styled financial institutions, such as exchange shop and money shop, whose operation is based on the financial strength of the boss, with credit lending as the way and the private interests of the minority people as the purpose, they comply with the old laws and do not know how to improve it. When the market is narrow and the

---

[33]*Ibid.*, p. 183.
[34]*Ibid.*, p. 66.
[35]*Ibid.*, p. 29, 40.
[36]*Ibid.*, p. 167.

economic changes are not dramatic, the inland's finance can be turned around. However, in the coastal business of large port and bulk import and export trade, they cannot work. Besides, as they pay much attention to people's credit, favoritism lending is very common, so the business is not stable. Since the market is expanding and the industrial and commercial changes are becoming more and more violent, they have become worse and worse."[37] On the contrary, in the new banking industry, most of the principals could build a new business to suit the needs of the social people; one can realize that the bank is a social institution and is responsible for the safety of the deposit. Therefore, the failure of the bank is far less than that of the money shop. In terms of management, "in view of the loss of the old financial institutions, the banking industry is committed to the operation of the limited organization to increase capital, accumulate various deposits and social funds, reduce credit lending, avoid excessive risk, promote documentary credit, stabilize business, and operate foreign exchange affairs, assist import and export trade, promote savings and trust business and expand the scope of services. Although all these methods imitate the operation of overseas banks, in our environment, it is the best way to get rid of old laws and adapt to our own environment; as a result, big progress is made. The reason why the banking industry has the spirit of creation is that the principals are responsible. They know that the bank is a social organization and has a considerable responsibility for the funds of the public, so they are prudent to serve the society and try to be useful. It is different from those of the old financial institutions, so the trust of the general people can be obtained and become a centralized organ of working capital in the country."[38] Chen summed up the breakthrough and a new path of China's banking industry based on six aspects. Banks have abundant capital, have accumulated social capital, avoided risks, assisted import and export, expanded the scope of services and managed to operate safely. To find out its root cause, Chen analyzed whether they had creative spirit service consciousness. As far as the environment in which the money shop was concerned, it was only suitable for the production of small commodities and the underdeveloped market. Therefore, in the face

---

[37] *Historical Data*, pp. 856–857.
[38] *Ibid.*, p. 857.

of the new environment, banks were in a muddle and struggled to cope; banks developed commodity economy and markets, taking to these concepts like the rising sun and a duck to water, and as a result, becoming the center of working capital. Chen's views on the advantages and disadvantages of the new and old-fashioned financial institutions may be contentious, but his general understanding was appropriate and profound.

In the same way, as far as banks were concerned, even for the same bank, in different environments, in order to make progress, the business needed to adapt to the environment; otherwise, it could not get rid of the punishment of natural law. In July 1935, when Chen analyzed the transformation of financial environment, he pointed out that the environment in the past 20 years could be summed up by the word "loose". He expressed this in three aspects: The first was the looseness of the financial market. Most of the surplus silver was flowing into China. New financial institutions were full of money and new businesses were making progress. The second point was about the looseness of the financial organization. The banks and money shops were self-reliant, and the central bank had not yet implemented their duties. Under ordinary circumstances, banks only competed with each other in a variety of uneconomical methods; when the market was short of money, two or three big banks maintained the situation and at most there was no serious flaw. The third point was about the looseness of financial management. The central bank failed to do its duty and the national currency was not unified. Banks and money shops gained several advantages, for example, money shops could collect bills, banker's notes and *Yangli*, while banks could issue money and receive remittance fee. They were not deeply concerned about their respective businesses, so they did not investigate credit loans and did not know the market situation and the general trend of the economy. Good institutions wanted to assist industry and commerce, but they lacked a thorough understanding of individual businesses. Poor institutions blindly speculated in real estate, foreign exchange and securities, with little attention paid to their own business. In the banking industry, "eating bad debts and closing them" become "a routine business". Although the number of institutions increased, there was no improvement in management techniques (methods). On this basis, Chen called on everyone to be vigilant. "We need to know that this environment has changed greatly today, and this transformation has been achieved in a very short time. What used to be a 'loose' environment is now a 'tight' environment." His so-called "tight" can also be understood from three aspects. First, the financial market was tight. Influenced by the US silver purchase policy, there were three inevitable results after deflation. Prices continued to fall and bank failures continued leading to financial panic. Second, financial institutions were tightly governed. At first, there was no intervention of the government; but later, it was promoted by the government, "Last year, the government banned foreign exchange speculation and put into practice the savings bank law. This year, three major banks were reorganized, the central bank law was announced, and Bank of China opened the savings bank recently, and the Central Bank set up a Central Trust." It can be seen that the unified issuance previously abandoned by the Central Bank, which set the interest rate and the right to exchange notes, was about to be withdrawn. This trend "should be endorsed by us". Third, financial management was tightly governed. "In this situation, we should try our best to prepare for the occurrence of unexpected events and we must not be careless in doing business as before." In order to adapt to this new environment,[39] Chen proposed to correct the lax organization, and the Bank of Shanghai was also to implement the organizational control. He urged everyone, "only by making the bank more organized can we adapt to the environment of financial control and have a way to survive and progress. So, in addition to the spirit of innovation and accountability that we have, we must possess a spirit of governance."[40] As he pointed out in another place, "we need to find new ways to develop urgently", otherwise, "commercial banks are not easy to exist."[41] Thinking ahead of the storm and preparing for the rainy day is one of the sources of Chen's thought that put him in an invincible position.

After the victory in the War of Resistance, the operation of the Bank of Shanghai continued to change with the change of environment. In February 1945, Chinese victory was imminent. When Chen Guangfu set up a plan for the demobilization and development of the Bank of Shanghai,

---

[39]*Ana*, pp. 166–167.
[40]*Ibid.*, p. 172.
[41]*Historical Data*, p. 867, 869.

he looked forward to the trend of the world's development and thought, we are out of line with the tide, and the tide will eliminate us. That's what makes me especially nervous. In recent years, the whole social thought in China has violently changed to an unprecedented stage with the general trend of the world. There were three main points in the economy that needed to be noted: moving (1) from the premise of private profit to the principle of public welfare, (2) from the form of free competition to the policy of planning control and (3) from commercial and financial means to industrial production. These three trends were just direct blows for business enterprises. Moreover, due to the integration of these three trends, China's social structure showed new development. Most importantly, under the three major trends in the economy, the government created a large-scale network of banks, set up factories and absorbed the talented people, and the scholars also had a chance to do something beneficial. The first combination of idealism, science and real creation in Chinese history formed a "new intelligent class", which was different from traditional bureaucrats and other figures. "Its strength and role had a strong and far-reaching influence on the future of new China."[42] Under the new conditions of social trend of thought and social intelligence competition, the Bank of Shanghai was "not be able to avoid a dilemma even if its talent level remains the same as before." To this end, from the development strategy, talent and many other aspects, Chen proposed the design, especially the education program, requiring "bright eyes, courage, modest and have sincerity to save himself".[43]

In the early 1930s, Chen accused China of having no financial system. He explained, "why is there no financial system? Our country today has no currency system, which means no currency system and business security."[44] This was only the first aspect, which led to the following disadvantages. Second, there was no central bank. "We have a central bank", he said, "but to this day, everyone understands that it has its difficulties and, in fact, it can't carry out the duties of a bank's bank."[45]

---

[42]*Ana*, pp. 218–220.
[43]*Ibid.*
[44]*Ibid.*, p. 67.
[45]*Ibid.*, p. 86.

Therefore, "the big drawback of our banking sector is that there is no center", "no solidarity, every bank seems to be a small world".[46] As a result, the reserve fund of the bank was 80% in the United States. "The United States has a Federal Reserve Bank, which can be the support force of other banks, and there are some other auxiliary organs, that is, when in a financial strait, they can also be the supporters. China does not have such auxiliary agencies. As a result, the reserve fund is 27% in China. When money market is loose, there is no need for a lot of silver. When money market is tight, the reserve cannot make ends meet. The fundamental drawback is that there is no monetary standard and no financial system. Besides, banks compete with each other and don't get touched."[47] In the face of the danger that affected the whole situation, such as financial emergency and market panic, banks could not unite and generate capital strength for adjustment to cope with the hardships. So, Chen predicted that "in the future, capital will still flow into foreign banks." There were numerous banks in China, but "it is impossible for them to get the most powerful institutions to support industry and commerce." China had a different bank organization and a different way of doing things. There were bank-style money shops, money shop-style banks and bank-style banks, but no bank's bank for regulation, as well as no system.[48] It was a mess.

2.2. The tenet of the Bank of Shanghai

Chen Guangfu "has strong mind and firm action".[49] "First of all, we must serve the community and can't draw water to our mill. This is the foundation of today."[50] He spoke about this whenever he had a chance.[51] In 1927, in the last part of the "Letter to Colleagues in 1927", entitled "Our Common Purpose", he wrote clearly, "as we work together, we must have a common purpose and concentrate on it, and then we will have a long

---

[46]*Ibid.*, p. 73, 85.
[47]*Ibid.*, p. 68.
[48]*Ibid.*, p. 73, 87, 140.
[49]*Ibid.*, p. 205.
[50]*Ibid.*, p. 217.
[51]*Ibid.*, p. 206.

career. It is not specially designed for profit making. The main purpose is to serve the society, where there is facilitation to the customers, and we should try to make it. For domestic industry and commerce, we should assist them. For foreign banks in China, we should try to eliminate it and save the country. If we want to achieve this goal, we must strive hard and never cease to improve ourselves."[52] As a lifelong goal, it was an unremitting pursuit. Chen hoped it could become the common goal of all members of the Bank of Shanghai. This yearning spirit, strong cohesive force and noble pursuit became a powerful driving force for the Bank of Shanghai, which was unmatched by other banks. In 1930, after describing the various effects and trends of the 15-year establishment of the bank, Chen said, "fortunately, due to the social sponsorship and the efforts of our colleagues, our bank can survive in hardship and repeated difficulties. We are able to expand business in a steady way, and achieve our three purposes: serve the society, assist industry and commerce and develop oversea trade. Social reward is gained."[53] This constituted the basic motto of the Bank of Shanghai. The premise of the motto was serving society. For domestic society, it meant assisting industry and commerce and serving the society; however, it was constrained by the social and economic conditions of China. Serving the society was neither an obligation nor a mercenary plan. Due to their different starting points and different means of achieving the goals, the results obtained were different.

Speaking of the service, Chen associated the Beiyang Government with borrowing and selling bonds to support themselves. Banks were forced to be responsible for the maintenance of the government. If someone hesitated, they were accused of being unpatriotic. In his view, borrowing and patriotism were two different things. Offering loans to the government was not necessarily patriotic, and vice versa. He believed that one must not regard the maintenance of government expenditure as a yardstick for measuring patriotism, nor could one deny that it was not patriotic because it did not maintain the government's funds, as "government funds should be budgeted, and they should live within their means

---

[52]*Ibid.*, p. 7.
[53]Song Chunfang, *First Draft of the 20 years history of Chen Guangfu Commercial Savings Bank*, (2), p. 17.

rather than depending on borrowing money. I've been investigated in the US and Europe, there is no such thing."[54]

Chen's understanding of service was "the purpose of opening a bank. People deposit money in the bank because of trust, so the bank should take care of it. Although the bank can borrow money to others for profits, it always has the responsibility of repayment, this is the so-called service. This is my purpose."[55] The service of a bank was to keep depositors' money and repay it at any time as entrusted by depositors. At the meeting of the general manager's office in October 22, 1932, he gave a specific in-depth explanation: "our bank focuses on service". "To serve, we must first protect the trust of the depositors and the capital of the shareholders. For the society, we should bear in mind it needs service, for example, bank assists rural economy and industry and commerce." "Other stores also regard service as the main idea, thus serving is a means of livelihood rather than a blind alley."[56] In his view, "bank business, unlike other stores, can be chosen by the display of goods, the goods of the bank are service, so we have nothing to rely on, but the spirit of service."[57] Therefore, colleagues "should know that the lifeblood of our bank is service. We neither have the right to issue notes nor any other special rights."[58] His words were clear and reasonable, plain and simple, and real and moving. Service is the creed, mission, life element, survival way, fundamental position and great aim of the Bank of Shanghai. His repeated publicity not only showed his great attention but also attracted the attention of all the colleagues. It became the new idea of the bank, the new spirit of the work, the new attitude toward the society, and thus established the new position of the Bank of Shanghai in society. The new concept of serving society was very strange to most Chinese at that time. For the Bank of Shanghai, serving the society, whether for the top management or the grassroots staff, was about self-restraint, self-sacrifice and blending with personal interests. "The bank is me, I am the bank", "you have me,

---

[54]*Ana*, pp. 79–80.
[55]*Ibid.*, p. 80.
[56]*Ibid.*, p. 117.
[57]*Ibid.*, p. 46.
[58]*Ibid.*, p. 18.

I have you"; that is a good banker. It was the common goal and pursuit of the Bank of Shanghai to work hard, respond quickly, treat others sincerely, be polite, give customers a good impression and serve them wholeheartedly.

There were three background factors for the Bank of Shanghai advocate serving society: The first was a way of survival for the Bank of Shanghai. To gain a foothold in Shanghai's financial sector, one had to introduce new ideas to get people's goodwill and social support. It was important to know that the Bank of Shanghai had a "bitter origin," "To recognize serving the community as the first goal and strive for progress is the foundation of today."[59] That is, "regarding serving the community as the motto, attaining and improving the status of our existence in the service of society, and serving the society with our improved existence."[60] When Chen made a speech at the management conference in July 1933, he looked back at the difficulty of founding the bank. The reason why the Bank of Shanghai was able to stand and develop quickly was that it believed in "regarding serving the society as the purpose rather than regarding profit-making as the only goal." As the financial power in Shanghai at that time did not have positions for Chinese people, Chinese banks and money shops all looked up to foreign banks, while foreign banks and their compradors were very proud and difficult to work with. In this regard, Chen had a profound understanding. In the board of directors of the Bank of Jiangsu, most of the directors were compradors of foreign banks. While the Chinese wanted to cooperate with them, they were too arrogant and unapproachable. At HSBC, the Chinese could only enter through the back door; both the compradors and accountants could not be seen, and were not allowed to talk to each other. After 18 years of operation, the Bank of Shanghai finally established itself as the foundation of financial business in Shanghai's financial sector. The Bank of Shanghai, for the first time, advocated to serve society. "By our promotion, other banks all regard serving society as the goal, as well as cigarette factories, big or small shops, even schools and political circles. Our financial power can also occupy the position in distress and business withering, that is,

---

[59]*Ibid.*, p. 65.
[60]*Ibid.*, p. 208.

the achievements of our past service."[61] "At the beginning of our business, we decided that the way to survive is to first serve the society, not to seek profits. Our today's foundation is gained by working together, uniting as one."[62] The pride in the words also reveals the sense of responsibility. The second was that in order to remain invincible in the financial sector, the Bank of Shanghai still needed to serve the community without being negligent. In November of the same year, Chen wrote an article and at the beginning, he stated, "In the past 18 years, there has been a saying, 'serving the society', we should keep firmly in the mind. These words are really the elements of our survival and our second life. No matter how the political situation changes, how bad is the environment, how the thought direction changes, and how the world changes, those theories that were regarded as a novelty 18 years ago becomes unfashionable. However, the spirit and application of the 'service society' are consistent and unchanged, as only truth can last forever in the world." Until September 5, 1945, in the face of the new conditions after the victory of the War of Resistance, Chen said earnestly in the US, "during the war, our colleagues drift from place to place homeless and miserable, their life is unstable. Although our business is affected by the war, our spirit of serving the society should not be changed. Our colleagues, no matter work in occupied area or free area, can rectify themselves and do their duty. We should carry forward the mission. We must understand the environment, identify the objectives of our work, and make every effort to achieve our goal. The basic creed and the mission are to serve the community."[63] The next year, when he spoke to colleagues in Tianjin, he stressed that "when the bank was opened 30 years ago, the slogan of 'serving the society' was set. We should stick to the goal as it is right and suitable for current situation, as well as the future situation." This was "incontrovertible truth and you should practice what you preach."[64] This slogan was confirmed by the history of the Bank of Shanghai; meanwhile, it was obeyed by Europe and the United States economy. It was precisely this idea that led to the unquestionable and

---

[61] *Ibid.*, pp. 138–139.
[62] *Ibid.*, p. 217.
[63] *Ibid.*, p. 155, 200.
[64] *Ibid.*, p. 224.

unwavering mission and spirit of the Bank of Shanghai. That is, "In order to build a business, we must have a great purpose in addition to financial resources. We started the business with 100,000 *yuan*. Our today's achievements depend on serving the society sincerely, not just for making profit. 'Serving the society' is the great aim. Our today's position is gained by social support."[65] The third was that social development was irreversible. In the papers published by an American magazine, Chen received spiritual support and belief, especially from capitalism, which needed new ideals to survive. This new ideal, "in a simple word, is serving the society". "A celebrity once said 'I'm here to serve the people'. All private industries, financial institutions, large enterprises, etc., please remember this firmly, otherwise their destruction, in any case, cannot be avoided." This further strengthened Chen's conviction: "our conclusion is that if economic organization can't satisfy most of the citizens, it will fail without question. If you shut your eyes and think about it, what a happy thing it is. If we can build the industry based on the new ideal, we must take 'serving the society' as the premise. As far as workers are concerned, it is better to be more humane than to be cruel and mercenary."[66]

The great aim of serving the community was not only a thought and idea for Chen Guangfu but also a criterion of action and the primary goal. This was reflected in every word and action of the staff, and directly related to the survival and development of the Bank of Shanghai. Yao Songling explored the reason behind the rapid progress of the Bank of Shanghai and the wide range of businesses, which was rare among Chinese and foreign banks, in his book *The Life of Chen Guangfu*. He wrote, "Chen can obey the creed of 'serving the society' and continue to promote its business scope. The most important reason is the service method and spirit instructed by Guangfu earnestly and tirelessly, which are: first, don't tire of being cumbersome; second, do not avoid fatigue; third, don't expect substantial profit; fourth, do what others don't want to do; fifth, start small; sixth, always think of new ways. In fact, if Guangfu does not engage in financial undertakings, his spirit and opinions will

---

[65]*Ibid.*, p. 154–155.
[66]*Ibid.*, pp. 155–156.

make him successful in any enterprises."[67] All the bank staff had to abide by this highest pursuit; however, this was not enough to guarantee the realization of the main purpose of "serving the society". The following four requirements had to be met: "don't be complacent; treating guests equally; having the courage to move forward; having compassion." "First of all, don't be complacent. In spite of the social credit, the bank still needs to be vigilant, not to be proud of it, to seek development in progress, to exert its ability to serve the society as far as possible, only in this way can the bank wins the praise of the society. This is the basis of our business."[68] Yao Songling criticized the wrong idea that the Bank of Shanghai was very strong and had a lot of deposit. This wrong idea was an expression of ambition, which he said should cause deep concern among people. Otherwise, one might take a perfunctory action to service. In this way, one could not make progress. After the victory of the war, Chen said in "To Colleagues" published in New York that he was well aware that his colleagues could obey the main creed "serving the society", and he hoped that "they can apply this creed to every business. Being prudent and thoughtful, strictly avoiding arrogance and rashness."[69] He quoted the old sayings and warned that "colleagues should be 'humility' in their life. 'Work as respectfully and conscientiously as the reception of distinguished guests and command the people as carefully as the service of great sacrifices.' No matter big or small thing, we must adhere to the attitude of 'self-improvement'." "The Book of Changes" points out that a noble man should strive with perseverance. "Meanwhile, it also teaches people to be humble. If we can see the beauty of life from humility, we can avoid the mistake of exaggeration and rash action."[70] "Secondly, treating guests equally. We should treat people with equal eyes and not show the difference in hospitality due to the distinction between rich and poor. We should know that no matter who is willing to be close to our bank, it is the glory. That is the real spirit of 'serving the society'."[71] Chen advocated

---

[67]Shou Tongyi, *Chen Guangfu and the Bank of Shanghai*, p. 2; it is recorded that Chen Guangfu forms principles of serving the society, which are similar to this.
[68]*Ana*, p. 18.
[69]*Ibid.*, p. 206.
[70]*Ibid.*
[71]*Ibid.*, pp. 18–19.

that banking services should be equal to all customers and one should not treat different customers with different standards. He also exemplified that if a farmer who had a torn coat wants to talk to someone, he would invite the farmer to the manager's room and treat him with a kind and sincere attitude. He required that all the staff in the Bank of Shanghai should do the same. Third, be believed in having the courage to move forward. This was the spirit that he displayed for many years. Because psychologically speaking, many years after the establishment and construction of the Bank of Shanghai, the mentality and appearance of the bank in different periods was just like a person's youth and middle age, that is, "In the age of youth, they have the courage to make progress. Many years later, the financial community has established a solid foundation and a stable credit in society. Just like a man comes to his middle age with rich experience and precise vision, for the progression, he may weigh the stakes and proceed steadily. If you don't encourage yourself and turn to embrace pride, then your spirit will decline, you will pursue nothing. This is called blood depletion disease, which is a serious taboo of banks."[72] Fourth, he believed in having compassion. Chen thought that "banks need to be compassionate towards society, both customers and non-customers. In this world, even if you meet someone you don't know, you should be compassionate and help each other. In addition, the society's trust in Banks is the sympathy expressed by the society. We should show our attitude of serving the society with compassion. Colleagues should express their spirit of solidarity with compassion. If colleagues don't love each other, then the mutual understanding will be lacked, they don't help each other in urgency and their interests are separated. Colleagues should be careful about it."[73]

From a psychological point of view, Chen also elaborated that one should try our best to give convenience to people and create a lively atmosphere so as to embody the purpose of serving the society. He thought that it was not enough to treat our customers with spirit of equality; no matter big or small customers, one should treat them with one's heart. Besides, "for those who don't have business with our bank, we should treat them with respect, let alone those small customers? As long

---

[72]*Ibid.*, p. 19.
[73]*Ibid.*

as they come, we should thank them for their kindness. Our bank's aim is to serve the society. For customers, we should try our best to offer convenience, for businessmen, we should get close to them, for business, we shouldn't seek short-term benefit. We should make counter's customers lively. They prefer crowded place, where is trusted by the public, therefore, we shouldn't have the heart of the envy due to futile effort. Serving the society is our duty, not for profit. The things we do may bring profit. People laughed at me when I advocated the prescribed minimum deposit is one *yuan*. But years later, people who had laughed at me started learning from me. I hope that you can bear in mind the aim and promote it, so as to establish Qingdao Branch as a strong position."[74] He also criticized that "rigid face is the common failing of Chinese people. This may cause by old moral codes. We have to change it and always smile at others, in this way, can we leave a good first impression to others."[75] As he had analyzed in his conversation with the national bank manager in Xuzhou, in the past, "bank managers, with bureaucratic habit, live in the high hall deeply and puffed up with self-importance. Managers treat customers with pride and a cold attitude, like they are subordinates. The officials rely on their power and position to be proud and ridicule, yet stingers are still sniffed at them. What should we rely on to be proud and ridicule as a banker? Therefore, this long-standing practice should be eliminated at once."[76] This is the meaning of "harmony leads to wealth", which is the interpretation of the older generation's important motto in the new era. Under the new historical conditions, the new explanation of the new financial institutions had only injected new meaning and vitality into the new environment, so that it could reappear in splendor.

How could Chen's unchangeable and deeply believed concept of serving the society adapt to the changed environment with a fresh outlook? He said, "We must not only pay attention to ourselves, but also to society and the environment, we must therefore serve meaningfully, and above all, strive to improve the system."[77] He also said, "Ancient philosophy

---

[74] *Diary*, p. 115.
[75] *Ibid.*, p. 132.
[76] *Ana*, p. 32.
[77] *Ibid.*, p. 69.

preaches that you should have your pursuit when environment is changed. That is, you should carry out the central meaning and basic principle of life that you believe, thus something must be done and things must not be done and finally to reach the position of invincibility before the storm falls. A group, like a person, must pursue something."[78] "Serving the society" was Chen Guangfu's ultimate goal for the Bank of Shanghai. Under different environmental backgrounds, the meaning also changed; it could not be grasped with the characteristics of the times. Chen believed that, first, in the past, serving the society might have been a personal choice, but it had become a necessary requirement for the society since then. After World War Two, "the trending thought of the world has entered a new stage for all enterprises. In the 19th century, the idea of 'pure profit' has been unable to stand on its feet, while 'public welfare' has been recognized as the premise of any enterprise. From now on, if any commercial organization fails to supplement public welfare, it will become a target of public criticism. Any commercial organization can only survive in serving the society. In other words, we could choose not to serve the society in the past, but now we will be excluded if we do so. Service has become the condition of the bank's survival." Second, "in the past, serving the society could be passive. Now, the initiative attitude must be taken. Passive attitude means customer's requirement can be met, while initiative attitude means visit and encouragement should be made before they come. In the other words, we should be more diligent. We must strive to learn, open our eyes and pay attention to the new technologies, tools, methods and trends. We must pursue new possibilities all day long and address our unique policies and practices before the general public has thought about them. Today, when it comes to serving the society, every entrepreneur must have the skill of a politician."[79] "In the past, the consciousness of serving the society only requires you to sit here with tidiness dress, treat guests with polite and unruffled attitude, as well as fluent answers; since then, the serving the society means that we must step forward our own threshold, go out of the counter and go to the enterprise and countryside, actively understand their needs, and continue to take out new ideas, new tricks,

---

[78]*Ibid.*, p. 205.
[79]*Ibid.*, p. 208.

new products and new tools, realize self-breakthrough in service consciousness, turn passive into initiative, be prepared in danger and take precautions. It is necessary to understand and grasp the service object from the large environmental background at home and abroad and make corresponding adjustments to our operating strategy and operating methods. This requires that we not only keep a foothold in China and take the whole world in view, but also that we should keep a foothold at present and take the future in view, thus we can make timely integration. This not only reflects the requirements and characteristics of the times, but also follows the trend of development and fits the characteristics of its own cultural customs and habits, which are accepted by the people and the society." This was the key to the success of the Bank of Shanghai's service tenet.

The spirit of continuous self-renewal needed constant improvement; besides, one should work with a humble and respectful attitude, as well as "striving for 'loyalty and humility' to strengthen group cooperation". Chen said, "loyalty can overcome selfishness, thus being loyal to the others, to ideals, causes and groups can lead to success. Honesty can overcome duplicity; we should be loyal to ourselves and to others. Humility can overcome greed, thus leading to less desire and less demand. Being courteous can overcome the obstacles arising from being egocentric and profit-centered." He refers to exercising the accumulation of traditional Chinese culture in modern financial institutions under new conditions. This moral admonition is necessary for team cooperation. He made a personal statement: "Recently, I have witnessed the wisdom of the world, and the more I understand the ancient people's daily moral precepts, the truer they are. Morality is a necessary condition for maintaining teamwork. Loyalty, honesty, humility and comity are especially related to business groups. The greater the scope of the business, the greater the difficulty of cooperation is. Moreover, the bankruptcy of the general moral habits in the current Chinese society can affect the maintenance of the inherent tradition of the bank." He criticized that the war "has caused the bad habits of ordinary people: selfishness, duplicity, greed and bully. With these four bad habits infiltrating into any group, the group will disintegrate at once." "At the time of this flood of turbidity, the slightest little bit of inattention can let you taint with them. The way of prevention for the public is to control them unremittingly, and keep in mind the four words: loyalty, honesty, humility and comity. Finally, loyalty is essential to any group, and humility is learned by any business people. The former word is obvious, while the latter is subtle. Businessmen are busy with reproduction and making money, while 'I' control them only with the spirit of humility, for those who seek benefits, 'I' get along with them in the spirit of 'comity'." "Simplicity can control the tedious, while quietness can control restlessness; this is pleasure and the source of success. Comity comes after humility, and harvest comes after comity. Fighting for it, you will lose it, while comity is the way to get it. I hope that our colleagues can understand it."[80] Although Chen was not a philosopher, he was a banker with a philosophical mind, which not only inherited tradition but also organically integrated Chinese and Western culture that complemented each other. He not only avoided sticking to rules strictly and making no progress but also prevented venality. It was the crystallization of his decades of life experience and careful observation in business.

In Chen's view, loyalty and humility were the "basis of our colleagues to 'develop our talent'. With the main body, our talent can be useful and we can serve the society." "We should actively serve the society to get an immortal position."[81] Talent development was the premise, while cultivating people was the basis. Group tenets and behavior, such as code of conduct, speech and deportment, manner, mental attitude and service attitude, cultivate people. They complement each other and determine the success or failure of a career.

The relationship between serving and profit-making is "to seek benefits in service, in other words, it is what we now call the combination of economic benefits and social benefits" (*Zi Yaohua*). Chen opposed the idea of making profits only, but that did not mean that he was against making profits. He only opposed those who cared for nothing but money, regardless of whether it was legitimate or reasonable. This understanding was most clearly expressed during a dinner and conversation with Shanghai compatriots on February 5, 1931: "When I set up the bank, serving the society is regarded as the first creed. People laughed at me and said

---

[80]*Ibid.*, p. 207.
[81]*Ibid.*, p. 208.

that banks are aimed at making profit, how can a bank make money by unrealistic service? What they don't know is that the purpose of our bank is to exchange reward by service. We get paid for serving customers to their satisfaction, it is called legitimate benefit. If the benefit is not legitimate, we will never take even a penny, while others may pursue profits only and not care about the interests of customers."[82] He further stated that he "holds the purpose, serves the society, heaven helps those who help themselves, the interests are already in it."[83] A bank was not a charitable organization, of course, so it had to consider the problem of profit; however, there are legitimate profits and improper profits, and Chen had a deep understanding of it. On the basis of safeguarding the interests of customers, it was a legitimate interest to receive remuneration through service, otherwise it was improper interest. "Blindly making profits is not the way out, but service is."[84] His incisive views were really penetrating. In November 1928, Chen said, "banking is only one kind of business. Today there is a sudden situation of standing out from the crowd, which is caused by the society."

"People in society only know that banks are rich. People's life is difficult and money worship is all over the country, I fear that 1 or 2 years later, the suffering day for banks will come."[85] This was Chen's unique wisdom and extraordinary brilliance among China's national capital bankers.

In February 1949, on the eve of the founding of the People's Republic of China, in his diary, Chen analyzed the motive and purpose of private enterprises in the past as nothing more than making profits and personal enjoyment; the standard of success or failure was mainly based on its profit. The Western enlightened capitalists had been different from this. China's private enterprises had not yet claimed to serve the society. After the War of Resistance, China's private enterprises generally attached more importance to profits; therefore, the wind of speculation aroused the world's unprecedented abhorrent to businessmen. Some businesses

---

[82]*Ibid.*, p. 46.
[83]*Ibid.*, p. 15.
[84]*Ibid.*, p. 117.
[85]*Diary*, p. 89.

called for serving the society; however, they unconsciously lost their original purpose. In order to survive, there had to be some compromise and perfunctoriness. Due to the uncertain situation, for security and self-protection, even if there was surplus, it would not be shared with shareholders and society; in the process of expansion, the metamorphosis of personnel was inevitably accompanied by the phenomenon of "anti-elimination" in sociology: the upright people perished first, but the speculators lived and prospered. Therefore, "private enterprise in China had become a social burden and bark beetle and lost its value in existence."[86] Therefore, Chen wrote touchingly, "the world and the history of China have shown that blind profit-making institutions will not last forever and that the 'ideal' factor must be incorporated into private enterprise for their survival. What is this ideal? In other words, 'offering what you have for what you need', that is, stay away from undeserved benefit. It was easy to say and hard to do because the first difficulty we encountered was few listeners. The nature of the service staff has changed. According to the old adage, 'A man lives with his work, when a man dies his administration will be cast away', only with ideal and knowledge and no talents, it makes no difference to the matter."[87] Of course, because such expressions can be interpreted differently, there is no certain way of defining the exact meaning. So nowadays it is of only referential value indeed.

2.3. His theory on bank management

2.3.1. Management philosophy

On October 25, 1949, Chen wrote in his diary, "The purpose of my bank is to fight with the harsh environment, and to increase production to improve people's living standards. For decades, I have done the same. Unfortunately, as no good government has been encountered, it has been hit for repeated times."[88] It could be seen that the purpose of his business was to increase production and improve people's life while struggling with environmental

---

[86]*Ibid.*, p. 215.
[87]*Ibid.*, p. 216.
[88]*Ibid.*, p. 235.

conditions, that is, to serve the community. Therefore, consistent with the main purpose of the Shanghai Bank, its management philosophy had to be fully put into practice and not violated. In 1930, this idea was fully expressed in the conversation with the manager of the branch in Jinan. Chen said, "Competing with others should stick to righteousness. While others are just for self-interest, I should serve the community. While they act like bureaucrats, I should kindly treat them as equals. While they are guilty of degeneration, I should keep upright. While they are guilty of being lazy and luxurious, I should be diligent. While they fight for short-term profits, I should be far-sighted. While they detest trivial matters, I prefer to take on tedious tasks. Keeping respectfully aloof from bureaucrats and being close to businesspersons must be observed. If we follow this matter and work hard to advance … without a war, the progress of the bank can be predicted. We should try our best to occupy the first place and gain a firm position."[89]

Here, Chen proposed that they should stick to seven principles: serving society, treating people as equals, keeping upright, being hardworking, striving for long-term profits, preferring tedious work and being close to businesspersons. In the fierce market competition, he was not only being tough on himself but also demanding that all his colleagues adhere to these seven guiding principles. On the contrary, Chen opposed mercenary behavior, associating with bureaucrats, putting on official airs, degeneration, idleness and luxury, competing for short-term gains and detesting trivial things, which he believed should be refrained from by the Shanghai Bank. In general, he held that the Shanghai Bank should uphold seven operating principles and be opposed to another seven opposite ones. He got these by drawing lessons from history, which were both from experience of exchange banks and from the development of the Shanghai Bank itself. Therefore, in the early 1930s, among the nationwide commercial banks, the bank's deposits leapt to the first place from the fifth place in 1927, boasting the largest volume except for the Bank of China and the Bank of Communications. In 1933, the deposits exceeded 100 million *yuan*. When analyzing the reasons for this achievement by Communication No. 65 of the Shanghai Bank, it was believed that the first element

---

[89] *Ana*, p. 34.

for depositing was security, followed by interest rate. It might not be so impressive for banks with large capital to attract deposits, whereas it was impressive for those with smaller capital to so. "It depends on the management and whether the banks can be believed by the public."[90] The belief and the management did relate to business philosophy and were determined by it. The seven principles put forward by Chen were not only beneficial to customer service but also conducive to gaining the trust of the community.

Chen's philosophy of operating banks can be boiled down to several aspects, among which the salient points are as follows: The first is "the purpose of establishing banks deep into society instead of the other way around."[91] For serving the community, the Shanghai Bank had to follow the tenet of "serving externally", which meant that the bank could not just provide service for large stores, big companies, and key customers but also offered door-to-door service to "grocery stores and small fruit shops". Therefore, multiple institutions of the bank had to be set up in the same area, as well as around the country. On the contrary, a small credit loan quota of 500 *yuan* with an interest less than one point could be released with two guarantees, and most temporary borrowing was available for those with the urgent needs for marriages, funerals and medical services to avoid exploitation of high-interest loans.

Second, "it must be achieved that the Shanghai Bank is what the people need based on the masses".[92] Chen repeatedly exhorted his peers in the bank to conform to the natural law and not to be eliminated by changes in trends, and he taught them to dedicate themselves to realizing the needs of the clients. "Whether rich or poor, only clients are treated equally without discrimination and the most common ones are provided with service can purpose of the bank be achieved",[93] he said. After the victory of the War of Resistance Against Japanese Aggression, he also proposed, "If we do not strive to enhance the well-being of the community, we will truly be sinners of the times. Specifically, after the war, China must strive for

---

[90]*Historical Data*, p. 402.
[91]*Ana*, p. 27.
[92]*Ibid.*, p. 29.
[93]*Ibid.*, p. 56.

industrialization and increasing international contacts. How we serve the community must be within our capabilities, and we should promote industries to increase people's prosperity. At the same time, the scope of our work should also extend from being domestic to international."[94] Developing the national economy and enhancing the overall strength of the bank lay in making people prosperous and assisting society instead of exploiting it. It was also required that the Shanghai Bank increase foreign exchanges, go abroad, develop an export-oriented economy and grasp the context of the times, thus making itself an indispensable part of the nation.

The third point was the progress of operating technology. "With operating technology improved, the liquidity of funds can be permanently maintained".[95] He criticized the warlords, "They don't know that the money in banks that equals to the liquidity in the market should be utilized for production in turns. Financial managers are expected to be responsible for this rotation and then they can live up to their duties."[96] He also criticized banks for having paid less attention to their management in the past. Banks had launched unsecured loans without related knowledge or investigation; they had also offered mortgage loans, without knowing market conditions and economic potential. "Despite hoping to assist the industrial and commercial industry, the former lacks thorough understanding of the industry; the latter is blind to speculation in real estate, foreign exchanges and securities, focusing less on their own business. Therefore, it has become a matter of routine for the banking industry to suffer bad debts. It can be seen that although financial institutions saw an increase in their number, there has been no improvement in the technology."[97]

After the victory of the War of Resistance Against Japanese Aggression, Chen set forth three management guidelines for the Shanghai Bank: First, it should be noted that the bank "is not a way for a small number of people to seek prosperity, but for the general public to seek financial convenience to promote trade and industry and benefit the national economy. Our bank has always been the customer's bank in the past, and it should be the same

---

[94]*Ibid.*, p. 209.
[95]*Ibid.*, p. 201.
[96]*Diary*, p. 8.
[97]*Ana*, p. 167.

especially in the future. After World War II, the global trend indicated that any business must focus on the welfare of the people and the so-called capitalist economy has evolved into a welfare economy. The contribution of services should be regarded as the premise for the source and application of financial resources because financial institutions keep close relationships to the public, together with their causes. Besides, services are also the responsibility of individuals for the community and play as the foundation of all outlooks on life." The second was striving for fund security. A small portion of the bank's funds was capital while most was in deposits. With the increase of deposits and the enrichment of funds, the bank's function of serving society expanded. How can one increase deposits? "The bank must adopt the most prudent management method that enables depositors to have an unwavering belief in our bank's operation. As the idiom goes, the peach and the plum do not speak, yet a path is born beneath them; as long as we pursue improving the bank's reputation with each passing year, our service range can gradually expand. Thus, all methods of operation must give top priority to fund security."[98] The third was cultivating the credit of the bank. To cater to needs of the community, the Shanghai Bank established travel agencies, insurance companies and so on, but the foundation of all business just lay in the bank itself. "We must not incur the sluggishness of bank funds due to the operation of sideline business, nor must we neglect the business of the bank itself. The banking system in China has not gotten on the right track. … Any bank must maintain the liquidity of funds by virtue of its own technology but mustn't neglect the flexibility of funds employment although investment loan is a sideline business of our bank. In addition, there are legal restrictions on running landslide business in the banking industry around various countries, which is also witnessed by China. Therefore, in the future, all efforts of our bank primarily aim at cultivating its own credit."[99] The management goals of today, including profitability, security and liquidity, were also of concern to Chen. According to specific conditions of that time, he issued some guiding opinions. The difference lay in that the profitability that we now pay special attention to was precisely replaced by services,

---

[98]*Ibid.*, p. 200.
[99]*Ibid.*, p. 201.

and was elevated to the level of creed and mission without any changes at any time by him. It was tantamount to saying that he persisted in the principle of serving society so that he could cope with shifting events by sticking to a fundamental principle. The Shanghai Bank aimed at avoiding being bent on profits that emphasized materialism rather than spirit, so that the position of finance in the national economy would not shake. It embodied the traditional Chinese thought that a man should do what deserves to be done, symbolized exchanges of proper service to social service and it was the reason why the bank was so successful.

Chen's specific techniques for business management were as follows. Considering deposit and loans, domestic remittance and documentary bills, and foreign business, Chen proposed that "the soundness of loan is closely related to the growth of deposits."[100] If the bank wanted to resume deposit, loans and expand the service scope, it had to increase its deposits. In the same competitive environment, attracting deposits depended on the bank's efforts, that is, "the trust of customers entails prudent service and the security of deposit interests. In the inflation this time, savings of clients with fixed time deposits for a long time finally disappeared. Our bank should try to provide relief for the depositors who have trusted us for a long time so that they will not lose too much, which is in the pipeline. It is also discussed that to facilitate collection and payment and reduce work cost, the accounting department of the bank should adopt new machines as far as possible to complete procedures quickly." With regard to lending, "sometimes in the past, we couldn't see how things will develop from the first small beginnings and didn't prepare in advance. While nowadays, we must learn from the history to guide the current situation, reflect on our service, strive to understand the situation and deal with it carefully. Besides, we must ensure that the bank's credibility doesn't shake due to rumors, and then we can stabilize the foundation of the bank. ... In the future, if we hope to strengthen the bank's reputation, learning how to improve loaning skills carefully will be necessary." The post-war economic construction and changes in industrial and commercial industries were closely related to economic trends at home and abroad. "Anyone involved in loans must be clear about both domestic and overseas

---

[100]*Ibid.*, p. 202.

economic dynamics, have a deep understanding of the level of the trust in and the management methods of industrial and commercial banks, and mustn't regard hearsay as the basis for loan. … Besides, loaners ought to improve their status, as well as the intellectual level as much as possible. Moreover, special attention should be paid to research on domestic and international finance. In addition, it's not only necessary to increase the knowledge of loaners, but also to make the research results contribute to industrial and commercial business, which means advancing the business and connecting it with finance closely."[101]

Chen's thoughts on domestic remittance and documentary bills were as follows. "Although the remittance is rarely profitable, it is not excessively risky. Our bank should … contact major Chinese and foreign commercial firms, such as those that distribute kerosene, tobacco, cotton goods, fertilizers to develop domestic remittance and documentary bills. Also, it should rely on the low charge of remittance and perfect service to win the trust of customers. Such kind of service can increase deposits and also promote loans. As for remittances in two places, payables have been deposited into our bank while other dues might be deposited into the account, which will result in an increase in the bank's deposits. Another example is the documentary bills of a large amount of goods, which is the loan during the period of transport that can assist the flow of materials. This should still be an important business of our bank after the war and always be promoted."[102]

On foreign business, Chen said the following. He believed that all businesses needed to be resumed after the victory in the War of Resistance Against Japanese Aggression as foreign business had stagnated for a long time during the war. In the wake of the currency reform, as the exchange rate was expected to remain stable, attention had to be paid to foreign export documentary bills, establishment of the letter of credit and the discount of commercial papers. Predicting that the post-war domestic currency system would be stable, he proposed to subordinate buying and selling recent and the long-dated foreign exchange. As the Shanghai Bank had been establishing a reputation in America, it was expected to take on

---
[101] *Ibid.*, pp. 201–202.
[102] *Ibid.*, pp. 202–203.

more agent receipt and payment business from foreign banks in China. With the disappearance of privilege of foreign banks in China, their credit might be worse than before, and then the bank might assume greater responsibilities for foreign trade turnover.

Chen attached much importance to economic research. When deploying the post-war management guidelines, he particularly valued the experience of operating the Shanghai Bank for three decades. Chen specifically urged, "Our desire for improvement in operating technology calls for frequent observation of domestic and international economic movements and constant research in the trends of commerce, industry and finance. Based on the research results, advancing business is like sailing on the sea where you must obey instructions of the compass, and then you will be free from drifting in the sea. ... I am increasingly convinced that continuously studying economic dynamics at home and abroad is the only way to improve our bank's management standards and to eliminate future rumors. Knowing the enemy and yourself, you can fight a hundred battles and win them. Here, knowing the enemy means studying the economy while knowing yourself refers to rectifying the personnel, and this applies to each business but not just operating banks. In the future, economic relations between China and every country will be more and more closely related, so any economic changes in the world will affect both our bank's major works and sidelines. Therefore, our bank must pay special attention to economic research, and it is necessary to enhance the functions of researchers in a way that enables their direct participation in the business, so that their knowledge and practice can be combined together to achieve mutual assistance."[103] Chen not only analyzed the relationship and mutual assistance between research and business but also insightfully pointed out the role and function of research, as well as the treatment and the role of researchers.

2.3.2. Management style

According to what Chen said at different times and on various occasions, the management style of the Shanghai Bank could be simply concluded as

---

[103] *Ibid.*, p. 203.

prudent management, unremitting self-improvement, mutual assistance, investigation and research, and practicing what it preached. In short, the bank enjoyed the spirit of unremitting self-improvement.

Spirit was crucial to Chen.[104] "A man must have a spirit to do everything". He held that it was the same whether you have a server or not for a meal. Likewise, though sweeping barefoot, one still had the ability to do it, which could be "regarded as the true spirit that gave one methods to avoid being defeated."[105] In the same way, he believed that "Spirit was superior to material",[106] and advocated that "The spirit only came from hardships, and as 'enjoying pleasure is equal to drinking poisonous alcohol to commit suicide, it can't be intoxicated with'."[107] That allusion derives from *Zuo Zhuan — The First Year of the Reign of Emperor Min*, in which Guan Zhong warned that indulging in a life of pleasure and comfort was just like drinking poisonous alcohol. Unfortunately, many people did not understand this truth. Obviously, he advocated that people must have spirit and they must be well prepared to work hard to get involved in business and entrepreneurship, while comfort and pleasure could be harmful. The spirit of a country's citizen was the sign that reflected the progress or decline, success or failure of the nation. Chen reckoned that "As for world civilization, materials are important, but spirits and moralities should especially be focused on." Confronting menacing and arrogant Japanese militarism, "Chinese people have become increasingly united in recent years, which can't be rivaled by previous years … let alone their enthusiasm. Only with this spirit can we find a new path." He encouraged his fellows and expressed his feelings, "A man must be self-reliant rather

---

[104] In Li Peide's *On China's Financial Entrepreneur Spirit — With K. P. Chen as an Example*, "entrepreneurial spirit", also known as "entrepreneurial ability", is generally interpreted as taking risks and carrying out corresponding reforms for profits. Chen's entrepreneurial spirit can be divided into broad and narrow aspects. The former includes reforms and strategies for various organizations and institutions, while the latter includes opening new types of deposit services, operating foreign exchange business, introducing new-style accounting methods and training systems for the bank's staff and expanding the Shanghai Bank's business to the mainland.
[105] *Ana*, p. 36.
[106] *Ibid.*, p. 190.
[107] *Ibid.*, p. 59.

than appealing to others, and if he can work relentlessly with the spirit like a stream that never stops flowing, how will he suffer from the lack of foothold?" After the Battle of Shanghai on January 28, 1932, the loss of homes of many staff in the Shanghai Bank made them constantly frown with no interest in doing business. They kept talking about "their own affairs, or complaining about the difficulty of keeping the livelihood, or worrying about having no way to make money." On the contrary, quoting from others, Chen said that China would eventually win and the hope would exist in Asia instead of Europe after 100 years. "The civilizations of European and American countries have a heavy emphasis on materials but are too indifferent to spirit and morality, which will gradually step down like water",[108] he also said. His opinion came from the fact that international organizations had extremely greedy hearts for rights without moral restrictions. European and American countries had forgotten the ideology of Jesus, and the prevalent nationalism was too focused on individual countries' interests, which caused the global situation of that time. After the First World War, as they did not learn their lessons, the European economy was in a sluggish state in the 1930s resulting from moral decline. Chen emphasized the power and role of spirit and morality. It is also worthwhile for us to think highly of the fact that while absorbing European and American banks' methods, he did not ignore the history of China. In 1946, he commented that Americans held even stronger material desires than before, and criticized those Chinese who talked about their aspirations without actions and who seemed to have the ambition to save the nation, because they enjoyed the life of the United States after they got there, totally forgetting the sense of "propriety, justice, honesty and honor".[109] According to Chen, the Shanghai Bank "should not be afraid of competition and being busy. It would see progress and not fall behind only if the busier, the more vibrant it is. … The two regions and branches in different regions should be required to take the head office as the one to admire and follow, thus establishing the bank's solid foundation in the

---

[108] *Ibid.*, pp. 91–92.
[109] *Ibid.*, p. 217.

financial world."[110] With the experience of the War of Resistance Against Japanese Aggression, he further strengthened his convictions, "The most important meaning for life is that spirit is superior to material, which proves that it is the same case with countries and business, so in such a confronting situation nowadays, we should own the spirit of fighting just like that against the war." After careful studying, he gave a very concise and straightforward definition to the anti-war spirit: "It is nothing but loyalty to the duty and the bank's duties in wartime are not much different from usual." In general, the bank should undertake three duties: First, "it should strive to protect the fund entrusted by depositors and shareholders" and "do its utmost to ensure fund security." "As the fund is the sweat of the Chinese, if we can keep it, it will increase the strength of the country and indirectly enhance the power against the war. Therefore, the importance of this fund is above all else."[111] Second, "if possible, it should offer convenience to depositors with the purpose serving people but shouldn't make things difficult for them in case of reduced trust in itself. Nowadays, considering that under legal restrictions, depositors are very painful, we should show sympathy and provide hospitality for them, so that there will be unnecessary panic for the peace of mind." Third, the bank ought to work hard to circulate goods, so that the funds will not be sluggish, and the minimum activities needed in industry and commerce can be ensured. In order to prevent industry and commerce from "permanent sluggish, we must study wartime traffic channels and methods of safe transportation, which allows the goods intensive in war zones to circulate to the Mainland. In this way, on the one hand, accidental losses can be avoided, and on the other, industry and commerce can be promoted, thus consolidating the economic foundation in the rear." He specifically called on all the staff in the bank: "The three duties, though normal, are particularly essential in the war."[112] In fact, those three duties are the so-called payment agency, credit intermediary and financial service. At that time, because the credit creation function had not yet been established, neither did the Shanghai

---

[110]*Ibid.*, pp. 54–55.
[111]*Ibid.*, p. 190.
[112]*Ibid.*, p. 191.

Bank have the right to issue banknotes nor did the Central Bank really play its role. Therefore, it is not surprising that it was not mentioned and not been discussed.

According to Chen, "the bank used to be temperate".[113] "For future progress, our bank should adhere to this rule, gradually advancing with a method that is prudent and sound."[114] In the early 1930s, a time of crisis, China's market was unstable, and the Shanghai Bank "has always served the society except politicians and warlords with a sincere attitude, so if it can't be protected by local laws when the ransom occurs, it can close at any time and open again at the right moment."[115] Although the bank would lose interest for no bank notes issued, it could avoid risks and also reduce losses. It promoted credit to objects rather than to people, thus reducing the risk resulting from loan. It also stood out for being rarely involved in investing in real estate stocks and bonds at that time. Besides, it paid special attention to research and had a good knowledge of the managers from firms that participated in the loan market, which reduced bad debts. Moreover, the accounts taken by all institutions of the Shanghai Bank were unified and could only be dispatched by the head office. When it came to "drawing, the bank coped with it successfully each time thanks to its robust management and sound preparation".[116] As stated by Chen, "The Bank's operation is based on the protection of shareholders' capital and social deposits, adequate preparation and good application standards. Secondly, the bank must be operated in accordance with rules and assist those who have hope for development, thus improving society and reducing unemployment. The bank does not seek substantial profits but strives to make progress in order to repay the trust of the community instead. Otherwise, without setting up branches in various places, only buying and selling public debts can also support its operation."[117]

Chen's principles of sound operation were as follows. By learning from the advanced experience of foreign countries and summing up the

---

[113]*Diary*, p. 30.
[114]*Ana*, p. 16.
[115]*Ibid.*, p. 28.
[116]*Ibid.*, p. 201.
[117]*Ibid.*, p. 104.

lessons learned in China and the Shanghai Bank, the principle was embodied in the following words by Chen: "careful, earnest, thoughtful and practical". He concluded, "Major causes all arise from painstaking effort, which is, being careful, earnest, thoughtful and practical. The success depends on these words whether it was the unprecedented industrial and financial situation created by the British entrepreneurs in the 19th century or the success of Mitsui and Mitsubishi of Japan. On the contrary, the empire run by the Meiji government for decades was toppled by the Japanese warlord in no more than 4 years for acting rashly." The current situation in China needed special care. After the victory of the War of Resistance Against Japanese Aggression, he said, "In this era of great turmoil, we should be awed as if we are treading on thin ice and shouldn't make a move without the most careful thought. The inflationary situation in the past 8 years has caused the speculative atmosphere and exaggerated style in which gamblers who bet handsomely claim to be the predecessor of the era." The Shanghai Bank performed well for decades to lay a solid foundation, which entailed being careful, earnest, thoughtful and practical. "Over the past 30 years, the cooperation of my fellows, trust of the community and careful management have formed the foundation of present business. ... I am deeply aware of that all the colleagues in the Shanghai Bank are cautious and conscientious and I hope that they can take this attitude toward everything. At the same time, it's a necessary for them to be careful, earnest, thoughtful and practical to refrain from common problems of frivolity and arrogance, so that they can avoid breaking the boat on the sway of 'desire for great achievements and rash actions'."[118] Being careful, earnest, thoughtful and practical only emphasized the scientific and thoughtful attitude instead of being too cautiousness to act, and on the contrary, it advocated self-improvement, creation and pioneering.

"Deliberation can bring about new methods and the inventors of all ages, at home and abroad, come from the utmost considerations. It's fortunate that my peers are work hard for it."[119] "If they employ a new method of remittance and transfer, they can improve the current situation, handling complex things in simple ways and being busy without a

---

[118]*Ibid.*, p. 206.

[119]*Ibid.*, p. 58.

mistake, so that the work can be done within eight hours every day."[120] Chen once brought up Louis Pasteur, a Frenchman who had found the way to rule out microorganisms in wine, and Thomas Edison, an 84-year-old American electrical inventor who made materials of substitutes for rubber, to his colleagues. He said, "These two people can be taken as examples for you to constantly strive for self-improvement and in-depth research to progress with each passing day." The revival of business was illustrated by examples of the remittance fee charged by the domestic exchange department, changes in Chinese and foreign currency markets, the collection department using its notes to redeem documentary bills, and different accounts and liaisons, "and then they could become departments of real service".[121] He criticized China for people's bad habits at that time, stating that people were "irresponsible and being onlookers. Even when they want to say something, they are not willing to speak it out but make others to do it and depend on them. The reason why the Chinese lack independent spirit may be that they are used to it due to thousands of years of oppression, which is unknown."[122] As a result, he put forth that the Shanghai Bank should "cheer up with new spirit". Then, "what is new spirit? The so-called bringing about new spirit are nothing but the removal of old stains and the reform of all stale bad habits, which is also the best result. However, it's always easier to say than to do it as to comprehensively implement it, how could it be effortless? The old saying goes that the butcher who lays down his knife at once becomes a Buddha, in which the butcher's knife represents stale bad habits; if he can get rid of them, he can turn into a saint. However, we are all mortals, not the sages and immortals, and don't enjoy such attainment. Therefore, the so-called new spirit refers to that we aspire to reform bad habits and make up our minds to realize it with practical actions. Maybe we are able to reform one-10th to two-10ths of the habits in the future, but if we say it can be completely accomplished, that will be empty words ending in failure."[123] Chen was not only a successful banker with glorious ideals but also a pragmatic

---

[120]*Ibid.*, p. 57.
[121]*Ibid.*, p. 44.
[122]*Ibid.*, p. 64.
[123]*Ibid.*, p. 45.

idealist who embraced ambitious goals when facing the harsh reality. He knew how arduous the bank practice would be and how difficult the reform would be and his success lay in persistence and catering to the trend of social development and people's needs. However, due to the limited options provided for him, it took a longer while to realize the changes that he wanted to make to the old policies.

Of course, he repeatedly used service spirit, struggling spirit, new spirit, innovative spirit and work spirit to motivate his fellow staff to struggle, advance, innovate, reform and do practical things. At the end of 1931, he said at the meeting of the Shanghai Bank, "This year, influenced by various factors, all of you have worked hard to eliminate obstacles in the way in struggling spirit, and in the following year you should further do your best to resist the harsh environment. Those who score eighty points for the fighting spirit this year should work harder in the spirit of one hundred and twenty points in the next year, which can indicate the particular unity spirit of our bank. Besides, you ought to be engaged in the clarification of new methods to seek your own progress."[124] In September 1932, to comprehensively interpret the spirit of constant self-improvement, Chen first started with the three steps (founding, reform, and success) of reform of the Shanghai Bank, and summed up that "the spirit of the bank not only lies entirely in reform but also in successive reform. The spirit of creation also completely comes from reform and from continuous reform." In the end, what does it mean to be constantly striving to improve oneself? He said, "It is not surprising that one boasts the founding spirit, whereas he should have the spirit of bold reforms. That means one is supposed to reform one thing after its foundation, which will lead to success, and reform again after being successful, which will also lead to success, so founding, reform and success will run in cycles and constantly progress. That is the so-called self-improvement spirit."[125] It is known that according to Chen, the constant self-improvement spirit includes entrepreneurship, reform and success, which constitute an organic combination. He said that under the conditions of mutual support and mutual foundation, one must integrate the enterprising spirit and continuously press ahead

---

[124]*Ibid.*, p. 75.
[125]*Ibid.*, p. 114.

to ensure that the causes one engaged in, the ideals one pursued and the Shanghai Bank all made progress. Then, reform would naturally be contained, which of course, needed tireless study, concentrated research, and strive for progress in order to achieve success.[126]

Learning can be investigation (domestic and foreign, including inspection), training and reading. For different people, Chen advocated adopting different forms to teach them, but one thing was common: reading. The most important career in life is learning. If one wanted to study, one had to first read. As he said, "Of all our causes, we must give top priority to study that is based on reading. If we study, we can not only build character, improve our virtue and refine our achievements, but also inspire ourselves by melting the opinions of others. No matter which kind, knowledge all comes from reading. ... So the more books you read, the better you are. ... That means opening a book is always beneficial."[127] At the management meeting of the Shanghai Bank, he also talked about the importance of reading with himself as an example, "especially in the past months, I felt that learning was necessary to work and the source of learning is to study. I'm afraid that some of you do not have such habits. If you seldom read, you must first cultivate the habit of reading before it gradually takes effect."[128] He considered reading as very important and the understanding of the necessity of reading could be deepened in four aspects. "Provided that common folks want to broaden their vision and increase their knowledge, reading should be taken as the most important way." "Against the backdrop of global competition, it is necessary for the workers to improve their knowledge for with more knowledge, their ability to do business will be superior."[129] The trend where only the fittest can survive in natural selection of the times forced people to fight. "Reading is the only way to struggle. ... If one can preserve regardless of the bad environment, he will push forward with knowledge, which equals to the advancement of the status ladder. ... As for learning and experience, they

---

[126]*Ibid.*, p. 97.
[127]*Ibid.*, p. 100.
[128]*Ibid.*, p. 127.
[129]*Ibid.*, p. 49.

are equally significant, but experience can also be derived from learning."[130] He integrated the pursuit of learning with one's material life, family and status, and combined practical efforts and long-term interests closely to encourage young people to study. "Reading should always be the basis for it can directly increase knowledge and can improve the status indirectly."[131] Second, to gain new knowledge, one must read. "Since the current academic thinking is changing with each passing day, one can't be better than others if he lacks brilliants ideas and foresight. Therefore, study and reach in fact is the strategy to deal with social affairs, that is, people should also study the research on agricultural conditions and business status that are less relevant to banking business. It can be called as losing opportunity and having no desire for entrepreneurship in view of the fact that salespersons in present banks often take advantage of personal friendship to seek economic support rather than understanding the details thoroughly."[132] He regretted and hated that Chinese people always muddled on and did not know to introduce or embrace new methods, different from that of the English and the Germans. He also envied that those foreigners would enter school to study and seize the opportunity, so he thought it was necessary to encourage reading. "As for reading, we must pay more attention to culture. Given that mottos in respect of self-cultivation of our country mainly focus on the fact that we are not fond of wealth, we seem to have cultivated our culture with it as the basis. There is an adage goes that: 'A gentleman makes money through honorable means.' We can see that a gentleman does not necessarily love wealth but he won't take any ill-gotten gains. Though working in the Shanghai Bank can't make a fortune, you can live without any worries about problems of food and clothing."[133] "Third, for the prospect and culture cultivation instead of for the clients, you have to read." He held that "the old habits of the Chinese people are deep-seated. In terms of the staff in our bank, they are able to cope with the trends in the next five decades. However, the latecomers will be more eager to catch up quickly, making fast progress, and then we should

---

[130] *Ibid.*, p. 106.
[131] *Ibid.*, p. 64.
[132] *Ibid.*, p. 47.
[133] *Ibid.*, p. 128.

tirelessly try our best to step forward but we will still worry about being left behind, let alone not striving for progress."[134] "Lacking self-cultivation, one will directly show what he felt, like pleasure, anger, sorrow and joy, and change his facial expressions accordingly. The customer ... will be disgusted with that for taking that as intentional contempt. That is not the service philosophy of our bank."[135] "Maybe the bank would have changed the monthly salary in the future and even if there was no lack of talent, they would have only employed erudite people even at a high cost. At that time, it would have been too late to reply on the excuse of 'for the sake of living', and the bank would have been powerless to render assistance. Therefore, you can only find a way in reading and learning."[136] For the sake of order, it is necessary to study. "Coming from reading, culture brings about order and without clear order, people can't do anything. ... The so-called 'order' is not specific to oneself but also refers to the ability to say and listen to others, and the ability to make complex thing simple. For example, if someone talks with complicated words, one can inquire whether it is the case in the simplest and the most concise language and then reply in plain language, which is the order gotten from culture."[137] At the same time, work quality and efficiency can be improved.

With respect to his learning attitude, Chen abided by the Chinese tradition that one must not pretend to know what one does not know, and one should not be ashamed of what he does not know but should be ashamed of not seeking knowledge if he has the opportunity. He reminded young people that they should not be full of ambition and be arrogant. If they think that they know everything of all sorts of science because of their seemingly outstanding academic achievements and are complacent but know nothing about the ways of the world, it just exposes their empty brain, which is a morbid condition in study. With reading as a treatment, he believed that young people more than 20 years old should work hard and should not follow others' mistakes and lose time.[138] Commercial

---

[134]*Ibid.*, p. 50.
[135]*Ibid.*, p. 49.
[136]*Ibid.*, p. 50.
[137]*Ibid.*, p. 51.
[138]*Ibid.*, p. 107.

banks must take actions in concert with market conditions, and only with everything they do being commercial can they live up to the word "commerce". He said frankly, "Banking is a new business from abroad and since Sheng Xuanhuai established a bank by imitating European and American institutions, many banks have gradually been established. So far, although it enjoys a history of 34 years, discounting markets, clearing houses and banker's banks have not yet been established as for the banking group and there's no one calculating the service cost as for inner management of banks."[139] Despite the fact that banks had grown from scratch in China, their system was still not perfect and internal management was not perfect. What they still needed to do was study earnestly, improve sincerely and even designate someone to go abroad to practice on the ground and truly understand the skills.[140] In February 1946, he recalled that, three decades ago, when Western industrial civilization had just entered China, Chinese people (referring to "intellectuals with learning culture and career aspirations") "only had the ideal of saving the nation by industry with no academic research on industry, or they only had academics without skills to realize their ideals and practice their academics. At this time, my colleagues were the first to put partial Western academics into practice to the banking industry, thus creating the Shanghai Bank. Taking the lead in this industry, we created new organizations and novel methods to meet the basic need of the public, which was the reason why our bank achieved recognition and support from the community."[141] Learning and imitating still required sophisticated research that could not be swallowed in a simple way. It was necessary for the staff to study whether the society needed the Shanghai Bank and to understand its environment and social situation. They also carefully sought innovative management methods so that the bank could lead all industries, and be thoroughly known and trusted by each business and the community. Afterward, the bank could achieve its purpose through implementation of efforts.[142] "Instead of totally based on foreign approaches,

---

[139]*Historical Data*, p. 775.
[140]*Ana*, p. 216.
[141]*Ibid.*, p. 219.
[142]*Ibid.*, p. 41.

the Shanghai Bank introduced various foreign regulatory procedures and conducts for sophisticated research while selecting those that were suitable."[143] This kind of research was regarded as "the life of the Shanghai Bank", which was one of the reasons why Chen could lead the bank successfully. Rather than studying foreign banks separately from studying local incorporated banks, he incorporated them, bringing out the best in each system. While imitating European and American banks, he earnestly studied the fine tradition of the exchange shops of Chinese unincorporated banks, and by virtue of bank management experience and social relations, he conducted research first, followed by loans to industrial and commercial units gradually. Besides, at first, he reduced discount on notes and then he exempted it, as well as reducing the interest of delinquent loans to compete with unincorporated banks. The bank's branches outside Shanghai also employed local people as their managers and staff members, which could make use of the local advantages and the strong points of the unincorporated banks. As Tang Shoumin pointed out, "The knack of the bank's management lies in one word — 'learning', both from foreigners at the trade port and the unincorporated banks in the mainland."[144] "Since the Central Bank regards that I can be an example to help it correct its errors, I should also take it as a good mentor and a helpful friend",[145] he also said.

"While doing business, a better choice is to learn from European and American practice. If you hold fast to your old ways, you will not succeed. Even if you cannot set the trend, you should not be following in others' footsteps. For this reason, the development of new trends should never be ignored." "Before the occurrence of a new trend, there must be a long incubation period and once the impetus came into being, it will be giant. If you conform to the trend, you will be lucky while if you run counter to it, you will be unfortunate." In Chen's view, everything of the Shanghai Bank was still in progress, so people should study carefully and gradually improve it without any thought of being perfunctory in the future. The tide of trends cannot be reversed, nor can competitions stop. The Shanghai

---

[143] Quoted from *Modern Chinese Financial Industry Management*, People's Press, 1990, p. 145.
[144] *Historical Data*, p. 83.
[145] *Ana*, p. 43.

Bank had a long way to go for development and "to achieve success, everyone must rack his brain every day. If you figure out a way per day, you will get 365 ways per year. With half of the ways abandoned, over 180 ones will be left; with the half abandoned again, over 90 ones will be left; with the half abandoned again, over 40 ones will be left. For those who don't think and waste time, their intelligence will disappear at a fast speed."[146] He believed that the improvement of the Shanghai Bank was not just owing to him, although a man must be self-reliant and should not appeal to others. However, with the spirit like the never-ending flow, if one could try his best to work, he would not have to worry about his foothold. It was necessary that the staff of the bank should make concerted efforts, work hard and study meticulously to figure out innovative new methods. Since "I can still think", there will be nothing to worry about the novel products. According to him, if "everyone sitting here" (more than 30 people who participated in the bank's meeting at that time) thought to find a method, there would be more than 30 methods proposed. At the time of doldrums when there was not enough work for too many staff to do, he opposed passive layoffs and wage cuts. Instead, they advocated active measures such as careful training for the sake of the future. He also advocated that the staff on the one hand should contact foreigners, be extraordinarily courteous and respectful, and on the other, they should be self-employed as salespeople and try their best to drum up business. It can be widely known that everyone works with others to work for the bank, has the obligation to introduce customers, unites as one, cooperates with each other and is in high spirits, which will be beneficial to the bank's business.[147] While actively advocating the safe deposit box business of the trust department, he proposed that it could be experimented by the preserving department first and then be copied by each department. "You should find new methods to do everything because only new thought can contribute to development, otherwise you will feel bored. Each salesperson is required to provide a new method in the dining party on every Friday for a brighter future of the bank. … During the period of doldrums, everyone must work harder instead of doing no business, namely, wasting time, for

---

[146]*Ibid.*, p. 33.
[147]*Ibid.*, p. 92.

he thinks it is a time of national crisis."[148] In his diary, one day, he devoted a great deal of space to discussing self-improvement, learning and improving business principles, reforming the bank's business and working hard to implement them. He impulsively wrote, "Research is the mother of success. Studying if the community needs the Shanghai Bank requires summing up the environment of the bank and social conditions and carefully pursuing leading and novel methods of management to make sure that the bank becomes more and more important in society. … It must be based on sound brainpower and new knowledge to improve business policy, meet needs of the community and avoid being replaced by new comers. … New methods must be provided for management to meet the needs of the community. … Integrity and honesty are especially required. … You should carry out sophisticated research, study how to reform and adapt to the trend, work together to develop the bank, and constantly improve yourself. For one thing, you can form a good outlook on life; for another, you can complete missions and duties of the society."[149] Self-improvement is a spirit and Chen's adherence to and publicity of it aimed at nothing more than creating, reforming and expanding business of the Shanghai Bank, so that the bank could keep its vitality, continue to conform to the trend and lead the ethos to achieve the purpose of serving the community.

To realize that goal, Chen repeatedly promoted the spirit of mutual support for he believed that without the tenet of coordination within the country, the purpose of external services could not be realized. He said, despite the fact that people should pay much attention to advanced management and external services, there was no time to be lost for them to strengthen coordination in China. The so-called *he zuo* in Chinese can be translated as "Cooperation" in English, but what he was actually talking about was "Coordination". Coordination means when performing duties, people should coordinate with others rather than considering that the whole work has been finished just because they have done their own parts. Then, it can be described as true coordination. Taking receipt and payment of the depositing department as an example, only if they coordinate with the cashier and accounting parts can the procedure be fast with no mistakes. In a highly competitive environment, what he was afraid of was not

---

[148]*Ibid.*, p. 93.
[149]*Diary*, pp. 142–143.

competition but uncoordinated staff who could not satisfy the clients. Therefore, they could not fail to coordinate themselves and should cheer up.[150] He believed that "social principles were based on mutual assistance."[151] People who had no friends could not stand on their own. As the staff in the Shanghai Bank were in the same boat, they knew each other well, so how could they be indifferent to each other? The weekly dinner party of the bank aimed at achieving an emotional connection within the staff and showing the spirit of solidarity, too. Otherwise, if they were in a state of disunity, it would be especially inappropriate. Chen hoped that to seek the spirit of solidarity among the staff, they should start by getting to know each other, then they could make friends, and at last, they would love each other.[152] The staff could benefit from mutual assistance that arose from making friends within the Shanghai Bank and affection from friends. The spirit of mutual assistance and constant self-improvement would reinforce each other. In Chen's view, the common folks can achieve the effect of coordination only when there is a spirit of concerted support and mutual assistance. No matter if it is a government, a group or a smaller family, it cannot maintain the status quo and step forward without coordination. Moreover, coordination is not necessarily related to one's own interests. Even if it is someone you do not know or something has nothing to do with your interest, "you must try our best to do it if you are able to help. With this spirit promoted around China, it will find many ways to be prosperous and strong. … You are expected to constantly improve themselves and make concerted efforts to achieve progress in the bank's business. Those are my suggestions for you and I am looking forward to yours for our bank because drawing on the wisdom of the masses is my hope."[153] In the pursuit of setting a good example, this kind of mutual assistance expected someone to set an example to give full play to coordination, so that the spirit of self-improvement can be invigorated in the entire bank. He also exhorted his fellows, "All of you should not be tempted by the degraded environment, but should pay undivided attention to hard work. If any one of you degenerates or fails to

---

[150]*Ibid.*, p. 54, 94.
[151]*Ibid.*, p. 94.
[152]*Ibid.*, p. 58.
[153]*Ibid.*, pp. 31–32.

improve himself, he should be urged and encouraged. The colleagues are as close as brothers and family members, so anyone making a mistake deserves exhortation."[154] His good intentions and sincere feelings showed what he felt and he put his thought into practice to set an example for others, which demonstrated that what he said was by no means empty words. In 1937, he specifically advised his fellows to "exert the service in their own positions, with the view to helping each other and seeking benefits for the community and the country. Given the current situation, being dependent will not be harmless to commercial banks but will contribute to their progress instead. The key just lies in 'conducting ourselves well'."[155] After the victory of the War of Resistance Against Japanese Aggression, he predicted that China would take the road of industrialization and its international contact will increase. He thought that the Shanghai Bank ought to choose the right path to serve the community according to its own abilities and advocate industry to enrich people's wealth. The bank should also gradually expand its service from China to foreign countries, quickly make good preparation for international trade and finance and grasp the needs of the times, thus making itself an indispensable part of the nation. "If you cooperate with each other while being cautious and prudent, the bank will take root in this ever-changing world and enjoy a promising future."[156] He said that the Shanghai Bank should change its service in the light of the environment but should never change its mission and spirit, and that was feature of Chen's financial thought.

Setting oneself an example to others was Chen's demand for himself and his colleagues. In terms of reading, he said at the management meeting, "If we want to promote reading, we must first practice it; while if we want to make everyone in each department willing to read, department heads ought to make themselves as examples. Otherwise, how can reading be effective if the leaders don't do what they need others to do?"[157] That is because the power of the example is infinite and the leader's actions are the most appealing, showing the meaning of affecting others quietly. After

---

[154]*Ibid.*, p. 37.
[155]*Ibid.*, p. 185.
[156]*Ibid.*, p. 209.
[157]*Ibid.*, p. 127.

the victory of the War of Resistance Against Japanese Aggression, when formulating the post-war management policy, he once again stressed, "Especially my colleagues at the higher levels who have been working for many years must continue to play exemplary roles, be upright and selfless, persuade each other with the spirit of loyal soldiers and form the social ethos. Then there will be no limit to the bank's future."[158] It can be seen that setting oneself as an example for others was a matter of the bank's ethos. It was necessary for the leaders at high levels to make themselves examples in keeping upright, selfless and loyal if the bank wanted to seize opportunities, take its own path, unremittingly provide services for the community, improve its management standards through stable operation, reduce rumors, and maintain its business by followers. Also, all the leaders of the Shanghai Bank had to be examples for others. "For example, employees in unincorporated banks should know the market condition and bankers should know all knowledge that they ought to know, such as economics, domestic and foreign history and geography, laws, Chinese and foreign exchange, psychology, organization, management, world politics, and industrial knowledge, and then they can benefit from that."[159] He promoted travel agencies to be pioneers of banks. He required that in travel agencies, "the general manager and the receptionist should share the same value for the purpose of serving passengers. Besides, there are many opportunities for receptionists to be constantly close to passengers every day, so it's appropriate for travel agencies to be the pioneer."[160] That was also the basis for him to be the example for others and the ideological foundation of making concerted efforts with his fellows. Therefore, he mentioned, "We have enjoyed far more than ordinary people, which is given by the community, and given how generous the community is, how can we don't seek a way to reciprocate."[161] Keeping that thought in mind, he believed that there were still a lot to learn from others about the bank's business and since the bank needed improvement, he would stay alone every day to warn himself not to be complacent with any compliment. He

---

[158] *Ibid.*, p. 204.
[159] *Diary*, p. 13.
[160] *Ana*, p. 29.
[161] *Ibid.*, p. 33.

thought that it was necessary to study hard and figure out a better method to improve the bank's business.[162] Otherwise, the bank might be left behind just like a boat sailing against the current, either swimming or sinking. As mentioned earlier, he encouraged people to read, inspired them to learn and persuaded them to make progress. Besides, he guided reading, exchanged reading experience and pointed out directions by recommending new books and new articles. Moreover, he influenced and motivated the staff to invigorate their ideas in various ways such as writing or speaking, thus forming a positive atmosphere for learning in the whole bank. For example, the publication of his book *Ana* was also for people to observe, so that they would know how difficult it was to start a business and maintain the achievements, how to practice what they preached and how to carry forward established rules.[163] In January 1929, he set up the monthly magazine *Sea Light*, which was also "for comrades to communicate with each other and promote their relationships. It also published various banking knowledge, as well as words that can encourage people both mentally and physically and cultivate their characters, hoping that readers could cultivate themselves and put the knowledge into practice, which was extremely meaningful."[164] In the winter of 1932, through reforms, the magazine stood out conspicuously in the publications of the financial community. In the circular letter to the shareholders in March of the following year, Chen talked about his publication again, "Considering that the financial business is increasing and the service scope of the bank is expanding year by year, I am worried about the fact that even if you have enough experience, your knowledge is insufficient. As the world changes too fast to deal with, I established the monthly magazine *Sea Light* in the past for you to observe and learn. We are now inviting erudite scholars to engage in writing and enriching the magazine with real examples. It concerns content from the world's economy, domestic financial conditions and the bank's management policy to methods of moral cultivation and gossip at one's leisure. In general, all contents that can enrich people's knowledge, broaden their horizon and add their interests, no

---

[162]*Ibid.*, p. 33.
[163]*Ibid.*
[164]*Ibid.*, p. 99.

matter significant or trivial, will be included in the magazine. The significant content can be drawn on to make the development plan while the trivial can help his fellows improve their service spirit and form good habits."[165] The magazine aimed at spurring the staff in the Shanghai Bank to undertake their responsibilities consciously and providing them with mental nourishment to enrich their minds and freshen them up, so that they can make every effort in their positions.

Chen advocated publicity of everything, simplicity and frugality. He preached frugality from different perspectives, such as bankers, youth and the old, which was well targeted and highlighted the importance of this issue. According to him, bankers should dedicate themselves to being temperate and frugal instead of promoting luxury. It was urgent for them to be prudent ideologically, be simple and frugal in everything, seek truth from facts rather than upholding empty talks and try their best to perk up, but those could only be practiced through assistance of all the staff rather than by oneself.[166] Frugality was not only a matter of style but also the state of mind and spirit, which related to luxury, reality or even the spirit state of the whole bank, so the staff should start from coordination of their ideology, let alone impeding or delaying the business. Penetrating the bank's business, frugality must be carefully studied to produce good effects. At the beginning of 1932, he put forward that "For thrift this year, we must earnestly take practical actions to study the ways to save with the idea of thrift going before that. There is no need to seek new tools if the old one is available and we must try our best to defeat three groups including the so-called elderly gentleman, great master and young master because the first is approaching death (except seniors with the spirit of doing things), the second doesn't know the hardships, and the third is bureaucratic."[167] The maxim about frugality that "Every grain comes from hard work" was what one learned from one's teacher as young children and was a good suggestion for the youth. He talked about frugality from office stationery, and as little strokes fell great oaks, it was necessary to

---

[165]Quoted from Song Qingfang's *The First Draft of the Shanghai Bank's Twenty Years*, 6, p. 4.
[166]*Ana*, p. 66.
[167]*Ibid.*, p. 78.

pay attention to trivial things. At the dinner party on July 30, 1937, after asking the staff if they had read *Master Zhu's Homilies for Families*, he talked about what he had learned from that book. "I thought that what Master Zhu said in the book is quite useful today. The key point of the book lies in frugality, which to be specifically is that frugality can bring about self-control and then self-control brings about self-restraint, and the spirit of being strong and resolute comes from self-restraint. Besides, we should think how difficult it is to get food and clothes."[168] What he said made others see big things through small ones and checked erroneous ideas at the outset, which was not just about "frugality" but would affect the future and destiny of a person, a unit and a nation. It was neither a joke nor alarmism.

2.3.3. Personnel management

For operating and management, Chen considered personnel work of paramount importance. "All businesses with outstanding personnel will thrive and when it comes to the supersession of the old by the new, only those talented successors can maintain the prosperity of the business in the long run."[169] At the bank's meeting in 1938, Chen said affectionately, "The real strength of the bank lies in the soundness of its personnel. At the beginning, the Shanghai Bank had only a capital of 100,000 *yuan* but it had the sound personnel who make the bank strive forward to such as position today. According to my experience of more than 20 years, I am increasingly aware of the supreme significance of the sound personnel in banking. The rejuvenation of the bank in the future will just lie in improving personnel quality."[170] One can say that Chen's personnel system, including the selection, molding storage and management of talents in the Shanghai Bank, was the biggest concern for private commercial banks in China and the most elegant and successful one. In 1944, before the victory of the War of Resistance Against Japanese Aggression, he proposed early, "Everything depends on discussing personnel to be successful and the personnel need to be trained in advance to take effects. Otherwise, if you gather unprofessional

---

[168]*Ibid.*, p. 60.
[169]*Ibid.*, p. 204.
[170]*Ibid.*, p. 196.

employees, when something crops up, you can't do anything right. Since now there is a trend that time will not wait for me, if you want to be farsighted and well thoughtful, you must consider about that, and then you should make detailed plans or be well prepared."[171] Putting it more vividly and more appropriately, what he said at the bank's meeting in 1935 was, "The bank has made good preparations now and to do it in the future, money plays a 30% role while personnel plays a 70% role."[172] Anyone can use money, so it should not have been entrusted to the bank. The reason why people entrusted money to the bank is that they are able to gain interest with the money returned to them at any time. All that depends on the dedication of the bank's operators, so the most important preparation is personnel. With regard to modern knowledge and banking experience, specialized talents are essential, whereas with managerial talents in various fields, the same thing can be done well. "However, the Chinese were unable to manage banks, thus causing the aggression and persecution of invaders."[173] After the victory of the War of Resistance Against Japanese Aggression, the biggest difficulty for the Shanghai Bank was nothing but the lack of talents and it was the key to development. "Factors of ups and downs of a group are complicated but the key one is personnel. With talents, a laggard group will certainly flourish but without personnel, even a thriving group will certainly decline." At that time, what the Shanghai Bank lacked was not internships for daily business but some leaders who could "recognize the times with adaptable ability and it was really urgent for the bank to cultivate this kind of talents. In other words, the needs of society have changed with the times, but most of the people left their ideas and styles behind. If we are out of touch with the trend, we will finally be eliminated by it. That is what I worry about most."[174] "Wheels of history are rolling forward, if we can't make clear of the situation, find the target, invite the participation of insightful people, work hard to make strategies, cultivate talents, endeavor to catch up with the forerunners, we will be eliminated by the trend sooner or later." Chen's anxiety was due to his sense of responsibility.

---

[171]*Ibid.*, p. 199.
[172]*Ibid.*, p. 164.
[173]*Ibid.*, p. 59.
[174]*Ibid.*, p. 218.

The real power of personnel and talent lay in a sound personnel system. "We must try hard to improve the personnel system." "In the future, the personnel of the bank must be disciplined and law-abiding, correct their shortcomings, but they shouldn't be dispirited. It is extremely necessary to make sure that fraud will no longer occur."[175] In order to achieve this goal, Chen believed that it was needed to intensify training, manage the bank strictly and order the staff to learn as much as they could, which also showed that a gentlemen would care for others with virtue.[176]

With regard to management, it was required to rectify the discipline. For example, the attendance work not only needed the attendance book managed by the personnel department but also the department's cooperation with others to inspect the staff and particularly keep fraud in check. The most important way to save expenses of the bank was to increase the efficiency of the staff and, particularly, cultivate their spirit of hard work and self-motivation. "For instance, if the waiter who takes charge of cleaning the bank buys snacks for his colleagues, he will violate the discipline and that behavior must be rectified. Considering the bank's future environment, I am not afraid that there will be losses or nothing to do but the staff may lack spirit, knowledge, experience and cultivation. As much distress regenerates a nation, in such a hard time, I hope that all of you will work hard spiritedly to build a wall of iron and steel to accomplish the mission of nation rejuvenation in the future."[177] In brief, one must strictly observe discipline, cheer up, rectify the bank's style, follow the rules, be responsible for one's own duties and ensure that everyone can be able to preserve their moral integrity when the bank is in a difficult environment. In 1935, before the war, he prepared for the personnel work, demanding that it should be made for the general situation at any time and for specific

---

[175]*Ibid.*, p. 197.

[176]Therefore, his assistant, Wu Kejia, who was responsible for the personnel affairs, summed up the two major tasks of the personnel department. One was to meet the needs of the present and the other was to prepare for the future. There were four tasks, including dispatch and assignment, employment, reconciling emotions and implementing discipline, which also paid great attention to welfare (health, saving pension, etc.), so that the staff of the Shanghai Bank would work hard at ease and cooperate with each other, which in fact were the driving force for the bank's development.

[177]*Ana*, p. 197.

circumstances in the light of the situation at that time, especially for specific items needing close attention. There were three preparations for the big circle, including trying one's best with integrity, getting rid of bad, outstanding debts and avoiding fraud. There were also three preparations for the small circle, which were being extremely calm and cautious, cutting expenses and collecting bad debts. Trying one's best with integrity meant that "All responsible people should be courteous and honest and dedicate themselves to the Shanghai Bank instead of taking advantage of their positions to seek personal gains." The bank's rapid development had made them confident, which was really a comfort for him. Next was getting rid of bad debts. For loan lenders, "The debt should be guaranteed with its recovery. … The highest principle of banking is that loaning can get rid of bad debts. If you suffer from bad habits, you have to admit that some people will brew up wicked plots, which needs our endeavor to improve."[178] The occurrence of bad debts was related to the downturn of the environment, and the business preparations accumulated over the past years by the bank were enough to offset bad debts. It was only one aspect of the problem, but it was equal to giving rise to bad debts and abandoning the highest operating principle. Therefore, one should do the utmost and managers should exert their wisdom and talents to plug the leaks, and defend desperately, so as to ensure that the losses are minimized. Fraud was not just a matter of money loss but also what influenced a bank's credibility that could not be recovered in a short period. With painstaking thinking, one should pay close attention to the absolute prevention of fraud. The staff's being extremely calm in face of business affairs comes from customers' trust in the bank and they must not express irresponsible remarks about unidentified things. It was not worthwhile to worry about rumors from outsiders but those from the bank's staff who do not know the truth but create lies. If the rumor is from the staff, everyone will listen to it with all his ears, so in this case, the staff members "can't be too cautious in order to avoid all sorts of doubting behaviors. … That means the staff should be trusted through their words and attitude by the clients. Assuming that all members can deal with that perfectly, they will become the source of trust, and then there will be no need to worry about rumors".

---

[178]*Ibid.*, pp. 164–165.

Next was trying to cut expenses. People are supposed to be able to live in bad days as well as good days and know when to advance or retreat, so that they can deal with incidents. There must be a spirit of cost-saving in order to be able to save money. Next was trying to collect bad or outstanding debts because everybody knows that "tightening loaning is enough to reduce deposits". "When others are tightening loaning but I'm not, it will inevitably lead to the lack of deposit security while when others are collecting loans but I'm not, the loans will necessarily be lost." Therefore, he believed that "it is necessary to collect loans early so as to increase the security of deposits". While facing difficulties and environmental hardships, "you should have a spirit of preparation and research in particular, think carefully before you act and adapt yourself to the changing circumstances, so that you are able to cope with everything successfully."[179]

"It's particularly hard to be bankers because they must not only possess the knowledge about astronomy and geography, but also coordinate with people." This is Chen's only basic requirement for bankers. Observing the astronomical phenomenon enabled bankers to directly survey the agricultural harvest and indirectly predict the market's development and financial conditions. "It's necessary to know geology because, given the different provinces and regions in China, production, demand and transportation of agriculture and industry can't be studied separately to formulate business principles. Besides, bankers have to pay special attention to price fluctuations in the market, in order to temporarily determine the deduction standard of loans." Coordination refers to "the trade situation of each business and individual economic condition, credit history and current situation, which originally should be investigated practically. In particular, getting in touch with friends and dealing with difficulties can't be achieved without coordination". Therefore, "nowadays, only bankers who do possess the knowledge and ability will be perfectly qualified for this job."[180] It may be difficult to require the same person to conform to 3 standards but if the work is divided to be finished through cooperation in a way that "gathers and consolidates people's advantages, it won't be difficult anymore. If you perform your own

---

[179]*Ibid.*
[180]*Ibid.*, p. 101.

function and accomplish your duties without mistakes or delay, and affairs of the whole bank will be free from mistakes and delay. Besides, studying the work of each person to attain its improvement and development plan, we will be able to improve the overall business of the bank."[181] That was no nonsense, nor was it dumb talk of the learned. It was indeed a summary of Chen's experience, and one of his important insights was that the integrated individuals could form collective intelligence and wisdom to exert their maximum energy. After reading the previous year's business report of the Bank of China in 1933, he sighed, "It was easy to be a banker in the past but it is not easy now." In the past, bankers only needed to have common sense or they just needed to behave properly and carefully and then they would not necessarily cause troubles. Different from the past, the bankers must also have a precise understanding of relevant banking affairs and even be able to participate in the discussion about economy and politics or know things besides their own business. "What a banker needs to know should cover everything."[182] At the dinner party of the bank's staff, he also said, "Bankers should dedicate themselves to being temperate and frugal instead of promoting luxury. It was urgent for them to be prudent ideologically, be simple and frugal in everything, and seek truth from facts rather than upholding empty talks and try their best to perk up, but those could only be practiced through assistance of all the staff rather than by somebody oneself."[183] Since Chen determined to regard service as his objective, he had to study culture. He contributed to civilization either by writing to spread knowledge or by introducing foreign books, machines and various good methods. "Accordingly, bankers are required to shoulder the obligation of introducing culture besides loaning to assist the community."[184] The prerequisites for the quality of bankers were precisely what the modern society demanded from leading figures in the banking sector. It also reflected the fact that the special status and the role of banks in society, economy and the market had witnessed great changes, not

---

[181]*Ibid.*, pp. 101–102.
[182]*Ibid.*, p. 130.
[183]*Ibid.*, p. 66.
[184]*Ibid.*, p. 112.

merely in the intermediary but also in the omnipotent monopolist and the hub of national economy.

The bank's requirements for the quality of talents determined its success. The banker should serve the customers with a benign countenance to win their sympathy; otherwise, if he is arrogant or inattentive, the customer will hesitate and repel the bank.[185] It is mentioned here that the first impression is very important, but it is not enough because credit is the first priority of the bank. Therefore, "only sound talents can develop. The sound talents enjoy five elements: the first is faithfulness and reliability, the second is progress, the third is skill, the fourth is being able to assist the bank's development, and the fifth is being able to focus on bank affairs. My colleagues with these five elements are the sound talents of the bank."[186] For the Shanghai Bank, being faithful to one's duties was a necessary condition, an essential spirit for one to do business and the basis for its revival in the future. To follow the trends and stand undefeated in the competition, one should make progress in the spirit of self-improvement, perseverance, being enterprising and being unwilling to fall behind. Skills were what one specializes in, and as the trend evolves, one should keep up with the situation and master the most advanced ones so that one can lead. Based on the first three items, the staff should play their due role in their own positions, which will undoubtedly contribute to the Shanghai Bank's development. In addition, it was necessary for one to concentrate on the bank's business. It seems that reversing the order of the fourth and the fifth elements is more logical.

In terms of talent cultivation, Chen stressed that the Shanghai Bank should first identify the way to go, make sure that the staff unite as one and keep the practical and hardworking spirit, which helped it pull through several difficult periods and gain such a foothold. "The bad habits cultivated by the business community during the War of Resistance Against Japanese Aggression are eroding the Shanghai Bank, so if we don't seek remedies as soon as possible, I'm afraid that the cause of our hard work for 30 years may be put off in 2 or 3 years. The key is talent and the

---

[185]*Ibid.*, p. 47.
[186]*Ibid.*, p. 193.

biggest crisis in our bank is the lack of internal talents."[187] However, facing three major trends (popular welfare principles, planned control policies and industrial production methods) and the new situation formed by the new scholars (intellectuals with academic cultivation and enterprising aspirations), he instructed the bank's staff, "You should be foresighted and brave enough to admit that the bank is decadent, and then you will earnestly desire to vitalize it."[188] The basic principle was the three attitudes of the staff toward conducting themselves and doing things and there was an internal "soul launching office", which played the role of eliminating bad attitudes. In addition, the education plan was the top priority of the bank at that time. Specifically, it should establish a school of economics and "studiously cultivate a group of thinkers and industrialists who will reform free enterprises, correcting mistakes originating from the past of the capitalists. While at the same time, by virtue of its independent status and automatic functions, the school can continue to exert our great and necessary functions in the mainstream of the control system in China's future."[189] He adhered to the capitalist path for private enterprises, but opposed oppression, looting and deprivation from outside. He asked for independence, implementing a welfare economy system, supported the dominant status of control economy and pursued the freedom of innovation. The contradictions and conflicts between his ideology and practice just reflected the state and characteristics of Chinese national capitalism.

At a dinner party with his fellows on December 26, 1930 in Tianjin, Chen publicly announced that he had decided to increase the capital by another 2.5 million *yuan*, with a total of 5 million *yuan*. The original shareholders could subscribe half of the new shares with another half for the bank's staff. "It aims at tightening the relationship between the bank and its staff and encouraging the staff to do things in a straightforward manner," which indicates the meaning of the bank's slogan, "The bank is me and I am the bank."[190] At a tea party in Wuhan with his fellows in the following year, he made a further announcement. He said, "Making all of the staff

---

[187] *Ibid.*, p. 218.
[188] *Ibid.*, p. 220.
[189] *Ibid.*, p. 221.
[190] *Ibid.*, pp. 26–27.

shareholders and implementing labor-management cooperation, the strength of unity will be increasingly consolidated."[191] In the opening speech of the training class, he asked each one to "follow the banks to serve the country with the determination that 'The bank is me and I am the bank' kept in mind. ... It is definitely not allowed that after you are employed by the Shanghai bank, you don't think about progress anymore, believing that since you have already gotten a job, you can feed yourself without hard working and muddle on as for studying and doing things."[192] To reflect the notion "The bank is me and I am the bank", the Shanghai Bank decided to adopt a shareholding system for its staff, "to achieve the goal of all employees being shareholders and implementing labor–management cooperation. We hope that the spirit of solidarity between the two parties will be more strengthened". Then, the staff would be shareholders, so that each member will possess the idea that "the bank is me and while I am serving the bank, I'm also serving myself and the community. Therefore, the purpose of cooperation can be achieved to assist domestic industry and commerce and develop international trade."[193] While formulating the management policy after the victory of the War of Resistance Against Japanese Aggression, he put forward that "In the future, hoping to make progress in the Bank's business, we must take the reinforcement of personnel training as our top priority. The bank must appropriately protect the staff's life as their welfare is the welfare of the Bank, too. While for all of the Bank's business, you must do your utmost as the future of the bank is also the future you. Integrating the bank with yourself may benefit you both privately and publicly."[194] It was a truly rare and lovely to combine the Shanghai Bank with its staff, the big family with the small family, the greater self with the individual, and integrate them into one in order to optimize the bank's performance. The labor–management cooperation and the staff's being shareholders were specific means and different steps for Chen to realize his ideal.

As for Chen's specific ideas on talent cultivation, research, etc., we will not go into details here.

---

[191] *Ibid.*, p. 38.
[192] *Ibid.*, p. 127.
[193] *Diary*, p. 138.
[194] *Ana*, p. 204.

3. The financial thought of Ma Yinchu

Ma Yinchu (1882–1982), courtesy name Yuanshan, was from Shengxian County, Zhejiang Province. He was China's first overseas scholar specializing in economics, and also a renowned economist, demographer and educator at home and abroad. He graduated from Peiyang University in 1906 and studied in the United States. He received a master's degree in economics from Yale University and a doctorate in economics and philosophy from Columbia University. After returning to China in 1915, he taught at Peking University, Hangzhou Finance School, Shanghai Jiaotong University, Central University, Soochow University, Zhejiang University and the Business School of Chongqing University. He was an adviser and general secretary of the Bank of China, President of China Economics Society, Zhejiang Provincial Government member and Chairman of Finance Committee, member of National Anti-smoking Commission, Legislative member of National Government, Chairman of Finance Committee of Legislative Yuan and Chairman of Economic Committee. He later joined the Democratic Alliance. He was aggressive, progressive and fearless, publicly attacking the four families and supporting the patriotic student movement. Imprisoned by the Kuomintang government in December 1940, he was freed in the winter of 1944 and later taught at Chongqing University, Shanghai Chinese Vocational School and Shanghai Institute of Commerce and Industry, and was also a member of the academic deliberation Committee of the Ministry of Education. As an academician of the Academia Sinica, he took part in politics in Beijing in the first half of 1949 through the Northeast. After the founding of the people's Republic of China, he was first deputy director of the Finance and Economic Committee of the Administrative Council, vice chairman of the military and political Commission of East China, and then president of Zhejiang University and Peking University, standing Committee of the National People's Congress, standing Committee of the National Committee of the Chinese People's Political Consultative Conference and standing Committee of the Bank of China. In 1960, he was criticized for publishing the New Population Theory and was forced to leave Peking University. Nine years later, he was rehabilitated. In 1980, he served as Honorary President of the China Population Society. His major works include *Ma Yinchu Speech Collection, Ma Yinchu Economic Proceedings, Wartime Economic Proceedings, Foreign Exchange of China, Bank of China, China's Economic Restructuring, China's New Financial Policy, New Currency Theory, Introduction to Economics, My Economic Theory, Philosophy, Thought and Political Stand* and more. *The Complete Works of Ma Yinchu* published by Zhejiang People's Publishing House is widely read in the world even today.

In the 1920s, he taught courses in applied economics, such as banking, insurance, and exchange studies, at Peking University. He often gave speeches and discussed issues with his audience. At a time when people generally paid little attention to economic problems, he used short articles to present his ideas instead of lengthy books;[195] considering that "this is the first time to study books about exchange in China and abroad, businessmen and students did not know the wonders of it. In fact, China and foreign exchange have countless mysteries, even those who are proficient in the money industry and banking do not know their essence."[196] Therefore, he used the convenience of being a consultant of Zhejiang Industrial Bank to collect information. In 1925, he wrote the book *Foreign Exchange of China*, introducing the basic knowledge and methods of international exchange between China and foreign countries. For the same purpose, he believed that the importance of banks to society is like that of the human body. To dissect, it is necessary to construct the structure, and it is imperative for the enterprise to understand the business of the bank. Moreover, banks are particularly closely related to finance. To understand China's finance, it was required to understand the principles of China's banking industry. Considering that China's economic departments of domestic universities and business specialties of business schools were setting up banking studies, the selected textbooks were all from the West with no Chinese input. However, banking studies "should discuss the facts of the country and introduce examples from the country so that both theory and practice can be involved." Only then can domestic students "not only acquire a kind of knowledge about the basic

---

[195] *Complete Works of Ma Yinchu*, vol. 13, Zhejiang People's Publishing House, 1999, p. 2.
[196] *The Bank of China*, Commercial Press, December 1934, p. 1.

principles, that is, the environment and relation of the basic theory, but also have a glimpse of it."[197] In a strong sense of mission, a sense of responsibility in 1929, he published the *Theory of the Bank of China*. Based on the principles of banking and China's national conditions, this paper probes into the essence, function, type, specific work of banking business as well as the financial system and shortcomings of China, the environment and relationship from which it comes into being, the influencing factors and the causes of underdevelopment. The second edition was published in 1934 because of "(1) the implementation of the abolition of the two reforms, (2) the emergence of the joint preparatory system of the Shanghai China Bank, (3) the creation of the clearing house, all of which are of great importance." "If you are wealthy, you will change. In addition, there are many reforms in the central bank, but the financial system is still negotiable."[198] Four new chapters were added, namely, *Abolishing the Two Reforms, Joint Preparation, Exchange of Notes* and *China's Financial System and Its Shortcomings* as well as a brief rectification of *Central Bank*. It was Ma's consistent thought to compile textbooks that suited China's national conditions. In August 1948, the preface of the Business Edition of the *University Series Finance and Chinese Fiscal-Theory and Reality* continued to elaborate this view. "The foreign language books are written according to the actual situation of the foreign country, the social environment, and the historical background, and are used in Chinese universities. It is not easy for students to comprehend, and there are great abuses." Ma also compared the Chinese and American banking businesses. As an example, the United States had two parts: the collection and payment courses. In China, regardless of the deposit or payment procedures, it was classified as a cashier. In the United States, there was only one formality, and in China it was divided into two formalities. There were more people in the bank, and customers had to wait for a long time. If there was a need to divide into two formalities, it was attributed to the role of the system and the balance. "To make two jobs, that is, two formalities, under such circumstances we can prevent fraud. The intention is good. This is beyond doubt. The national

---

[197]*Ibid.*, p. 2.
[198]*The Bank of China*, Commercial Press, December 1934, p. 1.

conditions are like this. The China Economic Transformation of 1934 and the New Financial Policy of China of 1936 are related articles. The former answers the question of 'how to produce various products', that's the economic aspects of production. The latter answers the currency problem in Chinese production and the currency as the payment instrument, that is, the exchange medium of the total products purchased by the society ('Easy')." During the War of Resistance Against Japanese Aggression, he published an economic collection that advocated a stable currency and opposed hyperinflation. He emphasized that the wartime currency should remain independent. He believed that China's War of Resistance was military on the one hand and economic on the other, that is, in addition to military wars, there were also currency wars. Moreover, he believed that China's participation in the Yen Group was equal to self-investment. In 1944, New Theory of Currency was released. He focused on the theoretical basis for China's consolidation of currency in the future and made a new summary of the evolution of currency systems and the evolution of currency theory after World War I. From the two aspects of theory and policy, that paper discussed all kinds of adjustments of currency in various countries, including methods and steps, comparing advantages and disadvantages for China's postwar adjustment of currency system advice. After the victory of the War of Resistance against Japan, he opposed the civil war and inflation, urging the levying of property and capital taxes, and he criticized Jiang Jieshi as a "vacuum tube". "The Chinese people must struggle with imperialism and feudal forces in the study of economics. We must fight with bureaucratic capital," and "the sound economic construction must take the suppression of civil war as a prerequisite," he said.

After the founding of New China, he enthusiastically praised the superiority of the socialist system and the tremendous achievements of economic construction. He discussed the essence and harm of inflation with a rigorous and scientific attitude, the characteristics and superiority of the new China's financial system. He conducted in-depth discussions on various aspects of the national economy, various sectors, regions, fiscal balance, price stability and made constructive comments. In 1955, he published *The Characteristics and Superiority of the New China's Monetary System*. In 1956, he published *Contacting China's Reality to*

Talk about the Theory of Comprehensive Balance and the Law of Proportional Development. In 1957, he published *Contacting the Reality* and *The Theory of Comprehensive Balance and the Law of Proportional Development and the Rise of Prices of Two Different Natures*. In 1958, he published important theories such as *My Economic Theory of Philosophy and Political Position*.

Ma's economic theory was based on the Western countries, but he focused on comparison. He compared the differences and similarities of the currency system, financial system and policies of Britain, the United States, Germany, France and Japan. At the same time, he compared the West with China, Chinese tradition and modernity. He did a specific analysis. He neither plagiarized nor maintained his prejudice by emphasizing particularity. This is worthy of our full affirmation and serious study.

Ma Yinchu's financial thought in the old China period covered his views on old China's monetary theory, credit system theory, banking theory, financial market theory, foreign exchange theory and the use of foreign capital. The following is only a brief and preliminary introduction.

3.1. Monetary theory

Ma witnessed different periods of the Beiyang government and the Kuomintang government. The Kuomintang government has also experienced the reform of the currency system before the war (the two stages of the abolition of the yuan and the legal currency policy) and the maintenance of the legal currency during the war. Later, a fight against counterfeit currency took place. Afterward, there was the process of sorting out the legal currency and issuing a voucher for gold after the victory of the War of Resistance Against Japanese Aggression. Therefore, Ma Yinchu's monetary theory can be divided into three periods: the 1920s, 1930s and 1940s. The first phase of the discussion focuses on the first volume of *Ma Yinchu Lectures* and *Economic Papers*. The masterpieces of the second phase are *China's Economic Transformation*, *China's New Financial Policy* and *Wartime Economics Collection*. The masterpiece of the third stage is *New Theory of Currency* and *Introduction to Economics*. It is described as follows.

In the 1920s, Ma focused on the reform of China's currency system. He realized that "the reform of the currency system is a fundamental problem, without which there is no hope of commercial development."[199] "If the currency system were to be reformed, bank problems can also be solved, exchange is also easy to do."[200] To reform, scholars and practitioners must sit together and study each other in order to achieve twice the result with half the effort. One should study carefully, proceed with caution and carry out reforms before one begins to do so. He cited two foreign experts coming to China as an example to illustrate the different ideas and practices, the final results of which were completely different. Jenks, an American, had a Ph.D. in economics. When he came to China, he preached the false gold standard, used gold for external purposes and used silver locally. However, he did not understand the situation in China and thought that India was good at using the virtual gold standard. However, he did not think that only India could use the virtual gold standard. Chinese people used silver, and silver dollars could be seen everywhere. Therefore, China had to unify the currency system first, and then carry out the virtual gold standard. Adams, a foreign expert who studied China's unified accounting system, followed another route. He first invited those accountants of each system to discuss the issue, including the German system presenting the northern section at that time; the British system in the southern section, the Belgian system of Beijing and Han Road and the French system of Zhengtai Road. After a year of planning, China's accounting law was unified.

China's currency system was not perfect. According to Ma's analysis, there are three reasons: The first was "the investment cause of the bank notes in Beijing is the most beneficial."[201] The Ministry of Communications and the Ministry of Finance were two departments of the same government, and they were in conflict with each other. The second was that the bank note also had done a bad job in bookkeeping, which had a great impact. The price of Beijing Banknotes rose and fell, and foreign currency

---

[199] *Collected Lectures of Ma Yinchu*, vol. 1, Commercial Press, 1924, p. 18. Hereinafter referred to as *Collected Lectures*.
[200] *Collected Lectures*, vol. 1, p. 15.
[201] *Ibid.*, p. 18.

and Beijing Banknotes could not be combined at the time of bookkeeping. The total number after the merger was not certain. The bookkeeping needed to be redone, which was neither economical nor appropriate.[202] Third, the use of silver was not convenient. Silver was generally divided into foreign currency and silver. The inconveniences of foreign currency include the following: First, foreign currency is not uniform, there is no unified bank, the value of foreign currency is not fixed, moving up and down; the higher its value, the cheaper it is and the lower the price, the more the money is worth. When you pay, you can always earn a few cents. Second, the exchange of cash is inevitable. The day of the rule is not cancelled, and the foreign currency cannot be cancelled one day. Banks will also suffer extreme pain. Third, it is not convenient to count. The goods are made of silver and can be used in foreign currency. Two different things cannot be added together. Fourth, the adjustment is inconvenient. The amount of money owed by different regions can be offset by each other. No one wants to do this. Both are due to the differences between foreign currency and silver. Fifth, the calculation is inconvenient. The market price is changing every day, and there is no way to go ahead. "How to calculate the cost! The calculation is probably wrong, and it needs to be reviewed. It is troublesome to review. So the currency system is not perfect, time, labor and energy are wasted, which is very uneconomical."[203] Fourth, Chinese use silver, foreigners use gold, and the change is big. The government borrows foreign debt. If the value of silver is lowered, the value of gold rises and the government will lose money. Then, the value of silver was high; the value of gold was low, under such circumstances speculative things happened.[204]

After analyzing the reasons for the currency disorder, Ma believed that there were roughly the following reasons: First, the silver dollar was not uniform. The color and weight of various silver *yuan* were different from factory to factory. The price was uncertain and fluctuating. Several mints made a lot of coins, and there was no standard, which was getting worse. Second, money cannot be freely cast. Money supply and demand were not

---

[202]*Ibid.*, p. 24.
[203]*Ibid.*, p. 32.
[204]*Ibid.*, p. 33.

compatible. If one can cast freely, all kinds of disorders can be eradicated. The price of foreign currency was variable, and it was necessary to fold it every day. Foreigners used the rules as a standard for business accounting, as the standard currency. Different accounting banks had been born in various places, such as the Guiyuan of Shanghai, Hanghua of Tianjin, the Public Funds of Beijing and the Foreignization of Wuhan. He believed that in order for foreigners not to adopt the regulations, the price of the silver dollar had to be stabilized. However, there were no ups and downs and the non-performance of the national currency regulations allowed the people to freely cast. According to his opinion, China did not have a local currency at the time. Because the price of the local currency was certain, it could not rise or fall. The price fluctuations were on goods rather than currencies. However, by only paying attention to coins and setting the banknotes while disregarding other issues one cannot solve the problems. At that time, the banknotes were officially issued (such as Hubei tickets, the official documents of the three provinces) and privately issued (bank exchange vouchers). The former was already indiscriminate, and it was still in full swing. The latter had gone to extremes. There were many different types and a wide variety of names. The government could not ban any of them, and the bank guild had no right to interfere. In the long run, it must be the same. To unify the currency, one must implement free casting, especially the paper money and the mints in the provinces. So, he warned, "If the Chinese government does not quickly organize the currency system, unify the currency, adopt the gold standard system, then when speculation is innocent, panic is endless." Finishing the currency system, he believed that the procedures were complex and one needed to achieve it on a step by step basis. The first step was to take back the indiscriminate banknotes in each province; the second step was to unify the various foreign currency markets; the third step was to abolish the Shanghai exchange money; the fourth step was to open the Shanghai Mint and build more foreign currency. In the fifth step, there were more foreign currencies. The regulations were to be abolished. On the contrary, outsiders would be asked to use foreign currency. After the sixth step of Shanghai abolishing silver, others would follow. The reform was introduced and the foreign currency was changed. In the seventh step, the currency system was unified, so the silver standard was changed to the gold standard.

At that time, the Association of Banks advocated the use of silver coins and foreign currencies. The Money Industry Association did not approve of this claim. Ma believed that it was not against the use of both, but rather that it was not feasible. Huashang Bank was powerful, but it was not as good as other banks. Foreign businessmen manipulated China's trade power and foreign banks had deposits. Mainland businessmen and banks had business dealings. Huashang Bank had no support, so the bank agreed to use foreign currency and silver coins, and the foreign bank customs were also to be checked. How was one to solve this problem? Instead of solving it, it was better to implement free casting in a straightforward manner and solve the problem fundamentally.

Some people argued that China should go through the gold exchange standard and then enter the gold standard. However, Ma believed that the gold standard must be unified before the implementation of the gold exchange standard. At that time, the silver standard was very complicated (names, scales and fine colors were extremely inconsistent). If the gold exchange rate was not used in advance, the gold standard would be added to the silver standard and financial disorders would intensify. Moreover, Chinese law was not strict. The police were not working. Private casting institutions were not easy to crack. This was the first point. Second, most of the gold was prepared to be kept abroad. Once there was a contradiction between China and foreign countries, whether it was possible to transfer money back to China was a problem. In the event that other countries did not have a uniform legal price for gold and silver, this system had no meaning. Third, the reserve fund was divided into six or seven countries, and the establishment of the exchange institution was not enough to win trust. If one hired an outsider, it was tantamount to asking for trouble. Fourth, most Chinese workers did not have a concept of exchange. Under the virtual gold standard system, the silver dollar was never handed over to the government at a statutory price, and the light silver coin was exchanged.

Some people advocated changing the gold standard from the customs side in order to determine the external debt. Then, the remaining plan should be implemented. Ma Ze pointed out, "Why the silver standard is not unified? Because the customs cannot switch to gold goods." Since the loss of the government caused objections and complaints from the outsiders, the standard was uncertain, with virtual and real distortion, and investigation was difficult. Violation of economic principles ("rich people pay more taxes, but now less, the financial resources should pay less, but now more") thus gave profiteers a lot of chances. The banking sector advocated the abolition of the rules with freed casting. Ma believed that this view was unreasonable and that people had forgotten that the rules were unchanged. The removal of the regulations will not fix the value of the silver dollar. Therefore, free casting had to be carried out first and then the rule will be eliminated by itself. Therefore, Ma proposed a method of unifying silver coins in three steps: waste dual-use *yuan*, unified mint and free casting ("the local currency is freely cast by the people, and the coin is cast by the government").

It was difficult and dangerous for China to issue banknotes at the time. Without an issuance system, the right to issue banknotes was easy to obtain. There were many laws and regulations, and there were no legal restrictions. China's banking business was not developed, there was no discount, deposits were only limited by current money, and all banks were trying hard to find a way to exercise distribution rights. The banknotes were naturally increasing in number, and the danger of banknotes was gradually increasing. There were many reasons for the outside world to make banknotes more difficult and dangerous. First, they discussed with banks and exporters to obtain benefits. In the case of a sudden run, the bank would close down. Second, the traffic was inconvenient, and it was impossible to quickly gather the necessary response. Third, the location of the mint was not good. Fourth, the circulation was limited to the prosperous business district, and the bank could not be slow. Fifth, it was customary to use silver, and it was difficult to issue banknotes. Sixth, the reserves were excessive, while the funds were stagnant, and they were not developed. The seventh point was that merchants were used to doing tricks. They did not talk about morality or hire talent. The eighth point was that the situation was turbulent. Therefore, Ma came to the conclusion that it was necessary to take five powerful measures, such as "stretching the power of the national currency and abolishing the silver".

Ma said that there were three ways for the government to raise funds — through tax increases, debt collection and banknotes. The United States used the first and second methods. The UK did not adopt the third method. Germany, France and Russia adopted the second and third methods. In China, the first and second methods were not used, but the third method was adopted. "Virtually, the third seems to be different from the first one, but once researched, the two are exactly the same. That is, banknotes are a substitute for taxation. So we call it indirect taxation; but the drawbacks of indirect taxation It is much larger than direct taxation." The government had various interests in replacing banknotes with paper money. Banknotes were easy to popularize and the issuance procedures were simple. The people did not feel that they were suffering, and the government was not fully responsible. However, in terms of the people, the harm was greater than tax. "Indiscriminately issuing banknotes will inevitably expel cash and silver outside the circulation market, causing expensive prices, commercial and people's livelihood, and both suffer." In the case of warlords, the issuance of public debt was not the general trend and the profits were low. The issuance of banknotes was a trend and a high profit. The warlords knew that these principles were bold. As a result, provinces set up provincial banks to issue banknotes. Therefore, warlords also ran banks, and banks were the source of financing. In fact, it was a transaction in which paper money was exchanged for goods, not foreign currency. Commercial banks were truly at a loss, and their finances were mixed. "I advocate the implementation of the policy of not converting banknotes." Drawing on foreign history, "nearly no country is not affected. And this impact involves 100 years. Once implemented, it is not something that reforms can change in decades." If one took the UK with the most developed banking system as an example, the finances were not confused. The most important business item of the bank was discounted promissory notes. The more prosperous the business, the more positive the bank was to exchange cash. Bank deposits increased one after another, and there were no concerns. Therefore, the financial sector was stable and the industry was settled. In comparison, the fundamental weakness of the Bank of France lay in the government's financial constraints, in the face of bad luck and poverty. The issuance of banknotes was not due to commodity trading, but due to the government purchasing military supplies. Therefore, all kinds of dangers were revealed one after another, and the financial industry was born with indiscriminately issued banknotes, banknotes falling in price, prices increasing, people's living standards suddenly decreasing and workers living a hard life. The number of strikes and competition for assets increased. Speculative flight took place, the foreign exchange price was up and down, the business was stagnant, the market was not declining, the family was defeated and the capitalists (unwilling) invested. Productivity was getting worse. The people were weak and there was national financial embarrassment. It was seen that "China's abuse of banknotes is not only enough to disrupt finance, but also bring disaster to the society. Destroy the government's credit and trap the state property in bankruptcy. Such a plan is too crazy." The rescue strategy was no better than that of the Bank of England. It was a matter of the financial industry issuing banknotes and the government not interfering. "Banks must eliminate all financial interference from the government and do not have to wait for the big boss to decide."

In terms of the right to issue paper currency, there were two ways: centralized system and collective system. The biggest reason for using the centralized system was summarized by Ma in four points: First, the credit of banknotes was completely different from the credit of checks. A check has two layers of credit. The cheque grantee needs to be familiar with the personality credit of the issuing party, and have sufficient confidence in whether the bank has the ability and willingness to pay. Second, banknotes were a kind of promissory note. Ordinary promissory notes were only commonly accepted by merchants; banknotes were forced, not arbitrary. Third, banknotes were liabilities in banks, similar to borrowing. It was just that the banknotes were cashed without regularity and no interest. The issuer was not profitable. If it was not honored, it made no sense; the more banknotes were issued, the more widespread it was. If there was panic, people stop switching. Fourth, the issuance of banknotes for legitimate loans could be said to be no danger. Regardless of the purpose, as long as someone borrowed, someone will dare to lend. Therefore, in order to avoid the drawbacks before the recovery, the value of the currency could fall and the price could rise. The financial panic caused the government to need serious supervision. "It is necessary to adopt a centralized system to restrict the qualification of issuance, and blame it on the central bank, so that the government has an easy supervision opportunity. And the central bank issues banknotes, there is room for expansion, and the total number of banknotes issued by him is easy to understand." Ma believed that there were also drawbacks to centralization, that is, the government grants the central bank the privilege of centralized distribution. Banks would be particularly good for the government. Financial difficulties in the country may involve financial and economic organizations, and financial credit was thus destroyed. The Bank of China was nominally the central bank at the time. It was actually a majority system. Banks and money houses had distribution rights. Therefore, first, the bank could obtain distribution rights under the name of industry. Second, the sponsors were being supervised by the army, retired celebrities, and their names were still there; in society, celebrities were omnipotent. If this habit was not changed, China could not make progress. Third, Chinese–foreign joint ventures or outsiders-alone hold banks, relied on international forces to win distribution rights. Fourth, money was omnipotent and so was bribery. Up to 30,000 *yuan* could be approved by the Currency Board. Fifth, one had to be well prepared. The difference between the gold business and the banknote was nominally prepared. In fact, the Currency Bureau knew that it was illegal, but the power of money was greater than the power of the law. Sixth was the transfer of public debt tickets. According to the banknote regulations, half of the cash and half of the public debts were required. China's issuance of public debts was often eligible for bank preparation. Seventh was the reduction of the interest on loans. There must be more loans, and the distribution will be indiscriminate. The bankers were not responsible for the various consequences of indiscriminate action. After the bank's bankruptcy was suspended, the capitalist had already withdrawn from the bank. The civilians were still responsible and suffered. As for the public library system, Ma thought that he could make up for it by various methods. However, it would be difficult if the warlords were not evicted. Even if it was done, there would be no good results.

In the 1930s, different views were taken in the face of major measures to reform the currency system such as the two reforms (1933) and the French currency policy (1935). In response to Liu Wei's ability-based theory, Xu Qing's virtual food standard theory, Yan Xishan's property securities, Huang Yuanbin's property and silver merger policy and Zhang's compensation currency, Ma Yinchu made comments and changed his original gold standard. He eventually advocated for the exchange standard.

For the US government's silver policy, he analyzed in detail and proposed corresponding countermeasures.

The US silver policy had triggered a big discussion on China's currency reform proposal. The opinions could be roughly divided into scholars and bankers. The former was represented by Gu Jigao's gold standard, Huang Yuanbin's corrective silver coin, as well as Adron Lewis and Zhang Lvluan's compensation currency. The latter thought that as long as the balance of payments can be balanced, everything can be solved. After the abolition of the two reforms, Ma believed that it was necessary to make the Chinese people deepen their faith in the silver dollar, and it was not too late to solve the gold standard. Because "the United Kingdom, Japan and the United States, which are most closely related to China, they have gradually abandoned the gold standard. China's adoption of this system at this time is a meaningless move. Moreover, China's prices have gradually fallen. If the gold standard is changed, prices will fall even more. The industry is more difficult to maintain. If you use the virtual gold standard, you can learn from the history of each country and avoid mistakes." Therefore, the currency standard of China could not be solved.

At that time, Yan Xishan was preparing to issue product securities in Shanxi, while Ma set up a special chapter in *China's New Financial Policy* to judge it. The first was that the value of a property security was itself worthless, and the value of a commodity price was measured by the value of a property security, which was tantamount to measuring one's own value by one's own property. How could it be justified? Mr. Yan's statement was not trapped in the dilemma of circular theory. Detailed analysis is provided below. Second, the issue of distribution could not be confused with the currency standard. It was very difficult for property securities to be recognized by non-economists across the country; distribution according to work meant that capitalists would automatically realize everything. This was simply equivalent to taking off the tiger's fur. In the international situation of the time, it would be even more difficult for friendly neighbors to understand this. This move could not be implemented. The Soviet Union issued the ruble in a simple and easy manner, because it manipulated the money in a man-made manner and did not spam the banknotes, so the value of the currency did not fall. In Ma's view, the banknotes issued by the Soviet Union were almost the same as the management currency. Therefore, of course, it was not necessary to use extremely troublesome property securities. Third, the lack of chips and the lack of capital could not be mixed into one. Yan Xishan mistakenly believed that the disease in China was not a lack of capital, but that property could be turned into a banknote. The government thought that it would be possible to open a factory with capital, but the government did not know that if it was productive but could not produce money, the factory would still close down. These problems were not caused by the lack of capital, but because production could not be turned into cash. Ma specifically pointed out that China's rural bankruptcy was not due to lack of chips, but was really due to lack of capital. Lack of transportation, poor seed quality, poor fertility of the land and lack of water were all capital issues, not currency issues. Fourth, under capitalism, there was overproduction and the people were not willing to increase consumption. It was not that "gold represents value", it was really due to "capital ownership". Under the capitalist system, the fruits of production were privately owned, and the income of laborers was far less than that of capitalists. The capitalists reinvested in their production with surplus income, but the laborers had low income and hence low purchasing power, and they could not afford to consume many finished products, so there was a phenomenon of overproduction. Moreover, the production efficiency of modern machines was great, and most workers were unemployed after being replaced by machines. The purchasing power of society was weak and the phenomenon of overproduction was becoming increasingly obvious. "This point is very big. If the cause of industrial panic is really 'capital private', not 'gold' value, then Mr. Yu's theory will soon collapse. … It mistakes the result of 'capital private' as 'gold'. The problem of 'value' is the biggest flaw of all theories. I think that 'private' and 'golden value' should be discussed separately and should not be confused." The fifth was that "Mr. Yan's theory is in a loop." The details are as follows: First, property securities replaced gold and silver. The intention was to give property securities, which were valueless in themselves, the function of exchange medium and value scale. Only the state gave the property securities the legal goods qualification, so that it became the exchange medium and the value scale, then the gold and silver could be taken instead. Second, the property securities were in the form of cash units, more or less as the standard. For example, if there was a photo of a property, then it was just a photo of one thing; but the pound was based on the transaction volume. As a result, the pound is the medium of exchange instead of the photo. "This difference is very big. The number of property securities and property increases at the same time, and it is inevitable that there will be inflation." Third, how was the property value stipulated? Once the name of the property securities unit was stipulated, the fluctuation of the silver price and the property securities would always be separated from each other. "How is the market price of the property expressed? I don't know how the market price of the property can be paid for the property securities?" Fourth, the biggest role of property securities was for the trading medium, which was a trading medium, and it must have its own value. The value of the property was equal, and it was not a photo of the property. It must be qualified for independent survival. From this one can see that "the fundamental theory of property securities cannot be established. If you want to be the measure of the value of the goods, you will not have the value of independent survival. You must use the value of the goods as the value, and you should measure the value of the goods by your own value. Isn't it in a circular inference? Therefore, property securities cannot be replaced by today's exchange standard or paper standard."

Liu Mianzhi[205] and Xu Qingfu[206] were two major people who advocated not to issue banknotes to save the country. Their solutions were different and they had confused the credit card as capital. Moreover, they did not know the role of credit vouchers or collateral. Ma mainly criticized their arguments in three aspects: First, it did not conform to the principles of economics. "Banknotes and goods must cooperate with each other. That is, the goods must be delivered after the payment is made. The goods can be collected when the goods are delivered. ... There is a ticket stub

---

[205]Liu Mianzhi (1872–1944) styled himself Wenchang. He was from Xiangtan County, Hunan Province. In 1904, he stayed in Japan. After returning to China, he became a professor in the Hanlin Academy. In 1913, he served as a special member of the Ministry of Finance and a member of the Senate.

[206]Xu Qingyu (1879–1966), formerly known as Dingnian, courtesy name Qingfu, was from Hang County (now known as Yuhang), Zhejiang Province. He used to be the head of the Bank of China in the three northeastern provinces, and the branch president and the finance minister of the Bank of China in Qingdao and Hangzhou.

for the goods, and the ticket must be attached to the goods. This is so-called finance. Now the warehouse violates the rules, once the good is not sold, the money is still transferred. it is not compatible with economic principle if there is no receipt for the goods." Second, there was the possibility of inflation. Xu Qingyi prepared for the release of real estate. The quality of products could not be unified, there was no unified market. It was difficult to exchange items. Neither could the rules be changed nor could they can be divided. If the banknotes can be exchanged for goods, the management of the goods was inconvenient and the disposal of the goods was difficult. In the end, it was impossible to maintain the stability of the currency ("fare"). Third, they mistook Sun Yat-sen's coin revolution as their theoretical basis. They believed that they were advocating not cashing out banknotes. Ma thought that they "only (knew) one of the theories and (were) ignoring other facts. Therefore, their theory has a lot of loopholes and fails to be scrutinized." The Prime Minister "is definitely not determined." Since then, "they quote money as evidence, stating that ordinary people only think highly of money, but never know how to make best use of it. Though he introduced the benefit of coupons, he never held opinions against money. It's like the capital needed in the material construction, and banknote has not been created to solve the problem."[207]

Huang Yuanbin put forward a silver correction strategy, supposing that China's cheap silver or expensive gold did no harm, but the high silver price would be unstable. Raising the price of silver will cause China to be hit by a double blow; on the one hand, exports will be hit hard, emerging industry would not be able to stand on its feet and, on the other hand, world prices would falling increasingly, and China would be bound to fall into an incorrigible place. Therefore, the "silver correction strategy" was of profound significance, "but there are also negotiable points". The first was to rectify the prices. This was an average figure based on the export–import price index and may not be consistent with individual prices. Even the price of gold was not necessarily in direct proportion to the rise and fall of prices. In Mr. Huang's words, "this is not something I can do. If a silk merchant is to benefit from a trade, but tea merchant gets a loss, it will not be easy to solve. But from the businessman's point of

---

[207] *Reforming China's Economy*, p. 412.

view, individual prices and average prices are valued by the businessman rather than the latter." Second, the exchange rate and silver price fluctuated in different proportions to each other. The exchange rate was not only affected by the sale of goods but also by the other balance of payments, as well as by intangible income and expenditure outside international trade. "Therefore, the price of silver and the exchange rate may not be complementary to each other." That is to say, the exchange rate between China and foreign countries did not have to be related to the price of silver fluctuation in the same case.

Adron Lewis, a foreign expert, and Zhang Lvluan advocated the adoption of Compensatory Currency (a mercantile commodity). That is, when the silver was expensive or cheap, the rate of increase or decrease would be based on the rise and fall of the price index to offset the impact of the US increase in silver prices on China. Ma thought it was reasonable, but there were many difficulties. The biggest shortcoming could be analyzed in five aspects, the crux of which lay in the fact that "the United States is the gold standard, or is able to coordinate with its countries, while China is a silver standard country, with no hope of coordination with other countries. It is even more difficult to implement such a system."

Ma's third period currency representative *New Theory of Currency*, had 24 chapters, and held that "After World War II, China's construction, whether internal or external, the construction of the currency must be put in the first place. There are many ways to adjust the currency, and since the First World War in Europe, other countries have adjusted their monetary policies as a reference for us. The intention of the book is that all the new doctrines invented after the First World War will form the basis for the theory that China should sort out its currency for the future. All the ways and steps of adjusting the currency with the post-war countries, those who can help China to sort out the experience of the currency, have written a monograph, making a trickle-down contribution to the present great era. As to the theory and process of the establishment of the French coin policy, we can refer to the New Financial Policy."

Ma reviewed the concept of the Chinese people's currency and frequently commented on the price of silver. Although China used to use the silver standard, there was no silver market in China at all. The largest silver markets in the world were in London and New York, which were in two gold-based standard countries. The Chinese saw silver as an ordinary commodity, and the price of gold indicated the price of silver. In China, the silver coin issue had not come to an end until the French currency policy. However, for this dispute lasting for several decades, one had to study and could not avoid that the price of silver being compared with gold; the bright and dark side of China's industry and commerce, workers, debtors, and trade exports; or the reason that America bought silver and gold and its effect on China. To say that the United States fought against China, all it had to do was to buy silver and collect it at an appropriate price. Then which does more harm, inflation or deflation? "Choosing the option that delivers most good or least harm." The ceaseless inflation would cause immeasurable loss. In today's world, the gold standard does not suit big industrial and commercial countries, just as the silver standard does not suit China. After the First World War, "for the cash flow in the United States, the deep credit expansion and price increase brought them a lot of trouble." "So they took cash away to make it not work. ... The inflow of gold was no longer outflow, and the gold standard has lost the role of automatic regulation."[208]

Ma put forward that "The gold standard changes internally and maintains externally. The paper standard system changes externally and maintains internally. In other words, a sacrifice of internal price is to maintain foreign exchange; or a sacrifice of foreign exchange to maintain the internal price."[209] In comparison, "it is better to sacrifice the external price to maintain the internal price, than to sacrifice the internal price to maintain the external price."[210] "If under managed currency, the amount of currency can be as large as possible, the authority may gradually raise the discount rate to the limit if it believes that there is a risk of excessive inflation. And don't worry about the outflow of cash, because it can be handled with ease. If so, not only will interest rate movements be small, that is, the frequency of such changes will be small, and prices will be able to attain a steady rate of return."[211]

Ma argued for the reasons why foreign exchange and domestic prices could be stable at the same time, pointing out, "It is good to have a stable

---

[208] *New Discussion of Inflation*, p. 14. The Commercial Press, 1999.
[209] *Ibid.*, p. 15.
[210] *Ibid.*, p. 47.
[211] *Ibid.*, p. 50.

domestic price but it is better to have a good balance of foreign exchange. Only by making the domestic price stable and keeping the power in our hand can things be easily controlled. If the price is to be stable, it must be based on the stability of the domestic price of a foreign country. It is not easy to do so because the power is in other people's hand. If China were rich and strong in the future, it could negotiate with the United States, which means China could not have been on an equal footing with the United States at that time. Also, China had to bend down for it's in the position of a supplicant." "When China implemented its legal currency policy, it publicizes the exchange rate between the fiat ticket and the British currencies, and the exchange rate between fiat ticket and American currencies. For the stable rate of these two countries, so our fiat ticket exchange rate can be fixed at the same time. The United Kingdom has three important ways to remedy changes in foreign exchange: futures foreign exchange, the establishment of a Foreign Exchange Stabilization Fund and the Government's assistance in purchasing foreign exchange futures. China's Stabilization Fund differs from Britain's, China is in a special situation. On the one hand, it enforces exchange control and on the other hand it maintains a black market by means of stabilization funds. Its purpose is to maintain the confidence of the people in the enemy-occupied areas in the fiat ticket and their credit with the outside world."

Based on the analysis of the relationship between the internal price and the external price, one could draw the following conclusions about what was the cause and what was the result and how to apply the remedy to the case. "The internal price of a country's currency varies according to the circumstances of the domestic agriculture, industry and commerce. Its external price is subject to change in the international situation. Therefore, it was thought better to separate the internal price and the external price.

The better way to separate the two was to establish a Foreign Exchange Equalization Fund (FEEF). According to the International Short-term Capital Flows (e.g., capital runaway, speculation and trading) and the difference between gold and silver, the risk of exchange rate fluctuations was borne by the FEEF. If the central bank reserves were not affected in any way, the discount rate would not fluctuate from one direction to the next.

Agriculture, industry and commerce in China could ride out the storm. Not only could the internal price be stable but the external price also did not fluctuate very much, because the domestic price and the external price complemented each other. The central bank's central reserve and the FEEF coexisted and operated simultaneously. The former maintained the internal price, while the latter maintained the external price. This was so that the domestic inflation and deflation risk, foreign speculators, the activities of the capital evader and the national financial policy would not damage the domestic economy, and internal and external stability could be achieved and the two sides could be balanced. At this point, Ma lamented, "The currency dualism is the most valuable new invention in finance today." However, the Foreign Exchange Stabilization Fund could only be used to resist minor disturbances. If a country's import and export trade was in excess and there was no invisible excess to offset it, then the Stabilization Fund would not be able to withstand it.

Economic life is a moving life, so in terms of motion, there are five forces that can make society change with each passing day, and stay in a static state. Ma combined the history and the current situation, especially in the light of the situation in China to make an interpretation:

1. **Population reproduction.**
2. **Capital increase:** China's lack of capital and high interest rates made it hard to get a lot of money in its cities except for Shanghai. The flow of funds from places with low interest rates to places with higher rates was natural. The greater the amount of capital, the lower the marginal productivity of capital and the lower the interest rate, but the greater the total production and interest. This was the power of capital expansion.
3. **New inventions or discoveries:** They can enhance the marginal productivity of capital or labor and resist the marginal productivity that is reduced by capital accumulation or overpopulation.
4. **Progress in management:** Scholars called the industrial revolution of the 18th century and the management revolution of the 20th century progress.
5. **The change of desire:** The higher the growth of the culture, the more developed the education, the more desire the human beings have; it is the most obvious phenomenon of dynamic society.

Therefore, "The so-called stable internal price will not change the nonfixed reserve. In the long run, nothing can go wrong. In terms of China's foreign trade, the total value of imports and exports in the early years of the Republic of China was no more than 100,000,000 *yuan*, and in the July 7th Incident, it exceeded 200,000 *yuan*. So reserves have to be increased or decreased from time to time. If we look at it from a long-term perspective, it is bound to increase."

Central bank reserves: Ma analyzed that the organization of the People's Bank of China, like the Bank of England, was divided into two parts, issuance and sales. So, for the preparation of issuance, the central issue department prepared for the issue. The Central Bank of China Issuance Department provided for 60% cash and 40% guarantee. With the introduction of the new monetary policy, reserves were largely in the form of foreign bullion notes or bills of exchange, except that the amount of silver required under the law was not less than 25%. There was one great difference between the British and Chinese approaches to preparation. The UK was a guaranteed reserve. Any issue in excess had to be financed entirely in cash. In China, for example, for every additional issue, only 60% of the cash reserves would be increased, while the remaining 40% would still be guaranteed reserve. Compared with the rigid system in the UK, it was more convenient.

However, the UK was the most creditworthy, with 88–90% of transactions made by cheque. Only a small portion of the transactions were carried out in the medium of banknotes, of at least five pounds for plain bills, which was not convenient for small transactions as they were made in silver coins. If the Bank of England issued more notes, the Sales Department would exchange cash for it. This was tantamount to expanding the credit of the Sales Department. It would only issue more cash and withdraw it from the Equilibrium Fund.

Most of the world's gold was in the hands of the Americans, and the rest of the world had a shortage of it, which was the reason to abandon the gold standard. Only after giving up the gold standard, "countries are willing to keep substantial cash reserves in order to shore up their creditworthiness for non-convertible notes." "Therefore, on the one hand, the balancing fund is responsible for regulating foreign exchange, and on the other hand, it is also the source of increasing reserves. Now, if we go further and say that the Exchange Balance Fund is not enough, what will it do to help the poor? If the exchange balancing fund cannot solve this problem, the whole currency problem remains unresolved."

To keep the Exchange Balancing Fund intact, Mr. Ma stressed the need to abide by the principle of both outward and outward remittances. The Fund would not be reduced, but would also have a large surplus. During the War of Resistance against Japan, China controlled not only foreign exchange but also reduced the need for foreign exchange, at the same time increasing the supply of foreign exchange for relief purposes. "A two-sided deal would balance our foreign exchange. But in the period of post-war construction, whether the two-tier system can continue to exist is a question." After the war, Mr. Ma thought that the foreign exchange market would not suddenly and completely restore its freedom, depending on the economic system to be established.

"Not to resort to extreme planning but to perpetuate foreign exchange control as the best method, it is necessary to take into account the following points: (1) In order for the controls to be effective, the State shall constantly enforce strict controls on incoming and outgoing mail, (ii) persons entering or exiting the country shall also be inspected, (iii) all external trade and financial activities shall be subject to official approval. Regulation has exposed some of the least politically intrusive places to political interference. It cannot coexist with a very sensitive international commodity market. The wide discrimination against international trade, which is not regulated directly and openly by tariffs, would be due to the approval of foreign exchange and to the marginalization of the MFN clause. Foreign exchange controls cannot, therefore, be regarded as a permanent regime."[4] Ma's discussion of foreign exchange control as a system that could not last forever was undoubtedly rational and correct.

In the gold standard, money and deposits had to be prepared with gold, and when countries gave up the gold standard, gold was excluded from the monetary standard. Without a moment's hesitation, Ma pointed out, "Gold can be regarded as dirt. The value of gold (when it is the price, Ma does not make a distinction, often confuses, notes) can be controlled by manpower. Under the paper standard, countries can manipulate the need for gold, if they want more, they get more; they want less, then less. All is controlled by men, and the authority of the gold will naturally fall to the ground. Therefore, the relationship between gold and currency is different now and then. In the past, the currency was dominated by gold, and the value of the currency depended on whether the gold was ready or not for transfer. Today gold is dominated by currency. The value of gold can be manipulated by manpower. If it is higher, it is higher; if it is lower, it is lower." Compared with the monetary standard system, the gold standard system had great advantages, but its disadvantage was that the value was unstable, fluctuated and changed constantly, that is to say, it caused price instability.

"As a result of falling prices, entrepreneurs have been the first to suffer. Debtors, the import merchants, the government and so on all have an unfavorable position. On the other hand, as a result of rising prices, consumers are the first to be harmed, and creditors and exporters are all adversely affected. The man with money should be regarded as a medium of exchange and a yardstick of value."

The value of money was such that it was not worthy of its mission. So, one had to change the status of gold. "Reduce the percentage of reserves, change from scattered reserves to centralized reserves, and even abolish the capital funds. All this can reduce the need for gold, so that although the supply of gold cannot be controlled, the need for gold has been controlled. If it can be well used, it is not possible to achieve the goal. ... Around the world today, without the United States, there is no country can take the responsibility. The United States is also doing its utmost to advance toward this goal. ... Now the United States ... although the gold flowed in, the currency is not ready, the currency will not inflate and prices will level off. Assuming that the United States wants to lend to foreign countries, it will not be drawn from the reserves of the Central Bank. Instead, it will be financed from the sealed coffers. There will be no deflation, and prices will not fall. This is indeed the key to the success of price manipulation in the United States. But he who is not rich is as far as America is concerned."

Next, Ma further stated, "The old school of monetary science could no longer explain the currency phenomenon in the world today. However, the paper standard of every country in the world today is derived from the gold standard, and still has a causal relationship with the gold standard. If we want to understand the function of the paper standard, we must take the gold standard as the starting point. Therefore, the old school of monetary book still has the value of selecting and reading. The United States does not hesitate to sacrifice large amounts of gold to manipulate domestic prices, but its power is so great that it does not control the prices at home. The United States controls the prices of all the countries in the world, and the United States should regard itself as complacent." According to Ma, "In the old days, the value of currency was decided by gold, but today the value of gold is determined in paper money. In other words, the value of gold is expressed in terms of the value of currency and cannot determine the value of currency."[4]

"The price of gold in Britain is really governed by the price of gold in the United States. The price of gold in the United States is governed by the currency of the United States, so the price of gold in Britain is governed by the currency of the United States too. It is wrong to associate Chinese coins with British coins from the very beginning." Affected by the currency policy of the United States, domestic prices had to be restrained, then the UK was the first to be affected. "If the United States wants to stabilize the prices of other countries as the United States, countries that refuse to do so will get harmed by the United States." For example, if the prices of country A rose and the trade with the United States exceeded the price, the price of gold would flow into the United States and the trade would turn out to be superior. The gold would flow back, the price would rise and fluctuate, which would be deeply harmful, even to the extent of no relief. The outflow of gold would be from the United States, which "is isolated from prices and unaffected", and they would use a discount policy to stabilize prices across the country.

Accordingly, Ma concluded, "World prices follow the United States, the price of commodity in the United States follows the discount policy and the discount policy follows the natural interest rate. So the natural interest rate is a golden mean phenomenon in China, the so-called 'Tao', the so-called 'Heaven's law'. The natural interest rate must be one that is appropriate for economic policy. If investment is increased, savings are increased, investment is reduced and savings are reduced, then the natural interest rate can remain unchanged." Most of the above comments were indeed shared by Professor Ghazal of Sweden. But Dr. Corker and Wallis had quite different opinions from that of Ghazal: "Whether the US joint reserve banks can use the discount policy to directly stabilize domestic prices and indirectly to stabilize the world remains questionable. If investment equals savings, and the monetary interest rate should converge with the natural interest rate, there is no problem."[2]

Keynes said that investment was equal to savings. Ma thought that saving was the basis of lending. Because of the high prices, the people had to cut down the saving, so this involuntary saving can be called compulsory. By reducing the discount rate, the central bank advocated lending to producers in order to increase social investment. Those who were not engaged in business or did not dare to expand their business because of high interest rates will now start or expand their businesses. "If money saved or saved under the campaign is not consumed by part of the people, it will not be used for investment purposes until the price of the goods is directly or indirectly sufficient to keep them from falling."

"Therefore, at this point in time, social savings will increase, investment will increase and savings will still equal to investment. This is the result of the Central Bank's application of the discount policy."[3] "If investment is to be equated with savings, prices should not rise or fall, and price stability should be used and currency neutrality should not be used." Ma then warned that consumer happiness can be increased in line with the position of economic progress. "As the income of consumers remains the same and prices fall, the purchasing power of their currency income increases and the standard of living increases greatly. This is the reward for technological progress, and it is advisable to adopt the Chinese currency theory. But this is an ideal situation, and it is in fact very difficult to do."

The British sacrificed foreign prices to maintain domestic prices. China's legal tender was linked to the British currency, pegged to the exchange rate to maintain the foreign currency, based on the purchasing power parity theory and derived from the exchange rate as the natural exchange rate. If the exchange rate between the two countries was either high or low, it would be harmful and lead to a currency war. It would be better to let nature take its course and make a balanced point, that is, the balance of purchasing power, and settle the two interests. In his article The Review and Criticism of the International Monetary Scheme in the UK, US, Canada and France, Ma was quite outspoken: "The book does not advocate a currency standard, so the system is not only enough to upset domestic financial and price levels, but also to make China lose financial control. Is it ... not the case that our currency is pegged to the currency of an advanced country? On the one hand, too much reliance on one country will lead to the loss of its country's friendship; on the other hand, the exchange rate of a country may not necessarily be able to stabilize it at the same time, to the detriment of trade relations with other countries." Ma revealed that the position of UK and America was contrary to that of China.

"The plain fact is that our gold is not as good as that of the United States, our trade is not as good as that of the United Kingdom, and our entry into the Anglo-American Plan must be followed by them. Their greatest focus is on stabilizing short-term exchange rates and promoting trade, and our interests in increasing production for the exploitation of long-term foreign investment. In order to tap the sources of wealth to increase production, we should include the capital gap outside trade. British and America focus on expanding the market abroad, and our focus is on developing the sources of wealth at home. Their problem is how to increase consumption; our problem is how to increase production. The two purposes are different and the natures of the two are different, so we can't expect British and America to provide long-term reconstruction or development of the funds." Ma's insight was so calm, objective and focused as to grasp the vital point.

Ma talked a lot to introduce price indices, comparing purchasing power parity with the monetary quantity theory, and Fisher, Keynes and Pigou's quantity theory of money. He reviewed the new theories invented by the countries after the First World War, which formed the basis of China's theory of monetary system later on. At the same time, he narrated the outline of currency consolidation in the post-war countries of Europe, "The basis of experience in currency collating system."[1]

Finally, Ma believed that after the War of Resistance against Japanese Aggression, China should do "some sort of work to stabilize the domestic economy, restore monetary credit, and then accept an invitation from a clearing union or foundation and take participate actively? It doesn't matter whether it is good or not, as soon as the agreement is established, China will participate in the agreement. That is, a scholar who does not rule money also knows that the latter law is not feasible." As for the method of sorting out the currency, Ma advocated the use of the austerity method to organize the legal tender. After the legal tender was withdrawn from circulation, and contracted later, the war money "should come from taxes, and most of the taxes should be placed on those who have make a fortune during country's difficult time. So that currencies will not have greatly inflation; prices will not rise sharply because of the violent inflation, and those who have made a fortune during this period will be suppressed slightly. ... Quietly watching today's trend, it is feared that this trend will come from the expansion of Germany and Russia. On the day of sorting out, another new coin will be issued. Then make an exchange rate and take back the old money, and then contact the international currency with the new currency. But in this case, the losses are totally put in the common people, and those who have made money during country's difficult time can go unpunished and ride out peacefully. As a witness to history, the national government headed by Chiang Kai-shek did so, and the flames of the people's liberation war sent the Chiang government on the road of no return." "Can those who made money like that give their ill-gotten money to their next generations peacefully? Things in the world can never be that simple."

3.2. On the credit system

In papers like "Similarities and Differences of Credit System between China and Foreign Countries" and "A Comparison of the Banking Industry between Europe and America", Ma analyzed the similarities and differences between Chinese and foreign credit system, the development stage of Chinese credit system and the comparison between Chinese and European banks.

In order to analyze the similarities and differences of Chinese and foreign credit, he pointed out that the economy can be divided into three historical periods according to the development situation: barter, currency and credit time. The credit age can be divided into two different stages of development: bookkeeping and billing. The former was to buy goods without cash, and only on the basis of their own credit, the seller recorded it in the accounting book as "cannot be transferred, if commercial paper can be discounted in circulation". The debts would only be cleared off at the Dragon Boat Festival, Mid-Autumn Festival or the end of the year. "Thus the freezing of Chinese funds is due to the lack of credit chips." There were few foreigners using this method, and it was more common to use the bill, which required three main elements: capital, character and trust. Not a single one could be omitted. A bill includes promissory notes and bills of exchange and also cheques and notes.

"There is neither bill nor discount in our country, then the deposit cannot come from the discount, the note cannot be issued by the discount. Each bank in our country only obtains the loan. Where a promissory note exists, the general rule is to keep accounts. There is no discounting except the bank ticket discount. Using goods or contingent securities as collateral was called loan on security by bank accounting." "Chinese deposits and banknotes do not occur by discounting, but by the lender." "The discounted item has been sold, and the mortgaged item has not been sold. Not only is there no expiration date, but the bank has to take great risks, and because the goods are sold out, there is no market for them. If there is a market for them, why should they be lent again?" This is the fundamental difference between discount and loan.

In the case of the discount of the bill of exchange, the mortgage was indeed safe. Discount was the safest, the bank made the seller flexible and transferred the financial, "it's totally different with item mortgage loan in China". The risk was of non-sale on behalf of the buyer by the lending bank, financial stagnation, failure to promote the flow of goods and loss of financial security; risk-taking by the forwarder was the duty of the insurance company, while the agent waiting for the transfer of financial resources was the responsibility of the commercial bank.

At the stage of development of China's credit system, Ma believed that it was still in its infancy and capital was in danger of being scarce. Its striking characteristic was that as the interest rate rose, the interest rate in a developed country, which has high credit, will reduce. Ma pointed out that there were four original reasons: First, China's currency system was not unified. In addition to the silver dollars, there was also the silver tael. The silver dollars were self-saving. The items were so numerous that it was impossible to set a price for them. As for the evolution of credit, Ma prompted that it should begin with money, banknotes, checks and discounts, so as to accept notes finally, which was stage five. At that time the

European states had reached the height of stage five. The United States was still in its fifth stage of development. China was in transition accounting, with large losses and high interest. Second, the credit organization was not complete; the investigation machine was in shortage. The lending of money was different between the United States and countries in Europe; for Europe taking the bill of exchange was the primary choice, but the United States chose discount.

"We dare not hope that China would adopt the European way. Should we want to follow the American practice, we don't have a complete setting-up of all the facilities and laws involved. As a result, banks have to be very careful when granting loans and public debt is the most secure. The increase in interest is the last resort." Third, China's banks were concentrated in the metropolis, so it was impossible to absorb the floating capital from the mainland, and the disorder became one of the reasons for the high interest rate. Small mainland businessmen only relied on banks for their money. Therefore, interest in the mainland was higher than that in the city, and money shops were larger than banks. Fourth, capital was scarce, oversupplied in some places and inadequate in others.

The poverty of workers in China and the increase in population ensured that the capital could not increase instantaneously. Without the prospect of development, people suffered from hunger and cold. Even if the government did not issue a bond within a few years, the interest rates would go up rather than down. "Less supply and more needs will bring the high price, which is an unchangeable principle in economics." From this, one can see that to ask for a lower interest rate is simply to look for fish from a tree. How can that be possible? "Therefore, it is the disadvantage of the bad credit organization that fools us into thinking that China's market interest is rising."

Comparing the financial industry of Europe, America and China, "Europe comes first, the United States second, China third. If Europe, the US and Asia are compared, China should step down and let Japan be the third one." Japan already had a central bank and a foreign exchange bank, which were naturally superior to those in China.

"The banking business of our country mainly deals in bonds." Ma thought there were four reasons for this, both domestic and foreign. **Foreign reasons:** First, the foreign exchange business was not easy to operate. With China's overseas shipping, cargo insurance and import and export business, foreign exchange was mostly operated, manipulated or monopolized by outsiders, the interest rate for foreign bills of exchange was low, and China had no ability to compete.[5] Chinese businessmen were not familiar with the foreign trade situation. Second, foreign currency trading was not easy to do. Nobody did the foreign exchange business generally, because its operation was not easy. Even if it was in good operation, such as the one in Shanghai, even Zhejiang Industrial Bank would not linger there. Third, less domestic remittance business was done.

The Chinese people stress human relations, so the bill of lading is usually not as reliable. The ships sailing on the Yangtze River would often be troubled by thieves and robbers, and the chaotic situation in other places would also lead to disputes and arguments. Fourth, the mortgage loan did very little to help people, as Chinese businessmen looked upon mortgage as a shameful thing. "Industry is weak, because foreign goods compete, society is unsettled, and tariff does not have the autonomy, but is in jeopardy."

Domestic reasons: First, it was easy to sell bonds. Second, as the bond was issued for the provision, there was an interest income, which could make up for the issue fee. Third, the silver price was low, and so it could only be sold when the price was high, in order to prepare the loan. Fourth, the most important motivation was the high interest rate for the purchase and sale of government bonds (loans of between 1.2 and 1.5 cents, and bonds of up to 2 cents).

"The government bond has low price and high profits. Neither discount nor lending can compare with it." "After realizing this brilliant plan, the bank realized that its capital was being used and was making huge profits. Could itself operate it and become rich? So it raised the interest and borrowed it from the usurer, and bought and sold the bonds. That's why China has such a high interest."

Even in terms of bond sales, the United States and China were different. First, the United States used its surplus (reserve for deposits and idle deposits, loans, remittances, etc.) while operating most (50% or 60%) of its bank funds. Second, the United States took advantage of brokerage, and banks had double safeguard for the risk: one is the issuer, the other is the broker. In China, banks were the only ones held responsible for it.

Third, the shares and bonds were purchased by the United States as companies, railways, mines and various industrial companies. China relied on the British balance in its hands. There were three dangers to this: the government broke up the fund, foreigners set aside the foreign debt and the price of gold was adjusted ($3.10–$2.80 each), leaving the gap to run out. It could be seen that China's finances lagged behind that of the United States and were even more backward than Europe.

3.3. On the banking system

3.3.1. Chinese banking system

Ma's discussion can be divided into three aspects: China's banking system, the operating mechanism and the repression by foreign banks in China with regard to the Bank of Commerce in China.

First, the banking system in China was disordered. At the end of 1927, at the annual meeting of the Economic Society, Ma delivered a keynote speech on China's Banking System. There were three points that deserve attention: First, China had no real central bank. The idea was that financial panic was originally caused by a lack of borrowing, and people were afraid of unexpected issues. If, at the outset, there was a real central bank that borrowed money on the basis of reliable collateral, and the financial sector had to be transferred, the bank would fall immediately. Would it not be beneficial to the whole community as a whole? Being a true central bank, the first condition was to have great influence. At that time, the three central banks of China (Guangzhou, Wuhan and Shanghai) acted independently and could not manage each other. Ma thought that they should be united. There had to be unity of capital, talent, credit and the value of the currency.

Second, foreign banks were too powerful. To be powerful, a central bank must have control both internally and externally. "All our financial affairs are in the hands of foreign banks. There is a special market for these foreign banks which deal with Chinese nationals but have little to do with Chinese businessmen." When China's imports were large and the money was tight, no matter how much money was taken up by foreign banks, the Chinese market will be shaken immediately. Third, "the scope of action of banks or money shops in China is narrow and partial. The society at lower levels can't borrow money from them. As a result, the society at lower levels can't find any advantage at all. It's called the Agricultural Industrial Bank, but it's really just a commercial bank. For example, there is an Agricultural Industrial Bank in Beijing. The person who borrows money is always a local tyrant. These local tyrants, with one or a few per cent interest, lend money out of a bank and then lend it to farmers at 2 or 3 cents a share, and in a second hand, make a profit several times over, while the real farmer still can't get the benefit. So now banks are only banks of high society, not banks of ordinary people. The benefit of banks is for only large businessmen, not poor farmers and workers." Ma advocated setting up a real agricultural bank to lend money to farmers at the lowest interest rate (0.6%, 0.7%) to help them improve agriculture. This would be a credit cooperative. Only in this way would the problems of the 80–85% of the population in China, the majority, be resolved and society would be safe. In this respect, both Japan and Russia were well-developed, and China's Zhili (Hebei) and Huayang Yizhen Conferences could also be used as examples of propaganda. Of course, in the final analysis, the banking system issue "is actually closely related to the foundation of society". This was true and universally applicable.

In terms of operation, in the first and second decades of the 20th century, there were four problems in China's banks. First, because "there is no reserve for deposits", "the bank in China is not exactly a bank". Depositors were not allowed to draw large deposits unless they negotiated with banks. Small deposit banks had to give in and bulk deposits did not negotiate with the bank first, and did not make withdrawals. Because the small depositors didn't have much to depend on, their withdrawal of the money had to be satisfied. On the other hand, large depositors had usually had better ways of coping, so their withdrawal of their deposits were often not immediately dealt with. Some corrupt officials' money was illicit so they did not dare speak loudly. Some banks might ask the directors to use their position to clear the withdrawals. The second was more indirect loans to merchants. With regard to indirect loans from banks, the more hands-on it was, the greater the interest rate. As they were not as well acquainted with the borrower's credit and trustworthiness as money shops, banks were often reluctant to make loans. A businessman could dispose of funds to the bank, from the first to the second, to facilitate the transaction, regardless of the week, without guarantee or collateral. As a result, the bank would dismantle money and give it back to the merchants. The third was less preparation for banknotes. This was a common problem in banks. If there was a risk, the crisis would be indescribable. Unlike the United States law, the National Bank was obliged to accept money from other national banks. As long as the banks accepted it, it could no longer be used in the market. The fourth was the reserve fund. China had two kinds of foreign currencies and silver, and it was all stored in the private bank in Hankou. In Shanghai, it was mostly deposited in private banks and foreign banks. "The benefits of advances are high, and the interest on deposits is low. Today, the bank borrowed money from the bank as a lender, but because of low interest rates, the bank deposits its peers." Ma criticized that this "fabrication is almost comical, and life is extremely impassable." The Western Central Bank's interest was high, and ordinary banks had lower profits. In contrast, China was the same as Japan. Ordinary banks needed the help of the central bank, and the central bank had no spare funds for relief during a panic. In the West, the Central Bank did not compete with ordinary banks under ordinary circumstances, and when the central bank was in a panic, it had support.

In 1927, Ma Yinchu pointed out, "The big problem in China's financial sector is that the forces in the Central Bank are too weak." When other banks were powerful, they may not rely on the central bank's heavy discounting or the orders of the central bank. Even if the central bank raised interest rates, they may ignore them. At that time, the Bank of China, which had fulfilled its responsibilities as a central bank, had no ability to contain the financial market. It was nothing more than a loss of a single distribution right and could not be incorporated into the China Bank. The exchange rate could not be increased to prevent the export of cash. At that time, foreign countries would invest silver in China, not only would they not flow out but would also flow in. The central bank should not have the right to issue a single banknote, and "there is no big capital that does not work. ... It is a financial institution on which industry, commerce, mining, and agriculture depend." Dividends were used to limit their profits but could not control their capital. For example, "The Federal Reserve Bank of the United States has a large capital, but it is very modest. Dividends are profitable at an annual rate of 0.6%, and each year it is profitable. After deducting the dividend from the common reserve fund, it is all stateowned and not distributed to shareholders." In *Chinese Banking Theory*, Ma suggested that China's banks, which are based on basic principles, should be reformed for three reasons, so that they can fulfill their responsibilities as the central bank and achieve a multiplier effect. In *China's New Financial Policy*, he pointed out that the central bank already had more real power in acting as a treasury, but it was a far cry from unified distribution right and centralized reserve. The concentration of reserve funds was not realized until 1936. For the exchange of Shanghai notes, deposits had only been made between the Bank of China and Bank of Communications in the past, and liquidation reserves had been established for each bank. The two banks paid deposits of 70% and 30%, respectively. After the establishment of the Central Bank, it did not join the clearing house because of the sensibilities. Afterward, due to the excellent performance of the exchanges, they also condescended to teach and participate as members, and only made new adjustments according to the ratio of 40%, 40% and 20% and deposited them in the three banks. It was clear that the central bank had limited credit, and the Bank of China had a higher status than the central bank, and the central bank was unworthy of its name. Then, in terms of inter-bank deposits (banking money deposits with each other, and can be withdrawn at any time), in 1935, it became known that the central preparations were not yet in the central bank, but in the Bank of China. British experts encouraged China to be as free from government intervention as the Bank of England. After inspection, Ma pointed out that the independence movement of the Bank of England was not an independent movement. Therefore, he advised the People's Bank of China to be independent. "Some fear that the Chinese government will not have sufficient budget and will use the bank to use the extra to make up for the deficiency." "Bank of England does not obey the orders of the National Assembly and it's in contrast to the government every time. But, in fact, it is unable to become independent. As the pound sterling credit falls, the strength of the Bank of England is indirectly weakened. Of course, the independence of the Central Bank of China has the significance of diplomacy and sovereignty, but it is in fact difficult to achieve. We can catch a glimpse of the difficulty from the composition of the board of directors of China's central bank. Among the 17 board members, 9 are from the government, constituting a majority; the power is naturally controlled by the government, reflecting the gradual implementation of the government's economic control policy. From the government's point of view, it is difficult for the independent Bank of China and Bank of Communications to be under the control of management and make the controlled central bank independent again. If so, how to deal with fraud and policy conflicts? Then the government will have to worry about it." Even so, Ma still believed that "whether in theory or in practice, it is not appropriate for the Treasury Secretary to serve as an officer". Because the council had been manipulated by the government, why should it be assigned to serve concurrently? In addition, "of the central bank's heavy staff, there are many people with profound experience who are very experienced and who may be promoted as senior officials." There was no need for a self-appointed president.

As for the disadvantages of old-style Chinese private banks, in the book *China's Economic Restructuring*, Ma pointed out that, "China's old-style financial industry has a relatively long history. Its business habits, specially emphasize on human credit and emotional color is very strong. In the country, there are no banking regulations to follow, and the method of bookkeeping is crude. Once it is closed down, the processing of its debts is often based on customs, especially emphasizing emotions, and most of them are not settled by legal procedures." Since the launch of Sino-foreign trade, the old-style financial industry in China had come to a standstill and was unable to make progress to adapt to the new environment. Emotion was emphasized. There was shop insurance, and there were bill contracts. Special emphasis was placed on double-named bills that were inconsistent with the modern banking industry policy. Credit lending was outside the law and also considered immoral. The creditor's rights were not guaranteed. There were many dangers and it was difficult to develop. Because of the protection provided by banks, interest on loans could be reduced. Traders were happy to use them. The speed of development of the banking industry was amazing, and the improvement of the credit system was the driving forces. Foreign banks applied new bookkeeping, and all creditor's rights and debts were handled in accordance with the laws and regulations. With strong bonuses, credit confirmation, opportunity to take advantage of private deposits, custody of government revenues and foreign currency exchanges in operating, China's interests were invaded.

From the perspective of Ma, China's new type of financial industry, eliminating human relations, paid attention to the mortgage payment and regarded the general public as a business object. The old pattern of foreign banks monopolizing the Chinese financial industry had been broken or was still being replaced.

As China's credit system gradually approached modernization, Ma believed that foreign banks were always using Chinese capital, and Chinese and foreign banks had gradually merged, and there were at least two shortcomings: First, the credit insurance industry had not yet commenced. Although there was Shanghai First Credit Insurance Co., Ltd., guarantees were still partial to individuals, different from foreign countries that specialized in the guaranteeing business. However, because some insured person thought that, as he paid a premium, he could do whatever he wanted, all risks were borne by the insurer. Because the premium was too expensive, it was not yet developed. Second, trust deposits were not yet developed. As the custodian, "he will be subject to the order and command of the client to act, if not to comply with the order of the principal, he will be freely disposed. If there is a loss, not only should he bear civil liability, but also bear criminal responsibility due to misconducting responsibility." Therefore, it was safer than ordinary deposits, and the Trust Department, which was established in Shanghai at the time, was the executor of the will, the manager of public and private property and proceeds, and had also traded government bonds and real estate for current accounts. However, it was somewhat speculative and "not exactly the same as intention".

Finally, Ma said that China's financial industry had been suppressed by foreign financial forces. There were inequalities in terms of name, status and strength. In terms of nominal status, for banks in Shanghai of the 1920s, China and foreign countries had mutual exchanges, but they were not equal. If the Bank of China was to borrow money from abroad, it must have collateral and be returned by China's bank. Conversely, not only was the mortgage not emphasized but also as a deposit, the deposit receipt was issued by the layman and had to be returned by the Bank of

China. The most unequal and important one was the circulation of foreign banknotes in China. Ma generously said, "Hong Kong Dollar is a great force in the domestic financial community, and it really makes people indignant! ... In the domestic financial community ... the recognition of this force has not been stipulated in the treaty, and it cannot be defeated by armed weapons. The only basic approach is to cancel foreign currency and adopt a standard currency system which is just as creditworthy as Hong Kong Paper. But this is by no means easy!"

Idle domestic currency was concentrated in foreign banks. China's financial institutions could not absorb deposits and keep interest rates high. As a result, the country's industrial and commercial sectors suffered greatly. Ma dissected the designated agent of foreign banks that wanted to invest in China. The property of wealthy old people of China was kept in foreign banks for safety considerations. It also attracted a large number of inter-state payments, such as the amount of money loaned to the Chinese government by countries such as Britain, Germany, Russia and France, and the income from collateral, the tariff, salt tax, etc. For example, HSBC had a huge amount of money of salt tax and tariff from the government. General corrupt officials also deposited huge sums for protection. As a result, "if funds are concentrated in the concession, the mainland's finances will gradually fail to strait, and the poor's life will suffer. ... Although foreign banks take extremely low interest rates, such as 0.1% or 0.2%, they do not hesitate to repay 0.5% or 0.6% of profits (Chinese banks would often charge a monthly interest of 1.5% or 2%) to open a factory industry with foreigners. Our peoples' money is exploited by our funds. With most people being ignorant of this, how could I not be sad?"

As for the relationship between China's banks and foreign banks, according to Ma, China's banks "have to be dependent on foreign merchants' bank". Shanghai's bank capital, with only as much as two or three hundreds of thousands and as little as dozens of thousands, had poor financial strength. If there was surplus capital, HSBC would lend to the Shanghai bank, so the banknotes of HSBC would remain in the hands of the private bank. Once the foreign bank reclaimed the money, the bank would panic. Therefore, Ma stated loudly, "If the government of our internal affairs doesn't become more transparent, the power of HSBC would become even bigger." Japan's economic power in China was no less than that of the United Kingdom. In terms of finance, the exchange between the three eastern provinces and Tianjin and Shanghai depended on the Bank of Japan. If one bought the golden ticket of the Bank of Korea, and remitted it to Japan, Shanghai Bank would sell the gold in Japan and sell it in Shanghai to recover the amount. In this way, Japan would be able to hold the key of the exchange between China's three eastern provinces and Shanghai. The exchange rate had skyrocketed and the foreign banks had profited; the economic exchanges between Hankou and Shanghai were close, and the period of customs clearance and payment had to be remitted by Hankou's foreign bank to buy Shanghai's regulatory *yuan*. Once the situation was tense, *Shenhui* had risen sharply and had gone up. In general, Chinese quotations were not eligible for purchase, and the official hall prohibited the bank from leaving China. There was no guarantee for the Shanghai businessmen, so they had to seek help from foreign banks. As a result, Chinese businessmen suffered a lot and foreign banks made a lot of money. Therefore, Ma angrily said, "There is no other way. If we are truly talking about breaking off relationships, the exchange of the three provinces in eastern China and Tianjin and Shanghai must be ended first."

It was on the eve of the War of Resistance against Japan that foreign banks still performed foreign exchange business all the time, resulting in China's financial power being swayed by outsiders. In *China's New Financial Policy*, it was pointed out that "If China can completely manipulate foreign exchange, it would be very easy to prevent imports. Since the importer must handle the purchase of foreign exchange through the three banks, they can refuse if they think it's unnecessary". China's importers were often subjected to foreign trade, and the three banks could not refuse. No foreign banks used foreign exchange. Therefore, at that time, the three banks could not prohibit foreigners from making foreign exchanges. "It is far from manipulating foreign exchanges, let alone talking about it prevents foreign dumping, so it has to be affected by the panic of the world economy."

3.3.2. *Restructuring of China's banking system*

In 1927, in the speech "Financial Problems under the New Economic Policy", Ma proposed the following: (1) He insisted upon a uniform currency system. A Shanghai Mint was to be built with free casting, scrapping *liang* and adopting *yuan*, unifying the currency system and implementing a gold standard. This view was completely consistent with that of Liang Qichao. (2) The central bank had to be given the right to issue banknotes. Only dividends could be used to limit its profitability, and its capital could not be controlled. (3) It was expected to establish a low-rate agricultural and industrial bank.

In 1937, with the title of *China's Banking System*, Ma proposed the "ideal banking system", which was to establish a "strong central authority that allows the supply of currency to be flexible and achieve the purpose of trading media". He discussed eight issues in two levels. The first level had four issues that were to completed or would be completed in the near future. The second level had other related issues. He concluded that after the establishment of the Kuomintang government, China's banking system improved through the cooperation of the government and the people. What had already been completed or could be completed in the near future was as follows: First was unified issuance. After November 4, 1935, a legal currency policy was adopted. The three banks had unlimited rights to issue banknotes, but there was absolutely no danger of running on it. Finally, the banknotes in Bank of China and Bank of Communication needed to be withdrawn, leaving only the central bank's banknotes ready for circulation. In 1937, the Kuomintang Government Legislative *Yuan* passed the Central Reserve Bank Law and the Central Bank's reorganization of the transitional approach and made it clear that the issuance of banknotes was the central bank's privilege, and that all other issuing bank vouchers would be fully recovered within 4 years after its publication. However, Ma believed that the banknotes issued by the two banks had been issued when the Beiyang Government borrowed money. At that time, the government had a plan without compensation. It seems that it could not be ordered to withdraw, so it was not easy to do so. The second was the unified treasury. When Song Ziwen headed the Ministry of Finance on January 1, 1929, he recovered the customs deposit rights and deposited it with the salt revenue of the central government revenue into the central bank. From this time, the state treasury was unified. The central bank "monopolized on one side and has managerial treasury on the other side. Its power is getting bigger and can become the bank of banks." The third was expected to reduce market interest rates. For the change in interest rates in foreign countries, when it rose from 3% to 3.5% to 4% in a short period of time, the increase, though only rising by 15–33%, was considered unusual. While in China, money could even be borrowed for no interest. In emergencies, the maximum interest was 7 *qian* (per 1,000 *liang* of silver), and the interest rate could rise from 2 or 3 *qian* to 6 or 7 in a few days, which was no less than 200–300%. "The fundamental reason is that no central bank has implemented the method of rediscounting as a back-end for commercial banks. ... Now that the central bank has implemented heavy discounting, general commercial banks have no worries and rich sources of funds, and interest rates are naturally not very high. The fourth is to control the exchange rate. Since the implementation of the legal currency policy, China has actually become the gold exchange standard system." "The extent of foreign exchange changes is limited", and English exchange was no more than 1/4 pence. The United States was not allowed to pass 50 cents. Countries "adopt more paper-based standards, and China's legal currency is also the same. Governments of all countries can manage banknotes. The government must not spam and can manipulate currency exchanges. Therefore, to manipulate currency exchange is to manipulate the legal currency, because you must make the currency not fall, and foreign exchange is not reduced." In the book *China's New Financial Policy*, Ma pointed out that the control of foreign currency exchange rates was "a certain range within which the government can customize and scale". However, in his view, the difficulties in controlling foreign exchange were many, because imported goods were contracted by foreign companies, foreign shipping, foreign insurance companies and foreign bank financing. This was what the Chinese government had no power in changing at the time. Constrained by the jurisdiction of the consular governor, it was just starting with the internal control system. In addition to the partial control of trade (such as foreign rice, tea, etc.), transport, currency, and industrial and commercial organizations had to be first controlled. The first two items "have made considerable progress through the efforts of the government", while the latter "is in the shade, so they should be paid special attention".

The second level of issues that Ma elaborated on related to some conditions of the Chinese banking system: The first was the status of private banks in China's banking system. Private banks were one of the three components that made up Shanghai Bank Group and were gradually losing power. Due to the weak financial strength of private banks, it was not enough to cope with the large-scale demand for a large number of businesses. Then, the shareholders of the bank had joint and unlimited liability. Therefore, the trust level of the bank depended on the elements of the shareholders and the managers, and it was not reliable because they relied only on a few interpersonal relationships to maintain their business. On surface, there was an unlimited liability system. "In fact, there are very few implementers. In case of failure, shareholders flee. ... There is no claiming responsibility. Normally, it is ended by mediation." Although foreign banks in China were big, they were far behind. The development trend of banks in industrial and commercial metropolises was as described above, while urban enterprises in the Mainland still needed banks to fit in, and there was a temporary value. This insight was realistic.

The second point was the relationship between legal currency and silver coins. China had a long history of silver use. The concept of coins had not been eliminated. When coins and paper money were used in parallel, people preferred to use coins first and then paper money. Song Ziwen pointed out that banknotes of the three banks had now become popular, and the country could stop the use of *Guiyuan*. Ma believed that legal currency was "compulsory in nature, and silver is prohibited from circulating. Silver is illegal and subject to severe punishment. People have to use the legal currency, and it does not fully prove that legal currency is welcomed." The reason why paper money of the three banks was generally popular was that cash silver was concentrated in the three banks. The transfer of a large number of depositors from the general commercial banks to these three banks was a psychological effect of depositors. It was sufficient to prove that the current concept of silver had not been eliminated. As for the actual conditions of the three banks in preparation, people would not know that. In the view of Ma, "the currency exchange standard has been implemented today. ... Silver coins are useless, and they are stored in large quantities. That is not economical. They are better to be sold to foreign countries for foreign currencies draft as remittance. Therefore, today's hope for the legal currency does not have to be seen as much for its depository and silver reserves. It only depends on the maintenance of its foreign exchange rate."

The third point was to improve the requirements of the central bank. The central bank's "principal owner must not be steadily operating, can only go on track, otherwise it is very dangerous". First, banks could only rely on operating loan-raising operations. They could not directly operate their own businesses, or they could violate the principle of bank operations. Second, the central bank's "business with other banks should be clearly understood, so that general commercial banks also have room for survival, which is a good strategy." Otherwise, it must be "a path to a sound banking system." Third, no banknotes could be made. Theoretically speaking, "The Government's reliance on issuing public debt to seal up for a while is already dangerous. If you make a note today, it is even more dangerous. Covering more banknotes is equivalent to spamming and banknotes. Foreign exchange cannot be maintained. Foreigners lose credit for China's legal currency and foreign debt will not be easily borrowed. There is no way to start large-scale economic construction." Of course, Ma also admitted that at that time that China was waiting to be treated, and all kinds of things were flourishing, such as industry, defense, culture, education, transportation and water, but not construction. A small amount of domestic funds could only be reserved for the development of light industry, and large-scale heavy industry could not use foreign capital. The success of the US–Japan construction was all the result of the use of foreign capital. If China wanted to build its achievements, it had to use foreign capital, that is, it had to stabilize the exchange rate and not spam the banknotes. It also had to be ensured by a balanced budget. However, in June 1937, immediately before the July 7th Incident, Ma clearly recognized the severity of the situation. He wrote, "Today has come to the Great Divide, and everyone should have the spirit of sacrifice. Balance of the budget is impossible, the budget cannot be balanced, and banknotes cannot be made infrequently. For the use of foreign capital, it is not much of an obstacle."

The fourth point was the method of balancing the budget. Because it is not related to the matter at hand, we would not mention it here.

For foreign banks in China, Ma's attitude was that only foreign exchange can be made and deposits cannot be absorbed. When he drafted the new Banking Law of the national government, he made a clear statement of his position: "According to the new Banking Law, the banks of

China were unable to operate due to various restrictions. And foreign banks can do anything. Therefore, the Banking Law should provide that foreign banks can only make exchanges and cannot absorb deposits, otherwise I can guarantee that corrupt officials' property must go to the warehouses of foreign banks. We must pay attention to bureaucratic capital". This kind of strict vigilance was necessary and valuable.

3.4. Theory of financial market

Based on the principle and practice of Western financial markets and the reality of China, Ma pointed out that China's financial market was incomplete, analyzed the reasons for this, and pointed out the direction of development. Discussing the differences in bills, he pointed out that the key point is not the existence of bills, but the types and main reasons for change. In the securities, the representative of Chinese characteristics was public debt, while the corporate debt had no market. He explored the causes of the situation and examined the bourses and China's interest rate cuts.

3.4.1. Financial market in China

Before the War of Resistance Against Japanese Aggression, China's financial market was incomplete. There was only a currency market (Ma called it money market) and no capital market; even the currency market was incomplete. He wrote, "China has not only no capital market, that is, the financial market is also incomplete, because there is no discount market." The former was a short-term capital market. Common commercial banks financed capital for industry and commerce. They were rapidly circulated as the most valuable source of deposits. Long-term deposits could be used for long-term loans, which could avoid the loss of funds. Short-term deposits for short-term loans could guarantee flexible turnover. Otherwise, if the short-term deposits were used for a long period of time, the banks would be trapped in poor circulation, long-term funds would be used for short-term use, and time would be wasted. The procedures would be extremely annoying. The latter referred to a government building railway, issuing public bonds and the repayment period was not fixed for 30–40 years. The handling agencies were industrial banks and trust companies. If one wanted to build a factory building, buy a machine, etc., one had to only use the annual operating surplus as a back-up, and one should not lend to ordinary banks. At the time, China's ordinary commercial banks had a heavy workload on short-term lending and high interest rates. The government issuance of public debt had to be a capital market business, underwritten by a bank, and the Anglo-American investment bank was a capital market.

China's non-discounted markets were all due to the fact that "the central bank does not emphasize discounting, nor do the ordinary commercial banks dare to run discounted businesses, and fears that the funds will be stranded". Business and commercial loans to banks were less convenient than discounting. In Shanghai, there were joint ventures between the company and major banks. If there was a stack sheet, a promissory note issued on the basis of it could be submitted to the bank for discounting after requesting the bearer to bear. However, the bearer was the bearer of the request. "It is still necessary to obtain a substantial amount of collateral, so the discount market can only be called promotion, but it does not begin to substantiate the financial market."

In order to develop a discounting system, China had to first develop a bill system. Ma stated, "Commercial paper is the object of discounting. With the development of the instrument, the bill market must follow up, the bank can transfer it at any time, and fund activities can be prepared. The role of discounted bills is the second line of defense that banks see as a reserve. It allows the financial industry's investment activities to realize real-time opportunities. Whenever the financial emergency is ready to be emptied, the ordinary bank can re-discount the bill to the central bank. The usual preparation amount may be reduced to the minimum, the stored bill remains in interest, and a large amount of cash can be created with a small amount of cash." Then, if necessary, the central bank could publicly sell the absorbed bills in the discount market, "absorbing the market's surplus capital and suppressing speculation are truly the vital line". Discounted bills, central bank rediscounting, and discounted markets were complementary to each other, and they formed a perfect discounting system. Otherwise, the funds of banks and industry and commerce would be difficult to exercise.

The loss of both parties would be self-evident, and the role of discounted bills would not be able to play or hinder the normal development of the discounting business. At that time, China's billing habits were paid in three quarters, which was quite convenient. It was a major obstacle to the development of discounting. If short-term bills were used instead, they could only be introduced gradually. It might have also been advisable to start with a new business. The gradual approach of this kind of differential treatment, starting from reality, was worth learning from.

3.4.2. *Issue of note*

In March of 1921, when China Public University lectured on "Important Philosophy in Economics", Ma talked about the application of domestic trade promissory notes and pointed out that "promissory notes have the ability to integrate society". This discussed the relationship between bills, starting from the following eight aspects. First, there had to be "a legitimate commercial transaction, or when it is really easy to release the goods as the basis for the issue of banknotes. Otherwise, it must not be arbitrarily issued". The second was when the promissory note was discounted to the bank. Banknotes or cheques were substitutes for promissory notes. Banknotes and deposit checks could be circulated in the society, while notes or cheques were active. The third was discounted bills; in fact, the bank guaranteed for merchants, because the banknotes could be required to pay cash to the bank. Fourth, bank reserve was very important to prevent the banks from being run due to poor market or financial tightness and declaring bankruptcy because there was no cash. Fifth, regardless of the variety of transactions, or how their notes and checks were mixed, the promissory notes issued had to be cleared and the banknotes had to be recovered. When the society had a promissory note that could not fulfill its obligations, it would have no effect on the entire society. However, when there was a failure in the same type of business, other types of business would be affected. Sixth, the promissory note was the endurance of finiteness. The banknote was universally accepted. This constituted the reason why the promissory note had to be discounted at the bank. Seventh was the time relationship between banknotes and tickets. The banknotes posted to the bank were deposited in the bank and caused the payment of the banknotes. The bank was able to withdraw the banknotes during the period. So, the time taken for banknotes to go back and the duration of the promissory notes went hand in hand, and then fluctuated. Eighth, "credit system is a disguised form of exchange of goods and materials" and "at different places, it's just time and trust". It was not necessary to exchange at the same time. There had to be a sense of trust and only then would transactions be possible.

In his article "China's Commercial and Banking Circle Should Give Due Attention to Commercial Paper", Ma said, "There are two major types of negotiable instruments, namely, the promissory notes and the money order. The promissory note is issued by the drawer, and the payee (the drawee) shall get the money on a certain day." Consequently, only two parties are involved in a promissory note relationship. For the money order, there were three parties involved: the drawer, the drawee and the payee. So the two types of negotiable instruments are slightly different in nature.

The distinction between Chinese and Western negotiable instruments lay mainly in their categories. A majority of the promissory notes in circulation in China "are issued by private banks and normal banks. Traders who issue them and circulate in the market are rare. The promissory notes of the money shops could be discounted at the bank, while the merchant's issued notes did not appear to be discounted by banks. ... When a businessman asks the bank for accommodation, there is only one way to make a mortgage loan". Similarly, bills of exchange that are circulated in the market, such as cheque bank drafts, "are also sent to banks and bankers. What is issued to merchants and circulated in the market is rare". "Merchants send out to merchants (not to banks); however, there are few who ask for bank discounts, and those that are circulated in the market are rare." The reason for this was that merchants' credit was far less than that of money houses, and traders were mixed. If there were one or two empty tickets, the banks would not dare discount them. Therefore, "to make my country's banks implement discounted commercial paper, we must first make businessmen pay attention to credit, and in particular, must make businessmen attach importance to the paper."

The reason why China's commercial paper was underdeveloped according to Ma was the settlement method of commercial transactions in China. At that time, Chinese merchants bought and sold goods mostly to account for expenses and repaid it on a monthly basis. Some of the money was not repaid until the Dragon Boat Festival. If it was not paid until the Dragon Boat Festival, then it would be repaid by the time of the Mid-Autumn Festival. In June and August, the outstanding goods would be paid on the Mid-Autumn Festival. In any case, once a year everything was closed and all outstanding debts had to be settled. "In view of this, our businesspeople communicate with each other and all of them count as accounts. The creditors can collect debts from the debtors, and it is unclear that issuing a bill of exchange to the debtor is their payment to third parties. Therefore, if there is an urgent need for our country's businessmen, we can only collect debts from the debtors, and we cannot make a draft, and the debtor will be required to admit it and ask the bank for discounting. However, the collection is extremely slow, and discounting can raise funds at any time." In Ma's view, Americans also have the habit of collecting money, but businessmen can use the uncollected books as collateral to borrow from the bank (not universal, but there is implementation). Our country does not, and our country's collection method is extremely inconvenient for businessmen. If it can be changed to discounting, it is more difficult for the business community to be fortunate than to be used to it. It is naturally very difficult to reform it. For the future, we must change it. If we think that the discount atmosphere is not open, I am afraid that it is not easy to act. In fact, as long as businessmen value the bills and pay attention to credit, discounting is the expected result. This habit is limited by the scale of circulation and the banking system. Ma's understanding seemed a little bit inappropriate.

With regard to the comparison of Sino-Western Securities, in May 1920, Ma made a speech on the crisis prevention of economic circles at Peking University. He discussed securities, stocks and bonds. "One of the companies' methods of guaranteeing dividends in China is the interest rate system. No matter if you make a profit or lose money, the company must pay the official interest. This system is the worst and most dangerous." It was very difficult for a company to make money during the founding phase. It had to pay the government interest from the capital, so the capital was reduced and the business scope was narrowed to the point of bankruptcy. "Recently, the company's business has not been able to develop or bankrupt. The official interest rate system is the main reason." In China, "the scale of companies is small and the organizations are in short supply. Therefore, there are few reliable stocks and very few types of non-special stocks, that is, corporate bonds are also unique." In contrast, as for foreign companies, "there are many companies and there are many types of stocks. Bonds also include corporate bonds and public bonds. Public bonds also include local government bonds, provincial government bonds, and central government bonds. Therefore, the range of securities transactions is large and the business is complex."

As for gambling and speculation, some people thought that the two were similar, but Ma criticized it. "In fact, the speculation and gambling of brokers are two things." "Gambling, if it is not necessary, may not be a gamble, and the business is different. It is subjective and objectively impossible to avoid danger. If a broker does not have to bear it, you will have to bear it. Gambling is making people get poorer, and brokers' speculation is getting richer. Gambling makes the value of winners and losers different from one another. As a result, one party is wasted, one party suffers, and sooner or later it suffers from a painful situation. Therefore, it should be prohibited. The speculators' speculation can keep prices stable and avoid the danger of skyrocketing commodity prices. The brokers, after collecting at low prices and selling them at a high price, have brought prices not far apart. Moreover, speculation is forbidden and will not be effective. Therefore, gambling is harmful to society. Brokers' speculation is beneficial to society and they occupy an important position in international trade in the financial sector. Speculation in Europe and the United States is very popular, so the country is very rich, and European and American countries rely on brokers to buy large securities, otherwise, how they can do this business!"

To understand China's securities, it is necessary to first know China's public debt. Because of its close relationship with society, Ma's analysis in 1925 posited the following three reasons: First, bonds were issued on the market only by the central government; then high and low public debts were introduced, thereby leading to an increasing in number of transactions. Second, there was no real central bank in China. Bank interest rates did not matter. Discounting was minimal and it was equal to zero. It was not as good as that Britain's focus on financial markets at the Bank of England and interest rates. China only had public debt. Third, the wealthy people in the south took the capital and lived in Shanghai. They believed that exchange trusts were not safe and they did not dare to invest in them. Reliable investment channels only worked with public debt for buying and selling securities, both spot and futures (1-month, 2-month, etc.). "In theory, the national public debts should not be opened for futures markets, because futures make the market uneasy. As for futures, they are all short selling in China, in fact, the settlement is probably not yet 1.2%. So people all do futures business, which is more harmful than gambling." The first reason was that the chief financial officer could start rumors to manipulate the market, and encourage market prices to increase, so as to obtain profits from them, or to say that there is no interest, and the market price would drop so that they can buy from them. This practice could have been dealt with according to the law. The public debt had never been dealt with in accordance with the law. The second was that to get money from public debt was called earning money, which sounded better than winning money. Third, public debt can be used for more. Sometimes, although there was no money, it could also be used as a public debt, leading to losses for many. Fourth, the public debt transaction did not require personal contact, as long as there was a phone. Fifth, both men and women can do it as morality and money will inevitably have a relationship. Sixth, the fee for the public debt was only 0.05%, which was lower than gambling, but more harmful. Therefore, futures trading had to be prohibited. Ma's conclusion was only one-sided. On the contrary, objectively, public debt and futures had reasons for existence. From the buyer's point of view, there were regular income earners who were afraid of the instability of borrowing money from others and saw little profit in bank storage, thereby choosing to buy debt bonds. Even if it was useless, but as long as the price was appropriate, it would be expected to sell, though buyers feared that prices would fall the next month. "The introduction by the broker led to the transaction between the buyer and the seller."

There were two types of investment: investment and speculation. For the credit consolidation of the former, the price was often fluctuating between 96 percent to 99 percent of the value, and those who held it could not be cut off, and rare transactions occurred in the market. Relying on various legends, the price of the latter changed drastically, soaring and falling, with speculators being extremely active.

As for the buying and selling market, in terms of territoriality, there were only two locations, that is, Shanghai and Beijing had different market prices. Ma said, "But its interest must be more than the sum of interest on shipping dates and the total cost of shipping." As a result, the prices of the two places could be leveled out, so it was quite useful. Shanghai had two kinds of stocks and futures. Beijing had more stocks and fewer futures. Public debt speculation was required to be well informed. For example, if one person called for trading in financial bonds, one looked bullish and one looked bearish. Bullish thinking was that public debt will be drawn by lottery. "Of course there are speculations on the part of sale and purchase of public debts, but most of them depend on news. Well-informed people swear in left vouchers. Failure to do so will result in failure and can be asserted." "Furthermore, all countries in the United Kingdom and the United States have speculative activities, and most of them are specialists. In China, there are all walks of life. The bureaucrats are also in it." If the officials of the Ministry of Finance bought it, they must "retreat from it and become increasingly overspending, and the public debt is also extremely affected". In 1924, there was a strong reason for the vigorous trading of public debt in China. According to estimation of Ma, financial bonds were bought at a discount of 40% (RMB 384 for public bonds with a nominal value of 640 *yuan*, and RMB 10 for each). Lots were still available with an interest rate of 6% and interest of RMB 60. After the annual repayment of principal and interest, the principal and interest totaled 288 *yuan*. "That is, after the signing, there is still more than one silver. If this is the case, then besides taking back some of the RMB 384, the remaining RMB 288 will be real, and the resulting benefit will be RMB 124. All two-thirds will be strong, and the benefits will be known. Trying to fill in the unsigned votes, and increasing their profits more frequently, they have borrowers to pay public debt."

As for the issuance of public debt, both China and the United States issued directly, but the banks were subject to different conditions. Ma said that in China, it was "quite strange that it uses public debt to make payments to banks." Ma's concern regarding this issue was that it was a debt crisis in our country. "The public debt relationship is financially large. If the Fund breaks down, the victims will be banks, schools, charitable organizations, orphans and widows, and all those who have the debt, especially the banks. Because the bank is the issuer of banknotes, the bank prepares public debt for its issuance. If the public debt fund breaks down, the bank will fall; if the bank falls, then the banknote will certainly become waste paper. The general victimization of the people will cause great social disruption." "The security and destruction of China's financial community and the survival of millions of people in China all boil down to the responsibility of a British person. Who is he? F. Aglen, the general customs commissioner." If one continued to keep the fund, the public debt will be safe. If the public security was safe, then the banking sector will be safe. Then China will be safe. If one ignored it, or even refused to pay it, and used it to repay the unsecured debt, the public debt would be in danger of bank collapse. Ma said with pain, "F. Aglen has such a large force. The government respects him as well as the business community. Huge amounts of customs duties and customs remain in HSBC. In the past, there was no interest, but today it is only 2%." Later on, Ma once again pointed out, "The most dangerous problem now in China is foreign debt without definitive collateral, while domestic debt is the second highest. If the foreign debt is not returned, there is a danger of bankruptcy; if the internal debt is not returned, the credit of the country will be lost." Ma also specifically analyzed the cause of the soaring market price of China's public debt since the spring of 1924, and the lessons learned from corporate bonds. The market price of public bonds had skyrocketed, especially financial and the whole six. In addition to various reasons such as the richness of tariffs, reliable balloting, and political changes, there were 12 studies on economic changes. Four of those are as follows: First was the investment in insurance premiums. Taking the life insurance company as an example, the annual premium collection was very large. Except for death compensation, Ma estimated that there was a large surplus, but the investment was narrow. Only the purchase of public debts was practical, so there was a greater need for public debt, which would lead to a surge in its price. The second was the guarantee reserve for rechargeable securities. Ordinary banks and money houses must be able to issue redemption vouchers on behalf of their clients, that is, "vouchers", for which they must pay 50% or 60% of the cash to banks that have the right of distribution, ensuring that 45% of the funds were prepared. The remaining 30% could be paid off with public debt, so the use of public debt was large, and its price rose. The third was the investment source of the postal savings funds. There were 10,000 depositors. Large-scale deposits could be used to buy public debts and profits were excellent. The fourth was the target of pension investment. As long as the pensions raised by the customs post were no less than 50,000 *yuan*, they all used public debts to earn a living, for example, investment in school funds, speculative development, personal sales, purchase of products and deposits. For example, Jiaoji Railway's use of debt bonds as a substitute for the exchange's evidence gold, as well as the pending public debt exchange and other factors, contributed to the surge in demand for public debt bonds. The involvement of financial institutions was a fundamental factor, and was also the main reason.

In early 1936, when Ma concluded that domestic corporate bonds had no market, the reasons were as follows. First, people were not aware of the contents of the company. Chinese companies had always kept secrets and refused to show people the internal workings, so people did not trust the company. Second, after the trust company and exchange crisis, the accident of Sugar Corporation of the Republic of China, people lost faith in the company, and it is not easy to restore it. "If the company wishes to entrust an exchange to open a stock market, it must make a detailed report on its internal conditions, business conditions, and real estate prices, submit it to the Exchange Registration Committee for review, and only after the approval of the committee does it begin to take charge. Therefore, the exchange has the responsibility of the introducer. It is not prudent to do anything about it." Corporate bonds instead of factory base payments had interests for both the issuer and the investor. There were three interests for the issuer: First, there was greater flexibility. Shares were easy to increase and hard to reduce. Debt tickets could be recovered at any time and the issuance was the most convenient. The second was to increase the number of debtors without interfering with the company's business. Creditors could not attend shareholders' meetings. Third, it was more convenient than borrowing money. The maturity of the bond and the maturity of the settlement were set by the issuer. There were two benefits to investors: one was the use of cash, which could be sold at any time; the second was that the collateral was indeed reliable. The issue of debt papers concerned more banks, and the banks were willing to bear them. The guarantees had to be reliable. According to the provisions of the company law, the company must issue conditions and standards for the issuance of bonds. If the bank bore it alone, it will be the same as the lending. As a result, the bank funds would still be frozen. Therefore, if the bankers were liberated, they must sell the bonds. As long as the business was frequently buying and selling, the agent could be notified by telephone at any time. If it took only one or two weeks to trade once or twice, there was no possibility of being sold at any time. There were three reasons why the company's debt was not as good as the market. First, the public debt must be greatly reduced, and the company must be able to afford the burden. If it was sold at a 30% discount, the actual payment would be 30 *yuan*. In the future, the company would have to pay 70 *yuan*. The second was that even if the company wished, it could raise the ex-factory price. Third, banks found it extremely difficult to bear, as they had two kinds of concerns; one was the fear of losing money and the other was fear of loss of reputation. When the price was high, the bank lost money. If the price was low, the company was unwilling to do so. The direct issuance suffered a large loss. In the downturn of the market, the company's stock had always fallen more or less, so it was better to have no market. Ma's conclusion was, "A detailed consideration of all aspects and the issuance of corporate bonds is all the more unpredictable because there are still many preparations that have not been completed yet." The preparatory work meant that the company itself was open and honest, revealing the inside story so as to arouse people's belief in the company. This war of commerce was not the same as the war of arms. It was announcing the company's financial accounts as much as possible. It allowed one to send another accountant to investigate, as it should be creditworthy. This was true insight.

On exchange, in December 1920, Ma gave a speech titled "China's Exchange". He clearly pointed out, "Is the exchange a big casino? Are the people on the exchange the gambler? Is regular trading a bet? China has no exchange. There is one since the beginning of last year. ... People should clap their hands to celebrate and should not be slandering it. Even if exchange has shortcomings, people should point them out one by one to encourage the parties involved to carry out reforms." He also explained the process of regular trading, and the insider's story revealed that it was not like a casino. "If there is no cargo, it is speculation. Like horse racing, everyone goes to bet on this horse win. The horse wins. If it wins, you can get profit. This is the bet. The exchange is obviously a transaction. How can one bet? The casino is the first bet and then there is a win or a loss, but the price change is that we can't make it. So it's a big mistake to say that the exchange is a casino and the people who trade are gamblers. He pointed out that the exchange is a highly developed product economy and the latest product of world civilization. Modern society cannot live without it. It is a symbol of world progress." "Without them, big business can't be done, and the world will not make progress. Therefore, the more civilized the world, the less able the brokers and the exchanges are to save. All kinds of exchanges, either jointly or separately, are important; because they have a certain status in the economic community, they cannot be viewed by gamblers." He also made further efforts in the speech delivered in Shanghai in April. He said that the exchange "has more good than harm, it can be asserted". He said it was certain that "we cannot say that among the exchanges, no one gambles, and neither their directors nor brokers are fraudulent." He does not dare to say that there is no one who speculated among the banks. However, despite its many disadvantages, it was always a "commercial market where traders' brokers gather, reciprocal opinions, and exchanges of knowledge, so the message is smart." And he pointed out incisively that "exchanges are the tables of the cold of the society, and banks are the lifeblood of society." He argued that the exchange was born "in response to this highly competitive world", and was "the indispensable part of society". If there was disruption in the world, the first thing affected would be the exchange. With the news of the exchange being agile, although the bank was able to enjoy all kinds of news, it still needed to pay special attention to the exchange. "As soon as the stock market crashes, the bank receives a scale payment, the merchant has goods and cannot be detained, and borrows money from the bank, so the livelihood of the society is very low. … The number of buyers is also reduced, and the price of goods will fall increasingly. … On the contrary, after the resumption of peace, all countries traded with each other, and the economic circles gradually became lively. ... Various industries thrive, prices of various stocks in exchanges rose, banks raised their prices, made loans, and increased livelihoods in the market. If there are goods, there will be live assets, and if there are goods, there will be fresh money, and if there is live money, people will be able to handle new goods. The price of goods will go up, and the surplus will be greater (high price has surplus). The people at all levels of society are very pleased with each other." He also pointed out with regret that China's current exchanges did not yet have such an effect because they were still in the "naive age" and there was no market for stocks and various commodities in various industries. Therefore, the relationship between banks and exchanges was not very close. "However, today's banks buying and selling public debt securities comply with the exchange's market conditions."

At that time, there were many transactions in the exchange, which were extremely significant. Combined with China's national conditions, Ma assumed that broker A had stock and was short of cash. Broker B had cash and was short of stock. The two were able to communicate with each other and implement delivery. The second type was borrowing after the selling was over. Borrowing and repurchasing were different, and they had the same effect. One was in and one was out, and two were offset. There was no need to pay for the stock. Therefore, after the closing of a foreign transaction, two brokers or loans were exchanged, and the delivery was erroneous. The borrowing of foreign stocks and the lending of government bonds in China become a phenomenon of securities trading. Why did a broker borrow money from a bank? First, the bank's interest rate was earned by its peers. Second, the procedures for bank borrowing were very easy to understand. Third, the borrowers in the industry could go straight out without discounting. Those who lacked the securities, if they threw too much speculation, were unable to make up for a moment, and had to take a debit. Those who had stocks to borrow could offer harsh conditions. In addition to swapping securities in cash, people had to put interest on it, so that the annual interest rate was 18 points (180%). In the absence of cash, Party A commissioned the agent to purchase the government bond at C. The cash was not settled. If he can get a bank loan, it is necessary to pay public debt in cash. It will be difficult for them to advance or retreat. Party A had to borrow from the bank's credit, or find another guarantee. During this period, some banks took a risk. Because there was no bank law, they were not aware of whether they were illegal.

The characteristics of China's foreign debt was the topic of Ma's lecture in August 1924. The content was vast. There were eight points: First, there must be collateral. There was no collateral for borrowings from each other in Europe and the United States. Second, China's foreign borrowing, public or private, all used diplomatic procedures. The governments of Europe and the United States must go through diplomatic procedures. The government and other countries' private borrowers will directly negotiate with private individuals. After an outsider signed a contract with China, he often failed to perform it. If the rights in the contract were resold to others, the contract could be fulfilled at a high price, otherwise it will be ignored. Third, all countries borrowed from China, all represented by banks. The Japanese representative had three banks, the United States had two, the UK had two, France had three, Russia had one and Germany had one. In terms of financial benefits, the bank was the treasurer and repayment of debts must be handled by the bank. The fourth was the priority of the loan. If one borrowed from a country the last time, the next time the loan must be offered to the country before they can borrow from other countries. Fifth, all countries had their sphere of influence. In order to borrow within their sphere of influence, a country also needed to first approach another country. Sixth, where a property or tax source was used as collateral for borrowing, an income was managed by an outsider and an auditor general office or branch office was established. It was operated by an outsider and all income was deposited in a foreign bank. Seventh, all the debt claims were deposited in foreign banks. The tight monetary conditions in China were related to the cash income of China's domestic foreign banks and China Merchants Bank, and were not the same as the cash inflows of domestic banks and foreign banks. If the railway was used as collateral, the railroad's procurement of materials, construction of roads, designation of the chief accountant's general accountant and supervision of the railway after its completion were all within its scope. The cause of China's foreign debt was the issuance of bonds, including the underwriting with foreign banks, which led to the fall of China's director general, who was restrained by the people, due to which the directors suddenly held full powers. Eighth, loans from foreign countries were all due to political ambitions for China, such as Japan in South Manchuria, Russia in Dongqing and the Xiyuan loan from four countries. Therefore, Ma came to the conclusion, "China cannot borrow foreign debt at this time, and domestic debt is also difficult to raise, leaving only the spam bill."

3.4.3. *The issue of interest rate cuts in China*

In the three lectures on *The Problem of China's Emphasis on Heavy Interests* in 1922, Ma analyzed the causes, related problems and solutions to China's heavy interests.

The reason for the heavy burden of interest in China was as follows. *The Beijing News'* editor wrote about the issue of interest, which attracted worldwide attention. Wang Heng, a member of parliament, thought that the interest could be reduced by legal enforcement. Ma thought that "heavy burden of interest is the natural trend of the economy and cannot be enforced by man-made laws." According to Western academic theory, he believed that there were three explanations. First, there was no saving. Second, there was a lack of capital. Third, the Chinese valued the current and looked toward the future. "China's savings (for one hand) are difficult, and the production business (on the one hand) needs to be developed. It is too demanding. If the demand is too high, the interest will be high. This is because of the natural relationship." However, he also pointed out, "China has its own reality, foreign countries have their own reasons, and there is something that cannot be applied. ... There are various special situations in China. ... Taking China's facts as a precondition, it is not a theory that can solve the various problems." The reason why China's interest was heavy was based on academics and empirical evidence, and the fundamental problem of heavy profits was that there were many kinds of interest. Pawnshop interest rates were 25%, public debt was 20%, bank lending was 15%, and bank demolition and bank houses were 2%. There was no standard interest rate at all. There were various reasons for various kinds of interest, not only purely for profit. In detail, first, it was about improperly obtained money and nothing else. The interest rate differed from bank to bank. The bank only worked for two days (in Shanghai). If the deadline for reimbursement was near, and the procedures were troublesome, the interest could not be low. The second was the bad currency system. The lenders must avoid losing money to prevent losses. Third, the traffic was inconvenient and the freight rate was high. Fourth, the contract (such as rent) was expensive. How could the interest not be high? Fifth, China's customs salt tax revenue was stored in foreign banks, resulting in less cash and greater demand. Sixth, there were many fixed assets (houses), and the market was increasingly lacking in jobs. Seventh, the public debt was used for military expenditure, and social wealth was lacking. Eighth, foreign banks in China absorbed more leisure payments from China. Once China's domestic demand increased, taking out deposits from outsiders would have led to an empty treasury and interest would therefore increase. Based on this, Ma believed that the legally enforced claim "has no use for facts".

However, looking at it from a social perspective, the roots of heavy interest were as follows: First, there was insufficient capital. The level of interest should be regarded as the amount of capital. If China wanted low interest, it must first increase capital. The positive approach was that everyone had savings. The negative approach was to use foreign capital for production needs. At that time, China was feeling a lack of capital. Due to the adjustment of the law of supply and demand, wages were low and interest was high. "According to the phenomenon of evolution, interest rates have been declining, and wages have been rising. Our country is just the opposite of this phenomenon." It was because of the shortage of capital. "Interest is paid for capital, not for money now; money is just the media ear of exchange." Most people in China mistakenly believe that interest was born because of borrowing money. In fact, it was not money but capital. The second was insufficient chips. There was more demand and less supply, leading to slower currency flows. To increase the number of chips and speed up the flow of goods, everyone had to use notes and cheques. In the UK, 97% of the means of payment was cheques, with the corresponding statistic in the United States being 95%. Banknotes had become a thing of the past. To develop the habit of using cheques in China, it was necessary to first solve the problem of banknotes. The drawer must trust the arbitrators and believe in the bank, and the banknotes only needed to be trusted by the bank. In order to solve the problem of banknotes, it was necessary to take the lead in planning a unified currency system and establish the local currency so that the currency can be used in the same way as the current ocean and realized in a timely manner. Therefore, it must follow the laws of the United States and provide for full cashing. For example, "the National Bank of the United States has the obligation to accept banknotes from other banks, but it does not have the right to use bank notes from other banks. The banknote falling price will not happen. Everyone has developed the habit of using banknotes, and cheques can also become common gradually. Therefore, the credit system is well developed. There are fewer money uses, and the number of chips increases, and the interest rate can be low." Otherwise, there was no hope of low interest. Promissory notes and bills of exchange can be discounted abroad and can be circulated, but not in China. "In the big deals, some of them need to be delivered on credit, and they must use cash. ... The demand for cash is high, the supply is low, and the interest rate is high." Chinese villages do not use banknotes but use cash. "If there is large need for cash, then the status of money rises, so people who borrow money need to use high interest to borrow money." The military used to occupy the mint, "in order to seek profits. ... China cannot freely cast money, so for the time being, there is an urgent crisis." "All provinces prohibit the export of money" and "Chinese villagers are happy to hide the money". By the time of the "liquidation, they would use the current money and could not keep accounts." "So the interest rate is related to the system, but not to politics."

In short, "interest is capital remuneration and has nothing to do with stacks (money). It is related to the stacks (money), but not only the price. So the level of interest depends on the number of capital. Therefore, the level of interest depends on the number of capital; the price level depends on the amount of money; if the money is more, its status will be lowered, the status of money will be reduced, and the price will rise and vice versa. However, money acts as a medium of exchange (chips). When the media are not fully allocated, the borrower is willing to pay high interest to borrow it."

In his important speech in January 1922 and his article "China's Banking Problem", which was published in 1925, Ma discussed the issue of heavy interests. Ma talked about the level of market interest rates, the backward bookkeeping law, the unlimited repayment period, unsafe trading, the debtor's sense of responsibility, excess of capital to buy, interest rebates and troublesome procedures that affect market interest rates. The credit system was naive, there was a lack of capital and there were insurance premiums in interest rates, as mentioned above. The high interest rate in China was also owing to arbitrage. In June and July, the bank bought silver dollars in silver and used those to buy the latest (7 months) public debt, while selling long-term (9 months) debts. Due to the recent long-term expense, the bank sold more silver dollars. The double interest of the public debt was due to the calculation of interest being more than two points, because the bank loan interest had to be more than two points. "It can be seen that the high interest rate in China is due to the bad habits of bookkeeping, bad credit systems, and interest rates that contain insurance premiums. In more detail, our country's laws are incomplete, politics are not pragmatic, and monetary systems are not unified." "The failure of the credit organization, the degeneration of the people's morality, and the infringement of commercial transactions are all the main reasons for the improvement of market interest. Yan said that banks bought government bonds and exploited the government to raise the interest rate. This is only one of the reasons." There were many reasons, but there were also differences between the primary and secondary systems, mechanisms, and political, economic, military and cultural differences.

If the above is an analysis of the internal reasons, then the following is an analysis of the external causes. Ma pointed out that "the level of the Bank of China is not confined to my hand and it is in the hands of outsiders. London is the world's financial center, and the price of silver is decided by it. Even if banks are to be restricted by law, their power cannot be compared with London." "Our country uses silver, other countries use gold. Silver's low status means more exports, while silver's high status means more imports … and the price of silver is set by London. Therefore, the level of the bank is set by London, not my own. … Therefore, if we want to solve the problem of high interest in our country, we must study various situations at home and abroad. However, if we rely on arbitrariness and not tell the truth, I have not seen it."

In 1936, in the book *China's New Financial Policy*, Ma made a special topic to discuss the issue of interest rate cuts. This was an analysis of the reasons for the high interest rates after the implementation of the currency exchange policy. One of the reasons for this was the speculation on China's investment. Previously, it was public debt, real estate and gold bullion. After the implementation of the legal currency policy, the speculative capital outflow was far less successful than in the past. However, the mainland needed extensive funds. After the increase in the price of silver, there was a lot of money going to foreign countries. Therefore, bank deposit interest rates were still falling, and Shanghai bank deposits were transferred into the three major banks. From the perspective of social capital supply, which was less than the past, the three major banks released very little. If they could give up more, the financial market would be loose and the interest rate would not be difficult to lower; otherwise, "while one wants to reduce interest rates, one concentrates deposits with the National Bank. How could it be?" Second, China lacked a capital market (industry, bank, trust company, etc.). According to the natural divide of the financial industry, short-term deposits were used for short-term loans, and long-term deposits were used for long-term loans. At that time, China did not have a real investment bank or savings bank. "China's ordinary commercial banks are also engaged in both short-term lending and long-term lending. The responsibility is heavy and interest rates are naturally high. The road to relief is designed to quickly create a capital market." Third, China's capital market organization is incomplete. "No discount market. ... Now banks are only making mortgage loans. ... But why banks are not willing to operate discounting, then the central bank is not going to reassert it now."

Ma also discussed the need for interest rate cuts, the difficulty of banks in cutting interest rates alone, the relationship between interest and credit, pawn shops, legal interest rates and market interest rates, and the advantages and disadvantages of reducing interest rates.

On the need to cut interest rates, high interest rates were thought to be a major obstacle to China's economic construction. Although there was little benefit in reducing interest rates, if one could improve the production technology and use large machines, it would be possible to urgently reduce interest rates, so that the national economy will gradually thrive and the national economy will prosper. The government's revenue would increase, and it would not be difficult to balance the government's budget. "From this point of view, reducing interest rates to balance the budget is also a passable approach."

High interest rates were not conducive to the development of letters and pawn shops. All countries had trust companies, of which the United State's was the most developed. Although China had a trust company, its operation was very lax. The reason was that it had high interest rates. Assume that the market interest rate is reduced, so that the return on deposits is not as good as investment income. Everyone is happy to invest and the trust business will flourish. The relationship between Chinese pawn shops and the civilian life on the mainland was close. Even the economically developed countries in the world, such as Britain and Japan, had not been eliminated pawn shops, not to mention China, which had such a debilitating economy. Since there was a need for the pawn industry to exist, it was imperative to improve its organization and business. The main point of improvement was in the reduction of interest rates, which indicated that "high interest rates not only make production difficult, but consumption is also not easy. There is also a need for reduction."

Chinese people often held the view that higher interest rates resulted in cutting down expenses, further saving money and promoting the development of factories, which was also the doctrine that orthodox economists believed in. But Ma argued that it was not always true. As one of the costs of production, higher interest rates would lead to higher production costs and lower profits for entrepreneurs. Everyone was willing to earn profits from deposits and unwilling to engage in new businesses, so how could enterprises develop? Without the development of enterprises, the workers had no opportunity to work, causing an increase in the number of the unemployed, which was unfavorable to labor and capital. However, with the separate interest rate reduction of bank, if the high interest rate was not moved and the interest rate was only reduced, the bank would find it difficult to maintain itself. If the deposit interest was reduced simultaneously, the depositors will not save to pursue higher profits, which will reduce the bank deposits and affect the bank's business. There was no influence on the foreign banks in China, resulting in domestic bank deposits flowing abroad. Therefore, it was difficult to hope for interest rate cuts alone in banks.

Legal interest rate and market interest rate were discussed, and Mr. Ma believed that the interest rate cuts could not be enforced. It was even more difficult to do so if the government explicitly cut interest rates. At that time, the civil law stipulated, "If the interest rate exceeds 20%, the creditor has no right to claim interest beyond part of the interest rate." Therefore, the monthly interest rate of 2% was the ceiling. But the mainland lending rate was often 3% or 4%, which was illegal and was evaded by offenders. Some people thought that the law was inconsistent with the facts, so it was better not to prescribe to it. Mr. Ma pointed out, "Although the law cannot be consistent with the facts, the law should be set due to its legal restrictions to facts." In his view, the government had no right to force the factual debtor to accept. However, "The law should stipulate limits for the standard of the ordinary human." There was no point in the provision of the minimum threshold, as the financial market could be allowed to float when the funds were loosened. So, a maximum limit was necessary without a minimum requirement.

The advantages and disadvantages of reducing interest rates were compared and Mr. Ma believed that there were respective strengths and weaknesses. In terms of profits, entrepreneurs can save money. It could do nothing for the already fallen entrepreneurs, but was beneficial to those who were on the edge of bankruptcy. Then, investment and saving were the supply and demand of capital, respectively. Their expansion and decline were determined by interest rates. The relatively large savings indicated that the supply of capital was larger than the demand and interest rates should be reduced to encourage investment; on the contrary, interest rates should be raised to limit the investment. The interest rate of the balance of investment and savings was called the natural interest rate. In 1939, he further pointed out that reducing interest rates had many benefits. The working efficiency of workers would not be affected, and the purchasing power of the people could be maintained and all disputes could be avoided. The disadvantage was that creditors suffered losses, and long-term investments will be affected. "Despite the reduction of nominal interest rates, real interest rates may be higher." It was a common phenomenon that the nominal interest rate was reduced and the market price of public debt fell with higher real interest rates, resulting in people's panic, a more serious fall of market price and even higher real interest rates. Therefore, compared with advantages, there were more disadvantages.

In the case of disadvantages, where were the outlets and where were the remedies? In November 1922, Ma proposed two aspects internally and externally: "(1) The number of chips in the game should be increased with the development of credit system. Everyone develops the habit of using banknotes. Common banknotes are necessary for the circulation of checks. The banknotes, cashing should be stipulated by the law and the monetary system must be unified. (2) The external money standard must be changed." After the implementation of the legal currency policy, in the face of new changes, he pointedly proposed, "It is necessary for the central bank to reduce the discount rate for the nation. So that effectiveness is large. In terms of long-term decrease of interest rates, creative savings, increasing production, and the rapid expansion of the people's financial resources are of great significance." In 1939, in the paper on the reduction of interest rates, he said it should be based on the general economic situation, and proposed that it was necessary for the government to consider the general economic situation. "For the pawn loan to the civilian population, it is inherently necessary to reduce the interest rate, and the loan rate of financial authority to the producer (the factory, the business name) should be set based on inflation. The corresponding policy adjustments should be made with the changes in the situation. It is necessary to not only fit with the requirements of the new situation, but also play an active role in interest."

3.5. Foreign exchange and foreign investment

3.5.1. Foreign exchange problems in China

In *China's New Financial Policy*, Ma distinguished the role of two different concepts of balance of payments and international trade imports. He pointed out that the former was greater than the latter, because it included the following two types of income and expenditures: (1) Income beyond trade, such as income from business and (2) revenues beyond financial, such as personal income from non-businesses (e.g., heritage rent). The so-called trade deficit of China over the years was not about the total number of international payments, but about the income and expenditure of international tangible trade. Whether the number of over-entry differences was reliable or not was based on the accuracy of customs records. However, there were many omissions in China's customs statistics, such as the following: (1) Border trade on land was often missed. For example, in the past, the records of the import of Japanese goods and Russian goods in the three eastern provinces and the trade between Yunnan and Vietnam in ancient times were often incomplete. (2) There was an underestimation of smuggling and cargo price. Due to the increase of the tariff rate in China, the smuggling of foreign goods from the customs had proportionally increased. There were still some people who had smuggled goods and were not caught. In terms of China's export of goods, businessmen preferred reporting more than actual numbers. From the perspective of the country, there were two reasons for export underestimation: First, the price of export goods was reported higher than the actual price. Second, the value of export goods in terms of numbers was the average. This average was set based on the prices in the spring, summer and autumn, which were lower than the actual price, and did not include the freight costs from the mainland port to Shanghai. (3) The value of foreign goods imported by China was greater than that of goods exported by China. That is, the value of foreign imports was calculated by gold, and the value of Chinese exports was calculated by silver. If the Chinese goods imported by foreign countries were converted into silver prices, there would be three situations in which the value of Chinese goods imported by foreign countries would be greater than the value of China's exports: The first was the increase of foreign price with China's export price being stable. The second was that foreign silver price was reduced. The value of foreign goods entering China was converted into silver coins, which was greater than the value of Chinese exports. The third was that foreign prices and silver prices had risen. The latter had risen less than the former, and then the foreign purchases converted into silver prices were greater than the Chinese export prices. China's export prices could not increase with it, because China's export trade agencies were different from foreign countries. First, silver was used in China and gold was used in foreign countries. The silver price fluctuation was not consistent with export prices (When silver price rose, export prices might have been low. When silver prices fell, the price might have been high.) Second, although few Chinese exporters handled the export business, they were mostly foreign businessmen. The ship insurance was also done by outsiders. Then, China Merchants Insurance was also limited to the domestic market. Therefore, export trade was completely manipulated by foreign businessmen. There were favorable opportunities for exports when foreign prices rose or silver prices fell. Foreign businessmen benefited from this and Chinese could not control it. (4) The input of army force supplies was not counted by the customs. Although there was no investigation, the number was not small.

Therefore, there were two reasons why China's actual export value was less than the value of exports: One was that exporters were overstated, and the other was that foreign prices rose or silver prices fell. Due to the manipulation of foreign trade, export prices could not react immediately. Domestic prices had to take considerable time before they could catch up. On the contrary, if foreign prices fell, domestic prices would also decline. Based on this, Ma believed that at the time, it was necessary to correct the misconceptions of the past. First, China's trade deficit was different from that of other countries. Second, China's export trade was often lower than foreign import prices. Several scholars only knew that China's trade deficit was related to export underestimation, but did not know that foreign banks held China's export trade and controlled the difference between foreign price rise and silver price fall, which had to also be corrected.

Faced with the intensification of Japanese militarism against China, Ma Yinchu was particularly concerned about its economic aggression against China. He revealed that there was serious smuggling activity in North China since August of 1935. According to official reports, from August 1, 1935 to April 30, 1936, China's tariffs had lost an average of about 8 million *yuan* per month, and had lost about 10 million *yuan* each year. Another statistic was that China's daily loss was about 500,000 *yuan*, which was more serious than shown in official reports. He also pointed out that smuggling in North China was an economic weapon that supported Japan's military aggression against China.

Based on this, Mr. Ma proposed to make up for the unfavorable balance of trade. He believed that gold and silver declaration export and privatization exports, foreign investment in China and credit loans, overseas remittances and foreigner's costs in China could all be regarded as essential elements of compensation. There was still room for discussion of the number. This could be illustrated by foreign tourists traveling to China, overseas remittances, gold and silver exports and foreign investment in China. Every year, the US accounted for 1/4 to 1/3 of tourism in the world. China had to take advantage of the phenomenon. China was famous for its vast land, historic sites and scenic spots. If transport was more convenient, the country would be quite attractive as a tourist destination, which would contribute to the annual revenue of intangible exports. "Why don't we take action?" Overseas Chinese remittances had been greatly reduced due to the panic of the world economy. Besides, they had been suppressed everywhere, further reducing the remittances. In the past, remittances were operated frequently with large numbers. In the future, remittances were expected to decrease sharply. Therefore, the funds exchanged from remittances had to be used to invest into production and increase exports to meet expectations of the diaspora. Gold and silver exports would not be able to continue beyond 10 years, and foreign exchange restrictions should be imposed to remedy them. There were many precedents for using foreign capital to rejuvenate the country. In the past, foreigners invested directly in China with the protection of consular jurisdiction, and were not subject to Chinese control. All were determined by the willingness of investment country rather than the planning of the Chinese government. China was trapped in foreign capital with unspeakable pain. This was fully proved by the fact that the British borrowed to build the Shanghai–Hangzhou–Ningbo Railway. The Belgians wished to build the Jinghan Railway. In contrast, China's trade deficit with Japan was not compensated by China's export of silver, and most of it was invested into China by the Japanese. During the more than 20 years from 1907 to 1930, Japan's total investment in China was 2.53 billion yen, while Japan's export surplus to China was over 2.42 billion yen during the same period, which was almost the same. Therefore, with such a great amount, the problem of China's trade deficit to foreign countries was really serious, which greatly affected the survival of the country.

3.5.2. Issues concerning the utilization of foreign capital

In a chapter of *China's New Financial Policy*, Ma suggested that using foreign capital was necessary for China to balance with other countries in the world. The use of foreign capital and relying on the League of Nations were not wise. There were many difficulties in borrowing from Britain and the United States. It was impossible to ask for a guarantee of the Federation and lend to the international community. It can be seen that there was no way to use foreign capital. Some people suggested the use of domestic resources. Ma believed that the existing domestic industries were light industry, with no need for huge amounts of capital. Although the number was numerous, it was not sufficient to demonstrate that domestic capital could be used. "If we want to set up a heavy industry and build a railway, domestic resources will be insufficient, and savings will be slow and unusable. Taking advantage of savings and using domestic capital seems a good way. It's easier to say it than to do it. It can only be realized when people implement forced savings, save daily consumption, and reduce living standards with the spirit of sacrifice. It is impossible for most Chinese whose life is extremely hard to have savings. If you follow the example of Soviet Russia, the hardship of the people will be even more serious." Therefore, it was virtually impossible to use domestic capital. As a result, Ma adjusted his thinking to the world currency market and did some intensive investigations. In terms of financing, he always kept the country and the nation and even the government in his mind.

Ma took Britain and the United States as examples to show that stabilizing the exchange rate was conducive to stabilizing prices, while stabilizing the exchange rate needed to be related to international investment. To prevent excessive international borrowing of China, South American countries (Chile, Peru, Bolivia, etc.), Poland, Austria, Germany, Hungary and Egypt after World War I were presented as the examples. The aim of Japan's large investment in China was thus more obvious. China only had a monetary market and no capital market. Therefore, long-term funds were mostly from the monetary market. There were many people represented by Zhang Naiqi and Yang Yingpu who advocated the opening of the capital market. The National Government claimed that the Ministry of Finance was also planning to open up capital markets and establish various investment banks. Ma thought otherwise and pointed out that it could not be achieved for a while.

According to Ma's investigation and research, the Anglo-American capital market also formed gradually, with the bank established first and then the bank law rather than first the regulations and then the establishment of banks. The silver company should be built as the foundation of the investment company first, and then gradually expanded, resulting in a capital market. In order to prevent the disadvantages of excessive investment due to competition, the United States had set up the Securities and Exchange Commission of 1933 for investment in foreign countries. China should have the corresponding countermeasures. Ma analyzed the dangers of excessive international investment and borrowing, and its prevention. He believed that regulation was necessary. First, the organization of the capital market should be simplified. Second, banks that operate long-term investments should cooperate in division of labor to avoid competition. Third, the supervision of the government should be conducted. Then the excessive investment could be avoided. It was reasonable in China at that time. He thought it unwise for China to borrow directly from Britain and the United States or rely on the League of Nations. The credibility of the League of Nations had been destroyed. It could be seen that there was no way to use foreign capital. British commercial banks would not make long-term investments. There were other investment banks making long-term investments. The banking law promulgated by the United States in 1933 stipulated that a long-term investment bank was not allowed to be a member of the Federal Reserve Bank. The boundary between the two was strict. Banks in continental Europe were often engaged in both business and investment because of their strong capital. The use of bank capital for operating and utilizing short-term deposits for long-term investment was different. The investment industry had to be supervised by staff, with relatively smaller risks. China's commercial banks also double the long-term loans, industrial loans, and mortgaged the factory bases and machinery, whose value was declining due to depreciation. Besides, the funds were increasing due to interest. The two were running counter to each other, so the lending would have failed. China's banks were often exposed to short-term deposits and long-term deposits with factories, which were very dangerous. It was proposed that the base machinery of the factory should be offset to issue public debt and absorb social capital. The interest on the company's debt should be guaranteed by the bank. If the surplus was sufficient, it could be slightly distributed. In this way, it was not difficult to create a capital market. The investment banks in the United Kingdom and the United States were very few. Talents, sufficient resources, special wisdom and experience were all necessary. They had to be familiar with the legal habits and local conditions of various countries. The kind of investment that is favorable and safe must be considered comprehensively. It was already common in the United Kingdom and the United States. In China, considering the failure of investment in the past, it was thought best to avoid competition, divide the scope and take care of them to avoid the excessive investment. In addition, the establishment of specialized organizations and the placement of specialized talents made long-term investment much more stable than earlier. Moreover, the capital market still needed a sound organization. Under the investment agency, there were brokerages and classics with companies in various countries. Wholesale could be dispersed throughout the country. As mentioned earlier, in China, it was still necessary to organize bank groups to work together.

With no hope of borrowing from the world capital market and the difficulty of using domestic capital, only the world currency market was accessible. There were different benefits for both parties with the use of foreign capital, namely, international investment. Ma believed that if foreign capital was available and various industries were held, the opportunities for people to work would increase with higher income and greater living standards. The world was a community. The economy in all countries could not be separated from the international community. All countries had to work together to be prosperous. However, the disadvantage of the use of foreign capital was that the investing country could abandon it halfway and the creditor countries might suspend the loan. The debt could not be deposited and the previously borrowed money had to be repaid with interest. In this way, the debtor country could only increase exports to repay the loan. The creditor countries feared that their own industry was threatened and thus resisted it. Therefore, they reduced the value of the currency, increased the tariff and adopted a quota distribution system so that the goods of the debtor country could not be imported. The debtor country could neither borrow foreign debt nor increase exports to repay the old debt, resulting in the repudiation. After the demonstration, Ma thought that China should follow the example of Soviet Russia and borrow short-term funds from the United States to purchase production tools (capital assets) from the United States. The effect would be the same as capital.

China's use of foreign capital in two different ways, tangible and intangible, was compared. The tangible way meant that the borrowers and the lenders had agreed upon the conditions for borrowing. The intangible way meant that bankers had securities. Ma pointed out that the latter was very simple on the surface, but it was quite complicated and could only be conducted by experts. "First, national securities markets and foreign exchange markets should be obtained to determine whether there is interest to countries. Second, we must be familiar with the situation of securities in national markets. Third, we must be familiar with the habits of national exchanges. Fourth, we must know the representation of securities markets in various countries. Fifth, it is important to know that the purpose of the securities market units in various countries is only to make profits, to move funds among various countries, to promote the purchase of low places, and to sell at high places and obtain spreads." The function was to adjust funds all the time and balance the interest rates of various countries. The result was that the international economy was based on the principle of division of labor. If capital could flow freely, capital remuneration had to be uniform. The industries were backward because of the lack of capital and the number of workers in poor living conditions and high capital rewards. Without intervention, developed countries would be willing to send the rest of their capital to backward countries to develop the industries in backward countries, which would significantly increase the capital reserves and decrease the interest rates. So, people's living standards would improve and the international economy would be balanced. "It is not difficult for the world to be united." On the contrary, it was advocated that capital should remain in the country and that foreign investment was a deterrent and counter to development. At that time, governments of all countries found it difficult to interfere with securities, which was quite effective in balancing world interest rates. The profit difference was small, so huge profits could only be obtained with great numbers. The scope of the set was not limited to two countries, that is, trade could be conducted among three or four countries, but the matter was very complicated, and was better conducted by those rich in experience and knowledge. There were two ways in which this could be done, one of which was joint venture. For example, a British bank and a US bank could establish a contract, joint venture arbitrage and share profits and losses every month. The other was sole proprietorship, such as entrusting foreign banks with representation, where they should carry the burden of profits and losses alone, but must be responsible for agency remuneration. Setting up securities was not as good as excessive borrowing of tangible capital to prevent excessive investment or excessive borrowing. The circulation of intangible capital was not harmful, but was difficult to manage.

Ma treated the research on the capital market with caution. He not only paid attention to the derivation of theory but also emphasized the feasibility of practical operation. He introduced the practices of advanced foreign countries, and dealt with problems according to China's national conditions. He was commercially minded and had a clear political and national position, which deserves further study.

3.6. The relationship between China's monetary finance and traditional economic ideas

Ma studied the relationship between monetary finance and financial economy under traditional Chinese economic thinking. Because the traditional economic thinking maintained the existing policy path, the acceptance of domestic and foreign prices was unknown. What type of monetary finance could be accepted considering people's customs and psychological literacy? Ma said, "Most Chinese are deeply affected by old ideas. It is impossible to change their way of thinking entirely. Therefore, we should make them change gradually."

Ma held that the focus of China's traditional thought lay in the middle ground and peace, which were valued by the Chinese for more than 2,000 years. Confucius believed that people worried about uneven distribution rather than being allocated fewer goods and they paid more attention to peace than wealth. It can be noted that the middle ground and peace were more important for them. This kind of thinking was not suitable in Ma's time. But it was impossible to completely remove this thought due to its long history. Introducing new ideas and new organizations and at the same time acknowledging the traditional and original thoughts were equally important.

Ma believed that all kinds of nations and societies were influenced by traditional ideas. Western thought was influenced by ancient Greece and Rome, whose most prominent theorists were Socrates and Aristotle. China was a country with the longest recorded history in the world and the influence of traditional ideas on China was even greater. In the long history of human beings, a nation could be ruled by different rulers, the government was reorganized and the capital was moved, once or twice, even dozens of times. Moreover, foreigners entered the Central Plains and were virtually influenced by traditional thinking and assimilated into the Han nationality. It can be noted that the traditional thinking goes deep into people. Therefore, one should clearly understand the traditional thinking. What should be left and what should be removed need to be reassessed. It should be related to the entire national spirit and cannot be dismissed overall. This is because the traditional thinking of the nation referred to beliefs of one or more theories in history and people were inexorably dominated by them without awareness. All kinds of nations and societies cannot escape the domination of their traditional ideas.

After comparing traditional Chinese thought and Western ideas, Mr. Ma pointed out that China's traditional thinking focused on peace, which was different from the westerners who weighed on strength. The Chinese people focused on self-reliance, and relative safety was important to interpersonal relationships. Everyone was afraid of something. A so-called big issue was transformed into a trivial matter, and a small matter was transformed into nothing. Disputes between people were always resolved by mediation. The Chinese were most afraid of involving the courts, thinking that it may hurt each other. The state focused on policing. In ancient times, policing was the first evaluation index for the performance appraisal of local officials. "Foreigners are different from us." In western countries, individuals focused on self-reliance, and people were mutually reinforcing, and the country focused on self-prosperity. "Therefore, in this world, we only seek peace instead of strength, which is not sufficient for self-preservation. But peace should not be forgotten when we struggle for our life. Extremes of the strongest will surely cause violence. There will be no humanity and the human civilization will be destroyed. China is balanced and not rich, while westerners are rich and unbalanced. If Chinese and Western thought can be exchanged with each other, then conflicts can be reduced and saving themselves can be achieved. As shown in "The Canon of Emperor Yao" in the *Shangshu*, the management of China is based on the principle of security. Chinese national spirit lies in peace and has become an indelible force in Chinese society. The paths of Chinese Confucianism and Taoism doctrine are different from each other, but seeking peace is the same target. Laozi's philosophy stressed that the natural course cannot be disorganized by humans, which includes peace inside. Confucius said: The benevolent is full of love and peace. The benevolence means that the two people complement each other. Therefore, peace is of significance among people. He also pointed out that the spirit of peace is the foundation of the Confucian philanthropic theory of Chinese social organizations. Considering five kinds of human relations and principle, Yao Dian pointed out that peace is vital in daily life. Mencius said: Charity begins at home, but should not end there. Of course, parents and strangers are different. Outside of five kinds of human relations and principle, all men on earth are human brothers. Similar to Christianity and Buddhism, although times have changed, this thought has not been destroyed." In Ma's view, the principle of peace was expressed in politics, diplomacy, religion and the armed forces. "Even if the foreign people enter the Central Plains, China can accept them with peace. In the nearly three decades of the Civil War, most people considered it had nothing to do with it. Religion can also be accepted with peace. The political monarchy is mainly demised rather than usurpation. Tender policy is used in Diplomatic activities. Confucius said: If others do not obey, we should attract them with great culture and further comfort them."

China's economic thinking for thousands of years could be expressed as the middle ground and peace. Peace can be realized through the middle ground, and the middle ground is the purpose of peace. State order, land governing, self-cultivation and family regulation all follow the principle.

China had a system of communal wealth (the property owned by the father and the sons and the husband and wife), a system of sub-finance (brothers had the right to co-finance and also the right to sub-finance) and a system of financial assistance (the principle of seeking compensation was applied in the relationship between relatives and friends). Based on the principle of average, Chinese families divided properties through agreement. The Chinese people attached great importance to wealth, but did not collect wealth. The result was the lack of big capitalists, and the dispersal of property from one individual, which depended on their financial resources. Wealth was divided among all people, and there were no rich or poor classes. This kind of social organization had been maintained for thousands of years because the ancient fiscal policies advocated the distribution of wealth to the people. As the saying goes, "the financial dispersion means the people's gathering, and the financial gathering means the people's dispersion." Low taxes were thought to be moral and high taxes were thought of as a form of tyranny. Official business was also considered evil by the society, with the thought that it should not compete with the people. Both the government and the society in ancient times advocated small capitalist enterprises. Each enterprise operated as a sole proprietorship without organization of joint-stock companies. The scope was small, and there was no panic. There were small peasants for generations without big landlords. Mechanical work was not advocated in the industry. Strange tricks were banned for generations. There was only the family-based industry, but there was no factory industrial producer, and no product surplus. The concept of ethics was deeply entrenched. There were many poor people and few rich people, who all paid attention to the middle ground. The rich has the responsibility of dividing wealth. Due to the large number of people, rich families were declining.

The above was China's method of maintaining a wealthy society and family-based social organizations, which spread to thousands of years. Considering the modern economic theory, most of the previous ideas were wrong. In the past, all were concerned with distribution. First, most people did not know that production was more important than distribution. Second, in the past, it was advocated to be poor and with no attention paid to life. These two points were contrary to the economic thinking of the West. Since then, traditional ideas had to change. However, in order to change the traditional ideas, traditional ideas needed to be studied and then reformed. A new economic organization was created on the basis of the old economy. Descendants could not be satisfied with poverty again. They had to pursue the average wealth to realize inner peace and mutual peace. Then one could realize one's own dreams.

4. The financial thought of Zhang Naiqi

Zhang Naiqi (1896–1977), also known as Jiasheng, was a native of Qingtian in Zhejiang Province. He was a famous economist, a financier and a wealth manager in modern China, and he was good at banking practice and financial management. In 1918, he graduated from the First-Class Business School of Zhejiang Province and was sent to Hangzhou Zhejiang Local Real Estate Bank as an intern. After the Spring Festival, or Chinese New Year festival, he went to Beijing Jing Zhao Agricultural Bank of Industry and Commerce as the director of the business department. The next year, he was promoted to the position of Assistant General Manager while also holding a concurrent position of business director. In 1920, he transferred to the Sino-American Industrial Company as Chief Accounting Officer and left in anger because of the imperious attitude of the manager. He reentered Zhejiang Local Industrial Bank in Shanghai in 1927 as the Business Director. At the same time, he ran his own semi-monthly *New Review*, and criticized the Kuomintang's policy of killing warlords. In order to safeguard the dignity of the country and the rights and interests of the banks, he treated both domestic and foreign banks equally without discrimination, so he won praise in the field of Shanghai finance. He was then promoted as Deputy General Manager and Chief of the Inspection Department. In June 1932, in consultation and liaison with the heads of the Bank of China, Bank of Shanghai, Xinhua Bank and Industrial Development Bank, he started the first China Credit Bureau, chaired by a Chinese for the first time ever, and became chairman of the board. In 1935, he was appointed professor of Shanghai Kwang Hua University, Shanghai Business School and University of Shanghai. During the War of Resistance Against Japanese Aggression, in December 1935, in order to join the national salvation movement, Ma Xiangbo and other patriots initiated the organization of the Shanghai Cultural World Salvation Congress. They signed a manifesto and raised a political proposition, "Stop the civil war and unite the outside world". Soon, the Shanghai All Circles National Salvation Federation was established, in which Zhang was responsible for finance and publicity, and was called "propagandist" by colleagues. The following year, the All-China National Salvation Federation was set up to publicize the work, and he also took a concurrent job as the editor of the *Survival Line*, *Storm* and other publications of the Society. He published the weekly magazine *National Salvation Intelligence*, condemning Chiang Kai-shek's policy to "put the inner peace ahead of keeping out of outer enemies". He was determined to save his country and decided to resign from his bank's preferential duties and devote himself entirely to the campaign to save the nation. In November 1936, he was arrested with Shen Junru and other people, which caused the "Seven Gentlemen Incident" which attracted the attention of the whole nation. After his release from prison on 31 July 1937, he continued to carry out rescue activities, took part in the Public Debt Advice Committee, initiated the China Industrial Cooperation Association with friends from the international community and members of the domestic industry and culture, and organized the relocation of coastal factories to develop wartime production and employment. In February 1938, on the invitation of Li Zongren, Chairman of Anhui Province, he successively served as Secretary-General of the Provincial People's General Mobilization Committee and Head of the Provincial Finance Department. He conducted a thorough investigation of the situation, and laid stress on the implementation of the policies of "eradicating corruption" and "economizing on waste". The creation of the Goods Inspection Office, the collection of goods inspection tax, the issuance of provincial bonds and the issuance of small banknotes of 2 million *yuan* enriched the province's extremely depleted payment tools and revitalized the market. He set up a lively financial system to solve the difficulty such as the financial panic in the province, financial exhaustion and the shortage of cadres. He also subsidized the New Fourth Army on a monthly basis, sent much-needed medicines and cultivated a large number of clean and honest financial cadres. The achievements of the province were beyond the reach of any other province. In April 1939, Chiang Kai-shek removed him from his office in the Finance Department of Anhui Province. Determined not to be a Kuomintang official, he wrote wartime economic articles for newspapers such as the

Ta Kung Pao. He founded the Shangchuan Industrial Company in Chongqing in June 1940. After his quitting in the following year, Shangchuan Enterprise Co., Ltd was established by a share offer, he was also elected Executive Director of the Qianchuan Factory Federation, he established the China Institute of Industrial Economics with Wu Yunchu and Wu Mei, and he advocated the introduction of foreign capital and the launching of competition in the market. In August 1945, he contacted Huang Yanpei, Hu Juewen and so on to form the Democratic National Construction Association with the industrial sector as the main body and was elected Executive Director. In February 1946, he was the main target of Kuomintang agents' false accusation attacks in the gate of the Chongqing school affair. In the autumn of 1947, he founded the Hong Kong and Kowloon Real Estate Company in Hong Kong. Shangchuan Enterprise Company invested in Lianhua Film Arts Co., Ltd. to make progressive films and obtained great success. In November 1948, he was invited by the Communist Party of China to come to Peiping via Northeast China from Hong Kong to attend the preparatory conference for the New China People's Political Consultative Conference. After the liberation of Peiping, he was recruited as an adviser to the People's Bank of China. After the founding of New China, he was appointed as a director of the official shares of the Bank of China and was elected as executive director, a member of the standing committee and the head of the financial affairs bureau of the national committee of the Chinese people's political consultative conference. He took up the post of administrative committee member and director of the establishment examination committee of the institutional structure of the administrative council and the member of the financial committee. He was also the Vice-Director of the National Democratic Construction Association and was in charge of publicity and education, and later the Vice-Director of the All-China Federation of Industry and Commerce. He was elected as Minister of Food in the Council of State in August 1952, until 31 January 1958, when he was removed from his post. In the meantime, in December 1967, he wrote more than 10,000 words on "The Seventy Self-Report", and he had no complaints about the political situation. His main works include *Where Does the Chinese Monetary System Go* (with Qian Junrui, *et al*.), *Swift Current* (1935), *The Problem of Financial Integration of Chinese Currency* (1936),

On the Transformation of Chinese Economy — Detumescence, Decorruption, Transformation (1952), and now the two-volumed *Collected Writings of Zhang Naiqi* is still in print.

Zhang's monetary and financial exploration and thinking mainly focused on the major issues concerning the monetary and financial system under the conditions of China's changing situation. He made a thorough and superficial empirical analysis and theoretical research, and put forward corresponding policy suggestions, such as abolishing the Two Reforms, the French Currency Policy, the Financial Central Bank, the Contingency Measures Concerning the Major Policies of China's Monetary and Financial Policy, the Currency System after the War of Resistance and the Monetary and Financial Policy of New China. From the point of view of national survival and social development, he devoted his energies and talents unreservedly. In the following sections, we analyze Zhang's financial thought from the aspects of the monetary system, currency war and financial system in the period of the Republic of China.

4.1. Zhang's theory of monetary system

4.1.1. The role of money and its system

Zhang's so-called monetary function refers to the role that money plays in social and economic life, or in the economic system, but not from the pure theoretical research. In the 1920s and 1930s, he faced the changes and developments of the world and the currency system in China and renewed his recognition of the use of currency. In February 1934, *The Monetary Policy of the Countries on the Eve of World War I* was published in order to show that the countries of the world were using monetary policy to prepare for the great war. It is necessary to explain the three different functions of money that ordinary people usually pay no attention to: first, it differs from person to person; second, it differs from place to place; and third, it differs from time to time.

The so-called variance from person to person means that the same silver coins are different for factory owners, workers and peasants. The flour mill owner will profit, but the peasants and the workers will earn their wages which they are paid in return for their labor. Therefore, "under the different application of the currency, a small number of people become rich day by day, and their productive capital expands day by day, and most of the rest of us — farmers and workers — are getting poorer by the day". The problem here is that the distinction between money and money capital is not thoroughly revealed or concisely stated, and there is no mention of the reasons for the distinction. He only made a simplistic statement of money and money capital as the general equivalent of exchange media. In the following discussions, there is also such a tendency, but we won't mention that again.

The so-called regional differences, depending on the conditions of production technology and equipment, lead to the division of production costs and productivity, and low-cost dumping: "In the international competition, China's factory owners are also in an oppressed position. The productive capital of the colonized and semi-colonial countries declined day by day because of their weak ability to withstand the oppression of the imperialist capital forces. The inability of the national capital industry to raise its head is indeed a fatal wound in a colonial and semi-colonial society."

As for the time being, it means that in times of prosperity and panic, the role of money is different. In times of prosperity, "the activities of money can be manipulated. Not only does money have great authority, but it is also popularly accepted as a kind of securities instrument that represents money." Combined with credit expansion, productivity will expand on a much larger scale, while on the other side, as a result of the advanced machinery, millions of workers will lose their jobs, lose their purchasing power altogether and create economic panic. On the surface, it is overproduction, but in fact, the masses of workers and peasants have no money and cannot buy the products. At this point, the currency is hidden in the banks' coffers. The industrial and commercial sectors have been unable to get enough currency to support them. As a result, factories and shops have been shut down, which has led to an increase in the number of unemployed and a deeper sense of alarm. "The big financial capitalists, on the other hand, have enormous amounts of money and retain supreme authority. Those who are unable to obtain ransom money from the factory or land shall be confiscated or auctioned and shall become their property directly or indirectly. And a lot of small banks, also died in this storm." It was the pre-World War II period of deepening economic panic and can be called "a period of currency change".

At the same time, Zhang pointed out that in capitalist society, money is "a magic weapon". "The activity of monetary base is the hub of all economic activities under the capitalism. Currency war is the bottom line of many economic wars." Gold is the most precious metal in the world and the main tool of international payments. "If we win the war by the power of gold, we can win more gold after the war by way of reparations."

In the book *Chinese Society Reflected in Monetary Finance* in 1935, Zhang explained the usual method of currency stripping. The first step is to replace the heavy copper with the light copper, which is found most frequently in Sichuan. The second is the issuance of low-quality silver coins, which can be represented by Guangdong Province. The third is the issuance of low-quality silver circles, which should also be considered to be the highest development in Sichuan Province. The fourth is the development of paper money. The most advanced of these developments is the Eastern Provinces. The way to exploit paper money is to rob people's coins by using paper money. In the process of reducing the price of paper money, the exploitation of paper money will be gradually completed.

The following is an overview of the reform of the monetary system in the last 5 years, 1929–1933. In his book, *The Currency Policy of Countries Before World War II*, Zhang recounted the period from December 1929 to September 1931. The international financial markets were shocked by the sudden cessation of the gold standard by the British, which was called the Finance Empire. The British Crown Dependencies and Colonies (except South Africa) subsequently abandoned the gold standard, and in March 1933 the United States also terminated the gold standard. So far, in the nine countries which claimed to maintain the gold standard, the gold standard had remained, but they were being deceived by Hitler. Germany was under serious trade control, exchange control and currency management, with gold reserves of only 2%.

"Why should America abandon the gold standard when it has so much gold?" This is seen from two aspects, as Chang pointed out. As Roosevelt came to power, on the one hand, "Many people gauged the need for currency reform, swapping dollars for foreign currencies or buying foreign securities, which caused a serious capital flight" and there was a "great financial panic in welcoming Mr. Roosevelt." On the other hand, inflation was the only way to drive up prices. There were no other options. So, the gold standard was finally forced to give way, and at the same time was deliberately abandoned.

After abandoning the gold standard, Mr. Zhang pointed out that inflation was bound to follow. Some were for financial shortage, others for the need to devalue the currency because of currency wars. "The technology of inflation is greatly improved at present; even for the sake of fiscal inflation, the indirect means of issuing bonds are often used instead of the direct hand segment of issuing notes. In fact, I am afraid that only inflation for fiscal purposes is a relatively complete expansion." When most countries abandoned the gold standard, a few maintained it, mainly because the European countries, suffering from inflationary pains after World War I, were reluctant to try again. However, in Zhang's view, the gold standard could be abandoned at any time once the situation changed, or the war began. Can inflation scare the economy? Zhang answered, "It's just 'inflationist's one-sided fantasy'." "They "tend to increase the amount of money only in terms of the quantity of money — the reduction of the gold component in the United States is a more progressive method."

Inflation is a form of exploitation for domestic workers, but a fatal blow to colonial and semi-colonial societies. Zhang revealed, "Under 'currency dumping', it is not only China's national industrial capital that has been hit hard, but also Chinese farmers who are gradually going bankrupt under the dumping of cheap agricultural products from foreign countries. In this way, the labor and colonial people have been the victims of a bottom-line inflation." What it creates is not a revival of prosperity, but an embryo of greater panic. Because the patient "didn't stop bleeding from his body. Some of the buying power of ... will soon be wiped out by the exploitation of profit." At this time of inflation, Zhang said that the rulers of Europe and the United States all knew that "Only war can eliminate fear. So there is a close connection between monetary policy and future wars".

Moreover, the monetary system of the colonial and semi-colonial countries is an important means to intervene, manipulate and control (dominate, control) the political and economic lifeblood of the country by the suzerain. In December 1934, in *The Financial Panic and the Currency Crisis*, he pointed out that the currency system of a colony must be under the same monetary standard as that of the suzerain. Then the financial power of the suzerain can obtain economic and even financial control in the colony. Because of this, Japan established the Puppet Manchukuo State in Northeast China and advocated the unification of the Japanese–Manchurian currency system. Had the 1918 gold standard plan of Cao Rulin and the "Gold Coupon Ordinance" based on the political and financial forces of Japan been forgotten? In this sense, it is not difficult to understand the far-reaching implications of America's silver policy. The logic was that after the United States acquired a considerable amount of silver, the price of silver would rise. Naturally, the price of silver should be further stabilized; if silver could be stabilized at a certain rate against the United States dollar, "China's bottom silver standard currency can be completely changed in line with the dollar base price changes. In this way, China has naturally joined the US dollar group?"

Zhang concluded that issues like the current international trade, the internationalization of currency and the circulation of money were all corrected by the law of supply. These issues have been distorted into "production under the 'self-supporting' 'closed-door' doctrine, which has become the extreme nationalism, and the currency has become nationalism in the same way. Money now is not merely a matter of leaving the field of the metal or the legal school and is under the full control of political means." This insightful analysis and judgement shows that Zhang was totally familiar with the concept and had a clear understanding of the monetary system, monetary policy and the political intentions of governments, the greatest interests, and the relationship between economy and politics and military affairs.

4.1.2. Changing Liang into Yuan

In 1914, the Beiyang Government promulgated the *National Currency Ordinance*, in which it intended to change *Liang* into *Yuan* and unify the practical silver dollars of the past. Because of the weak government, the opposition of banks and the imperialism of banks in China, the proposal of the new type of banks, the industrialists and economists was delayed for a long time, and the inconvenience and loss of the merchants were ignored. The coinage spread out more widely, the right to issue paper money became more prevalent, the currency became overrun with money and the value of the coin fell. Far from improving, the chaotic currency system intensified. On March 2, 1933, the Ministry of Finance issued the Decree on the Abolition of *Yuan* Reform, deciding to start with Shanghai on the 10th of the same month. The transaction was made illegal after April 6 in the whole country. In June 1932, the Shanghai Banking Association agreed in principle to abolish the *Yuan*. However, the Government proposed a strategy of delaying money for a period of time in order to prepare for taking the attack as the defense. It then decided to cancel the commission for the exchange of silver dollars and Yuan from August 6. In the meantime, Zhang continued to publish *The Question of Abolishing the Liang with Yuan and the Last Struggle of Abolishing the Two Reformers* on August 2, 2007, in which a total of 13 questions were covered, which can be categorized into five areas.

The first was the timing of replacing the *Liang* with *Yuan*. In Zhang's view, "In the past, it was only a question of financial currency and silver but today, it has become a very serious social problem in general." "Those who live on wages are seriously affected by gold, silver, and base, and are affected by high price of *Liang* and low price of *Yuan*. Before you know it, income has dropped by 5%, and the economy is on the rise again. To eliminate the man-made boundary between different silver currency, to stabilize the price of currency, to secure the society and the people, is the urgent task of the moment." According to Zhang's analysis, it was a good time to replace *Liang* with *Yuan*. At that time, the Shanghai Bank had an unprecedented record, and the Central Mint equipment was finished, so the supply of silver dollars was not in danger of being exhausted. The market price of the silver dollar was so low as to contain the real value of the silver, and there was no difficulty or dispute about the exchange rate of silver and the exchange rate. Taxes were not in short supply; there was a possibility of absolute centralization of currency.

The second was the obstacle of replacing *Liang* with *Yuan*. In the past, Zhang thought that it was difficult to move. There were four sides, one was the shortage of silver. Second, the price of the silver dollar was higher than the real value of the pure silver. Third, the Customs may not be able to comply on the ground which may affect tax revenue. Fourth, there was no centralization of the right to make money, and there was no real protection for the quality and weight of the products. Before the formal change of policy, the currency policy which has no causal relationship between the two parties was forced to join forces with the replacement of *Liang* with *Yuan*, and take it as an excuse to resist. Chang exposed the fatality of these people, "the idea of cupidity is enough to cover one's conscience; The so-called overall situation can't be reached by others. However, if we confuse the abolition of the *Liang* with the currency policy, then it will be as incongruous as the mouth of a horse on the head of an ox." The so-called "replace *Liang* with *Yuan*" must first organize the coin, which was actually the reversal of cause and effect. The so-called paper money was particularly comical and paradoxical. The so-called Silver Standard was simply a non-matter of fact and was simply not understanding the meaning of monetary value. Some celebrities were so completely unsuspecting that they lashed out at the people, "Financial leaders, who hold a prominent position in the economic field, may weep over such a statement which disregards the general situation and does not know what is right and what is wrong. Knowledge of the weakness of the grounds for objections is not a sufficient means of delaying time by deliberate discussion on the basis of long-term considerations." Zhang lamented, "The discussion on the replacement of Liang with Yuan has been going on for more than 10 years. After repeatedly studying, there are many outcomes. How can we call this not careful? What is more compelling?" Objecting to the procrastinator's intent, he said "to exploit the chaos of money, to exploit the people for their own benefit; then his sin is not the illegal activities like smuggling cigarette; one day it will come to an end." Therefore, he issued a warning, "My money industry has repeatedly stated that *Liang* and *Yuan* exchange's benefits are not valued, it should not be a time for further confusion." In the end, Mr. Chang spoke to celebrities, including military politicians, bureaucrats who would intervene and talk about everything, "Finance is by no means the way for a specialist to pry open-minded. China's great trouble is that there are too many omnipotent people, and too few who are really capable of doing so. The celebrities should not stand in his own place, but in his country's … know what one really understands." Moreover, Britain did not have a three-tier system such as the Conservative Party, the Liberal Party and the Labour Party, which resulted in partisan disputes. There were no 10 parallel currency metaphors in Germany because of the number of parties.

The third was the concrete idea of substituting *Liang* with *Yuan*. Zhang believed that one must first sort out the formulation of the silver dollar to silver conversion ratio, "The most appropriate standard, 7 dollars per *yuan* of compliance." Because of the provisions of the Regulations of the Republic of China in the 3 years, "The actual value of the sterling silver contained in each dollar is six dollars and nine cents and 3.4 cents per millisecond and four cents per millisecond besides casting. Compared with current market prices, there are so many things that can be said to be fair. And the numbers are neat, easy to calculate." And the price was about one percent higher than the market price, so it was considered a favor to those creditors and silver possessors. In the implementation process, there will be no obstacles. The second was the weight and fineness of the new coins; the most appropriate and advantageous method should be that the containment of pure silver in each *Yuan*, reducing the cast fee and taking it as a standard. Suppose the cast fee is 1%, then the Containment of Pure Silver in each silver *Yuan* should be 23.284107. Compared with the original legal amount of sterling silver per dollar, the reduction is 18 per thousand. If the weight is constant, the fineness shall be reduced to 87.1. Therefore, in this way, Zhang said, "If the amount of 18 per thousand pure silver is reduced while casting is being changed, the cost of casting will not be a problem. There are still a number of surplus." The third was the centralization of seigniorage and free casting. In order to avoid the recurrence of the currency system confusion, Zhang put forward that "The right to seigniorage to be concentrated in the Shanghai Central Mint is appropriate." The plates for coinage should be temporarily held in suspension of service. It was also necessary to first improve the organization and maintain close liaison with the Central Mint on various important matters such as administration, technology and laboratory tests. When there was an agreement between the two sides, it could be used again. As for the issue of free casting, Zhang believed that "it seems inappropriate to imitate the British precedent by the government. It is more appropriate to entrust the central, China and communications banks to act as agents for the issue of new currencies." Fourth, issues central mint organization should pay attention. Its director "must be a financial currency expert and must not take changed politics as advance and retreat." "Managing administrative matters within the plant" was his position. In addition, the weight and fineness of money must be upheld in accordance with the principles of openness. The commission for inspection of currencies was organized, including representatives of the municipal chamber of commerce and the money industry association being invited to carry out the work of testing, preferably once a week in a public laboratory, and the results disclosed at any time. The government enacted an organization law, and the related group organized a demonstration of its independence. The fifth was the circulation of new currencies. The first step was whether circulation will be blocked. He thought, "the establishment of monetary credit, in the weight of the neat one, with the weight of a permanent protection." A good example was the replacement of the Longyang silver *yuan*, which was 90 percent silver, with the new silver *yuan* of 89 percent silver. The latter was more readily accepted because it was more perfectly organized and better authenticated by the government. Second, on the new currency issue, allowing the existing silver dollars to be used, there would not emerge the phenomenon of bad money driving out the good. "The old coin was privately melted down. Because most of the circulation is the weight of the messy Prime Minister like silver, privately melting. If you are not sure about it, you will not dare to do it easily. Finally, I am worried that the new coins will be included in the currency value of the casting fee to the new currency. It is feared that foreign exchange will not be as cost-effective as regular dollars." "We should note that the Shanghai and New York silver prices are still subject to cash transfer points. ... The cost of casting is not important ... and the regulatory element is not foreign silver. Bank trust, in terms of 'foreign exchange' calculations, has been deliberately undervalued. ... Therefore, it is necessary to purchase foreign currencies by regulating the yuan knot. The more cost-effective theory is absolutely groundless."

4.1.3. *Comments on the reform of the currency of different schools*

On October 24, 1935, Zhang Naiqi wrote a special article, "Introduction and criticism of the theory on the reform of various monetary systems", which focused on Xu Qingfu's "virtual grain standard", Liu Mian's ability standard system, Yan Xishan's "the product negotiable securities", Chu

Fucheng's "the theory of monetary revolution", the management of money and the switch to the gold standard, and then had comments on these views.

According to Zhang, the Chinese currency has a strong feudalist character, which is not only an obstacle to the development of national capital but also an obstacle to the imperialist exploitation of the Chinese market at times. "For example, there are different attitudes towards the feudal *Yin Liang*, which stands for the Shanghai Regulation, to foreign banks and trading houses. The former, for *Yin* and *Liang* are already under their control, and they can profit from the name of 'adding water', they must oppose the abolition of *Liang* with *Yuan*. The latter, because of the trouble of calculation and the loss of 'add water', should agree with changes. However, foreign businessmen in China are unanimously opposed to the obstruction of the Mainland's variegated currencies. In particular, they are sponsoring China to adopt the gold standard for the convenience of importing their capital and commodities into China. Therefore, the issue of China's currency reform has for decades been the subject of discussion among 'people from China and foreign countries'." But the talk from Hurd and Wu Weide to Cao Rulin and even Kemal's plans were a thing of the past. Ever since 1930, when the Expensive Gold and Cheap Silver Tide took place, the enthusiasm for domestic research was unprecedented, which had just a few main points.

Xu Qingfu proposed to replace gold and silver standard with "virtual grain standard", and the government set up a public trust center to concentrate all the gold in the country for the balance of payments. The public trust gave them the property (real estate, movable property and currency) of the people, within the credit limit, and a check could be issued for payment. So that the government could pool the money for balance of payments, and the people can also live without the worry about the depletion of chips. Liu Mianzhi's "competency-based system" advocates that the people should obtain the ability to issue general certificates as long as they can provide guarantees from the committee. Only the natural person were entitled to this privilege, but the country and local authorities and the public welfare institutions were the exceptions. The quota for each person should not exceed 1/10 of their yearly income, and the quota for the country and local authorities and the public welfare institutions were below 5/10 of the yearly income. noticeable among these were the property certificates issued by the Yan Xishan government in Shanxi Province, which were used by the government in exchange for the products of the people. Zhang supported the issuing of exchange certificate for products to the peasants to relieve the countryside finance. In *The Future of Chinese Currency* (1935), Zhang says, "This currency, in Shanxi Province, is already a good currency; using this kind of currency to replace the original one is already a progress; if it is to be carried out in the place where the coin is used, it may not be possible." With the grim situation of war threat, if the issuing of reserve funds could not help the government much, there is the need of considering many other factors since there is also a cash shortage. The factions that govern monetarists are also very divided. Some people base their efforts on stabilizing the value of currencies, and advocate using the living index as the standard, or advocate using the price index as the standard. There are people who think that the Pound is the most managed currency in the world, and advocate the adoption of the Pound standard, while others advocate maintaining the silver standard, unify the domestic currency system and concentrate the power of the whole country to cope with the great war in the future." However, their "common point is the so-called problem of the purchasing power of money. This means what they are advocating are largely based on the quantity of money. At present, money experts tend to emphasize the relationship between money supply and demand, and neglect the relationship between the supply and demand of goods." The problem was that prices were falling. Therefore, the general monetary manager's direction of management was to reduce the purchasing power of the currency by increasing the number of currencies. This is what is called limited inflation. In theory, if prices rise, the amount of currency should be reduced to increase the purchasing power of money. But that is often empty talk because the loss of the so-called consumer masses is not accounted for.

Zhang further pointed out that the switch to the gold standard was the currency reform theory that was popular at that time. In *The Financial Panic and the Currency Crisis*, he asserted, "In fact, it is impossible for China to establish a true gold standard at present." "Japan, the master of the Far East, could not 'stop making progress'." But Japan's financial power was still too new, its foundation in China was too weak, and its currency system was not sound. So he thought that Japan and the United Kingdom will sing the tune of cooperation in the Far East. Who can say that they are disadvantaged by their power and friends? The question is insightful and hits the point. In the *Two Fronts in the Economic Debate*, Zhang revealed that the gold standard is the consistent proposition of currency internationalization. He argued that since the Monetary Reform of November 4, 1935, such claims have been fully realized. "However, the National Bank's unlimited purchase and sale of foreign currencies in the Currency Reform Bill has led us into a trap of imperialism, on the basis of which the classical school of liberalism has been theorizing." Because of this condition, "China's currency reform will completely lose the role of wartime economy!" Zhang's analysis of imperialists using investment as bait states, "in order to eliminate the surplus commodities of various countries, the international equilibrium can be re-established under the conditions of international excess capital and surplus goods." He goes on to point out, "If China joined the Sterling Group, it would make the United States and Japan unhappy and create diplomatic difficulties." Japan intensified the establishment of a puppet regime in Northeast China, and the United States depressed the price of silver by 1/3, causing China to lose 300,000,000,000,000 yen! "The rise and fall of the value of our reserves is in the hands of the United States; but we have no buyers besides the United States for all our silver sales. If the deposit is sold to the United States, the future overseas preparation will naturally be US dollars, and China will naturally fall into the dollar group. But the UK will not let go easily!" As history can testify, it was indeed as Zhang guessed. The Internationalization of currency would lead to the outflow of capital. The silver privately transported by way of Japan was said to amount to 200 million *yuan*. After the reform of the currency, the policy of stabilizing the exchange rate guaranteed the interest of capitalists. The reformed currency system was fragile for the war-time economy and dangerous for the peace time. For the better development of industry and commerce, there should be a mild inflation. But the emergence of inflation would lead to the danger of capital outflow. Only by extreme austerity and high interest rate could the outflow of capital and crisis be avoided. However, under these pressure, the economic crisis was becoming worse day after day. That was due to the influence of liberalism. The state banks under the practice of currency internalization were buying and selling foreign currency without any restriction, giving the privileged few the freedom of capital outflow while depriving the national economy of its free development. In the face of the internationalized claims, Zhang expressed that people do not stand for isolation or against freedom, but that one should fight for national liberation and freedom. People stand on the national front and oppose all capitulation-style internationalization! In respect of currency, "China's currency should be under the principle of maintaining independence, unifying the domestic currency system, and concentrating the strength of the whole country to cope with the war in the future."

After introducing the above-mentioned domestic currency reform argument, Zhang pointed out, "It should be admitted that China has its relative characteristics, but we disapprove that it is absolutely contrary to other countries. If the currency reform cannot solve the social problems of other countries, can we hope that it can solve China's social problems?" That is, China's social problems cannot be solved through currency reform. Until China's social problems are completely resolved, it would be impossible to place too much hope on China's currency reform. Otherwise, it would be difficult to achieve the desired goal.

In the eyes of Zhang, Xu Qingxuan and Zhu Xishan advocated the use of currency reform as the main means to solve land problems and implement state-owned industrial management. At the time, "the depletion of rural finances, whether due to the decline of productivity, or the exploitation of exotic products, industrial products, and warlords, bureaucrats, and heroes, was a huge problem." Because of the development of price-cutting on input and output, there was a decline in import prices. It was not as good as export prices. "We can understand that the exploitation of imported goods is deepening in the rural areas. In the development of the scissor-shaped prices of industrial products and agricultural products, the decline in the prices of industrial products is not as good as that of agricultural products. We also know that industrial products have deepened rural exploitation." In addition, the increase in tariffs and salt taxes, the introduction of taxation and the various forms of local taxes have been heavily exploited. Farmers' burden of taxation is probably enough to constitute a rural capital outflow, which is even greater than the decline in productivity of farmers.

Based on the above analysis and understanding, Zhang proposed that if one cannot reduce foreign exploitation of peasants or control the prices of industrial products and agricultural products in order to prevent the exploitation of peasants by industrial products and reduce the burden of peasants' taxation, then one should give them some money that can be used for production, so that they only suffer some losses. Similarly, if people want to use inflation to solve the panic of the urban economy, people must also cover the basic crisis with the issue of the festival. The so-called urban economic crisis is nothing but special attention. In this context, in the words of Zhang, people have come up with substantial and crucial conclusions: "This unprecedented crisis of the whole nation means that we can use the currency reform method to rescue people. We have such an easy thing in the world." All kinds of monetary reforms in China cannot avoid the theory of inflation. The so-called grain-based, capacity-based and item-based all focus on rural finance. Their common goal is to try to get people to get money before the product or labor has been sold, so that the finance will not dry up. The other kinds of currency reform proposals are mainly focused on the decline of urban prices and the financial difficulties of the government; their common goal is to suppress the currency price, raise prices, stimulate people's purchasing power and allow the government to reform the currency system. Li, through the current financial difficulties, would be able to use cheaper capital markets in the future, reduce the burden of interest on debt and facilitate the issuance of new debt. This commentary of Zhang's remarks only addresses the arguments about the currency system and the currency and talks about currency. The point of view is the only difference. The starting point is exactly the same. Without touching the actual political, economic and international relations, it is only necessary to consider the future and destiny of the nation, that is, the so-called "overestimating the role of currency, or raising money issues to erase more fundamental issues, we naturally should oppose".

In this case, was it not necessary to reform the currency? Not that it was. According to Zhang, the significance of the currency reform lay in the fact that for the benefit of farmers and national industries, the price of coins should be reduced to raise prices; for the relative balance of import trade, the exchange rate should be kept low to limit input and stimulate output, also in defense. Shanghai's depository became a deposit abroad. "However, the effects of these kinds of species are all temporary. If we do not have a strong national policy as the backbone to liberate the Chinese people from the aggression and exploitation, then the role of this kind of pinpointing force will become 'relentless'." In another article, he emphasized, "We are not trying to oppose the currency revolution, but we are not saying that the monetary revolution will not be able to achieve satisfactory results under fragmented national power." The Chinese financial industry is still struggling with the frontline of "solidarity and self-salvage. ... At home, the independence of the bottom of the currency still exists; and this kind of currency transformation is relatively natural in the situation rather than chaos." "If China is to strive for national liberation, we should argue that: China needs to have an independent currency standard and a stable monetary value; this is the idea of using its own money to manage it." With such an ideal as a goal of struggle, one would naturally hesitate to follow and seek to strive. In the article The Future Of China's Currency on September 10, 1935, referring to the ideal currency standard, Zhang said, "Speaking of the issue of currency prices, the most ideal currency standard in the world is probably the purchasing power standard. The so-called 'compensated currency' (compensated dollar), but under the state of anarchy, the complete implementation of this system is impossible." As for the management of currency, he said, "For the use of their own management I still have some opinions on the idea of currency. I think that our ideal currency must not only have a higher degree of independence, but also be able to achieve national unity internally." The combination of independence and unity was the basic idea which he had repeatedly emphasized and elaborated, a principal that he always adhered to.

The main conditions for the reform of the Chinese currency were summed up Zhang. One was the connection with foreign currency. As long as it did not establish relations between Chinese currency and other currencies in the form of statutes or treaties, it only used exchange policy to stabilize the future standard, which is about the currency value of customs units and other countries, "but still has not given up on currency. The autonomy of value manipulation is not much hindrance". Because it did not have any statutory or contractual constraints, the independence and autonomy of China's currency were not subject to threats and violations. The second problem was the storage of overseas reserves. If overseas reserves and other countries set the depository relationship in the form of a treaty, "then, even if the exchange rate is not tied to the treaty … the exchange rate will still become a liberty." Third, it was the issue of the handling mechanism of the exchange policy. As long as the currency exchange policy was manipulated by people, monetary rights could not remain independent. Therefore, Zhang had been very opposed to "the Central Bank and HSBC Bank cooperating to maintain the exchange rate". The fourth was for personal investment. Although they did not oppose the investment of foreigners in China, they could not blindly or unconditionally welcome foreign investment. Politically, attention had to be paid to the purpose and conditions of borrowing and economic development must be reserved for ethnic enterprises. "We cannot allow foreign capital to take advantage of the situation". The fifth was to improve the financial market. "The bill market and the industry securities market must be established very quickly, so that there will be modern short-term funds and long-term capital markets in the national financial system." Otherwise, the inflationary currency would, as usual, "increase speculation on real estate and public debt in the concession." The degree of depressing the price of the Chinese currency should not be too great, and it should not cause major oppression of the people. On the contrary, the government should "make use of natural fruits to balance the budget". Using inflation as a means of fiscal expansion was not suggested; otherwise, the country's credit vacillation and currency reform would fail. China's currency reform program could neither be copied from the United Kingdom nor from Japan. "We have great natural strength, but we lack a prescription to develop it." It was only necessary to recover the domestic market and recover the lost territory. "When the child comes back, we only need to recoup the lost purchasing power from the enemy's hands and try our best to maintain the power of inflation. And only in this way can we achieve the final success of the currency reform." These two could be regarded as follow-up conditions, and, after solving the external autonomy, one should pay attention to the internal elements.

In the end, Zhang still stressed that this was just a matter of monetary currency, and it was naturally not enough for the nation's future. It was undeniable that the currency reform did indeed contain the role of national defense for the sake of the liberation of the nation. It only required conditions and was indispensable for both the internal and external political and economic foundations.

4.1.4. Currency reform and inflation

On July 1, 1935, in *The Evolution of the Financial System in Financial Panic*, Zhang Ming clearly stated, "The purpose of currency reform must be economic rather than fiscal." The specific requirement was, "if we were to establish the management standard, what criteria we should use to settle our currency value". The easiest method was to reduce the percentage of the current silver coins, while the ideal method was to use the living index as a standard to settle the currency value. However, this had its drawbacks. Therefore, Zhang personally thought that the more feasible method was to lower the value of the currency by using gold as a standard and under the cover of the gold standard system.

On November 15th of the same year, after the Currency Reform, Zhang's criticism of the Chinese currency after the Renminbi Reform was on the so-called Money Management. When the banknotes were circulated in the country, the international exchange rate was stabilized by the National Bank's business means. The exchange rate and the pound sterling were linked at a rate of one shilling and two statutes per one half of the Chinese legal currency. Although there was no statutory provision, it was said that there was no shackle of the treaty. In fact, China had already joined the sterling group. He further criticized, "The fiscal authorities told us that this currency reform is not inflation. In fact, the management of money is the use of inflationary policies; in academic terms, scholars in various countries often do not say that they are inflationary. In an extra cautious way, or we might say: It is a limited inflation."

Prior to this, Zhang wrote articles and analyzed the role of inflation from multiple perspectives of economy and politics. In terms of economy, "inflation has no problem in raising prices ... another effect is to make financial relaxation; this, within certain limits, can also raise prices." Inflation "can stimulate purchasing power, but it cannot generate purchasing power; it can stimulate prices, but it cannot stabilize prices." The fundamental reason for price fluctuations was still the relationship between supply and demand for commodities. According to Zhang's view, inflation had caused prices to rise, in part because of the reflection of the decline in the value of the currency. This was partly due to speculative purchases. "People with more money bought futures from the exchange, and cotton, cotton yarn, wheat, flour. ... It would fly up; people with less money would buy large quantities of daily necessities from shops, so as to avoid future price increases, they would not be able to buy cheap goods." This was the purchasing power of revenues and expenditures. It was ahead of purchase power and could not be sustained. This kind of purchasing power was a stimulating purchasing power, not a real purchasing power, because speculators not only had no meaning in buying but they also had no intention of selling when they bought futures, and they would sell futures after the price rose. The original transaction was settled and an intermediate profit was gained. When the wave of speculation passed and the purchasing power of the people did not increase, production would still be in surplus and prices would still fall. Here, he criticized the arguments that the unknowing economists shied away from light. The benefits of financial relaxation could only be found in industry and commerce, but not in the consumer. Industrialists could use this to purchase more raw materials and increase production. Merchants could thus import more goods. If the purchasing power of the consumer did not increase, prices would continue to tumble after rising. Zhang's analysis of the reasons why inflation could not generate purchasing power was based on different social strata. He pointed out that if the wage did not increase, the purchasing power would not increase; instead, in the case of high prices, the purchases would only be cut back. Whether unemployed workers could get jobs and increase purchasing power was also a problem. The main component of the national industry was the textile industry. If the purchasing power of farmers did not increase, the sales of cotton yarn would not prosper; cotton yarn export would also require less cotton yarn prices. Otherwise, the benefits of the falling exchange rate would be offset by the rising losses of cotton yarn. The increase in purchasing power of farmers, which accounted for 80% of the country's population, was a more serious problem. If the price of agricultural products did not rise as much as industrial products did, the purchasing power of farmers would only decrease. From the general trend of view, agricultural products' falling prices were often much lower than industrial products, and when prices rose, they tended to rise less than industrial products. Therefore, when inflation stimulated prices to rise, the purchasing power of farmers would not increase. This was Zhang's analysis of the economic role of inflation.

As for the political impact of inflation, according to Zhang, "In plain words, it can make it easy for the government to solve financial difficulties." In the context of financial relaxation, the interest rate in the market would be reduced. The government could issue low-yield new bonds to replace old public debts to reduce the burden on the state treasury. It could also issue more new public debts to relieve financial difficulties. According to the experience of various countries, after inflation, the power of support lay with the colonies and the government. The former was the United Kingdom, and the latter was the United States and Japan. For the monopoly of the colonial market, it was naturally necessary to increase international conflicts and trigger new colonial strategies. Japan had already said to Britain, "If you can't open the gateway to Great Britain, let's be tempted to block the Far East portal." Germany and Italy also said, "You have locked up the vast colonial market. We have to invade the new colony." Therefore, Zhang came to the conclusion, "The means to support inflation through fiscal expansion will inevitably lead to war." Both Japan and Italy used the slogan of exploiting the territory as a reason for fiscal expansion. In particular, Japan could not speak without emphasis. First, since the Mukden Incident in Shenyang, the British also gave up the gold standard. Under the slogan of "extreme time", it continued to swell. The national debt jumped from 6.3 billion yen at the end of 1932 to 9.3 billion yen at the end of September, 1935. The government purchased large quantities of munitions; unemployed workers regained purchasing power and

Japanese prices, instead of falling, rose considerably. This was the so-called Military Prosperity of the smell of gunpowder. Before the Mukden Incident, several Japanese prime ministers resigned due to deficit budgets. After the Mukden Incident, due to the effect of extreme time, the wartime budget would not have to be balanced; they released public debt in "a perfect excuse". Japan used the "implementation of the mainland policy" to stabilize the people in the country and cover up the financial crisis. Northeast China was in Japan's hands at no cost. In 4 years, the Japanese budget had been expanding day by day and the government's credit could be supported by the "partial success of the mainland policy". At the same time, it could also "expand the future of the mainland policy" to require more military spending. As a result, "Japan's fiscal expansion has become an evil practice, and Japan's mainland policy has also been caught in a dilemma."

Inflation itself is an economic war. "Inflation can not only eliminate panic but also promote war. It can also be said that inflation is a wartime currency system." Zhang Naiqi also emphasized that the people of the country should make it clear that the colonial people, especially in China, "We are not just suffering from the loss of a currency war, but also the loss of military aggression." Because inflation is a currency dump in terms of trade, using currency devaluation as a means to compete for the market, this is the so-called currency war. In the currency war, the colonial and semi-colonial people were the biggest victims. There were no tariff barriers, no great capital front; that miserable industry was only destroyed in the currency war. Since China's inflation in the world in 1931, prices continued to decline under the dumping of various currencies; under the imperialist economic and military aggression, the industrial base was shaken and bankrupted. There is no strong overall policy, nor is there a strong political foundation. When people talk about currency revolution, they mean "Saving the country has become a deception of the people and does harm to a country!"

The problem was unconventional economists whose opinions were contrary to economists with a sense of justice and national responsibility. Zhang observed that "Facts have proved that the theory of a vulgar economist is to cover a large scale, to avoid serious problems, to be hypocritical, and to be a fraud." Therefore, "they are accustomed to raising a small element of the economic panic and magnifying it to mask the fundamental elements of panic and mask the seriousness of panic." In China, they raised the issue of silver even higher than heaven, thinking that all emotions and joys and sorrows were based on silver and gold; and the semi-colonialism, the entire imperialist forces and the serious imperialist military aggression were placed second. The raging of all kinds of domestic feudal forces had been opened up. They also believed that we only needed to balance the payments, the budget and the currency system, and thus all problems would be solved. Zhang pointed out sharply, "In order to fight for China's currency rights, imperialism can help China reform its currency system. For the export of capital, it can borrow money for China, but it must not listen to China's management of currency exchange or even control trade. They all demand a balance. Where are their excess goods dumped?" When it comes to the balance of the budget, Zhang believed that it should recognize and reduce the excess revenue, and the original main source of taxes would be reduced. The main source of new tax sources was inheritance tax and income tax. The former could not be effectively implemented in Shanghai in the heritage base because of the tax, and the latter could not be implemented because the foreign industry was not subject to Chinese ordinance control. The income tax waived the main source of industrial profits. It only expropriated the wage earners, and it did not make much progress. Under the separatism of feudal forces, could one talk about the balance of international payments, the balance of budgets or the unified currency system? Obviously, this was all in vain.

On March 14, 1935, Zhang published a research report on industrial and commercial finance jointly with Yang Yinji and Zhang Youmei. After analyzing inflation, their conclusion was, "China's current economic needs are the expansion of credit, and it is not yet a currency. Inflated. ... In China, the notes and securities are all in the bud. ... If you can catch up, seize the opportunity, and create a tool for the search for credit; while in the current situation, creating tens of millions of dollars in Shanghai is achievable. The financial industry's flexibility in discounting bills can relieve tensions. The issuance of industrial securities can't be expected to be developed in the present or in the near future; the scale and establishment of the foundation will not be limited to the future after the financial relaxation."

4.1.5. On hyperinflation

On the hyperinflation during the War of Resistance of the Japanese invasion, Zhang published his article *On Hyperinflation* on September 24, 1939, which discussed seven aspects. First of all, what is the analysis of hyperinflation and its causes? As Zhang saw it, it "is not a policy, but a dead end in wartime finances that have been helpless." Since no government was willing to expand viciously, no one will advocate hyperinflation; but, when it does occur, no one can put an end to it. Its formation is often due to the expansion of military demand. Its most significant characterization was that it was "involuntary". Therefore, one could draw a conclusion that it should not be a policy. Military procurement and military payments were too much, and there had been a sharp drop in the number of commodities and a surge in the volume of currency in the market. Meanwhile, wartime productivity, instead of increasing, tended to drop; after a sharp drop in the quantity of commodities, the price would skyrocket; this would induce speculation and a surge in military payments. At the same time, the government failed to absorb surplus foreign currency through the use of taxation, debt-raising and mandatory savings, thus encouraging speculative purchases and waste, and failing to cope with the surge in military payments. It would be reliant on the printing of banknotes, embarking on the dead end of malignant expansion. "This works as both cause and effect and would continue endlessly. Inflation, price and military payment seem three wild horses, chasing one another frantically but ending with no one catching up with others. In the end, they all fell down out of exhaustion." The second was the crisis of the malignant expansion of the enemy and the fact that people did not want vicious expansion. Comparing the enemy's finances and economy, analyzing the advantages and disadvantages of the enemy, one can "understand each other better". He believed that "every enemy's disadvantages are congenitally deficient, and resources for human and material resources are poor; and its advantages are political organizations, economic organizations and social organizations. If they are more progressive, they will be much more powerful. ... Which day will it lead to a vicious expansion? It depends on its plot to 'raise and fight' and when it goes bankrupt." From the aspect of military expansion, by the proportion of national savings and public debt issuance, it could be estimated that the malignant expansion was imminent; however, according to the Japanese bank's banknote issuance figures, after the war, the increased issuance was 120 million yen, and it was still possible to struggle for life. For a certain period of time, the increase in payments due to the increasing circulation of notes in wartime was actually needed. In terms of productivity, a country with a population of 70 million needs to mobilize 2 million people to support the war. The decline of production was unavoidable. More than 40% of non-governmental farming horses had been recruited for the military, which was a very serious blow to agricultural production. The expansion of the military demanded more than the people could afford, the issuance of public debt was higher than the total savings of the people and wartime production was absolutely incompatible with the consumption of war. These three factors had made Japan viable and inflated. It was struggling with the more advanced state organizations. It also adopted a new trick of "cultivating and fighting for war". This plot was not only a "debilitating agent for malignant expansion, but also a renewal soup for the Japanese warlord regime!" It was "the only source of external forces".

How to deal with the conspiracy of Japanese militarism to sustain wars by means of wars? Mr. Zhang pointed out that "we must pay serious attention to the enemy's plot of sustaining wars by means of wars, that we must be vigilant and prevent ourselves from turning our 'vast territory and abundant resources' into the enemy's, and we should guard against the enemy's passing on their "natural inadequacies" to us. Only when we see through their plots, strengthen ourselves, and try our best to take advantage of all possible resources, could we defeat the enemy's evil deeds. In principle, we are "the War of Resistance Against Japanese Aggression with the founding of the country at the same time, a special countermeasure is to fight against economic and economic construction behind the enemy."

On the issue of China's malignant expansion, Zhang confidently stated, "I dare to say that the expansion of China's military needs is very limited. ... Comparing enemies cannot be done on the 'same day' because

China is an agricultural country. At that time, the decline in productivity was originally lighter than that in industrial countries. ... China's national savings are not mainly in banks, but in the general public. We have only 270,000 *yuan* in public debt issued during wartime; the wartime public debt of the 10,100-yen is really very small amount compared to. ... We can know that in the three aspects of expansion of military demand, public debt issuance and productivity, we don't have the crisis of malignant expansion. The malignant expansion is the price issue." However, in Zhang's view, "Since the malignant expansion began, prices will certainly rise, but rising prices are not necessarily indicative of malignant expansion." He observed prices from two aspects. "First of all, he must not be overly anxious about price issues, and he must not ignore price issues. A few rear cities, such as Chongqing, Kunming, and Guilin, have skyrocketed in price, but it does not represent the rise in overall prices. The price of food in these cities has not risen so much, but in the vast rural areas it has fallen instead. In the majority of poor people's living expenses, food expenditure accounts for more than 80%. Therefore, it can be asserted that the current price increase will affect the lives of the majority of citizens. On the other hand, the high prices of industrial products are common, the lack of industrial products, the former is more moderate, and the intrusion of counterfeit goods is a fact that cannot be ignored. Due to the stringency of the blockade, there are serious problems with the sale of agricultural products, and they will do harm to the grain. Agriculture has even become abandoned in the rear area, due to the lack of raw materials, technology and workers, the costs of production are high and the speed of production slow. At the front, the enemy might have the plot of supporting war with war, while the prices of commodities in the rear area are often under much influence. Therefore, he suggested that one must pay attention to how to grasp inflation and even use inflation. With regard to grasping the inflation problem, Mr. Zhang affirmed some measures that had been taken during the war. For example, the decree restricting the deposit on finance had received immediate results. Financially, people failed to keep up with taxation, debt collection or other means. As a result, the expansion of commercial capital and consumer capital had affected the price of goods; therefore, people had been accumulating money in the direction of inflation in terms of fiscal revenue and saving money in the direction of inflation. The financial resources will not be exhausted, while the currency system will be particularly stable. China's problem was that "economic and social organizations are weak and it is indeed more difficult to work on it." What made Zhang quite confident was that "the mobilization of people's strength in wartime can remedy this defect". The financial sector could also use further expansion to increase production. It was more important and fundamental to consolidate economic barriers. However, one must not be afraid of vicious expansion. One must not bind one's hands or feet, and weaken the power of lasting resistance. The explanation of reasonable expansion by Zhang was that it was for production; as long as it could expand for production, the expansion of one dollar could often increase the productivity of several thousand dollars. The balance of expansion was to transfer the power of expansion to the vast number of enemies, that is to say, to expand the area. He believed that the region had expanded and the danger of malignant expansion had naturally disappeared. For the expansion, he was particularly concerned about "the necessity to prevent the outflow of the legal currency". He came up with his own opinions.

After the founding of the People's Republic of China, in order to eradicate the legacy of old China, Zhang discussed the inflation of old China, and wrote in sorrow, "Inflation in the past 12 years has brought about new illnesses. The expansion of the number of households is even faster. The most important thing is that if you work on a production business, you can also make up for it and become a 'famous seller and a good seller'. ... Therefore, the number of light industrial households that have become easy to swell will also greatly expand. It is speculation, and it is also speculative for consumers to import more supplies. ... The purely speculative business of gambling has also greatly expanded. ... If you make easy money, you may wish to let go of your hand, and the industries that consume everything are also greatly inflated." The aftereffects of inflation and the strange phenomenon of all the people being involved in business were vividly demonstrated in front of everyone. For his own reasons, Zhang believed that there was no need to make a fuss. In the inflation period, throwing out currency to buy commodities was a stable and profitable way. There was no need for and there would be no plans to do business. There was no need to have specialized experience nor was there any need to plan. As long as the company's bank number was set up to obtain legal protection, the intermediaries and companies that had business between them might be able to get mixed up. Even repayment had been greatly improved. The bank "can use their money to pick their own goods, and they can also take advantage of usury ... to make money in a steady way ... usury can still make profits ... colluding with large and small bureaucrats capitalists, you can make huge profits." "The biggest beneficiaries are the four big families. Inflation, after all, is the issue of printing paper to collect people's supplies, which is extremely cruel exploitation. Therefore, the people's wealth and the purchasing power are still reducing day by day. The wealth of the four big families was more than US$10 billion, among which the majority is derived from the exploitation of inflation."

The speculative business and finance industry had inflated day by day with the help of the poor, relying on their hard work. According to Zhang, "a bloated morbid condition is a more serious condition than a bloated face". In the most concentrated and most conclusive way, it showed the evidence of the inherent negation of capitalism by the development of itself. That was "the decay and bloatedness, which have developed into their flashpoint, are precisely the economic basis of the collapse of the Kuomintang's reactionary rule. This incurable economic root is doomed to its collapse as well."

4.2. Theory of currency war

4.2.1. Overview of currency war

"Currency war is a new term that has been used in recent years. It is a change in monetary policy as a means to compete for commodity markets and financial markets."[212] On June 1, 1936, in the article *The Current Situation of the Foreign Currency Wars Against China*, Zhang Naiqi pointed out, "For the struggle between imperialists and the imperialist invasion of colonies and semi-colonies, what is on the surface is race of political power. In fact, it is the struggle of the economic forces. The

---

[212]*Ibid.*, p. 335.

political forces were competing for economic interests, while the struggle developing from the economic forces themselves is actually the biggest part of the international struggle. ... About struggle in economy, what we once knew is only the term 'trade war'. ... In fact, after imperialism transferring from commodity export into capital export, the object of international competition is not only commodity markets, but also raw material markets, labor markets, and financial markets, resources, and transportation. This kind of fact. ... The classical school of surrender is unwilling to raise these questions."[213] In another article, he said, "The outward contradiction developed by internal contradictions — currency war, judging from the relations between imperialism, it is the final scene of the economic war, followed by the military war. Speaking of the relationship between imperialism and the colonies, it is the cruelest exploitation of the colonial people. On the one hand, it is extracting the only purchasing power of colonial peoples, and the other is destroying the childish productivity of the colonies."[214] This is the most persuasive expression of the nature of the currency war.

In the way of struggling in the commodity market, Zhang pointed out that it is usually a dumping of falling prices, and government subsidies are used to compensate export merchants for their losses of prices falling and dumping. "It is establishing a no-most-favored-country exclusive tariff treaty with other countries to gain monopoly over the market." In the most intense phase of the struggle, currency wars became necessary. A currency war manifests itself in the use of state laws to reduce the value of money in the commodity market, to reduce the cost of domestic commodities in overseas markets and to fight for the market. That is the so-called currency dumping. In the fight for financial markets, the role of currency war is even greater. Internally, imperialism maintains an international financial center, as a base for economic strategies, and externally uses carrot and stick to seize currency power in backward countries.[215] The superior position in the world of London, which was formed by the British Pound group, and its rivalry with New York in the United States, was enough to

---

[213]*Anthology of Zhang Naiqi (Part 1)*, p. 335.
[214]*Ibid.*, p. 331.
[215]*Ibid.*, p. 336.

overwhelm Paris in France, which was the best demonstration. "The purpose of the currency war has also evolved from a simple market competition to a competition for currency rights, which has caused the sharpening of the opposition of international currency groups."[216]

As for the cause of the international currency war, according to Zhang's analysis, from the perspective of phenomena, in the crisis of capitalism, it was the only way for capitalists to broaden their overseas markets. This is because capitalism in its later stages has not been able to advance human evolution as it did during its earlier stages of growth. In terms of currency, the trend has changed from maintaining the value of the currency to basing the value of the currency on the commodity prices. "On this occasion, the bourgeoisie, in order to safeguard its own interests, has violated human evolution and disregarded human happiness, only has the actions on purpose of raising prices. In essence, the bourgeoisie has monopolized the commodity and monopolized the currency. From the intent of maintaining private ownership, it is impossible to spread the currency to the public to increase purchasing power, and it is impossible to disperse commodities for consumption by the general public. Therefore, it will inevitably result in a stalemate that the money in its hands will directly purchase the goods it has, but there will be no corresponding consuming power. For this reason, the bourgeoisie has to use inflation to increase the amount of money. If the money after the increase still cannot flow into the hands of the general public and become real purchasing power, the speculative purchases and false prices reflected in the stimulus will not be sustainable. In this case, the only way out capitalists have is 'Only using the low exchange rate when the value of the underlying currency has fallen, to carry out their overseas markets by using currency dumping, which begins the international currency war'."[217]

With regard to the tactics of currency war, Zhang said, "The most highly technical application in all economic wars is relatively profound. The development inside is dialectics."[218] Regardless of whether

---

[216]*Ibid.*, p. 332.
[217]*Ibid.*, p. 331.
[218]*Ibid.*, p. 336.

consciously or unconsciously, whether it is a conviction or a skeptical attitude, it had to be applied. For example, Zhang explained that the first is giving up the gold standard and implementing the legal currency policy; the concentration and control of precious metals is a very important strategy for currency war. However, if it exceeds the limit, an oppressive country will abandon the metal standard and will implement the legal currency. The use of US gold policy resulted in the United Kingdom giving up the gold standard first, and the US silver policy made China give up the silver standard. The second is that the currency falling prices will cause capital to disappear. However, when the price drops to a certain limit, the capital will return and make the price drop an advantage rather than a disadvantage. Before and after the British renounced the gold standard, capital largely fled. After a certain period of time, the capital returned in abundance. "Up to now, many people think that the British currency has once dropped its price, and it will not be in danger of falling prices any longer. Compared with French currency, which has fallen after the big panic, British currency is less dangerous. As a result, capital often flees from France to the United Kingdom. And the devaluation of the currency has become a favorable condition for Britain. These are all 'yes-no, no-yes' and 'quantitative change leads to qualitative change'. For a person who only understands formal logic, he must think that favorable is ultimately beneficial. It is impossible to grasp this phenomenon of change."[219] Therefore, Zhang reemphasized that "China cannot join any currency group. This will not only be necessary to maintain the independence of currency power, but also necessary to avoid unnecessary disputes."[220]

On the way of currency war, Zhang thought that it was full of tricks and became a profound tactic that was not easy to understand. Until that time, "There are already many ways as abandoning the gold standard, reducing the currency fine, buying gold, buying silver, and buying other currencies."[221] The sharpening of the international group movement was a feature of the eve of war. As the currency war developed, international

---

[219]*Ibid.*, p. 337.
[220]*Ibid.*, p. 337.
[221]*Ibid.*, p. 332.

group movements became even more superficial than customs wars. Under the circumstances, the situation of opposition between the three currency groups of the British pound, the US dollar and the Franc was already very intense. A currency group is often tied with tariff groups to strengthen its power. "Ambitious Japan. ... After all, because of its slow development of financial capital, it still cannot form the so-called 'Japan Gold Group'. ... Therefore, there has recently been an advocacy of 'Silver Group'."[222] After analysis, Zhang's conclusion made it impossible for one to have a sense of the "coming" of the Second World War! Unfortunately, the development of the situation proved that he was right. It is clear that Zhang's vision was incisive and the judgment was accurate.

4.2.2. The Far East currency war among Britain, the US and Japan

After a detailed analysis of the European currency war, Zhang turned to a currency war between Britain, the United States, and the Japanese imperialists in China. He pointed out that the three countries of "Britain, the United States, and Japan are fighting for the currency power in China. ... The ultimate goal of the US silver policy is to bring China into the US dollar group ... Britain proposes to use 10 million pounds of borrowings to exchange the Chinese currency right ... Japan's ... use of 'retreat for advancement' ... in addition to armed struggle and commodity dumping, does not cooperate with other imperialists to compete for the Chinese currency right."[223] On April 16, 1935, in his article *Anglo-American Currency War in China*, he exemplified that China's currency joined the US dollar group. "A unit of China's national currency is equal to a percentage of the US dollar, so the exchange between China and the US will be very stable, and even if there are some fluctuations, it will usually not exceed the cash point. Therefore, Chinese importers and exporters will feel that buying and selling goods to the United States will be less risky. Only the risk of price fluctuations and the risk of no exchange rate will make the US's

---
[222] *Ibid.*
[223] *Ibid.*, p. 334.

trade with China exceptionally well-developed. It is particularly evident in the investment aspect that the instability of the exchange rate often becomes a major obstacle. Once gold becomes precious and silver become cheap, China will suffer a loss, and no one will forget the loss of foreign debt exchanges in the past. Political borrowing may be quenching the thirst with poison, and no one will not dare to try commercial borrowers. On the contrary, the Americans have to exchange their own dollars into Chinese currency to lend to the Chinese, and they also have to bear the risk of such exchange. Creditors cannot afford to lend money to others." "If China joins the US dollar group, this problem would naturally be solved. Financial capital of the United States can be imported into China in large quantities to create its advantage in China."[224]

The Far East Currency War, which aimed at plundering Chinese currency rights, had already begun very early. Since 1930, the consultative group headed by E. W. Kemmere traveled across the oceans. The advancement in the Far East, especially the investment in the northeast provinces, was a factor contributing to Japan military assault on China.[225] Roosevelt's silver policy continued Hoover's struggle for new capital in the Far East. Zhang thought that the comments of many writers on Roosevelt's silver policy were to please the "Silver senator who represents the interests of the silver miners. This is correct, but it is not enough". The ultimate goal of the silver policy was to obtain the currency power of China, including the currency power of the three provinces in the East, and to control the currency power of the South American and Far East by the virtual gold standard. It was to open up vast investment markets for a financial capital in South America and the Far East, and to open up vast commodity and raw material markets for an industrial. Only such a silver policy for the benefit of its entire bourgeoisie could get the approval of the majority in the parliament.[226] This was indeed an incisive argument which was based on the overall scope of the global political economy and economic benefit. It was of great significance to study the US silver policy of that year.

---

[224]*Ibid.*, p. 321.
[225]*Ibid.*, p. 322.
[226]*Ibid.*, p. 323.

4.2.3. Silver policy of the US and the silver issue of China

The United States' silver policy unexpectedly felt the unprecedented financial panic in China. Zhang thought that it would be wrong to blame the US silver policy completely. It was in fact the result of the Anglo-American currency war in China. After the United States announced its silver policy, it not only became a big buyer of the world's silver but also became a supporter of London's silver market. London's silver brokers had to wait for Washington's calls to buy in order to open the market. When the United States stopped buying silver in London, London's silver market almost became a dead market. At this point, the United Kingdom had no way to grab China's overseas reserves.[227] In order to cope with the US currency wars, British Business HSBC first shipped a large amount of silver to Shanghai. This not only prevented the Chinese government from interfering with silver exports but also gave the United States and the Chinese government a warning. "China must join in the pound sterling group to rebel against the United States. It must also abandon its attempt to set a currency exchange line by balancing the tax."[228] Britain's tactical intimidation, which was full of "retreat for advance", was indeed large and had an effect. The United States stated that it had taken steps to ease the price of silver, that is, it had to lengthen the process of seizing Chinese currency power. China also sought help from Britain and was in the process of negotiating big loans. Although the attitude of the British capitalists in China was not very consistent, they tended to be slightly different in tactics, but they could also be used strategically to "use for each other".[229] In *The Future of the Chinese Currency* on September 10, 1935, Zhang suggested that, "If the United States can lend us a large sum of money, it is not difficult for China to maintain the silver standard for the stable silver price in the United States. This is what Japan opposes and the United States does not dare try when the Pacific military forces are not enough to overpower Japan. At this time, there was a suggestion to change the virtual capital standard. Its content was to use the UK for 20 million

---
[227]*Ibid.*, pp. 338–339.
[228]*Ibid.*, p. 325.
[229]*Ibid.*, p. 326.

pounds as a preparation for the launch. Naturally, the UK is willing to take the lead before the United States has stabilized the price of silver. In order to worry about Japan's opposition, the UK proposed in March 1935 that the international community jointly resolve the Chinese currency system and jointly borrow money to China. Japan, which insisted on monopolizing China, at this time put forward the slogan of 'China–Japan Economic Cooperation' and reject the proposal of Britain, and then they will step back and send financial experts to China. Japan naturally assumes ownership of the East Asian masters. Of course, Japan cannot ignore the Anglo-America currency war in China. In fact, for the development of the Anglo-America currency war in China, Japan's attitude is a decisive factor. Japan's financial capital is still very naive. Its currency foundation is particularly fragile. Since it cannot yet assimilate the pseudo-Manchu currency, naturally it will not have the assumption of assimilating the entire Chinese currency. The forces available for Japanese imperialism are only military forces and commodity dumping forces. Its superior military forces in the East and West Pacific Oceans may prevent any of the great powers in the Chinese economy from advancing.[230] The United States has to take steps in the military, and Britain has to compromise with Japan. At bottom, the era is radical and there is no independent currency standard guaranteed by independent regime. This is an unprecedented crisis that is currently faced. 'In addition to the competition of Britain and the US for China's currency power, Japan also has the 'East Asian currency group' and the 'Silver Group' proposed. In the latter plan, Japan will change the currency system to the silver standard and form a 'silver group' together with China and the pseudo-Manchu. For these reasons, these two proposals cannot escape the part of the so-called economic alliance between China, Japan and 'Manchukuo'."[231] It is necessary to know that, the "China and Japan's economic support" arrived in late February of that year. The Japanese Ministry of Foreign Affairs resolutely opposed the Anglo-American international assistance campaign in March. Zhang revealed that Japanese attempts to monopolize China contributed to the UK's joint response to Japan's situation. Therefore, since that time,

---

[230]*Ibid.*
[231]*Ibid.*, p. 371.

monopoly and co-management have become sharp confrontations. Afterward, they were preparing to hold an international currency conference in Nanjing but gave up because of Japan's objections. "Then there are British, American, French and Italian financial experts to China. The first to be sent was Britain's representative, Frederick Leith-Ross. At that time the attempt of Japan to monopolize China was already launched with great strides.[232] The Japanese–British relations have changed with the changes in the European situation. If the war in Europe is inescapable, Britain may have to make concessions to Japan. The relationship between the United States and Britain and Japan is as long as the United States can calmly enrich the military power in the Pacific. Until the day when it can completely overpower Japan and terrorize the United Kingdom, it quickly completed its silver policy and obtained China's currency power. The easing of Japan–US relations can be achieved as long as Japan is single-mindedly attacking the Soviet Union. International anti-Soviet wars were being highly brewed, and the world's general trend has the potential to change dramatically."[233] Zhang's prediction in Europe was indeed confirmed by history, but it was inappropriate to use it in Asia, especially in East Asia.

In *Current Situation of the Foreign Powers in China's Currency War*, Zhang specifically exposed Japan's despicable tactics of politics and economy of fighting against Britain to compete for Chinese currency rights, its engagement in evil activities devoid of conscience, launching another "the North China Event" and establishing the Luandong Puppet Organization and the Administration Committee of Hebei Province. It also further protected the development of the ronin smuggling voyages, in addition to the 20 million yen of silver that was shipped out and the 30 million yen worth of goods smuggled in. This not only hit China's currency base but also undermined China's fiscal base. "The 'smuggling' issue is widely reported. On the one hand, it can be said that the Japanese imperialists have always adhered to the policy of aggression against China. On the other, it is intended to overthrow the British Customs administration in China as a revenge for the currency war. In addition,

---

[232]*Ibid.*, pp. 329–330.
[233]*Ibid.*, p. 330.

the rejection of silver by the Japanese Bank in China and the blocking of southbound transportation of silver form the North China can be described as a wave of currency war."[234]

Zhang's asked the question, "How should we save the currency power of China? This is not a separate currency issue, but rather a national issue."[235] "If China is to strive for national liberation, we should argue that: China must have an independent currency standard and a stable currency value. This is the advocacy to switch to using our own currency."[236] This is the conclusion that Zhang Naiqi arrived at after careful consideration.

In the *Current Silver Issue* of August 22, 1934, and two related articles published on November 9 and 15, Zhang Naiqi made the following comments. In 1930, a "wave of gold being expensive and silver being cheap" occurred and unexpectedly after 4 or 5 years, a "wave of silver being expensive and gold being cheap" occurred. When others "have surplus silver", China, which is "controlled by others", can be their reservoir. When "silver of others is insufficient", they can be their "outside warehouse". "Under these two 'tasks', the 'wave' is naturally extraordinarily large."[237] On July 15, 1949, Zhang wrote an article to review several "silver disasters" that China experienced from 1926 to 1935. The first time was from 1926 to 1932. At that time, the world's silver price plummeted. The silver price of New York fell from 69 cents per ounce in 1925 to 28 cents in 1932. China's silver was in excess of import, causing a disaster of inflation, rising prices, speculative activity, economic and social chaos, and the devastation of people's lives. "This time the silver plague was directed by British imperialism. It presided over the currency reform of India and changed from the silver standard to the virtual gold standard of the pound sterling. China has become the warehouse of silver and suffered a scourge." The second was from 1933 to 1935, when the world's silver price soared. The silver price of New York rose from an average price of 28 cents per ounce in 1932 (the lowest price was 24 points) to 81 points in April 1935. "Three times stronger in 3 years.

---

[234]*Ibid.*, p. 338.
[235]*Ibid.*, p. 327.
[236]*Ibid.*, p. 371.
[237]*Ibid.*, p.346.

China's silver turned over and was excess in export, creating a serious situation of deflation, sharp drops in prices, collapses in industry and commerce, and unemployment. This silver disaster was directed by US imperialism. It launched the International Silver Conference, established the International Silver Agreement, issued the Silver Purchase Act, and further announced the state ownership of silver by 1934." The silver that had been excluded from coinage in the past was first restored in the United States to some uses of coinage and currency reserves. The treasury could buy domestic and foreign silver at a price. The rise and fall in the price of silver was completely manipulated by the US government. "In these two 'Silver Disasters', the financial giants of the United States and Britain benefited, and the main victims were people in China and India. Because of the collusion with the Anglo-American imperialists, Chinese bureaucratic capital has gained many benefits and laid their foundation in the people suffering."[238]

In the spring of 1935, the United States raised the silver price and led a tide. According to Zhang's analysis, by the end of June, silver from a port in Shanghai had export surplus of just more than 30 million *yuan* in half a year. In July, the situation suddenly became serious. By the beginning of August, the United States announced its silver policy and the situation was extremely tight. The export of China's silver was rapidly in surplus. Shanghai's silver deposits amounted to 594 million *yuan* in May of that year. It had a huge export of 43.9 million *yuan* on only one day of the 20th. Such a large number of shipments of several tens of thousands of *yuan* a day was unbearable. As a result, "the financial sector was suddenly uneasy; on the day of the securities market price, a drop of 2 or 3 *yuan* was found: on the 21st, a new rate of 1 *jiao* and 1 *fen* was found. In the lax financial market, suddenly there was a sense of 'a cloud on the horizon'!"[239]

After the United States announced the nationalization of silver, it would have a great impact on China's financial economy. Zhang accurately analyzed the reasons for this — silver outflow caused financial depletion and disorders. "Because the US government artificially raises

---
[238]*Ibid.*, pp. 599–600.
[239]*Ibid.*, p. 347.

the price of silver, overseas silver prices will inevitably rise faster than China's silver prices, and lower-priced Chinese silver will quickly flow overseas. At the same time, because the Far East War is filled with war clouds, the wave of export bans has once again been very high, and there has been silver outflowing for the 'refuge', causing the trend of silver outflows to be particularly serious. The reason why China's silver outflow problem is serious is that silver is China's standard currency metal. As a result of the constant outflow of local currency metal, there is bound to be a panic of financial depletion. In recent years, most of the financial industry in Shanghai has sighed that 'the rich have nowhere to put', and the deposit of China merchants' banks has not decreased, and the panic caused by 'false alarm' has already appeared." "The short-term interest rate on the deposit suddenly rose from the usual *fens* to more than 1 *jiao*. The public debt market has also started to fall. The unorganized financial market once again exposed weaknesses."[240] In this situation, "opinions varied", and Zhang used this metaphor to refer to the confusion at the time of the discussion, which can be broadly divided into three aspects: laissez-faire, interference and indirect interference. "If China adopts a policy of direct interference, most of the import trade must be stopped (60%, according to trade statistics in recent years, exports account for 40% of imported goods), equaling to the elimination of import surplus. This is very favorable from the point of view of the national economy, but from the financial point of view it is a fatal injury. Since the central government's revenues relied on import taxes, and it's afraid that it must account for 40%. How can the government take a 40% tax revenue a knock? The Chinese government cannot make the import trade get affected. It is certainly not advisable to adopt the policy of direct interference, while the policy of laissez-faire will also be a big threat to the finances. According to the year (1934), the central government had a shortage of 140 million *yuan*, and it was necessary to issue public bonds of 200 million *yuan* to make the income and expenditure appropriate. The outflow of silver, the financial depletion, and the fall in the prices of government bonds will make it very difficult to issue public debt. In the same year, local fiscal revenues were severely hit by floods and droughts several times across the

---

[240]*Ibid.*, p. 349.

country. Local governments' attempts to issue provincial bonds or to use provincial debt to borrow money may also fail. After all, the impact of laissez-faire policies on finance was indirect, while the impact of interference policy was direct and the indirect impacts also had all sorts of fantasies about self-comfort. Therefore, the authorities initially adopted a laissez-faire policy. In a short period of time, the fantasies 'completely vanished' and indirect interference must be adopted in the middle of no solution. However, in the situation that silver has become a commodity in the world market again, the silver delivery point will inevitably evolve in accordance with China's international payments." "If China's export continues to be in excess, and the balance of payments continues to make ends meet, silver will inevitably be constantly outflowing."[241] The effect of the exchange system's production must also have been based on whether the import surplus can be eliminated and the balance of payments can be balanced. Zhang "always advocates the interference policy."[242] Faced with the outflow of silver, it could only be proposed that China should prepare to build a sound and strong basis of interference policy. Financial sources cannot always rely on several ports. Financial centers cannot be always established in Shanghai. A currency system that can handle any incident is also needed.

On the far-reaching intentions of the US silver policy, Zhang said, "The aim is to make the Chinese currency system a member of the 'US dollar group', but the core explanation is to make China vassal to the US." Zhang then said, "If it is said that it aims to undermine China's financial currency system, it will be excessive. It is correct to say that it aims to increase its output to China, but it is not enough."[243] As the silver proponent of the US Wheeler said, "the increase in the cost of Chinese industrialists makes us very uncomfortable."[244] The steps taken by the United States, in Zhang's view, were after silver was bought to a considerable extent and the price of silver was raised to the appropriate standard, when it was naturally necessary to further stabilize the price of silver. "If silver

---

[241] *Ibid.*, p. 353.
[242] *Ibid.*
[243] *Ibid.*, p. 362.
[244] *Ibid.*, p. 366.

can stabilize its price with the US dollar at a certain rate, China's silver-dominated currency can fully follow the changes in the price of the US dollar, so that China will naturally join the US dollar group."

According to Zhang's view, the US silver policy inevitably included the following three functions: The first was internally winning over the feelings of silver soldiers who represented the interests of a silver master. It was a blow to the Chinese economic community. Otherwise, "China's price in terms of silver will not collapse."[245] The second was to externally compete for China's commodity market. This was mutual for the powers. "However, the ideals of the American silver proponents to raise the purchasing power of the Chinese people by raising the price of silver have apparently failed." This was "a quote to win over common American industrialists. The immediate result is precisely the sacrifice of the interests of the general industrialists in the United States in order to maintain the interests of the silver miners. ... If China is forced to adopt measures to increase the US tax rate on major export products to China in order to boycott US silver policy, it is particularly a blow to the general industry in the United States." The third was to further stabilize the price of silver so that China would naturally join the US dollar group. Zhang pointed out that it was pointless to be disappointed with the results of the situation (1935.4) because there was more than just America in the fight for Chinese currency power. Even if "China's currency power is in the control of the United States, what benefit would the US have with China becoming utterly impoverished?"[246]

Around 14 years later, Zhang further pointed out that the United States has concentrated a large amount of gold and silver and those were the two major weapons that controlled international finance. "The US Treasury concentrates more than 244.6 million US dollars' worth of gold, which equals three-fifths of the world's reserves. This is a financial weapon that controls Western Europe and other vassals." At the same time, it also concentrated more than 2.78 billion ounces of silver (data at the end of 1948). "US capital also controls 66% of the world's silver production. US capital controls 75% of silver from the world's largest

---

[245] Ibid.
[246] Ibid., p. 367.

producer, Mexico. Therefore, from the standpoint of the United States, in order to safeguard economic interests, it must control the world's silver market and actively control the politics of countries in North and South America and the Far East. So, it can use the silver policy as a financial weapon. This is precisely the weapon that controls the world's silver producing countries, especially the many countries in the Far East and the Near East who are happy to store silver. On the one hand, US imperialism has the world's largest productivity, boasting that it can sell whatever you need. On the other hand, it has the most gold and silver in the world, boasting that it can lend money to you. The conditions for selling are the exploitation of the blood and sweat of peoples in countries. The conditions for lending further control the sovereignty of all countries and interfere in the internal affairs of each country."[247] The ugly face of the US imperialism was portrayed vividly. The silver policy, as an organic component of the US global strategy, was revealed profoundly.

4.3. China's financial system theory

4.3.1. Finance and politics, philosophy and life

In April 1935, in the article *How to Study China's Financial Problems*, Zhang pointed out that the financial issue was not easily understood in economics. However, just like other problems in economics, it could not escape the scope of people's daily life. Studying financial problems can be realized by the facts in daily life and one can easily know how to start. For example, "evil money can drive out good money, and good money cannot drive out evil money." This is an explanation of an important law in monetary science. It is better to take the silver coin, silver auxiliary coin and copper coin as examples. When it comes to silver coins, the lower-grade national currency replaced the high-grade Ying Yang coin, the inferior Guangdong double replaced the higher single and double-angle silver auxiliary coins, and the low-quality copper coin also replaced the higher quality copper coin. By doing this in an indirect way, with the immediate examples illustrating profound principles, it will surely attract people.

---

[247]*Ibid.*, p. 600.

According to Zhang, the social age representing China was, of course, different from that of the advanced capitalist countries. "The present China is a semi-colonial country; the special nature of the semi-colonial countries is a combination of imperialist and feudal forces that hinder the independence and evolution of the nation." He thought that these were all relatively profound topics and somewhat difficult to understand. However, current examples can give them a clear explanation.[248] Regarding the answer to the question of development, because of the development of currency management, bad money driving out good money has become a historical term. In the course of establishment of capitalism, this law is also often used as a means of uniting currency, that is, the issuance of a unified lower-grade currency to expel the higher-quality currency. From capitalism to the era of imperialism, the concentration of capital led to the concentration of cash. As this was the only means of currency management, that is, the current means of reducing the value of the currency, it does not matter whether it is bad money or good money, which shows the last crisis of capitalism.

Regarding the prerequisites of finance, in the *Two Fronts in Economic Debate*, Zhang proposed that philosophy and politics be closely linked with finance and play a role in the administration of jurisdiction. He said, "After all the theoretical discussions have reached the highest level, they must be linked to philosophy. When all the theoretical struggles reach the top of the tension, they must be linked to politics. To put it more precisely, we have philosophical knowledge, and then we can have a profound cultivation of the theory of a certain department; we must have a very intense theoretical struggle for the tense of political issues."[249] This became the main principle of entire theoretical study of Zhang's work and is fully reflected and tested in his literary theory.

As far as the Chinese academic circles were concerned, Zhang pointed out clearly that "in the late Qing Dynasty, it was mainly a struggle between those in favor of reform and conservatives, but in recent years, it is a struggle between those supporting revolution and those anti-revolutionary people. So there is a great change indeed." The old-schoolers will be judged to be 'historical traitors', theoretically 'minor philosophies' and

---

[248] *Corpus of Zhang Naiqi*, I, p. 239.
[249] *Ibid.*

'traitorism philosophy'!" "They have mixed up with the various foreign classics and vintage thought to become the whole counter-revolutionary front. ... Under the protection and cooperation of imperialism, they struggled with the new and progressive revolutionary forces. This is an important department in the Chinese national liberation struggle — the cultural sector; it is sharpened with the sharpening of China's national liberation struggle."[250] Zhang believed that in the field of economics, there was also such a struggle. Claiming "Chinese learning for the essence and Western learning for practical use", the leftitsts of the conservatives were introducing Adam Smith's *The Wealth of Nations* into China; it was not until the May 4th Movement that the new economics was introduced to China; it immediately carried out a great deal of power in terms of revolutionary theory. During the Great Revolution in 1926–1927, the debate between the two factions "still remained a purely theoretical struggle during the maintenance of capitalism and the assertion of socialism."[251] From the failure of the Great Revolution in 1927 to the "September 18th Incident" of 1931, it was the heyday of the British and American imperialist forces. They paid attention to turning public opinion in China, especially paying attention to the cultivation of imperial economics. So, liberalism, individualism and vulgar economics that neglected political significance and analyzed the state of affairs floating on the table became their most ideal tools. On the contrary, progressive elements were committed to the critique of reality and collided with scholars of classical school and vulgar economy in the fiscal area, finance, trade, industry and other sectors of the agricultural economy. Therefore, many people expressed their progressive views to expose the deceptive nature of the "Customs Report", *Commerce and Finance*, an English newspaper, and Arnold, an American commercial counselor in China. After the "September 18th Incident," the imperial tools were internally divided into pro-Japanese, pro-European and pro-American factions, and disputes arose. Many political awareness changes occurred in the mercenary economists. Some of them firmly stood on the national front, and the opposition of the instrumentalized classical school united with the progressives who advocated the national revolution and

---

[250]*Ibid.*, p. 239.
[251]*Ibid.*, p. 240.

became a broad national front. "In this way, the times and the environment have caused the sharp opposition between the imperialist front and the national front in the Chinese economics circle."[252]

As for the affirmation of the historical value of the classical school, Zhang fully affirmed that at the end of the 18th century, after the collapse of the feudal system in Europe, the invention of the steam engine brought great new ways to human productivity. Mankind took drastic actions in production activities under liberalism and individualism. Personal development became the development of human civilization. The interests of individual were the interests of the entire society. "Under this new world, it is indeed correct."[253] Britain, the advanced country of the industry, and the most powerful country in the world in the 19th century with the most powerful economic forces, called for a world with free trade. The strength of its industrial production and financial capital was sufficient to fight against any country. It wanted the possibility of plundering other people without the possibility of others plundering it. The international division of Adam Smith's theory and the ideal of the world were used "to complete the special status of imperialism in the world."[254] "In recent years, Britain's tariff barriers have been as high as those of others; the scope of tariff barriers has expanded to all colonies. This is like the robber in the village. It has changed from one family to three or four. The new robbers are only two or three, and they are even more fierce than the original one. The original robber did not dare to open the door at this time. Instead, they closed their doors. Everything in the international era of the times is just such a thing!"[255]

Zhang moved his focus to China at the time and painfully disclosed that the imperialist economics of emperors in China obeyed the will of their masters and imported liberalism into China. The liberalism used in semi-colonialism was nothing but imperialist predatory freedom. "Under liberalism, the imperialist front in China is to be carried out with the overall subject of internationalization … is: internationalization of production,

---

[252] *Ibid.*, p. 241.
[253] *Ibid.*
[254] *Ibid.*, p. 242.
[255] *Ibid.*

internationalization of markets, internationalization of transportation, and internationalization of currency."[256]

4.3.2. China's credit system

Zhang Naiqi believed that the development of a credit system was an element of capitalist performance. It made "financial capital able to complete the monopoly of current capital and become the characteristic of its 'peak generation'. … The credit system is the backbone of modern financial capital. The reason why credit system can promote productivity is because such currency, used as medium of exchange, underlies credit system, it has developed the scale of large-scale production." Before the credit system was created, the payment instruments were only a limited number of metal currencies (coins). Since the credit system was created, there were credit instruments, bills and securities that had the largest number of banknotes (soft currency). With the issuance of banknotes, the amount of money could be greatly increased at the time of free exchange. "Under the present unrealized monetary system, there is no limit to the increase in the amount of money."[257]

Zhang compared the original form of credit system with the capitalist form, and found that under the original credit system, the use of loan disbursement enabled producers to engage in reproduction before goods were sold, thus playing a role in promoting commodity productivity. "However, this lacks the use of credit instruments. With the advancement of credit system, the first kind of credit instrument — negotiable instruments has been generated. Under the way of discounted bills, the goods can be produced before they have been sold. In this way, the product productivity will be further promoted. Afterwards, the credit system was further advanced. The second kind of credit instruments — industrial securities (stocks and corporate bonds), were created." "The producer can obtain new capital when capital accumulation is not completed and engage in larger-scale production. Such method will enable product's

---

[256]*Ibid.*, p. 243.
[257]*Ibid.*, p. 159.

productivity to reach the highest level."[258] This was the development of capitalist advanced countries' industries, which depended on the development of the company's organization, "depending on the issuance of industrial securities, the establishment of large capitals and large-scale production organizations, and on the purchase of industrial securities, the gradual concentration of industrial capital — large capital households buy up industrial securities and absorb small-scale industrial institutions to become a monopoly. On the one hand, industrial capitalists naturally become financial capitalists during the process of the trusts. This shift is necessary for the convenience of capital absorption and utilization, and activeness of the securities market. On the other hand, financial capitalists have developed the organization of the Holding Company during the purchase and acceptance of industrial securities, and have collected many industrial companies in their own hands."[259]

Zhang's in-depth comparative study of credit instruments concluded that industrial securities were a very important tool. "In essence, negotiable instruments are still just a way for commercial capital to reach its highest form. What it can solve is no more than short-term floating capital — a commercial capital that has changed in the industrial capital society. Its foundation is limited to the area of existing production capital; the quantity of production is limited and cannot exceed the total amount of existing commodities and claims. Industrial securities are tools for the most basic and long-term fixed capital in industrial development. Its production is unlimited and mass production, and can be adapted to the mass production of commodities. Its foundation includes future capital — so it can create new capital." From 1924 to 1929, the credit expansion of industrial advanced countries was based on industrial securities as an important tool. Only in this way could credit be expanded to an endless limit.[260] In times of prosperity, the expansion of credit, the mass production of money and commodities were adapted to each other, and they were all anarchic. After the outbreak of panic, it was initially an excess of commodities and after a considerable amount of time, there was a surplus of funds.

---

[258]*Ibid.*, p. 160.
[259]*Ibid.*
[260]*Ibid.*, pp. 160–161.

Zhang believed that "if we do not have a sound credit instrument — the credit chip,[261] we will not be able to get cheap capital; if we don't have the proper credit instruments, obtaining funds will not benefit the national economy."[262] However, "the preciousness of finance lies in the circulation, and the loan of funds are the interests of the financial community itself. As long as the security of financial industry is guaranteed, there is no fear of sluggishness in its own funds, then there is no doubt that the financial industry is willing to lend.[263] A sound expansion of credit means instead of an unsound means of inflation will increase credit chips compared to the issuance of currency notes. The use of creditor's rights on account books is not yet covered by the issuance of currency notes. Since the abolishing of the silver tael and the establishment of *yuan* as the sole monetary unit, the greatest progress in China's financial industry can be maintained and sustained."

According to Zhang, the mode of operation of banks must be adjusted accordingly. In his book *The Evolution of Financial System in Financial Panic*, Zhang wrote, "I think that the banking industry must not accept the payment of factories and machinery and should instead issue corporate bonds. The bank may wish to bear its own corporate bonds first, and then gradually transfer it to general investors in the securities market. In this way, the banks' assets will not be easily frozen, and industrial and commercial businesses may also receive funds with lower maturity and lower interest rates."[264] In addition, he called on the government to amend the company law and relax the corporate bond issuance quota. He also

---

[261] Nine people such as Zhang stated in the "Opinions on increasing the number of chips": "The chips are also called tools. The chips in the financial market are divided into two categories: credit chips, i.e., credit instruments, which are credit objects for the financial industry. Securities, bills, etc. belong to this category. The second is payment chips, i.e., payment instruments, are the means for the final settlement of creditor's rights and debts. Coins and banknotes fall into this category. Now that ordinary people are using a bargaining chip, they ignore the difference between credit and payment chips. However, the difference between the credit chips and the payment chips cannot be calculated in the same way." (*Ibid.*, p. 454)
[262] *Corpus of Zhang Naiqi*, I, p. 419.
[263] *Ibid.*, p. 453.
[264] *Ibid.*, p. 422.

proposed to organize a joint acceptance office for industrial papers so that the industry can discount accepted notes with bank to solve short-term funding problems. Until September 1943, Zhang's article continued to stress the bank's lending to industry. "From the national monetary policy and the source of industrial funds, it is a palliative." "The implementation of industrial securities and bills is the solution to the root causes." He pointed out, "Now in advanced countries, the industrial sector needs long-term capital, not mortgages to banks, but issuance of stocks, or corporate bonds, which are first underwritten by banks. In the future, banks can sell on the stock market, recoup the amount of money they have paid for underwriting, and add some profits. On the other hand, if it is a mortgage, the bank cannot sell it to someone else. The bank must use its own money. Although it can transfer the mortgage, it does not have a good face. If it is a security, you can sell it when you are willing to sell it. No one will notice it." "The problem in China is that there are some industrial securities, but no industrial securities market. As a result, industrial securities are not easily developed."[265] This is like an actor with good skills but no theater to give full play to his talents, thus limiting his development. "Although modern credit instruments have been crudely shaped, they cannot be fully developed because they lack a securities market and lack a platform for active circulation. As modern direct financing means cannot obtain the platform conditions to give full play to its advantages, the modernization of China's economy will be constrained and lag behind."

4.3.3. Financial markets in China

Zhang gave a concise answer on the concept of financial markets, covering different markets, different utilities, methods and traits. He said, "The so-called financial markets originally included two abstract markets, namely (1) the money market and (2) capital market. The utility of the money market is to provide funds for an activity; its main method is the discounting of bills. The utility of the capital market is to provide capital for an industry; its main method is the investment in stocks and corporate bonds. Whichever modern financial market we analyze, we have both markets."[266]

---

[265]*Ibid.*, pp. 551–552.
[266]*Ibid.*, p. 70.

He introduced the financial markets of the United Kingdom, which did exceptionally well in the money market, and Germany, which was just as good as the capital market. In the current situation in China, although there was a money market with its working methods of only original loans and deductions, discounting of bills was really difficult to meet. Zhang believed, "A bill money market without bills discounting naturally cannot be considered a modern money market." As for the "capital market, it is still not even in embryo." "Although we have a securities market, the securities market only buys and sells government bonds. If we analyze the European and American securities markets, we will find that what they do is mainly the sale of stocks and public debt, because only investment in stocks and corporate bonds can transfer money to production capital." Therefore, "a market without stocks and corporate bonds cannot be considered a capital market." In Shanghai, there was a public business office run by foreign merchants, specializing in the sale of foreign companies' shares and public debt in China. It can be seen that "China's production business is still in the hands of foreigners; it can also be said that foreigners will think about investing Chinese people's money in their industries, but Chinese people have never noticed that the money of Chinese people is being used in production."[267]

Zhang advocated that "to complete the responsibility of the modern money market, it should be our banking community to take responsibility for doing it." Taking the lead in "trying to cancel delivery receipts, using promissory notes or bills of exchange to pay for the purchase price; turning dead claims on the books of account into circulating notes" and "the work of building a capital market — or can be said to complete a securities market — the responsibility of the trust industry is heavier than the banking industry."[268]

In building the capital market, why is the responsibility of trust industry more important than the banking industry? Zhang believed that it was necessary to have a sound business; that is, for the issuance of stocks and corporate bonds, the financial industry first took it down and then gradually dispersed into the society through the securities market. On the

---

[267]*Ibid.*, p. 71.
[268]*Ibid.*

contrary, it was also possible that the introduction of non-governmental finances and financial services had been invested in the production industry through the purchase of stocks and corporate bonds. Accepting business was a tool for countries to develop their industries. "If we have a tightly affiliated organization, we will not have the rubber stock crisis and trust company and exchange crisis in the past. The financial industry's acceptance of stocks and corporate bonds is naturally subject to rigorous examination. Therefore, unreliable stocks and corporate bonds will naturally not be accepted by anyone. In a society with a developed business, there is naturally no one who dares to invest in stocks and corporate bonds that the financial industry refuses to accept. Therefore, the financial industry's endurance and unbearability will give the general public an indicator."[269] "The content of undertaking business is mainly to judge: (1) Is the business run by a company that issues stocks or corporate bonds embarking on a prosperous stage, or is it entering a declining stage; (2) whether the company's organization, equipment, and business conditions are promising? (3) Are the directors and officers of that company good people? As long as these conditions are clearly analyzed, problems that cannot be sustained will be solved. The risks, benefits, efficacy, and organization of this work, and the reconciliation of other types of business and occupation, were analyzed and introduced by Zhang. He thought that "If the trust industry and the banking industry can unite to hold such a vigorous trust business at this time, most people will immediately recognize the great significance of the trust business; the misunderstanding of the trust company in trust company and exchange crisis will be cancelled once."[270] The trust business naturally blossomed. This was indeed a good thing for the country, society, finance and the trust itself. "Foreigners have already done it there. Shouldn't we still catch up with it?"[271]

Zhang particularly valued the status and role of monetary finance in the social economy. In the article *The Chinese Society Reflected by Currency Finance*, he proposed, "Monetary finance is a very important sector in social economy, and most scholars consider it to be a social and

---

[269]*Ibid.*, p. 72.

[270]*Ibid.*, pp. 73–74.

[271]P. 74 of the Corpus of Zhang Naiqi (I).

economic hub. Therefore, I dare to say: They are very representative."[272] Zhang thought, "Commercial capital is a factor destabilizing the feudal system. However, it itself is still one of the things under the feudal system; sycee is no exception."[273] Such understanding was also very important to grasp the nature and development of China's traditional economy and modern economy. "It has enabled us to have a standard that will make us open eyes and see clearly." In terms of finance, he specifically analyzed the financial market in Shanghai, which is the center of modern China's financial market. It includes three groups, the Foreign Merchant Bank Group, the China Merchants Bank Group and money houses, which represent three kinds of forces, namely, imperialism, new capital and feudal forces. Zhang made a detailed and in-depth analysis as follows.

"The money houses, in fact, represent pure commercial capital. ... The mainland money houses are undoubtedly the suppliers of business capital of usury. It is the Shanghai bank house, and their birthplace is Doushi Street in northern part of the city. ... It is a financial institution that supplies miscellaneous grain to capital. Probably in semi-colonial countries, the more advanced feudal forces are inevitably collaborating with imperialism. Therefore, the money house in Shanghai will inevitably become in 'oneness' with the comprador of foreign bank. With respect to the lending of surplus funds, China Merchants Bank needs house to be their medium; and in the circulation of the '*Zhuangpiao*' (promissory note used in the Qing Dynasty), the money house needs the 'favor' of the comprador of foreign banks, and in the financial integration, it also needs the backing of comprador of foreign bank. ... In addition, the sycee and Huayang (a non-convertible silver note) created by money house ... the guild system inherited by money house."[274] This meant that it represented the feudal forces. Of course, Zhang also fully affirmed the long history and rich experience of the bank house in the Chinese financial market, and its closer ties with industry and commerce, and repeated the same words as Chen Guangxuan in a tone of approval that the money house "is not eliminated in any way". As far as the future development was concerned,

---

[272]*Ibid*., p. 257.
[273]*Ibid*., p. 264.
[274]*Ibid*., pp. 266–267.

so far he had made it clear that their future operation should never aim at the substitution of banks. From the macro perspective, he started from the analysis of financial capital organization and reached this conclusion. It could have been applied more than 10 years ago, but now it is time to make new adjustments. At that time, he said "In the organization of the financial market, it can be said that others are taking the initiative!" Zhang explicitly stated that "funds in the financial market should be concentrated at higher levels."[275] In his view, the general banks did not have a lot of money in their hands, and would not abuse it. "The National Bank concentrates the hot money for the financial industry and decides interest according to financial industry. At present, the situation in Shanghai is just the opposite. The National Bank does not ask ordinary commercial banks for their needs. Sometimes they put funds into their deposits. Hot money from ordinary commercial banks is also slammed into the money houses, also without asking them what they needed." "In this way, the funds of financial industry are dispersed downwards so that naturally no one will know the whole situation of finance. The money houses have no way of knowing what happened to us or what kind of nature is the money deposited to them?"[276] Seeing too many funds will naturally lead to spamming, and all speculation will be brought about. In such a situation, it is absolutely impossible to expect a rigorous financial organization. Zhang also analyzed the bank's credit deposits at the micro level, and pointed out that the bank accepted the money on the one hand and gave it to the merchants on the other hand to earn a few percent of the interest. In fact, the money house became the middleman of bank lending. Although the bank did not rely entirely on its money, it was a huge business. The shortcomings were as follows: "First, there is no guarantee for credit money released by money house; second, there is no guarantee for the bank's money to be paid to money house; and third, the bank's money to money house cannot meet the needs of money bank."[277] It turned out that although the bank raised the signs of human credit, most of their foundations were based on real estate credits. In the money market, they were based on shareholder's

---

[275]*Ibid.*, p. 29.
[276]*Ibid.*, p. 30.
[277]*Ibid.*, p. 31.

real estate credits. When they were short of money, they could borrow money from others to solve the problem of money transfer. For foreign banks, it is "using a shareholder's ownership of the real estate's deeds, which is mortgaged when the funds are requested, which solves the problem of the liquidity of deductions. The reuse of this remittance organization and the two turnovers of turnover made it impossible for China merchant bank to entrust with the settlement of affairs of agents and to absorb the reserve of China merchant bank in order to create the invincible forces in the past."[278] Zhang put forward his own opinion on the way out of the money house, a bill brokerage or a bill acceptance office, because "in the past 3–4 years, I have constantly put forward two slogans: 'Complete a modern money market' and 'Create a modern capital market'. I hope our financial community can go all out."[279] In terms of specific measures, "If we have a bill market and the money house on the one hand uses a discounted method to lend money, and on the other hand uses the rediscount method to finance the bank, isn't it a solution to all the problems? If the bank finds a way out on this, it can be said that it is very easy to learn. Their business, and there is no major change compared with the present, but their future status will be higher than the ticket brokers in New York and London."[280] This was written in July 1, 1935, and compared with the words of May 24, 1932, it is more specific, more thorough and feasible.

On the China merchant bank, Zhang pointed out, "The new China merchant bank, on the surface, naturally represents the new national capital. However, in the past, many China merchant banks have the background of warlords and bureaucrats. It is at this moment that the provincial banks in various places … the issuance system is disorderly and a new situation is being unfolded. This is just as same as the popularity of provincial controlled economy. We can only estimate the feudal forces to embark on a new stage, and we must never be optimistic about its decline."[281] "Some of the bank's business is developing in terms of

---

[278]*Ibid.*, p. 421.
[279]*Ibid.*, p. 420.
[280]*Ibid.*, p. 31.
[281]*Ibid.*, p. 267.

commercial capital. The other part is developing financially. The investment of commercial banks in real estate is probably the highest level of development in China. This kind of abnormal business development is still typical of commercial capital as well as a result of financial development. It has created a new pattern of high-income loans in public debt investments.[282] Are the immediate problems of China's banks and the dangers of bank operations as simple and slight as the average person thinks? Zhang thinks it is the opposite. Obviously, the bank's fixed assets are relatively small; however, the bank's contractual responsibilities are limitless. The collapse of several banks is only for the purpose of several speculative trading contracts; in a bureaucratic bank that does not have strict organization and management, speculative trading contracts will not be properly limited and audited. In addition, the issue of legal responsibilities, the issue of fraud by the executives, etc., are enough to shake the banking foundation."[283] If there was no turning point in economic panic, the future of real estate would be very pessimistic. The oversupply of national debt was bound to become the bane of the banking industry. For the "developing banking industry, if we continue to use real estate and national debt as the bottom-line business objectives, it is bound to have no future." In demanding "funds for agriculture", two conditions must be met: First, it must be used for production, not for consumption. Otherwise, the peasants would be "drinking and quenching thirst" and "extinguishing their lives", trapping themselves in danger; second, interest cannot be higher than the peasants' profits, otherwise it would be an exploitation added to the peasants, not a relief. At the same time, it was still necessary to ensure a steady income for farmers, that took into consideration floods and droughts and the dumping of foreign agricultural products and industrial products. "As far as the actual situation is concerned, when farmers do not finish their work, they are reluctant to pledge 'ancestral estate'." At the same time, productive borrowing was not easy to implement in China, where the "farmers have no other fields" and where the farming system has become popular. Therefore, "it is probably a good term for the return of funds to agriculture; it is impossible to plan a way out for the rural

---

[282]*Ibid.*
[283]*Ibid.*, p. 402.

economy, nor can it find a way out for bank funds." From this, Zhang's conclusion was, "I'm sure to say: Unless the general economy can be surprised by an accidental boom, the current development of the Chinese banking industry is a field with no future."[284] *The Current Financial Issues* in March 1935 described the problems of stopping the bleeding and blood leakage in China's financial industry. From the exchange control system to the credit control system, from account claims to par claim, and between banks, these four aspects concluded that "if politically there is no other way, there can be no economic solution."[285] Zhang believed that if there was no clear policy, it would be difficult to govern financially. To manage finance, one must first start with governance politics. In July of the same year, the article "The Evolution of the Financial System in Financial Panic" argued against "financially speaking only to finance" and considered it "impossible". "When we talk about financial issues, we must think of the more fundamental currency issue; we cannot but associate it with the problems of balance of payments and trade balances, and we must also be involved in diplomatic issues." In this way, "from the point of view of the currency system, the problems of distribution, banking system, market organization, preparation distribution, and rural finance are mentioned in turn. China may have to involve diplomacy and general politics."[286]

Regarding foreign merchant banks, Zhang believed that there was no doubt that it represented the forces of imperialism. Until the 1930s, it still had the power to overwhelm the China merchant bank. From the comparative figures of deposits and the large volume of silver exports by foreign merchant bank during the period of the "Silver Crisis" shaking the foundation of the Chinese currency system, it was concluded that "the development of China merchant banks in Shanghai in recent years can be said to be a great leap forward". The article "The Current Situation of China's Fiscal Finance" also said that comparatively speaking, it was "a great leap forward". The number of national banks was around 150 in January 1935, and there were about 100 general branch offices in Shanghai; by the end

---

[284]*Ibid.*, p. 403.
[285]*Ibid.*, p. 408.
[286]*Ibid.*, p. 409.

of 1933, the paid-in capital was about 265 million *yuan*, which was unmatched by the US Citibank's 127 million *yuan*. It was also dwarfed by the huge sum of 295 million *yuan* of Japanese yen by Japan's Zhengjin, Mitsui and Sumitomo Bank.[287] However, in this Silver Crisis, "it can be seen that this seemingly flourishing weather can't stand up to imperialism's working in collusion." "After abolishing tael for silver dollars, the currency system in central China has also become more stable and unified. However, in this trend, the currency system is not only shaken, but also feels helpless."[288]

Zhang performed an analysis of the securities market. "The first is the comparison of the two securities markets. One is the Shanghai Stock Exchange organized by foreign companies, and the other is the Chinese stock exchange. The former is mainly engaged in industrial securities." By July 1934, there were 98 brokers (havens), of which nine were Chinese. There were 155 kinds of its market order, almost all of which were issued by foreign companies. They belonged entirely to foreigners in China, and most of them were Jews. Zhang cannot help but lament, "On behalf of a capital market, and the Chinese stock exchange can only barely be called as 'financial market' — this is unique to China. ... None of the securities bought and sold are issued by Chinese companies, which tells us very clearly what kind of backwardness the Chinese national capital is."[289] The Chinese stock exchange mainly operated financial securities. The stocks began to shoot, and they were once very lively in trust company and exchange crisis in 1918. What started out was an abnormal speculative trading and no real industry stocks. In the future, there were occasional stock market transactions, but the number of transactions was minimal. When compared with two and three million shares of monthly turnover of the Shanghai Stock Exchange, it was incommensurable. In January 1935, Zhang disclosed in the article that more than 80% of holding component of public bond bank probably belonged to financial industry. In 1932, the securities of 28 Chinese domestic commercial banks amounted to

---

[287] *Ibid.*, p. 282.
[288] *Ibid.*, p. 267.
[289] *Ibid.*, p. 442.

240 million *yuan*, and it could be estimated very conservatively that 80% of it was public debt.[290] It can only be counted as a "financial market". This is one aspect. The second is the overall impression. Zhang thought that "China's production capital is almost entirely under the imperialist power; slight national capital can be described as insignificant."[291] After the "September 18th" Incident, there was a kind of waning misery everywhere. However, "the issuance of industrial capital by imperialism in China will reach a large number of 100 million *yuan* in 2½ years."[292] Not only does it mean that China's national capital was underdeveloped but it also means the colonization of China's financial capital. "Some people think that this is a way of attracting foreign capital; however. … In fact, most of the money absorbed is still Chinese people's money; 69% of the owner of Shanghai Electric Power Company's preferred stock, according to the company's 1933 annual report, was Chinese; buyers of municipal government bonds, as far as I know, the Chinese were afraid to account for 80% of the total.[293] Third, it is worth noting. Foreign investors issued property securities in China, and investors are mostly Chinese. It is an avenue of collusion between the Chinese warlords and gentry and imperialism outside the bank deposits of foreign merchants. … At the same time, the number of securities that China merchants bank has invested in foreign merchants is not small; this means that without the development of ethnic industrial capital, the national financial capital that serves as the basis for business operations will also contribute to the impetus of the imperialist capital forces in China."[294] The fourth is a miracle discovery. Zhang set his sights on the spreading of the two securities markets. "The annual value of government bonds on the China Securities Exchange is 6%, the market price is 20%, and the income is usually more than one-two points; Well-known bank shares, occasionally found that the market also said that more than 1 point. The Shanghai Stock Exchange's usual revenue is only

---

[290]*Ibid.*, p. 280.
[291]*Ibid.*, p. 269.
[292]*Ibid.*
[293]*Ibid.*, p. 442.
[294]*Ibid.*, pp. 269–270.

56%, and the interest rate of 60% of the bond market is often above the premium." "After 1932, the bonds with the highest interest rates in the Shanghai Stock Exchange were 7% per annum, the lowest was 5%, and the majority was 6%. Their most recent market price was 108 *yuan*, and the lowest was 99 *yuan*. Most of them are between 104 *yuan* and 106 *yuan*. At the same time, the market rate of 6 centi-years for the revenge of government bonds on the China Stock Exchange has recently reached an all-time high price, which was only 83%. On the one hand, this indicates that the expansion of central government has already surpassed the market's needs. However, the expansion of capital is still far below the market's needs. On the other hand, it also indicates that the status of capital of the two financial markets in Shanghai–China merchant financial market and foreign merchant financial market is incommensurable."[295] "Under this serious interest rate differential, it can be seen that China's national industrial capital cannot compete with the imperialist capitalists."[296]

China's financial barriers were fragmented. On January 15, 1935, Mr. Zhang clearly and accurately pointed out the problem of fund stagnation in Shanghai on the premise of the rapid development of the commercial banks in China and the increase of deposits. Then there was the suggestion of "capital for farming". However, under the dual exploitation of feudal forces and imperialism, "capital for farming" could not be realized. In 1933, the cash flow from the mainland to Shanghai was more than 70 million *yuan*, while the loans of farmers in Shanghai were only about 1 or 2 million *yuan*, which would be a drop in the bucket. The United States regulated that silver is state-owned, raising the price of silver, resulting in the US dollar bill being cheaper in the Chinese exchange market and the American goods introduced into China having a bad effect on Chinese national goods. Then the silver outflow situation was caused. Therefore, the essential issue for China finance was not "capital for farming", but "capital outflow abroad". "Then, in October 15th, the export tax rate of silver dollars was increased, which invites the protest from foreign businessmen. Under the pressure from foreign businessmen, the balanced tax rate is

---

[295] *Ibid.*, pp. 442–443.
[296] *Ibid.*, p. 270.

reduced. There is still a 2.3% interest for the export of silver. In the one and a half months from the beginning of the tax rate increase to November, there still exists 11,000 *yuan* silver export. At the same time, the number of private exports is also startling. From October 15th to the end of November, the number of silver from Shanghai to ports in North China, South China and the middle reaches of the Yangtze River was 27 million *yuan*." "There still exist serious silver problems due to the public export and private transport. The main two destinations of China's capital flight are Dalian under the control of Japanese imperialism and Hong Kong under the control of British imperialism." "When the North China silver comes out of the Great Wall, the price is raised by more than 15%, almost as much as the export tax. In Hong Kong, the outflow of capital can be realized not only by exporting but also through the method of remittance. As an important operator, HSBC might have transferred all its reserves to Hong Kong." Mr. Zhang questioned, "Is it possible for foreign banks to be the medium of capital escape in an independent country? Could foreigners carry out private transference of money in China like the Japanese ronins? Under such a broken financial barrier, the monetary and financial bases can be built through effort. However, it is also very easy to be destroyed by someone else in a short time." It was the imperialist force that had the greatest impact on China's finance and the feudal force had a destructive impact on China's rural finance. Mr. Zhang and other enlightened Chinese were concerned about the future of China under the pressure of two forces.

On February 15, 1936, Mr. Zhang pointed out that it was unreasonable to manage foreign exchange without making full use of the power of the people. He stressed that only the rise of the people's anti-war sentiment and the close organization of the people's National Salvation Front could make most of them discover patriotic enthusiasm and not do anything to escape the capital. If there were some heartless people, the public will naturally accuse them and punish them. In Zhang's view, "even if we reissue twice the bill and issue 10 times the debt, our financial base will be always solid as long as we have an organization. The only thing we can do is to call on and organize the people under the slogan of the National Liberation War, making the nation an organized nation." For this, he was full of confidence and his opinion was confirmed by history.

4.3.4. China's financial system

Finance is meaningful because it is the pivot of economic society. Zhang Naiqi described vividly and vulgarly that gold is a hard and fixed material and melting is the meaning of melting and circulation. Finance plays an important role in turning the hard-fixed gold into a melting state of circulation. How can gold be melted? It depends on the burning of credit. Sometimes, "the fire of credit" burns too hard, and the melting gold boils over, resulting in pouring out the "the fire of credit". Then the melted gold cools and freezes. The panic phenomenon is caused by the excessive expansion of credit, which is the so-called frozen asset. Therefore, the important significance of finance is to promote the circulation of money and to stop its stagnation and freezing. Besides, Zhang believed that finance was the basis of the economic society and was the pivot of all trades. In a report with Yang Yingpu and Zhang Xiaomei, they suggested that finance is to the economic circles what blood is to mankind. Blood stagnation is serious, but blooding is also fatal. Accordingly, the direction of credit expansion is necessary, that is, the results of credit expansion, which can reduce the outflow of funds negatively, and actively stimulate the overflowing of funds. There is no doubt that financial capital can dominate everything in modern society. Finance is built on the top of all trades, which is supported and constantly maintained by the industry and commerce. Therefore, the ups and downs of financial industry should follow that of the industry and commerce. However, the opposite situation occurred in China. "Rural bankruptcy is more and more serious. The general industrial and commercial panic in the city is spreading day by day. While the banks are growing more and more prosperous and the bank's profits are still not reduced. The special phenomenon of banks is caused by the abnormal development of China's banking industry. The reason for its development is the parasitic plant's flowers and the warp of the national economy, which is harmful to the national economy and its prosperity. It promotes the colonization of the Chinese nation and further develops itself." In China, finance was depressed under the oppression of imperialism. There was no bright future.

Despite decades of struggle, China's local financial capital had not completely divorced from the parasitic form of international financial capital in China. In the past, with abundant funds in foreign financial groups, the accommodation of capital had an influence on the national financial system, which caused the so-called "parasitic form". Since August 1934, foreign banks in China sent deposit funds to overseas countries. Besides, they reclaimed the hot money invested in the national financial system. They also used "arbitrages" to increase their interest rates and banknotes, and absorbed funds in national capital finance, which caused credit bloodletting. Credit is precious. The bloodletting almost extinguished the credit fire. Banks stopped making mortgage payments, and old-style Chinese private banks stopped paying their debts. This was the homeopathy caused by leakage of blood. Therefore, Mr. Zhang put forward the stepwise governance strategy. "Firstly, the leakage of blood should be stopped, which means the stop of outflow of cash. There is no other way but to take credit control, which is the typical situation in the colonial country like China." As far as Mr. Zhang could see, this was the second-best regulatory solution. "Because foreign banks are mainly engaged in inward bills and cannot set up branches in the mainland, they have no rights to handle foreign exchange from the port to the mainland. It is difficult for them to make a loan to the Chinese wholesalers directly for the reason that they are unfamiliar with the situations in China. The accommodation of funds for wholesalers, retailers and comprador are all dependent on the Chinese Merchants Bank and the old-style Chinese private banks. If the accommodation of funds is controlled, the foreign goods will have no access to the mainland, with the meaningless transportation of the foreign goods into the port." Mr. Zhang believed it wise for Shanghai Banking Industry not to lend money to foreign businessmen, especially luxury merchants. "Credit control aims to expand and specify the principle. Even if the fundamental method is adopted in the future, and the tranche system is replaced by the bill discounting system, the whole or one part of this method should be maintained. It is reasonable for the financial industry to put forward the method under the current panic situation." "Secondly, the credit loan is replaced by bill discounting. At the same time, the accounting system itself is a doubtful investment because the financial industry has no information about the business of the borrower. Once the market is in a hurry, it is necessary to stop accommodation due to suspicion, causing panic. As far as the financial industry is concerned, discounted bills can be supplemented by rediscounted funds, where book debts can be circulated on their own." Therefore, it was necessary to create a discount market and an industrial securities market to fit in with the modern money market and modern capital market. The above two points were of great significance.

There was the problem of central banks which means a bank in the banking enterprises. Mr. Zhang suggested that the two words *Zhou Zhuan* in Chinese that equal "turnover" were meaningful. *Zhuan*, meaning "turn", refers to circulation. *Zhou* means "endless flow". The circulation should be fluent without blood stopping and leakage of blood. With the leakage of blood, there will be stagnation for the circulation. Thus, the heart of the circulatory system is of great importance for blood regulation, which plays an important role as a bank in the banking enterprises. Mr. Zhang expressed that it was the task for note brokers that the commercial paper is discounted to the ordinary bank, and that the ordinary bank rediscounts it to the central bank. At the same time, the bank's reserves should be deposited into ordinary banks, and ordinary bank's reserves are redeposited into the central bank. In this way, panic will not easily occur with the very strict system for loans and reserves. However, these two issues cannot be separated; obligations and rights are mutual, not one-sided. "It seems to be possible that funds are returned to the central bank soon after the rediscounting, as long as the reserves can be concentrated in the central bank and it can reduce the serious outflow of nation's funds. After we have cured the bleeding and stop blood, we must finish the task of establishing the heart of the bank's financial system of the bank in the banking enterprises." As early as November 17, 1931, Mr. Zhang wrote an article about lacking spirit of cooperation in financial industry. Considering the theory and the foreign advanced countries, he believed that there was no strict leadership and no organized organization for the financial industry. For finance, circulation is the most important, in which unification is of the significance. A central force, which contributes to the fluent and unified circulation of the finance, is necessary for the unification. Finance is based on credit, which is the original driving force for circulation. If there is no credit, the people collect their own cash. Although there are millions, its effect is equal to zero. There must be a center for credit, which can be trusted by the industry and can also deliver the credit consciousness to them. In this way, cash can be concentrated and a unified financial market can be established. "This central power is presented as the national bank in Europe and Japan, while in the United States it is the central preparatory bank. The so-called state banks are subject to the authority of the government and have the right to represent the treasury and issue banknotes. And for the society, they afford to maintain the burden of financial markets. Our financial industry is still immature, and the banking system is much more diverse. Besides, the central force has not yet been established. Once there is an incident, everyone preserves himself and the circulation of finance is stopped with the coming of panic. Therefore, there is a pressing need to build the center of finance. When the market is loose and ordinary banks abuse the credit, the National Bank, namely the Central Bank, raises the discount rate and reduces the outflow of funds as a precaution. When the financial emergency occurs with the shortage of ordinary bank's funds, loans should be kept down to ease the situation. In this way, the credit system will not be damaged and the financial circulation will remain constant. As far as the current situation is concerned, the Central Bank of China is the National Bank in law. In reality, the two banks Bank of China and Bank of Communications have the largest circulation of banknotes. The three banks have been concentrated and can become the central forces of our financial industry enough. At present, a special organization is necessary to be the center of the financial industry. The organization should complete above-mentioned important tasks in silver and further provide strength according to the size of its issuance to manipulate the financial market." He thought it impossible for the powerful organization to lose its financial power. It can be seen that the establishment of a strong financial central bank in China and the formation of a strong national financial center were the consistent thought of Zhang Jing. It was the ideal pursuit of his dream, that is, the formation of China's financial strength, the resistance to foreign capital invasion and the development of the native agricultural and commercial base.

On August 24, 1932, in the article "Lessons from the Past Mistakes in the Financial Industry", Mr. Zhang criticized the financial community for being far away from the track. He believed that financial circulation was similar to the blood cycle. "There is no real National Bank, which can play the role as the center of the financial market in Shanghai. It can be said that the circulatory system has lost its heart and the blood unsystematically flow. The results of turbulent flow sometimes lose too much components and sometimes flow out too little. Too much flow is the so-called credit expansion, encouraging investment. Too little flow is the so-called credit crunch, which causes panic." When it comes to China's financial system, he thought that legislation was complete. However, in fact, it was on the road to an ordinary commercial bank. "For the so-called ordinary commercial banks, there are speculations of real estate and securities, loan collateral, the preparation for investment of the standard goods and standard money, bond ticket, and lease agreement." Mr. Zhang believed that a crooked stick will have a crooked shadow, meaning that the foundation was not strong. The undesirable system and environment were the primary cause. "To improve the situation, we must thoroughly study it and correct it, otherwise, it is useless and futile. Of course, the bank's business policies, organization of affairs, and employment also need to be improved."

The banking enterprises must be strong enough to build a sound financial system, which was put forward by Mr. Zhang in the article the evolution of the financial system with financial crisis in 1935. He not only learned from the experience of Britain and America, but pointed that the shortcomings of China's financial system lay in the decentralization of issue and preparation. "The malady of the decentralization of issue not only lies in the decentralization of preparation, but also in the unfair competition and its destruction to the distribution system. What's worse, the formation of unlimited inflation is more dangerous. In the whole issuing system, the multi issue system is also a dangerous thing. The decentralization of so-called distribution is not only scattered among several issuing banks, but also scattered in other financial sectors. The preparation for distribution is absolutely impossible for both purposes, and can never be used for commercial purposes through old-style Chinese private banks. The situation has been improved since the establishment of the Shanghai clearing house. But this is a serious problem recently. The bank has got the unneeded funds and has to let it out. As soon as the money is not retracted, the old-style Chinese private banks cannot bring back the money in a timely manner. The banks also cannot bring back the money from the old-style Chinese private banks. This phenomenon has been exposed continuously since the '128 incident'."

Mr. Zhang affirmed the situation in which the three banks contact and restrict each other. For the government, official stocks can be increased. For the issue banks with problems, official stocks, practical assistance and supervision should be provided for them in the way of reorganizing the personnel. Whether such a concentrated movement can be carried out thoroughly is debatable. But it is a fact that the movement was developed to some extent. He believed that "unified issuance is impossible at the moment, while concentrated preparation and restrictions the abuse of issue right is possible."

Commercial preparations for ordinary banks were also proceeding rapidly. Mr. Zhang believed that the development of this work was caused by reality rather than the policy. After several consultations by the banking industry, the commercial preparation of banks was concentrated in three national banks through clearing house instead of being scattered across the old-style Chinese private banks.

"The concentration of financial forces can come to an end after the concentration of distribution preparation and business preparation. What we should do next is to use and maintain the forces. Here, in addition to the use of privileges, it is necessary to perform the task. The three banks should take responsibility for the appropriate relief to the market and appropriate accommodation for the financial industry, which can make the power more concentrated, and make the strength of the maintenance possible. Self-defense forces, especially financial self-defense forces, are necessary to deal with the counter attack of the balance of payments firstly and to cope with the attack of military forces of other countries secondly. Balance of payments is a complex problem, in which the most important thing is to reduce the surplus. Besides, increasing the import tax rates is also viable."

There was also the problem between bank and law. Zhang Naiqi believed that banks were the organs that served the society, and banking was a very broad and profound subject. In 1933, the monograph in banking and law noted that banking is a very expansive subject and there were no other disciplines with so broad a scope like banking. "For example, the people who serve in the financial sector are indispensable to the knowledge of finance, economics, philosophy of life, psychology, statistics, law, business and commodity, calculation and ethics. If the bankers are unfamiliar with the economics, they cannot understand the change of the society. Without the knowledge of monetary science, they cannot deal with the changes in the financial market. It is necessary to understand the philosophy of life and psychology in the process of dealing with customers. Statistics will contribute to the understanding of the trend of market and the change of business. To handle affairs, protect interests of their own and customers, they must have a good knowledge of law. So, in a narrow sense, banking is relatively simple, while in broad sense, banking is very profound. The profoundness of banking is reflected in the different status of bankers and scholars. Even if there are mistakes of scholars' opinions, the effect of their comments is relatively small. If the bankers' thought and judgments are wrong, unfortunate results in the economic and social numbers will occur immediately. So bankers cannot just be complacent with themselves if they only have a smattering of relative knowledge. The bankers should be able to thoroughly study and really find the core of the problem. What he particularly valued is bankers' practical operation ability and market judgment ability, which can be tested by practice. Respecting the experienced financial practitioners is of great significance, because they have rich practical experience, the ability to accurately grasp the market, currency, prices, market, and resist credit risk. Their experiences are far more authoritative for the employees of the banking industry to put into practice than that of the boastful boasters who talk big and do nothing." In Zhang's view, the experienced financial practitioners were indeed conservative and could not be summed up systematically. "However, they often had an excellent view of the market and the ministry. Although they have not studied economics, the essence of the money is often experienced through their practices. Without reading economics, they have kept the principles of economics in their minds."

In the discipline related to banking, "the knowledge of law is the basis, especially in the current situation. In the bank, employees of upper, middle, and lower levels all should understand the law. It is a legal act for the superior to preside over the investment and lending work. It is also a legal act for the mid-to-lower staff to deal with collection and payment, send and receive letters. The ability of a clerk depends on whether he is suitable for dealing with affairs. 'Legitimate' and 'illegal' account for an important position in evaluating so-called 'appropriate' and 'inappropriate' significance. There are so many bankers suffering losses due to the shortage of legal knowledge. First of all, there are several cases each year because of the endorsement of the guarantee. Secondly, trading with foreign businessmen is often a great loss because they do not understand their legal status. After the promulgation of the bill law, there are two potential troubles in the bank's handling procedures. The first may be caused by crossed cheques. It may be discovered that the checks were taken in bad faith by an unidentified bank account holder with family names with crossed cheques, which has a bad effect on banks. The second may be caused by the mortgage of real property. According to the promulgated civil law, a broker cannot set a mortgage on real estate unless he has a written power of attorney. If the manager of the company wanted to detain the company's real estate, his authorization must not be checked."

Mr. Zhang made sharp criticisms against the two wrong ideas of the law of the bank officials in China at the time. One was lawlessness and the other was fearlessness. He compared the former to a warden who treated customers as prisoners. "These workers always speak as the judge and command others. They often argue with customers or even deliberately make things difficult for customers. Their attitudes are greatly different from those in European and American banks. With more and more banks in even fierce competition, banks don't treasure customers and customers have also more choices. Once the bank discovers that the staff he hired has a bad effect on its business, the staff will be fired. Meanwhile, many countries without laws have also revised many laws. From then on, lawless agents should also lose their prestige." He believed that the latter type of people mostly understood the power of the law, but they did not know the content of the law, or only knew how to use it, but they did not understand it thoroughly. For example, "when young people under the age of 20 come to make deposits, they think that they have no guarantee of law, but don't know that there is no problem as long as they have no debts." Seeing the customer deposit cheques lined with the words "prohibit transfer", they are afraid to accept responsibility, but do not know the customer is the trustee rather than the transferee. They think that losing the customer's receipt is as serious as losing a promissory note. In addition, they claim that no endorsement will be guaranteed because of a problem with the warranty endorsement. They think it unnecessary to add trouble to business due to limited knowledge. They maintain that only thorough research will give us a safe and secure path. In the face of thousands of legal studies, practitioners should stick to five points. The first one is goodwill, which is a moral issue. The staff should take care of others. The second one is prudence, which is a condition for the protection of the law but is not equal to non-action. The third is to maintain routine. Fickleness is taboo in banking, which serves the society. It is obligated to observe the rules and regulations of the industry, and even the procedures must be consistent. The status of customary law can be obtained. The fourth is to pay attention to the contract. Many troubles and losses can be avoided as the contract or exchange formality is written. The fifth is to employ a legal adviser. In addition to the preparation of legal books, legal advisers are also very necessary.

At the end of March 1933, Zhang wrote a special article with various questions concerning the bill law and its enforcement method and proposed, "Any fruitful discussions have been transmitted to the bank's trade associations and distributed the banks. There are still a few points, or there are articles whose meaning is not clear, or where there are many obstacles, or if other countries already have judgments, but in our country, the interpretation of the provisions is still questionable." He had drawn up 14 items, which were supplemental and paid for discussion.

There still existed financial problems in rural areas. In the article on evolution of the financial system in the financial panic, Mr. Zhang suggested that the relief rural area was originally a part of the financial industry in rural areas. However, before the liberation of the nation, the financial industry of the Chinese businessmen had sluggish tens of millions in funds to help the industry and commerce. It was said that there was the loss of millions of *yuan* in the relief of the rural areas. If the power of the state could not protect the interests of the peasants, "the financial industry is also in vain to relieve the countryside." "People will have the doubt whether we can have a tariff barrier or any national policy to protect the interests of industry and commerce and farmers."

Mr. Zhang paid attention to the Chinese farming with regard to two key aspects. First, the investment of the bank must be guaranteed, otherwise the capital will become land, or even turn into an account, and the capital will be unsustainable. The focus here is in the flow and accommodation. Second, farmers must borrow for production rather than consumption. Otherwise, it will be useless for banks and borrowers, and it will also be meaningless to society. These two aspects must have a common premise, that is, the price of agricultural products should be stable and the farmers' income should be guaranteed. If the income of the farmers is completely unprotected, the borrowed funds are used for consumption, resulting in the loss of guarantee for bank lending. However, in terms of specific operation, Mr. Zhang pointed out, "Except for agricultural products, I always object to commercial banks' direct investment in rural. I think the relief of rural finance must go through bonds, that is, commercial banks invest in mobile bonds, and special banks will lend money to the countryside. There are Chinese Agricultural and Industrial Bank, the farmer's Bank of China, Local Agricultural and Industrial Bank and Local Famer's Bank. The issuance of the bonds should be in charge of the government, and the funds can be put on by them." Moreover, under the condition that the land problem in China was not properly settled and the gentry' forces in the countryside still existed, the financial industry in rural areas would not have good results. The most fundamental solution was to talk less and practice more.

4.3.5. *Chinese credit agency*

On January 1, 1933, in the four months since the establishment of the Chinese credit agency, Mr. Zhang noted that a cooperative credit investigation organization was established since the plan made in March, 1932. Aimed at building the Chinese credit agency, the academic body of Xingxin Community in China was established. The purpose of the project was to describe 10 issues such as the origin, organization, work patterns, business principles, business summary, business progress, editorial list of the credit industry and industry bank, and the social outlook and prospects of the Chinese credit agency.

Mr. Zhang's thoughts on the purposes, principles, policies and requirements of the Chinese credit agency are as follows:

He thought that the nature of the credit agency was one of the businesses of China Xingxin Community, and was a public service organ for credit investigation work. It was a public institution, a non-productive profit-making institution that openly provided services to credit investigation, which determined the nature of credit agency.

"The purpose of the credit agency is to serve the members. The service object is its member, while the non-member is not its service object. Services provided for members are nonprofit. While non-members are only provided services when profits are available. Therefore, a factory firm or individual who wishes credit agency to do the investigation work for him is usually a member of the credit agency. Non-members may also ask the agencies to do the investigation, but the cost is very expensive and the procedures are very troublesome. Members are divided into several kinds, depending on the amount of payment. Those who pay more initially can pay lower report fees later and have more numbers of entrusted investigation cases. The basic members range from the initial opening of 12 to the 18 later. The ordinary members are divided into three levels of A, B, C, whose total number is 29, including 22 overseas businessmen, and seven Chinese businessmen. There are important staff members from 18 basic members participating in Xingxin Community in China. Three to five officers are promoted by China Xingxin Community to guide the work of the Chinese credit agency. At the same time, the design committee and the review committee are organized. In the former committee, except for the members as the ex officio, six members are recommended as committee member. The latter committee is designed to review the investigation report, the internal accounts and the publication of the text."

The principle of the credit agency is based on "all the cause should find a way out from the active aspect". Mr. Zhang insisted on the spirit of continuous learning and firmly opposes mixing "keeping the household" and "doing business". He thought that wasting time in passive throttling and delaying the positive development of the business were silly. He strongly opposed the belief that vigorous public institutions are made as the ancient temple. He believed that many careers were destroyed due to being negative. Therefore, he specifically emphasized that people, whenever and wherever, should be active in their career rather than passive. Actively raising funds, employing staff and conducting business are all carried out in a positive and aggressive manner. Therefore, the belief of the credit agency is embodied in "perfect work performance equals to the life of the business." Only the credit agency with the wonderful work performance and reasonable costs will be accepted by the society. A negative credit agency, on the contrary, will be eliminated and destroyed.

The work rules of the credit agency were actually guidelines for business work. Mr. Zhang suggested that "the law of the work of the Chinese credit agency is usually divided into the following three types: (A) prudence for 'true', and (B) in detail for 'beauty', and (C) faithful and fair for 'good'." He explained that truth is the right meaning, which is the most important condition for investigation. "There is no doubt that the reports after strictly investigating, reviewing and examining are true. The so called beauty lies in the exhaustiveness and clarity of the reports. The content of the report should include more facts and less criticism. The insignificant micro words and inconspicuous digital records should be included to give the chance for readers to judge by themselves. To avoiding the confusion of people, the arrangement of data must be clear with reasonable arrangement, which is very vital. Goodness is a faithful and impartial moral creed, which is the embodiment of 'open and honest attitude', 'loyal and fair air' and 'strict organization'." "Therefore, the colleagues in the credit agency must abandon the bad habits and old habits, and work hard. It is no problem to be good with strict organization to maintain their interest and belief in work."

There are many misunderstandings in society about the credit agency, such as it is the organ that introduces the investment of the loan and whether the contents of the Chinese industrial and commercial entrepreneurs will be told to non-members. Mr. Zhang gave a clear explanation for that. He hoped that in the future the credit agency would promote the development of all the technical institutions and would lead the Chinese people to use the scientific means, and abandon the past judgments by the emotion and the superstitious means of dealing with the problem.

After the founding of the People's Republic of China, Zhang published many positive, confident and vital articles on a series of issues concerning currency, monetary policy, finance and old-style Chinese private banks. They are as follows: "Where the private banks are going", "The future of private banks", "Transformation of the surplus private banks", "Restoring to the silver standard system", "The future of industry and commerce with the stability of the currency system", "The transformation of the economy — the swelling, the corruption, and the birth",

"Speculative traders stopping their evil practice quickly", "Using their own bookkeeping principles to keep accounts", "Reusing the principle of applying their own bookkeeping principles", etc.

5. The financial thought of Li Da

Li Da (1890–1966), formerly known as Ting Fang, styled himself as Yongxi and Heming with several pen names: Lida, Jiang Chun, Hu Qing and Li Te. Li was from Lingling in Hunan Province. He was a famous Marxist theoretician, one of the earliest pioneers of disseminating Marxism in China and one of the founders of the Communist Party of China (CPC). In 1909, he was admitted to the Advanced Normal College of the Imperial University and turned his attention to saving the country through industry from education. In 1913, he studied in Japan and his hopes of saving the country through industry were dashed. Then, he turned his attention to the Bolsheviks, began to study Leninism, namely Marxism, and think about the salvation road. After returning to China in 1920, he participated in sponsoring and organizing the Communist Party of China and edited the party's first publication *The Communist*. In the First National Congress of the CPC, he was elected as the director of Publicity Department of the CPC. He presided over the founding of the party's first secret publishing agency — People's Publishing House — and was responsible for writing, translating, soliciting and proofreading contributions as well as issuing work. He established the Shanghai Civilian Female School and also served as the principal. With great enthusiasm and effort, he engaged in the study of and advocated Marxism–Leninism theory, participated in the attack of the Research Clique and criticism of anarchism, and instilled scientific socialism in workers. In November 1922, he was the president of Self-Study University of Hunan and taught classes. He edited the school magazine *New Age* to train cadres for the revolution. He gave lectures on historical materialism in the Public and Law School of Hunan, Hunan University and Hunan First Provincial Normal School. He returned to Shanghai in the summer of 1923. However, serious disputes on the Kuomintang–Communist cooperation emerged between Chen Duxiu and him. He failed to adhere to Chen's opinion in the correct way and he left the party. Thereafter, he continued to study and spread the Marxist theory to assist party organization work. In October 1926, the Northern Expeditionary Army occupied Wuhan. He served as the chairman of the editorial board of the Political Department of the National Revolutionary Army, as well as the instructor and acting chief in Central Military and Political School. In the spring of 1927, the General Political Department established a discussion committee on peasant issues. He was appointed as a member of standing committee. In the spring of 1928, he was wanted by the authorities. In winter, he founded the Shanghai Kunlun Bookstore. In the summer of 1930, he participated in the Shanghai Left-wing Social Scientists Union. Later, he worked at Shanghai University of Political Science and Law, Jinan University, Law and Business department of Peiping University, Peking University, Guangxi University, Sun Yat-sen University, Hunan University, etc. He taught such courses as Marxist Philosophy, Political Economics, Sociology, and Monetary and Social Development History in the Kuomintang-ruled areas. He was the most renowned leftist theorist, the most popular professor and was also blacklisted by the government authorities and could be arrested at any time. After the founding of New China, in December 1949, he rejoined the party and successively held the posts of the first vice president of Central University of Political Science and Law, the president of Hunan University and Wuhan University, a member of Social Sciences Department of the Chinese Academy of Sciences and the first president of the Chinese Philosophical Society. He was elected as a member of the first and second sessions of the National Committee of the Chinese People's Political Consultative Conference, a representative of the 1st and 2nd National People's Congress, a member of the 1st Standing Committee of the National People's Congress and a representative of the 8th National Congress of the Chinese Communist Party. His major works included *Modern Sociology*, *Outline of Sociology*, *Outline of Economics* and *Introduction to Monetary Theory*. His translations mainly included *An Interpretation of Historical Materialism*, *Marxist Theory of Economics*, and *A Critique of Political Economy*. Now, the four volumes of *Collected Writings of Li Da* are available on sale.

Outline of Economics and *Introduction to Monetary Theory*, which are representative works of Li Da, are symbols of outstanding results achieved by early Chinese Marxist theorists who were involved in the field of economics. Based on studying Marxist philosophy, Li turned his research focus to political economics and monetary studies. In 1932, Li served as director of the Department of Economics in the School of Business and Law of Peiping University. In order to teach economics, he compiled a lecture entitled *Elements of Economics*, which was printed by the School of Business and Law of Peiping University in 1935. Li sent the book to Mao Zedong. Mao recommend it to the Yan'an theoretical community and said that he had read it three and a half times and was prepared to read it 10 more times. Prior to this, Mao had studied Li's *Elements of Sociology* 10 times and made notes in the margin; the book had an influence on anti-Japanese revolutionary bases and individuals and youth at that time. The book's Introduction and the first part were issued by Shanghai Bookstore in January 1948 with the title of Theory of Capitalist Social Economic Formation, and were included in the third volume of *Collected Writings of Li Da* in the 1980s. Later, Wuhan University Press issued an offprint.

As for *Introduction to Monetary Studies*, it was recorded that Li Da began to write in 1934, completed it in 1937 and finalized the version in May 1949 after he returned to Peiping. As one of the "Series of New China's University", it was published by Shanghai Sanlian Bookstore in July of that year and reprinted the following year. In the third volume of *Collected Writings of Li Da*, it was considered "the main work of Comrade Li Da in economics in the 1930s". The information cited in the book was roughly from 1936. The range of this book was from the end of the 1920s to the early 1930s, when it was the phase of the collapse of the world's gold standard. "It is the panic of capitalist countries' currency, which is the inevitable result of the current third phase of the capitalist panic. ... In order to strongly criticize various misperceptions, we must fundamentally establish a correct view, must study Capital and carry forward the theory of economy and currency in Capital. I want to write such a book that currently in China is not accessible yet. Such a book is needed."[297]

Based on Marxism, Leninism and national conditions of the country, the book comprehensively introduced and discussed the basic concepts

---

[297]Cited in *An Intellectual Profile of Li Da* by Ding Xiaoqiang and Li Lizhi, Beijing Library Press, 1999, p. 82.

and theories of relevant currencies from the elementary to the profound. The topics involved such knowledge as the nature and function of currency, fiduciary money, currency system, currency circulation, inflation, financial panic and related credit banks. Rigorous in structure and complete in content, the book consisted of nine chapters as follows: (1) Nature of Currency, (2) Functions of Currency, (3) Various Currency Theories, (4) Credit and Credit Currency, (5) Currency System of Capitalism, (6) Financial Panic and Currency Circulation, (7) Currency Movement and Exchange Rates in the World, (8) Inflation and (9) Collapse of the Gold Standard System. The book basically followed Chapters 1–3 of Marx's *Critique of Political Economy and Capital Volume I*, namely, Commodity, Exchange Process, and Circulation of Currency or Commodities to elaborate on the nature and functions of money, and the critique of various monetary theories; then expounded credit, commercial credit, capital credit and bank credit, credit currency (commercial bills, bank vouchers), and capitalist monetary system from the view of Bank Capital Components, Monetary Capital and Real Capital, and Circulation under Credit Systems, Currency Principles and British Banking Legislation in 1844 and Precious Metals and Exchange Rates in Chapters 29–35 of Volume III of Capital, and some descriptions about bank and bank roles in Lenin's book Imperialism is the Highest Stage of Capitalism, financial capital and financial oligarchs, capital output. Basically following the structure of Marx's *A Critique of Political Economy*, the book elaborated on the nature and functions of money, and the critique of various monetary theories. After that, it applied the principles of the third volume of Capital and Lenin's *Imperialism, the Highest Stage of Capitalism* to discuss such issues as commercial credit, capital credit, bank credit, credit money and the monetary system of the capitalist world. The last part was about the finance panic and the collapse of the golden standard in the capitalist world. At that time in China, it was a masterpiece that expounded monetary theory by Marxist principles. Even in the world, it was the best book on Marxist monetary theory at the time. After the founding of the People's Republic of China, as one of the "Series of New China's University", it had long-term impacts on China's political economy and monetary banking research from a theoretical point of view to content structure.

The five aspects are briefly discussed as follows:

5.1. Nature and functions of currency

Following Marx's thinking, Li Da first analyzed commodities and studied the emergency of currency to explain the nature of currency. Just as he said, "the nature of currency, its internal contradictions, and the source of its movements must be explored from commodities. That was to say, we must first analyze commodity before searching for the nature of currency."[298]

Li Da analyzed the duality of commodities and pointed out, "the duality of labor was hidden in the duality of commodities. The duality of commodities was the reflection of the duality of labor."[299] Goods are directly exchanged in the market, which reflects the equivalence between different things. In fact, behind the equivalence of things (goods), "the equivalence of various types of human labor that adopts abstract labor forms is hidden. Therefore, values do not represent the equivalence of commodities (i.e., things). Instead, it represents the equivalence of labor spent in the production of each product."[300] He explored the process of the development of commodity value patterns and revealed the emergence and development of currency.

Under the topic of History of Currency, he wrote a section of text on ancient Chinese currency and arrived at the following conclusion: "What kind of commodity could first become general equivalent and was even used as fixed currency commodity was determined by historical, social, and geographical circumstances."[301] The explanation of Marx's theory by Chen Qixiu and Shen Zhiyuan, writers of Marx's theory at that time, was not only lacking theoretical integrity but also a tentative connection with China's historical situation. Therefore, generally speaking, it was not as profound and clear as that of Li Da.

---

[298] *Collected Writings of Li Da*, vol. 3, People's Publishing House, 1984, p. 517.
[299] *Ibid.*, p. 522.
[300] *Ibid.*, p. 524.
[301] *Ibid.*, pp. 540–541.

Li Da carried forward the essence of Marx's monetary theory, unequivocally revealed that money was the veil that covers social production relations between commodity producers and mercilessly criticized currency fetishism. "The phenomenon of taking money as an idol and bowing down to pray as god of wealth is called currency fetishism."[302] "As currency can be exchanged with any commodity, people's dependence on money is more obvious than that of commodities."[303] Finally, he reached a historical conclusion that "in the limit of commodity economy existence, currency will never be eliminated. Neither will currency fetishism."[304] It also revealed a fact that those who regarded currency as the root of all evil, advocated abolition of gold and silver currency and did not preserve private assets, advocated to maintain the production of commodities and abolish the currency, maintain the currency and preserve goods production did not fully understand currency history, which was not worthy of being criticized. Because he thought that the reason was self-evident and there was no need for further refutation, which was a waste of energy and time. However, the tragedy of history repeats later in China. After the accomplishment of socialist transformation of the means of production, there was again the trend to eliminate commodity and currency, which was a profound lesson indeed.

In terms of currency functions, Li Da discussed each one by one, and then explored the relationship between money and capital, money and commodity production, especially the process of capital capitalization in capitalist society. Li also explored currency issues in ancient times, the feudal era and modern society. Li concluded that "money still existed in socialist countries. However, currency in socialist and capitalist countries was different in nature, and its role in classes had another meaning."[305] In fact, in a class society, money was an important tool for a particular class to conquer, plunder, exploit and control other classes, and a tool for the exploiting class to exploit the exploited class. Just like language and weapons, they can not only become weapons and tools used by ruling

---

[302] *Ibid.*, p. 547.
[303] *Ibid.*, p. 550.
[304] *Ibid.*, p. 551.
[305] *Ibid.*, p. 614,

classes to rule the ruled but also weapons and tools of the ruled against the ruler. Currency was only a medium for exchange, a fixed general equivalent, and was indispensable for every member of the commodity society. Therefore, according to Li Da, currency in a commodity society became a concentrated manifestation of will and interests of the ruling class in a class society, or a representative. In modern society, if the commodity economy were greatly developed, currency would become a tool of great powers to conquer, enslave and oppress colonies, which was plausible and easy to understand and accept. Therefore, one could draw a conclusion that money had a class character and is "explicitly apparent"[306] in modern society. Mainly based on credit means of circulation, circulation rules of currency can be enumerated briefly from eight aspects. It is concluded that the "money is the tool used by the imperialists to slaughter weak peoples and to conquer the hard-working people. The law of currency movement is a reflection of the dying capitalist relations of production. ... Finally, money still exists in socialist countries. However, currency in socialist countries and capitalist countries is of a different nature and the class role of money has another meaning."[307] This led to other doubts, and several debates in academic community took place. However, Li Da was one of the earliest people in China who proposed that currency had a class nature.

5.2. Various currency theories

In order to deepen the understanding of currency, Li Da used Marx's monetary theory to analyze and criticize metal theory of money, nominal theory of money and quantity theory of money. Li pointed out that when money functions as value scale, circulation method or payment instrument, it is the unity of the existence of money and material, the unity of the nature of the physical and the spirit, the unity of value and use value, and the unity of abstract labor and specific labor. "Generally speaking, both metal theory and nominal theory are based upon physical and divinity of money, and are confined by monetary phenomenon. They do not

---

[306]*Ibid.*, p. 613.
[307]*Ibid.*, p. 614.

know that the nature of money could be understood from the perspective of commodity production relation. They merely put one or two functions of currency on an absolute position and ignore other functions of currency, which leads to a one-sided monetary theory."[308] "The above facts lie in dialectics of money itself, namely looking only at the surface of things and missing the essence of things, only paying attention to the existence of money concept, or only the material existence of money, or missing the forest for the trees. Therefore, economics of the orthodox school and its descendants do not understand the dialectics that currency has two existence forms, the interrelationship between two forms and transformation from one to the other, thus creating various monetary theories that distort the reality and disguise the truth. The so-called metal theory of money, nominal theory of money, and quantity theory of money are the representatives of this kind of money theory."[309]

When criticizing metal theory of money, Li Da pointed out, "metalists knelt upon the physical and divinity of money, floated on the surface of phenomenon and explained the mystical ability of currency from the natural nature of gold and silver of money materials."[310] They studied from the established currency but did not know the origin and development of currency and regarded currency as pure precious metal. Because they did not understand the nature of money, they neither understood the history of monetary economy nor the history of commodity production relations. They only saw the relationship among things or between people and things, and could not see relationships among people. "The use value was treated as value, and the special use value of metals was considered as the value of money. Therefore, what they called value scale referred to scaling the use value of other commodities by the use value of money."[311] It is only the revelation of the relationship among things. It was Li Da who was more critical than Chinese contemporary scholars when criticizing metalism. Li Da said that metal theory originated in the 16th and 17th centuries and was assumed to have free competition feature of the time as

---

[308]*Ibid.*, p. 619.
[309]*Ibid.*
[310]*Ibid.*, pp. 621–622.
[311]*Ibid.*, p. 622.

the theory argued that the state did not interfere in currency. In the era of financial capitalism, it had been replaced by another monetary theory, namely, the nominal theory of money.

Regarding the nominal theory of money, Li Da said, "the origin of the theory was very early. Aristotle in the Greek era had established the proposition that 'currency is the result of everyone's consent'. In medieval times, some jurists had long held the view that 'money was a symbol and the value of precious metals was entirely imaginary', and supported kings of the entire medieval times to counterfeit coins."[312] If measured by this standard, the metal theory of money can be dated back to ancient times.

Li Da's review of modern nominal theory was that "modern nominalism explained currency from existence forms of currency concept instead of king's notice. Moreover, and nominal theory emerged in the final stage of capitalist commodity economy, reflecting that it had its progressiveness."[313] He keenly pointed out that the representatives of modern nominalism "were subjectivists. Their nominalism was closely related to the concept of economy in their hearts." They "interpret currency as a symbol of value, or as a means of calculating ideas, or as a means of payment for tickets. The common point was that currency has no value. It was not a commodity and only stood for value or a symbol."[314] There was something different about Li Da analyzing the essence of nominal theory of money from the idealism of the entire economic theory of nominalism. In the same way, Li Da also analyzed the background of nominal theory based on social and economic factors. First, they held that banknotes were the key to understanding currency, denying currency as a commodity and claiming that money had no value. Second, development of capitalist commodity economy at home and abroad led to unbridled development of credit transactions. With the growth of bank capital and banking services, the cash settlement portion of general transactions had been decreased gradually, while settlement without currency (referring to cash settlement) developed rapidly. A large number of realistic

---

[312]*Ibid.*, p. 625.
[313]*Ibid.*, pp. 625–626.
[314]*Ibid.*, p. 626.

representations generated such thinking that money was only an abstract calculation unit in its essence. In this unit, the price of a commodity and labor value could be calculated. Third, with the development of exclusive capitalism, precious metals had to be given exclusive prices by the monopoly. Due to this fact, nominalism underwent an upside-down phenomenon, as if gold and silver were priced by currency. After analyzing the content of the nominal theory, Li Da summed up the main points of the famous theory. There were four points. First, he claimed that money was a product of people's will and the laws they stipulated. It was by no means the result of spontaneous development of commodity economy. Second, the real currency was paper currency. Third, currency had no value, so it was not a commodity. It was only a unit to measure the price of a commodity. Fourth, money was created by the country and its legal system and its legal value was given by the legal system. In connection with the actual social economy, he turned his attention to the mid-war period of the First World War. The nominalists "affirmed inflationary policies and used the monetary system as a means to exploit the working people. The rising price caused by inflation and the relative reduction in wages actually decreased the labor value."[315] As a result, the theoretical flaws, the political one-sidedness and the limitations of the class position in nominal theory of money were exposed clearly.

Regarding the quantity theory of money, Li Da analyzed its origin and made comments on modern quantity theory of money.

First, he summed up general characteristics of the quantity theory of money as follows: "Currency has no inherent fixed value. The value of money was formed in circulation. The purchasing power of money was directly controlled by the quantity of money. The purchasing power of money was inversely proportional to the quantity of money. If the quantity of commodities and the speed of currency circulation did not change, the change in the quantity of money would directly cause a proportional change in price. ... Therefore, if the quantity of money increased, the purchasing power of money would decrease while the level of commodity prices would increase. If the quantity of money decreased, the purchasing power of money would increase, and the level of commodity prices would

---

[315]*Ibid.*, p. 633.

decrease."³¹⁶ Therefore, the level of commodity prices or the value of money was regulated by the quantity of money.

Second, he pointed out the fundamental reason why David Ricardo failed to implement his proposition of labor theory of value and then turned to say that quantitative theory did "not understand the nature of money, that is, the duality of labor."³¹⁷ Labor, that Ricardo referred to, was the specific labor that created use value, not the abstract labor that created value. There was no abstract labor category in his economics. What he noticed was only the amount of value, not the quality of value. Even in modern quantity theory of money, these erroneous ideas were the same.

Third, after introducing Fisher's equations, he pointed out that the fundamental theoretical fallacy in quantity theory of money lay in "reversing the causality, taking the quantity of money as a reason, and viewing the low purchasing power of the currency and the rising price level as the result."³¹⁸

Fourth, the mistakes in the understanding of paper money by the currency quantity theory were that "they did not understand value and the nature of money". "The so-called value of paper money was determined by quantity. It did not mean that the amount of paper money alone can determine value, but it means that gold and silver were the first and fundamental things; only when the paper money represented a certain amount of gold, did the number of paper money determine its value."³¹⁹

Fifth, in the face of modern panic, Fisher, Cashier and Keynes had different opinions and ideas, but they all tried to overcome the panic based on the same principles. They all advocated the implementation of credit systems and other schemes of the monetary system, such as changing the discount rate to control the credit, finance and price movements. The objective effects of these methods had been proven to be unsuccessful. Because the bank was still in bankruptcy, gold still flowed from one

---

³¹⁶*Ibid.*, pp. 633–634.
³¹⁷*Ibid.*, p. 636.
³¹⁸*Ibid.*, p. 641.
³¹⁹*Ibid.*, p. 644.

country to another. Prices were still low, which meant that "they did not and even did not want to understand the real reason of the panic."[320]

In the end, Li Da summed up the similarities and differences between the quantity theory of money and nominal theory of money, and the core and essential characteristics. He pointed out the essential characteristics and methodological features of quantity theory. "In investigation of circulation process, money was seen as a certain thing with a finished form. The most important feature was that they observed all phenomena from the perspective of exchanges. ... Because of this insight, they regarded money as the root cause of all changes in the capitalist economy and thought that as long as the monetary issue was solved, then all economic problems could be solved." "This method was characterized by antihistoricism. ... They regarded the capitalist system as ideal permanent things."[321] "The social class mission of quantity theory was to uphold the capitalist order and attempt to carry out all the capitalist economic controls by currency management, with a view to averting or alleviating panic and reducing panic. This claim, on the other hand, maintained capitalist profits and increased the exploitation of surplus labor."[322] In old China, this was a powerful theoretical weapon for educating people and making them aware. Today, it is still an effective theoretical method for observing and analyzing monetary issues.

5.3. *Credit, credit currency and monetary system*

To study the collapse of the gold standard, we must first study the capitalist credit system and monetary system. The capitalist credit system covered commercial credit, capital credit, bank credit and its credit tools and operating agencies. Li Da explained them in turn.

He initially analyzed commercial credit, capital credit and bills. He said that commercial credit emerged under pre-capitalist conditions, but "commercial credit in a pure commodity economy was only an accidental phenomenon, and commercial credit in capitalist society was a universal

---
[320]*Ibid.*, p. 646.
[321]*Ibid.*
[322]*Ibid.*, pp. 647–648.

inevitable phenomenon."[323] Commercial credit can achieve the continuity of capital circulation, and at the same time shorten the time for capital stagnation in circulation. Therefore, the obstacles to the movement of capital's deformation can be ruled out, the necessary monetary capital in circulation can be reduced and money capital can be liberated to expand production. "It seemed that commercial credit was on the one hand the realization of commodities, and on the other hand, it was the lending of capital, which was the duality of commercial credit."[324] Commercial credit was closely linked with the reproduction of capitalism. Its role and characteristics were expressed by Li Da accurately.

He analyzed capital in two situations, namely, stagnating in the form of currency and in a resting state. However, some industrial capitalists lacked capital and needed to inject capital to produce surplus value. Therefore, the possibility and necessity of debit and credit emerged. Once debit and credit were established, "the loaned capital was called lending capital, and the interest received was called lending interest. The lending of this capital was called capital credit."[325] Commercial credit was payment credit, and capital credit was established by money transfer. It was different from payment credit and had different functions. Capital credit was established in the financial market, and interest rates were determined by market profitability. The average rate of profit varied between capitalist developed countries and backward countries. The movement of currency capital among international countries formed an international average interest rate.

A bill was a certificate of credit. "When a credit grantor provided credit, he always asked the debtor for a security as a guarantee of payment."[326] Bills could be divided into two types, promissory notes and bills of exchange, which were protected by law, maintained the rights and interests of creditors and implemented easily. States formulated the bill law to assist creditors to obtain the par value from the debtor. As long as the signature was stamped on the bills, money must be paid. This approach

---

[323] *Ibid.*, p. 649.
[324] *Ibid.*, p. 650.
[325] *Ibid.*, p. 651.
[326] *Ibid.*, p. 653.

made the bills easily encashable. The bill "was the most important form of credit, and its significance was profound. As the bill made the capital easy to circulate and made calculation easier, it could eliminate the need for cash".[327] Discounting of bills "could expand credit scope and contribute to the credit's sensitivity".[328] The role and significance of bills, especially bill discounting in the economy of modern society, were obvious.

In Li Da's view, commercial credit and capital credit were intertwined with bank credit. In order to illustrate the credit in capitalist society, it was necessary to explain bank credit. Bank credit involved a special credit agency — bank. He used concise words to explain that in the process of capitalist development, emergence of banks made credit more flexible, eliminated various obstacles in direct credit transactions and expanded the possibility of credit behaviors. He quoted a large section of classic text in "Credit and Fictitious Capital", Chapter 25 of *Capital,* to explain that "a bank was an intermediary between a person holding a rest currency and a person who needed money". Li pointed out that the dual role of banks in the primary era of capitalism encouraged the accumulation of capitalist production, the growth of the wealth of a handful of capitalists and the extraction of the working masses. With the development of banks, the process of monetary capital being left out of functional capital developed and, the nature of parasitic capitalists was strengthened. These contradictions had been deepened. In the era of imperialism, with the development of banking business and its accumulation in a small number of institutions, banks had changed from the intermediary industry to the monopoly of one country or several countries.[329] The banking industry developed and mainly focused on a small number of institutions. With this expansion and development of business operations, banks transformed from ordinary intermediaries to universal monopolists. It was clearly expounded by Lenin as second major issue in the *Highest Stage of Imperialism*. Li Da explained the relationship between bank credit and commercial credit. Commercial credit developed earlier in history was the precondition of bank credit and the basis of the entire credit system. However, there was

---

[327] *Ibid.*, p. 654.
[328] *Ibid.*, p. 655.
[329] *Ibid.*, p. 657.

a difference between bank credit and commercial credit. "Commercial credit was the lending of commodity capital invested in the process of reproduction." The purpose of lending was the realization of commodity capital, while the payment for the grant of capital was of secondary significance; "it was only implemented in reproduction among people."[330] Bank credit was not in the reproduction process and its only purpose was to obtain interest. Bank credit was the credit relationship between lender capitalists and industrial capitalists. Business credits and lending capitals were latently integrated with commodity capital. Without its own movement, bank credit would be expressed as a more profound development of the contradiction between industrial capital and monetary capital. Commercial credit "adopted a contradictory movement pattern of production and circulation, which was a method to shorten the circulation period and expand production, and was also a form of capitalist reproduction."[331] "Bank credit showed the process of capitalist expansion and reproduction."[332] Business credit and bank credit were two forms of capitalist credit, and they are the manifestations of the two development stages of the contradiction between all capital and functional capital. The two formed a unity. "The development of banks was combined with the development of monetary capital. Because of the advent of banks, credit had been the center of organization, then developed and become a complex credit institution system that affected social development."[333] There were many kinds of banking activities and types. Li Da basically summed it up as "credit service that implements collecting and allocation of currency capital".[334] "It can be divided into two major categories. The first was borrowing money, which was the bank's passive business; the second was lending money, which was the bank's dynamic business." A bank's passive services were mainly deposits (current and fixed deposits) and borrowing of current loans. According to the bank's experience, except for keeping a certain amount of reserves for depositors' withdrawals, the remaining deposits could be released. A bank issued checkbooks to

---

[330]*Ibid.*, p. 658.
[331]*Ibid.*
[332]*Ibid.*, p. 659.
[333]*Ibid.*, p. 660.
[334]*Ibid.*

depositors to facilitate the use of current deposits. "Depositors used checks to make banks act as currency tellers." As money capital was accumulated, the "bank did not need to increase cash reserves, and could use purely technical means to expand the accumulation of money capital. Therefore, the expansion of reproduction isolating from practical currency, that was the constraints of accumulation, were getting more flexibility. At the same time, the possibility of excess production had increased as well, thus panic easily occurred."[335] The dual role of bank in its contribution to promoting development and brewing fear could not be ignored and deserved further investigation and study.

Among credit currencies, commercial papers, promissory notes and bills of exchange, and checks due to commercial credits could, to a certain extent, replace currency circulation. They also had certain limits and scopes. Credit currency issued by the bank, namely, bank vouchers, was also subjected to such restrictions. Li Da deliberately pointed out, "bank vouchers were taken as a credit by person who received bank vouchers".[336] "Bank vouchers and the credit of issuing bank were maintained by reserves of cash." Reserves for issuing bank vouchers consisted of bullion or gold and silver coins, securities and commercial bills, but the latter were not "reliable and it was clearer during panic or unrest periods." "But the bank did not need 100% of the reserve for issued bank vouchers."[337] In modern capitalist countries, such issuing banks often became "banks of banks" or central banks. In this regard, Li Da made a special explanation. The state "used to use issuing banks to relieve financial and financial issues. For example, the issuing bank was obligated to bear the national debt. It attempted to apply interest rate policies to regulate national economy, and assisted exchange banks and other special banks, as well as relieving capitalists in panicking state, etc. All were making full use of the issuing banks."[338] As a result, a country's responsibilities, which were limited to one or more issuing banks, and the identity of banks of banks and central banks were all explained.

---

[335] *Ibid.*, p. 661.
[336] *Ibid.*, p. 664.
[337] *Ibid.*, p. 665.
[338] *Ibid.*, p. 666.

Credit played an important role in the reproduction of capitalism. Li Da made an overview and analysis from four aspects, namely, helping to equalize the rate of profit, accelerating the speed of currency circulation, realizing the mobilization of capital and subsidizing the organization of stock companies. He explained in depth the analysis of the latter role, suggesting that "with the development of stock companies, the contradiction between the sociality of production and the privateness of possession had become more acute."[339] Thus, credit played a dual role in the production of capitalism: On the one hand, it promoted the development of capitalist production, and on the other hand, it expanded the contradiction of capitalist production. It "actually was the manifestation of the contradiction between private ownership and productive society".[340] Li Da clearly revealed to the Chinese people — who were struggling to find a road that could enrich the country, become independent, help in survival and boost development — that the tremendous productivity of capitalism was the reason why the source of energy was not exhausted. At the same time, Li also predicted a cyclical crisis of capitalist economy. As a proletarian revolutionary theorist, he consciously shouldered the historic mission of a Marxist theoretical worker.

Based on the above arguments, one would naturally establish the following proposition: "the capitalist monetary system was based on gold, and closely related to gold; on the basis of gold, there were metal currency and paper stamps with insufficient value."[341] It explained why the gold standard system was adopted by the capitalist countries from among the gold standard system, the gold and silver recovery standard system, the parallel standard, limping standard and the silver standard. "There was no gold standard country yet except for national or semi-colonial peoples. These countries, because of its weak financial power, could not really adopt the gold standard system, and suffered huge losses."[342] This of course included China. China could not use the gold standard system to analyze its losses. Against the painful collision, Li Da conducted further

---

[339]*Ibid.*, p. 669.
[340]*Ibid.*, p. 670.
[341]*Ibid.*, pp. 673–674.
[342]*Ibid.*, pp. 674–675.

investigation and study. He pointed out that "before the emergence of a general equivalent that is better than gold, the plan of all the bourgeoisie countries to abolish the use of gold as currency is never implementable. In other words, gold would continue to serve as currency until the elimination of commercial economy."[343] "Thus, in domestic circulation, even gold could not be seen, it did not mean that domestic circulation did not need gold." He insisted that "in capitalist countries, a certain amount of gold must be provided for domestic circulation. Otherwise the chaos of circulation could not be avoided."[344] He further pointed out that "the so-called plan to abolish the use of gold as currency would never be made possible by any agreement between countries."[345] Before World War II, real gold still circulated internationally, which reflected the fact that abandoning the gold standard system was not to abolish gold as currency. "The so-called abandonment of gold standard system only announced to use banknotes as a domestic currency substitute to stop cash payment. However, in fact efforts were still made to concentrate gold in the hands of the state to ensure the circulation of domestic banknotes."[346] "Bimetallic standard was theoretically false and practice showed its failure."[347] However, the United States tried to return to the bimetallic standard. "Silver Purchase Act" was nothing more than to increase silver price, increase the purchasing power of China, South America and other Asian countries, and expand the domestic goods market to control the finances of the silver-using countries. "For the domestic market, we could rely on the purchase of silver to increase currency and inflation, in an attempt to solve the panic problem."[348] How could Li Da not get angry that the suffering motherland was being plotted against and played by other powers! He seized the crux of the problem and went straight to the American silver policy, exposing the American hypocrisy to the world! What an exciting

---

[343]*Ibid.*
[344]*Ibid.*, p. 698.
[345]*Ibid.*, p. 675.
[346]*Ibid.*, p. 675.
[347]*Ibid.*, p. 676.
[348]*Ibid.*, pp. 676–677.

matter it was! As for the history of pounds, US dollars, francs and yen, he also made a brief statement.

The issue and circulation of bank vouchers can be classified into normal conditions and extraordinary conditions. The circulation rule of bank vouchers under normal conditions is "subjected to the circulation rule of gold in the real currency."[349] The circulation of bank vouchers increases or decreases as the necessary amount of currency circulation increases or decreases. The issue of bank vouchers can be roughly classified into the following three cases: "First is the occasion where central bank accepts the gold from the gold owner as reserves to issue bank vouchers; second is the occasion of issuing bank vouchers to general banks; third is the occasion of issuing loans to the government and issuing bank vouchers."[350] In short, under normal conditions, "the circulation of bank vouchers is determined by capital and commodities circulation." In contrast, the Central Bank is forced to undermine the credit principle itself, which issues more bank vouchers under such cases as financial panic to relieve the financially distressed banks, and when a government issues deficit bonds to solve fiscal deficits and borrows large sums of money from the Central Bank; a country's capitalists also get plenty of gold because of trafficking a large number of goods into belligerent countries or from the interest earned on foreign investment. Based on the above situations, Li Da believed that "if the number of bank vouchers exceeded the necessary amount, those surplus bank vouchers would flee from circulation and convert into rest capital, which would increase the capital for loans. As a result, the interest rate on lending decreased."[351] The increase in lending capital and the decrease in lending rates would lead to the following two phenomena. One was the flight of capital and the other was active commodity trading and the increase in production.

Li stated that the basis of circulation rules of bank vouchers was the gold circulation principle. Bank bonds could not be separated from gold, not only in the world market but also in the domestic market, as only bank vouchers that could be freely transformed into gold were considered the

---

[349] *Ibid.*, p. 684.
[350] *Ibid.*
[351] *Ibid.*, pp. 685–686.

real things. "So bank vouchers were also called vouchers."[352] And, "maintaining redemption was the guarantee of maintaining the circulation rules of bank vouchers." He believed that "the issue of bank vouchers must be guaranteed by gold. It was the first condition of bank vouchers." Actually, if banks issued bonds worth one billion *yuan*, it was not necessary to prepare gold for guarantees as long as there was a certain amount of gold guarantees. Other parts of bank bonds could be used as credit guarantees. "The characteristics of bank vouchers existed in such point. Therefore, the guarantee of credit was the second condition of bank vouchers."[353] Because a part of bank vouchers was issued on the basis of reliable discounted bills, it was suitable for actual commodity trading of a certain period during the reproduction process, reflecting that it was safe. He pointed out, "under two guarantees of exchange and credit, banks could not use force to put excess bank vouchers into circulation, nor can they forcefully withdraw the necessary bank vouchers from circulation." A bank's voucher was not allowed to be redeemed. If it could get the guarantee of a country's credit, it could become a general circulation method. For example, at an extraordinary time, the government or the central bank would announce the termination of exchange, but people trusted the government and the central bank.[354] In such cases, bank vouchers still circulated as usual. Bank vouchers could still become a storage method as gold coins, so the circulation of bank vouchers did not exceed the necessary amount. Of course, if bank vouchers were declared to be suspended, and unviable bank vouchers became unexchanged papers, it would be subjected to the laws governing banknote circulation. Therefore, Li Da held that "inflation of bank vouchers in the banking system occurred only under such situation that vouchers inflation was taken as banknotes inflation."[355] Provision for issuing bank bonds in the early days of capitalism, during the emergence of banks and with the formation of the world market and different phases of the central bank, had different forms. The reserve function maintained by the central bank

---

[352]*Ibid.*, p. 688.
[353]*Ibid.*, p. 689.
[354]*Ibid.*, p. 691.
[355]*Ibid.*, p. 692.

generally had three aspects: international payment, domestic circulation and exchange reserve. If the reserve was sufficient, it seemed that nothing would occur. "But in today's world economy where national economies fight against each other, the bourgeoisie of any country strived to obtain ample reserves. As a result, battle for gold among capitalist nations occurred. ... This kind of capitalist production contradiction would inevitably cause panic and war, so battle for gold would be increasingly more acute."[356]

Li also elaborated on issues of irredeemable bank vouchers and paper money of bank vouchers. He warned that "the economic exchangeability of bank vouchers was determined by the credits of bank vouchers."[357] As long as the aforementioned credit relationship of bank vouchers was not lost, bank vouchers would not lose their economic exchangeability. Irrespective of whether bank vouchers stopped redemption or not, the legal exchangeability was lost. Therefore, the so-called economical exchangeability "was the nature of banknote that had not lost its credit and the circulation nature as gold, namely the nature that could be exchanged with gold and silver."[358] It was still a bank voucher instead of banknotes, and still governed by the rules of bank vouchers instead of the banknote circulation rule. The fact that bank vouchers lost credit, Li believed, was generally due to the converted reserves falling below a certain percentage. It occurred under two conditions. The first was the situation in which large amounts of gold continued to flow out under the state of crisis. The second was the occasion where the circulation of bank vouchers had dramatically increased.[359] For example, it would occur under special emergency conditions, when banknotes were issued due to the exchange of short-term public debt, or banknotes were issued due to the need of state finance. Banknotes that had been bankrolled were subjected to the laws governing the circulation of banknotes, and they were bound to reduce their prices. "Thus, the degree of price reduction, from the very beginning, was more

---

[356]*Ibid.*, p. 694.
[357]*Ibid.*, p. 695.
[358]*Ibid.*
[359]*Ibid.*, p. 696.

intense than the ratio of paper coupon circulation."[360] It was caused by the difference in the nature of the two.

In order to confirm the correctness of the above viewpoints and deepen people's understanding, Li introduced the principle of the bourgeois bank voucher system, especially currency principle, banker capitalism, currency control system of Britain, the United States, France and Japan, and the exchange system among bank vouchers. Therefore, it was concluded that "systems controlled all currencies of capitalist countries were governed by the fundamental laws of currency circulation. The ultimate purpose was to maintain the existing gold and fight for a large amount of gold in order to stabilize the country's local currency and get favorable conditions for extracting the colonial or independent people and all the working people. So struggles among capitalist countries were thus manifested in the war for gold. ... The unbalanced law of capitalist development appeared in the uneven distribution of cash preparation. Several major imperialist countries had secured most of the world's cash reserves, which weakened the foundations of the monetary system of all other countries. Therefore, currency's vacillation was on a global scale. The universal collapse of the gold standard reflected this fact."[361] With acute eyes, sharp strokes and thorough analysis, Li Da made his conclusions of guiding value, which was the aim of Chinese Marxist theoreticians.

5.4. *Financial panic and the collapse of the gold standard system*

The relationship between currency circulation and financial panic was first analyzed.

Li thought that "financial panic was the outward manifestation of industrial panic".[362] Panic was the characteristic of capitalist reproduction. The reproduction of capitalism presented a kind of periodicity, and

---

[360]*Ibid.*, p. 697.
[361]*Ibid.*, p. 710.
[362]*Ibid.*, p. 712.

the power of panic could shake the foundation of the capitalist economy. Panic was characterized by disruption of circulation, poor sales, low prices, commercial stagnation, factory closures, bankruptcy and unemployment of workers.

He analyzed the causes of the panic. First of all, it was the contradiction between the use value and value developed due to the contradiction between commodity and currency. The possibility of panic had been lurking in the division and isolation of sale and purchase. This possibility had arisen from the circulation function of money. In the payment function of money, there was a direct contradiction. The independent existence of currency as exchange value appeared as an absolute commodity. This contradiction itself bred the possibility of panic. The contradiction between the production sociality of capitalist reproduction and the privateness of possession was the root cause of panic. On the one hand, imbalances in production and consumption were shown. On the other hand, imbalances in the production sectors were also manifested. In other words, the production department of production means and the production department of consumption materials were interdependent and infiltrated into a unified body. Under the private ownership system, they were separated and independent of each other. That is, the possibility of unbalanced potential was lurking. Capital was increasingly concentrated in the production sectors of production means, and the capital invested in the means of production of consumption data was relatively reduced. As a result of the above contradictions, there was a contradiction between the need for unlimited expansion of production for the capitalists and the reduction in the need for the ability of the working people to pay. Panic was bound to occur.

Li also proposed the cyclical nature of panic, which lay in the cyclical nature of capitalist reproduction. When it was active in the early stage, the market had more capital for lending and the interest rate was lower. "When the industrial and commercial frenzy developed, banks were willing to provide credit to various enterprises and boldly implement lending, and thus continued to issue a large number of bank vouchers. As the bank's profits increased, they competed to expanding credits. In terms of business and stock exchanges, they were constantly providing credits, even more than the total amount of deposits. Under such prosperous conditions, prices were rising, capital turnover was rapid, and capitalists were able to obtain large profits. ... Capitalists seemed to be mad and tried to make full use of this prosperity to produce large quantities of commodities, while they were unwilling to consider the needs of the market. At this time, speculative fever had dominated all capitalists, and the trend of excess production had lurked for a long time."[363] Li further pointed out that the cyclical nature of panic was not a simple circular movement but a spiral movement. Every crisis had its own special form and adapted to the reality of capitalist economic development stage.

Financial panic, Li believed, was an inevitable phenomenon in the circulation of industrial panic. It can be classified as general or special. The general financial panic, namely, credit panic, is the phenomenon of industrial panic. The special financial panic is "the kind of panic involving activities in banks, exchanges and finance, with monetary capital as the center."[364] It is the result of the departure of the movement of money capital from the reality of capital movement. It often happens at the banks and exchange institutions and will disrupt the reproduction process. Financial panic includes credit panic, bank panic, currency panic, exchange panic and currency-based panic. "The industrial panic arising from overproduction first emerged as a credit panic."[365] The method of banks to maintain the minimum reserves is to increase interest rates and reduce credit extensions. As a result, most companies lack funds. The development of credit panic will inevitably lead to the panic of the banks. "If banks failed to work well, all depositors are eager to withdraw deposits, and banks cannot but suspend business. ... The closure of a bank will affect other banks. Bank closure spreads one to another and from one place to another, which leads to a panic among banks across the country."[366]

In times of panic, currencies that perform various functions will change. Money circulation as a circulation method will shrink, and money circulation functioning as a payment means will expand. The total

---

[363]*Ibid.*, p. 718.
[364]*Ibid.*, p. 721.
[365]*Ibid.*, p. 722.
[366]*Ibid.*, p. 723.

amount of currency circulation, that is, the total amount of bank notes, will either remain unchanged or reduce. However, at the moment of panic, the rate of increase in the currency used as a means of payment will be higher than the rate of reduction of the currency seen as a means of purchase. Therefore, the amount of currency that functions as a purchasing instrument is reduced, while the total amount of currency can be increased.[367] When credit panic erupts, the credit is frozen while the cash system is revitalized. Capitalists sell goods at a low price. People holding the papers demand that they must be honored as soon as possible. When market demands bank voucher urgently, it is withdrawn from circulation and converted to the storage currency. Thus, the currency panic is formed. Li warned us that currency panic was a common phenomenon when credit panic occurred. Because there are many legal restrictions on issuing bank voucher, a large number of bank vouchers cannot be issued casually, and in fact they are afraid of affecting cash preparation. So, currency crisis is difficult to avoid. In particular, he pointed out that it was impossible to confuse the differences between money and capital, and the differences between the phenomenon and the nature of panic. The currency that the capitalists lack is actually the currency in currency form because they cannot recover the money in the capital form. The reason for the panic does not seem to be a reduction in the purchasing power of the general public. In fact, it is due to the fact that the total amount of money obtained by the general public is lower than the total price of the goods produced for the general public. He further described the capitalists during the panic, "not only asking for all the bills, all the securities, and all the commodities, to exchange for bank vouchers, but also further demanding that all bank vouchers should be exchanged for gold."[368] "This unexpected request that turns all wealth into gold is something must happen to the credit system itself." Li Da issued a warning that "at the time of credit collapse, issuing banks were often involved in chaotic whirlpools."[369] The gold redeemed by capitalists not only acts as a means of storage but also as a means of payment for international trade.

---

[367]*Ibid*., p. 724.
[368]*Ibid*., p. 725.
[369]*Ibid*.

Especially in this case, the difference used to compensate for international lending cannot be paid without gold. The pillar of the credit system is the issuing bank. "If cashing was stopped and gold export was banned, the currency standard would lose its function as a standard. It is the so-called panic phenomenon of stopping the gold currency standard."[370] He conducted a study and introduction of capitalist countries that wanted to give up the gold standard.

At the same time, Li Da introduced the exchange panic. He said that "when the credit was persecuted, it often began with an outbreak of panic at the exchange."[371] Here, he discussed the stock exchange panic. In credit crunch occasions, if speculators of buyers could not get credit, stocks would definitely fall. When the share price decreased, banks that had previously paid for stocks with high-priced stock collateral would require debtors to increase collateral. However, most debtors in the speculative sector could not make it. Hence, banks had to sell the share of the collateral. As the supply of stocks suddenly increased, prices fell even more. This declining trend was further reinforced by the seller's massive sell-off. So, the stock plummeted, causing new credit restrictions, which in turn led to the stock reselling. The plummeted share price produced a panic in the exchange.[372] It was directly induced by changes in the currency market, namely, due to the increase in interest rates. It became a precursor to excess production panic.

Under the title of *International Financial Panic*, Li Da expressed clearly that in the capitalist world, financial panic often evolved into an international-scale financial panic. The evolution of panic generally performed as the opposite phenomenon of the peak of the booming period, that is, the expensive commodity representing prosperous domestic sales. Cheaper foreign goods were constantly input and gradually exceeded the output, reflecting the flowing out of gold. In the credit crunch period, the outflow of gold would affect the central bank's cash preparation. In order to cash the bank vouchers, the central bank must ensure the safety and one of the methods was increasing interest rates. However, this had affected

---

[370]*Ibid.*, pp. 725–726.
[371]*Ibid.*, p. 726.
[372]*Ibid.*, p. 728.

credit relations and had become a sign of credit panic. On the contrary, at the peak of the boom, interest rates were soaring and speculative, which would attract capital input from other countries. When other countries' economies entered the culmination of prosperity, they would withdraw the capital they invested. Thus, it led to two forms of outflows: "first was the outflow of payment balances in foreign trade, and the other was the outflow in the form of currency capital (foreign securities bought by foreign capitalists were sold out as gold and brought back to the country). Therefore, the country's credit panic and exchange fears were bound to become more serious. This country, due to the outflow of gold, opened veil of panic and caused outbreak of panic, thus promoting the outflow of gold. ... The same thing happened in the second country in turn. ... Spreading from one country to other countries, all countries were involved in the swirl of panic."[373] Li further revealed that people faced severe gold outflow during a panic state. "The government or the central bank must not neglect the bankruptcy of private companies and only tried to save their own crisis by unusual methods. For example, the suspension of bank vouchers and the ban on gold exports were implemented under these conditions."[374] He criticized those vulgar economists who, in times of crisis, were only concerned with the phenomenon of slow currency circulation and money deficiency. They could not further examine the nature of the crisis and put forward various theories as a basis for banking legislation, attempting to eliminate the panic of finance equaling credit panic. However, because of the existence of industrial panic, the panic of finance equaling credit can never be eliminated.

On exchange rate issues, Li Da explained in detail about the formation, nature, types and changes of the exchange rate, as well as the analysis and criticism of the purchasing power parity theory. First of all, he started with currency exchange to explain the international movement of gold and silver and the international flow of commodities and capital. Countries that experienced low levels of production, regardless of their rich natural resources, could only export raw materials and became markets for advanced countries to sell their goods. Thus, capitalist countries

---

[373]*Ibid.*, pp. 730–731.
[374]*Ibid.*, p. 733.

would destroy small industries of backward nations and turn into places for selling goods and collecting raw materials. "So countries across the world were divided into industrial and agricultural countries, and formed the precondition for the circulation of international commodities. ... Thus, the interdependence of nations became more and more close. ... It was the sign of sociality of production expanded to the world scale."[375] In the era of imperialism, "great powers adopted new methods and tools — capital output to compete for market and raw material production."[376] Capital output has two forms. One is the form of loan capital for obtaining interests, such as purchasing bonds issued by foreign countries, stocks and other investments; the other is the form of industrial capital for obtaining corporate income, such as enterprise investment on foreign industries. Loan output is often combined with industrial capital output. Domestic banks set up sub-branches abroad and use sub-branches to manipulate the finances of the host countries and control their industries. Powerful banking branches collect domestic commodity selling, and the local raw materials become financial institutions. He also cited the ways in which lending capital was often borrowed and loaned to foreign governments, which had a political role, and interest rates were usually high. Even if they did not extract high profits, they must have other requirements, such as obtaining certain rights or purchasing goods from the country. Such kind of money borrowing was common in China. This is truly a sharp accusation in the guise of theoretical analysis. He also stated that the period after World War I was characterized by the output of short-term capital. The status of London in the international financial market declined, and the status of New York and Paris increased and they became the world's two major financial centers.

We know that the exchange rate is centered on the mint parity, and the cash transportation fee fluctuates around the center. In this range, the exchange rate often changes according to the international lending relationship. In the explanation of the examples, Li pointed out that the calculation method of the current silver transportation points was slightly different in the currency exchange between the gold-based and

---

[375] *Ibid.*, pp. 737–738.
[376] *Ibid.*, p. 739.

silver-based countries. Taking China as an example, the market price of London's large bars changed somewhat. China's cash transfer points often changed with silver prices. There were three reasons for the changing of the exchange rate. One was the difference in the expenditure on international lending, the second was the decrease in the value of a country's currency and the third was the change in the relative price of gold and silver under the conditions of the free import and export of gold and silver and the ban on exports. The above three factors had an impact on the changing of the exchange rate. The exchange rate was essentially "the price of a bill of exchange converted in national currency. It adapted to changes in the demand and supply of bills of exchange and changed in a certain range. ... It was because the world economy did not have a uniform price standard. ... It was a contradictory product of world economy."[377]

Li criticized the theory of Purchasing Power Parity (PPP). The theory of PPP was advocated by Gustav Cassel and supported by Keynes and other people. The exchange rate determination theory in paper-based countries means that the exchange rate between two paper-based countries is determined by the purchasing power of two countries' currencies. Li Da wrote something about Cassel's main viewpoint and the formula he invented, "the key of the purchasing power parity theory was to determine that the bill of exchange is determined by the difference between the general price level between A and B. Therefore, the price of the bill of exchange is only determined by the price level of two countries, has nothing to do with the relationship between supply and demand in financial market, and has nothing to do with the balance of international borrowings and the balance of payments."[378] "The fundamental meaning of this theory is that price stability is a direct method of stabilizing exchange rates. ... It is essentially the thought of 'organized capitalism'."[379] However, the productivity development of various countries is unbalanced. Eliminating this imbalance is only an illusion. Therefore, the purchasing power parity cannot be established if one wanted to rely on

---

[377] Ibid., p. 750.
[378] Ibid., pp. 768–769.
[379] Ibid., p. 769.

price stability to stabilize the exchange rate. After analysis, Li came to the conclusion that "they did not know that price was a manifestation of the movement of productivity, and claimed that price was the result of inflation and parity depreciation. Therefore, creating the so-called price difference was the only reason for the exchange rate change, which was a vulgar description of the exchange rate obviously. Hence, the purchasing power parity theory can be said to be a hypothetical theory based on the premise that it cannot be established."[380]

At the same time, Li Da revealed that "the fundamental purpose of the discount policy was making the balance of payments balanced so as to improve the exchange rate."[381] It was the financial policy of central banks before World War I, "which aimed to use the discount rate to automatically prevent the outflow of cash and then adjust finance and stabilize the exchange rate."[382] For certain capitalist countries, it was indeed a weapon to consolidate cash reserves, balance payments and improve exchange rates, and also an effective weapon for foreign exchange policies and lending capital management policies. However, it was not the only weapon of the lending policy. For the interest rate policy, when the panic was severe, it was difficult to achieve the above effect. Moreover, this kind of international credit on foreign exchange was based on gold. Issuing banks of various countries "all fought for gold to consolidate the local currency as a central task." "When credit was shaken, all real wealth was suddenly required to be transformed into gold."[383] This reflected that "the nature of monetary commodity was gold".[384] This understanding was objective and scientific, profound and real at the same time.

5.5. *The collapse of the gold standard*

Li Da thought that his description of the first seven chapters of *The Introduction to Monetary Theory* was about elements, functions,

---

[380]*Ibid.*, p. 770.
[381]*Ibid.*, p. 771.
[382]*Ibid.*, p. 770.
[383]*Ibid.*, p. 773.
[384]*Ibid.*, p. 774.

movement patterns, interconnections, characteristics, roles and contents of the law of currency movement. What was to be elaborated was "the monetary phenomenon (the movement pattern of the currency and the commodity's connection) caused by countries' use of artificial methods to destroy the monetary movement rules."[385] It involved the collapse of inflation and the gold standard system.

The first chapter was about inflation. Li discussed two aspects of inflation and its negative impact and negative performance. He described inflation as "the phenomenon of currency chaos caused by capitalist countries' violation of the law of currency and excessive circulation of currency."[386] Inflation can be divided into three forms, namely, inflation of banknotes, exchange rate and credit. "Among these three forms, inflation of banknotes originally meant inflation and was a narrow inflation. For the other two forms — exchange inflation and credit inflation, they were a broad inflation."[387] He further stressed that gold was circulated because of its value, and that paper money obtained value because it represented gold in circulation. When the amount of paper money coincided with the amount of gold coin for circulation, people would not feel the law of the actual movement of the paper money. Otherwise, people would feel the movement. He described the law of banknote movement as, "if the number of banknotes did not exceed the circulation necessary for the gold coin it represented, banknote would represent the value of the gold coin. This was the movement law of banknote. So the law of paper money was just a reflection of gold and silver equals to the law of currency movement."[388]

Li believed that the paper money was put into circulation by a state's mandatory common power. The paper money issued by the bourgeois countries had to have a class nature. It was very clear that the benefits of paper money belonged to bourgeois countries. When the circulation of banknotes was not completely exchanged, the class nature of the banknotes was apparently exposed. Once the issuing of banknotes

---

[385] *Ibid.*, p. 776.
[386] *Ibid.*
[387] *Ibid.*, p. 776.
[388] *Ibid.*, pp. 779–780.

exceeded the limit, it would lead to vicious and mandatory borrowing. It was a taxable means and a borrowing certificate that did not need to be repaid. It was the root cause of the deterioration of public life and fiscal disorder. "In the era of the general crisis of capitalism, during the times of the war and in the post-war era, bourgeois countries used the issuing of banknotes method on an unprecedented scale as a means of redistributing income to raise funds during panic and war. The purpose of the redistribution of capital and the raising of large capital was strengthened the exploitation of the public."[389] "Toward the peak of world panic, the bourgeoisie was almost advancing toward the inflationary path of banknotes."[390]

Li further pointed out that in a time of panic or war, because of financial difficulties, the state would no longer be able to provide financial resources, and its only method would be to continuously increase the number of paper money to meet financial needs. "When government continued to issue bank vouchers through bank issuance, which resulted in the loss of bank vouchers and the conversion of bank vouchers into bank notes, the phenomenon of banknote depreciation and price exuberance would occur, namely the phenomenon of banknote inflation."[391] He summarized the law of inflation. According to him, "after the destruction of the law of the circulation of banknotes, the inflation of banknotes takes place and then develops into the stage of breaking down. The tendency of occurrence, development and breaking-down is the law of banknotes inflation."[392] The inflation of banknotes could be divided into three stages. The first was the stage of occurrence, and it could also be called the latent stage of inflation. The credit of the banknotes was lost, and the part that turned out of circulation to become a means of storage had increased abnormally. The second was the stage of development. It could also be said to be a period of pseudo-prosperity of inflation. Prices were extremely high and the exchange rate was declining to a significant degree. On the one hand, speculation was particularly popular, production and consumption

---

[389]Ibid., pp. 780–781.
[390]*Ibid.*, p. 782
[391]*Ibid.*, p. 789.
[392]*Ibid.*, p. 790.

increased, and many men of wealth emerged. On the other hand, the gradual decline in the living standard of the general public and the process of plundering and engulfing of the general public continued to develop during this period. Third, during the break-up phase, the flood of paper money flowed sideways. When the last obstacles were encountered, the public would rather return to the state of self-sufficiency in the exchange of goods and would eventually bring about an overall economic and political crisis.

Li made a distinction between exchange inflation and banknote inflation, and proposed that because the international borrowing and loan balance continued to show a negative tone, it imposed a ban on gold exports and stopped cashing. However, if the balance of payment could not be turned back, the exchange rate would continue to decline and the price of goods in proportion to it would rise to an unlimited degree. As a result, currency would be inflated to an unlimited degree as well. This kind of inflation would occur due to the low exchange rate and high prices. It was called exchange inflation.[393] It seemed to be the same as the banknote inflation, but the causes and developments of the two were different. However, the two was interlinked and passed on to each other so as to overlap. The trend of prices would also overlap. "Prices were swift on the one hand due to the low exchange rate, and on the other hand, they would be devalued due to the reduction in the price of banknotes. At the same time, the low price of exchange rate was also overlapping, which was due to the fact that payment was more than offset by changes in parity with the banned gold exports. On the other hand, the reduction of banknotes led to the low price of the exchange rate."[394]

It could be seen from the above that while exchange rate inflation could be converted into banknote inflation, banknote inflation could also be converted into exchange rate inflation. The two kinds of inflation were different from each other, but there was a certain degree of inevitability between them, which was the performance of a dangerous conflict between the two functions of the reserve.[395]

---

[393]*Ibid.*, p. 794.
[394]*Ibid.*, p. 795.
[395]*Ibid.*, p. 796.

Li also analyzed credit inflation. If credit under certain conditions expanded indefinitely, for example, the general bank's lending exceeded its total deposits, or if the central bank's lending exceeded its reserve amount, then excessive issuing bank bonds would lead to a huge amount of short capital and a majority of credits would be granted to those who had no ability to pay, leading to the phenomenon of excessive price inflation caused by excessive expansion of credits formed as the inflation of credit.[396] Moreover, "capitalism was developed into an exclusive stage. Once credit inflation occurred, it would cause panic to erupt. Not only would it not be completely liquidated and would not return to a state of balance, it would be followed by another recurrence of credit inflation."[397] Credit inflation could not be stopped and could be mitigated in latent form. "The method of mitigation was that the dominant exclusive capitalist sought relief through the government. There were two methods of relief: the first was the direct remedy of creditworthiness for companies that would go bankrupt. The second was that the government received credit from the central bank to prevent price from falling through setting up enterprises."[398] Li reviewed the role of credit inflation in panic and its effects. The first method of remedy was for the government to give excessive credit to the companies and banks that were in bankruptcy through the central bank or indirectly through other banks. After banks obtained bank bonds, they could repay their debts to avoid bankruptcy. "The credit chain that had already gone bankrupt was therefore newly repaired, and the overall development trend of financial panic could also stop."[399] However, it could not end the industrial panic, but it would make it prolonged and chronic. Because of the surplus of resting money and capital, and declined interest rates, abnormal financial stagnation occurred. On the one hand, it caused speculation on securities, thus raising the price of securities; on the other hand, it only restrained the acute decline of prices, and surplus products could not be sold out, thus prolonging the panic. The

---

[396]*Ibid.*, p. 797.
[397]*Ibid.*, p. 798.
[398]*Ibid.*
[399]*Ibid.*

second method of remedy is for the government to issue bonds and banks to issue exchange bank vouchers. Through establishing civil engineering and expanding military industry, unemployed workers were directly relived and capitalists were indirectly relived. However, during the panic period, capitalists selling civil materials and military materials preferred to free up production equipment rather than expand equipment. Whenever a customer customized a commodity, the capitalists only strengthened the labor of the original worker or prolonged the labor time, and were never willing to hire workers. If the government wanted to reduce excessive fiscal deficits, it would increase taxes, leading to the burden passing on to the working masses and the public's purchasing power would definitely be reduced. Since 1929, the relief inflation policy implemented by President Hoover of the United States had not had the effect of overcoming panic, which was the most obvious explanation.

Li Da revealed that the quantity theory of money was the theoretical basis for the credit inflation policy. Miersel, Keynes and David Home were the representatives. They believed that the reason for the panic was the lack of lending capital. Therefore, they advocated using the credit inflation policy to overcome the panic.[400]

Li Da also introduced credit inflation during the boom period and during the war and the characteristics of these three forms of credit inflation. He believed that their common feature was currency stability. That is, currency would not be depreciated.[401] This was where credit inflation differed from exchange inflation and banknote inflation. The three types of credit inflation each had their own intrinsic characteristics. The main manifestations were as follows. First, inflation during the boom period occurred due to excessive credit among private capitalists and banks, which could promote price increase. Second, the credit expansion in the panic period occurred because of a country's excessive credit. It could stop the acute decline in prices and sometimes it could cause prices to rise slightly. Third, the credit inflation in the wartime period was due to the excessive credit of the state, private capitalists and banks. It could promote the rapid rise in prices. "The three types of credit inflation, in the

---

[400] *Ibid.*, p. 801.
[401] *Ibid.*, p. 805.

course of its development, had the possibility of shifting inflation among others."[402]

As for the social impact of inflation, Li Da analyzed different strata of the capitalist countries and conducted an investigation of the three social dimensions from the bourgeoisie, the small producers, the pay producers and the working masses. "In the course of inflation, the monopoly of capital received the greatest interests. Other small and medium-capital capitals could develop into larger capitals, and some would decline. Landlords, agricultural capitalists and rich peasants could also obtain considerable benefits."[403] Small producers and small makers in the city were completely bankrupt. The rural peasants below the middle and lower peasants were in the same situation. The difficulties of the average salaried people were greater with the progress of inflation. The working people suffered a double blow in inflation. They had to bear the reduction of their nominal wages, endure higher prices, paying wages and bear the loss of banknotes falling. As a result, the rising nominal wages could not catch up with the price of necessities.

Although inflation was a means of multiplying value by dominating exclusive capital, it had to be broken if it reached a certain extent and reduced populations to great hunger and turmoil. In view of this, after discerning and summing up the views of the modern popular currency quantitative theory and the labor theory of value economists, Li Da pointed out that one must explore the characteristics of inflation from the nature of money, the laws of the movement of money and the class nature of money. Again, the inflation could be defined as follows: "Inflation was the dominant bourgeoisie who, for the benefit of his own class, utilized the issue of currency to depreciate the worker's real wages and redistribute the national income, resulting in the collapse of capitalist economy's production institutions and commodity circulation."[404] Li Da affirmed that inflation was a monetary phenomenon, which utilized the currency issuing method to redistribute national income, dismantle existing production institutions and commodities. It was the root of the problem. Or one may

---

[402] *Ibid.*
[403] *Ibid.*, p. 813.
[404] *Ibid.*, pp. 822–823.

say it was the key and essence of the problem. Regarding Li Da's request for resistance on behalf of the aggressor countries, the oppressed classes and the enslaved nations, when revolutionary theoretical arms were needed, it was understandable to limit the definition of inflation to the capitalist economy and the bourgeois category. However, one must point out that that it also showed his historical limitations. In ancient societies, inflation served the imperial court, the emperor and the interests of the ruling groups they represented. Inflation occurred in modern times also. It was also serving the government representing the interests of the ruling group. Inflation does not belong only to the bourgeoisie class and the capitalist economy, but that was beyond Li Da's understanding.

Li Da predicted the transition from inflation to deflation, proposing that this was the only method of exploitation after the collapse of inflation in the exclusive capital.

Finally, Li Da discussed the collapse of the gold standard system. He first reviewed the whole process of the inflation of countries during and after World War I and, and the collapse of the gold standard caused by the panic of gold standard currency. As for the collapse of the pound, yen, US dollar and gold franc, he conducted a detailed investigation. He also analyzed the background of the collapse of the gold standard, the particularity of the so-called third-world panic, such as the exceptionally large scope, the degree of deepening, the particularly prolonged period, the unbalanced development, the increase in the number of unemployed people, the agitation of the agricultural industry and the world's most intense panic in the United States after the first post-war imperialism, thus stating that "the inevitable outbreak was the third period of international fierce currency-based panic."[405]

The local currency panic, he stated, "performed as the bank vouchers stopped cashing, gold export was banned, the currency price reduced, paper currency was inflated in various form."[406] It was a stage of the general economic panic, causing price cuts in credit circulation and a fierce credit system panic. He also analyzed the four changes of the local currency panic. One was the change in post-war credit composition. After

---

[405]*Ibid.*, p. 861.
[406]*Ibid.*

the war, the total amount of international short-term credits (bank deposits, bills of exchange, government bonds, stock certificates, etc.) increased and long-term credits decreased. The second was the fragility of the gold foundation of the national currency system. The unbalanced reserve of the world's gold was expressed as an imbalance of the world's monetary system. Third, the Versailles system caused international currency and credit relations to sway. The *Treaty of Versailles* exerted tremendous pressure on the economic and financial conditions of Germany and Austria. What's more, it also influenced very much the development of the financial panic, especially the panic over the standard currency. The fourth point was the national financial difficulties after the war. In order to raise funds, in addition to aggravating taxation, governments issued additional domestic public debt. With the onset of world panic, in order to fill the deficit budget, it was imperative to use banknote printing machines, which caused the panic of local currency.[407] These various opportunities were the cause of the panic of the local currency on the basis of the general crisis of capitalism. Li Da therefore came to the conclusion that "the world's standard currency panic was no other than the result of the fierce crisis of the entire capitalist system."[408] That was his historic conclusion.

---

[407] *Ibid.*, pp. 862–864.
[408] *Ibid.*, p. 864.

Epilogue

At the end of the 1980s and the beginning of the 1990s, I wrote an outline of *A History of China's Financial Thought*. At that time, I felt that China, a great country with 5,000 years of civilization, should have its own history of financial thought in addition to its history of economic thought and history of monetary thought (theories). As a teacher in the financial field, I had the responsibility and obligation to shoulder this task. So I made up my mind to use my spare time to draft such a book. After four or five years' endeavor, I finished the first draft and had it published by the China Financial Publishing House in October 1994. After the publication, I felt rather happy, because the book was sold out within a year, which was a good indication of the need for such a book. In the second year, the book was awarded the first prize among the fields of philosophy and social sciences in Beijing, because it filled in an academic gap. However, I felt uneasy because my academic accumulation was shallow. Some of the financial thought was not explored in the social environment of its emergence and there wasn't any comparative analysis either. There were some things unsaid, some things unclearly expressed, some things too demanding of the ancient scholars and some things farfetched in my writing. In addition, there were quite a few wrongly used or inappropriately omitted words, some of which were key words. As a result, readers might have found it hard to comprehend or would easily have misunderstood the text, which could lead to confusion or cause trouble. Moreover, in the postscript to the first edition, I mentioned that I had planned to write about the time before the founding of the People's Republic of China. But that edition stopped at the May Fourth Movement. My promise to the readers is a debt to be paid off as quickly as possible. During the past 16 years, though I have been quite busy making preparations and amendments, my diligence has not been enough for the task ahead. In this revision of and addition to the first edition, I implemented the following ideas.

First, for each historical period, I have presented the most advanced or representative ideas of the time. I have not made a general introduction. Instead, I have combined key points and less important points to introduce to the readers a more comprehensive picture. For example, during the Wei, Jin and the Northern and Southern Dynasties, the currency minting ideas of the Northern Dynasties were not advanced at all, but they were characteristic of the time and indicative of the unstoppable quality of the trend. Although there were twists and turns in the process, it was impossible to resist the landslide trend forward. Without an introduction, no one would be able to reflect on that historical development. The dispute over money drought beginning in the Tang and Song Dynasties was related to monetary policy. I had bookishly thought that such a dispute was not academic or theoretical, and a description of such a phenomenon was a profane act. However, ten years of administrative experience changed my naive ideas. I came to realize that while it is important to have pure theoretical or academic enquiry, policy and management thought are of equal importance. On the one hand, Chinese people have never stopped their exploration of problems in the economic and financial fields. Otherwise, the flourishing time of the Han and Tang Dynasties could never have existed, and there would never have been paper money in the Song Dynasty, which circulated in the whole country in the Yuan and Ming Dynasties and even in foreign countries, lasting for five to six hundred years. How can we turn a blind eye to these and think nothing of our forefathers' contributions? Talking always of Western financial thought is lamentably like forgetting our ancestors. On the other hand, Western countries and China have their respective advantages. In the past one hundred and fifty to sixty years, the Western countries became stronger while China fell behind. That is also true as far as economic thought is concerned. How should we sum up the lessons from our experience? Only when we can correctly treat our history and the present can we have a better understanding of the future and the world, especially in our dealing with the relationship between the East and the West as well as that between the North and the South.

Second, instead of being simplistic and crude, or being subjective, we should study the background and the unique environment of the financial thought carefully and intensively. I was impressed by the way Chohachi Itano, a Japanese scholar, studied the economic thought of Sima Qian. He analyzed Sima Qian against the background of the Yellow Emperor and Zhuang Zi, maintaining that he respected nature but supported some decisive measures to retain the dignity of the Han government, because he was a royal historian. That analysis was simply convincing. In my writing, I often wanted to challenge myself and tried to get rid of the simplistic way of thinking. I was determined to learn from masters in this field and followed all convincing suggestions. Unfortunately, I was often beset by my stupidity and ignorance.

Third, regarding citations, in the first edition I tried to be concise in my quotations and avoided, where possible, longer ones. Now, I have changed my way of thinking and think that this book is not only for myself but also for other people. It is to serve the needs of the readers and offer them a chance to make independent judgment and deeper enquiries. So there is indeed no need to impose my views on other people. Without much adjustment to the overall structure, I have tried my best to cite more quotations and added my understanding and interpretation when the need arose. The effect of doing this shall be determined by the readers.

Fourth, the thirty years from the May Fourth Movement to the founding of the PRC, though seemingly short, was a period of great change. In order to strive for national independence and prosperity, there had been attempts to save the country by education, science and industry. With many active minds, there had also been different strategies and methods emerging, such as the clash between Marxist and non-Marxist beliefs, the conflicts between old and new ways of thinking, and the collision between internal and external forces. Such a scene was magnificent and unprecedented. As far as financial writings were concerned, research papers not included, monographs, collections of published articles, textbooks and popular writings were already voluminous. According to Hu Jichuang's *A Sketchy History of China's Contemporary Economic Thought* published in 1982, there were already 60 monographs, textbooks and collected writings. 10 years later, in the financial part of the general bibliography in the Beijing Library of the Republic of China, it was roughly estimated that there were at least 200 similar items. If books related to the reform of currency were also included, there would be more than 300 of them. In part I want to supplement that I could only add those representative people according to the ancient standards. No matter whether they were famous prime ministers, financiers, thinkers, writers, scientist or industrialists, they had to have an innovative understanding of finance, a superior consciousness and a spirit of the time. Their pedigrees or ranks would not count. Their viewpoints had to influence policy decisions or the thinking of one or several generations of people. In addition, I also paid my tribute to those people whose deeds were grand and spectacular. Among the four representative figures, two of them had come back from their study in the USA. Chen Guangfu was a representative of the national bankers in the contemporary Chinese financial field. Ma Yinchu was a renowned economist and patriot, known to be tough as nails. Zhang Naiqi was a self-taught banker and financier, one of the Seven Gentlemen in the Anti-Japanese Salvation Movement, and a firm ally of the Communist Party of China (CPC). The last one was one of the founding members of the CPC and the one of the first to spread Marxism in China. These four people were basically positively viewed and so far I think no one has outdone them. It also seemed unnecessary to pick out one or two scholars for reverse reviews, at least not for the time being. The validity of this pioneering effort still needs to be tested over time. Besides, their financial thought was only introduced vaguely and the comments were also very brief, to be elaborated on in the future.

Fifth, it is challenging to complete the task of combing through the long history of financial thought of at least 2,500 years, during which the Chinese currency evolved. In ancient China, there was officially run credit in addition to usury. Besides, there were such ways of exchange as *bianhuan* and *feiqian*, for the purpose of avoiding hardship and the risk of long-distance transportation. As a matter of fact, there were different methods to avoid risks and the money drought. The local restrictions on the cross-border circulation of currency exacerbated the shortage of money, during which *feiqian* emerged. It still needs to be clarified whether the development of credit catered to the need of money drought or if something else played a decisive role in the process. The learning from this was that as long as credibility and other technical conditions were present, even if the transactions were carried out in different places and at different times, and the transactions were not in a cash-on-delivery mode, *feiqian* and paper notes would surely emerge, taking the place of coins and functioning as the media of exchange. The key point here was that the credibility of the issuers of these credit instruments should be unquestionable. Otherwise, cash would be required and they could not be used as the substitutes. As a result, it might be safe to say that China's commodity economy was unusual in some regions, such as large cities, political and economic centers, and key waterway and frontier places. Although the whole economy was still a small agricultural economy that was only self-sufficient but not very developed, in these regions, the commodity economy and currency economy were extremely active and developed rather quickly. The advanced development of credit, the vast territory of China, the needs of the border war, the supply of food and fodder, the government procurement and the concentration of taxes all needed corresponding solutions which were suitable for the national conditions of China. If we are oblivious to the achievements of our forefathers, how can we talk about our Chinese characteristics? How can we make other people understand the history of China's financial thought with our vague narration? For the convenience of writing, in this book I used currency to refer to cashable money and paper notes to refer to uncashable money. But both these kinds of moneys were different from the kind of currency issued by Western banks or Chinese banks in later years. There were also differences between the face value and the market value of the currency. Inevitably, there would also be people who manipulated the market and engaged in speculation and profit-seeking activities. In my opinion, we might conclude that the stock market in ancient China was thus born. Besides, because of the prominent feature of the Chinese government-run credit, something similar to trust institutions seemed to have also emerged, though insurance institutions had never appeared. It still needs to be clarified whether that had anything to do with the officially run feature of credit. I think this is probably due to the difference between Chinese and Western cultures, to which we must pay enough attention. On account of these reasons, I am deeply aware of my lack of learning, inability to conduct a comparative study and superficiality of my grasp of China's history of financial system and history of thought, not to mention things abroad. But I also firmly believe that as long as researchers, me included, start to do research in this field, there would be no need to worry about future success. That day will surely come.

With a somewhat reasonable knowledge structure, I could only turn for help to my predecessors, colleagues and students. I sincerely appreciate the time I am living in. Before the end of the Cultural Revolution, my courage and determination had been tempered, so I am not afraid of hardships and difficulties. Since the Cultural Revolution, we have been living in an era of emancipating the mind. This extremely active atmosphere brought about fruitful and flourishing academic outcomes. Classical literature, which used to be difficult to get, is now easily at hand. Chronicles, biographies, commentary upon people and various other research achievements keep coming out, to the extent that one cannot finish reading them all. The convenience resulting from the compilation of ancient literature made me strive all the more, being afraid that I am not diligent enough. The publication of *Quan Song Wen*, *Quan Yuan Wen*, *Xu Zizhi Tongjian Changbian*, *A Collection of the Writings of Kang Youwei* and *Complete Works of Ma Yinchu* came about so successively that my eyes seemed fully occupied. The *Selected Literature on the History of China's Economic Thought*, compiled by Wu Baosan, presented the literature from the pre-Qin period to the Ming and Qing Dynasties, benefiting researchers in this field and contributing immensely to the study of the history of China's economic thought. The collation and publication of various collections of writings provided firsthand information for research and made it convenient to carry out objective research from a historical materialistic perspective, thus getting rid of the possibility of being wrongly informed or doing ineffective study. We should not treat the ancient scholars as we wish and pay no respect to their thought. We should also not regard history as a little doll to be dressed up any way we like. Instead, we should adopt an attitude of historical materialism and carry out our research without any bias. For that reason, I have revised many problematic points, which were mostly too demanding of the ancient scholars or too imprecise about the general background of the introduction. In general, my basic viewpoints remain unchanged, which is also one of the reasons why there is not much comment in the newly added chapter.

Speaking of *A History of China's Financial Thought* and the revision and supplementation of this book, I should first of all thank the related leaders and members of the Ministry of Education for their understanding and support. At the beginning of 2003, when a leader of the Ministry of Education talked with me, I submitted my request for my withdrawal from the administrative post to concentrate on teaching and research. I they could grow up in practice. With my requirements satisfied, I could only make good use of the time and do my best to repay such good will.

I also want to thank Shanghai Jiao Tong University Press. The press presented me the chance to revise and supplement the original work and publish this book. At the time of the compilation of *A History of China's Financial Thought*, Feng Qin, the editor, telephoned to inform me of their intention to republish the book, for which I was very grateful. I had mixed feelings because I intended to make revisions but could not start the work at that time. Mr. Feng, the editor, was very tolerant and assured me that there was no hurry. Disappointingly, I dragged on until it was very late to submit my final version of the book. After a thorough reading, I still found many unsatisfactory points, for which I felt very apologetic to the press and the enthusiastic readers. On reconsidering, I realized that my limited scholarship could not be improved within a short time. So I could not keep putting off the publication of the book.

I want to add that I must thank the Central University of Finance and Economics, of which I have been a member, and to be more specific, the school of finance I am teaching in. Since I came back in 2003, I have not been assigned any specific tasks except the tutoring of my graduate students. I have been offered a very comfortable, quiet and relaxed environment in which I could concentrate on my research. I would like to take this opportunity to express my thanks to the young teachers in the school. They shouldered the heavy task of teaching, scientific research and all kinds of pressure from their families, leaving me a quiet and undisturbed environment. It is only natural that I should say a sincere "thank you" to them.

In the course of writing, my students and my family members offered me help and support from different angles, which encouraged me substantially and could only be repaid by my intensified efforts.

On the publication of this revised edition, I want to say that I am not afraid of being laughed at. My intention is to be a stepping stone for others, so that we can all accumulate experience from such an endeavor. Consequently, I'm looking forward to suggestions from the readers, especially specialists in this field.

Yao Sui
July, 2010, revised in October, 2010

Postscript*

The writing of this book was under the encouragement of Professor Yu Tianyi, my advisor, and Professor Ye Shichang. The first draft was finished in October 1991, but the change in the nature of my job kept me extremely busy and unable to complete it. During those days, Mr. Jiang Hongye, head of the Financial Research Institute of the People's Bank of China, read through the book in the midst of his busy schedule and put forward valuable suggestions. During the process of editing and publishing, Mr. Xu Shuxin, Mr. Mao Chunming, Mr. Deng Ruisuo and Mr. Zhou Zhandi, of the China Financial Publishing House, contributed their enthusiastic support and help. In the process of collecting related materials, Mr. Mao Jinghua of the library of the Chinese Academy of Sciences and members of the Reader Services Department of the China Bookstore voiced their concerns and offered me much assistance. I would like to extend my sincere thanks to all the teachers and friends who have supported the composition and publication of this book.

    I had intended to conclude the book with the part of history before the founding of the People's Republic of China. However, due to the slow progress of data collection and analysis, the book shall end at the May Fourth Movement of 1919, with the unfinished part to be continued in the future. In the process of writing, I have always felt that my theoretical

---

*This was originally in the edition of *A History of China's Financial Thought* published by the China Financial Publishing House in 1994.

inadequacy and insufficient scholarship were a hindrance to the quality of this book. Therefore, it is not clear whether this little book presented to the readers can achieve the purpose of simplicity, popularity, systematicness and scientificness. It is unavoidable that there will be problems or mistakes in opinions expressed and references cited. I am sincerely hoping that readers, especially experts in related fields, could offer suggestions without any reservation so that the book would be better revised later.

Yao Sui
October 2, 1993